The Book of Memory

The Book of Memory is a wide-ranging and amply illustrated account of the workings and function of memory in medieval society. Memory was the psychological faculty valued above all others in the period stretching from late antiquity through to the Renaissance. This study by a literary scholar draws upon insights from a variety of disciplines, including modern hermeneutical theory, art history and codicology, psychology and anthropology, the histories of medicine, education, and of meditation and spirituality. It will be important to students in all these fields who value interdisciplinary approaches to historical material.

Mary Carruthers begins by examining two governing models whereby memory is conceived in terms of a tablet awaiting inscription or a storehouse or inventory. She discusses memory systems as a kind of artificial intelligence, and considers carefully the ethical and literary values attached to memory training in medieval culture. Her examination of the scholastic and early humanist adaptations of classical mnemotechniques introduces medieval writers such as Hugh of St. Victor, Albertus Magnus, and Thomas Bradwardine; while Dante, Chaucer, and Thomas Aquinas provide recurring examples.

The medieval assumption that human learning is above all based in memorative processes (rather than the communication of information that we now tend to emphasize) had profound implications for the contemporary understanding of all creative activity, and the social role of literature and art. Dr. Carruthers explores such implications, examining the ways in which the written page was understood to be a memory device, how mnemonic techniques affected literary composition, and how reading was itself regarded as an activity of the memory.

CAMBRIDGE STUDIES IN MEDIEVAL LITERATURE

This series of critical books seeks to cover the whole area of literature written in the major medieval languages – the main European vernaculars, and medieval Latin and Greek – during the period *c.* 1100–*c.* 1500. Its chief aim is to publish and stimulate fresh scholarship and criticism on medieval literature, special emphasis being placed on understanding major works of poetry, prose and drama in relation to the contemporary culture and learning which fostered them.

The Book of Memory

A Study of Memory in Medieval Culture

MARY J. CARRUTHERS

CAMBRIDGE
UNIVERSITY PRESS

PUBLISHED BY THE PRESS SYNDICATE OF THE UNIVERSITY OF CAMBRIDGE
The Pitt Building, Trumpington Street, Cambridge, United Kingdom

CAMBRIDGE UNIVERSITY PRESS
The Edinburgh Building, Cambridge CB2 2RU, UK
40 West 20th Street, New York, NY 10011–4211, USA
477 Williamstown Road, Port Melbourne, VIC 3207, Australia
Ruiz de Alarcón 13, 28014 Madrid, Spain
Dock House, The Waterfront, Cape Town 8001, South Africa

http://www.cambridge.org

© Cambridge University Press 1990

First published 1990
First paperback edition 1992
Tenth printing 2002

Printed in the United Kingdom at the University Press, Cambridge

British Library Cataloguing in Publication data
Carruthers, Mary J.
The book of memory: a study of memory in medieval
culture
I. European civilization ca. 400–1500
I. Title
940.1

Library of Congress Cataloguing in Publication data applied for

ISBN 0 521 38282 3 hardback
ISBN 0 521 42973 0 paperback

IN MEMORIAM

Morton W. Bloomfield
E. Talbot Donaldson

quid esse potest in otio aut iucundius
aut magis proprium humanitatis,
quam sermo facetus ac nulla in re rudis?

(Cicero, *De Oratore*, I. viii)

Contents

Illustrations

List of illustrations

Acknowledgements

This book, to an extent greater than any other work I have undertaken, has been the result of many conversations.

I would like first of all to thank the two scholars to whose memory this book is dedicated. Morton Bloomfield gave me much-needed advice on where to begin in a lengthy afternoon's conversation in June 1983, and continued to encourage my research until his sudden death in 1987. Talbot Donaldson was the first person I talked to about what I wanted to do; he continued to be interested and encouraging until his death in 1987, one day before that of Morton Bloomfield.

Conversations with other scholars were also most helpful to me, even though they may not remember the occasions as well as I do. Malcolm Parkes, Derek Pearsall, and Derek Brewer each read the prospectus of the book and made good suggestions; Derek Brewer also helped me to unravel some of the intricacies of the Fitzwilliam Museum's reading room. My Chicago-area academic colleagues have shown a continuing interest (not that they had much choice in the matter), especially Sylvia Huot, Clark Hulse, Christina von Nolken, Richard Kraut, Susan Cole, and, while he was there, Winthrop P. Wetherbee. Marjorie C. Woods shared her knowledge of the glosses on Geoffrey of Vinsauf's art of poetry. Jeanne LaDuke helped me with matters related to the history of mathematics. Martha Driver, Lucy Sandler, Robert Hanning, and Marshall Leicester all shared their thoughts with me over lunches in New York. Elizabeth Kirk and Judith Anderson provided attentive ears, encouragement, and fruitful argument, especially in the early stages of my project.

I have also gained much from presenting parts of this book as talks to various professional organizations, whose members have provoked me by their questions to constructive revision and rethinking. Before I began my serious research, I profited from attending a colloquium on "La mémoire," sponsored by the Institut d'Etudes Médiévales of the Université de Montréal in the spring of 1983, especially from conversations there with E. Jane Burns, Paul Zumthor, and Eugene Vance.

The research for this study was helped immeasurably by year-long Fellowships from the University of Illinois at Chicago Institute for the Humanities, and the National Endowment for the Humanities-Newberry Library Fellowship program, which I held concurrently in 1984–85. My

Acknowledgements

study of manuscripts held in European and British libraries was aided by a Grant-in-Aid of Research from the American Council of Learned Societies in the summer of 1985. I would like to thank those invaluable funding institutions for their financial help, which, together with a sabbatical leave, freed me from other responsibilities for the better part of two years. I also profited from many conversations with the other 1984–85 Fellows at both the Newberry and the UIC Institute for the Humanities.

I wish to thank the staff and resident Fellows of the Henry E. Huntington Library, especially Daniel and Elizabeth Donno, and the Library's former Director, James Thorpe. Other research libraries have also been most hospitable: the Pierpont Morgan Library; the Houghton Library at Harvard; the Bodleian Library, Oxford; the libraries of the Fitzwilliam Museum, and Emmanuel and Trinity Colleges, Cambridge; the British Library; and the Biblioteca Medicea Laurenziana in Florence. The University of Illinois at Chicago Library staff was most helpful in searching out and getting material for me.

But I was particularly fortunate in being able to work at the Newberry Library in Chicago, without whose extensive collections in medieval and early Renaissance rhetoric I could not have managed, and whose staff have been true colleagues. Mary Beth Rose and Richard Brown made sure I had the space and support I needed, and listened patiently to my various plans. Paul Saenger gave me valuable advice about manuscripts and shared his ideas on medieval reading habits. The Newberry's frequent seminars and conferences gave me the opportunity to learn from and ask questions of such experts as Jürgen Miethke, R. B. C. Huygens, and Jonathan Alexander.

I am particularly indebted to Paul Gehl, the Custodian of the John M. Wing Collection at the Newberry Library. Paul listened at length to my embryonic ideas, put me in contact with people of kindred interests, and suggested much helpful bibliography. Having fostered my project in so many ways, he also read the last draft of the entire manuscript and made many useful suggestions and corrections.

The careful vetting of the manuscript by the two readers for Cambridge University Press, Michael Camille and an anonymous second, was extremely valuable to me. My editors at Cambridge, Kevin Taylor and Josie Dixon, have been most helpful, prompt, and professional. I was glad to have the opportunity to work directly with them and other members of the editorial staff in Cambridge during September 1989. Mrs. Dorothy Dosanjh prepared the index; Patrick Deer helped me in checking the bibliography.

Many friends and the members of my family have been unfailing in their encouragement, and eased my life considerably by their continuing interest. Finally, I want especially to thank Erika Rosenfeld, for help in translating early Italian, and for gladdening my life during work that is always solitary and often seems without end.

As the above list partially demonstrates, I have inevitably relied upon the experience and counsel, both oral and written, of specialists in a variety of disciplines whose knowledge connects with the subject of this book, for *memoria* was elementary in medieval life. My indebtedness to these specialist "clerkes" will be apparent from the notes and bibliography: here I would like to emphasize with Chaucer's Parson, that

> nathelees, this meditacioun
> I putte it ay under correccioun
> Of clerkes, for I am nat textueel.
> I take but the sentence, trusteth weel.

Note to the 1992 edition

My translation of Thomas Bradwardine's "Ad Memoriam Artificiale Adquirenda" is based on the version of the text in the Fitzwilliam Museum, Cambridge MS. McClean 169. After typesetting, I found a previously unknown copy in British Library MS. Harley 4166. I have now prepared an edition of the Latin text from the Harley and McClean manuscripts, which will be published in the *Journal of Medieval Latin* (York University, Ontario) vol. 2 (1992). The readings of this edition supersede in several places the version that formed the basis for translation printed in Appendix C.

Abbreviations

AASS	*Acta Sanctorum*
Ad Her.	Cicero, *Rhetorica ad Herennium*
Avi. Lat.	Avicenna (Ibn Sina) Latinus
CCSL	*Corpus Christianorum, series latina*
CHB	*The Cambridge History of the Bible*
Conf.	St. Augustine, *Confessiones*
CSEL	*Corpus Scriptorum Ecclesiasticorum Latinorum*
CT	Geoffrey Chaucer, *The Canterbury Tales*
De orat.	Cicero, *De oratore*
DTC	*Dictionnaire de Théologie Catholique*
Du Cange	C. Du Cange, *et al.*, *Glossarium mediae et infimae latinitatus.* Graz. 1954–5
EETS	The Early English Text Society
Epist.	*Epistolae* (various authors, as indicated)
Etym.	Isidore of Seville, *Etymologiae*
FQ	Edmund Spenser, *The Faerie Queene*
HF	Geoffrey Chaucer, *The House of Fame*
Inst.	Quintilian, *Institutio oratoria*
JMRS	*Journal of Medieval and Renaissance Studies*
JWCI	*Journal of the Warburg and Courtauld Institutes*
MED	*The Middle English Dictionary*
MGH	*Monumenta Germaniae historica*
OED	*The Oxford English Dictionary*
Ox. Lat. Dict.	*The Oxford Latin Dictionary*
PG	*Patrologia cursus completus, series Graeca.* Edited by J.-P. Migne. Paris, 1857–66.
PL	*Patrologia cursus completus, series Latina.* Edited by J.-P. Migne. Paris, 1841–64.
Sent.	Isidore of Seville, *Sententiarum libri* III
ST	Thomas Aquinas, *Summa Theologiae*
STC	*A Short-Title Catalogue* (Pollard and Redgrave)

Introduction

When we think of our highest creative power, we think invariably of the imagination. "Great imagination, profound intuition," we say: this is our highest accolade for intellectual achievement, even in the sciences. The memory, in contrast, is devoid of intellect: "just memorization," not "real thought" or "true learning." At best, for us, memory is a kind of photographic film, exposed (we imply) by an amateur and developed by a duffer, and so marred by scratches and "inaccurate" light-values.

We make such judgments (even those of us who are hard scientists) because we have been formed in a post-Romantic, post-Freudian world, in which imagination has been identified with a mental unconscious of great, even dangerous, creative power. Consequently, when they look at the Middle Ages, modern scholars are often disappointed by the apparently lowly, working-day status accorded to imagination in medieval psychology – a sort of draught-horse of the sensitive soul, not even given intellectual status. Ancient and medieval people reserved *their* awe for memory. Their greatest geniuses they describe as people of superior memories, they boast unashamedly of their prowess in that faculty, and they regard it as a mark of superior moral character as well as intellect.

Because of this great change in the relative status of imagination and memory, many moderns have concluded that medieval people did not value originality or creativity. We are simply looking in the wrong place. We should instead examine the role of memory in their intellectual and cultural lives, and the values which they attached to it, for there we will get a firmer sense of their understanding of what we now call creative activity.

The modern test of whether we "really know" something rests in our ability to use what we have been taught in a variety of situations (American pedagogy calls this "creative learning"). In this characterization of learning, we concur with medieval writers, who also believed that education meant the construction of experience and method (which they called "art") out of knowledge. They would not, however, have understood our separation of "memory" from "learning." In their understanding of the matter, it was memory that made knowledge into useful experience, and memory that combined these pieces of information-become-experience into what we call "ideas," what they were more likely to call "judgments."

A modern experimental psychologist has written that "some of the best

The book of memory

'memory crutches' we have are called laws of nature," for learning can be seen as a process of acquiring smarter and richer mnemonic devices to represent information, encoding similar information into patterns, organizational principles, and rules which represent even material we have never before encountered, but which is "like" what we do know, and thus can be "recognized" or "remembered."[1] This is a position that older writers would have perfectly understood.

I think it will be useful to begin my study by comparing descriptions of two men whom their contemporaries universally recognized to be men of remarkable scientific genius (assessments which time has proven correct, though that is only partly relevant to my discussion): Albert Einstein and Thomas Aquinas. Each description is the testimony (direct or reported) of men who knew and worked intimately with them over a long period of time. The first is by Leopold Infeld, a physicist who worked with Einstein at Princeton:

> I was very much impressed by the ingenuity of Einstein's most recent paper. It was an intricate, most skilfully arranged chain of reasoning, leading to the conclusion that gravitational waves do not exist. If true, the result would be of great importance to relativity theory . . .
>
> The greatness of Einstein lies in his tremendous imagination, in the unbelievable obstinacy with which he pursues his problems. Originality is the most essential factor in important scientific work. It is intuition which leads to unexplored regions, intuition as difficult to explain rationally as that by which the oil diviner locates the wealth hidden in the earth.
>
> There is no great scientific achievement without wandering through the darkness of error. The more the imagination is restricted, the more a piece of work moves along a definite track – a process made up rather of additions than essentially new ideas – the safer the ground and the smaller the probability of error. There are no great achievements without error and no great man was always correct. This is well known to every scientist. Einstein's paper might be wrong and Einstein still be the greatest scientist of our generation . . .
>
> The most amazing thing about Einstein was his tremendous vital force directed toward one and only one channel: that of original thinking, of doing research. Slowly I came to realize that in exactly this was his greatness. Nothing is as important as physics. No human relations, no personal life, are as essential as thought and the comprehension of how "God created the world." . . . one feels behind [his] external activity the calm, watchful contemplation of scientific problems, that the mechanism of his brain works without interruption. It is a constant motion which nothing can stop. . . . The clue to the understanding of Einstein's role in science lies in his loneliness and aloofness. In this respect he differs from all other scientists. . . . He had never studied physics at a famous university, he was not attached to any school; he worked as a clerk in a patent office. . . . For him the isolation was a blessing since it prevented his thought from wandering into conventional channels. This aloofness, this independent thought on problems which Einstein formulated for himself, not marching with the crowd but looking for his own lonely pathways, is the most essential feature of his creation. It is not only originality, it is not only imagination, it is something more.[2]

The following descriptions are excerpted from a life of St. Thomas Aquinas, written shortly after his death by Bernardo Gui, and from testi-

2

Introduction

mony taken at Thomas's canonization hearings from his close contemporary, Thomas of Celano, who also knew Reginald, Thomas's *socius*, or friar-companion.

> Of the subtlety and brilliance of his intellect and the soundness of his judgment, sufficient proof is his vast literary output, his many original discoveries, his deep understanding of the Scriptures. His memory was extremely rich and retentive: whatever he had once read and grasped he never forgot; it was as if knowledge were ever increasing in his soul as page is added to page in the writing of a book. Consider, for example, that admirable compilation of Patristic texts on the four Gospels which he made for Pope Urban [the *Catena aurea* or "Golden Chain"] and which, for the most part, he seems to have put together from texts that he had read and committed to memory from time to time while staying in various religious houses. Still stronger is the testimony of Reginald his *socius* and of his pupils and of those who write to his dictation, who all declare that he used to dictate in his cell to three secretaries, and even occasionally to four, on different subjects at the same time . . . No one could dictate simultaneously so much various material without a special grace. Nor did he seem to be searching for things as yet unknown to him; he seemed simply to let his memory pour out its treasures. . . .
>
> He never set himself to study or argue a point, or lecture or write or dictate without first having recourse inwardly – but with tears – to prayer for the understanding and the words required by the subject. When perplexed by a difficulty he would kneel and pray and then, on returning to his writing or dictation, he was accustomed to find that his thought had become so clear that it seemed to show him inwardly, as in a book, the words he needed . . .
>
> Even at meal-times his recollection continued; dishes would be placed before him and taken away without his noticing; and when the brethren tried to get him into the garden for recreation, he would draw back swiftly and retire to his cell alone with his thoughts.[3]

It might be useful to isolate the qualities of genius enumerated in each of the above descriptions. Of Einstein: ingenuity, intricate reasoning, original-ity, imagination, essentially new ideas coupled with the notion that to achieve truth one must err of necessity, deep devotion to and understanding of physics, obstinacy, vital force, single-minded concentration, solitude. Of Thomas Aquinas: subtlety and brilliance of intellect, original discoveries coupled with deep understanding of Scripture, memory, nothing forgotten and knowledge ever-increasing, special grace, inward recourse, single-minded concentration, intense recollection, solitude.

As I compare these two lists I am struck first by the extent to which the qualities ascribed to each man's working habits are the same. In both, one gets a vivid sense of extraordinary concentration on problems to the exclusion of most daily routine. Infeld speaks of tremendous vital force, Bernardo of intense inner prayer, but both are describing a concentrated continuous energy that expresses itself in a profound singlemindedness, a remarkable solitude and aloofness. Each also praises the intricacy and brilliance of the reasoning, and its prolific character, its originality. It is important to appreciate that Bernardo values originality in Thomas's work – he praises its creativeness just as Infeld praises that in Einstein's.

3

The book of memory

What we have, in short, is a recognizable likeness between these two extraordinary intellects, in terms of what they needed for their compositional activity (the activity of thought), the social isolation required by each individual, and what is perceived to be the remarkable subtlety, originality, and understanding of the product of such reasoning. What is strikingly different is that in the one case this process and product are ascribed to intuition and imagination unfettered by "definite" tracks, in the other to a "rich and retentive memory," which never forgot anything and in which knowledge increased "as page is added to page in the writing of a book."

My point in setting these two descriptions up in this way is simply this: the nature of creative activity itself – what the brain does, and the social and psychic conditions needed for its nurture – has remained essentially the same between Thomas's time and our own. Human beings did not suddenly acquire imagination and intuition with Coleridge, having previously been poor clods. The difference is that whereas now geniuses are said to have creative imagination which they express in intricate reasoning and original discovery, in earlier times they were said to have richly retentive memories, which they expressed in intricate reasoning and original discovery.

We know a good deal about the actual procedures that Thomas Aquinas followed in composing his works, thanks in part to the full accounts we have from the hearings held for his canonization,[4] and in part to the remarkable survival of several pages of autograph drafts of certain of his early works. Both sources of material have received a thorough analysis from the paleographic scholar, Antoine Dondaine.[5] Dondaine's work confirmed the existence, alluded to many times in the contemporary accounts, of a group of three or four secretaries who took down Thomas's compositions in a fair hand from his own dictation. The autographs are written in *littera inintelligibilis*, a kind of shorthand that fully lives up to its name (Dondaine says that the great nineteenth-century editor, Uccelli, lost his eyesight scrutinizing these drafts) for it was not designed to be read by anyone other than the author himself. As Dondaine has reconstructed the process of composing the *Summa contra gentiles*, an early work for which a number of autograph leaves exist, Thomas wrote first in *littera inintelligibilis* and then summoned one of his secretaries to take down the text in a legible hand while Thomas read his own autograph aloud. When one scribe tired, another took over.

But no autographs are found of the later major works. Dondaine remarks this fact as curious, because one would expect these autographs to have been treasured at least as carefully as those of earlier works. He suggests that their nonexistence is due not to loss but to there having been none in the first place to save. "Le fait qu'il n'y ait plus d'autographes des ouvrages postérieurs invite á penser que saint Thomas ne les a pas écrits, sinon peut-être sous forme de brouillons, et qu'il les a dictés en les composant."[6] Dondaine points out the tedium and waste of time involved for Thomas in writing out a complete text, even in shorthand, and then reading it aloud for it to be written again, this time in a fair hand.

Introduction

There is good evidence in the remembrance of his peers that, certainly later in life, Thomas was not accustomed to write his thoughts down himself, even in *inintelligibilis*. Two incidents in particular suggest this habit. There is the famous story of Thomas at dinner with Louis XI, Saint Louis. Though seated next to the king, Thomas was still preoccupied by an argument he was composing against the Manichees. Suddenly he struck the table, crying, "That settles the Manichees!" and called out to Reginald, his *socius*, "as though he were still at study in his cell . . . 'Reginald, get up and write!'"[7] This incident must have occurred between the springs of 1269 and 1270; the work in progress was the Second Part of the *Summa theologica*.[8]

The second incident occurred in conjunction with the writing of his commentary on Isaiah, a work for which an autograph of five chapters exists (Vatican MS. lat. 9850).[9] Thomas became puzzled for days over the interpretation of a text:

At last, one night when he had stayed up to pray, his *socius* overheard him speaking, as it seemed, with other persons in the room; though what was being said the *socius* could not make out, nor did he recognize the other voices. Then these fell silent and he heard Thomas's voice calling: "Reginald, my son, get up and bring a light and the commentary on Isaiah; I want you to write for me." So Reginald rose and began to take down the dictation, which ran so clearly that it was as if the master was reading aloud from a book under his eyes.[10]

Pressed by Reginald for the names of his mysterious companions, Thomas finally replied that Peter and Paul had been sent to him, "and told me all I desired to know." This tale, among other things, suggests that some of Thomas's work was composed in a mixture of some parts written out in shorthand and then read to a secretary and some mentally composed and dictated. The contemporary sources suggest strongly that the entire *Summa theologica* was composed mentally and dictated from memory, with the aid at most of a few written notes, and there is no reason to disbelieve them.

Around 1263, Thomas wrote a compilation of patristic texts on the Gospels, the *Catena aurea*, which Gui describes, in the passage I just quoted, as "put together from texts that [Thomas] had read and committed to memory from time to time while staying in various religious houses."[11] Chenu accurately describes it as a "concatenation of patristic texts cleverly coordinated into a running commentary"; it includes a number of Greek authorities as well, which Thomas had had translated into Latin in order to add these extracts, "being careful to place the names of the authors before their testimonies" in the proper quotational style, whose purpose, as we will see in chapter 3, was certainly to aid memorial retention.[12] The *catena* or "chain" is a very old medieval genre of scholarly commentary, used widely by the monastic scholars as part of *lectio divina*.[13] The authorities are chained, or hooked, together by a particular Biblical phrase. Thus the commentary entirely follows the sequence of the main text, each chapter division of the Gospel book forming a division of the *Catena*, and each verse (actually its unnumbered phrases and clauses) quoted separately with a string of relevant comments following it.

The written organization of the *catena* simply reproduces its memorial organization, as each bit of Biblical text calls up the authorities attached to it. For example, on Mt. 2:9, Thomas Aquinas first gives us a bit of Chrysostom on Matthew, then Augustine from two sources, then the ordinary gloss, then Ambrose on Luke, then Remigius, and then the gloss again. It is important to note that in writing this work Thomas did not look up each quotation in a manuscript tome as he composed; the accounts are specific on this point. The texts were already filed in his memory, in an ordered form that is one of the basics of mnemonic technique. And of course, once the texts were in his memory they stayed there for use on other occasions.

I am not suggesting that Thomas never made reference to manuscripts – on the contrary, we know that he did. We also know that one task of his secretaries was to copy manuscripts for his use.[14] But the picture we are often given of Thomas pausing while dictating in order to check a reference in a manuscript seems to me contrary to the evidence. For we are told over and over again that Thomas's flow to his secretaries was unceasing: it "ran so clearly that it was as if the master were reading aloud from a book under his eyes." He dictated "as if a great torrent of truth were pouring into him from God. Nor did he seem to be searching for things as yet unknown to him; he seemed simply to let his memory pour out its treasures." And again, "When perplexed by a difficulty he would kneel and pray and then, on returning to his writing or dictation, he was accustomed to find that his thought had become so clear that it seemed to show him inwardly, as in a book, the words he needed."[15]

That unceasing torrent, that clarity as though reading from a book before his eyes, that quality of retaining whatever he had read and grasped, can be understood if we are willing to give his trained memory its due. Thomas himself stresses the importance of concentration in memory, and we are told many times of his remarkable power of deep concentration, often approaching a trance-like state in which he did not feel physical pain. Thomas communed with his memory constantly, certainly before he dictated, and only when he clearly had "the understanding *and the words required*" (my emphasis) would he lecture or write or dictate.[16] (This, of course, is not to suggest that his works were dictated always in the absolutely final form in which we have them today; Dondaine gives much evidence of revision and reworking in the autographs and between the autographs and the fair texts. For some works, he left notes which were to be worked up later; the *Supplement* to the *Summa* is an example of such a practice.) I am even inclined to take somewhat seriously his comment to Reginald that Peter and Paul spoke with him and instructed him in his difficulties with the text of Isaiah. Their words were certainly intimately in his mind, among the many voices in his memory, intimate colleagues to his own thoughts. Moreover, subvocalization, a murmur, was a persistent and apparently necessary feature of memory work. One of his secretaries, a Breton called Evan, told how Thomas would sometimes sit down to rest from the work of dictating and, falling asleep, would continue to dictate in his sleep, Evan continuing to write just the same. What Evan took for sleep may have been an extreme form of Thomas's concentration. Or perhaps we should credit the story as told; since the matter had been worked out beforehand in Thomas's memory, perhaps a kind of mental "automatic pilot" took over in times of extreme fatigue.

Most remarkable is the testimony of all his pupils and secretaries, including Reginald, that "he used to dictate in his cell to three secretaries, and even occasionally to four, on different subjects at the same time."[17] Gui comments, "No one could dictate simultaneously so much various material without a special grace." Dondaine is inclined to discount this story as the evidence of the single Breton secretary (are Bretons especially credulous?).[18] But Gui ascribes the testimony to *all* those who wrote to Thomas's dictation.

Moreover, as Dondaine himself notes, such stories have been told – though rarely – of other historical figures, notably Julius Caesar. Petrarch tells the story about Caesar as an instance of trained memory ("ut memoria polleret eximia"), that he could dictate four letters on different subjects to others, while writing a fifth in his own hand.[19] Whether the tale is factual or not is less important for my analysis than that Petrarch understood it as evidence of the power of Caesar's *memory*, for Petrarch himself had a significant reputation as an authority on memory training. Thomas's biographer, too, understood a similar feat to be enabled by powerful memory. But it is not achieved by raw talent alone; indeed natural talent will not produce such facility or accuracy. Memory must be trained, in accordance with certain elementary techniques.

The nature of these techniques and how they were taught is the subject of much of my study. *Memoria* meant, at that time, trained memory, educated and disciplined according to a well-developed pedagogy that was part of the elementary language arts – grammar, logic, and rhetoric. The fundamental principle is to "divide" the material to be remembered into pieces short enough to be recalled in single units and to key these into some sort of rigid, easily reconstructable order. This provides one with a "random-access" memory system, by means of which one can immediately and securely find a particular bit of information, rather than having to start from the beginning each time in order laboriously to reconstruct the whole system, or – worse – relying on simple chance to fish what one wants out from the murky pool of one's undifferentiated and disorganized memory.

It is possible for one with a well-trained memory to compose clearly in an organized fashion on several different subjects. Once one has the all-important starting-place of the ordering scheme and the contents firmly in their places within it, it is quite possible to move back and forth from one distinct composition to another without losing one's place or becoming confused. As an experiment, I tried memorizing a few psalms (texts that come to us with a divisional system already in place) in accordance with an elementary scheme described by the twelfth-century teacher, Hugh of St.

The book of memory

Victor – a scheme that I analyze in detail in chapter 3. That scheme enabled me to recall the texts in any order I pleased. If one so novice and unskilled as I am can recite without difficulty three psalms "at the same time" (that is, going easily from one psalm to another, verse to verse, backwards or forwards or skipping around at will) a memory as highly talented and trained as Thomas's could surely manage three *quaestiones* of his own composition at the same time. The key lies in the imposition of a rigid order to which clearly prepared pieces of textual content are attached. Both the initial laying down of the scheme and its recollection are accomplished in a state of profound concentration. Proper preparation of material, rigid order, and complete concentration are the requirements which Thomas Aquinas himself defines in his discourses on trained memory, and as we will see are continuously emphasized in all ancient and medieval mnemonic practices.

Scholars have always recognized that memory necessarily played a crucial role in pre-modern Western civilization, for in a world of few books, and those mostly in communal libraries, one's education had to be remembered, for one could never depend on having continuing access to specific material. While acknowledging this, however, insufficient attention has been paid to the pedagogy of memory, to what memory was thought to be, and how and why it was trained. Nor can the immense value attached to trained memory be understood only in terms of differing technical applications, though these are basic.

It is my contention that medieval culture was fundamentally memorial, to the same profound degree that modern culture in the West is documentary. This distinction certainly involves technologies – mnemotechnique and printing – but it is not confined to them. For the valuing of *memoria* persisted long after book technology itself had changed. That is why the fact of books in themselves, which were much more available in the late Middle Ages than ever before, did not profoundly disturb the essential value of memory training until many centuries had passed. Indeed the very purpose of a book is differently understood in a memorial culture like that of the Middle Ages than it is today.

A book is not necessarily the same thing as a text. "Texts" are the material out of which human beings make "literature." For us, texts only come in books, and so the distinction between the two is blurred and even lost. But, in a memorial culture, a "book" is only one way among several to remember a "text," to provision and cue one's memory with "dicta et facta memorabilia." So a book is itself a mnemonic, among many other functions it can also have. Thomas Aquinas makes this assumption about books in a comment on Ps. 69:28, "Let them be blotted from the book of life":

A thing is said metaphorically to be written on the mind of anyone when it is firmly held in the memory . . . For things are written down in material books to help the memory.[20]

Andrew of St. Victor, writing over a hundred years earlier, comments similarly on Is. 1:18: "Though your sins be as scarlet, they shall be white as snow":

Introduction

According to Jewish tradition, the sins of all men are preserved in writing on a shining white substance . . . Grievous sins are written in red and other colours which adhere more faithfully to the parchment and strike the reader's eye more readily . . . When sins are said to be written in books, what else does it mean but that God remembers as though they were written?[21]

In the early twelfth century, Hugh of St. Victor, instructing some young students on how to remember, explains clearly the mnemonic utility of manuscript page layout and decoration (appendix A). Repeating traditional advice about always memorizing from the same written source, lest a confusion of images caused by seeing different layouts make it impossible for the brain to impress a single image, he says:

it is a great value for fixing a memory-image that when we read books, we study to impress on our memory . . . the color, shape, position, and placement of the letters . . . in what location (at the top, the middle or bottom) we saw [something] positioned . . . in what color we observed the trace of the letter or the ornamented surface of the parchment. Indeed I consider nothing so useful for stimulating the memory as this.

Much later, in a fifteenth-century French *ars memorativa*, similar advice is given by its author, Jacques Legrand, to pay close attention to the color of lines and the appearance of the page in order to fix the text as a visual image in the memory:

wherefore one best learns by studying from illuminated books, for the different colors bestow remembrance of the different lines and consequently of that thing which one wants to get by heart.[22]

Throughout this study, my concern is with educated memory. All my evidence comes from learned works, most of them written in Latin, from about the fourth through the fourteenth centuries; the few vernacular poets I cite are themselves learned, working within a highly educated group. *Memoria*, as these writers understood and practiced it, was a part of *litteratura*: indeed it was what literature, in a fundamental sense, was for. Memory is one of the five divisions of ancient and medieval rhetoric; it was regarded, moreover, by more than one writer on the subject as the "noblest" of all these, the basis for the rest. *Memoria* was also an integral part of the virtue of prudence, that which makes moral judgment possible. Training the memory was much more than a matter of providing oneself with the means to compose and converse intelligently when books were not readily to hand, for it was in trained memory that one built character, judgment, citizenship, and piety.

Memoria also signifies the process by which a work of literature becomes institutionalized – internalized within the language and pedagogy of a group. In describing the truth of Holy Scripture, John Wyclif argues that God's text is contained only in a sort of short-hand form in books, language, and other human artifacts "which are the memorial clues and traces of pre-existing truth"; because of this, the actual words are five times removed from Truth itself, and must therefore be continually interpreted and adapted to what he calls the *liber vitae*, the book of life in the actual person of Christ.[23] This

9

opinion is a commonplace; Wyclif attributes it to Augustine, but we find it earlier than that, for the idea that language, as a *sign* of something else, is always at a remove from reality is one of the cornerstones of ancient rhetoric. This idea gives to both books and language a subsidiary and derivative cultural role with respect to *memoria*, for they have no meaning except in relation to it. A work is not truly read until one has made it part of oneself – that process constitutes a necessary stage of its "textualization." Merely running one's eyes over the written pages is not reading at all, for the writing must be transferred into memory, from graphemes on parchment or papyrus or paper to images written in one's brain by emotion and sense.

It should be clear from what I have said so far that I am not concerned with what has traditionally been the subject of studies of "the rise of literacy" during the Middle Ages, although I have, inevitably, run up against other scholars' distinctions between "oral" and "literate" societies in the course of my work. As a historian of literature, my emphasis is on the function of literature in particular societies – and "literature" is not the same thing as "literacy." The ability to "write" is not always the same thing as the ability to compose and comprehend in a fully textual way, for indeed one who writes (a scribe) may simply be a skilled practitioner, employed in a capacity akin to that of a professional typist today. The distinction of composing (or "making" in Middle English) from writing-down continued to be honored throughout the Middle Ages. Similarly, learning by hearing material and reciting aloud should not be confused with ignorance of reading. Especially in describing the Middle Ages, when the criterion of being *litteratus* was knowledge of Latin, one should be careful to remember that some degree of bilingualism (Latin and a vernacular) was a fact of every educated European's life, and not confuse apologies for "illiteracy," meaning "unable to compose fluently in Latin," with an apology for being unable to think or write clearly in any language.[24]

Historians of literacy have been concerned with normative channels of communication in societies. An "oral" society is thus one in which communication occurs in forms other than written documents, and in which law and government are conducted on the basis of orally-preserved custom. For such an historian, much of the best evidence comes from studying the changing ways in which legally persuasive evidence was thought to be established.[25] In the medieval period, such studies have focused on the ways in which the tribal cultures of Germanic, northern Europe became acculturated to the literate norms of late Roman law and education, preserved primarily in Italy and in the institutions of the Roman church. Because oral cultures must obviously depend on memory, and hence value memory highly, such valorization has come to be seen as a hallmark of orality, as opposed to literacy. This has led to a further assumption that literacy and memory are *per se* incompatible, and that a "rise of literacy" will therefore bring with it a consequent devalorizing and disuse of memory.

Introduction

It is this assumption that my study calls particularly into doubt. For the cultivation and training of memory was a basic aspect of the literate society of Rome, and continued to be necessary to literature and culture straight through the Middle Ages. This privileged cultural role of memory seems independent of "orality" and "literacy" as these terms have come to be defined in the social sciences, and it is dangerous to confuse those terms with a literary and ethical concept like medieval "memory."

Indeed, I think it is probably misleading to speak of literary culture as a version of "literacy" at all. The reason is simply this – as a concept, literacy privileges a physical artifact, the writing-support, over the social and rhetorical process that a text both records and generates, namely, the composition by an author and its reception by an audience. The institutions of literature, including education in the arts of language, the conventions of debate, and meditation, as well as oratory and poetry, are rhetorically conceived and fostered.

The valuing of memory training depends more, I think, on the role which rhetoric has in a culture than on whether its texts are presented in oral or written forms, or some combination of the two. For the sake of definition, I will distinguish here between fundamentalism and textualism as representing two polar views of what literature is and how it functions in society. These two extremes are always in tension with one another; one can analyze many changes in literary theory as efforts to redress an imbalance of one over the other. (For example, some Biblical scholars of the thirteenth century stressed the literal "intention" of the text in order to redress what they saw as an excess of interpretative commentary on the part of earlier exegetes – in my terms, this would be a dash of fundamentalism injected to offset too excessive a textualism.)

Fundamentalism regards a work of literature as essentially not requiring interpretation. It emphasizes its literal form as independent of circumstance, audience, author – of all those factors that are summed up in rhetorical analyses by the word "occasion." Legal scholars speak of "originalists," those who believe that the "original intention" of a written document is contained entirely in its words, and that all interpretation is unnecessary and distracting. The kinship of this position to religious fundamentalism is apparent. True fundamentalism understands words not as signs or clues but takes them as things in themselves. It also regards works exclusively as objects, which are therefore independent of institutions – perhaps that is why fundamentalism was so frequently a component of medieval heresies.[26]

Fundamentalism denies legitimacy to interpretation. Instead of interpreting, a reader is engaged at most only in rephrasing the meaning of the written document, a meaning which is really transparent, simple, and complete – but which the detritus of history and linguistic change has temporarily concealed. (It is significant that the Southern Baptist fundamentalists have allowed the publication of only one Bible commentary, the Boardman Bible Commentary, which purports simply to clear up inadvertent obscurities produced by history.) Fundamentalist translations are considered to be merely restatements of an inerrant truth that is clear and non-ambiguous – they are not adaptations or interpretive readings. Fundamentalism ideally should produce no gloss or commentary. Thus the role of scholarship is solely to identify the accumulations of interpretive debris and to polish up the original, simple meaning. It is reasonable, from a fundamentalist attitude, that God must be the direct author of the Bible. This belief holds true as well among secular fundamentalists writing about literature, who postulate a God-like author who plans, directs, and controls the meaning of his work.

But texts need not be confined to what is written down in a document. Where literature is valued for its social functions, works (especially certain ones, of course) provide the sources of a group's memory. Societies of this sort are "textual communities," in Brian Stock's phrase, whether those texts exist among them in oral or written form. The Latin word *textus* comes from the verb meaning "to weave" and it is in the institutionalizing of a story through *memoria* that textualizing occurs. Literary works become institutions as they weave a community together by providing it with shared experience and a certain kind of language, the language of stories that can be experienced over and over again through time and as occasion suggests. Their meaning is thought to be implicit, hidden, polysemous and complex, requiring continuing interpretation and adaptation. Taken to an extreme, of course, textualism can bury the original work altogether in purely solipsistic interpretation. Beryl Smalley, who spent her scholarly life reading medieval commentaries, once remarked wryly that "choos[ing] the most arbitrary interpreter of Biblical texts of the Middle Ages would be rather like awarding a prize for the ugliest statue of Queen Victoria."[27]

In the process of textualizing, the original work acquires commentary and gloss; this activity is not regarded as something other than the text, but is the mark of textualization itself. *Textus* also means "texture," the layers of meaning that attach as a text is woven into and through the historical and institutional fabric of a society. Such "socializing" of literature is the work of *memoria*, and this is as true of a literate as of an oral society. Whether the words come through the sensory gateways of the eyes or the ears, they must be processed and transformed in memory – they are made our own. Thomas Aquinas was a highly literate man in a highly literate group, yet his contemporaries reserved their greatest praise not for his books but for his memory, for they understood that it was memory which allowed him to weave together his astonishing works.

Memory also marked his superior moral character; it should not go unnoticed that the praise heaped on his memory came at his canonization trial. In fact, prodigious memory is almost a trope of saints' lives. One thinks of St. Anthony, who learned the whole Bible by heart merely from hearing it read aloud (the fact that he never saw the words written is what astonished his contemporaries); of St. Francis of Assisi, reputed by his followers to have a remarkably exact and copious memory. Tropes cannot be dismissed as "mere" formulas, for they indicate the values of a society and the way in which it conceives of its literature. The choice to train one's memory or not, for the ancients and medievals, was not a choice dictated by convenience: it was a matter of ethics. A person without a memory, if such a thing could be, would be a person without moral character and, in a basic sense, without humanity. *Memoria* refers not to how something is communicated, but to what happens once one has received it, to the interactive process of familiarizing – or textualizing – which occurs between oneself and others' words in memory.

Many historians will wonder why I have avoided assigning Neoplatonist or Aristotelian labels in my discussion of memorial technique and practice, especially given the role of memory in Neoplatonist philosophy. But my decision is deliberate. A currently accepted picture of the intellectual history of the twelfth and thirteenth centuries is one of movement from a Neoplatonist matter/spirit dualism, influenced profoundly by Augustine (though not identical with his thought), to an Aristotelian hylemorphism articulated most successfully by Thomas Aquinas. But to associate an interest in memorial practice with one of these schools more than the other is misleading, as I discovered early in my study of the subject. While the Neoplatonist–Aristotelian distinction is crucial in some areas of medieval culture, it is not, I think, when it comes to this one. In fact, intellectual history, as traditionally practiced, is not the best way to go about studying the role of memory in medieval culture.

Memoria is better considered, in the context of my study, as *praxis* rather than as *doxis*. Practices are sometimes influenced by ideas (and vice versa) – chapter 4 describes one major instance of this in later medieval mnemotechnique – but they are distinct, and follow different patterns and tempos of change. Historians of rhetoric have sometimes described Memory as one of the two "technical" parts of their subject, along with Delivery, distinguishing it thereby from the "philosophical" areas of Invention, Arrangement, and Style. This classification may well have contributed to the impression that *memoria*, being merely technical, was limited in its applicability to the conditions of oral debate, as was Delivery.[28] But as the practical technique of reading and meditation, *memoria* is fundamental in medieval paideia, having even greater importance in that context than it does as a "part" of rhetoric. If my study achieves nothing else, I hope it will prevent students from ever again dismissing mnemonics and mnemotechnique with the adjective "mere," or from assuming that memory technique had no serious consequence just because it was useful and practical.

The historian Lawrence Stone has wisely remarked that all historical change is relative. Within any given period, we may stress differences or continuities. Most historians of the Middle Ages are now engaged in detailing the differences that existed among Western peoples during that immensely long stretch of time, geography, and linguistic and institutional developments that we hide within the blanket designation "the Middle Ages." In this study, I stress the continuities, though I am aware of the differing circumstances that separate the various scholars and poets whose work I discuss. I am concerned with elementary assumptions and the commonplaces which underlie the practices that are the subject of my study.

My method is, I hope, made legitimate by the nature of the topic I am studying: *memoria*, in the rich complex of practices and values that word acquired. It is also justified by the elementary nature of my subject, whose training began in one's earliest education and was basic to both reading and composition. And while this study lays some foundations, it is in fact the first of three. It must be complemented by a full study of how mnemotechnique changed over the medieval centuries (I glance at this aspect of my subject in chapter 4). The third study would consider *memoria* not as a technique but as a cultural value or "modality" (in the sense developed by A. J. Greimas) of literature, and this aspect of it is touched upon especially in chapters 5 and 6.[29]

I begin this book with an examination of two of the governing models for the operation of memory in respect to knowledge, expressed as two families of related metaphors: memory as a set of waxed tablets upon which material is inscribed; and memory as a storehouse or inventory. These models are complementary; they are also archetypal Western commonplaces. The next two chapters examine the workings of memory itself. Chapter 2 begins by considering memory's psychosomatic nature in classical and medieval psychology, its intermediary relationship between sensory information and intellectual abstraction, and its identification with habit in the ethical realm. Next, chapter 2 considers the ethical imperative attached to memory training, and ends by examining a parallel between the ancient memory system based upon placing images mentally in architectural places and the case history of a "memory artist" described by the Soviet neuropsychologist, A. R. Luria.

Chapter 3 describes several elementary schemes taught for designing a trained memory, which utilize the principle of a rigid order into which short pieces of material are placed, and consciously supplied with a network of associations, the aim being to provide a securely accessible "library" (as it was often called) known by heart. In chapter 4, I examine the circumstances in which the ancient mnemotechnique described in the *Rhetorica ad Herennium*, attributed to Cicero, was revived in the scholastic setting of the universities and by the early humanists, and examine carefully three scholastic arts of memory that seem to show how an essentially medieval mnemotechnique was married (somewhat awkwardly) to principles of the ancient architectural scheme. I have provided, in appendices, English translations of three medieval texts that are not easily available now, but are important descriptions of various memory techniques. They are Hugh of St. Victor's preface to his elementary Biblical *Chronicle*; a discussion of the nature of memory and memory technique by Albertus Magnus; and an "Art of Memory" by the English cleric, Thomas Bradwardine.

The last part of this book turns from the theory and practice of mnemotechnique itself to examine why it was held in such esteem. Here I define in detail the important institutional role of *memoria*, first in relation to reading and then in the context of the activity of composition. These related discussions in chapters 5 and 6 clarify how literature was thought to contribute to the ethical life of the individual and to the public memory of society. Finally, in chapter 7, I examine how the memorial needs of readers and the memorial nature of literature affect the presentation and layout of the text in the physical book itself.

I would like to acknowledge at this point certain works whose influence on my opinions came as I was working out the earliest parts of this study, and is consequently more profound than may be entirely evident from my notes: Paul Ricoeur, *The Rule of Metaphor*; Jacques Derrida, "White Mythology"; Wesley Trimpi, *Muses of One Mind*; Gerald Bruns, *Inventions*; Richard Rorty, *Philosophy and the Mirror of Nature*; Clifford Geertz, *The Interpretation of Cultures*; A. J. Greimas, *On Meaning*; Jean Leclercq, *The Love of Learning and the Desire for God*; the studies of ancient and early medieval education by H.-I. Marrou and Pierre Riché; and Brian Stock, *The Implications of Literacy*. I have raided the footnotes of many scholarly studies, but none more fruitfully than those of Richard and Mary Rouse. Finally, and most importantly of all, any work on artificial memory systems must begin with the studies of Frances Yates and Paolo Rossi; though mine ranges far from theirs, I could not have done without them.

Citations in the footnotes give only the author, title (or short title), and page references to works; the reader is referred to the bibliography at the back of this volume for complete reference data. I have generally used the Oxford Latin Dictionary when discussing words only within a classical context; I have used Lewis and Short's Latin Dictionary, supplemented by various word-lists and dictionaries of medieval Latin and/or the *Thesaurus linguae Latinae*, when discussing Latin words in later contexts.

My subject is complex and multifaceted; I have tried to keep my analysis adequate to it, though I know I have simplified some things, perhaps overly so. I must ask for some patience from my readers, as I follow out various strands of what is, actually, a skein. If I seem to be digressing unconscionably, I hope that they will bear with me until we come back to the main subject, enriched in understanding. (And perhaps some of the memory techniques described in my early chapters will help in remembering the parts of this discussion.) For this book can be read in at least two ways: as a history of a basic and greatly influential practice of medieval pedagogy, and as a reflection on the psychological and social value of the institution of *memoria* itself, which is in many ways the same as the institution of literature.

Models for the Memory

Readers who are familiar with a current opinion that there are radical differences between "oral culture" (based upon memory) and "literate culture" (based upon writing) may be puzzled by the very title of this book, and even consider it self-contradictory. My source, however, is Dante,[1] who was newly articulating a very old observation. Even the earliest writers I discuss did not operate within a culture that could be described as truly "oral." Yet for all these writers, memory is a central feature of knowledge – its very basis in fact – whether through "recollection" (as for Plato) or as the agent building "experience" (as for Aristotle). This emphasis upon memory persists, shared by societies varying widely in the availability of books to readers: that is, in their "literacy." (I am adopting here Eric Havelock's useful definition of "literacy" as coterminous with "book-acquiring public.")[2]

In none of the evidence I have discovered is the act of writing itself regarded as a supplanter of memory, not even in Plato's *Phaedrus*. Rather books are themselves memorial cues and aids, and memory is most like a book, a written page or a wax tablet upon which something is written. Cicero writes about the relationship of writing to memory in his elementary text, *Partitiones oratoriae*:

[M]emory . . . is in a manner the twin sister of written speech [*litteratura*] and is completely similar [*persimilis*] to it, [though] in a dissimilar medium. For just as script consists of marks indicating letters and of the material on which those marks are imprinted, so the structure of memory, like a wax tablet, employs places [*loci*] and in these gathers together [*collocat*] images like letters.[3]

The metaphor of memory as a written surface is so ancient and so persistent in all Western cultures that it must, I think, be seen as a governing model or "cognitive archetype," in Max Black's phrase.[4] In the passage most familiar to the later Middle Ages, the image is used by Aristotle in his treatise *De memoria et reminiscentia*. A memory is a mental picture (phantasm; Latin *simulacrum* or *imago*) of a sort which Aristotle defines clearly in *De anima*, an "appearance" which is inscribed in a physical way upon that part of the body which constitutes memory. This phantasm is the final product of the entire process of sense perception, whether its origin be visual or auditory, tactile or olfactory. Every sort of sense perception ends up in the form of a phantasm in memory. And how is this "mental picture" produced? "The change that occurs marks [the body] in a sort of imprint, as it were, of the sense-image, *as people do who seal things with signet-rings*" (my emphasis).[5] In this particular passage, Aristotle uses, in addition to his usual word phantasm, the word *eikón* or "copy," which he qualifies by calling it "a sort of *eikón*." His language here derives in turn from Plato, who uses several of the same words in his own descriptions of what constitutes the physiological process of memory. As Richard Sorabji notes, for Plato, too, recollection involved "the seeing of internal pictures" which are imprinted upon the memory as if with signet rings.[6]

The idea that the memory stores, sorts, and retrieves material through the use of some kind of mental image was not attacked until the eighteenth century.[7] It has recently been vigorously revived by certain cognitive psychologists, some of whose experimental work provides startling apparent corroboration of ancient observations concerning what is useful for recollection.[8] According to the early writers, retention and retrieval are stimulated best by visual means, and the visual form of sense perception is what gives stability and permanence to memory storage. They do not talk of "auditory memory" or "tactile memory" as distinct from "visual memory," the way some moderns do.[9] The sources of what is in memory are diverse, but what happens to an impression or an idea once it gets into the brain is a single process resulting in the production of a phantasm that can be "seen" and "scanned" by "the eye of the mind." This sort of language is constant and pervasive in writings on the subject from earliest times. Albertus Magnus, for instance, writes that "something is not secure enough by hearing, but it is made firm by seeing." And he quotes Horace to the effect that "things intrusted to the ear / Impress our minds less vividly than what is exposed / To our trustworthy eyes."[10]

A major source of confusion for proponents of the opinion that a "literate consciousness" replaced an earlier oral one lies in their frequent failure to distinguish this very matter, the generic cause from the physiological cause (if I may, on the verge of an Aristotelian analysis, freely adapt some Aristotelian categories). In discussing the acts of memory, we can be concerned with three quite separate matters: first, what is the actual origin of information entering the brain; second, how is that information encoded, and is it in a way that physically affects our brain tissue; and third, how is its recollection best stimulated and secured, or what kind of heuristic devices are necessary for us to find it again once it has been stored? As I have already indicated, according to the Greek tradition, all perceptions however presented to the mind are encoded as *phantasmata*, "representations" or a "kind of *eikón*."[11] Because they are themselves "sort-of pictures," these representations were thought to be best retained for recollection by marking them in an order that was "readable," a process the ancients thought to be most like the act of seeing.

Evidently, at least in the context of this metaphor, reading was considered to be essentially a visual act, despite the fact that most ordinary social reading, at least, was done aloud by someone to a group of listeners, throughout antiquity and until the Renaissance. None the less, as they understood the process, whatever enters the mind changes into a "see-able" form for storing in memory. Jerome describes it well and typically in his commentary on Ezekiel 40:4 ("And the man said unto me, Son of man, behold with thine eyes, and hear with thine ears, and set thine heart upon all that I shall shew thee; for to the intent that I might shew them unto thee art thou brought hither.") "Nothing," Jerome writes, "that you have seen or heard is useful, however, unless you deposit what you should see and hear in the treasury of your memory. When indeed he says, *all that I shall shew thee*, he makes his listener attentive, and also makes (these things) prepared for the eyes of his heart, so that he may hold in memory those things shown to him, *for to the intent that I might shew them unto thee art thou brought hither*."[12]

Material presented acoustically is turned into visual form so frequently and persistently, even when the subject is sound itself, that the phenomenon amounts to a recognizable trope. Guido d'Arezzo, the eleventh-century Benedictine music master whose annotation schemes profoundly influenced the writing of music, likens the values of the chord to the letters of the alphabet – one writes with each: "Just as in all writing there are four-and-twenty letters, so in all melody we have seven notes."[13] The note recalls a *vox* or sound, just as the written letter does. In his *Teseida*, Boccaccio describes how Palemone's prayer to Venus takes on human shape as his words rise up. This "shape" walks around the gardens and temple of Venus, and petitions the goddess, while the speaker himself remains corporeally below (Bk 7, 50–69). And in Chaucer's *The House of Fame*, gossip-spread tales pass through the House of Rumour until, acquiring a feathered body, they "creep" through a window and "fly" away (*HF*, iii, 2,081–2,087).

I want to distinguish very carefully here between "pictorial" and "visual."[14] Memories could be marked by pictorial means; the ancient system described in *Rhetorica ad Herennium* was precisely that. But pictures are not the only sorts of objects we can see. We also see written words and numbers, punctuation marks, and blotches of color; if we read music, we can see it as notes on the staff; if we play the piano by ear, we can see music as the position of our fingers. Moreover, we can manipulate such information in ways that make it possible to bring it together or separate it in a variety of ways, to collate, classify, compose, and sort it in order to create new ideas or deconstruct old ones.

One accomplishment which seems always to have been greatly admired by both ancient and medieval writers was the ability to recite a text backwards as well as forwards, or to skip around in it in a systematic way, without becoming lost or confused. The ability to do this marked the difference between merely being able to imitate something (to reproduce it exactly) and really knowing it, being able to recall it in various ways.

Such reports are common enough throughout the period of my study. For example, Augustine describes a school friend named Simplicius:

an excellent man of remarkable memory, who, when he might be asked by us for all the next-to-last verses in each book of Virgil, responded in order quickly and from memory. If we then asked him to recite the verse before each of those, he did. And we believed that he could recite Virgil backwards. If we desired a commonplace concerning any topic, we asked him to make one and he did. If we wanted even prose passages from whatever of Cicero's orations he had committed to memory, that also he could do; he followed in order however many divisions [*versus*] we wanted, backwards and forwards. When we wondered (about his abilities), he testified that he had not known God could do this before this proof from experience.[15]

Notice that what is unusual to Augustine is not that Simplicius knew all of Virgil and much of Cicero, nor that he could manipulate these texts, but the *degree* to which he could do so – pulling single verses of Virgil out of context, composing commonplaces on any topic, running extensively backwards as well as forwards through various lengthy texts. The proof of a good memory lies not in the simple retention even of large amounts of material; rather, it is the ability to move it about instantly, directly, and securely that is admired.

To produce this facility, memory must be trained as though it were a kind of calculative ability, manipulating letters, bits of text, and commonplaces in addition to numbers. Such manipulation can only be accomplished if the materials can in some sense be internally "read." Try the following two exercises. First, recite from memory the first verse of Psalm 23 ("The Lord is my shepherd; I shall not want") in normal order, and then backwards word by word. Next, whistle a short phrase from "Mary Had a Little Lamb" in normal order, and then backwards note by note. It is possible to scan both the words and the musical phrase backwards, but the music must be rendered in a form that makes the relations of pitch able to be "read" in a way similar mentally to reading the words backwards. For instance, if one assigns the musical values of the first phrase to the three joints of one finger, one will find that one is as easily able to perform the musical exercise as the recitational one. This is the principle of the so-called "Guidonian hand," associated with Guido d'Arezzo (though probably older), in which the musical values of the gamut are assigned to various locations on the left hand. Drawings of it appear in many musical texts through the late Renaissance.[16] Visual coding, like writing, allows the memory to be organized securely for accurate recollection of a sort that permits not just reduplication of the original material, but sorting, analysis, and mixing as well, genuine learning, in short, rather than simple repetition.[17]

It might be useful to pause a moment here in order to clarify certain terms I have occasion to use throughout this work. First, I wish to clarify the distinction between memory understood as the ability to reproduce something exactly ("rote") and memory as recollection or reminiscence. Second, and related to the pre-modern understanding of reminiscence, I want to clarify the distinction I make between the adjectives "heuristic" and "hermeneutical."

Modern experimental psychology, focusing on the behavior and capacity of "short-term" memory, has encouraged an understanding of memory that identifies it with the ability to reproduce exactly the items in a series, carefully excluding from its concerns the ability to reconstruct such information, whether logically or by a mnemonic scheme.[18] This is not at all what pre-modern writers meant by "memory." The distinction is clear in Albertus Magnus's commentary on Aristotle's *De memoria et reminiscentia*. Albertus says that the iteration, or rote repetition, of knowledge is not at all a task of *memorial* recollection or "memoria." He defines reminiscence or recollection as the "tracking-down" (*investigatio*) of what has been "set aside" (*obliti*) through and by means of the memory; this process differs in nature from "rote repetition" (*iterata scientia*). Recollection occurs consciously through association: one finds or hunts out the stored memory-impressions by using other things associated with it either through a logical connection or through "habit" (*consuetudo*), the sort of associations taught by the various *artes memorativa*. Rote repetition, since it is not "found out" by any heuristic scheme, is not considered recollection or true memory (*memoria*).[19]

Chaucer's Summoner is a familiar example of mechanical, rote reiteration (*CT*, I, 637–643); he can repeat a few Latin phrases heard in court, but Chaucer comments that a jay can cry "Wat" as well as the Pope can – the Summoner's "memory" is of that sort. Notice that the Summoner is compared to a bird; animals were considered to have no true memory. It is also worth noticing that Chaucer does not use the word "rote" in connection with the Summoner's mimicry, in contrast to what he says about the trained legal memory of the Sergeant of Law (I, 323–327), who has every statute "pleyn by rote" in his memory; this made him formidable in "termes," or negotiations, because he "hadde" all cases and precedents from the time of King William on.[20]

The "art of memory" is actually the "art of recollection," for this is the task which these schemes are designed to accomplish. They answer to principles that define and describe how reminiscence occurs, what it is, and what it is supposed to do. And among those tasks, iteration *per se* was clearly not considered vital. The crucial task of recollection is *investigatio*, "tracking-down," a word related to *vestigia*, "tracks" or "footprints." All mnemonic organizational schemes are heuristic in nature. They are retrieval schemes, for the purpose of *inventio* or "finding." The word "heuristic" derives from a Greek verb meaning "to find," and I use it to mean any scheme or construct that is "valuable for stimulating or conducting empirical research but unproved or incapable of proof" itself (in the definition of Webster's *Third International Dictionary*).

Distinct from "heuristic" are the words "hermeneutic" and "iconographic." These latter two, as I use them, both refer to interpretation rather than retrieval. *Hermeneutic* refers to the methods and content of textual interpretation, especially of the Bible, and *iconographic* to the "illustration of a subject by pictures" (to quote *Webster's Third* again). The heuristic schemes might well take advantage of certain hermeneutic and/or iconographic conventions in constructing mnemonically valuable markers, but such meanings are not intrinsically necessary to mnemonic schemes. In fact, such received meanings can be more of a hindrance than not, and every writer on the subject urges students to form their own "habitual" schemes rather than relying on those of others. For the mnemonic scheme's basic function is only heuristic, to retrieve not to interpret.[21] Recollection can occur either "naturally" ("ex parte rei," as Albertus says, though we would probably use a word like "formally") or "artificially" ("ex parte consuetudinis," or as we are more likely to say "associatively"). The latter sort is generally more useful because it can organize a mass of otherwise unrelated material, like texts or sermons. The former is restricted to material that is in itself formally congruent, like a logical proof. But both sorts of schemes are heuristic, inventive, and investigatory in the classical sense.

Thinking of memory as wax or a waxed surface on which "sort-of images" are inscribed involves us in two distinct, if related, questions: what is the physical nature of such "images" and in what sense do they "represent" that which they "copy"? In the discussion which follows, I am going to reverse the order of these questions and focus first on the representational character of the memory-likenesses and then on their physical nature. Directing my analysis is the ancient observation that I have just discussed, that memory is a process most like reading written characters.

The earliest explicit use of the seal in wax model for cognition is in Plato's *Theaetetus*, although the image is not original to Plato, who says that he was developing a metaphor already implicit in Homer. In fact, Socrates is at some pains to say that his way of describing the memory as being like seals (*sémeia*) made by a signet ring is not new, but really very old. This is important because it is a model based upon how the eye sees in reading, not how the ear hears. In recollection, one *looks* at the contents of memory, rather than hearing or speaking them; the mediator is visual. Socrates says:

Imagine . . . that our minds contain a block of wax, which in this or that individual may be larger or smaller, and composed of wax that is comparatively pure or muddy, and harder in some, softer in others, and sometimes of just the right consistency. . . . Let us call it the gift of the Muses' mother, Memory, and say that whenever we wish to remember something we see or hear or conceive in our own minds, we hold this wax under the perceptions or ideas and imprint them on it as we might stamp the impression of a seal ring. Whatever is so imprinted we remember and know so long as the image remains; whatever is rubbed out or has not succeeded in leaving an impression we have forgotten and do not know.[22]

Plato's choice of phrase, "kérinon ekmagéion" (block of wax) is significant, for the noun *ekmagéion* has a long career in philosophical writing. Aristotle used it to mean "matter as a recipient of impressions" (for example, in *Metaphysics*, 988a1); it is used as a verb by Plato (in *Theaetetus*) and other philosophers to mean "mould" or "impress." It can also mean "model," and is so used by Plato in *Laws*, 800b.[23] The tablet on which the wax is spread, thickly or thinly or "just right," is the pair (though sets of as many as ten have been found) of wooden slabs fastened together, familiar to every ancient student; it was one of the oldest surfaces for writing known to the Greeks, and representations of such tablets have been found in eighth-century B.C. reliefs from Western Asia.[24] They served for memoranda of all sorts – ephemeral and occasional writing, like school notes and exercises, sketches of compositions, bills and accounts.

The root Plato uses for "seal" is *séme-*, which means "sign" or "a mark by which something is known"; it has several other more restricted meanings related to the basic one, like a "signal" as in battle, or a "badge."[25] It is significant, it seems to me, how emphatic Plato is about the "sign"-nature of his metaphor, for he repeats the idea three times in three words: the phrase translated "as we might stamp the impression of a seal ring" is in Greek "ósper daktylión sémeia ensemainoménous." So the "seal in wax" is basically a model of inscription or incising, as writing is incised upon a clay or wax or stone surface. Moreover, the forms incised symbolize information and thus are "representations" that serve a cognitive purpose, as do the representations of words, whether by phoneme or syllable or unit of sense, used in writing systems. In other words, to borrow some terms from the cognitive psychologists, the "representation" in memory is "verbal" rather than "pictorial" in nature.

The underlying implication of the metaphor of the seal in wax receives one of its fullest expressions in Cicero's *De oratore*, one of the major vehicles through which the image came to later writers like Quintilian, St. Augustine, Martianus Capella, and others. Later still, writers of the scholastic Middle Ages found it anew in the *Rhetorica ad Herennium*, ascribed by them to Cicero, and in the Latin translations and commentaries on Aristotle's *De memoria* that became available during the thirteenth century.

In Book II of *De oratore*, Antonius discusses with his friends the value of memory training. He recounts how Simonides first discovered the principles of the mnemonic technique of placing images (*imagines*) in an orderly set of architectural backgrounds (*loci*) in his memory because one day he had just left a banquet hall when the roof collapsed on it, killing all who were still there. He was able to reconstruct the guest list by recalling the location of each person's seat (*sedes*) at the table. Antonius goes on to say that sight is the keenest of all our senses (*sensum vivendi*).[26] Therefore, perception received aurally or by the other senses, or objects conceived through thought alone, "can be most easily retained in the mind if they are also conveyed to our minds by the mediation of the eyes." Of course, many things and events are of a nature that we either have not seen or cannot see what we wish to remember. In these cases, we should make them visible by marking them with a sort of image or figure (*quasi et imago et figura*).

These "mental images," the ancients say, are *sort of* figures and similitudes. The qualification is crucially important, for reasons well defined in modern philosophical discussions of the nature of mental images. Following suggestions of Wittgenstein, J. T. E. Richardson defines the representational aspect of mental images functionally rather than mimetically. What defines a mental image is not its pictorial qualities but whether its user understands it to represent a certain thing. As J. A. Fodor has written of this same subject, if asked to make a picture of a tiger I can paint a realistic portrait or I can draw a stick figure, but in both cases I understand the result to represent a tiger. "My images . . . connect with my intentions . . . I *take* them as tiger-pictures for the purposes of whatever task I have in mind."[27]

The mental image which an individual makes often has little to do with "objective" reality. Donald Norman reports on experiments with mental imaging which he has conducted, and notes that most people, when asked what city in North America is most directly across the Atlantic Ocean from Madrid, Spain, construct a mental map on which most of them say they "see" that Madrid is somewhere south of Washington, D.C. – Richmond, Virginia, or perhaps Cape Hatteras. In like manner, most place London on a line with Boston, and Paris with New York. A glance at a map shows that this mental image is clearly "wrong" as an "accurate" representation of the "real" relationship of these cities.[28] For my part, I cling to my "wrong" images no matter how often I am "corrected," because the image functions cognitively for me not as a terrestrial map but as a cultural one. I know that Madrid is "south" in Europe, and so I place it "south" in the United States. Paris, London, and New York (lined up in a row in my mental image) are aligned because they are all three cultural capitals. Given its cognitive function for me, my cultural map is perfectly "correct," and I am right not to change it.

A functional definition understands the words "representation" and "image" in ways that I think are essentially compatible with ancient understanding embodied in words like *séme-* and its derivatives, and in the subsequent, continuous development of the metaphor of mental image as writing. The "likeness" between the two terms of the metaphor is one of cognition (as a word "represents" a concept) rather than the replication of form. The structures which memory stores are not actual little pictures, but are *quasi-* pictures, "representations" in the sense that the information stored causes a physical change in the brain that encodes (the modern word) or moulds (the ancient one) it in a certain way and in a particular "place" in the brain. This "sort-of" image is then used as the basis for cognition by a process (intellection) which understands it to be a configuration standing in a certain relationship to something else – a "representation" in the cognitively functional sense, as writing represents language.

Such a distinction between objective and functional representation probably lies behind Aristotle's analysis, in 450b 11–20 of *De memoria*, of how a memory-image, which is "like an imprint or drawing in us," can also cause us to remember "what is not present." He likens the memory-drawing to a painted panel: "the figure drawn on a panel is both a figure and a copy . . . And one can contemplate it both as a figure [*zoón*] and as a copy [*eikón*]." As a figure or picture it is "an object of contemplation [*theorema*] or an image [*phantasma*]. But, in so far as it is of another thing, it is a sort of copy [*oion*

23

eikón] and a reminder [*mnemóneuma*]."[29] If, for example, there should pop into my mind a delightful composition of the letters and numbers "Psalms 23:1," I may regard it simply as a picture that I can think about for its own sake. But if this "picture" also reminds me of the words, "The Lord is my shepherd; I shall not want," then it is a signal or cue for remembering, and it "stands for" those words as a "sort-of copy" of them.

The distinction between "figure" and "copy" continued to be emphasized in both Arabic and scholastic comment upon Aristotle's text. Avicenna and Averroes address it as the distinction between regarding an image as a picture or as a portrait. What is involved in remembering is the association and recollection of previously impressed material when the original is no longer present to us. If the object should become actually present to our senses again and we can compare our mental image to it for accuracy, we are engaged in a process of *recognizing* rather than of remembering or recollecting. We might, in such a situation, be momentarily embarrassed that our mental stick-figure bore so little resemblance to the actual lineaments of the tiger we see before us. At such a moment, we are regarding our mental image as a "picture," to be judged as good or bad according as it presents a *recognizable* likeness of the original we see. As portrait, however, the mental image calls to mind someone who, by definition, is not present; its function in such circumstances is to remind or recollect to us its original. As picture, the formal characteristics of the image itself are all-important; as portrait, its recollective or heuristic *function* is paramount to everything else.[30]

The distinction which philosophers of language are now making between "formal" and "functional" views of linguistic representation is useful also as a modern restatement of the ancient distinction between "philosophical" and "rhetorical" concerns.[31] The extreme idealist or formalist thinks of language in terms of how completely it represents the tiger, and since it can never fully get that right, would rather lapse into silence than speak. The rhetorician or pragmatist, having to speak, accepts that words are all more or less in the nature of crude stick-figures, but can be used meaningfully so long as speaker and audience share a common cultural and civic bond, whether that of *civitas Romana* or *civitas Dei*, a bond forged by the memories of people and their texts. Where classical and medieval rhetorical pragmatism diverges from modern, I think, is in assigning a crucial role to a notion of comunal memory, accessed by an individual through education, which acts to "complete" uninformed individual experience. This notion is basic to Aristotle's view of politics as the life of the individual completed in society. Such assumptions put the civic bond on a historically continuous basis, and make the notion of shared meaning less arbitrary and merely occasional than most modern "functional" theories of language tend to do.

If we, in Paul Ricoeur's phrase, unpack the metaphor incorporated in the scholastic dictum, "veritas est adaequatio verbi et rei,"[32] we find that it embodies what is basically a rhetorical view of the "representational" relationship between word and thing (and we must always remember that the

Latin word *res* is not confined to objects of our senses but includes notions, opinions, and feelings) – that is, a view based on the principle of decorum.[33] *Adaequatio* is a word of relationship, "adjustment," "fitting" a word to what one wants to say. The prefix is crucial to its meaning, not a "dead" metaphor. *Aequatio* and its adjective, *aequalis*, convey the notion of iteration, "equal," identity of a formal, quantifiable sort. But in this dictum, truth contained in words is always *ad-aequatio*, getting towards identity but never achieving it. Although *adaequatio* is sometimes applied even by medieval logicians to the sorts of mathematical identities one derives from truth-tables, that is a specialized use of the word which ignores its root metaphor. *Aequatio* conceptually admits only of true or false; *adaequatio*, being a matter of relationship and not identity, admits of many grades and degrees of approximation. *Aequalitas* is an absolute and necessary state of affairs; *adaequatio*, being a matter of more-or-less, requires human judgment. *Adaequatio* is a likeness between two non-identities, and it thus has more in common with a metaphor or a heuristic use of modeling than with an equal sign.[34]

Partialness is also a characteristic of memory. This is true not only because memory and recollection proceed by means of *imagines rerum* rather than the things-themselves, but because a part of the original experience is inevitably lost or "forgotten" when the memory impresses the *imago* of a *res*. This position is common to both Aristotelians and Platonists, those who believe the mind stores and makes use only of *phantasmata* derived from the sensory mediation of "objects," and those who believe the memory also has been truly stamped by divine ideas, which humans have "forgotten" because of original sin or simply in the act of birth. Albertus Magnus writes that since recollection is of past experience, there is a "break" between the original action of memory that impresses the sensory image and its recollection. This "break" means that the original experience itself is lost, wholly or in part. Recollection thus becomes a reconstructive act, analogous to reading letters that "stand for" sounds (*voces*) that "represent" things in a more-or-less adequate, fitting way.[35] This is also to say that human understanding occurs in an occasional setting; it is not universally and eternally fixed "for ever." By their very nature signs are sensible, practical, worldly, belong to the traditional realm of rhetoric and must be understood within its procedures, most particularly the process of decorum, of fitting a word to a thing in terms that an audience will understand.[36]

Without getting too far into the intricacies of medieval signification theory, upon which much excellent work has been done in the past thirty years,[37] I would stress that the assumption behind all the theory is that signs can be meaningfully judged and interpreted. Because it recalls signs, reminiscence is an act of interpretation, inference, investigation, and reconstruction, an act like reading. But in pre-modern thought, signs only have meaning as they refer to something else. They are not also (as in most modern linguistic philosophy) inherently meaningful as parts of a self-generative, self-sustaining "system" of grammar that is universal to all human beings. In pre-modern thought, the memory phantasm is not a picture of what it represents, but neither is it "language," as modern philosophers use this term,[38] for it has no "grammar," no necessary structure of its own. The task of the recollector who is composing (and, as we will see, recollection is commonly described as an act of composition, a gathering-up into a place) is to select the most fitting and adequate words to adapt what is in his memory-store to the present occasion. Language is shaped to thought (rather than causing understanding) or, as Chaucer wrote, "The wordes moote be cosyn to the dede" (*CT*, I. 742) – cousin, not parent.

This view of the matter, so characteristically different from our own, is well demonstrated in Augustine's notion of the "inner word" or understanding, "the word which shines within" illuminated by grace, and which then must find expression in words "spoken without" in human tongues conditioned by particular times and places. Because of its very nature, the relationship between the inner truth and its human expression in language will be inexact, unequal; like the pagan orator, the Christian will also have to seek a decorum, a mean or "adequacy" or plane of congruence between these two ine-quivalencies.[39]

Most pre-modern writers thought of knowledge as a collection of truths awaiting expression in human languages, and fitted, as appropriate, to various occasions. These truths are general but can never, with the exception of a limited set of mathematical axioms, be universally or singly expressed.[40] Ethical truths especially are expressed not singly but "copiously." When one examines a typical entry in a medieval *florilegium* one finds not generalized definitions, together with illustrative citations, as in a modern dictionary. One finds under a heading such as *justicia* dozens of *dicta* and often *facta* or exemplary stories as well, each of which is a definition, or, more precisely, a way-of-saying (*dictum*) "justice." Copiousness, like decorum, is an essential part of a rhetorical understanding of the nature of human speech; indeed, copiousness and decorum are in a relationship analogous to symbiosis. The memory of an orator is like a storehouse of inventoried topics that ideally would contain all previous ways-of-saying ethical truths like "justice," "fortitude," "temperance," from which he draws in order to fit words to yet another occasion, requiring another way-of-saying. But this storehouse should be thought of as a set of bins that are empty when we are born and get filled up with a lot of "coins" or "flowers" or "nectar," whose aggregate is a meaningful if only partial "speaking" of "justice," or whatever. And each "speaking" of "justice" adds to the common store.

Thus "justice" has no single or simple meaning, but it is not thereby without meaning. It is a principle, a "starting-point," or a *res* (which in this context might best be translated "notion") one holds within oneself either through accrued experience, both individual and comunal, or through some combination of that and indwelling divine grace (to adopt Augustine's notion). This inner *res* needs to be spoken "without" in human language adjusted to occasions throughout time. Such occasional speaking will not coincide with, be fully extensive with (for a spatial notion is part of the root meaning of Latin *aequus*), the universal aggregate of "justice" that God alone knows, and in that sense it will be partial, lacking, and imperfect rather than complete. But, if its expression is "adequate," justice can be usefully, and in that sense truthfully, applied within a particular human situation. Words used by a wise speaker are the means of this application, words drawn from the copious inventory of *dicta et facta memorabilia* in the educated person's memorial *loci*.

The problem of how words "represent" *res* is related to but not identical with the question of what form the mental *imagines* or *phantasmata* take in the brain. In my next chapter I will discuss at greater length the physiological process by which such images were thought to be produced; this will get us closer still to understanding what they are, though not completely to an answer (indeed, the ancients themselves never completely defined their nature).[41] It is apparent from the metaphors they chose to model the processes of memory and perception that the *imagines* were thought in some way to occupy physical space. They are "incised" or "stamped" into matter, they are "stored" and can be recalled or reconstructed by means of memorial storage. And because each memorial phantasm is in some way physically present in the brain, it can be given a particular "address" during the process of memory storage, associations that will "send" recollection to it. Whatever else the memory image may be, it is clearly in part material; as we shall see, the physical variations of individual brains were thought to be crucial to their "talent" for storing and recalling *phantasmata*.

This assumption concerning the material, and therefore spatial, nature of memory images also helps to account for why the ancients persistently thought of *memoria* as a kind of eye-dependent reading, a visual process. There simply is no classical or Hebrew or medieval tradition regarding an "ear of the mind" equivalent to that of the "eye of the mind." The exception is the famous invocation to the monks which opens Benedict's Rule: "Ausculta, o fili, praecepta magistri, et inclina aurem cordis tui," "Listen, my son, to your master's precepts and incline the ear of your heart".[42] The image is not a general trope, however, but a literary recollection of Ps. 44:11: "Audi, filia, et vide, et inclina aurem tuam." The same verse was invoked by Jerome at the beginning of a letter (*Epist.*, 22) on virginity, and Benedict was probably thinking of that famous precedent as well. The phrase "aurem cordis" seems to be his own; it was not used by Jerome. Perhaps Benedict employed it because the Rule was to be read aloud to the monks during *collatio*, the occasion which combines eating, listening, and meditation. Elsewhere in the Rule, Benedict does not hesitate to use a meditational aid that is visual and spatial in character, the mnemonic trope of Jacob's ladder, to help recall the stages of humility (chapter 7).

Memory advice stresses the empirical observation that remembering what is aurally received is more difficult for most people than remembering what is visual, and the consequent need to "fix" the one by association with the other. Aural reception, as has often been remarked, is temporal not spatial; yet, Aristotle says, even our ability to judge time-lapses depends on a mechanism of visual comparison like that by which we judge spatial magnitude. We must construct in our minds, he says, a kind of schematic diagram, by means of which we can judge relative durations just as we similarly use memory images to judge relative size.[43]

Antonius says in Cicero's *De oratore* that we "employ the localities and images respectively as a wax tablet and the letters written on it."[44] It is highly significant, it seems to me, that although his subject is the architectural *ars memorativa*, the process continues to be understood not as one of viewing a picture or sculpture, but of reading letters. Even the most apparently pictorial of mnemonic systems are based on principles governing the nature of signs rather than on iterative copying. Most require that the "picture" relate to the word or concept it marks for recollection via a pun or homophony. The earliest Greek memory text we possess, a pre-Socratic fragment called *Dialexeis*, relies upon a sort of visualized homophony in its advice about memorizing for both "words" and "things."[45] Thus to recall the name "Pyrilampes," we should "place it on" (i.e. connect it with) *pyr* "fire" and *lampein* "to shine." To remember "things," we recall a significant figure to represent the particular theme; thus, to remember courage we fix it with a representation of Ares or Achilles. The connection between what is to be remembered and the device used to remember it is fundamentally through language, not through picture, through sign and not through mimicry. When the ancients use the word "visual" to refer to the nature of the phantasm, it is the act of reading words that they have in mind. The point is well made by John of Salisbury: "Letters however, that is their shapes [*figurae*], are in the first place signs of words [*vocum*, literally "sounds organized into words"]; then of things, which they bring to the mind through the windows of the eyes, and frequently they speak silently the sayings of those no longer present."[46]

Cicero uses the wax tablet image itself a bit later in Antonius's speech. Metrodorus of Scepsis, a man famous for his memory, said that he wrote down things to be remembered in particular places in his mind, as if he were writing letters on wax tablets.[47] The contemporaneous *Rhetorica ad Herennium*, which gives us the most detailed description of the ancient architectural mnemonic, also contains the fullest elaboration of the metaphor that likens writing on the memory to writing on wax or papyrus:

> those who have learned mnemonics can set in backgrounds what they have heard, and from these backgrounds deliver it by memory. For the backgrounds are very much like wax tablets or papyrus, the images like the letters, the arrangement and disposition of images like the script, and the delivery is like the reading.[48]

The metaphor changes slightly over the centuries to reflect the most common form of writing materials, but its tenacity in Western thought is remarkable. Martianus Capella, writing in the early fifth century when the codex had supplanted the papyrus roll as the vehicle of choice for books, advises that "what is [sent] to memory is written into areas, as if in wax and on the written page."[49] Dante writes of a "book" of memory. Nor is the image exclusively Greco-Roman, nor only in rhetorical teaching, for there is a variant of it in Proverbs 3:3 (though Proverbs does show considerable Greek influence): "Let not mercy and truth forsake thee: bind them about thy neck; write them upon the table of thine heart."[50] The Hebrew words contain the metaphor, but of course it was the Latin that was known to the Middle Ages: *describere*, "write upon" or "incise", and *tabulae*, "wax tablets" of the sort used until paper tablets fully supplanted them in Europe sometime in the fifteenth century. The appearance of the metaphor in Biblical as well as classical tradition (so it would have seemed to medieval scholars) would have considerably enhanced its prestige as a governing archetype.

In addition to demonstrating that pre-modern scholars thought of remembering as a process of mentally visualizing "signals" both of sense objects and objects of thought, this metaphor also shows that the ancients and their medieval heirs thought that each "bit" of knowledge was remembered in a particular place in the memory, which it occupied as a letter occupies space on a writing surface. The words *topos*, *sedes*, and *locus*, used in writings on logic and rhetoric as well as on mnemonics, refer fundamentally to physical locations in the brain, which are made accessible by means of an ordering system that functions somewhat like a cross between the routing systems used by programs to store, retrieve, merge, and distinguish the information in a computer's "memory," and postal addresses or library shelf-marks.[51] It is Cicero again who makes clear both the physiological nature and cognitive function of these words. In *Topica*, a work he composed from memory while on a voyage without his library, he writes:[52]

it is easy to find things that are hidden if the hiding place is pointed out and marked; similarly if we wish to track down some argument we ought to know the places or topics: for that is the name given by Aristotle to the "regions," as it were, from which arguments are drawn. Accordingly, we may define a topic as the region of an argument, and an argument as a course of reasoning which firmly establishes a matter about which there is some doubt.[53]

Aristotle did indeed think of his *topoi* as structured regions in the mind where arguments, either general or subject particular, were stored. He advises his students in *Topica* (163b) to memorize these by number, for then they will be able to take a quick and sure mental look at them (the verb he uses is *blepein*) when composing their own discourse. Particularly in *De memoria*, Aristotle emphasizes the importance of order for storing the *phantasmata* in the memory, and recommends an alphabet-based mnemotechnique (evidently both number and alphabet were known to him as providing useful bases for mnemonic heuristics). In a crux that has proved very difficult for a number of commentators (partly because of a faulty text), but that has been considerably clarified by Richard Sorabji,[54] Aristotle describes the advantage of using the order of the alphabet to organize material in the memory. If one assigns a separate letter of the alphabet to distinct pieces of information, then one can move from one bit to the next using the rigid order of the letters to organize otherwise unrelated material. In recollecting, one can start with Alpha, if one wishes. But if one wants to remember something further on, one could begin instead at Theta. Or one could begin with Zeta and move easily to its "neighbors," Eta or Epsilon.[55] It is the orderliness of the "places" that makes it possible to "read" what is "written" in the "shapes" stored in memory.

Thus far, I have discussed this ancient metaphor of the waxed tablets as though its explanation of memory processes were modeled upon a previously familiar process of writing on a physical surface. In fact, however, both ancient and medieval authors reverse the direction of this metaphor. Ancient Greek had no verb meaning "to read" as such: the verb they used, *ànagignósko*, means "to know again," "to recollect." It refers to a memory procedure. Similarly, the Latin verb used for "to read" is *lego*, which means literally "to collect" or "to gather," referring also to a memory procedure (the re-collection of "gathered" material).[56]

Like reading, writing depends on and helps memory. The shapes of letters are memorial *cues*, direct stimuli to the memory. It has been remarkable to me, and I will have occasion frequently to recall the phenomenon during this study, that none of the texts I have encountered makes the slightest distinction in kind between writing on the memory and writing on some other surface. Writing itself, the storing of information in symbolic "representations," is understood to be critical for knowing, but not its support (whether internal or external) or the implements with which it is performed. All these early writers are agreed that writing on the memory is the only writing truly valuable for one's education, literary style, reasoning ability, moral judgment, and (later) salvation, for in memorizing one writes upon a surface one has always with one. And the corollary assumption is that what one writes on the memory can be at least as orderly and accessible to thought as what is written upon a surface such as wax or parchment.

At the end of his *Phaedrus*, Plato gives one of the best statements of this assumption in antiquity. Written words, says Socrates, serve only to "remind one who knows that which the writing is concerned with."[57] The trouble with a written composition is that it becomes detached from its author, and goes off on its own, so to speak, falling into ignorant as well as learned hands. The educational value of writing thus depends upon the knowledge and quality of the person who reads it, for reading can only remind readers of what is already imprinted upon their memories, of what they alone "bring to the text," as we now say. To Socrates, "living discourse" is best; the wise man will write only "by way of pastime, collecting a store of refreshment both for his memory . . . and for all such as tread in his footsteps."[58] Two living minds can engage one another, whereas in the solitary reading of a written text the mind encounters, he implies, only itself. But Socrates allows value to writing as a way of storing experience for oneself and posterity (in a phrase which, incidentally, suggests strongly that he is thinking of something along the lines of a *florilegium*).[59]

It is in this context that Plato introduces the myth of Theuth (Thoth) and Thammuz (called Ammon in some versions). Theuth is the Egyptian god who invented calculation, number, geometry, dice – and script. He came to the king, Thammuz, to introduce his various arts, most of which were well received, but when he extolled writing, Thammuz expressed skepticism. Theuth claimed that writing was a "recipe for memory and wisdom"; Thammuz replied that it hadn't anything to do with memory at all, but merely with reminding, and was thus clearly wisdom's semblance rather than the real thing. The danger in it was that men might begin to rely upon writing instead of truly learning things by imprinting them in memory first.[60] Socrates is concerned in the whole *Phaedrus* with distinguishing between true and apparent happiness, beauty, love, and – in the end of the dialogue – rhetoric. Full of finely crafted discourse itself, the dialogue is concerned to reveal the falseness of any teaching which suggests that rhetoric should be only a matter of knowing tropes, figures, and ornaments instead of having a firm conviction of truth and knowledge of philosophy as well. In context, Plato is specifically responding to the use of textbooks with a "cookbook" approach as a substitute for live teaching. So, Thammuz objects to Theuth's "recipe" for memory by saying that it is a mere gimmick which substitutes an appearance for the substance. Textbooks substitute writing "produced by external characters which are not part of [oneself]" for writing on the memory.[61]

The ancient observation that what we do in writing is itself a kind of memory, suggests an interesting correction to the popular idea that writing, defined as the use of an alphabet, and, consequently, literacy are essential human competencies (like the ability to add) rather than techniques (like digital computation) or technologies (like silicon chips). As M. T. Clanchy says of literacy, "It has different effects [on human societies] according to circumstances and *is not a civilizing force in itself*" (my emphasis).[62] The ancients began from the twin assumptions that the mind already writes when it stores up its experience in representations, and, as a corollary, that the graphic expression of such representations is not an event of particular importance, at least for "ways of thinking about things" – no more important than the sound of an individual's voice is to his or her ability to use language. From this viewpoint, the symbolic representations that we call writing are no more than cues or triggers for the memorial "representations," also symbolic, upon which human cognition is based. And to mistake one sort of thing for the other would be a significant error. Writing something down cannot change in any significant way our mental representation of it, for it is the mental representation that gives birth to the written form, not vice versa.

From this viewpoint also anything that encodes information in order to stimulate the memory to store or retrieve information is "writing," whether it be alphabet, hieroglyph, ideogram, American Indian picture-writing, or

Inca knot-writing. Writing is as fundamental to language as is speaking. We still habitually use "he said" to mean "he wrote"; though this idiom has been adduced as evidence of deeply-buried "aural residue," it seems to me it can equally well be interpreted as an acknowledgement that both writing and speaking are expressions of a more fundamental human competency.

Clearly various societies have felt variously a need to put systems of mental representation and organization down on some surface, but the impulse to do this, and the preserved form it may take, has more to do with the complexity of their social organization, the other groups with which they come in contact, the nature of materials used and their accessibility, than with the way in which a human being is able to form and organize mental "representations" for cognition, and to understand that they *are* representations (i.e. they "stand for" something). I will later discuss a case wherein a lag of well over a millennium demonstrably exists between the common use of a particular scheme of mental organization and its first appearance in written form. Similarly, neither the prevalence nor the form of written materials in a culture should, I think, be taken as any sure indication of those people's *ability* to think in rational categories, or of the structures those categories may take. I am not suggesting that technique and technology have no effect upon human culture; this study is concerned to identify and describe a number of distinctive features in medieval literary culture which are sometimes expressed in particular techniques, such as page layout. But I try not to reify technique, and in particular I think it very important to recognize that the form in which information is presented to the mind does not necessarily constrain the way in which such information is encoded by the brain nor the ways in which it can be found and sorted. The three are distinct. Classical and medieval philosophers recognized this when they said that all information, whatever its source or form, becomes a phantasm in the brain. And those *phantasmata* are retrieved by heuristic schemes that need bear little resemblance to the form in which the information was originally received.

The idea that language is oral, that writing is not a fundamental part of it, is a modern one, enunciated by such linguists as de Saussure and Leonard Bloomfield, and then generalized into a theory of culture and even of epistemology by the French structuralists, chiefly Claude Lévi-Strauss. It has become a canon in this theory that Western culture can be divided into periods characterized by "pre-" and "post-Gutenberg man [sic]," and the dividing line is marked by a "veering toward the visual," to use Walter Ong's careening image.[63] My study will make it clear that from the earliest times medieval educators had as visual and spatial an idea of *locus* as any Ramist had, which they inherited continuously from antiquity, and indeed that concern for the lay-out of memory governed much in medieval education designed to aid the mind in forming and maintaining heuristic formats that are both spatial and visualizable.

Models for the memory

The second major metaphor used in ancient and medieval times for the educated memory was that of *thesaurus*, "storage-room," and later "strong-box." Whereas the metaphor of the seal-in-wax or written tablets was a model for the process of making the memorial phantasm and storing it in a place in the memory, this second metaphor refers both to the contents of such a memory and to its internal organization. A version of the storage room metaphor occurs in Plato's *Theaetetus*, when Socrates, explaining how one is able to recall particular pieces of information, likens the things stored in memory to pigeons housed in a pigeon-coop. This occurrence attests to the antiquity of the idea; indeed, both metaphors, equally visual, equally spatial, seem to be equally ancient as well.

In his *Institutiones*, Cassiodorus describes the structured memory, this "mirabile genus operis" or "remarkable piece of work," as a kind of inventoried set of bins or animal-pens, into which observations and knowledge, all experience of the world however derived, are sorted and contained. One should think of each "bin" as a labeled "topic" or place into which a collection of appropriate items is gathered. This "piece of work," the "topica memoriae," structures the free and liberal intellect ("conclusit"); for whatever thinking ("cogitationes") the mind will have entered upon ("intraverit"), the natural intelligence ("humanum ingenium") falls into ("cadat") one or another of these places ("in aliquid eorum").[64] The relationship which Cassiodorus conceives between structure and its content is quite clear in this passage. First is the educational structure, laid out in "topica memoriae," "places of memory," appropriate to rhetoric, dialectic, poetry, and jurisprudence – this structure gathers into one place (the trained memory) everything human knowledge has gained of the world. One is not born with this structure, nor is it passively gained; one constructs it oneself during one's education. And whatever thoughts one has will necessarily be structured by this previously laid-out inventory of experience and will find their appropriate place, each contributing its "bit" to the general store. Without the sorting structure, there is no invention, no inventory, no experience and therefore no knowledge – there is only a useless heap, what is sometimes called *silva*, the pathless "forest" of chaotic material. Memory without conscious design is like an uncatalogued library, a contradiction in terms. For memory is most like a library of texts, made accessible and useful through various consciously-applied heuristic schemes. St. Jerome writes to Meliodorus that "by careful reading and daily meditation his heart (i.e. his memory) should construct a library for Christ."[65]

Modern scholars usually translate *cogitatio* as "thought," but this conceals a crucial difference in how pre-moderns conceived of what that is from how we conceive of it. Cassiodorus says literally that "the mind enters into thoughts"; a modern would much more likely say "the mind thinks." *Cogitatio* (con + agito, "move, rouse") is defined in rhetoric (and in Greco-

Arabic somatic psychology) as a combinative or compositional activity of the mind. It necessarily uses memory because it combines *imagines* from memory's store. One should therefore think of a single *cogitatio* or "thought" as a small-scale composition, a bringing together (*con + pono*) of various "bits" (*phantasmata*) in one's inventory. The *topica* provide both content and structure for these *cogitationes*. Aristotle, and all succeeding writers, distinguishes between "general" *topica* and "particular" ones; basically, in this context, the general topics are structuring devices solely, such as comparison, contrast, and the like, while the particular topics are the collected expressions of an ethico-political concept, such as mercy, wisdom, justice, and so on. A commonplace is described as being "made" or "manufactured" – Augustine says that Simplicius, when asked for a *locus communis* on some subject, would "make" it ("de quocumque loco voluimus . . . fecit.") One does not simply parrot forth some previously recorded *dictum* word for word by rote, but builds a "topic" or "(common-)place" out of one's memorial inventory.

The *topica* provide the construction materials for thoughts, for whether one takes a simple Aristotelian position that knowledge is composed of experience constructed from many memories, or whether one shares with the (Neo)Platonists the belief that knowledge is a process of remembering the imprints of hypostatized Ideas, thoughts cannot be made without the materials in memory. For whatever memory holds occupies a *topos* or place, by the very nature of what it is, and these *topica*, like bins in a storehouse, have both contents and structure. Every topic is in this sense a mnemonic, a structure of memory and recollection.

The image of the memorial storehouse is a rich model of pre-modern mnemonic practice. It takes a number of related forms and gives rise to several allied metaphors for the activity of an educated mind, but all center upon the notion of a *designed* memory as the inventory of all experiential knowledge, and especially of those truths of ethics, polity, and law, which are "copious" in their very nature. Synonyms of *thesaurus* which are also used for the memory include *cella* or *cellula*, *arca*, *sacculus*, *scrinium*, and the Middle English word *male*, used perhaps most famously in Harry Bailly's comment to the company in *The Canterbury Tales* just after the Knight has spoken: "This gooth aright; unbokeled is the male!" It occurs again, of course, at the end of the tale-telling, when Harry Bailly cautions the Parson to "unbokele and shew us what is in thy male."[66]

Zeno the Stoic (4th–3rd century B.C.) defines memory as "thesaurismos phantasion" or "storehouse of mental images."[67] *Thesaurus* is used metaphorically both in Romans (2:5) and the Gospel of Matthew (6:19–20) in the sense of storing up intangible things for salvation, the Greek being translated by Jerome as a verb, *thesaurizare*, thus: "Nolite thesaurizare vobis thesauros in terra . . . Thesaurizate autem vobis thesauros in caelo."[68] The *Rhetorica ad Herennium* calls memory the treasurehouse of found-things, "thesauru[s] inventorum" (III, 16), referring particularly to a memory trained by the artificial scheme which the author proceeds to recommend. Quintilian, also recommending a cultivated memory, calls it "thesaurus eloquentiae" (XI, 2, 2).

But these metaphorical uses, though they clearly demonstrate the pervasiveness and antiquity of the link between *thesaurus* and a trained memory, do not help us know how a medieval student, encountering the word, might visualize the object denoted. *Thesaurus* refers both to what is in the strongbox, the "treasures," as when Augustine speaks of the treasures of countless images in his memory, "ubi sunt thesauri innumerabilium imaginum" (*Conf.*, X, 8), and to the strongbox itself. When the wise men kneel before Jesus in Matthew's account (2:11), they bring out their offerings of gold, frankincense, and myrrh from opened *thesauri*: "et apertis thesauris suis obtulerunt ei munera, aurum, thus, et myrrham."[69] The *thesauri* of the wise men are portable strongboxes such as a merchant might carry.

Cella, the word used by Geoffrey of Vinsauf for the memory (which he calls a "cellula deliciarum"), also means "storeroom," as indeed its derivative form, *cellarium*, English "cellar," still indicates. When Chaucer's Monk threatens to tell numerous tragedies "Of whiche I have an hundred in my celle" (VII, 1972), he is more likely using the word to refer to his memory "cell" or store than to the cell he lives in at home. After all, a hundred tragedies housed in his cloister cell are not going to do him any good on the road to Canterbury and having to tell a tale or two, but stories in his memory-cell are a different matter. Therefore, though virtually every editor of Chaucer has thought the Middle English word needed no gloss, it does: the Monk is saying that he has a hundred stories tucked away in his memory. The gloss is underscored by the Monk's mention two lines later of the "memorie" of tragedies made to us by "olde bookes."

But the Latin word *cella* has a number of more specialized applications that links it complexly to several other common metaphors for both the stored memory and the study of books, as well as words like *arca* and *thesaurus*. *Cellae* are stalls or nesting-places for domestic animals and birds, and, by a transference of meaning, small rooms or huts for people (whence derives the word's monastic usage, invoked by Hugh of St. Victor as a metaphor for trained memory, which he likens in his *Chronica* preface to the *cellae* of a cloister or *ambitus*). In classical Latin, a dove-cote was called a *cella columbarum*.[70] The compartments made by bees for their honey are called *cellae* (still called "cells" in English). So Virgil in his Fourth Georgic describes the various tasks of bees: "aliae purissima melle / stipant et liquido distendunt nectare cellas," "others pack the purest honey and distend the cells with liquid nectar."[71]

Bees and birds (which pre-modern natural history thought of as closely-related creatures, "flying things") are also linked by persistent associations with memory and ordered recollection. Indeed there is a long-standing chain or, perhaps the better word, a texture of metaphor that likens the placement of memory-images in a trained memory to the keeping of birds (especially pigeons) and to the honey-making of bees. Trained memory is also linked metaphorically to a library. And the chain is completed by a metaphoric connection of books in a library both to memories placed in orderly cells and to birds and bees in their celled coops and hives. These links are extensive and commonplace in Greek and Latin, as well as later languages. I hope I may be indulged for a few paragraphs while I trace some of them. My method of demonstrating these links, though hardly constituting "proof" in modern terms, may be justified its place in this study as an example of a basic memory technique called "collatio," "gathering," which builds up a network, a "texture," of associations to show a common theme.

First, pigeons. The first-century Roman writer, Junius Moderatus Columella, whose *De re rustica* is a guide to agricultural practices, calls the coop in which pigeons were kept a *cella* or *cellula*. He also uses the word *loculamenta*, and describes how such "tiers of pigeon-holes" are constructed of boards and pegs to make a structure divided into separate cells or compartments suitable for each pigeon to nest in. This structure he calls "columbis loculamenta vel cellulae."[72] The word *loculamenta* was also used at this time for bookcases. Seneca so uses it for personal bookcases; Martial uses the related word *nidus*, "nest" or "pigeon-hole," for the place where his book-seller kept copies of his work. In one of his epigrams, he says that his works can be bought easily from a book-seller: "Out of his first or second pigeon-hole [*nidus*], polished with pumice, smart in a purple covering, for five denarii he will give you Martial."[73] Another word for Roman bookcases was *forulus*, a diminutive of *forus*, meaning a "gallery" or "tier," and used by Virgil for the tiers of cells that make up a bee-hive.[74] J. W. Clark concludes that papyrus rolls were kept in shelving against a wall, in which the horizontal shelves were subdivided by verticals into pigeon-holes (*nidi, foruli, loculamenta*) "and it may be conjectured that the width of the pigeonholes would vary in accordance with the number of rolls included in a single work."[75] The English word "pigeon-holes," meaning compartments in a desk or cabinet into which papers are sorted and filed, is a recent imitation of classical usage (OED's earliest citation is late eighteenth century).[76]

In the light of this ancient association between nesting birds and "nesting" scrolls, one might reconsider Plato's other metaphor in *Theaetetus* for memory, namely, "pigeon-holes," *peristereon*. A *perister* is the familiar domestic pigeon, *columba livia*, which inhabits buildings of every sort, whether especially designed for it or not.[77] The pigeons, Plato says, stand for bits of knowledge, some in flocks, some in small groups, some solitary. When we are infants, our coops are empty, and as we acquire pieces of information, we shut them up in our enclosure – this is called "knowing."[78]

Plato is clearly being partly playful, though *peristereon* certainly belongs to the large class of "store-room" images for the memory. Birds are a common image for souls, memories, and thoughts throughout the ancient world, both classical and Hebrew. "Feathered thoughts" and "winged memories" copiously flock in the Psalms, in Virgil, and many lesser texts, though one of the best and, in the Middle Ages, most remembered is that of Boethius, *The Consolation of Philosophy*, IV, prose and meter 1.[79] But here Plato refers specifically to pigeons, not (more abstractly) souls with wings attached, like angels. Given the fundamental ancient assumption that written material in essence is an expression or extension of memory, I wonder if this *Theaetetus* image has not something also to do with the use of words and phrases meaning "pigeon-holes" and "dove-boxes" for library-cases full of various sorts of written rolls. Perhaps Plato was fancifully playing with an established metaphor which the Romans later imitated, or perhaps this helped to establish later use. The point cannot be settled. There is, however, a curious use of the word *epistylion* in Aristotle's *Constitution of Athens*. The *epistylion* is the "architrave" on which, in the Doric style, rested the characteristic entablature of metopes and triglyphs. In context, Aristotle's use of the word is a metaphoric transference, which John Edwin Sandys, the nineteenth-century classical scholar, explains as follows: "I should understand it to mean a shelf supporting a series of 'pigeon-holes,' and itself supported by wooden pedestals, in the office of the public clerk. The entablature in Doric architecture, with its originally open metopes alternating between the triglyphs, may well have suggested a metaphorical term for a shelf of 'pigeon-holes,' used for the preservation of public documents."[80] While I am engaged in this wild speculation concerning the foundations of the pigeon-hole metaphor, I think one might finally consider that open metopes would make splendid pigeon-roosts, *columba livia* being no respecter of public buildings. I realize that these are slender reeds – but there they are.

The metaphoric relationship of birds, especially pigeons, to thoughts and memories persisted in the Middle Ages, probably aided by Boethius and the Holy Spirit, as well as the dove (*columba*) released by Noah from the Ark,[81] but medieval writers do not pick up the pigeon-hole/book/memory connections, probably because the idiom fell into disuse after the codex-book was generally adopted, for codices were kept flat on horizontal shelving without verticals, in a cupboard-like structure, free-standing or (more commonly) built into a recess in the thick medieval walls – called *arca*, *armarium*, *bibliotheca*, or *columna*.[82] Bees and honey-cells, however, are a different matter.

The earliest surviving occurrence of the trope is in Longinus, but Longinus himself suggests that he is using a well-established metaphor (as indeed the use of *loculamenta* and *forulus* for both "beehive" and "bookcase" would corroborate). Quintilian likens the orator, who makes eloquence from many arts and disciplines, to a bee producing honey, "whose taste is beyond the skill of man to imitate, from different kinds of flowers and juices"; the trope is also used by Seneca, in a version I discuss at length in chapter 6.[83] Richard de Bury, the fourteenth-century English humanist and Chancellor to Edward III, seems to have thought that the metaphor lay in some way behind Virgil's poem on bee-keeping, the Fourth Georgic, because of the mnemonic associations centering in the word *cella* and its synonyms, and the trope of readers as bees.

Richard de Bury's language (if it is his, though I see no real reason to saddle Robert Holcot, in spite of that friar's own extreme inventiveness, with the preciosity of *Philobiblon*[84]) is allusive (several less kind adjectives also present themselves). He is inordinately fond, by modern taste, of elaborate allegories and learned conceits, obscure allusions, unattributed echoes, and other devices that test or flatter the learning of his readers, a style he characterizes as "stilo quidem levissimo modernorum," "in the very playful modern manner."[85] An example of it is the following description of how to read a book:

> But the written truth of books, not transient but permanent, plainly offers itself to be observed, and through the translucent spheres of the eyes [*per sphaerulas pervias*],[86] passing through the vestibule of the common sense and the atriums of imagination, it enters the bed-chamber [*thalamum*] of the intellect, laying itself down in the beds [*cubili*] of memory, where it cogenerates [*congenerat*] the eternal truth of the mind.[87]

Bury is playing with a number of traditions here, among them the newly rediscovered ancient mnemonic based on architectural "places" of memory. Wisdom in books must be memorized to be useful and truth-producing – what more light-hearted modern way to state this old adage than by a witty play with the most learned and humanistic of mnemonic arts? Hence the process of turning a sense perception into a thought is imaged on the places of a classical house: *vestibulum*, *atrium*, *thalamus*, and *cubile*. But that is not all, I think. Bury also seems to me to invoke here the Fourth Georgic particularly, for Virgil speaks of the bees' cells as "cubilia" (42, 243), and of the bees retiring for the night in their bed-chambers: "iam thalamis se composuere" (189). "Honeycombs," "bees," and "bee-hives" figure commonly as metaphors for books, book-collecting, memory, and scholarship elsewhere in *Philobiblon*, and to catch the allusion here to Virgil's bees in a discussion of memory and books would, I think, please Bury immensely. It is exactly the obscurely lumbering sort of pedantic play he found amusing.

But if Bury is being allusive, he is playing with one of the commonest medieval metaphors for study, that of a bee collecting nectar with which she makes honey to pack her *cella* or *thesaurus* with wisdom. Rhabanus Maurus, writing at the end of the ninth century, says that "Divine Scripture is a honeycomb filled with the honey of spiritual wisdom."[88] Ever alert to a bibliophilic cliché, Richard de Bury likens the labors of those who collect books to bees storing their cells with honey: "industrious bees constantly making cells of honey."[89] It seems to me that this association of bee-cells and honey, with books whose wisdom is to be packed into the compartments, *cellae* or *loci* of an ordered memory, carries over also to the metaphors that liken books and memory to fields and meadows (*campi* and *prata*) full of flowers, which the reader must cull and digest in order to store the *cella* of his memory.

In other words, one should be alert in medieval discussions of honey-bees, for a trained memory may very well lurk within the meadows and flowers, chambers, treasure-hoards, and enclosures of the hives/books. The topic has a long history among people with a classical education. Francis Bacon likens a scholar-scientist to a bee in the first chapter of his *Novum organon*; in the eighteenth century, Jonathan Swift invokes the metaphor in his preface to *The Battle of the Books*, and Isaac Watts may also have been thinking of it, however dimly, in his poem "Against Idleness and Mischief," about the "busy little bee" improving "each shining hour." And it seems to me possible that the seventeenth-century Barberini pope, Urban VIII, was making a witty pun on this long-established trope when he fastened his family's insignia, bees, to the doors of the Vatican Library, that inventory filled with the meadows, flowers, and fields of memory.

Related to the concept of "treasure-hoard" is that of "money-pouch" or *sacculus*, the metaphor for trained memory used extensively by Hugh of St. Victor and other twelfth-century writers. In a variation of the seal-in-wax metaphor, Hugh likens the making of a memory image to a coin stamped by the coiner with a likeness which gives it value and currency.[90] Coins are kept in coin-sacks. The *sacculus* is not an ordinary sack into which one dumps things any which way, but a leather moneybag with internal compartments which sort coins by their type and size. Its outer shape is unclear from what Hugh says, though its compartmentalized nature is not; it may have been like a saddlebag or a leather-bound box tied onto a horse as "males" are described in Middle English, or it might have been a much smaller, wallet-like object, as the diminutive ending suggests. In his *Dialogues Concerning the Lives and Miracles of the Italian Fathers*, Gregory the Great tells how Abbot Equitius always carried the sacred codices with him in leather bags ("in pelliceis sacculis") hung from his left and right sides, and when he met someone he would tap the fountain of Scripture and water the meadows of their memories.[91] This suggests that a *sacculus* would be something rather larger than a purse, and was used sometimes to carry books as well as coin – very precious things, useful for nourishing memories.

The word *scrinium* denotes in classical Latin a letter-case or book-box, or any chest in which papers are kept. In the late Empire it came to mean the state archives; according to the sixth-century jurist, Julian Antecessor, who lived in the time of the younger Justinian, there were four state *scrinia* or repositories, the *scrinium libellorum*, the *scrinium epistolarum*, the *scrinium dispositionum*, and the *scrinium memoriae*.[92] Monasteries, churches, and the papacy had *scrinia* where documents relating to their rights and property were kept. More generally, *scrinium* was a synonym for *thesaurus* or *fiscus*, the treasury or mint, but in Christian usage it seems to have been associated with the keeping of all valuable ecclesiastical items, including records, books, and relics – things for remembering. These meanings are still present in the English word "shrine," which derives from the Latin. Spenser's historian, Eumnestes, "of infinite remembraunce," rightly lays what he records "in his immortall scrine," both his archive and his memory.[93]

The *scrinium* was presided over by an official called the *scrinarius*. The papal court had such an office, as did larger churches and monasteries. This person was an archivist, and he also wrote official documents; thus a document is authenticated, "Scriptus per manum Petri Scrinarii sacri palati."[94] A *scrinarius* is thus often synonymous with a *secretarius*, as a *scrinium*, at least in the earlier Middle Ages, was also a *secretorium*; the words suggest a repository for (written) things that are hidden and closed away as well as precious, as treasure is laid or hidden away, most notably (for Christians) in Matthew 13:44, where the kingdom of heaven is likened to treasure hidden in a field. The connotation of hidden treasure also links up to the common metaphor for memory as a cave or recess, which we see in Augustine and Hugh (*antrum, cavus*). I have already noted that Virgil calls the beehive, into which honey is closed, a *caveus*. Likening memory to an inner room or recess is also very common in antiquity, so much so that one cannot help speculating about its connection to the architectural mnemonic described in the *Rhetorica ad Herennium*. In meditational work, Quintilian says, one should withdraw both literally into a closed inner chamber, "clausum cubiculum" (x, 3, 25), and a mental inner chamber, "secretum" (x, 3, 30), where one can concentrate in intense communion with one's recollective and compositive faculties.

An early Christian *secretorium* is described by Paulinus of Nola. A part of the church, it contained at least the Bible, and these verses were inscribed: "Si quem sancta tenet meditandi in lege voluntas / Hic poterit residens sacris intendere libris."[95] One notes the allusion to Psalm 1:2 in the invitation to meditate upon the holy law; the allusion seems to have been fairly commonly used when talking about the reading of Scripture. *Scrinium* maintained its association with books as well as saints through the Carolingian period at least. Isidore had some of his verses written on the book-cases of the episcopal palace at Seville; among them were these: "En multos libros gestant haec scrinia nostra; / Qui cupis, ecce lege, si tua vota libent," "In many books these our sacred writings lie enclosed; / Which within their presses, if they should choicely articulate your pious prayers, behold, read."[96] These books, he writes in verses on another wall, are really meadows full of thorns and flowers; if you haven't the strength to take up the thorns, take the roses instead. Take and read.[97] (Notice again the persistence of memorial meadows.) Around 794, Alcuin, complaining of the heat and politics in Rome where he had journeyed on business, wrote to a student, "O how sweet was life when we sat quietly among the shrines of wisdom, among the abundance of books, among the venerable wisdom of the Fathers."[98] Thus, as used by Isidore and Alcuin, *scrinia* has become a metaphor for books themselves, not only their repository.

Especially in the earlier Middle Ages, books were decorated in the same way as shrines, like reliquaries of saints, another memorial object. Book covers with jewels, ivory, and other precious material were used to bind Gospels and other precious books, the material making literal the book's function as a *scrinium* for its contents. The Book of Kells, for example, is said to have been originally covered with gold beaten over wood, which was wrenched from it after it was stolen in the eleventh century.[99] And it is recorded in the Book of Durrow that a silver case was made for it by Flann (d. 916), son of king Malochy of Ireland. Many jewelled book covers still exist, however, for the practice continued into the sixteenth century.[100] As a motif of illumination, jewels – often pearls, rubies, and other stones mentioned in the Bible – were commonly painted into the margins of Books of Hours at the end of the Middle Ages, an allusion to their nature as memorial shrines and *thesauri* (see figure 1).

The Middle English word *male* (Modern English "mail") is a "travelling-bag" or "pack" of leather, for leather-makers constructed them.[101] Its immediate origin is French, but it is not a Latin-derived word; cognates suggest its origin to be Germanic.[102] One could carry various items in a "male," including clothing and other gear; in the *Romance of Sir Bevis of Hamptoun* someone takes bread and meat from his "male," and in the Towneley "Prima Pastorum" a shepherd takes a roasted oxtail from his "mayll."[103] But one also carried valuables, especially gold; thus in *Havelock*, someone carries gold in his "male" on his back; Chaucer's Pardoner carries his relics in his "male"; in *Piers Plowman*, Avarice goes a-thieving in the night and riffles some pedlars' "males"; and in the earliest recorded occurrence of the word, in Layamon's *Brut*, Gordoille (Goneril) tells a servant that her father can have a "male riche" of a hundred pounds.[104]

Males also had at least some internal compartments. Thus a fifteenth-century cookbook instructs one to season with various powdered spices "of þe male"[105] – obviously powders that were separately kept. There is a leather-covered small box bound with a buckled belt and cylindrical locks in Holbein's portrait of the merchant, George Gisze, now in the Staatliche Museum, Berlin – his strongbox or *male*.[106] Such a *male* is like a *sacculus*, divided into internal compartments for ease of sorting and changing money.

When Chaucer uses the English word figuratively in *The Canterbury Tales*, it is such a "male" as I have been describing, a leather strong-box bound with a buckle, that he has in mind rather than the "pedlar's pack" that Walter Skeat, and every subsequent annotator, gives as a gloss of this word. If it is understood in the sense I am suggesting, then the metaphor becomes an English version (indeed the first recorded) of the speaker-composer opening the organized compartments of his memory to disclose its store of riches. Chaucer's metaphor seems to have been immediately and widely imitated. Thus, in *The Tale of Beryn* "Harry Bailly" asks, "Who shall be the first that shall vnlace his male / In comfort of vs all, & gyn som mery tale?"[107] (I do not claim that it was *well* imitated.)

But it is Stephen Hawes who most evidently understood this image of Chaucer's as I am suggesting it should be. In *The Pastime of Pleasure* (1517), Dame Rhetoric, whose wise advice the narrator has carefully "marked in memory" (645)[108] (that is, "tagged" as well as "stored") gives instructions on invention (composition), interesting for being among the earliest presentations in English of mnemonic teaching. Invention needs the five inward wits, Rhetoric says, the hindermost of which is "the retentyfe memory" (750), the agency that gathers together all thought. The orator hears various tales, encloses them "in due ordre" (1258) in his retentive memory, and, when he needs material, he brings forth both a tale and its moral from his store, "his closed male:"

> Yf to the orature many a sundry tale
> One after other treatably be tolde
> Than sundry ymages in his closed male
> Eche for a mater he doth than well holde
> Lyke to the tale he doth than so beholde
> And inwarde a recapytulacyon
> Of eche ymage the moralyzacyon   (1247–1253)

There are a number of interesting matters in these lines, in addition to Hawes's use of "male" as an image of the trained memory. The image which the orator makes of the sundry tales he hears is "eche for a mater," that is, memory according to the *res*, the "matter." He holds these "one after other treatably," in orderly fashion; because the memorial imprinting is "in due ordre, maner and reson," everything comes forth "eche after other withouten varyaunce." These tales are held in memory according to both the "mater" (*ad res*) and their "moralyzacyon." Here Hawes means the moral category of virtue or vice under which inwardly one "recapitulates" each "image" – literally gives it a "re-chapter" (from Latin *capitula*, "heading"), or cross-reference. In other words, one stores the tale itself and also indexes it mentally under a subject classification, advice that also occurs in some of the early thirteenth-century *artes poeticae*.

This method of memory is learned in "the poetes scole" (1267), and Hawes calls it "the memoryall arte of rethoryke" (1269), which although at first obscure will be mastered "with exercyse" (1273). An art, for a medieval scholar, was a method or set of prescriptions that added order and discipline to the pragmatic, natural activities of human beings. Hugh of St. Victor remarks in *Didascalicon* that while people certainly calculated and measured, wrote and spoke, reasoned and played music before the *artes* were introduced, the arts gave them order and enabled them to be systematically learned. Harking back to Aristotle's definition, an art is a set of precepts deduced from many experiences, which in turn result from many repeated memories: "All sciences, indeed, were matters of practice [*in usu*] before they became matters of art [*in arte*] . . . what was vague and subject to caprice . . . [was] brought into order by definite rules and precepts."[109]

The final member of the group of metaphors which I want to discuss is *arca*, the commonest and in some ways the most interesting of them all. An *arca* is basically a wooden "chest" or "box" for storage, and, like the other items, it came in several sizes and was used for varying purposes. Small *arcae* were used for transporting valuables, including books.[110] And the chests or cupboards in which books were kept in early monastic libraries were sometimes called *arcae*. So the *Regula magistri* states that books should be brought for distribution from the "arca."[111] When Hugh of St. Victor says that wisdom is stored in the "archa" of the heart, and there are many compartments in this storage-chamber, he is taking advantage specifically of the long association of *arcae* with books. Memory is not just any strongbox or storagechest – it is particularly one in which books are kept, a powerful portable library. Indeed, as John of Salisbury wrote, "the memory truly is a sort of mental bookcase, a sure and faithful custodian of perceptions."[112]

But there is another meaning of *arca* which is associated from earliest times with the process of Scriptural *lectio* and study. As *arca sapientiae*, one's memory is the ideal product of a medieval education, laid out in organized *loci*. One designs and builds one's own memory according to one's talent, opportunities, and energy. That makes it a construction, an *aedificatio*. As something to be built, the trained memory is an *arca* in the sense understood by the Biblical object called Noah's Ark, the construction of which occupies some detail in Genesis, and the Ark of the Covenant, into which the books of the Law were placed: "Take this book of the law, and put it in the side of the ark of the covenant of the Lord your God" (Deut. 31:26).[113]

The double understanding of *arca*, "chest," as both the Ark of Noah and the Ark of the Covenant is clearly set out in a painting of the Deluge in the Ashburnham Pentateuch, a manuscript of the early seventh century, possibly from North Africa (B.N. MS. N.A.L. 2334), shown in figure 2.[114] The Ark, floating above a sea full of drowned corpses, is shaped distinctly like a wooden chest with feet, its sides curved and bound with strips of red, pink, and brown, that are shown nailed to the surface boards, as leather strips were nailed to the frame of an actual chest. It has a wooden door and wooden-shuttered windows cut into it, and a wooden cover set over the box like the lid of a chest.

Philo speaks of Scriptural study as being like constructing a building[115] and the metaphor is a common one for the method of exegesis developed during the Middle Ages, whereby one builds layers of interpretation according to allegorical, moral, and mystical senses upon the foundation of the literal. A well-known example of such analysis is in Gregory the Great's *Moralia in Job*: "For first we lay a secure foundation of history; next through typological signification [allegory] we raise up in the citadel of faith a structure of our mind; on the outside as well through the grace of the moral sense, we clothe as it were the superstructure of the edifice with color."[116] By *mens* in his phrase "fabrica mentis," Gregory meant the educated, trained memory; *mens* frequently is used by medieval writers to mean the whole complex of processes occuring in the brain, including memory, that precede understanding or intellection.[117] Hugh of St. Victor uses Gregory's description in *Didascalicon*, but his most original development of it is in his treatise on Noah's Ark, "De arca Noe morali," known in several manuscripts as "De arca Noe pro arca sapientiae," "De archa intellectuali" or "De quatuor archis."[118]

It was also an exegetical commonplace to regard the development of the moral life of a Christian in terms of building a temple or church; Jerome's commentary on Ezekiel's vision of the Temple contains an elaborate example of such exegesis.[119] Hugh of St. Victor's particular genius in "De arca Noe morali" is to bring together the processes of Scriptural reading, moral development, and memory training in the single image of Noah's Ark. "I give you," he writes, "the ark of Noah as a model of spiritual building, which your eye may see outwardly so that your soul may be built inwardly in its likeness."[120] His exegesis is on three levels (a fourth is developed in the separate treatise, *De arca Noe mystica*), though the major part of the treatise is devoted to the third: first, the historical ark built by Noah; second, the ark of the Church which Christ built; and third, the "arca sapientiae," which "every day wisdom builds in our hearts out of continual meditation on the law of God."[121] Hugh's words make it clear that it is memory he means by this last "ark"; *meditatio* is the stage at which reading is memorized and changed into personal experience, and "in our hearts" was understood throughout the Middle Ages to be an adequate synonym for "in our memories," as the injunction to "write upon the tables of thy heart" makes clear. Jerome, for instance, glosses the Biblical phrase "in corde tui" as "in memoriae thesauro."[122] Jerome's comments on Ezekiel 3:5, when the prophet is instructed to "eat the book," are also of interest: "Eating the book is the starting-point of reading and of basic history. When, by diligent meditation, we store away the book of the Lord in our memorial treasury, our belly is filled spiritually and our guts are satisfied."[123] Jerome then links this action of eating the book to the story of Samson finding honey in the lion's mouth (Judges 14:8) and to Proverbs 6:8 ("Go to the bee"), read as an admonition to store the honey of Scripture in one's own memory/heart. In this way, he concludes, one imitates the prudence of the serpent and the innocence of the dove (a verse usually understood as an exegetical emblem of Ethica). The passage is an astonishingly compact memorial "gathering" or chain (*catena*) of many of the major themes which I have discussed in this chapter.

The *arca sapientiae* is constructed in the mind of each student. Hugh compares it to the *arca* of the Church, built in the eternal mind of God. In human minds, time exists, and yet by disciplined thought we can withdraw from it and in some way imitate the eternal present of God. "Thus, indeed, in our mind past, present, and future exist in thought at the same time. If therefore by a difficult program of meditation we begin to dwell in our heart, then in a certain way we withdraw from time, and, as though made dead to the world, we live within God."[124] It is clear that Hugh specifically means memory here, for it is memory that holds time. Moreover, it is through disciplined training of and communion with our memory that we build the ark/chest/library of wisdom which allows us to dwell inwardly with God, "per studium meditationis assidue," "through the hard discipline of *meditatio*." "This," Hugh concludes, "is the ark you ought to build."[125]

The *arca sapientiae* is thus the process and product of a medieval education, both the construction process and the finished structure. The ark of complete understanding ("arca intellectualis") has three compartments in it ("mansiones"), and Hugh proceeds to detail at some length the characteristics of these rooms/way-stations. The ark is, on a grand scale, the compartmentalized, thoroughly filed, labeled, and addressed mental "storagechest" described by Cassiodorus, which every scholar could carry to a library, store with a *summa* of commentary and texts, and take away with him.

At the very end of Hugh's treatise, it is clear that the Ark, as an organizing metaphor for education, has become a book itself, indeed The Book, together with the whole program of study undertaken to comprehend its wisdom and mysteries:

This ark is like to an apothecary's shop, filled with a variety of all delights. You will seek nothing in it which you will not find, and when you find one thing, you will see many more disclosed to you. Here are bountifully contained the universal works of our salvation from the beginning of the world until the end, and here is contained the condition of the universal Church. Here the narrative of historical events is woven together, here the mysteries of the sacraments are found, here are laid out the successive stages of responses, judgments, meditations, contemplations, of good works, virtues, and rewards.[126]

The triple-tiered ark is the triple mnemonic of medieval Scriptural study: *historia, allegoria, moralia*. Within its compartments are placed in orderly fashion all the gloss and commentary, the many *interpretationes*, together with the literal texts upon which they build, so that as one pulls forth one thing, a great many others are disclosed, in a systematic concordance and index. This book/ark, constructed by each student, is an "apothecary" of diverse, yet orderly material. The word *apotheca* means "storehouse," originally for wine, but extended, by Hugh's time, to mean something like a "shop," a store full of precious things laid away in order, any of which the *apothecarius* can bring forth immediately in response to a request, and indeed, bring forth a host of related things too.[127] Hugh's *arca* is both a memory and a book, the common metaphor of "storehouse" collapsing the two objects to which it simultaneously refers, as so many other ancient and medieval metaphors of this type also do.

Descriptions of the Neuropsychology of Memory

All accounts of the workings of memory written after Aristotle separate its activities into two basic processes: that of storage (in a strictly defined context, the activity to which the words *memoria* and *mnesis* are applied); and that of recollection (*reminiscentia* and *anamnesis*). In broader and more common contexts than strict philosophical definition, *memoria* is used to refer to both storage and reminiscence; indeed, described as a part of rhetoric, it refers to training and discipline in memorial and recollective technique. Though the two activities are obviously closely related, the one being dependent upon the other, I prefer to follow ancient example and discuss *memoria*, at least to some extent, separately from *reminiscentia*. Thus, this chapter is concerned first with the nature of memory-storage, of what is stored and how, and then with the question of what recollection is and how it was thought to proceed.

A caveat to this discussion should be kept in mind: the monastic traditions of the early medieval centuries in the West are not primarily concerned with the definitional problems that later occupied the scholastic philosophers, but are directed towards the practice of meditational prayer. Gillian Evans has noted that "[t]he notion of memory poses a variety of problems which seem to have held few attractions" for pre-scholastic scholars.[1] This is not because memory was unused, but rather because *memoria* was thought of as the praxis of liturgical and devotional prayer. Thus, while there are virtually no medieval treatises "De memoria" much before the twelfth century, there are a number of writings on prayer, meditation, and the study of Scripture, which employ some basic features of practical memory-work that we find also in antiquity, without evidencing much (if any) interest in the concept of memory and recollection, philosophically conceived. But the physiological descriptions of memory and recollection, most fully articulated by Aristotle and his heirs, account for certain basic themes in medieval practice and for some of the terms used in rhetoric to discuss *memoria*, such as the notion of "places," the importance of "images," and the somatic-aesthetic emphasis given to the workings of memorial storage and recollective procedure. So, without wishing to label these general practices as "Aristotelian" in any ideological sense (they appear in quite un-Aristotelian and pre-Aristotelian works too), I will discuss the Aristotelian analysis of *memoria* at some length in this chapter, despite the fact that it was not known directly in the medieval West until the late twelfth century, because it most adequately explains how and why practical mnemotechnique was supposed to work, and glosses some of its basic terminology.

THE MEMORY IMAGE

Systematic philosophical and medical discussions of what we would now call the neuropsychology of memory are solidly based, in both late antiquity and in the later Middle Ages, on the familiar descriptions by Aristotle, found chiefly in *De anima* and the short treatises on recollection, sleep, and dreaming known collectively as the *Parva naturalia*. During the Middle Ages, the Arabic and Hebrew commentaries on Aristotle, chiefly of Avicenna and Averroes, were used extensively as well. What is said about memory in the first-century A.D. medical compendium of Galen reflects these same traditions, and was the basis for medical knowledge of the workings of memory. Memory is treated in these related traditions as the final process in sensory perception, which begins with the stimulation of the five senses and becomes the material of knowledge through the activities of a series of internal functions, known to the Middle Ages as the inward sense(s).

The development of the conception of the inward sense has been ably traced by several scholars, notably H. A. Wolfson in a 1935 essay in the *Harvard Theological Review*.[2] One difficulty shared by many of these modern accounts, however, is that in so carefully delineating the subtle variations among the accounts in Aristotle and his commentators, they inevitably leave the impression that the distinctions among the various "parts" of the interior sense are more precise and absolute than in fact they are in the texts. Even Avicenna, in some ways the most careful of the Arab commentators, varies in his own use of several terms, varies even in whether he refers to "interior senses" or "interior sense."

Wolfson's essay does an admirable job of showing the complexity and variability of medieval descriptions of the interior senses, but even he does not quite convey the dimension of the problem. His table of correspondences among Arabic, Hebrew, and Latin texts of the various terms for the internal senses demonstrates his apt observation of the "remarkable care and comparative uniformity with which the technical Arabic terms are rendered into Latin."[3] But the confusing inconsistencies that do indeed exist are found not primarily in translation or the specific enumeration and definition of the parts of the internal senses, but in the varying perception of the describer concerning the function of his definitions – as physician, as philosopher, as theologian, as rhetorician, as curer of souls.

The explanation given by the ancient and medieval writers for how the mind knows and what kinds of knowledge it is capable of must be understood in the context within which the various works on the soul were written. Even philosophical works are products of their time, and it is important to acknowledge their cultural matrix. Students of history have long recognized that philosophical answers are specific to time and place, but one needs also to keep in mind that philosophers have not, in fact, asked "eternal questions."[4] The questions themselves proceed from assumptions embedded deeply within a culture's habits of mind, those presuppositions about human and cosmic nature that are absorbed in earliest education and often survive to color in some degree all subsequent experience, even of the rarest individuals.

One fundamental assumption that lay behind the psychological questions framed by Aristotle's medieval heirs was that human beings have two distinct kinds of knowledge, of "singulars" or particular material things, and of abstract principles or concepts. Discussions of the "internal senses" address the problem of how people know their own experience(s) in terms of how we can come to understand abstract concepts when the input to our brains is in the form of individual sensory impressions. A second assumption within which psychological explorations were framed was that the whole sensing process, from initial reception by a sense-organ to awareness of, response to, and memory of it, is somatic or bodily in nature.[5] Finally, Aristotelians, in particular, assume that everything created, even knowledge, has an immediate, proximate material cause. Aristotle says that acts of recollection occur "because one change is of a nature to happen after another," either of necessity or by habit.[6] Such a statement makes sense only when read in the context of his belief that things are caused by and cause other things, one after another, contiguously or proximately.

The medical interest in the improvement and maintenance of memory is a continuing theme in ancient and medieval writings on the subject. One of the most popular Renaissance "arts of memory" was written by Mattheolus, a physician of Perugia. That memory and recollection could best be understood as a physical process involving physical organs is both fundamental to the whole idea of memory *training*, and quite foreign to much post-Cartesian epistemology: it will be helpful, therefore, to begin with the "anatomy" of memory. All the different interior faculties, wits, or senses described in ancient philosophical and medical literature after Galen are operations of one organ, the brain. Aristotle, and the medical tradition in which he wrote, supposed that two organs were involved in the production of memories: the heart, which received all externally-derived impressions, and the brain, to which this information was relayed and where it was stored.[7] The controversy over whether the brain or heart was primary was resolved medically in the Alexandrine schools. Herophilus of Chalcedon and Erasistratus of Ceos described (perhaps after human dissection) two parallel systems in the body, one of blood vessels that centered in the heart, and the other of spinal marrow and nerves that centered in the brain. To the brain was attributed sensitivity, motion, and neurological functioning and to the heart warmth and "vital spirit." This model of human physiology prevailed for nearly two thousand years.[8]

But, even though the physiology of consciousness was known to occur entirely in the brain, the metaphoric use of "heart" for memory persisted.

Descriptions of the neuropsychology of memory

"Memory" as "heart" was encoded in the common Latin verb *recordari*, meaning "to recollect." Varro, the second-century BC grammarian, says that the etymology of the verb is from *revocare* "to call back" and *cor* "heart."[9] The Latin verb evolved into the Italian *ricordarsi*, and clearly influenced the early use in English of "heart" for "memory." Chaucer often uses the phrase "by heart" as we still use it, and while he was perhaps echoing the medieval French phrase "par coeur," there are also much earlier uses of the metaphor in English. The Middle English Dictionary records an early twelfth century example of "herte" to mean "memory"; there is an Old English use of "heart" to mean "the place where thoughts occur," *cogitationes*.[10] Since the common Old English verb meaning "to remember" was made from the noun *mynde*, "mind," it seems probable that the metaphorical extension to memory of the English word *heorte* was made on the direct analogy of the Latin metaphor in *recordari* and its derivatives. Certainly, the existence of *recordari* in Latin is the justification for Jerome's assertion that, in the appropriate Biblical contexts, *cor* is a common metaphor for *memory*.

Neither Aristotle nor Augustine nor Thomas Aquinas had a conception of "mind" or "mental activity" like ours.[11] "Soul" is not always the same thing as "mind," as most moderns who are not philosophers are inclined to think. In an essay on the development of the "mind-body problem," Wallace Matson calls attention to Aristotle's comment in *De anima*, "If the eye were a living creature, its soul would be its vision [or its ability to see]."[12] Aristotle's fundamental understanding of "soul," which was preserved to a degree by his medieval descendants, was that it is not a "thing" (ghostly or not) but "a kind of organization and functioning that certain pieces of matter have." Prior to Aristotle, even the soul was thought to be a thing, "an interior double, which both pushes and orders the body around."[13] *Soul* is the whole complex of organization and function of a human being; *mind* is invoked to explain that aspect of its function relating to its ability to understand and to acquire wisdom.

For Aristotle, emotions and even judgments are in some sense physiological processes, though they are more than just that. Memory images, produced in the emotional (sensitive) part of the soul, are "physiological affections [meaning both "a change" and "a disposition to change in a certain way"], in some sense of 'is' analogous to that in which a house is bricks. But it is not 'simply' this."[14] These images "impress" the material of the receiving organ – that is a chief implication of the seal-in-wax archetype. Aristotle goes on to explain that young and old have poor memories because in each group the body is in flux and therefore does not retain images well (450a 32). Later he remarks that people whose humors are out of balance are sometimes better at recollecting than remembering or the reverse. Those who are melancholic are too fluid to retain images well and so recollect uncontrollably: "The reason for recollecting not being under their control is that just as it is no longer in people's power to stop something when they throw it, so also he who is recollecting and hunting moves a bodily thing in which the affection

49

resides." (453a 14). "Dry" people on the contrary form images more slowly but are better at retaining them, while dwarfs and people "whose upper parts are especially large" have poor memories because they have more weight resting on their perceptual organs (453a 31), and the images fail to persist.[15]

This conception of the essentially somatic nature of the memory's images continued through the Middle Ages. Medical recipes and dietary advice devoted to memory's maintenance and improvement are common. Many of these go back to classical and Arabic sources, and all reflect the basic Galenic anatomical description placing memory in the posterior ventricle of the brain. They follow ancient physiological theory in believing that the health of all organisms is best maintained through dietary manipulation of the balance of humors.[16] One of the most famous physicians of the late Middle Ages was Arnaldus de Villa Nova, Chaucer's "Arnold of Newe-Town," a Catalan who died in 1311. He translated many medical works from Arabic to Latin, and wrote several tractates of his own. His name is attached to one of the most widely printed medical compendia in the Renaissance, *Philosophi et medici summi*, though not all it contains is his.[17] He did compose a collection of medical aphorisms, "Doctrina aphorismorum," which contains some dietary prescriptions and recipes for aiding the memory, and a separate, brief treatise "De bonitate memoriae."[18] Many of the same prescriptions occur also in the fifteenth-century memory treatise which I have mentioned earlier, the "De augenda memoriae" by the physician, Mattheolus of Perugia.

Since the brain is moist and cool, it needs to be protected against overheating of all sorts. Drunkenness is especially bad, but so are all sorts of immoderate or superfluous activities, including sexual.[19] Too much *meditatio*, however, can also be bad; Arnaldus prescribes "temperate joy and honest delight" as beneficial for maintaining memory (and, as we shall see, the idea that the memory should not be crammed at one sitting, but fed temperately only until it is satisfied, not satiated, is a commonplace in teaching).[20] A diet which includes fatty meats, strong wine, vinegar and all sour things, legumes such as beans, and especially garlic, onions, and leeks is very bad for memory. (It is a wonder that Chaucer's Summoner has any mind left at all.) These are all very hot foods of the third or even fourth degrees.[21]

Generally, whatever is good for the health of the body also aids the memory, so various purges can be efficacious.[22] Mattheolus advises a seven-day regimen of drinking sugared water for several days instead of wine (since sugar was thought to have medicinal value perhaps it would seem to safeguard the water). Certain herbs, especially ginger and coriander, when chewed or taken in powdered form, are particularly good. Arnaldus and Mattheolus also suggest bathing the head in a concoction which contains laurel leaf, camomile, and a honey-derivative "de decimo in decimum diem," "every ten days" (some of these ingredients are still used in shampoos), and Arnaldus also recommends frequently bathing the feet in a similar potion.[23] Physical prescriptions, however, are secondary to the need for memory training and practice. Mattheolus's medical advice comes briefly at the end of several paragraphs devoted to the training advice of Thomas Aquinas, Hugh of St. Victor, and Cicero; Arnaldus says that the chief way to strengthen and confirm memory is through "concentration [sollicitudo] and frequent recollection of what we have seen or heard."[24]

In his discussion of memory as a function of the sensitive soul, Thomas Aquinas follows the outline of his chief sources, Avicenna and Averroes, and his master, Albertus Magnus. He enumerates the interior senses in the *Summa* during his discussion of human psychology, especially in 1a, Q. 78, article 4. Four powers are described: common sense; the fantastic (imagination: "as it were a storehouse of forms received through the senses"); the estimative; and the memorative. That power called estimative in animals is called the cogitative in humans, or the *ratio particularis*. In his "De potentia animae," cap. 4,[25] Thomas defines the powers more particularly, enumerating five this time: the *sensus communis*; *phantasia* (retentive imagination); *imaginativa* (the composing imagination); *aestimativa seu cogitativa* (called the latter in human beings and also *ratio particularis* or collectiva "intentionem individualium," the opinions, beliefs, prejudices, of a particular individual human); and *memorativa*. But the composing imagination (*imaginativa*) is elsewhere combined with *imaginatio* (or *phantasia*) and called simply *phantasia seu imaginatio*.

In addition to the memory of sensorily-perceived objects, Thomas Aquinas distinguishes a type of memory, which he calls "intellectual." This distinction arose in part to resolve the problem of how one could remember conceptions, since one's memory stored only phantasms of particular sense objects or composite images derived from particular sense objects. The type of memory which recalls abstractions, things created in thought rather than sensorily perceived, is a part of the intellect; Thomas defines it in article 6 of Q. 79 (*Summa* Ia), as "a power to keep thoughts in mind," rather than only individual things, and it is peculiar to human beings. Animals have memories too, but only of discrete experiences – they cannot generalize or predict on the basis of what they remember. But concepts "are not retained in the sense part of the soul, but rather in the body-soul unity, since sense memory is an organic act" (ad. 1). Human memory is thus both material, as it retains the impress of "likenesses," and yet more than that, for people can remember opinions and judgments, and predict things, based upon their memories.

The concept of "intellectual memory" is attributed by Thomas Aquinas to Augustine, although in *De memoria*, Aristotle distinguishes the two kinds of memory (449b 30ff), as he also does in *De anima* in his effort to qualify Plato's doctrine of recollection. Aristotle says that both concepts and "singulars" are known through images – sensory objects by the likenesses we get through our senses, and concepts by images which we associate with them. "Memory, even the memory of objects of thought, is not without an image. So memory will belong to thought in virtue of an incidental association, but in its own right to the primary perceptive part."[26] When we think of the concept "triangle," Aristotle says, we think of a triangle, even though

51

we understand our image to be a conceptual model, "as in drawing a diagram."[27] No human being is capable of thinking entirely abstractly without some sort of signifying image. Thomas Aquinas, though differing from Aristotle in how and where images for thought were retained, also believed that no human thinking could take place without some sort of image.

The two major faculties of the sensory soul which Aristotle describes in *De anima* are the common sense (*sensus communis*) and the imagination. *Sensus communis* is the receptor of all sense impressions (Avicenna defined it as "the center of all the senses both from which the senses are diverted in branches and to which they return, and it is itself truly that which experiences"[28]). It unites and compares impressions from all five external senses, but it is also the source of consciousness. It both receives the sensation of hearing a sound and realizes that hearing is taking place.[29]

While all animals have sensation, not all have imagination – yet imagination is not thought either. It is the process in all animals capable of learning (like dogs, horses, birds, and perhaps bees and spiders) whereby *phantasmata* are formed and move the creature to action. Human imagination, however, involves some quasi-rational activity, for humans are not just moved by imagination's products, but judge and form opinions about them. Human imagination is what Aristotle calls "deliberative" (*bouleutiké* or *logistiké*): "Imagination in the form of sense exists, as we have said [*De anima*, iii, ii] in other animals, but deliberative imagination only in those which can reason" (*De anima*, iii, xi, 434a 5ff). Pure sensation is always true, enjoying something of the status which contemporary philosophers accord to what some of them call "raw feels," but imagination can be false.[30] It therefore involves a slightly more "advanced" activity than the elementary sensory consciousness of the common sense.

Aristotle's definitions of the stages in the sensory/consciousness process can be classified in two ways: 1) whether or not actively conscious behavior is involved; and 2) as types of interior activity. According to the first kind of classification, *sensus communis* and imagination (in humans) are differentiated from one another; so too are "believing" and "thinking," and memory and recollection. In this classification, the "faculties" or interior senses are six in number, pairs of receptor (passive) and conscious (active) operations. But described as types of interior activity, Aristotle distinguishes only three: the activity of forming the mental images (*phantastikón*); the activity of reacting or forming opinions about these images (*dianoutikón*); and the activity of recalling those images and reactions (*mnemoneutikón*). The threefold classification of mental activity was authoritatively fixed by Galen's immensely popular medical compendium in the anterior, medial, and posterior ventricles of the brain, as described by ancient anatomists. Medieval encyclopedists, like Bartholommaeus Anglicus, often paired "passive" and "active" states of these three functions, ascribing them to these distinct areas in the brain, which were described as cavities or chambers of the brain's soft matter.[31]

Aristotle's great medieval Arabic and Hebrew commentators elaborated and, to some extent, continued to localize the somatic psychology of their Greek sources, to a degree that no student of medieval psychology can afford to ignore. Their description attempts to fill in (usually by complicating) that of Aristotle, both detailing more precisely the physical nature of the sensory process, including memory, and reifying the non-corporeal aspects of thinking, especially about abstract "knowledge-bodies" like concepts. Though they do not introduce an actual "mind-body problem," Avicenna and especially Averroes do seem to emphasize a mind-body split by their insistence that human intellect, as part of an independent "agent intellect," can directly consider abstractions. This characteristic of their psychology is usually related to the attempt, in late Alexandrine philosophy, to reconcile Plato (as Neoplatonism) to Aristotle.

Avicenna's long commentary/compendium of *De anima* and the *Parva naturalia* is the *Liber de anima*, composed in the early eleventh century and translated into Latin in the twelfth. In the fourth part, Avicenna details the powers of the soul that are involved in translating sense impressions (which he also thought to be in some way corporeal) into thought. First, there is the *sensus communis*, having the Aristotelian functions of receiving and combining external impressions and of basic consciousness (knowing that one is sensing). Next, he defines *imaginatio*, solely a retentive faculty: "that [power] detains the sensible form which is called *formalis* and *imaginatio* and it does not categorize [*lit.* separate] it in any way."[32] Scholastic writers sometimes called this function *vis formalis*, as indeed Avicenna himself does here. It is often paired with *sensus communis* and located in the paired front "ventricles" of the brain.

There is also, however, a "deliberative" kind of imagination (as Aristotle suggested), one which has a composing function, joining images together: "the construction out of images of things existent, new composite images of things non-existent, or the breaking up of images of things existent into images of things non-existent."[33] As Wolfson suggests, this is basically Aristotle's "deliberative imagination" (*phantasia logistiké* or *bouleutiké*), by which "we have the power of constructing a single image out of a number of images."[34] This power of composing an image in both humans and animals is joined to a power of judgment, whereby we form an opinion of the image we have composed. This was called in Latin *estimativa*, a translation of the Arabic word *wahm*, introduced into the classification by the Arabic Aristotelians.[35] Latin scholastic writers re-defined *estimativa* as something like "instinct" in animals, the reaction whereby a lamb, seeing a wolf for the first time, knows to fear it, or seeing its mother knows to follow her. They called the human power *cogitativa*, defined as a conscious, though pre-rational activity.[36]

Avicenna's scheme also distinguishes between the form and *intentio* of a sense-image, every such image being composed of both. Each aspect, form and *intentio*, of the sense image has its own apprehending faculty and a storehouse into which it goes. *Intentio* means opinion about or reaction to something. It also means something less definite, related to the concept in rhetorical and literary theory of "points of view." Since our knowledge comes to us through our senses, every image impressed in our memories has been filtered and mediated through our senses – it is not merely "objective." Our senses produce "affects" in us, physical changes such as emotions, and one of those "affects" is the memory itself.

Thus, to say that all memory-images are made up both of "form" and "intention" is to say that our perception of something is an inevitable, necessary part of every image we have. Our memories store "likenesses" of things as they were *when they appeared to and affected us.*[37] This analysis – we should note – requires that all memory-images have an emotional component, acquired during the process of their formation. Form and *intentio*, the completed phantasm, then are stored together as a single memory-phantasm in the *virtus custoditiva* or *virtus memorialis*, becoming the experiential basis of knowledge. Here again Avicenna is following Aristotle, who says in *Metaphysics* (i, i) that "Experience is formed of many memories."[38]

Thomas Aquinas shared the somatic psychology of his sources concerning the nature of human perception and the process whereby the soul knows; if anything, he insisted more completely than the Arabic commentators on the "embodiment" of all kinds of human knowledge.[39] All thinking utilizes the brain's phantasms: "Avicenna erred in saying that once the mind had acquired knowledge it no longer needed the senses. For we know by experience that in order to reflect on knowledge already gained we have to make use of phantasms, and that any injury to the physical apparatus underlying these will tend to prevent our using the knowledge we already have."[40] Thus all stages and varieties of knowledge for human beings, from the most concrete to the most abstract, occur in some way within a physical matrix. The phantasms are produced by *imaginatio*, the image-making power, which, like memory, is an "affection" (to use Aristotle's term) or "motion" (to use that of Averroes) of the soul, motions which are physiological although not simply that, in the way that a house is bricks but not "just bricks."[41]

In his lectures on *De anima*, Thomas describes the process of sensory perception as involving either "material" or "spiritual" change. He gives his definition in the context of his discussion of the operations of the five external senses. He says, as do his sources, that taste and touch perceive by direct contact with their objects, whereas the other three senses perceive through "media." But of those three, "the sense of sight has a special dignity; it is more spiritual and more subtle than any other sense."[42] The senses of touch and taste are composed of all four elements, as the body itself is, but the other three of air and water.[43] (Keep in mind throughout this discussion that the brain, while composed like all the body of four elements, is especially moist.) The act of perception for all the other four senses involves some kind of "material" change or addition; the organ receives material qualities directly from the object emitting them. So, in touch and taste "the organ itself grows hot or cold by contact with a hot or cold object," in smell, there is "a sort of vaporous exhalation," in hearing "movement in space" of reverberation.[44] But sight causes a wholly "spiritual" change, the likeness is received in the eye "*as a form causing knowledge*, and not merely as a form in matter."[45]

The likeness received by the eye is formed by light, the nature of which is crucially relevant to the way in which a visual "appearance" affects the eye. Thomas Aquinas says that light is neither wholly physical nor wholly spiritual, for "it is impossible that any [wholly] spiritual or intelligible nature should [fall within the apprehension of] the senses; whose power, being essentially embodied, cannot acquire knowledge of any but bodily things."[46] But light is not physical either, for it does not behave like a body having mass.[47] The likeness of an object, progressing to the eye through air, is formed by light and received "immaterially" in the following way:

the recipient receives the form into a mode of existence other than that which the form has in the agent; when, that is, the recipient's material disposition to receive form does not resemble the material disposition in the agent. In these cases, the form is taken into the recipient "without matter," the recipient being assimilated to the agent in respect of form and not in respect of matter . . . Aristotle finds an apt example of this in the imprint of a seal on wax. The disposition of the wax to the image is not the same as that of the iron or gold to the image; hence wax, he says, takes a sign, i.e. a shape or image, of what is gold or bronze, but not precisely *as* gold or bronze. For the wax takes a likeness of the gold seal in respect of the image, but not in respect of the seal's intrinsic disposition to be a gold seal. Likewise the sense . . . is not affected by a coloured stone precisely as a stone, or sweet honey precisely as honey.[48]

Once again, he says, the distinction between "spiritual change" as here described and "material change" is that in the latter case the recipient (a sense organ) "acquires a material disposition like that which was in the agent"; that is, it receives heat or cold or smell particles or reverberating air – some matter – emitted from what it is perceiving.[49]

The crucial features of Thomas's understanding of "spiritual" and "immaterial" in this context lie in his appeal to the ancient image of the seal in wax. For the wax does form itself to a physical likeness of the original seal. What he evidently means by "immaterial" is that the wax material does not become the gold or bronze of the original, *but not that nothing physical at all happens to it*. The seal's image is not ghostly like that of a photographic slide projected on a screen, but is an actual physical imprint that permanently affects the brain tissue. The phantasms are in some respect physiological; they are materially caused (in Aristotle's terms) by the physical nature of the brain. What Thomas says here he understood in terms of Aristotle's four "causes" (or aspects) of all created things: "material," "formal," "efficient," and "purposeful." What the eye takes from the object via air and light is its "formal" aspect but not its "material" one, and this aspect causes the eye to change physically, the change we call "sight." The change in the eye occurs in the same manner in which phantasms are recorded in memory, like a seal in wax.

A further context for understanding the quasi-physical nature of the phantasms is found in Thomas's comments on *De anima*, III.iii. Referring to Aristotle's statement (in William of Moerbeke's translation) that "these images dwell within and resemble sense experiences," he says, "images . . . 'dwell within' in the absence of sensible objects, as traces of actual sensations; therefore, just as sensations arouse appetitive impulses [emotions] whilst the sensed objects are present, so do images when these are absent."[50] The phantasms themselves are "movements started by actual sensations,"[51] and memory is, in definitions deriving from Aristotle, a "delayed motion that continues to exist in the soul."[52] Thus in some physical sense – just how is difficult to understand because the writers seem themselves unsure on this point – recollection involves a re-presentation of images imprinted in the matter of the brain's posterior ventricle,[53] which are then "scanned" or "seen" as objects by the intellect in some way analogous to that in which the eye perceived them in the first place. "The phantasms in the imagination are to the intellect as colours to sight; as colours provide sight with its object, so do the phantasms serve the intellect"; knowing differs from sight in that "understanding is an act proper to the soul alone, needing the body . . . only to provide its object [the phantasms]; whereas seeing and various other functions involve the compound of soul and body together."[54]

Thomas's description of how conceptual knowledge comes about is also instructive in understanding how he regards the bodily/"spiritual" nature of phantasms. We come to know a concept like "curvature" by means of an hypothesis, an "as though" proposition:

When . . . the mind understands actually anything precisely as curved, it abstracts from flesh; not that it judges the curved thing to be *not* flesh, but it understands "curved" without regard to flesh . . . And it is thus that we understand all mathematical objects, – as though they were separated from sensible matter, whilst in reality they are not so.[55]

We understand universals by considering "certain aspects . . . of sense-objects . . . in separation or distinctly, without judging them to exist separately."[56] Here Thomas rejects a Neoplatonic view that universals themselves are imprinted in the soul, and that in sense-objects we recognize or recollect these prior implantations; he also, clearly, rejects the Avicennan-Averroist view that direct knowledge of separately existing universals is possible. Indeed, he again shows himself to be a better Aristotelian than many of the commentators he was following. As Sorabji comments, Aristotle's belief that biological growth and conscious activity are both equally powers of the soul could lead to the sort of materialism which concludes that conscious activity is therefore simply another biological process. But instead, he (and Thomas Aquinas with him) "prefers to deny that biological growth is 'simply' a physical process – which is not however to say that it is a mental one [in the modern sense]. Growth is also a development towards an end. And desire, perhaps, is an efficient cause of action towards an end."[57]

Similarly, for Thomas, objects of thought (e.g. triangle, curvature, whiteness) are re-presented in the individual, psychosomatic phantasms produced by sense-objects, but they are not merely such traces in the brain. They are abstracted by a process of comparison and contrast, "related to a unity in so far as they are judged by one intellect."[58] But even in describing so purely "mental" an activity as abstraction seems to us to be, a physical analogy persists. Thomas, as we have seen, regards the production of phantasms as a process of physical changes ("motion"); thus in sight, "the colour-affected air itself modifies the pupil of the eye in a particular way, i.e. it imprints on it a likeness of some colour, and . . . the pupil, so modified, acts upon the common sense."[59]

We have followed the progress of the likeness, the seal impressed upon the stuff of *imaginatio* and memory, until it is presented to the intellect as an object of thought, not of sense only. And we have seen that Thomas regards abstracted ideas as being "as if" distinct, not as actually existing separately from the phantasms in the memory. But in his discussion of his process in *Summa theologica*, Thomas explains that because the phantasms are products and forms in sense organs, and are of individual objects, their "mode of existence" is different from that of the intellect – how then can they cause knowledge? They must somehow be impressed upon the receiving intellect as color-affected air modifies the pupil of the eye, an organ itself composed of air and water and thus able to be a medium between the light-generated, air-born likeness and the moist brain. The intellectual impression is mediated and formed

by the power of the active intellect, which by turning towards the phantasm produces in the passive intellect a certain likeness which represents, as to its specific conditions only, the thing reflected in the phantasm. It is thus that the intelligible species is said to be abstracted from the phantasm; not that the identical form which previously was in the phantasm is subsequently in the passive intellect, as a body is transferred from one place to another.[60]

Granted these serial processes are increasingly "spiritual" and "immaterial," it is still crucial to notice that for Thomas Aquinas the activity of thinking and the activity of having a sense perception are fundamentally analogous, not fundamentally different. Images, representative likenesses, are fundamental to knowing (one must have "knowledge of" something) even if they have to be produced in something which by definition has no matter to be formed. That this is so is a symptom of how basic the simile of the seal in wax was to Thomas's understanding of knowledge, perception, and memory. For St. Thomas, the soul is neither a "ghost in a machine" nor the machine itself. It is "embodied," as the form which "causes matter to be."[61]

The implications of this belief were well realized by Thomas Aquinas's great pupil, Dante, when, at the end of his *Paradiso*, memory and speech both fail him. Angels, say Dante, have no need of memory for they have continuous understanding,[62] but human beings must know by remembering physically-formed phantasms. Of direct knowledge of God, such as that indicated at the end of the *Paradiso*, the memory "can form no adequate image," in Gardner's phrase (we recall the scholastic aphorism, "veritas est adaequatio rei et verbi"), and so it fails the intellect, bringing back nothing but an inadequate shadow or impression of the vanished vision.[63] The bodily matrix of memory is also clear in Thomas Aquinas's belief that sensory memory does not survive death, for it has "no activity apart from the corporal organ."[64] The memory that is immortal is what he calls "intellectual memory," since the intellect does survive death. But this is not true memory. Intellectual memory is "the notion of memory" (a conception of having had a memory when one was still alive in one's body); after death, the soul can still regard past events which are preserved in its intellect, and it can recall these (for recollection is an intellectual activity). But it can form no new memories when it no longer has a body.[65] Because memory requires a body, the souls in Dante's *Inferno* are forever stuck in their pasts, unable to form memories or combine old ones into new thoughts (for which they would need bodily organs), yet cut off also from the continuous vision that nourishes the blessed souls and angels.

Other kinds of images were thought to arise from the imagination. It will be useful to consider these briefly, as a way of distinguishing them from memory images. Imagination produces a dream-image in a different manner, though from the same materials. Aristotle says that the mental images which come in dreams arise spontaneously, not in response to a controlled process like recollection; in fact this is their chief difference from the memory-images that are the subject of my study here. Dream-images are created by the *vis imaginativa*, as are all phantasms.[66] They are in the same class as "after images," hallucinations, and other irrational images, the product of aroused, imbalanced emotions (as perception is distorted by anger or lust) or of raw sense-data unformed by judgment (as when we "see" the land move as we ride past it). Such images are themselves just sense-data, *aisthémata*, rather than being the imprint of a sense impression after some time has elapsed, Aristotle's basic definition of a memory-phantasm. To put the matter in modern psychological terms, Aristotle does not consider that a memory is a memory until it has been securely stored in a retrievable manner in the "long-term memory." In sleep, the controlling *sensus communis*, the seat of basic awareness, "consciousness," is not functioning. So the external senses, if stimulated, produce unprocessed raw data; there are also residual "movements," effects, left over from material received during the day.[67] All of this uncontrolled material can stimulate the imagination, but with the *sensus communis* and all other judgmental activity in the inner sense suspended, the resulting mental images pose a special interpretive problem, for they must be judged after the fact, as it were, as to their truth or falsity, whether they are of divine origin, predictive of the future, or whether they are simply the body's way of adjusting the balance of humors, or the product of random, raw *aisthémata*.

While Aristotle acknowledges that some dreams can be "true," such things do not seem to interest him very much, and he says little about them. But

Descriptions of the neuropsychology of memory

Averroes and Avicenna are both greatly interested in prophetic dreams, which they regard as the province of those with especially well formed imaginations. Avicenna discusses the prophetic imagination, "that is, what is genuinely prophetic in the image-making power."[68] Dreams of the future result from a direct action of angelic intelligences upon the mind in sleep, acting upon the imagination. He also recognizes inspirations "which suddenly fall into the soul [*quae subito in animam cadunt*]," unrelated to previous knowledge or experience. Such inspiration is of various kinds, "sometimes it is from the intellect, sometimes by means of divination, and sometimes it is from poetry, and this happens according to aptitude and habit and custom."[69] These inspirations, Avicenna says, arise from causes

which assist the soul for the most part unknown and for the most part [they] are like sudden apparitions, which thus do not remain so that they can be recalled unless the soul should hasten to help them with an already-held recollection.[70]

Avicenna underlines here the relationship between the images formed in heightened states such as trances and epilepsy, in dreams, and those required in memory. The images produced during dreams and trances will disappear unless they are associated with images that are already in memory storage, already familiar and accessible to recollection. Thus even direct inspiration requires the immediate assistance of human memory, though in a way more mysterious than that of ordinary dreaming or consciously controlled recollection.

Meticulous mental imaging – mental painting, really – is a feature of trained recollection, even when one may be "recollecting" an experience recorded in someone else's words. In his *Epitome* of Aristotle's *Parva naturalia*, written about 1170, Averroes writes of individuals with peculiarly gifted powers of concentration, who can form accurate images of things only from their description by others: "In this manner, it is possible for a person to form the image of an elephant without his ever having actually seen one." Such a feat can only be achieved by all three faculties (imagination, cogitation, and memory) acting together, and is possible only for humans because it is an intellectual operation. Such concentration is "exceedingly difficult" and "will only occur in the case of those who exercise their minds in solitude." Averroes is speaking of *consciously controlled* procedures here, and it is noteworthy that he believes that the power of imagining predictively and originally can be achieved by conscious meditation as well as by sudden inspirations. But ordinarily it is in sleep or trance, or in particular cases like epilepsy, that the faculties will all unite and the dreamer "will behold the wonders of the world."[71]

Before turning the discussion directly to the processes of recollection, let me summarize for the sake of emphasis the chief features of a memory-image. Most importantly, it is "affective" in nature – that is, it is sensorily derived and emotionally charged. It is not simply an abstraction or a mental ghost, despite its critical usefulness to all rational processes. Nor does the language of computation adequately describe what a memory was thought to be – it is not a mere algorithm or schema of the sort that accounts for what a machine does, though, as we will see, many mnemonic techniques function, at least in part, like algorithms. But they are never just that. Successful memory schemes all acknowledge the importance of tagging material emotionally as well as schematically, making each memory as much as possible into a personal occasion by imprinting emotional associations like desire and fear, pleasure or discomfort, or the particular appearance of the source from which one is memorizing, whether oral (a teacher) or written (a manuscript page). Successful recollection requires that one recognize that every kind of mental representation, including those in memory, is in its composition sensory and emotional. Recollection *may employ* schemes, but it *is like* reading a book, that is, an event involving judgment and response (*intentio*) in addition to intellect.[72]

One other feature distinguishes a memory-image from every other sort. Aristotle says that, "Memory is of the past," and "all memory involves time."[73] Because time is bound into their nature – memories are presently-existing images of things that are past – memories differ from other sensorily-produced images, as recognition (of something present) differs from recollection (a matter which I discussed in chapter 1). Their temporal nature also means that memory's re-presentation is less importantly mimetic, or objectively reiterative of the original perception, than it is temporal, because it makes the past perception present. Aristotle says that we judge time-lapses and the relative duration of time by an imaging process similar to that by which we judge magnitude (449b 30ff and 452ab), by constructing a sort of scale model in the mind. Aristotle spends a good deal of his brief treatise on this particular problem, suggesting a solution which Sorabji describes in pp. 18–21. What is important to later thinkers about this discussion is Aristotle's insistence that memorial *phantasmata* are both representations of things (in the senses discussed in chapter 1) and "re-presentations" of experience no longer present. Time is a dimension of all images in the memory.

Thus, recollection was understood to be a re-enactment of experience, which involves cogitation and judgment, imagination, and emotion. Averroes and Aristotle both insist on this: "the one who recollects will experience the same pleasure or pain in this situation which he would experience were the thing existing in actuality."[74] Memory's success is heavily dependent on the recollector's skill in being able to form memory-images that are "rich" in associations, as "iconic" (to use another term from neuropsychology) as possible. All mnemonic advice stresses the benefits to be gained from forming memories as "scenes" that include personal associations. Hugh of St. Victor, for instance, stresses the need to impress the circumstances during which something was memorized as part of the associational web needed to recall it: the sort of day it is, how one feels, the gestures and appearance of one's teacher, the appearance of the manuscript page, and so on.

Descriptions of the neuropsychology of memory

RECOLLECTION

In his *Rerum memorandarum libri*, Petrarch gives the following account of the recollective abilities of one of his friends:

> It was enough for him to have seen or heard something once, he never forgot; nor did he recollect only according to *res*, but by means of the words and time and place where he had first learned it. Often we spent entire days or long nights in talking: there was no one I would rather listen to; for even after the passage of many years, if the same things were spoken of, and if I were to say much more or less or say something different, at once he would gently remind me of this and moreover correct the word in question; and when I wondered and asked just how he could have remembered it, he recalled not only the time during which he would have heard it from me, but under what shady tree, by what river-bank, along what sea shore, on the top of what hill (for I had walked long distances with him along the coasts), I recognizing each particular.[75]

Striking in this account is the friend's mnemonic use of unrelated, experiential detail to mark what we think of as "objective" information. Some contemporary psychologists are inclined to think that the memory used in reproducing information accurately (called "rote" or "semantic" memory) is unrelated to what is called "event" or personal memory, our ability to recall events from our own past, because personal memories are subject to re-creation and "inaccuracy," whereas the usefulness of "rote" memories (such as remembering that $6 \times 7 = 42$) depends exactly on their unchangingness. But in this account recollection of personal observations is used to ensure greater accuracy of memory, an accuracy which Petrarch recognizes when he acknowledges that his friend was able to correct Petrarch's own memory of the information – quotations and learning – they exchanged. Personalizing bits of information helps to distinguish one bit from another, and thus is an aspect of the "addressing" system itself. Each memorized bit, in this technique, is regarded in the first instance not as "information" to be reproduced but as a personal event, with full phenomenological status. Accuracy comes about through the act of recreating in memory the complete occasion of which the accurate quotation is a part.

The whole matter of memory error seems to be quite differently conceived by the ancients from the one that fuels modern anxieties about "making mistakes." For us, "making a mistake" of memory is a failure in accuracy, a failure exactly or "objectively" to iterate the original material. In antiquity and the Middle Ages, problems involving memory-phantasms are described as heuristic (recollective) rather than as reproductive problems, and are due to a failure to imprint the phantasm properly in the first instance, thus causing confusion and recollective loss. One must be careful to form one's *imagines* securely and distinctly in the first place, and by repetition and practice ensure that they are in "long-term" memory. One must make them sufficiently distinct from one another, and use a set order with a clearly-established beginning, like "one" or "A." One should not tire the memory by trying to memorize too much at a time, or too quickly, for this produces an over-loading problem. "Forgetting" is a technical error, due to such things as insufficient imprinting or mis-addressing, and errors of recollection are thus perceptual in nature, if the "eye of the mind" cannot see clearly or looks in the wrong place. But if one's images are clearly made, and if one's routes to them through the mass of individual phantasms stored in memory are properly marked, one will always safely and securely find one's place. As Quintilian says, "however large the number of [things] we must remember, all are linked one to another like dancers hand in hand, *and there can be no mistake* since they join what precedes to what follows, no trouble being required except the preliminary labor of memorizing" (my emphasis).[76] A common image for items associatively grouped in memory is that of *catena* or "chain"; perhaps the very notion of *texta* itself, which literally means "something woven," derives from the same mental phenomenon. And the language that describes the formation of associations as "hooking" material to other things leads to a metaphor of recollecting as fishing; as one pulls up one's line, all the fish on one's hooks come with it.

The idea also informs the common metaphorical extension in Latin of the word *silva*, "forest," to mean "a mass of unrelated and disordered material." Within his memorial "forest," a trained student, like a knowledgeable huntsman, can unerringly find the places (*loci*) where the rabbits and deer lie. Quintilian observes that:

just as all kinds of produce are not provided by every country, and as you will not succeed in finding a particular bird or beast if you are ignorant of the localities where it has its usual haunts or birthplace, as even the various kinds of fish flourish in different surroundings . . . so not every kind of argument [comes from just any place (*undique*) and for the same reason is not to be sought out in scattered and random places (*passim*)].[77]

The spatial nature of this mental search is clearer in the Latin: "ita non omne argumentum undique venit ideoque non passim quaerendum est." As the huntsman finds game and the fisherman fish, so the student finds his stored material – by knowing its "habits." Accuracy is a feature of the memory-image which is determined at the imprinting stage; Quintilian counsels having someone read aloud from a text so that one can check the accuracy of one's image of it during the process of "setting" it in the memory.

The first part of Aristotle's *De memoria* defines the nature of the memorial image and how such images are "stamped upon" the soul, like a signet ring in wax. The second part of the treatise deals with the process of recollection. For Aristotle, recollection is the active, intellectual process, distinct from the passive, receiving nature of memory. Sorabji (p. 35) suggests that Aristotle thought of it as distinct from memory in part because the Greek verb for "to recollect" is passive, "to be reminded of," and so the recollector must become the conscious agent, who associates ideas with one another, "one thing putting you in mind of something else." (Recollection does not "just happen.")

When we recollect "starting in thought from a present incident, we follow the trail in order, beginning from something similar, or contrary, or closely connected."[78] The important thing is to have a starting-point (*arché*), and to have the things to be remembered set in an order that can readily be searched: "whatever has some order, as things in mathematics do, is easily remembered."[79] This is what remembering from places (*apo topoi*) also affords, for "people go quickly from one thing to another, e.g. from milk to white, from white to air, and from this to fluid, from which one remembers autumn, the season one is seeking." The "places" Aristotle appears to be talking about in this passage are instances of individual visual or verbal associations. But another system of "places" discussed at greater length in *De memoria* is more consciously systematic.

Sometimes it is best, Aristotle says, in recollecting a series of things, to begin at a medial position because then one can remember either of the two things to each side of it. Evidently, as Sorabji comments, Aristotle is describing a mnemonic technique "done through some system of images."[80] The system Sorabji reconstructs is quite specific and elegant, in the mathematical sense of that word. Images are "placed" in threes, each triad containing (perhaps as its middle term) a numerical symbol (a similar technique is recommended in *Rhetorica ad Herennium*). The images are scanned when we need to recollect, but associating them in triads marked by an individuating device such as a number allows one to scan more quickly, by being able to skip over several sets until one arrives at a suitable starting-place; it also allows one to "visit the images that are next door on either side" ("neighboring," Sorabji's translation of *syneggus*), instead of going through a whole series one after another each time. Undoubtedly such a procedure would be useful in remembering a composition of one's own (which is the task most ancient writers on rhetoric address, as do their modern commentators) but it is equally useful as a technique for recalling the work of others, for "scanning" a treatise, for example, or a set of "common places" (*koine topoi*) which one had read and stored in one's memory library and which one wished to refer to in composing one's own work. Aristotle highly recommended the systematic cultivation of memory to his students in dialectic. According to Diogenes Laertius, he wrote a book on mnemonics, and he refers several times (notably in *De anima*, 427b) to a system of memory training, such as the familiar memorizing of "places" (*topoi*). In the *Topics*, he says he wants students to memorize arguments, definitions, and the *topoi* of argument as defined in *Topics*, II–VII; furthermore the *topoi* should be memorized by number so they can be quickly scanned during debate.[81]

It is the spatial, somatic nature of memory-images that allows for secure recollective associations to be formed, according to a variety of consciously applied techniques, training, and diligent practice. Recollection is like reasoning: Thomas Aquinas says that human beings not only have memory as animals do, as a spontaneous remembrance of things past, but they also have it in a particularly human way, as reminiscence, "a quasi-syllogistic search [*quasi syllogistice inquirendo*] among memories of things past in their individuality."[82] But because it is also a physiological process, recollection is subject to training and habituation in the manner of all physical activity. The most powerful associational connections are formed by habit, *de consuetudine*, rather than by logic, *de necessitate*. Logical reconstruction is universal to all human beings in all situations; six times seven is always forty-two, and seven times seven is seven more, or forty-nine. But, while "white" may remind me of "milk," it may remind you of "snow" and someone else of "lilies," and thus lead all three of us in different, unrelated associative chains, none of which is inherently (*de necessitate*) truer or better than another. Such chains are individually habitual, unlike 6×7. All ancient mnemonic advice takes this fact into account by counseling that any learned technique must be adapted to individual preferences and quirks. One cannot use a "canned" system, nor will every system work equally well for everyone.[83] The ability to recollect is natural to everyone, but the procedure itself is formed by *habitus*, training, and practice.

Aristotle demonstrates the associational nature of memory by observing that one sometimes can recollect something in one way and sometimes not. Sometimes, if we want to remember C, we can get to it via B, but sometimes B does not work, and we need to remember D in order to set up the "chain" that gets us to C. "The reason why one sometimes remembers and sometimes not, starting from the same position, is that it is possible to move to more than one point from the same starting point" (452a 24), for example from "white" to "milk" or "lilies." A "chain of succession" is set up in recollection, "for the impulses follow each other by custom, one after another" (451b 22). "By custom" (Sorabji's "by habit") translates the Greek "gar ethei," literally "by repetition."[84]

Thomas Aquinas and the other scholastics elaborated Aristotle's observations on the associational, "habitual," nature of recollection. Commenting on Augustine's discussion of the trinitarian nature of the human soul (memory, intellect, and will), Thomas Aquinas says that Augustine did not think of them as distinct powers but "by memory he understands the soul's habit of retention; by intelligence, the act of intellect; and by will, the act of the will." Memory is a proclivity or disposition ("habitus") of the soul rather than a power of activity itself. "As Augustine proves, we may be said to understand, will, and to love certain things, both when we actually consider them, and when we do not think of them. When they are not under our actual consideration, they are objects of our memory only, which, in his opinion, is nothing else than a habitual retention of knowledge and love."[85] The habit is a mediator between a power and its object, for "every power which may be variously directed to act, needs a habit whereby it is well disposed to its act."[86] All virtues and vices are habits, good or bad (see *ST* II–I, Q. 55). Defining memory as *habitus* makes it the key linking term between knowledge and action, conceiving of good and doing it. Memory is an essential treasure house for both the intellect and virtuous action.

In Aquinas's theology the influence of Cicero is apparent in his discussion of the four cardinal virtues,[87] whose names and attributes themselves are taken from "Tully's First and Second Rhetoric" (i.e. *De inventione* and *Ad Herennium*) though reference is also always made to *Wisdom* 8:7: "for [wisdom] teacheth temperance, and prudence, and justice, and fortitude, which are such things as men can have nothing more profitable in life."[88] Prudence, the first of them, is also called by Cicero *sapientia*, a word he used to translate the Greek *sophiá* of his sources.[89] Prudence, says the *Ad Herennium*, "is intelligence capable, by a certain judicious method, of distinguishing good and bad; likewise the knowledge of an art [*scientia cuiusdam artificie*] is called Wisdom; and again, a well-furnished memory and experience in diverse matters [*rerum multarum memoria et usus conplurium negotiorum*] is termed Wisdom."[90] Cicero himself defines prudence as:

the knowledge of what is good, what is bad and what is neither good nor bad. Its parts are memory, intelligence, and foresight. Memory is the faculty by which the mind recalls what has happened. Intelligence is the faculty by which it ascertains what is. Foresight is the faculty by which it is seen that something is going to occur before it occurs.[91]

As he adapts these texts in his own thought, Thomas Aquinas addresses the three basic meanings of prudence given in *Ad Herennium*. Classical rhetoric had defined as one aspect of prudence "the knowledge of an art," or what we now might call "know-how." In his general discussion of the nature of virtue, Thomas considers the question of whether art (artifice) can be considered as relevant to speculative knowledge or only to mechanical knowledge. He responds that even purely intellectual activities require art; for the construction of a sound syllogism, or of an appropriate style, or the work of measuring or numbering all involve something of artfulness, of craft. Art is here defined as knowing how to make something well.[92] All craft is acquired through habit (repetition), but it is an intellectual or "speculative" habit, not a moral one:

Since, therefore, habits of the speculative intellect do not perfect the appetitive part, nor prompt it in any way, but affect only the intellective part directly, they may indeed be called virtues inasmuch as they make us capable of a good activity . . . yet they are not called virtues . . . as though they ensured the right use of a power or habit. Because he possesses a habit of a theoretic science, a man is not set thereby to make good use of it . . . That he makes use of it comes from a movement of his will. Consequently a virtue which perfects the will, as charity or justice [or prudence], ensures the right use of these speculative habits [such as any art].[93]

Next, Thomas Aquinas distinguishes "know-how" from the ethical nature of prudence, thus departing from, or rather refining, as we shall see, this part of the classical description in order to emphasize and isolate clearly the essentially ethical character of prudence. As art is knowing how to make things well, prudence is knowing how to do well: "prudence stands in the same relation to . . . human acts, which lie in the effective application of powers and habits, as art does to external productions."[94] While the

definition of prudence is closely associated with that of art, in itself prudence
is a moral virtue, channeling the will and appetites, not perfecting intellectual
activities, although like all virtues it is under the control of reason. Prudence
is

a virtue of the utmost necessity for human life. To live well means acting well. In
order to perform an act well, it is not merely what a man does that matters, but also
how he does it, namely, that he acts from right choice and not merely from impulse or
passion . . . Man is directed indeed to his due end by a virtue which perfects the soul
in the appetitive part, the object of which is a good and an end. For a man to be rightly
adapted to what fits his due end, however, he needs a habit in his reason; because
counsel and choice, which are about things ordained to an end, are acts of reason.
Consequently, an intellectual virtue is needed in his reason to complement it and
make it well adjusted to these things. This virtue is prudence. And this, in consequence, is necessary for a good life . . . Art is necessary, not that the artist may lead
a good life, but so that he may produce a good and lasting work of art. Prudence is
necessary, not merely that a man may become good, but so that he may lead a good
life.[95]

Prudence involves both reason and will, an "intellectual virtue" which also
directs and "perfects" the emotional, desiring will. It requires knowledge but
it acts to shape up our ethical life so that we may live well, and not merely be
good, in the way that a carving or a building can simply "be good."

Prudence as *sapientia*, "wisdom," comprises the suitable use of all knowledge, practical and speculative – including, let it be noted here, the making of
poems. It thus includes dialectic, rhetoric, and physics, or knowledge arrived
at by arguing from probable premises, knowledge arrived at by persuading
on the basis of conjectured truth, and knowledge arrived at through demonstration.[96] This classification of all human knowledge as a part of prudence is
also found in later medieval writers, such as Brunetto Latini, who in his
Trésor states that prudence ("sapience") contains all sense and all teaching,
and it also knows all times ("tens"). Echoing *De inventione*, although he says
his immediate source is Seneca, Brunetto gives the definition of prudence we
have already noted: "c'est le tens alé par memoire, de quoi Seneque dist, ki ne
pense noient des choses alees a sa vie perdue; et du tens present par
cognoissance; et du tens a venir por porveance."[97] Prudence comprehends
not only all human knowledge but also temporality. The definition of it
given in *De inventione* makes this clear: its parts are temporally related,
memory being of what is past; intelligence of what is; foresight of what is to
come.

The temporal nature of prudence is stressed by Thomas Aquinas when he
comes to defining its exact nature; his first topic under the parts of prudence
is whether memory is one of them. He concludes that it is, for

Tully [*De invent.*, ii.53] places memory among the parts of prudence . . . Prudence
regards contingent matters of action, as stated above [II–II, Q. 47, art. 5]. Now in
such matters a man can be directed . . . by those [things] which occur in the majority
of cases. . . . But we need experience to discover what is true in the majority of cases:
wherefore the Philosopher says [*Nichomachean Ethics*, ii.1] that "intellectual virtue is

engendered and fostered by experience and time." Now experience is the result of many memories as stated in *Metaphysics*, i.1, and therefore prudence requires the memory of many things. Hence memory is a part of prudence.[98]

By memory, Thomas clearly means here not just the natural power of the sensitive soul described by Aristotle but trained memory, the memory which is a treasury of many memories.

Thomas's meaning is made apparent when one contrasts his quotation of these words from the *Metaphysics* with that of his teacher, Albertus Magnus. Albertus, citing the same *Metaphysics* passage in *De bono*, Q. II, a.1, writes that the power of experience is perfected by "multae enim memoriae euisdem rei" – many memories of the same thing – which is actually what Aristotle himself wrote.[99] When Thomas Aquinas, however, cites the same passage, he writes that experience results "ex pluribus memoriis," from several different memories. The memorial experience that founds prudence is not iterative but concatenative, "plural" in the sense of the motto of the United States, those many memories contained in the varied quantity of his sources. E K. Rand has written eloquently of their role in Thomas's compositional style:

St. Thomas has learned from many men of wisdom, but on the present occasion they are summoned to court [to discuss the nature of temperance], summoned from their chambers in his mind. I am not going to name them all, but they are hovering outside the courtroom in crowds, ancient Greeks and ancient Romans, members of all the philosophical schools, some of their poets, as we have seen, and Christian poets like Ambrose, doctors of the Roman church and of the Greek, Popes all down the line, saints and heretics – at least the mighty Origen – writers of the early Middle Ages from England, France and Spain, writers of the Renaissance of the twelfth century, writers of his own day, the Hebrew Rabbi Moses, or Maimonides, the Arabs with Averroes at their head, mystics, monastics, and metaphysicians, writers of lawbooks and decretals, Church councils and liturgy, yes, Holy Scripture, Old Testament and New and the glosses thereon.

The material from secular Roman authors alone quoted in the *Summa theologica* is remarkable: it includes Cicero, Juvenal, Ovid, Terence, Seneca, Boethius, Macrobius, Caesar, Livy, Sallust, Valerius Maximus, Varro, Vegetius, and Virgil.[100] It is an immensely rich set of memories, but it can be paralleled in any number of other medieval works. The point to realize is that Thomas's experience was consciously made up from them all, a mighty chorus of voices able to be summoned at will from the tablets of his memory. The very usefulness of memory as a treasury of knowledge and experience lies in its ability to be nurtured and trained. Memory is a "habit of retention," as Thomas says in *ST* Ia, Q. 79, article 7. Thus, "the aptitude for prudence is from our nature, while its perfection is from practice or grace. And so Cicero observes that memory not only is developed by nature alone, but owes much to art and diligence."[101]

The nature of the memorial phantasm as *passio* or *affectio animi* is important to understand, for this idea is basic to the notion of trained memory as the *habitus* that perfects, indeed makes possible the virtue of prudence or moral judgment, and to the corollary idea that memory is the faculty that presents (or re-presents) experience, the basis upon which moral judgments must be made. As the subsequent history of the words *passio* and *affectio* shows, the making and re-presentation of a *phantasm* is also closely bound up with the physiology of emotion.

Since each phantasm is a combination not only of the neutral form of the perception but of our response to it (*intentio*) concerning whether it is helpful or hurtful, the phantasm by its very nature evokes emotion. This is how the phantasm and the memory which stores it helps to cause or bring into being moral excellence and ethical judgment. Every emotion involves a change or movement, whose source is the soul, but which occurs within the body's physiological matrix: such "affects" are "movement[s] of the soul through the body," as Theodore Tracy happily translates *De anima*, 403a 24.[102] Thus the phantasm is "conceived as a controlling factor in the whole mechanism of emotion and action, with which moral excellence is concerned."

The word which Aristotle uses to classify the memorial phantasm is *pathos*, translated by William of Moerbeke as *passio*:[103] the *pathos* is what a sense perception causes in the soul as a kind of image, the having of which we call a memory.[104] Since it is a physical change or "affect," a phantasm is also an "affection" or *passio*. Memory itself is neither perception nor conception, but a "condition," *habitus* (Greek *hexis*) or "affection" (*pathos*) touched off by these, after some time has passed, and a phantasm has been formed.[105] Memory is *hexis* or *pathos* in that "it is a *state* or *affection* . . . that follows on perceiving, apprehending, experiencing, or learning" – all of which require the production of phantasms.[106] This basic connection between the process of sensation which ends in memory, and that of human emotional life is fundamental for understanding the crucial role memory was thought to have in the shaping of moral judgment and excellence of character.

In his *Nichomachean Ethics*, Aristotle says that ethical excellence, "character" (*éthos*), results from habituation or repetition (*ethos*).[107] The organism's *hexis* or *habitus* is developed by the repetition of particular emotional responses or acts performed in the past and remembered, which then predispose it to the same response in the future.[108] Vices and virtues are both habitual dispositions, formed in this way. What develops, as Tracy describes it, is a "moral organism" akin to and embodied in the physical organism.[109] Experience is made from many repeated memories, which in turn are permanent vestiges of sense perceptions: "Thus [a] sense-perception [*aisthéseos*] gives rise to [a] memory [*mnéme*], as we hold; and repeated memories of the same thing give rise to experience [*empeiría*]; because the memories, though numerically many, constitute a single experience. And experience, that is the universal when established as a whole in the soul – the One that corresponds to the Many . . . provides the starting-point of arts [*téchnes*] and sciences [*epistémes*]; art in the world of process [*génesis*] and science in the world of facts [*tó ón*]."[110] Experience – memories generalized and judged – gives rise to all knowledge, art, science, and ethical judgment, for ethical judgment, since it is based upon habit and training and applies derived principles to particular situations, is an art, and part of the "practical intellect," that is, directed to the world of process and change rather than of essence and unchanging Being (*tó ón*).

Quintilian defines *hexis* as that "assured facility" (*firma facilitas*) in any art which supplements and transcends the rules themselves, and constitutes what we call mastery. As the psychologist George Miller observed, learning can be regarded as the acquisition of "richer" and better mnemonics. Donald Norman describes a fine instance of this in posing the old problem of "cannibals and missionaries" who all want to get from one side of a river to the other, but have only a boat that carries two, and neither cannibals nor missionaries want to be left alone with one another. Their early efforts to solve this problem take his students many moves and much time, but gradually the problem is reduced to a few seconds and a half-dozen moves as the "rules" of the "art," derived from "many memories of the same thing," are worked out.[111]

Hexis is physiological, as the memory is trained to respond with certain movements, just as a dancer's muscles are, but it is also reasoned, for it is "facilitated" rather than "automatic" response. Thomas Aquinas makes this distinction between "automatic" and "considered" response the crux that differentiates the *prudentia* of humans from that of animals, for though animals have a certain kind of prudence, theirs is entirely by natural instigation ("ex eo quod instincter naturae moventur"), whereas the human virtue is "ex ratione," from considered judgment. And because this is so, human prudence requires both memory of the past and the ability to recollect it in a considered manner, for prudence (meaning something like "the ability to make wise judgments") can project into the future only because it also knows the present and remembers the past.[112]

The *hexis* or orientation of the moral organism which disposes it to act righteously is prudence. And this learned disposition or virtue in turn is the product of "repeated individual emotional responses [what I have called reactions, the *intentio*-part of each phantasm], leading to action in a variety of situations."[113] Hence, the ability of the memory to re-collect and re-present past perceptions is the foundation of all moral training and excellence of judgment. Moreover, the representation produces an emotional response; since it is an *affectio* it is experience as genuine as what initially produced it. Averroes writes of memory images, "Since that which is to be recalled is similar to the thing comprehended by [a person] in actuality, the one who recollects will experience the same pleasure or pain in this situation, which he would experience were the thing existing in actuality. It is as if he brought the thing to be recalled into effect . . . Accordingly pain can occur in connection with a thing to be recalled or pleasure too, in the same way as it would occur, were the thing existing in actuality."[114]

Trained memory (*memoria*) is "one of the conditions required for prudence," an integral or enabling part of the virtue.[115] Thomas Aquinas quotes

Tully, but he could also have quoted his own mentor, Albertus Magnus. Albertus's discussion is in some ways clearer and fuller than Thomas's, with respect to just how memory can be regarded as a habit and why it is an attribute of prudence; and so we might begin our discussion of how memory was trained in the late Middle Ages with Quaestio II, "De Partibus Prudentiae," articles one and two, of Albertus's treatise, *De bono* (translated in appendix B).

The first article of this question is "Quid sit memoria." Albertus quotes Cicero to the effect that the parts of prudence are memory, intellect, and foresight, corresponding to the three tenses. First, he considers in what way memory can be a part of prudence, since he earlier had defined memory as simply a function of the soul, not a trainable characteristic (a feature required of something that is a *habitus* and thus a virtue). Prudence is knowing how to do what is good or bad, a knowledge which in turn depends upon past experience, because we can only judge of the future by what is past. Memory can be considered in two ways, as the storage capability of the brain, or as the recollective process. As the store of what is past, memory is the nurse and engenderer of prudence and so a part thereof. As the process of recollection, memory is a habit; recollection is a natural function which can be strengthened through training and practice. This makes it truly necessary in order for prudence to exist. Albertus concludes this article by defining memory as "habitus animae rationalis," a trained facility of the rational soul.

He next considers more precisely in what way memory displays the characteristics of *habitus*, and this leads him directly to a lengthy discussion of "artificial memory," specifically the Ciceronian technique of places and images, *loci* and *imagines*, and of "memory of things" and "memory for words," taken from the "Second Rhetoric" of Tully, the *Ad Herennium*, III.[116] Albertus starts with Tully's consideration of the distinction (echoed in virtually every ancient treatise on the subject) between natural and artificial memory, that is, whether memory is a native talent merely confirmed by practice or whether it can actually be improved. He concludes, as the ancients had, that while artificial memory schemes cannot make a naturally poor memory good, they can improve and perfect the potential of a naturally sound, normal memory:

Therefore we say with Tully that the kind of memoria which relates to human life and justice is two-fold, that is, natural and trained or "artificial." That is natural which by virtue of its talent for finding-out things remembers easily something it knew or did at an earlier time. The "artificial," however, is one which is made from an orderly arrangement of images and places, and, as in everything else art and virtue are a perfection of natural talent, so also in this. What is natural is completed by training.[117]

By adopting Tully's definition of memory as a habit and the condition for prudence, which is in turn the repository of all liberal knowledge and ethics, Albertus Magnus and Thomas Aquinas both make the conscious cultivation of memory and the practice of the memorial arts a moral obligation as well as a scholarly necessity. The training of memory fits Thomas's definition of a moral virtue perfectly, such virtues being called "from *mos* in the sense of a natural or quasi-natural inclination to do some particular action. The other meaning of *mos*, i.e. 'custom,' is akin to this: because custom becomes a second nature, and produces an inclination similar to a natural one."[118]

The moral aspect of memory training is crucial to understand as we examine the role of memory throughout the medieval period. Memory could be aided by an assortment of tools, ranging from conscious mnemonic systems to written notes on wax tablets or even paper, but they were no substitute for conscious training. For the trained memory was not considered to be merely practical "know-how," a useful gimmick that one might indulge in or not (rather like buying better software). It was co-extensive with wisdom and knowledge, but it was more – as a condition of prudence, possessing a well-trained memory was morally virtuous in itself. The medieval regard for memory always has this moral force to it, analogous to the high moral power which the Romantics were later to accord to the imagination, genetrix of what is best in human nature. As I have noted, the memory feats of saints are frequently stressed in hagiography, even of saints who were not scholars (like Francis of Assisi). This was done not to show off their intellectual prowess, but to stress their moral perfection.

In this heavily Aristotelian chapter, I have, inevitably, concentrated on scholastic traditions in the theology of prudence and character. But scholars writing before the full revival of Aristotle also saw the connection between memory and the moulding of moral character, in terms explicitly of the seal-in-wax trope. Hugh of St. Victor addresses the moral education of novices in this manner:

For, [when a seal is stamped] a figure that is raised up in the seal appears depressed in the impression in the wax, and that which appears cut out in the seal is raised up in the wax. What else is shown by this, than that we who desire to be shaped up through the examples of goodness as if by a seal that is very well sculpted, discover in them certain lofty traces of deeds like projections and certain humble ones like depressions.[119]

The "dicta et facta memorabilia," exemplary deeds and words of others impressed into our memories like a seal into wax, shape our moral life in shaping our memories. One can recognize in this trope how thoroughly embedded in the neuropsychology of memory ethical action was considered to be, and how in stamping the material of the brain with both a "likeness" of sensory experience and a personal, "gut" response to it, a memory phantasm also shaped the soul and judgment.

THE ARCHITECTURAL MNEMONIC

The "places and images" scheme of artificial memory – which I call the "architectural mnemonic," a term more accurate than Frances Yates's "Ciceronian mnemonic" and less misleading than the Renaissance's "the art of memory" – is described most fully in *Rhetorica ad Herennium*, which is dated *c.* 86–82 B.C., just after Cicero's *De inventione*, and possibly composed by someone who had the same teacher as Cicero.[120] The basic system is now familiar to most scholars, thanks to the efforts of Frances Yates and Paolo Rossi, but a brief description is perhaps in order here by way of introduction. There are three chief ancient sources describing it: Cicero's *De oratore* (in which it is summarily described in Bk II, 350–360), the *Rhetorica ad Herennium*, Bk III (the most detailed account), and Bk XI of Quintilian's *Institutio*.

According to the account in *Ad Herennium*, III, the backgrounds are like wax tablets (*cerae*) or papyrus, and the arrangement of the images on them is like writing; subsequent delivery is like reading aloud. The backgrounds must be arranged in a series, a certain order, so that one cannot become confused in the order. One can thus proceed forwards from start to finish, or backwards, or start in the middle (one might recall here the artificial memory system described in Aristotle's *De memoria*, which also allows one to "scan," sort, and move about mentally in a similar way).

The formation of the backgrounds in the mind should be done with special care and precision, "so that they may cling lastingly in our memory, for the images, like letters, are effaced when we make use of them, but the backgrounds, like wax tablets, should abide." (III. xviii.31) One should practice daily seeing one's backgrounds and placing images on them. It is also useful, in order to keep track of where one is, to place a mark on every fifth or tenth one – a golden hand, or the face of a friend named Decimus. In memorizing backgrounds, one should avoid crowded places, because too many people milling about confuse and soften their outlines. Background *loci* should be well lighted but not glaring; they must not be too much alike but differ enough in form to be clearly distinguishable one from the next; they should be of moderate size and extent, "for when excessively large they render the images vague, and when too small often seem incapable of receiving an arrangement of images" (xix.32). (Notice that grouped images are placed in a "scene" on a single background.) If we are not pleased with the real backgrounds available to us, we may create some in our imagination and "obtain a most serviceable distribution of appropriate backgrounds" (xix.32).

These backgrounds should be viewed from about thirty feet away, "for, like the external eye, so the inner eye of thought is less powerful when you have moved the object of sight too near or too far away" (xix.32). Both Tully and Cicero use the word "intervallum" in articulating this rule, meaning "the distance between two points." I understand this word differently in the context of mnemotechnical advice from the way it is translated by Harry Caplan, the Loeb editor. He refers it to the distance between the background places themselves. Now, while one is advised to make these distinctive from one another in order to avoid over-lapping and confusion, the *Ad Herennium*'s author explains the need for this rule, quoted above, in terms of the viewer's ability to see an object clearly. This concern also accords with an aspect of mnemonic advice from the Middle Ages. So I understand "intervallum" to refer to the distance of the viewer from the background, optimally (according to Tully) thirty feet; it is thus a principle of perspective, the viewer's stance in relation to the background.

The images to be placed in these backgrounds are then described in detail. The principles governing their creation are consistent with ancient observations that recollection is achieved through association, and that images, especially visual ones, are more easily and permanently retained than abstract ideas. So we associate the materials of memory through a system of consciously selected visual-verbal puns or pictures, whatever will serve to fix the association of image with idea. One can use such a system to remember "things" (*memoria rerum*) or to remember "words" (*memoria verborum*). Remembering "things" means remembering the main words in quotations, the chief theses of an argument, the gist of a story, or the like. Remembering "words" means exact word-for-word memorization, and should be reserved for extracts from the poets (xix.34) – the author recommends the practice for children, and for adults only as an exercise to sharpen memory for things (xxiv). In each kind of memorizing, punning images are used to make orderly association, but he admits that word-for-word memorization in this fashion is cumbersome and burdens the mind; exact memorizing is better served by repeating a passage two or three times to set it in the memory before one begins to attach images to it (xxi.34).

Much the same advice is found in *De oratore* but more briefly because the subject "is well known and familiar" (II.87.358).[121] Visual images are the keenest of all and best retained by the memory; auditory or other perceptions are retained when attached to visual ones (87.357). Images are retained more easily than abstract thoughts, but they "require an abode," for "the embodied cannot be known without a place [*corpus intelligi sine loco non potest.*]"[122] One needs a large number of *loci* "which must be clear and [distinct] and at moderate [distances, *for* "modicis intervallis"], and images that are effective and sharply outlined and distinctive, with the capacity of encountering and speedily penetrating the mind; the ability to use these will be supplied by practice, which engenders habit . . . on the system and method of a consummate painter distinguishing the positions of objects by modifying their shapes [*modo formarum varietate locos distinguentis*]" (87.358), a phrase which Rackham, the Loeb translator, observes "denotes what we call 'perspective'."[123] One should remark here Cicero's important, though commonplace, comparison between the forming of images and painting; one should also remark that he acknowledges the importance of the viewer's perspective.

Quintilian has been sometimes regarded as skeptical of the whole idea of artificial memory, but as Frances Yates has observed this reputation is not founded.[124] He extolls memory highly – "our whole education depends upon memory [*omnis disciplina memoria constat*]" (XI.ii.1) – and believes, like all the authors of antiquity, that a natural memory can and should be cultivated by practiced techniques. "The power of memory alone brings before us all the store of precedents, rulings, sayings and facts which the orator must possess in abundance and which he must hold ready for immediate use" (xi.ii.1); it is the treasury of eloquence ("thesaurus hic eloquentiae").

Quintilian's skepticism is directed towards the image-making schemes to accomplish "memory for words," such as that described in *Ad Herennium*. How, he says, can such a cumbersome method enable one to grasp a long series of connected words, such as the five books of the second process against Verres (Cicero's *Verrine Orations*)? One cannot even represent every sort of word by an image (for instance, conjunctions). Quintilian admits that one might devise a method of shorthand symbols (*notae*) as Metrodorus is said to have devised, but he himself counsels learning a long work by dividing it into short sections, which one then memorizes one at a time, so that "by dint of frequent and continuous practice" one learns the words in each brief section, and then unites the fragments in order. He suggests embedding cues (*notae*) to stimulate the memory, especially in passages hard to recall – these cues could take the form of associated images or some other method (perhaps numerical or other *notae*). He also suggests learning a passage by heart from the same wax tablet upon which it was originally written down, thus effecting a transfer from the external tablet to the tablet of memory, and counsels reading passages aloud once or twice over "so the mind is kept alert by the sound of the voice" (ii.32–34). For memory work, the voice should not rise above a murmur, however. It also helps if another reads aloud to us so that we can test what we have memorized, identify hard passages, and mark them. By such means, he says, he has trained his own natural memory, which is not at all exceptional. And he ends with his famously skeptical assessment of reported feats of prodigious memory, such as those of Theodectes, supposed to be able to remember any number of verses after a single hearing: "we shall do well to have faith in such miracles, if only that he who believes may also hope to achieve the like" (ii, 51).

It is noteworthy that Quintilian's reservations are directed more at schemes which promise accurate memory for words than at memory for "things." This attitude is compatible with the basically ethical value given to memory training. Memory for words, like any merely iterative reproduction of items in a series, can deteriorate rather quickly into mere trickery, and is associated by Quintilian with sophistical rhetoric (a prejudice which extends at least into the thirteenth century, as we will see in chapter 4). Even Tully commends memory for words primarily as good exercise for memory for "things." *Memoria ad res* compels the recollector to actively shape up material for an occasion, whether as composer or viewer or reader, and thus is ethically more valuable, consistent with the moral emphasis given to rhetoric by Cicero, Quintilian himself, Augustine, and the traditions of monastic prayer. Especially in composition, memory for things is preferred to rote iteration, even when the speaker has accurate command of the original words. This is, of course, exactly the reverse of modern prejudice.

Quintilian's reservations concerning elaborate schemes of *loci* and *imagines* have reinforced our own modern puzzlement in the face of such an apparently cumbersome and odd procedure. Even Frances Yates, who studied these schemes so thoughtfully, confessed herself puzzled by their seemingly cluttered nature, especially that for *memoria ad verbum*. What purpose could they serve, except to show off "the vanity and boastfulness of a man who was inclined to vaunt his memory as being the result of art rather than of natural gifts," as Quintilian says of Metrodorus. Quintilian's criticism of the Greeks (and one should note that all the people whose extravagent claims he criticizes are non-Romans, though similar claims, as we know from Pliny, were current concerning the prodigious memory of Julius Caesar) is likely to have been in part a Ciceronian pose, that of the practical, sparely educated Roman, the persona adopted in *De oratore* by both Crassus and Antonius, the heroes of the dialogue, both men highly learned in Greek but affecting to despise "Greeklings." "Crassus," Cicero says, "did not so much wish to be thought to have learned nothing, as to have the reputation of looking down upon learning . . . while Antonius held that his speeches would be the more acceptable to a nation like ours, if it were thought that he had never engaged in study at all" (*De orat.*, II, 5). Quintilian, we recall, was modeling himself upon Cicero's example, against excesses of artifice and style he detected in Seneca and Tacitus. But though this literary context may help to explain Quintilian's skeptical pose regarding the Greeks, it does not help to ease our modern skepticism concerning how the system of backgrounds and images could work for many people, as it evidently did, being "well known and familiar" to Cicero's audience.

A remarkable demonstration of how it might work has come recently in psychological literature. The distinguished Soviet neuropsychologist, A. R. Luria, published a lengthy case study (*The Mind of a Mnemonist*) of a Russian journalist of prodigious memory, who became a professional "mnemonist" or performing memory-artist. Luria studied him over a thirty-year period, from the 1920s through the 1950s, testing him frequently and asking him in detail about the systems he had worked out for retention and recall. The system used by Shereshevski, the subject (whom Luria refers to as "S." in his study), was almost exactly that of the ancient architectural mnemonic, based upon "places" and "images," although he was entirely self-taught in memory arts. Luria himself seems unaware of the ancient system; at least he does not mention it. Moreover, Luria refers to an account of a Japanese mnemonist, who had also worked out a system of "placing" images very similar to that of S.[125] The study of S. gives valuable insight into the praxis of the ancient system.

Luria observes first that everything S. recalled was in the form of words (including numbers, nonsense syllables, and seen or described objects) and that he responded to hearing words by at once converting them into vivid and remarkably stable visual images. He did this on a word by word basis, so that to recall a long series of words he needed to find a way of distributing his mental images in an orderly row or sequence. He seems most often to have used a street which he visualized in precise detail in his memory, often a street in the town he grew up in but also streets in Moscow, where he then lived – Gorky Street served him often. As Luria describes the process: "Frequently he would take a mental walk along that street . . . beginning at Mayakovsky Square, and slowly make his way down, 'distributing' his images at houses, gates, and store windows. At times, without realizing how it had happened, he would suddenly find himself back in his home town . . . where he would wind up his trip in the house he had lived in as a child." (p. 32) This technique enabled S. to reproduce at will a series from start to finish, or in reverse order, or from any point. He could also tell at once, given one word in a series, which word occurred on either side of it, its "neighbors," so to speak (we recall Aristotle's similar description of this recollective phenomenon in *De memoria*).

His recollection of these visual images was so stable that when asked to recall passages or series he had memorized even years earlier he could do so promptly and perfectly accurately. Luria and his associates concluded quickly that S.'s memory was essentially limitless and gave up trying to measure its capacity. The key to this capacity was the stability of his images and places. As Luria concludes, "the astonishing clarity and tenacity of his images, the fact that he could retain them for years and call them up when occasion demanded it, made it possible for him to recall an unlimited number of words and to retain these indefinitely."[126]

Nonetheless S. did occasionally make errors. Luria determined, however, that these were not errors caused by loss but errors of *perception*. In revisiting his places, S. sometimes failed to notice or saw badly an image which he had placed in a poor location. As S. described these errors to Luria:

I put the image of the *pencil* near a fence . . . the one down the street, you know. But what happened was that the image fused with that of the fence and I walked right on past without noticing it. The same thing happened with the word *egg*. I had put it against a white wall and it blended in with the background . . . Sometimes I put a word in a dark place and have trouble seeing it as I go by. (p. 36)

His solution to the problem was as follows:

What I do now is to make my images larger. Take the word *egg* I told you about before. It was so easy to lose sight of it; now I make it a larger image, and when I lean it up against the wall of a building, I see to it that the place is lit by having a street lamp nearby . . . I don't put things in dark passageways any more . . . Much better if there's some light around, it's easier to spot then. (p. 41)

Crowds and noise confused him (p. 37) because they interfered with his ability to perceive his images and places, and stray noise confused his concentration. S. described his problem: "You see, every sound troubles me . . . it's transformed into a line and becomes confusing. Once I had the word *omnia*. It got entangled in noise and I recorded *omnium* . . . and the more people talk, the harder it gets, until I reach a point where I can't make anything out." (p. 39)

Descriptions of the neuropsychology of memory

S. had trained his memory "for words" rather than "for things," in the ancient sense. His grasp of entire passages of a text, his ability to form coherent images associated with the meaning of a long passage, was far from good. If a story were read to him, especially at a rapid pace (S. required a pause of 3–4 seconds between items in order to form and place his images), he would complain that since each word called up an image for him they began to collide with one another in a hopeless muddle (p. 65). He was best at recalling items in a series, or brief connected passages which he could remember as though they were parts of a scene. His capacity for recalling thousands of such series, however, was virtually limitless in space and over time; indeed, S.'s chief problem, especially after he became a professional performer, was how to forget, a problem which presented itself to him as how to erase images he had formed. He tried mentally burning an image sequence he no longer needed, and he tried writing it down (unwittingly putting to the test Thammuz's fears about the danger of substituting writing for memory). Thammuz need not have worried. Neither technique had the least effect on S.'s memory. Finally S. realized that he could simply will a specific series of images not to appear, and they would not come up (pp. 66–71). This clear indication of his conscious control was a great relief to him.

One test Luria set for S. was to remember the first four lines of the *Inferno*. S. knew no Italian, and so made images for Russian homophones of Dante's words. This was the method he described using to memorize the first line, "Nel mezzo del cammin di nostra vita":

Nel – I was paying my membership dues when there, in the corridor, I caught sight of the ballerina, Nel'skaya.

mezzo – I myself am a violinist; what I do is to set up an image of a man who is playing the violin [Russ: *vmeste*], together with Nel'skaya.

del – There's a pack of Deli Cigarettes near them.

cammin – I set up an image of a fireplace [Russ: *kamin*] near them.

di – Then I see a hand pointing to a door [Russ: *dver*].

nostra – I see a nose [Russ: *nos*]; a man has tripped and, in falling gotten his nose pinched in the doorway [*tra*].

vita – He lifts his leg over the threshold, for a child is lying there, that is, a sign of life – vitalism. (pp. 45–46)

His system for the other three lines was similar, though he devised a different "scene" of related images for each line. Sixteen years later, without warning, Luria asked him to repeat these lines for him and he did so, flawlessly and effortlessly.

S.'s technique for recalling after so long an interval is also discussed by Luria. It made no difference to him whether a series were presented orally or in writing. He had practiced his imagining technique to the point where he could find images quickly even for words he had never heard before; for common words, he tended to use the same images over again. Once remembered, he had no difficulty in recalling, whether the interval had been a day, a month, or many years. But he needed first to place himself mentally back in the situation in which he had first committed the series to memory. As Luria describes it:

S. would sit with his eyes closed, pause, then comment: "Yes, yes . . . This was a series you gave me once when we were in your apartment . . . You were sitting at the table and I in the rocking chair . . . You were wearing a gray suit and you looked at me like this . . . Now, then, I can see you saying . . . " And with that he would reel off the series precisely as I had given it to him at the earlier session. If one takes into account that S. had by then become a well-known mnemonist, who had to remember hundreds and thousands of series, the feat seems even more remarkable. (p. 12).

One final characteristic of S.'s method is worth remarking. Luria stresses that the highly intricate technique he had developed was at its basis entirely natural to him, essentially a matter of spontaneous recollection by his memory aided by consciously applied method. The "techniques he used were merely superimposed on an existing structure and did not 'simulate' it with devices other than those which were natural to it." (p. 63) The author of *Ad Herennium*, introducing his strikingly similar mnemonic, comments that "the natural memory, if a person is endowed with an exceptional one, is often like this artificial memory [*similis sit huic artificiosae*], and this artificial memory [*haec artificiosa*], in its turn, retains and develops the natural advantages by a method of discipline" (III. 16.29). The use of the demonstrative pronoun in the Latin text seems to me significant. *This* method, Tully is saying, builds upon the memory's natural dispositions. So too S.'s memory system – to say nothing of that of the Japanese mnemonist who used a similar one – was "natural," developed by practice but entirely self-generated and self-taught.

There are a number of ways in which Luria's study of S. can provide useful insight into the basic neuropsychology of the descriptions we have of the architectural and other mnemonic schemes. First, Luria was especially impressed by S.'s synaesthesia, or apparently simultaneous and "unsorted" sensory perceptions, especially of ear, eye, and nose (though all five senses were involved). He "saw" sounds as visual shapes, and his memory-images often produced sensations of vibration or smell for him, as well as sight. This natural tendency was greatly increased by his mnemonics, for everything coming in to his mind was turned into an image. The essentially visual nature of these images was psychologically crucial. Sounds were only confusing to S. unless they were translated into particular clear visual images. It was the images which provided the stability over time to S.'s recollective power.

Medieval memory advice stresses synaesthesia in making a memory-image. The Aristotelian description of how a memory-image is formed after data from all five external senses is processed in the *sensus communis* already implies a large degree of synaesthesia, and this – while according pride of place to visual factors – is reflected in mnemonic procedure. Memory images must "speak," they must not "be silent." They sing, they play music, they lament, they groan in pain. They also often give off odor, whether sweet or rotten. And they can also have taste or tactile qualities. I will have more to say about this later, but it is worth commenting on here, since synaesthesia was considered to be so vital to S.'s success.

In the second place, S.'s process of recollection was a process of perception; he mentally walked through his memory places and looked at what was there. This accounts for the essentially perceptual nature of ancient advice on the preparation of *loci*, that they be properly lighted, moderate in size and extension, different enough from one another in shape that they cannot be confused, not crowded, that the images in them be of moderate size and neither too large nor too small, and that they be made clearly distinct from their background.

Third, S.'s problem with "overloading," experienced when words were read to him too rapidly, or when he tried to grasp a lengthy passage as a whole, suggests why all the ancient Roman writers, from the *Ad Herennium* author through Quintilian, had their doubts about the ordinary utility of "memory for words" when tied to images like these. Fourth, and as a counterbalance to the previous point, S.'s ability to recall thousands of short series of words, even though he had trouble grasping long connected passages, sheds light on the ancient advice to memorize lengthy passages piecemeal, in short sections which can later be united. As Hugh of St. Victor writes, the memory rejoices in shortness ("memoria brevitate gaudet"); the experience of S. should caution us, however, against assuming that in saying this Hugh meant that only brief extracts of longer works could be retained in the memory. Any long work can be considered as a number of short series joined together – indeed, this is exactly Quintilian's advice. And as separate series, a virtually limitless number can be retained in a good, trained memory.

Fifth, and in some ways the most important for our purposes, S. was completely uneducated in mnemonics. The system he devised of backgrounds and images was self-taught, refined by trial and error. He never seems to have discovered the principle of "memory for things" that every ancient writer on the subject is at pains to emphasize as the key to the successful composition and delivery of an oration. This, surely, was because his prodigious feats of memory were treated as freakish, and he himself as a vaudeville act, his art perceived to be a mere curiosity without social usefulness and ethical value. The situation in the ancient and medieval worlds, needless to say, was far different. By providing such tantalizing parallels, S. can teach us how the memory system described in these treatises is true to human psychology, but there is evidently much about the actual use of memory in education and composition during the Middle Ages that S.'s experience cannot tell us.

3

Elementary Memory Design

THE NUMERICAL GRID

The architectural mnemonic was certainly not the only nor even the most popular system known in the Middle Ages for training the memory. In her 1936 study of the subject, Helga Hajdu mentions various alternative systems, including an elaborate digital method of computation and communication that also served mnemonic purposes, discussed in the treatise *De loquela digitorum* ascribed to Bede (*PL* 90, 685–702); various mnemonic verses that serve both scholars and laity, such as the university students' mnemonic for remembering the various types of syllogism ("Barbara Celarunt Darii," etc.) and the execrable rhyming hexameters used by lawyers as a mental index to the various collections of laws; and various counting devices, like the rosary and the abacus, which involve manipulating physical objects in a rigid order as aides-memoire in calculation.[1] There are rhyming catalogues of medieval libraries which were intended to be memorized by the monks,[2] and there are Alexander de Villedieu's 4,000 rhymed hexameters setting forth the rules of Latin grammar, the *Doctrinale*. One of the earliest and longest-lived poems in English is the mnemonic for the months of the year: "Thirty days hath September, April, June and November."

Interesting as these particular items are, however, they are too limited in purpose or too bound to a particular situation, such as the monastery or the law courts, to be of much interest in considering how memory was trained by a wide variety of people to retain and recollect a wide variety of texts and other material (what Albertus Magnus lumps together as "negotia," a word which usually means "business," but in the context of memory-training translates best as "matters" or even "stuff"). But other systems of memory training clearly rivaled that of the *Ad Herennium* both in their longevity and their broad applicability to all spheres of learning. And like the architectural mnemonic, they too were widely disseminated and find their way into vernacular writings on the subject of memory. In this chapter, I will be concerned with two simple schemes, taught at the beginning of memory training. They are based on the most common of heuristics, the order of numbers, and that of the alphabet.

The number scheme is most fully described by Hugh St. Victor in a text virtually overlooked by modern scholars, the Preface to his *Chronica*, also called "De Tribus Maximis Circumstantiis Gestorum," translated here as appendix A. Hugh's description is one of the fullest, and clearest, of any mnemonic system. The method utilizes psychological principles similar to the method using images in backgrounds, but in this case the "background" system is numerical and the "images" are of short pieces of text written into the numbered backgrounds, as though within a grid. The images of written text are impressed as they appear in the particular codex from which they were first memorized, including their location on the page (recto, verso, top, middle, bottom), the shapes and colors of the letters themselves, and the appearance of each page including marginalia and illuminations, to make a clear visual image. Finally, Hugh advises that the physical conditions under which one had memorized the original material should also become part of one's total memory of it.

The preface was composed about 1130, and is addressed to very young students beginning their study of scripture in the cathedral school of St. Victor. It precedes a Chronicle of Biblical history, set out as columns – seventy folio pages worth in the fullest versions – of names, dates, and places, which the students were to memorize as an elementary part of their education in *sacra pagina*, or the study of the Bible. The preface was unpublished until 1943, when it was edited by William M. Green and printed in *Speculum* (there appear to have been no previous printings at all).[3] The manuscripts suggest that the prologue, while having some local success, never achieved the wide dissemination of *Didascalicon*, the work which earned Hugh a reputation for being an important proponent of *ars memorativa* in the later Middle Ages and Renaissance. There are several manuscripts of the preface alone; Green comments that while portions of the Chronicle tables were "often omitted with much resultant confusion and variety in the manuscripts, the text of the prologue . . . is usually well preserved."[4] Thirty-four manuscripts of the Preface survive (compared to 125 of *Didascalicon*), nearly all written in the twelfth and thirteenth centuries, though there are two from the fourteenth, and one from the fifteenth century. Of those whose provenance is known, most are claustral.[5] The largest number of manuscripts is French, as we would expect, including several from St. Victor. So, the evidence suggests that this particular treatise was not regarded as major or original enough to deserve wide dissemination, despite its author's eminence; that it was never known much beyond the precincts of St. Victor; and that it sank into oblivion by the early fourteenth century, because it had been superseded by or incorporated into other pedagogical tools. Its very ordinariness, however, makes it important to my study.

The method Hugh describes for his young charges displays the principles basic to classical mnemonics, as we find them described by Aristotle, Tully, Cicero, and so many others. One must have a rigid, easily retained order, with a definite beginning. Into this order one places the components of what one wishes to memorize and recall. As a money-changer ("nummularium") separates and classifies his coins by type in his money-bag ("sacculum," "marsupium"), so the content of wisdom's storehouse ("thesaurus," "archa"), which is the memory, must be classified according to a definite, orderly scheme. Without retention in the memory, says Hugh, there is no learning, no wisdom. "The whole usefulness of education consists only in the memory of it."[6]

The example Hugh gives is how to memorize the Psalms. There are 150 in all, and to learn them one first constructs a series of mental compartments, numbered consecutively from 1 to 150 – in other words, a rigid system of backgrounds with a definite starting-point. To each number is attached the first few words (the *incipit*) of each psalm, so that as one visualizes the number "one", one simultaneously visualizes "Beatus vir qui non abiit in consilio impiorum"; upon seeing "xxii" one also sees the text "Dominus regit me, et nihil mihi deerit"; and so forth. In Hugh's scheme the images are the written words as they actually appear in a manuscript and the *locus* is simply a number, but the incidental difference of this scheme from the architectural one is less important than its fundamental psychological similarity; they both employ a system of consciously adopted, rigidly ordered "backgrounds" as a grid which is then "filled" with "images."

Hugh also counsels that this same method of numerical ordering can be used to learn the text of an individual psalm. Under number twenty-two, for example, one visualizes a subsidiary set of numbers, again beginning with "one" and proceeding in consecutive numerical order; to these one attaches the rest of the text, in short pieces (verses), however many one needs to complete the task. The crucial task for recollection is the construction of the orderly grid of numbers which one can see in the memory. This enables one "when asked, without hesitation [to] answer, either in forward order, or by skipping one or several, or in reverse order and recited backwards" whatever is in the memorized text as a whole. And it also enables one to construct mentally a concordance of the text, thus "compounding with interest the authority of some one psalm" by citations from a multitude of other, related texts.[7]

Moreover, this scheme will work for any book of the Bible (or for any text at all, for that matter). A long text must always be broken up into short segments, numbered, then memorized a few pieces at a time. We have some clue as to exactly how short "short" was from the length of verses in the medieval format of the Psalms, and from the number of words enclosed in *cola* and *commata* divisions. Obviously, optimal length varies slightly from one individual memory to the next, but the medieval texts of the Psalms generally contain more verse divisions than do modern texts. Psalm 23, for instance, is six verses long in the King James Bible, but has nine divisions in the "Paris" text of the thirteenth century. The longest of these is the first, containing thirteen words; by contrast the King James contains thirty words in verse four and twenty-two in verse five. The fewer number of words in the medieval format may well reflect the psychological realities of the relatively strict limits of short-term memory, that is, what one can take in during a single memorial *conspectus*, or glance (to use the terminology of the memorial *artes*).[8]

The advice to "divide the text" duplicates that of Quintilian, as it also articulates the experience of S., who had difficulty remembering long passages of connected words, but none at all in retaining an apparently unmeasurable number of short segments. Any long text can be treated as though it were composed of a number of short ones:

For the memory always rejoices [says Hugh] in both brevity of length and fewness in number, and therefore it is necessary, when the sequence of your reading tends toward length, that it first be divided into a few units, so that what the memory could not comprehend as a single expanse it can comprehend at least in a number.[9]

This is advice which Hugh repeated in *Didascalicon*. In this treatise Hugh extolls even more the dependency of all wisdom ("sapientia") and the liberal arts upon memory, training which is now sadly decayed because students do not learn proper habits:

We read that men studied these seven [arts] with such zeal that they had them completely in memory, so that whatever writings they subsequently took in hand or whatever questions they posed for solution or proof, they did not thumb the pages of books to hunt for rules and reasons which the liberal arts might afford for the resolution of a difficult matter, but at once had the particulars ready by heart. Hence, it is a fact that in that time there were so many learned men that they alone wrote more than we are able to read.[10]

This same contempt for the cumbersome, inefficient, and chancey method of turning the pages of a book to look for a text that one needs is found in Hugh's preface. Do you think, he asks his boys, that people wanting to cite a particular psalm turn over the pages of a manuscript hunting for it? "Too great would be the labor in such an task."[11] It is also striking that Hugh makes an exact correlation here between the amount stored in one's memory and the amount of written composition one produces.

But Hugh's most concrete advice in *Didascalicon*, a work which teaches the arts of reading as its title indicates, is to "gather" (*colligere*) while reading, "reducing to a brief and compendious outline things which have been written or discussed at some length."[12] Again the principle of dividing a long text ("prolixius") is to be observed, because, Hugh says, the memory is lazy and rejoices in brevity.[13] Therefore, we ought to gather something brief and secure from everything we learn which we can store away in the little chest of our memory.[14]

One should not assume that Hugh meant that one should retain only a compact summary of what one has read; what he means is that one should break prolixity, a long text, into a number of short, securely retained segments which can be gathered in the memory. This method of study certainly leads to florilegia, as it leads also to Bartlett's *Familiar Quotations* and *The Oxford Dictionary of Quotations*. The phrase "brevem ... et compendiosam summam," "a brief and compendious summary," might seem self-contradictory, except that Hugh is clearly giving the same advice he spells out more fully in his *Chronica* preface, memorizing a "compendious" summation of "brief" segments of the text one is trying to master – the scholar's method of note-taking, in other words, except written in the memory instead of on note-cards. It is worth recalling by those who might dismiss such advice as mere florilegiality, born of distaste for the comprehensive knowledge of a text, that note-taking and serious scholarship are not exclusive activities. How "compendious" the summation of a text might be would depend on the industry and talent of each individual reader, and the importance to him of a particular text.

This principle of grouping or "gathering" respects the limits of human short-term memory. While the storage capacity of memory is virtually limitless, the amount of information that can be focused upon and comprehended at one time is definitely limited, to a number of units somewhere between 5 and 9; some psychologists express it as a law of "Seven plus-or-minus two."[15] So one of the fundamental principles for increasing mnemonic (recollective) efficiency is to organize single bits of information into informationally richer units by a process of substitution that compresses large amounts of material into single markers. In this way, while one is still limited by one's capacity to focus on no more than 8–9 units at a time, each unit can be made much richer. As the psychologist George Miller has written (quite unconsciously echoing a favorite image of Hugh of St. Victor), if my purse holds only six coins I can carry six pennies or six dimes; similarly, it is as easy to memorize a list containing a lot of information coded into "rich" units as it is to memorize one containing "poor" units, for the limiting factor is the number, not the nature of each item. Miller describes "gathering" in this way:

The material is first organized into parts which, once they cohere, can be replaced by other symbols – abbreviations, initial letters, schematic images, names, or what have you – and eventually the whole scope of the argument is translated into a few symbols which can be grasped all at one time.[16]

This is exactly what Hugh counsels doing when he substitutes number-coordinates for the verses of a Psalm – the active memory first focuses on the number, and then that numerical "address" leads to the text "placed" there, itself composed of a few words at a time, grouped into phrases. In recollection, one first focuses on the informationally "richest" sign, say "Psalm 23." That "stands for" a set of six sub-units or verses (in the King James Version), and one might focus on one number amongst those, perhaps "two." That sign in turn both "stands for" and "leads to" the words "He maketh me to lie down in green pastures; he leadeth me beside the still waters," themselves grouped into five syntactic sub-units or "phrases."

Because of the substitution process that creates "rich" units, one can skip material, rearrange it, collate it, or whatever, simply by manipulating a few digits mentally – recalling the second verse of every psalm, perhaps, or reciting a couple of psalms by alternating verses from one with the other, maybe one in ascending order and the other in the reverse. Any number of impressive parlor-tricks (ancient and medieval pedagogy would have called them exercises) can be played, for one is actually just counting a few digits at a time. One can also use the ability conferred by this process for serious ends, such as concording texts on a particular topic, as Hugh suggests in his preface, by "proferentes numerum," "bringing forth the number,"[17] that is, memorizing only the number coordinates to a text under the topical key-word. These coordinates then trigger recollection of each separate text.

Two late Roman grammarians, Fortunatianus and Julius Victor, define these matters very clearly, and since each was quite influential throughout the history of medieval pedagogy, it is worth pausing over what they have to say.[18] Both are clearly disciples of Quintilian and Cicero (the Cicero of *De oratore* and *De inventione*, not Tully).

Julius Victor, more or less a contemporary of Augustine's, alludes briefly and disparagingly to the art of memorizing by *loci* and *imagines*. For him, memory as a subject in rhetoric is chiefly important for invention: "Memory is the secure perception [literally "gathering together"] in the soul of words and themes for composition."[19] He quotes *De oratore* I, 18 (a passage that became famous in the later Middle Ages) to the effect that memory is a treasure-house ("thesaurus") of everything an orator needs, safe custodian of the *verba* and *res* required in thought and invention. But Quintilian is his major source. Paraphrasing *Institutio*, II, 7, 2–3 and XI, 2, 37, he advises learning by heart both your own and others' written compositions, but recommends particularly, as Quintilian does, that one learn the best compositions of the orators, historians, and other worthies by heart, for then one will carry within oneself models for imitation and sources for substance and style.

For both written and purely memorial activities, *divisio* and *compositio* are most useful. He who correctly puts together the basic structure of an oration can never err.[20] This will hold true not only when one arranges the questions to be addressed, but in expounding them as well – if the first and second and so on are bound together correctly, then one will securely remember the whole following content. Similar advice concerning the advantages of properly dividing a theme for the sermon is a feature of late medieval *artes praedicandi*, as we shall see. *Divisio* means dividing a text into short segments for memorizing, and *compositio*, putting the segments together in order, arranging them properly from one to two to three, and so on.[21] The advice is a cliché of classical rhetoric, from the pen of a very ordinary professor of the subject, but it is a most valuable cliché.

One needs, as Aristotle said, a starting-place, a beginning marked "one." By dividing and composing, one is constructing a series of numbered sequences for each text one memorizes, whether it be one's own work or a set piece from one of the greatest stylists of the past. Quintilian's otherwise cryptic advice (*Inst.*, x, 7, 7) to orators always to have before them the "modus" and "finis" of their speech, "and for this division is absolutely necessary," makes some sense when one understands "divisio" in its mnemonic context. The order of numbers cues both the "modus" or "way" and the "finis" or "goal" for a speech; it allows for digression and all sorts of extempore speaking, while keeping one from losing one's way, forgetting how much one has left to cover, or one's chief points.

The mnemonic requirement for a firm starting-point also gives a practical context for the critical importance given in medieval commentary to the title of a work, an emphasis that often seems to us bizarre. "Titulus" is derived from "titan," says Remigius of Auxerre, because it is the illuminating "sun" of the entire text. The *titulus* was one of the basic "categories" or "circumstances" that every student had to know about a work. Mnemonically speaking, the "starting-point" of a text is its title; everything else both in the text itself and its accompanying commentary will be linked in an order from this point.[22] The Benedictine Rule required that each brother be given a codex at the start of each Lent, which he was to read "in order from the beginning."[23] "In order starting from the beginning" is a mnemonic requirement; as he makes the book his own in his memory, each monk must give particular care to the "starting-point" of the book for that is the key to its order, and thus to his ability to recall it. "Begin at the beginning" was made a moral duty in the Rule because of its fundamental mnemonic importance.

Fortunatianus, also of the fourth century, wrote an art of rhetoric in three books in the form of a dialogue. Fortunatianus relies almost entirely on Quintilian's advice in *Institutio*, XI, 2, for what he says about memory. Memory is a mixture of natural ability and artifice, or training; nature is served by art and art aided by nature. Simonides, Charmadas, and Metrodorus Scepsis taught the art of memory; what Simonides learned from his experience at the banquet was that memory is best aided by orderly marked-out places ("sedes") in the soul; when we have such places, we can bring things together, whether we compose in writing or mentally ("ad scripta vel cogitata").

Fortunatianus then says that the best procedure for memorizing is first to divide a long piece into sections. Next we memorize by constant and intense concentration ("continua et crebra meditatio"), and then we join one piece to the next in numerical order, until we have learned the whole. "What best helps the memory? Division and composition; for order most secures the memory."[24] Those passages we find hard to memorize should be additionally marked with *notae*. We should repeat often what we have learned, and write passages down on wax tablets. To exercise our memories, we should begin by memorizing poems, then orations, and then harder material such as legal writings. Reciting in a low voice or murmur is also a very useful technique ("voce modica et magis murmure"). We also retain better and recall more clearly what we have learned at night, when distractions are few. (Much of this advice is also in Martianus Capella; its antecedents are in Quintilian.)

One of the commonest and oldest distinctions made in memory advice is between memory for things and memory for words; we find it already in

Dialexeis. The meaning of "memory for words" is perfectly clear, even to us, for it denotes the word-for-word repetition that we identify with memorization. What exactly constitutes "memory for things" is somewhat less self-evident. The distinction drawn in *Ad Herennium* is probably the clearest of the ancient accounts. There, "memory for things" means organizing memorial cues by means of a composite scene of mental images associated with various key-words and subjects (illness, poison, heir, will, witnesses). "Memory for words" also involved constructing images, but seriatim, following the exact phrasing of the original.

Fortunatianus gives some illuminating examples concerning when to select one method or the other. Should we always learn word-for-word ("ad verbum")? Only if time permits; but if it does not we should retain only the matter, the gist ("res"), and suit our own words to it later, according to the occasion.[25] It is a very bad practice to have to excuse ourselves and refresh our memories by a prompt, or by reference to a book. If your memory is poor or time is short, do not tie yourself down by trying to speak word-for-word from memory, for if you should forget even one word in a series it will lead to an awkward pause or to silence. So it is best to remember *res* rather than *verba*, for one can suit words to the *res* as occasion demands ("de tempore") and not run the risk of needing prompting or forgetting altogether.

Word-for-word memorizing of a number of outstanding literary and Scriptural texts was also always considered to be essential for education. Quintilian advises acquiring such a memorial foundation in earliest education, and we have John of Salisbury's admiring account of how his master, Bernard of Chartres, set daily memorizing exercises of this kind for his pupils.[26] But many writers gave paraphrases of texts, even when manuscripts containing the complete text were available to them. The reason is not far to seek. They are quoting from memory "sententialiter," according to the matter or *res*, rather than word-for-word. The amount of material memorized by each method probably varied according to an individual's talent and time, as Fortunatianus here acknowledges. One finds even the poetry of the *Aeneid* sometimes quoted approximately. Pierre Riché cites two Merovingian examples: *Aeneid*, I. 90, "Et crebris micat ignibus aether," becomes "Crebris micantibus ignibus ex aethere," and *Aeneid*, II. 794, "Par levibus ventis volucrique simillima somno," is rendered as "Par levibus ventis similisque somno volucri."[27] In each instance of adaptation the chief words are remembered but the syntax is completely altered in the first, moderately changed in the second. Fundamentalists will object that the author's sense has also been altered, and they will be correct. But by late classical and medieval standards, the *res* in both instances is preserved, even though the *verba* are a bit changed.

The important thing to realize is that such alteration can result from a choice made consciously by the memorizer and writer – it does not automatically reflect poor training or a "bad" manuscript. On its face, alteration like this is completely neutral. Modern scholars tend to assume that accuracy of reproduction is a function of continual access to written texts, and thus that the extent of an author's reliance upon his memory can be gauged in inverse proportion to the fidelity of his quotations. I think this is a naive assumption. It is clear from what Fortunatianus says that he urged his students always to memorize in the first instance *ad verbum*. Only if one is pressed for time should one fall back on memorizing the *res* (it is also clear that *res* could mean anything from a summary aphorism to all the main words of a text). From advice in various early monastic rules, it is clear that students then were obliged to memorize important texts accurately and in full.[28] Monastic reading, of course, meant *meditatio*, as Dom Leclercq has so well described it: "The *meditatio* consists in applying oneself with attention to this exercise in total memorization; it is, therefore, inseparable from the *lectio*. It is what inscribes, so to speak, the sacred text in the body and in the soul."[29]

The Rule of Ferreolus observed, "anyone who wishes to be worthy of the name of monk is forbidden to be ignorant of letters; he must also hold all of the Psalms in his memory"[30] – "totos psalmos," "in their entirety" – a task that commonly took 2–3 years, though gifted individuals could manage it in six months. The mnemonic practice which informs this command also informs the admonition of the sixth-century *Regula magistri* that monks on a journey who had not yet mastered the Psalms should provide themselves with tablets on which the text was written, so that when they stopped they could sharpen their memory with the help of their companion.[31] This requirement is also derived from ancient mnemonic practice: recall Quintilian's comment, that it is of great value when one is practicing in order to fix one's memory, to have someone else read aloud the material, so that one can check the accuracy of one's recollection against the reading.

The book which Christians, both clergy and educated laity, were sure to know by heart was the Psalms. It has been observed that Augustine wrote not only in Latin but "in Psalms," so imbued is his language with their phrasing and vocabulary; the same could be said of any number of Christian writers. Nor was it only the Psalms which were so intimately known; Pierre Courcelle has shown the extent to which Gregory the Great and other writers might be said to write "in Augustine."[32] Such intimacy can be achieved only by long and thorough familiarity with a text as a whole, not just a few aphorisms. As Riché observes, "to know how to read was to know one's Psalter"; even Merovingian lay aristocrats, including the women, knew at least a few Psalms "verbaliter," word-for-word.[33]

Accuracy of recollection was a helpful skill to nurture in an age of few manuscripts, many of uncertain quality. The *Regula magistri* counsels that the Scriptures be retained in memory partly so that if a codex has lacunae or lacks the commentary ("textum lectionis"), the missing parts could be supplied or expanded from memory.[34] There is no point in debating whether or not their faith in the accuracy of memory was misplaced, for some individuals have highly accurate recollection and others do not. The point to understand is rather that one's memory was *expected* to be not only copious but accurate (the reverse, one might observe, of expectations now). Nor is this characteristic only of the period from the sixth through ninth centuries, when the availability of books was at a minimum. Writing his *Dialogus* while in exile in Munich and away from the libraries that nurtured him earlier, William of Ockham apologizes not for the inaccuracy of his memory but for the fact that circumstances prevent him from having access to all the latest documents in the ongoing controversy, and so his treatise is incomplete – imperfect in that sense. Thomas Aquinas, living in a century far richer in books than the sixth, still stored his reading from various libraries in his memory, to be pulled forth as a seamless golden chain, *Catena aurea*. The ability perfectly to replicate the contents of one's memory again and again, forwards, backwards, and in all sorts of combinations, remained a revered skill at least until the end of the Renaissance.

The "inaccuracy" we find so frequently in medieval citation is often, I believe, the result of a deliberate choice on the authors' part, either at the stage of initial memorizing or (and I think more frequently) at that of composing. Medieval scholars' respect for accuracy in copying texts has been repeatedly demonstrated (despite complaints about particular errors), and it is justly observed that without the labors in scriptoria throughout the Middle Ages virtually no ancient literature would be known to us today. Yet the same people who honored the exact copying of even non-Christian texts quote these same works erratically, at times precisely, at times so paraphrased and adapted as to alter them almost beyond recognition. The one sort of activity is a form of *memoria ad verbum*, the other *memoria ad res*.

The fourteenth-century English Dominican, Thomas of Waleys, a careful scholar of decidedly non-florid style (Beryl Smalley remarks that, unlike Robert Holcot, Waleys "seldom made a mistake" in the attribution of a source[35]), advises against rote memorizing of one's composition in his *De modo componendi sermones* (c. 1342), for:

Words easily pass out of the memory, and from such a trivial action, the memory of what one is saying is disturbed, because words, more readily than concepts, fail to hold together. Often, from forgetting a single syllable, one forgets everything. Thus, the preacher can be confounded because he has bound himself to the words rather than to their gist.[36]

Waleys also disapproves of relying on an overly polished style, composing the whole sermon in rhythm, or too many divisions of the text, for these devices also engender mistakes of recollection and the consequent confusion of the preacher. So too does citing too many authorities. Forgetfulness and its attendant embarrassment is the fault of the preacher who strives to excell in mere ingenuity ("qui in curiositate conatur excellere").

To ward off such preacher's perils ("periculum praedicatori") one should memorize not word for word, but according to the "sententia" of one's authorities ("sententiam auctoritatum plene et distincte retineat"). By this advice, Thomas of Waleys means that one should remember the most important words, but not worry about the lesser ones:

And if there are words in these authorities (i.e. the texts) which are singularly weighty in merit, one should especially strive to retain and speak them, caring less about the others. And it is certainly true that there are many authoritative texts of the saints which because of their length and obscurity it is better and more useful to speak according to their sense alone than to recite word for word. And given that they can be recited word for word [by the preacher], where the authorities are obscure at all, their meaning can be set forth in other clear words, for, when they are not understood by the listeners they miss all the fruit.[37]

Waleys makes several interesting distinctions in this section, beginning with a basic one between "sententialiter," "according to the sense-units," and "verbaliter," "word for word" – a variation on the ancient distinction between memory for matter and memory for words. His advice is directed toward the delivery of an already composed sermon; the preacher should retain his *sentence* and deliver his sermon with the aid of his *memoria* ("memoriter retinere et dicere"). This procedure is preferred to rote recitation for reasons of security as well as elegance.

Sententialiter may also have a technical meaning in the context of mnemonics, one that links the mnemonic value of the colon divisions marked off in a written text with the advice to remember "by the *sententiae*". A *sententia* was not merely an impressionistic division, but, according to a well-known definition of Isidore of Seville, coincides with a colon; it is a coherent though not complete semantic unit, and a number of such *cola/sententiae* make up the completed, distinct thought that is a *periodus*.[38] So remembering material *sententialiter* would mean to remember it in chunks the equivalent of colon-divisions, by its constituent "ideas" or *sententiae*, rather than by word-for-word reiteration. Two verbs, *retinere* and *dicere*, are used by Waleys with the adverb *sententialiter*; by contrast, the verb, *recitare*, is used twice with *verbaliter*. "Recitare" is the verb also used for the elementary school-room exercises, in which children train their memories first by rote, "word-for-word."

Essentially what Thomas of Waleys says here is also Cicero's advice in *De oratore* and elsewhere, that one prepare a speech for delivery by remembering it according to its topics and major parts, rather than word for word. For Thomas of Waleys, the fault of an overly ingenious preaching style is that one may literally lose one's way in it, for one must learn an ornate composition word for word, and that method risks losing everything in the memory loss of a syllable.

But, Thomas of Waleys is quite clear, one does not choose absolutely between *sententialiter retinere* and *verbaliter recitare*. Waleys says that the preacher knows his memorized texts "verbaliter," and then adapts them to the occasion and to the circumstances of his auditors – "dato quod verbaliter recitentur," "given that the texts can be recited word-for-word [by the preacher]." Whether or not we believe that all preachers conformed to this behavior, it is significant that Waleys expects it as a norm ("dato quod").

Fortunatianus gave similar advice: we should learn texts word-for-word whenever we can, but, so long as we are careful to convey the *res* of our original, we may accommodate it in our own words to the occasion. Those accustomed to medieval texts are familiar with the results.

Some years ago Theodore Silverstein recognized that Adelard of Bath had certainly had direct knowledge of Cicero's *De natura deorum*.[39] His demonstration depended on recognizing that Adelard had reproduced the *res* of a passage in Cicero, though he had not quoted it *verbaliter*. The Latin of the two texts, Silverstein wrote, is similar "in the way the ideas . . . march together step by step, but their language is not quite the same." Nonetheless, Silverstein boldly rejected the notion that an (unknown) written intermediary had to have intervened between Adelard and Cicero to account for these differences. He writes, "such a text . . . has thus far not appeared in evidence and will, one may guess, be difficult to find." Once the phenomenon of *memoria ad res* is recognized by modern scholars, the need for such genealogical speculation disappears.

Even Scripture is often altered to accord with the particular occasion a writer is addressing. An example occurs in a section of Hugh of St. Victor's *De arca Noe morali*. Hugh's theme is that the tree of wisdom is firmly rooted in faith, and he is chastising those sinners who flaunt their lack of faith, not fearing the Lord. He quotes Psalm 72:2–3, but slightly alters the text to make it emphasize his immediate occasion: "Mei autem pene moti sunt pedes, pene effusi sunt gressus mei; quia zelavi *in peccatoribus* pacem peccatorum videns."[40] The Vulgate reads "quia zelavi *super iniquos*." Frequently Hugh will add an "inquit" or an "autem" to a text to improve the transition between his words and those of a quotation (scholars still do this, of course), or he will change an inflection to fit the syntax of his own sentence. He also often incorporates fragments of text into his own words, making them virtually into items of his own vocabulary, the sense of quotation being almost lost. So Proverbs 8:31, where Wisdom speaks of herself "ludens in orbe terrarum; et deliciae meae esse cum filius hominum,"[41] is quoted as follows: "Haec est sapientia, quae aedificavit sibi domum, quia descendens *in* orbem *terrarum* delicias suas dicit *esse cum filiis hominum*." Such adaptive freedom is enabled by complete familiarity with the text, the shared memory of it on the part of both audience and author, and hence a delight both in recognizing the familiar words and the skill with which they have been adapted to a new context.

Memorizing *ad res* greatly increases the efficiency of recollection. George Miller has observed that a hypothetical sentence can be thought of as one hundred letters or twenty-five words or three phrases or one proposition. If one considers a sentence as one proposition, one will obviously be able to grasp it more effectively and securely than if one regards it as 100 letters. It is, says Miller, "those larger, subjective units, loosely called ideas, that we must count to determine the psychological length of any text."[42] This is exactly what ancient and medieval writers called *memoria ad res*.

Hugh of St. Victor, in *Didascalicon*, describes his own practice as a student, in terms of his favorite image of the trained memory as an orderly money-bag:

How many times each day would I exact from myself the daily debt of my bits of sophomoric wisdom [*sophismata*],⁴³ which thanks to the principle of shortness I had symbolized in one or two maxims in abbreviated form, so that indeed I held in my memory both the payouts and the numerical order of virtually all the propositions, questions, and objections which I had learned.⁴⁴

In this context, "solutio" refers to the information "paid out" from memory's store, as the skillful money-changer pays out coin. This store is in the form of "pieces of wisdom," "sophismata" or "dicta," the bits into which texts are divided. And they are "marked" for recollection (*signare*) by having been reduced, according to the rule of "brevitas," to one or two sayings "in abbreviated form" ("in pagina") and numbered in order.

Hugh uses the word *pagina* in a specialized manner here that is recognized only in dictionaries which cover late Roman and medieval Latin: Du Cange and the *Thesaurus linguae Latinae*. *Pagina*, like *(s)cedula* (discussed in the next part of this chapter) refers both to a type of physical surface and, by extension, to the sort of thing written on such a surface. Latin *pagina* is derived from the verb "pango," "to fasten," and refers to the rectangular boards covered with wax that, fastened together, made up a set of tablets.⁴⁵ The constraints of the surface required writing in columns. Obviously, *pagina* refers to such physically-shaped surfaces, as when Cicero, for example, writes of "filling a page [*complere pagina*.]"⁴⁶

But what one wrote on a *pagina* was what we call "notes," that is, ephemeral memoranda, abstracts, computations, the "rough drafts" of compositions that were to be fully composed later, either in oral delivery or written onto papyrus or parchment in fair hand. The meaning of "pagina" was extended in later Latin to include this other meaning – a "memorandum," something that is in an abbreviated, memorial form.⁴⁷ Du Cange cites a letter of Ambrose, in which he says to his correspondent that he is sending him a little present, this short letter, because his friend wanted him to *paginare*, "examine in brief and informal form," some things concerning the interpretation of the Old Testament.⁴⁸ Similarly, Paulinus of Nola writes that the laws of God were written on stone in "pagina," meaning "in essential or short form" without all the commentary.⁴⁹ In medieval Latin, one finds the word *paginator*, the person who ornamented the pages with pictures and drawings. This task is associated with the work of the "rubricator" or *miniator* (the word from which the Modern English "miniature" derives), the person who worked with red pigments to mark the text with short-form summaries, digest, and pointings of its contents, *in pagina*. It is worth noting that "rubricare" and its derivative, "rubric," had dual meanings also.⁵⁰

After one has divided a text in order to gather it and placed the segments onto one's numerical grid, the next principle, according to Hugh's preface, is to memorize each bit in such a way that one sees it clearly and distinctively.

Elementary memory design

One should always read a text from the same codex, so that the features of the page on which the particular segment of text appears become part of one's mnemonic apparatus. "Indeed I consider nothing is so useful for stimulating the memory as these," Hugh writes.[51] The layout of the many folio leaves of names, places, and dates which comprise his *Chronica*, was evidently designed by Hugh himself. Each page is in four columns, with headings in red introducing groups of ten (sometimes fewer) items (figure 3).

The lay-out Hugh adopted was clearly influenced by that of the Canon Tables of Eusebius, added to virtually all early medieval Bibles.[52] Compiled in Greek around 331, they were later translated into Latin. The elements in the design of these tables, which show parallel passages in the four Gospels, are very old and scarcely vary over their history (an example from the ninth century is reproduced in figure 4). Passages are cited by number (including numbers over 200 – instead of chapters and verses, Eusebius divided the Gospels into sections) without any written text.[53] There are ten tables in all, the first showing concordant passages in all four Gospels; the next three show concordances among three of the four, the next five those among any two, and the last one lists passages unique to each of the four. The tables are laid out in columns (one meaning, we recall, of "in pagina"), the numbers listed one after another vertically, and architectural columns are drawn to separate the four main vertical spaces on the page, together with arches and other architectural elements representing a classical facade.

It has been suggested that in this context, such an arcade motif may derive from the ancient mnemonic advice to use buildings, including "intercolumnia," "spaces-between-columns," as backgrounds for things to be remembered.[54] Certainly "intercolumnia" is one of the most enduring types of "place" advised in mnemotechnique. Within each rectangular space made by the columns, the name of the gospel is written at the top, and then the chapter numbers of the synoptic passages are recorded. Horizontal lines, sometimes colored, are drawn between every four numbers (in the Greek text) or five (in the Latin); the effect is to divide the page into a series of small rectangular "bins," none holding more than five items. Such a layout is clearly designed for mnemonic ease; as Hugh of St. Victor tells his students about his own similar design: "Now indeed you have enough to do to imprint in this fashion in your memory the matters which are written out below, according to the method and diagram for learning by heart demonstrated to you earlier."[55]

The presentation of the manuscript page in medieval Bibles provides one of the most interesting contexts for understanding Hugh's injunctions to his young pupils concerning the need to "divide," the mnemonic value of textual lay-out, and the requirement always to use the same codex. Typical of "Paris" format is an English Bible of the late thirteenth century, now in the Huntington Library (EL 9 H4). Each book is divided into numbered chapters, using Langton's scheme, with divisions by *cola* and *commata* as well. Each chapter begins with a colored initial, alternately red and blue. The text of each chapter is presented in prose form, unbroken except for the punctuation of the *cola* and *commata*. Each chapter is numbered, in Roman numerals with alternately red and blue colored elements. These numbers also have distinctively drawn colored pen lines and circles in them – these, plus the colored initial, for which there are two or three different forms for the commonest letters, give each folio opening a unique appearance. The running heads at the top of each opening are also distinctively colored and drawn with differentiated pen ornamentation. Since this Bible is a small one, the differences in the design of the running heads from one opening to the next are quite noticeable.

The Psalms, together with collections of maxims such as Cato's *Distichs*, were the elementary reading text throughout the Middle Ages, from late antiquity onward.[56] And Hugh of St. Victor evidently regarded their mastery as a beginning task, among the "puerilia." But in the majority of medieval Bibles, the Psalms, unlike the divisions in all the other books, are unnumbered. Moreover, whereas in Carolingian Bibles the Psalms are written in verses, Bibles of the thirteenth century and later characteristically wrote them out as units of prose. The reason for this change undoubtedly is that the Bible at this time began to be issued as a single bound volume, often quite small, even pocket-sized, whereas in the earlier Middle Ages it was usually issued in separate volumes of full folio size.[57]

However, in these later Bibles the verse divisions are indicated by colored initials, alternately red and blue. Each psalm begins with a large colored initial, sometimes fully decorated, other times just drawn large, red or blue alternately. It is interesting that the Huntington Library's manuscript of Richard Rolle's fourteenth-century English Psalter (HM 148) preserves this format for the Latin text of the Psalms written above Rolle's translation of it and of Peter Lombard's commentary. Each psalm's verse division has its initial letter colored alternately red or blue, the first initial of each psalm is a large blue letter with distinctive red pen decoration surrounding it, and the color scheme is repeated, like a color-code, for the English translation, and the commentary which follows. These markers alternate between red and blue. An effort is made in the writing of the book to distinguish each memory-sized "bit" as a unique visual image. Since in fixing one's images for storage (which required time, and at least two or three separate passes over the written text), one made sure to use the same codex – as all memory advice stressed – the mnemonic usefulness of such "decorative" elements is apparent.

Even what we hear must be attached to a visual image. To help recall something we have heard rather than seen, we should attach to their words the appearance, facial expression, and gestures of the person speaking as well as the appearance of the room. The speaker should therefore create strong visual images, through expression and gesture, which will fix the impression of his words. All the rhetorical handbooks contain detailed advice on declamatory gesture and expression; this underscores the insistence of Aristotle, Avicenna, and the other philosophers, on the primacy and security for memory of the visual over all other sensory modes, auditory, tactile, and the rest. Hugh as well insists that acoustically received material must be translated to visual terms and so fixed in memory. We recall that for the memory-artist, S., it made no difference whether material to be retained was presented to him orally or in writing – his visualization technique was the same.

The synaesthesia that S. naturally practiced is an articulated principle in medieval mnemonics. In addition to all the other sensory impressions that one should use to fix a memory-image, Hugh also recommends that one pay careful attention to the occasion ("tempus") on which we memorized something, a matter not only of the date (year, month, and day) but of the circumstances such as weather and time of day:

we [should] also pay attention carefully to those circumstances of things which can occur accidentally and externally, so that for example, we recall along with the appearance or character or location of the places in which we heard one thing or another, the face and habit of the people from whom we learned this and that, insofar as they are the kind by which they accompany their performance of an activity. All these things indeed are rudiments, but of the sort beneficial for boys.[58]

Although one cannot be entirely sure, it seems to me very unlikely that the *ars memorativa* so carefully explained in Hugh's preface was original. More likely he articulated systematically for his students mnemonic techniques well known for centuries. Several things lead to this conclusion. There are a number of other sources and practices current throughout the Middle Ages which indicate that both the numerical grid system and mnemonic value of page layout were well known; I will discuss several of these next. Then there is the fact that the manuscript evidence clearly shows that this particular text fell into disuse within a couple of centuries, though the grid method continued to be well known. Finally, and most persuasively to me, is the fact that Hugh wrote this for young students. The advice it contains is "puerilia," "kids'-stuff." The same cannot be said of the various medieval *artes* which adapt some features of the architectural mnemonic, or of the university-level mnemonics like that of Thomas Bradwardine, or of the even more elaborate arts of Raymond Lull or, perhaps, Roger Bacon.[59] Though the psychological principles are identical, these others are far more sophisticated, complex, and learned. The commonness of the number-grid is indicated by its use to format the Bible, and by its traces in other scholarly contexts, such as the style used to cite the Decretals and other non-Scriptural texts.

The numerical grid imposed on Scripture by its division into numbered chapters and verses was first printed in the Geneva Bible of 1560. But Scripture had been divided into brief segments before Jerome, and indeed dividing by chapter goes back to the scholars of the Masoretic text. (We should remember that ancient texts were commonly copied without any divisions except for the fixed number of syllables that constituted a line of writing – students learning to read were taught how to divide up the text on their own. This was the practice for writing texts through about the third century A.D.) Jerome divided in the classical fashion of *cola* and *commata*; so did Cassiodorus, who used not only these divisions of the text but chapter divisions and headings as well.[60] The late medieval Bible is divided into numbered chapters, using the thirteenth-century scheme of Stephen Langton, and the Cassiodorian division of the Psalms into *cola* and *commata*, which Alcuin had made standard. This late medieval format is called the "Paris" Bible. The essential utility of such division for memorizing the Biblical text was obvious to Langton, who glosses as follows Jerome's warning, made in his prologue to the Vulgate text of Joshua, that both reader and copyist should diligently preserve the divisions of the text: "by divisions, that is by chapters . . . which truly are most valuable for discovering what you want and holding it in your memory."[61]

Langton's chapter divisions superseded various earlier divisional schemes. This whole matter of the relationship between how scholars laid out a text in their memories, cited it when they made reference to it, and how scribes composed it on a manuscript page is well illuminated by a study of these habits prior to about 1200 A.D. The problem is important because some modern historians of technology seem to assume that there is a direct and simple correlation between the form something takes in writing and the way a person is able to think of it, in the same way that a washing-machine's design determines how clothes washed in it will be washed. The fashion for defining writing as a technological innovation of the same sort as television and the automobile, or the heavy plow and moveable type, seems to me fraught with difficulties. Why I think so will be apparent from the following study of citational habits, page layout customs, and the use of the mental numerical grid for remembering Scripture during the early Christian and Carolingian periods.

It is apparent from remarks of St. Augustine, who used the pre-Vulgate, Old Latin text of the Bible, that the Psalms at least were taught to him and his audience in an order that was numerically designated. In *Enarrationes in Psalmis*, he prefaces his comments on Psalm 118 (119), with an observation about his compositional habits. He apologizes for delaying so long his comments on his psalm, though he has expounded all the others, partly in sermons to the people, partly by dictating, but Psalm 118 is long and extremely difficult.[62] He refers to this psalm by number ("psalmum centesimum octavum decimum"). Of another psalm, 125, he says, "Now you remember, *according to the order taught to us*, this psalm is one hundred twenty-five, which is among those psalms whose title is 'A song of degrees'" (my emphasis).[63] From its manner of address, it would appear that this commentary was one of those Augustine composed for preaching, and he clearly assumes that everyone in his audience will know which is Psalm 125, "according to the order taught to us." Similarly, in commenting on Psalms 100, 104, and 105, he refers to them by number, though his usual habit is simply to begin by referring to "this psalm [*iste psalmus*]" without further identification. He does not seem to find mystical significance in these numbers; indeed, his attitude toward their numbering seems to me quite purely practical, a fact which suggests that he thought of the designation as a handy mnemonic tool, nothing more. Other early commentators, however, did find mystical significance in some of the numbers. It is worth remarking that *any* heuristic instrument, such as a number, can be reified. A mathematician once explained to me the difference between numerology and number-theory this way: "the one (numerology) wants to explain everything, the other explains nothing but itself."

This casual, matter-of-fact reference to psalms by number is not, however, Augustine's style of citation when marking a quotation. It was the universal custom in early medieval scholarly composition not to use numbers at all when citing sources. Passages from Scripture especially are often quoted without any attribution; the audience was expected to recognize the source from memory. New Testament texts may be introduced by a phrase such as "the Lord said" or "so the Apostle says," without naming the particular Gospel or epistle being quoted; prophetic books of the Old Testament are cited by name ("Isaiah says") sometimes, but the historical books often are quite unattributed. And the Psalms, perhaps the most frequently quoted of all, are almost always completely unattributed; even the phrase "ut ait in psalmis," "as it says in the Psalms," is unusual. Augustine was being quite untypical of himself when, in the *Enarrationes*, he cites a text as being "in Regnorum secundo libro," "in II Kings."[64] Occasionally he will introduce a quotation from a psalm by "in alio psalmo," "in another psalm," but usually he simply quotes a verse in complete confidence that his audience will know it.

Jerome often refers to the psalms by number, even in order to introduce a quotation from one. He also uses the less exact (from our point of view) citational style of Augustine, but, for example, he introduces a quotation from Psalm 44 by writing, "Legimus in quadragesimo quarto psalmo," "We read in Psalm 44,"[65] and one from Psalm 9 by "in nono psalmo . . . dicitur," "it says in the ninth psalm."[66] Books of the Bible, including the Pauline epistles and historical books of the Old Testament, are often cited by name, unlike Augustine's practice. Jerome does this not only in his commentaries, but also in his letters. For instance, in his famous letter (no. 53) to Paulinus on the study of Scripture, he introduces a quotation to Psalm 118 by its number.[67] Jerome also numbered and referred by number to the book-divisions of his own works; thus in the introduction to Book 8 ("octavus liber") of his *Commentary on Isaiah*, he refers to "books six and seven above."[68] Such variations in citational style continue through the early Middle Ages; Bede, for example, in his treatise on the patterns and tropes of Scripture refers to the Psalms by number. But Carolingian manuscripts are the first written books to indicate occasionally in the margin the name of the book from which a quotation is cited, although such information was frequently not copied by later scribes.[69]

It is clear, I think, from these early references to psalms by number, so at odds with the citational conventions then prevalent, that one should not presume that the form of a citational style limits the abilities of scholars and their audiences to conceive of and designate texts in other ways. It is obvious from the works of these fourth-century Christians that the Psalms not only had a fixed order, but that they were taught and memorized by number in that order. The earliest monastic rules, including Benedict's, discuss the order of the Psalms for divine office by referring to their numbers (e.g. chapters 9 and 18 of the Benedictine Rule). Indeed, the method described by Quintilian of dividing a long text into short sections, memorized seriatim or "per ordine," lends itself to just such a method of memorial storage, and suggests to me that the numerical grid principle is very ancient indeed. Quintilian's advice itself implies numbering the segments produced by *divisio* of a long text, so that one can join the second bit to the first, and so on (*Inst.*, XI, 2, 37).

There is also clear evidence that the verse divisions of each psalm were numerically designated as early as the time of Augustine, and certainly from the time of Alcuin (eighth century). The word "versus" is used by Augustine to refer to the divisions within the Old Latin text (though it was Cassiodorus who established the divisional scheme used in the medieval text of the Psalms),[70] and these verses have numbers. So, in his commentary on Psalm 6 (referred to as "in sexto psalmo" in the comments on Psalm 11),[71] he speaks of the first verse and second verse of the psalm. These verses are somewhat different from those similarly designated in the Vulgate text. Though the divisions themselves differ, clearly the principle of dividing by verses was known. These divisions were imposed on the text only in memory. They are not marked in the early Christian codices we possess – indeed even word divisions are not indicated.[72] It thus appears that versions of the numerical grid system described by Hugh of St. Victor for memorizing and mentally concording the Scriptural text were taught commonly at least by the fourth century, and probably were applied to texts well before then.

Alcuin regards the numerical order of the Psalms as so ancient and fixed that he indulges in some exegesis of the symbolism of a particular psalm's place in that order. In his commentary on Psalm 118, he begins by saying that one should first determine, for this longest and most difficult of all the Psalms, the reason for all the numbers contained within it. "That is, why are all the penitential psalms positioned [within the order] in a number containing sevens? and why is psalm 118 divided into twenty-two sections, of which each one has eight verses? or what is the reason for there being 15 psalms called in their *tituli* 'a song of degrees'?"[73] Invoking the text from Wisdom (XI, 21) that God created the universe (including Scripture) by number, order, and measure, he proceeds to analyze the mystical significance of the numbers in the format of Psalm 118. For our purposes, however, what is significant is the simple but profound fact that Alcuin thought of the text in terms of a numerical grid format, twenty-two sections of eight verses each, and that he also thought that the psalm, which itself had a number in the order of the whole book (118), incorporated subsets of numbered divisions in sections and verses. This is the mnemonic format which Hugh of St. Victor taught in 1130, and is in the tradition of numerically-designated divisions which we find in the fourth century.

But the first Bibles to write out the complete format of chapter and verse are mid sixteenth century, and virtually no medieval scribes wrote in the numbers of the verses in any scriptural book; chapter numbers were copied in routinely only beginning in the thirteenth century.[74]

There is, in other words, a lag of well over a millennium between the time the numerical grid was certainly in common use for "dividing" Scripture, and its first complete appearance on a physical page. It is clear in this instance that people had laid out the Bible on a grid in their memories for over a thousand years before they bothered to express that grid in writing, and for at least four hundred years before they thought it important even to suggest it in their scholarly citational habits.

In a treatise on sermon composition, Thomas of Waleys makes a comment that is illuminating of this whole matter. Advising preachers how to cite the Bible and patristic authorities during their sermons, Thomas suggests that although some cite the Psalms by number, others omit such numerical citation, referring instead generally to "the Psalter," since the Psalms are so commonly known:

Sometimes indeed a psalm itself is cited, and is referred to as the fortieth or thirtieth, or in another similar manner. Others however omit such citation, and only say: "This is found in the Psalter," and the reason is that the Psalms are commonly enough known.[75]

Themes taken from every other part of the Bible must be cited by chapter and book, however. This comment by Thomas would seem to explain why, even in late medieval written Bibles, the Psalms are commonly unnumbered while in all the rest of the books the chapter numbers are included.

It also indicates how widely used some sort of numerical grid was as a mental filing system. The style for citing the *Decretum*, used in glosses and other contexts throughout the Middle Ages, was according to the number of the large division (*distinctio, quaestio,* or *causa*) followed by the introductory word or phrase of the particular canon referenced, "xxxij c. multorum" or "xxiv c. cum itaque." If two or more canons in a given *quaestio* or *distinctio* began with the same words, they might be distinguished as, for example, "c. Si quis i, Si quis ii," etc. Similar forms were used for citation of the various volumes of decretal collections compiled after Gratian's catalogue.[76] Obviously a canon lawyer was expected to have pretty well memorized the entire set of Decretals in order to be able to use these references without a great deal of wasteful "turning the pages." William of Ockham, in his *Dialogus*, speaks of his relief at having stocked his memory with so much material, including all the decretals, when he found himself exiled in Munich; Peter of Ravenna, a fifteenth-century Italian lawyer, claimed, as we will see, that adopting his version of an alphabetical mnemonic enabled him to learn all the decretal collections.

Yet there were clearly risks in citing too many numbers while one spoke. Thomas of Waleys advises that supplementary authorities, Biblical and patristic, should not be fully cited by book and chapter number, but by book alone. If one insists on citing every chapter number it often happens, when bringing together a number of authorities, that a chapter number falls out of the preacher's memory, and one then could bring forth another text than the intended one. Wherefore, he says, he praises the practice of former times when preachers did not cite chapter numbers in their delivery, but only when they wrote their sermons down. He concludes, "I think their method was better because it was safer [*tutior*] than the modern method by which chapter numbers and books are cited together."[77] Before dismissing this as the advice of an irredeemable pedant terrified of being caught out by a colleague, let us consider it in terms of the practical difficulties attendant on the numerical grid as a method for recalling text. The grid serves essentially as a coding and filing system for the orderly and ready recollection of material. In using a mnemonic, however, one does not normally call out its coordinates, whether one's grid be the architectural places or this numerical one. The grid is essentially arbitrary, in the sense that it is not part of the material placed within it, any more than a file is part of what it contains. However, wrong coordinates will send one to the wrong text, the wrong part of the file, which could then cause a devastating mental loss of place. Thomas advises articulating only the name of the work cited, a safer thing to do since it isn't a part of the grid. It is not the file itself, only the name of the file. Indeed it is striking that he advises avoiding articulation of the code whenever possible, even of the Psalms if one can get away with it. Only in the more secure situation of a corrected, written version should the numerical grid be articulated, when any miscitation can be worked out. And his advice is given for *safety*'s sake.[78]

Not every preacher followed Thomas's advice in this matter; he himself suggests that it is a bit old fashioned, and of course the sermons we have preserved are all in written form, with all citations given. But it is a significant point that medieval citations are given *before* the text more frequently than after it. The anterior position serves to cue the mental grid. Our mode of citing after a quotation, in parentheses or a footnote, is designed solely to send a reader to a printed source that he or she must find elsewhere. Our citations are referrals, not access cues to a mental grid of texts.

Indexing systems devised in the monasteries and, later, the universities seem all to have served the dual function of being both tools for finding texts initially and also for noting them in the memory, as mnemonic "hooks." Not only numbers could serve such a purpose: the Dominican system, devised for the Bible concordance, of citing by book, chapter number, and letter (A–G) to indicate the position of a text within the chapter was widely disseminated. The Rouses describe a bookmark of the thirteenth century, which explains the key to the pagination scheme of the volume in which it is found, a Cistercian manuscript in which pages are marked with a combination of letters and dots.[79] One side of the bookmarker says: "Ut memoriter teneatur alphabetum taliter ordinatur: a .a :a a:," etc. Evidently this reference scheme was designed in part to provide a memory grid for the readers. On the reverse of this bookmark, the strip of parchment is divided into seven equal sections, marked A through G, the location scheme also used by the Dominicans within chapter divisions. One held this side against the edge of the page to provide the finely-tuned location for the text. A number of other such bookmarks are known.[80]

As Richard and Mary Rouse say of all these various coding and filing schemes, "they emerge with striking suddenness in the West, to the point that one may say that, probably before 1220, certainly before 1190, no such tools existed; and that, after the 1280s, the dissemination and new creation of such aids to study were commonplace."[81] Of the sudden proliferation of written tools there is no doubt; as there is also no doubt that the same order (the Dominicans) chiefly responsible for creating them is also chiefly responsible for the dissemination of the architectural mnemonic. It is also true that during the thirteenth century schemes for memory training were disseminated into the general culture via vernacular translations and adaptations of the architectural and other memory-training techniques. We therefore should not, I think, assume that these multitudinous study aids replace memory as a fundamental tool; instead, it seems to me, they often were thought of as memory systems first and manuscript aids second. This suggests that reading and memorizing were taught as they were in antiquity, as one single activity, and further, that the monastic understanding of what one does in reading, so well described by Dom Leclercq, not only persisted but became part of general culture in the thirteenth, fourteenth, and later centuries, for reasons that had as much to do with the moral value of *memoria* in meditation and prayer as with its utility. But this is a subject for later chapters.

Furthermore, the proliferation of written guides to these various heuristic schemes in the twelfth and thirteenth centuries, does not mean that there were no indexing mnemonics in use earlier. Hugh's preface describes an indexing scheme in great detail, long before 1190, and for reasons I have indicated, it seems most likely he was describing a well-known, persistent technique. Indeed it seems to me quite likely that all these schemes, numbering of chapters, alphabetizing (we know that the memory scheme which Aristotle described in *De memoria* was an alphabetical one), page indexing by number and/or letters, are medieval adaptations of schemes known since antiquity as memorial schemes. I myself suppose, as do the Rouses and other scholars, that a chief reason for the proliferation of written indexing schemes was that more people had need of organized textual material and that there were more texts to be learned after the twelfth century infusions from Spain and Sicily. Once the scholarly community was enlarged beyond the monastery, the need for written transmission was greater, and priests and friars who need to preach have need of preacher's tools. But this did not occur at the expense of memory; indeed the written schemes themselves are to be used as memory grids: "ut memoriter tenea[n]tur."

One other intriguing practice which indicates the tenacity and pervasiveness of the methods described by Hugh of St. Victor is the practice of quotation itself, and the related practice of what Hugh calls "gathering," *colligere*. The medieval verb *quotare* first makes its appearance, according to the *Revised Medieval Latin Word List*, early in the thirteenth century (which does not mean it was unknown earlier). Derived from the adjective *quot*, "how many," it meant to "number" a book, dividing a longer text into numbered subdivisions, such as chapters. Robert of Basevorn discusses quoting in chapter 31 of his *Forma Praedicandi*, written in 1322. After the prayer, the theme is restated and quoted, "quotandum quantum ad librum et capitulum." For authorities other than the theme, it is not necessary to give the chapter number "secundum modum modernum" (apparently, like Thomas of Waleys, Robert did not like the new custom of citing every authority by chapter number), though one may number books in a series (like I and II Kings), or one may also give a chapter number in a book which explains another book (Gregory's *Moralia in Job*, for instance). The correct form is, for example, "Gregorius primo, vel secondo, Moralium super illud Job." But masters and professors of theology may "quote" (numerically divide) anything:

It is permitted, indeed it is their prerogative, for masters and professors of sacred theology to quote everything in a carefully worked-out manner [*exquisite*], since in regard to this matter so much is held accountable to them by others, because of the testimony of their excellent teaching and display of humility regarding those matters in which they are accountable, and because of the dignity and honor of their rank.[82]

So the practice of quoting, marking and numbering a text for citation, seems to have been the special prerogative of the most learned members of the university, who alone are able to quote *exquisite*, "in a carefully worked-out way."

The verb also found its way into the medieval vernaculars. The earliest English citation (1387)[83] is to Trevisa's translation of Higden's *Polychronicon*, describing "Stevene þe archbishop," Stephen Langton, "who coted þe Bible at Parys, and marked þe chapiters." This usage clearly accords with the Latin verb, a restricted, technical meaning. A fifteenth century translation of Higden, also cited by MED, discussing how the Greeks numbered years, comments that at first they "cotede yeres at the glory of their victory from the captiuite of Troye." There is also a Middle English noun, *cote*, meaning "a part," but the meaning seems especially restricted to a numerical part; for instance, in Capgrave's *Chronicle*, the parts of the number six are discussed, which are 1, 2, and 3, each a "cote" of six because "in her revolving thei make him evyr hool" (that is, $1 \times 6 = 6$, $2 \times 3 = 6$, $3 \times 2 = 6$, and $1 + 2 + 3 = 6$, making six a mathematically perfect number). The earliest citations in the OED which show anything like the modern meaning of "quote" are sixteenth century. One interesting, transitional example is in one of Mercutio's speeches in *Romeo and Juliet*: "what care I / What curious eye doth quote deformities?" (I, iv. 30–31). "Quote" here means "number or mark mentally," a reference to the old numerical grid system for which quoting was designed.

But the Middle English meaning is clearly still as restricted as that of the Latin original, as a verb meaning "to divide a text into short, numbered segments" and as a noun "a part of a (numerical) whole." And evidently quoting was regarded as an activity requiring considerable knowledge and skill. Stephen Langton, Smalley writes, took thirty years to work out his chapter divisional scheme, perfecting it through classroom testing.[84] The quotation of patristic texts is a feature of thirteenth century scholarship, and made possible the compendia of authorities designed for sermon composition, such as *distinctiones* collections, textual *concordantiae*, and other *libri rerum memorandarum*. Often in these collections, each quote is cited by book and chapter number (and in some by the further refinement of A–G division), the two basic coordinates of the grid that serve not only to help find them in a complete text of their parent work but to place them in a memory file, so that thinking of Avaricia, for example, would bring forth a number of texts, each labeled in the mental grid of the file called "Avaricia." Indeed, for most friars working far from equipped libraries, the citations could have served only as memory coordinates. These collections were made for people without access to libraries, as preachers' digests; the likelihood of a friar who had learned his texts from one of these collections ever wanting (let alone needing) to check them out against a full library copy seems to me remote. The citations are rather, as Thomas Waleys characterizes them, the "chapter-headings" in which the *memory* could hold and file them.[85]

I think it likely, in fact, that the passion of the late medieval preacher for numbering sermon divisions – what has been called the "scholastic" or "university" method of the thirteenth century – is related to the nature of this numerical grid. Thomas of Waleys says that numerical division of the theme in the modern style is not just a gimmick, but most useful for both the preacher and his auditors:

Indeed if only one division of the theme be made, still that division will be beneficial as to those matters, as much for the preacher as for the hearer. For the moderns began not just because of the vogue, as others believe, to divide the theme, which the ancients did not customarily do. Truly it is useful for the preacher, because division of the theme into separate parts affords an opportunity for dilation in the farthest continuation of his sermon. For the hearer truly it is most useful, because when the preacher divides the theme and afterwards follows the parts of the division in order and clearly, both the matter of the sermon and the form and manner of the preaching is more easily understood and retained; that will not be the case if the preacher proceeds unclearly or without order and in a confused form.[86]

Of special interest in this advice is the assumption on Thomas of Waleys's part that both preacher and auditor relied on the numerical system for retaining discourse, for the key both to successful dilation and to retention is orderly division by number. This manual was written for a university setting, in which preacher and hearers were scholars, although the same method was used in preaching to the laity.[87] The fourteenth-century Dominican preacher, Giordano of Pisa, whose sermons were taken down by dictation while he spoke, uses the method of division constantly. Since he preached commonly two or three times a day, Friar Giordano often only got through the first few divisions of his sermons, though he always announces all of them in order in his introduction. When this happened, he would promise to continue where he left off at a later time – and he did, invariably picking up exactly where he left off. These sermons were taken down as they were preached; they were not corrected.[88]

Aristotle's *Topics*, after all, are both a logic and rhetoric text; Aristotle understood his text to provide a basic structure of *topoi*, "places," useful in composing particular arguments, and urged his students to memorize them as such.[89] The *Topics*, together with similar texts by Boethius and Cicero, was the basic medieval text in dialectic; its advocacy of a trained memory may well be the point at which dialectic and rhetoric meet and diverge in the liberal arts after the thirteenth century, especially since its method coincides readily with the numerical grid system that we have seen to be already in common scholarly use:

For just as in a person with a trained memory, a memory of things themselves is immediately caused by the mere mention of their *loci*, so these habits too [having a "thorough knowledge of premises at the tip of one's tongue"] will make a man readier in reasoning, because he has his premises classified before his mind's eye, each under its number.[90]

Notice how Aristotle sees a true relationship between logic and memory-work in terms of method and heuristic, as the same orderly numbering scheme that serves as a mnemonic hook for textual common-places in rhetorical *memoria* serves as a hook for the premises of logic. This functional connection between the two, and the definition of memorial arts as a kind of logic persists well into the Renaissance. For example, the fifteenth-century Perugian physician, Mattheolus Mattheoli, refers to Aristotle's *Topics* as an important memory text ("De memoria augenda," ii.recto).

Several excellent examples of how thematic division works mnemonically can be found in Robert of Basevorn's treatise on preaching. For a sermon on the Passion, Robert suggests the following "division" of the text: "Jesus iterum clamans voce magna emisit spiritum," Mt. 27:50 (I will quote the Latin text here because the word-play, essential to its mnemonic effectiveness, cannot be reproduced in an English translation):

Hic notantur: Passionis utilitas, *Jesus*; patientis potestas, *clamans*; humanitatis veritas, *voce magna*; patiendi libertas, *emisit*; separationis acerbitas, *spiritum*.[91]

This is the basic division into five, a portion of the theme plus a rhyming catchphrase which in some way (not always clear to me, I confess) abstracts the major idea to be developed from each of the five divisions.

Elementary memory design

Then comes the subdivision, also in five parts:

Subdivitur tunc sic: Quinque sunt vocales, scilicet *A E I O U*, quae omnem vocem faciunt. Sic quinque vulnera Christi omnem sonum, sive doloris sive gaudii faciunt. Vide *in manibus A* et *E*: [Jer. 31:3] "Attraxi te miserans" et: [Is. 49:16] "Ecce in manibus meis descripsi te"; *I in latere*: talem enim figuram imprimit vulnus lanceae, hoc est "ostium arcae" quod "in latere," etc. in Gen. [6:16] et in Joan. [20:27]: "Infer digitum tuum huc et mitte in latus meum, et noli esse incredulus," etc.; *O* et *U in pedibus*: [Ps. 8:6] "Omnia subjecit Deus sub pedibus ejus". Ideo ut consequaris dicas facto: [Job 23:11] "Uestigia ejus secutus est pes meus."[92]

No one will have any difficulty in recognizing this counsel to be at once typically "medieval" and, from a modern standpoint, bizarre to the point of intellectual decadence. Yet the scheme proposed is eminently sensible as a mnemonic both for composing and for delivering a sermon, as well as providing auditors with a clear structure within which they can grasp and retain the major points of the sermon.

This example, like many others, combines a variety of mnemonic structures, which in this case are also reflected in its compositional structures.[93] The theme is the Passion, and the preacher elects to divide by fives, a number with evident associations to his subject because there were five wounds in the cruci-fixion. A mnemonic rhyme composed of summary catchphrases organizes the main division in five. Then, in the subdivision, one remembers the five wounds, imposing upon the structure of those five another five, the five vowels, or "voces," perhaps used because of the word's punning association with "voce magna," the third division of the text which deals with the theme "humanitatis veritas." (One should, I think, notice how fundamental a prin-ciple homophony – punning of all sorts – is to these mnemonics; one encoun-ters what I have called "visualized homophony" throughout the history of written mnemonic advice, both as a principle for forming images and for asso-ciation of "ideas.") To each of the five vowels is attached a text whose initial letter is one of them, in their commonplace order. Five vowels, five wounds; the basic composition is complete, combining a scheme of *loci* and *imagines* that incorporates a numerical grid, on which are "placed" brief texts and other sorts of visual images. As hermeneutic, an interpretation of their meaning, attaching these particular texts to the five vowels is grotesque non-sense, but as an elementary device for retaining and recollecting them – as heuristic – it is both simple and effective. One can return to the theme of one's composition after a detailed exposition of any of its pieces and readily find one's place.

Robert of Basevorn's other examples follow the same principles. For a division into six of the theme, "Ego vox clamantis in deserto, parate viam Domini," he suggests using the six basic syllables of the chant, a pun on "vox clamantis." To these six notes – ut, re, mi, fa, sol, la – are attached the texts for the subdivision, as follows:

1) UT filii lucis ambulate; 2) REvertere, revertere, sulamitis, revertere, revertere ut intueamur te; 3) MIsere animae tuae placens Deo; 4) FAcite dignos fructus poeniten-tiae; 5) SOLve vincula colli tui, captiva filia Syon; 6) LAvamini, mundi estote.[94]

This is a most revealing application of the technique called "solmization," for it shows that Robert of Basevorn understood that the device was primarily a mnemonic, and could thus be utilized in non-musical contexts. It also suggests how much more broadly the function of a mnemonic was understood then than it is now (when we restrict it to simple reiterative tasks).

The principle of attaching a syllable to a particular musical value or "degree" of a chord or scale was known in antiquity, and indeed is found in virtually every culture.[95] It is most notably discussed in the Middle Ages in a letter of Guido d'Arezzo to the monk, Michael. There is evidence that solmization was used in medieval Europe before Guido, but the Benedictines were certainly happy to give him credit for having "invented" it, and the system he describes became the dominant one, indeed the foundation of what Westerners still use. Guido's syllables are taken from a hymn to John the Baptist, "Ut queant laxis"; these syllables then became the names of the six parts of a hexachord, at that time the unit organizing musical tones. As Guido writes to Michael:

You have therefore a system for learning unheard melody most easily and correctly . . . For after I began to teach my pupils this system, some of them were able easily to sing melodies unknown [to them] in less than three days, which with other systems would have taken many weeks.[96]

His system is designedly mnemonic, "for retaining each note in the memory,"[97] whether you knew the melody before or not, "quem scias vel nescias." For they are a kind of alphabet. Indeed, Guido's analysis of the purpose and function of musical notation seems to derive from Isidore of Seville's definition of the purpose of letters, that is, to hold things in memory, including what we do not already know. Just as the alphabet enables us to hear again and retain in memory the voices/words of those who are not actually present and whom we have never heard or seen in the flesh, so musical notation is, in this way, like an alphabet (and so says John of Salisbury, in a passage I will examine in the next part of this chapter).

Here as well as in any other medieval text, we can understand that "rules" were thought to be, as Aristotle says, built up from repeated memories, the principle being to recognize and organize likeness, even in things never seen before. This is not mnemonic in the restricted sense that moderns tend to understand it, but in the larger sense of how all learning takes place. Learning is regarded as a process of discovering more effective, efficient, inclusive mnemonics – for memory, as Hugh of St. Victor says, is the basis of learning. To learn the alphabet (and numbers were designated by letters of the alphabet, too, we should keep in mind) was to be possessed of a set of infinitely-"rich" mnemonics – not only a "skill," in the modern sense, that would enable one to read signs on a piece of vellum, but a key opening the door to the whole cultural complex of institutionalized practices signified in the word *memoria*. This is an analysis of learning that differs from our own in its emphasis upon memory and memorial cues, but it is very far from being simple rote.

Whatever the number of one's sermon division, Robert of Basevorn recommends attaching a set of symbols or markers that incorporate that number and can be used as a mnemonic for the subdivisions. For example, besides the two already described, Robert suggests the seven mercies of God, the eight Beatitudes, the nine orders of angels, the Ten Commandments, the twelve hours of the day. But eleven, he says, is almost never used, and never a number greater than twelve, for one will lose track. This observation is borne out in a catalogue of such numbered groups of items that was made anonymously and attached, as Book IV, to Hugo de Folieto's *De avibus*. Though many threes and sevens, fours, sixes, tens, and nines are listed, there are only two elevens – and nothing greater than twelve.[98] It is also useful, Basevorn says, to break up a larger number; for example, subdividing an initial division of nine into three sets of three, since there are so many threes that three presents no problem. Mary and Richard Rouse comment concerning a sermon of Alan of Lille on the Trinity that it is "an extravaganza of triplicity" – so too they well characterize the sermons of Innocent III as amounting to "a sequence of lists" of threes or fives or fours or sevens.[99] These items are the "singula" of which Hugh speaks, sorted and stored like similar coins in the properly numbered compartments of the memorial storehouse.

THE ALPHABET AND KEY-WORD SYSTEM

The number grid which Hugh of St. Victor describes was but one of several memorial heuristics taught in the Middle Ages. Memory training, we learn from Quintilian, was an elementary component of learning to read and to write. The numerical coding seems best designed to remember and be able to collate (that is, move discrete pieces of texts about in various combinations) longer works, like the Psalms, although it clearly can be used for a variety of other purposes as well. But in addition to such a task, a trained memory needs to have cross-referencing systems, and these also seem to have been taught among the educational basics.

Quintilian speaks both of memorizing a text in (numerical) order, and of marking the passages one especially wants or needs to remember with mental *notae*. *Notae* are discussed twice in relation to memory training. First, describing the system of *loci* and *imagines*, Quintilian suggests imprinting in orderly progression a spacious house with many rooms, and then marking the items to be remembered by a *nota*, either an associative sign (an anchor to remind one of navigation, for instance) or a key-word, "for what is slipping from the memory is recovered by the admonition of a single word." These *notae* are then placed in the orderly series of rooms. He prefers, however, a simpler system, yet one still using *notae*. After one divides a text into short sections, and has repeated these to oneself two or three times and perhaps written them down as well, one then marks passages one especially needs to recollect with *notae* which one has invented for oneself.[100] Martianus Capella some 400 years later also advises using *notae* to mark passages, and the word is found commonly in memory advice, and ubiquitously written out in the margins of manuscripts against passages that either the scribe or a later reader thought to be especially important for remembering.

It is unclear from Quintilian and other writers whether these *notae* or *notulae* are to be inscribed on the physical page or only in memory, as Hugh of St. Victor counsels; clearly some were made physically, for marginal marks do occur in manuscripts, copied by scribes evidently to help users of the books. But since every reader is advised to make *notae*, most mnemonic signs must have been devised mentally, especially when books were used by many different readers over several generations. In manuscript margins from the twelfth century on, one finds commonly the word, "nota," addressed to the reader. It is the imperative singular of the verb "notare," "make a note," and it points out an important or difficult passage that the reader might wish particularly to mark with a "nota" of some sort of his own to help remember it.

Mental marking is mnemonically advantageous because each individual makes up his own system of *notulae*, his own filing system, and as we know from *Ad Herennium*, one's own *notae* and *imagines* are to be preferred to memorizing a pre-existent system, because such exercise stimulates the memory more fully and fixes it more securely. Hugh of St. Victor describes a completely mental system; Robert Holcot, in a text we will examine again later, says that as he reads he imagines a memory image projected onto the particular text that he wishes to remember, and he gives detailed instructions in his commentaries for making these. Yet the written manuscript containing them is a plain one, rubricated but without any drawing or decoration. Only in the margin, opposite each verbal picture, is written the single word "pictura." Perhaps we might understand the word in this context not as a noun, but, on the analogy of "nota," as a command to the reader that he is to make a picture from the written description, evidently in his mind.[101]

At the end of the English Middle Ages, Stephen Hawes writes of the orator tucking into his memory "sundry ymages," not only for the "mater . . . lyke to the tale" but also in a "recapytulacyon" ("re-chaptering" or "cross-heading") of each image by its "moralyzacyon," a general ethical topic or "common-place" heading. Much material – how much would have to vary individually – seems to have been assumed to be filed away not as a complete text (or not only as a complete text) but as sets of extracts "noted" in the memory. The verb *tractare*, meaning to "draw out" or "extract," is frequently used of a process of reading as well as of a genre of composition. To "tract" a text while reading it means to pull out of it the various matters that one wishes to squirrel away in one's memorial inventory. Then, when "composing a tract" (William of Ockham uses the gerund form, *tractandum*, to indicate this activity), one begins by collecting on a particular subject all the material, together with appropriate commentary, that one had previously "drawn out of" one's reading and filed away under a letter or a key-word or some other *nota*.

Elementary memory design

A late but important description of memory-work by the fifteenth-century Italian jurist, Peter of Ravenna, who wrote one of the works on the art of memory most popular in the Renaissance, states that a well-trained memory is most like a book containing both text and glosses. "For I daily read all my lectures of Canon Law without a book; but if I should have a book before my eyes, I deliver the textual concordances [*textum*] and glosses from memory so that I should not seem to omit the least syllable."[102] It is evident that by this time a lecturer could expect to have a book open before him, but even so, says Peter – astonishingly, from our point of view – he uses it as a prop to cue his memory for its concordances and glosses. At the end of the fifteenth century, Peter still "reads" regularly without a book (though he boasts of this ability), and supplies his lecturing apparatus more accurately and completely, he says, from his memory than by depending on a book. Moreover, he continues, he holds all the concordances and glosses securely and permanently in his memory-places, both what he has collected together regarding some legal matter and the glosses he has taught "regarding locations," which I take to mean, in this context, the textual locations (*loci*) to which such material was attached, often by some sort of *nota*, even if it were no more elaborate than the red underlining of the key-word or phrase.

His memory-places, Peter says, are arranged alphabetically: "on the nineteen letters of the alphabet I have placed twenty thousand extracts of both sorts of Law." I will come back to this passage shortly to discuss exactly how he says he did this, but for now I want to stress his use of the alphabet as his ordering device. He uses, he says, the regular alphabet, but also "human figures in place of the letters and thus living, vivid images."[103] For the sake of vivid images, unusual ones of the sort memory can easily fix on, he can make use of a sort of human alphabet to indicate the various letters. He even suggests using the forms of enticing women in such a role: "illae enim multum memoriam meam excitant," "these greatly stimulate my memory," though, he adds, this is not a technique for those who hate women or who cannot control themselves.

Evidence that alphabets were commonly used as a mnemonic ordering device is scattered but persistent in both ancient and early medieval books. Aristotle describes (in *De memoria*) the use of letters of the Greek alphabet as an ordinary method for ordering memorized material. But if one is using an alphabet to file lots of different topics, one might well need more than one set of such "places" to accommodate one's material, lest one's memory be overwhelmed by trying to crowd too much into one place (a persistent warning in memory texts). To avoid this, one needs more than one set of alphabets, containing different forms though having still a rigid, easily-recoverable, order. That is what Peter of Ravenna was doing with his human "alphabets."

It is a curiosity (to modern scholars) of medieval books that tables of Greek, Hebrew, Coptic, runic, and even wholly imaginary alphabets are found side by side in a number of monastic manuscripts. It is also an insufficiently explained curiosity that books containing the Bestiary, mora-lized descriptions of animals both real and imagined, are found commonly in monastery libraries. Scholars have wondered what function such apparently puerile, unscholarly material might serve to justify its preservation. I will return to this question in chapters 4 and 7, to make my case more fully, but my hypothesis is that they functioned not only to delight and intrigue medieval students but to provide them with mnemonically valuable heuris-tics, orderly "foundations" or sets of mnemonic *loci*, which can continue to have value throughout one's education (a lifetime project).

Learning an alphabet is a part of grammar; this is also the point at which one lays down one's fundamental mnemonic apparatus. Mnemonic writers such as Thomas Bradwardine and John of Garland assume their students have certain "sets" of images already in their memories – in addition to the alphabet and numbers, these include the Zodiac and the "characteristics of animals, [*voces animantium*]" a collection of attributes that derives from the various versions of the Bestiary, a work that itself goes back to Alexandrine Greece. Ordered lists of this sort, I propose, were deliberately memorized in order to serve as potential mnemonic heuristics, "seats" into which one could place the variety of diverse material one would acquire in one's education and reading.

Morgan Library MS. M 832, a manuscript written and painted in the last half of the twelfth century at the monastery of Göttweig in Austria, contains in its first folio the letters of five alphabets – Hebrew, Greek, Latin, "Scythian," and Runic, taken from Rhabanus Maurus's "De inventione linguarum." The rest of the manuscript is a Bestiary. In light of the mnemonic role of alphabets and of the *voces animantium*, finding the two sorts of material together in a single manuscript makes some practical pedagogical sense, for such a manuscript would have served the monks by providing them with material to help them form sets of memory-places (indeed, it is hard otherwise to explain a practical reason for twelfth-century Austrian monks to learn such alphabets as "Scythian" or Runic).[104]

There is evidence of scholars using both imaginary and real alphabetical sets later in their careers. Robert Grosseteste's scheme of referencing symbols is derived eclectically from various alphabets, and many of his *notae* are imaginary. Boncompagno da Signa lists in his *Rhetorica novissima* (1230) a variety of signs and symbols that are useful as artificial aids to natural memory, including "deposita alphabeta," and describes as well how he has used an imaginary alphabet as a memory code. By this means, he claims, "within thirty days I have memorized the names of 500 students. And I also affirm, which will seem more remarkable, that in the sight of all I have named every one by his own name, not omitting his surname and where he was from: wherefore, together and singly, they were overcome with admir-ation."[105]

Boncompagno's feat may appear pallid in comparison with some of the feats of memory described by other scholars, but my concern is not with his talent but with his method – using an imaginary alphabet. Bernhard Bischoff describes some manuscripts from the ninth and eleventh centuries in which the names of the months and of numbers in Greek, Hebrew, and Coptic are given in parallel columns. Such lists, he says, "worked like magnets" in attracting names from other languages as well, but "I think . . . these lists and enumerations in general cannot be regarded as the result of, or as an attempt at genuine language study. They might rather be regarded as a symptom of a naive curiosity which manifests itself also in the collecting – it is a kind of collecting – of foreign and strange alphabets which can be observed in manuscripts from the eighth century on and continued to post-medieval times," collections which included, indiscriminately, both real and invented alphabets.[106] Such a long life, it seems to me, would suggest that readers found utility in these lists (after all *curiositas* or the useless collecting of knowledge was regarded as sinful); I suggest that they are collections of *notae* that might be useful in schemes for memory coding, and were provided to supplement, as a reader might wish, those with which he was already familiar.

For after all it was Isidore of Seville himself, that chief conduit of ancient pedagogy, who defined the function of written letters in terms of their memorial utility. Alphabets are a kind of *notae*, and these written letters were invented "in order to remember things. For lest they fly into oblivion, they are bound in letters. For so great is the variety of things that all cannot be learned by hearing, nor contained only in memory."[107] Writing is a servant to memory, a book its extension, and like the memory itself, written letters call up the voices of those that are no longer present. Two things are worth emphasizing in Isidore's definition. First, note that the emphasis on the primacy of memory over writing, which one encounters in a text like Plato's *Phaedrus*, is still present here in Isidore. Secondly, one should also note that writing and memorizing are regarded by Isidore still as essentially the same process: writing is an activity of remembering, as remembering is writing on the tables of the mind. And all textual *notae*, such as marks of punctuation, or editorial signs and the shorthand symbols and abbreviations known properly as *notataria*, are of the same class as letters. Isidore defines a *nota* as "figura propria in litterae modum ponita," "a distinctive shape used in the manner of written letters."

By defining the essential utility of written letters as being memorial in nature – writing is to keep us from forgetting – Isidore gives a remarkably succinct statement of a principle tenet of pre-modern pedagogy. A student in ancient schools (and these earliest accomplishments were the work of the nursery, according to Quintilian) first learned his letters, beginning with their names even before their forms, though Quintilian prefers, he says, that children learn the two together, endorsing especially the use of ivory alphabet-blocks for children to play with. In a custom deriving from Greek education, Latin letters were learned from A to X and then backwards from X to A, and then in pairs, such as AX, BV, CT, DS, and so on. Finally, breaking the order entirely, they were taught in all various combinations.[108]

Quintilian rightly stresses that such a method teaches children to learn letters individually, not just in rote order.[109] But the exercise also induces a facility for *calculating* with the alphabet, that is moving it around quickly and surely in all sorts of both common and odd combinations. Such facility is very useful for the kind of mnemonic "shuffling" necessary for composition, and would create an alphabetical heuristic as flexible as a numerical one. As Quintilian says, "the basics of grammar are solely a question of *memoria*";[110] he meant not only developing memorized content but, of equal importance, the capability for secure, rapid, and capacious system-building which characterizes trained *memoria*. "For memory is most necessary to an orator . . . and there is nothing like practice for strengthening and developing it. And at the tender age of which we are now speaking, when originality is impossible, memory is almost the only faculty which can be developed by the teacher."[111]

After individual letters, instruction proceeded to syllables (ba-, be-, bo-, bi-, bu-, etc.) and then to words; all this time, writing was also taught, the student doing exercises on his wax tablet to complement the mental exercises performed on the "wax tablet" of his memory. Reciting was part of the reading-writing process from the very beginning. Quintilian recommends that students learn reading, recitation, and writing from material that contains sound moral advice,[112] the sayings ("dicta") of famous men and lines from the poets. As Marrou says, "A la lecture et à l'écriture est intimement associé la récitation: l'enfant apprend par coeur les petits textes sur lesquels il s'est exercé, à la fois pour se former et meubler sa mémoire."[113] "To form one's character and furnish one's memory" – they were the same goal in educational practice and philosophy from antiquity throughout the Middle Ages.

Reading required careful preparation, including learning the proper use of punctuation. Marrou mentions traces of such student-originated preparation still observable on papyri (which were written without any sort of punctuation, even word-divisions), where strokes have been made, by students not the scribe, to separate the words and lines, and to cut words up into syllables for scansion.[114] *Cola*, *commata*, and *periodi* served a dual purpose; they marked the sense- and pause-divisions, and they also cut the text into the brief segments that could be memorized as a single unit. Quintilian says that a "period" should never be too long to be recited or read in a single breath. It also "must not be too long to be carried in the memory" as a single, intelligible unit.[115] A period contains at least two *cola*, Quintilian says, units that are not semantically self-standing but are "rhythmically complete," *numeris conclusis*.[116] The use of rhythm to define units of prose is also mnemonically valuable, of course, for rhythm serves the synaesthetic requirements of "rich" mnemonics. A basic memorial unit is the colon, a short segment of text that is coherent (it is, says Isidore, a "sententia" – "sentence," in Middle English), and is marked by a medial point in many manuscripts.[117]

Notae also included short-hand marks and abbreviations. Systems of such marks, numbering many hundreds, were taught as the *notataria* to ancient and medieval notaries and lawyers; students were taught the complex system of Latin abbreviations that we encounter in all medieval manuscripts. Thomas Bradwardine concludes his treatise on artificial memory (*c.* 1335) by saying that "whoever will learn the notatarial art will attain the highest perfection" in the craft of memory.

John of Salisbury's *Metalogicon*, written some fifty years after Hugh of St. Victor's preface, is particularly interesting for the light it sheds on what was thought to be the link between memory and *notaria*. Like Hugh, John of Salisbury characterizes memory as "the mind's treasure-chest, a sure and reliable place of safe-deposit for perceptions."[118] Memory is a natural gift, but, like all natural abilities, must be cultivated and trained (here he echoes both *Ad Herennium* and *De oratore*).

John of Salisbury especially laments the decline of training in *notataria*. He is discussing punctuation, and evidently thinking of what Isidore called the *notae sententiarum*, the editorial marks devised in antiquity for textual scholarship. These little notes, which "indicate the mode of what is written and show whether the latter is clear or obscure, certain or doubtful, and so on" were powerful tools, "highly effective for both comprehension *and retention*" (my emphasis). They are to reading and memory what notes are to the chant.

That such great import has existed in such tiny notations should not seem strange, for singers of music likewise indicate by a few graphic symbols numerous variations in the acuteness and gravity of tones [= pitch]. For which reason such characters are appropriately known as "the keys of music." If, however, the little notations we spoke of above gave access to such great science, I am surprised that our forefathers, who were so learned, were not aware of this, or that the keys to so much knowledge were lost.[119]

Two things at once are being spoken of here. First of all, he speaks about the particular system of editorial *notae* (obelisk, apostrophe, etc.) described by Isidore of Seville, which John claims is no longer taught, and the secret of which has been lost. John of Salisbury also recognizes the general importance of all kinds of *notae* for memory training, for he assumes that these strange marks, like all the other *notae*, are memory aids, necessary both for retention and comprehension. And though the knowledge of some systems of ancient *notae* and memory coding are now obscure, still grammar, including memory, must be studied at least from the books we do have. For "if all the books of the grammarians are not available, it is still very helpful, for the interpretation of what we read, to have fixed in our memory even this fragmentary survey" (the *Metalogicon* itself).[120]

That the *ars notataria* was associated specifically with advanced memory training is also suggested by a twelfth-century gloss on the *Ad Herennium*, the so-called "Alanus" gloss, which may be the work of Alan of Lille, although no one can say certainly.[121] Commenting on the passage in Book III, in which Tully cautions against those Greek works which offer lists of pre-formed "imagines verborum," because they are both inadequate in scope and less effective for memory than images one makes oneself, the glossator writes that the author "did not have the notarial art in mind."[122] He clearly knows, as did John of Salisbury, that *notae* are important for memory, and recognizes in his comment that the accumulation of *notae* that one learned in the advanced studies of this art helped to perfect the training of memory.

Memorial *notae* were commonly used for concording schemes. Of these, the prototype is an alphabetical heuristic, which has left many traces in the organization of written texts. The existing account of it, which describes its use with a degree of detail comparable to what Hugh's preface tells us about the number grid, is very late (fifteenth century). Still, what it describes is borne out by the actual design of medieval concordances, *distinctio* collections, and other preachers' tools. And we do have Aristotle's succinct account of an alphabetical memorial system in *De memoria*, Quintilian's reference to key-words to aid recollection, and certain other evidence which we will look at soon. This alphabetical system produces what is essentially a *catena*, in which a key-word or phrase acts as the hook for several bits of stored material, the indexing words themselves being stored alphabetically. The monastic practice so well described by Dom Leclercq, "whereby the verbal echoes [of Scripture] so excite the memory that a mere allusion will spontaneously evoke whole quotations"[123] is a version of this type of memorial organization.

The description occurs in the testimentary letter by Peter of Ravenna which I cited earlier in this discussion; it prefaces the memory rules which form the body of his book, *Fenix*.[124] As is the custom of such advertisements, the language is self-congratulatory and inflated, but the method itself is credible, and borne out by other evidence. Peter says he has "placed" 20,000 legal extracts, 1,000 texts from Ovid, 200 from Cicero, 300 sayings of the philosophers, the greater part of Valerius Maximus, 7,000 texts from Scripture, and other pieces of learning on 19 letters of the Roman alphabet. If he searches the letter A, for example, he is able to produce immediately texts and examples from learned sources on a variety of subjects, "de alimentis, de alienatione, de absentia, de arbitris, de appellationibus, et de similibus quae jure nostro habentur incipientibus in dicta littera A," "about provisions, about foreign property, about absence, about judges, about appeals, and about similar matters in our law which begin with the letter A."[125] Or, if a sacred context is wanted, out come texts on Antichrist, on worship ("adulatio") and other subjects. Or on natural history, texts from Ovid, Valerius, and Cicero can be produced on A-beginning animals. And when he gets all the way through, he can immediately go back and begin his lists over again. Even allowing for boasting, this is impressive and Peter clearly intended it to be so to his contemporaries.

But more interesting to me at the moment than the quantity of information held is the way it is organized. A letter of the alphabet acts as the primary key or *locus* or file. Then texts are placed in the file by a secondary key, a word beginning with the primary letter. In Peter's scheme, the key-words are themselves arranged also by general topic: natural history, sacred subjects, vices and virtues, etc. And the confirmation of his orderly arrangement lies in his ability to replicate his lists. In other words, the memory in this scheme is organized like a subject concordance of texts.

Peter of Ravenna says that though he stored his materials alphabetically, he pulled in from his memory both glosses and concordances according to their order (their "loci") in the text. A much earlier instance from which, I think, we can infer that an alphabetically sorted set of glosses is intended to be used in this same way, keyed to words as they occur in their textual order, is Jerome's index and gloss of the Hebrew names in the Bible. This, together with Eusebius's canonical tables, was one of the most familiar of scholarly tools. It was incorporated into a larger alphabetical glossary of the whole Bible from at least the thirteenth century (as part of the "Paris" format). But Jerome's original construction of the index applies the principles of the memorial heuristics I have described.[126]

In its written form, Jerome's index is first catalogued by a particular book of the Bible, beginning with Genesis and proceeding in canonical order. The Hebrew words occurring within each book are then grouped alphabetically. But they are not "fully" alphabetized, that is, not beyond the initial letter. Instead they are given in the order in which they occur in the actual text. So the first word glossed in Genesis, under A, is "Aethiopiam" (1:13), followed by "Assyriorum" (1:14), "Adam" (1:19), "Abel" (4:2), "Ada" (4:19), and so on. The first word under G is "Geon," the name of one of the rivers flowing from Eden in 1:13, followed by "Gomer," a son of Japheth mentioned in 10:2, "Gergesaeus" at 10:16, and the place-names "Gerara," "Gaza," and "Gomorrha," given in the order in which they occur in 10:19.

In a preface, Jerome describes how he came to make this index, and what his intention was. He says he was urged by two of his conventual brothers, who considered him to be notably proficient in Hebrew, to bring together and expand glosses and explanations of Hebrew names in the Old Testament that had been made by Origen and Philo; "and, excited by the usefulness of this suggestion, I hastily ran through one at a time each book according to the order of the Scriptures."[127] Each book at a time, following the order of the written text, is exactly what the extant index shows. But notice that Jerome considers this scheme to be especially *useful*, particularly user-friendly in contrast to the work of his predecessors. Other sorts of glossaries are known from early periods. For example, the "Old Latin" glosses of the Gospels, which were copied into the late seventh-century Book of Durrow, represent traditions independent of Jerome but even older. But these glosses in the Book of Durrow are alphabetized out to the second or third letter, not geared to their occurrence in the text as Jerome's are.[128]

The order followed in Jerome's compilation responds to the principle of mental concording, and the mnemonic principles which he assumed that its users would also have. Absolute alphabetical ordering is a scheme best adapted to the needs of readers working from a written codex physically open in front of them, the way readers now work. In such a circumstance, it is much easier to find words listed in completely alphabetical order, the way a modern dictionary is, than to find them in a partially or initially alphabetized list.[129] But for someone who is working from a text stored discretely in numbered memory bins, Jerome's system is actually much quicker and easier than a modern list would be, for one finds the glossed word in the order of its first occurrence in the text. To retain any of the glosses one needed, one could simply attach it as it came up, using the chapter and verse order of the text itself, as Peter of Ravenna centuries later described himself doing.

That this method, useful only to someone working primarily from memory, continued in use is indicated as well by a small continuous gloss on the whole Bible, including Jerome's prefaces, that is written out, after the fully-alphabetized dictionary of Hebrew words, at the very end of a French Bible of c. 1325 (Huntington Library MS. HM 1073). It is sometimes supposed that full alphabetization constituted progress so apparent that it inevitably replaced such methods as Jerome's (and is a sure indication of literacy driving out memory), yet in this manuscript of the late Middle Ages both sorts of organization appear, the one for a large amount of encyclopedic material, the other for a much shorter, more selective amount, keyed to long-familiar texts. The individual glosses are very brief (about one colon apiece) and each is marked by a red or blue paraph, colored alternately, and they follow exactly the order of the text from Genesis on. It would be a simple task to slip these glosses into one's memorial places, and bring them out at the proper "locations" in the text, as Peter of Ravenna did.

All of these schemes bespeak the assumption that a good memory is a library of texts, and a thoroughly catalogued and indexed one at that. And in this intimate relation between memory and page, the memory performs the greater part of indexing and organization. The structure of the various schemes is geared to the requirements of the memory. One might well wonder why Jerome bothered to classify the Hebrew names alphabetically at all; why not just give them in the order in which they appear in each book? If Jerome had composed with the understanding that his index would always be physically open before his readers, as they recited their way all the way through Genesis each time they used his list, he might have done such a thing. But since he expected his list to be used to compose a mental gloss that would be available to someone speaking from memory, he knew practically that such a scheme would not work, for it would overwhelm the active memory. "Memory rejoices in brevity"; one consequence of this is that individual items must be grouped and clustered into classifications and sub-classifications in order to provide recollection with the means of finding them surely and quickly. This fundamental psychological principle underlies all indexing systems. As Quintilian says concerning *partitio*, the orderly arrangement of all our propositions, "it follows nature as its guide" and is the greatest of aids to memory.[130]

Another interesting example of a subject concordance is the famous indexed "Tabula," compiled by the English Franciscans, Robert Grosseteste and Adam Marsh, around 1235–43.[131] The marginal notes Grosseteste habitually made in the books he owned are a striking feature of his work; his library, left to the Franciscan convent at Oxford, was valued for these annotations as well as for the books themselves. As R. W. Hunt has written, "More books containing autograph notes by him have perhaps survived than of any other medieval writer of comparable eminence."[132] Most of these marginalia are subject-headings or corrections to the manuscript; often they simply identify the source of a quotation in the text. But there are also extensive cross-references; for instance, in a copy of Boethius' *De consolatione philosophiae* Grosseteste added "a dozen references . . . to various works of Augustine,"[133] citing, as was the custom, by title and book number, no more. He also added punctuation divisions to this particular Boethius, which had been copied without them.

A typical page of one of his books, known to be annotated in his hand, is reproduced (from Bodleian Library MS. Bodley 198) as the frontispiece to D. A. Callus's *Robert Grosseteste, Scholar and Bishop*; the writing is a highly abbreviated cursive akin to the "littera inintelligibilis" used by Thomas Aquinas for his dictation draft of a portion of the *Summa contra gentiles*. Such notation, in similarly abbreviated writing, is sometimes found in other scholars' manuscripts. But Grosseteste's books are also filled with marks (*notae*) each of which is keyed to a particular topic, that serve as a subject index to the book's contents. The key to these *notae* was found by Professor Harrison Thomson, bound with a Bible now in the Municipal Library of Lyons (Lyons MS. 414). Fifteen folios preceeding the Bible contain a topical concordance of texts from Scripture and the Fathers, each topic being marked by a sign or *nota*. The first four pages of this concordance give an index of the signs; there are just over 400 of these, and Thomson comments that it would be "no inconsiderable task" just to remember them (though no harder than remembering the thousand-plus signs taught to Roman notaries). "All the letters of the Roman and Greek alphabets, mathematical figures, conjoined conventional signs, modifications of zodiacal signs, and additional dots and strokes and curves are pressed into service. There seems to be no recognizable system behind the choice of a sign for a given subject."[134] This last observation suggests strongly the nature of these *notae* as purely heuristic, deriving from a privately-devised scheme for filling discrete bits of information, of exactly the sort commonly advised for memory design.

The concordance of texts itself follows this directory in the Lyons manuscript. Nine major classifications were used, called *distinctiones*, but the copyist has written only "ad dist. vi et parum plus," "and a little more."[135] The main headings are divided into sub-topics, and the *notae* are keyed to these. Professor Hunt has transcribed a typical entry: "ℱ Quomodo philosophia accipienda sit a nobis." (The way philosophy should be received by us)[136] There follow the citations, first those to the Bible, and then, in a separate paragraph, those to the works of the Fathers and more recent theological writings. Citations to pagan authors are given off to the right, in a separate column. Thomson and Hunt both conclude that the purpose of the compilation was to serve as a subject index to Grosseteste's books. Hunt observes that the system continued to be used among the Franciscans in the second half of the thirteenth century, for other books so marked have been found.[137]

But how, for whom, and why was the compilation written out? The possible answers to these questions remain somewhat mysterious. Thomson suggests that Grosseteste uses the signs so that as he rapidly thumbed his books he could find appropriate passages on a given subject, without the bother of re-reading. "For an ecclesiastic as busy as Grosseteste was, the gain was considerable, but it entailed an initial reading and indexing that must have demanded extremely close attention."[138] To this observation of Thomson's, we should join the remark of the Franciscan regent-master at Oxford in 1316–17, William of Alnwick, who, in a disputation, challenged his opponent's reference to one of Grosseteste's marginal notes made in his copy of Aristotle's *Physics*. Alnwick says that Grosseteste wrote in the margins of his books "when some noteworthy thought occurred to him . . . so that it should not escape his memory, just as he also wrote many 'cedulae' which are not all [authoritative]. What he wrote disconnectedly in the margin of his copy of the *Physics* is of no greater authority than the other cedulae he wrote, which are all kept in the library of the Friars Minor at Oxford, as I have seen with my own eyes."[139]

It seems to me most likely that Grosseteste's indexing system was devised by him originally for his own use in designing his memory. The *notae* are both formed and used according to the familiar pedagogical principles, placed against passages of a text that one particularly wishes to remember, or are especially important or difficult to recall. Grosseteste is unusual only in having drawn his *notae* so systematically with pen and ink, instead of mentally projecting them as he memorized his passages (perhaps the fact that these were his own books rather than belonging to a whole community freed him to do this).

But we should be as grateful to Grosseteste's penwork as we are to Hugh of St. Victor's elementary preface, for it gives us an instance of just how the sort of memorial subject concordance which a medieval student was expected to devise for himself was put together. I myself doubt, given the compositional habits of the time, that Grosseteste thumbed constantly through his manuscripts to find material for his voluminous work. We may usefully remember Hugh of St. Victor's admonition: "Too great would be the labor in such a task." Thomson rightly observes that the initial effort to read and index the books was clearly immense; indeed that is so, but it is exactly the sort of concentrated, thoughtful *meditatio* required in medieval study to memorize, ruminate, and make one's reading one's own. At the end of it, Grosseteste had a mental concordance of considerable scope and power; his ability to cross-reference and "quote" (in the medieval sense) his Boethius, to compile his tabula, and indeed to compose all those tracts and commentaries and letters, scientific and pastoral works, in addition to his duties both at Oxford (a place with very few books in his day)[140] and as Bishop of Lincoln, attests to a memory supremely and securely designed, a remarkable, though by no means rare, realization of the ideal and goal of a medieval education.

Other evidence of the memorial function of the Grosseteste-Marsh tabulation, besides what is obvious from its method of creating *loci* by classification and sub-headings, lies in the fact that each entry follows a design that is almost, but significantly not quite, identical. First come the Biblical citations, in canonical order; then, in a separate group, the Fathers, beginning with the Latin Fathers (in the order Ambrose, Jerome, Augustine, Gregory), the Greek, and finally any recent theologians. Off to the side on the right are the references to pagan writers, Latin, then Greek, then Arabic.

But the individual works of authors such as Augustine (whom Grosseteste cites far more often and variously than anyone else) are not always given in the same order. I find this significant in establishing the memorial origin of the compilation. If it were being made from an indexed book open before the compiler, one would expect him to write down all the citations in the book, under their appropriate headings. This should have the effect of causing citations from a particular work to appear always in the same order relative to other works by that author. But this is not the case. Similarly, were the work being compiled from individual slips marked with a citation (an unlikely possibility), one would expect a constant order among the works cited, especially since all the numbers of the book- or chapter-divisions are given in order (as "Augustinus: ep. 9. 11. 15. 20. 38. 50. 57; De civ. dei li. 10, 11, 12, 13," etc.).[141] Why carefully order the one, but not the other, if one were organizing separate slips? That the design extends as far as authors, and then skips, as it were, to chapter numbers (the order in which a particular work is recalled), suggests to me that the citations are given in the order in which Grosseteste had stored them in memory, and not from a physically manipulated source.[142]

So why was the subject concordance written down (though incompletely)? Presumably to be of use to other scholars, as indeed it proved, for a long time, to be. Grosseteste's *tabula* amounts to a florilegium without the texts themselves being written out. A note in the manuscript tells us that Adam Marsh extended his master's signs and classifications; indeed, space is left under some entries in the Lyons manuscript, presumably for additional entries. This concern for expansion suggests to me that Grosseteste's system became "public," presumably when his library came to the Oxford Franciscans. The index guides a student with access to this particular library to making his own index by memorizing those passages to which the *notae* lead him.

Another interesting use of alphabetical organization is the second part of Book II of Albertus Magnus's treatise, *Mineralia*.[143] Here the chapter headings state the nature of the organizing principle: "De lapidus pretiosis incipientibus ab A," "Concerning precious stones beginning with A," and so on through Z. This would seem to reflect the way Albertus had organized his material mentally. Especially interesting is the fact that the names are not in absolute alphabetical order under each letter; so under B there are Balagius, Borax, Beryllus; under C, Carbunculus, Chalcedonis, Calcaphanos, Ceraurum, Celidonius, Celontes, Cegolites. Peter of Ravenna's lists also are not absolutely alphabetical; to me, this suggests someone arranging material mentally rather than alphabetizing written-out words with the aid of slips, simply because it is easier mentally to organize material using a few letters at a time than to alphabetize fully a number of long words. The latter is better done when one can manipulate written words physically, as anyone who has had to prepare an index will recognize. His method suggests strongly that Albertus is using a mental alphabetical heuristic, which he has simply transposed to a written document, writing on the page as he had written in memory before.

One alphabetizing principle that seems very odd and useless to us is employed in the index to a late-thirteenth-century manuscript of Sentences commentary by the Dominican friar, Richard Fishacre, who died in 1248 (New College, Oxford, MS.112).[144] The indexing words are arranged not according to initial letter but by their vowel combinations; in other words, by syllables rather than by letters. An explanation of the system is given (f.322):

this preceding index is arranged according to the order of the vowels in the alphabet, and according to the manner of their combinations [with consonants]; if you wish therefore promptly to find those things which are contained in the preceding book, take the subject concerning which the passage is made (principally) or should be made, and regard the vowel of its syllable, or of each of its syllables if it should be a two-syllable word; and having recourse to the index you should find the vowel or vowels written in the margin and ordered as previously said. And opposite the word you will find written the folio number, the page number, and even the line number in which you will be able to find what you seek; knowing this also, that "a" designates the first column [of the book opening], "b" the second, "c" the third, and "d" the fourth.

Accordingly, the index begins with monosyllables in "a" ("pax," "laus," "pars"); then bisyllables having "a" in each syllable ("adam"); then "a" plus "e"; "a" plus "i"; "a" plus "o"; "a" plus "u"; and so on through all five vowels singly and in combination. Only the first two syllables of multisyllabic words are considered for indexing purposes. This produces a list in which "locutio" and "pondus" both precede "locus," "pax" precedes "amor," and "terra" precedes "spera," for the initial consonants are not considered in the scheme.

Fishacre's indexer belonged to a culture that still learned to read Latin by recognizing syllables. They were the basic units from which words were thought to be built. Word-recognition and retention was basically a matter of syllable-recognition; Thomas Bradwardine's advice for word-memory is to make an image for each of the five vowels, and then for each possible combination of one consonant plus vowel. Remembering a whole word consists of stringing together the various images one has pre-formed for its syllables. The Fishacre index seems to me based upon a similar understanding of how words are recalled, simplified to a string of no more than two. Why the compiler virtually disregarded the order of the consonants accompanying the vowels is mysterious; evidently, in his mental arrangements, all the possible "a" syllables were grouped together, as Albertus Magnus grouped things by their initial letter. A scheme that groups by syllables is not inherently less useful as a mental heuristic than one which groups by initial letter; there were nineteen letters in the Roman alphabet (twenty-one if one includes "x" and "z," rarely used as initial consonants), but the Fishacre index allows forty-five groups altogether, so that there are actually many fewer individuals within each group than in the initial-letter schemes. It should be noted, however, that I know of no other index using this heuristic.

A mental library of *dictiones* and a library of physical books used the same heuristics. I have already discussed at length the enduring image of the trained memory as a library; to conclude this chapter, I would like to reflect briefly on their parallel cataloguing systems. The cupboard-like press in which medieval books were kept could be called an *armarium*, "cupboard," or a *columna*, "column," the word used in a library catalogue from 1400.[145] The books in these medieval *arcae* or *armaria* were labeled according to schemes of letters and numbers, sometimes used separately, sometimes in tandem. The sources we have for this information are library catalogues and sometimes the books themselves, mostly from the twelfth century and later. Typically, each book-press was assigned a letter, and each shelf (*gradus*) in it a number, starting from the bottom shelf to allow for expansion.[146] Sometimes another, subsidiary, number was assigned to each volume to indicate its place on its *gradus*. Alphabetizing as a heuristic scheme for libraries dates at least to the Alexandrine Library.[147] But the layout of the library imitates the design of the scholars' memories, as I have argued before; some of the best evidence for the similarity perceived between what is read and written in memory and in books is the way in which heuristic schemes taught for organizing one's memorial *arca* are also used, when collections are large enough to need them, to organize the codices in their wooden *arcae*.

4

The Arts of Memory

The mnemonic techniques that I have described so far are basic, their elementary nature attested by their ubiquity. *Divisio* and *compositio* are processes required by the physiology of memory itself, at least as the pre-modern world understood it. But it is important to keep in mind that in considering *memoria* we are dealing with more than just a set of techniques or a descriptive psychology, yet more specifically realized a value than those "ideas" (like "the Gothic") which modern students have attached to some philosophy or other, or to a metahistorical "mentalité." From antiquity, *memoria* was fully institutionalized in education, and like all institutions it was adapted to circumstances of history. *Memoria* unites written with oral transmission, eye with ear, and helps to account for the highly "mixed" oral-literate nature of medieval cultures that many historians of the subject have remarked. Yet it is clear that the later Middle Ages, from the twelfth century onward, was a far more "bookish" culture than the earlier medieval centuries had been. *Memoria* was adapted to that change, without – as a set of practices – losing its central place in medieval ethical life. In this chapter I will focus on this change by considering the revival in the thirteenth century of the ancient architectural mnemonic which I described in chapter 2.

Briefly, the history of the architectural mnemonic subsequent to its exposition in *Ad Herennium* and its espousal by Cicero in *De oratore* (both products of the first century B.C.) appears to be this: by the time of Quintilian (first century A.D.), the method of projecting images into architectural places, though still known, had declined in popularity and was considered cumbersome and gimmicky. This attitude persists in the rhetorical teaching of Julius Victor (fourth century). Medieval commentaries on the *Ad Herennium*, which date from the twelfth century or so, are usually silent on its mnemonic advice.[1] But in the thirteenth century, the architectural method enjoyed a revival, being commended as the best method by both Albertus Magnus and Thomas Aquinas.

It is clear from their remarks, however, that they understood the specific rules of Tully in the light of a medievalized tradition, the nature of which is the subject of my present chapter. The revival of Tully's art of memory occurred in the context of the classicizing fervor of the early humanists, among whom, for the purposes of this history, we must include the friars chiefly responsible for the Aristotelian renaissance that brought back into scholarly circulation his *De anima* and its appendices, the *Parva naturalia* including *De memoria et reminiscentia*. Aristotle gave a philosophical explanation for using arbitrary associations as a basic mnemonic tool; both Thomas's and Albertus's commentaries on *De memoria* use Tully as a prime example of the practical application of Aristotle's general precepts concerning the associative nature of the recollective search.

In addition to the Aristotelians, the "Ciceronians" of early humanist Italy played an important role in the revival of the architectural mnemonic; indeed, some evidence points to the circle around Brunetto Latini as one agency of this revival. And it is, it seems to me, the identification of this particular mnemonic scheme with humanism that led to its dominance in the memory texts of the Renaissance, which emanate from a provenance that is Italian and also Dominican. To that story, however, I will return after examining more particularly medieval schemes.[2]

The sources of the specific medievalness of "the arts of memory" I will discuss now are not, so far as I can determine at present, attributable to textual sources, such as some (unknown) non-Ciceronian body of rhetorical precepts. It seems related instead to manuscript painting conventions, the *Bestiary*, and various conventions of pictorial diagrams. In the early Middle Ages, *memoria* is discussed most often not in the context of rhetoric but rather in writings on meditation and prayer, in which a diagram-like "picture" is created mentally which serves as the site for a meditational *collatio*, the "gathering" into one "place" of the various strands of a meditational composition. A particularly illuminating and complex example utilizing the principles of medieval memorial "picturing" is Hugh of St. Victor's "De arca Noe mystica," which I discuss at length in chapter 7. That text is not, however, an art of memory; in this chapter I will discuss in particular three texts which purport to be "arts of memory," written by John of Garland, Albertus Magnus, and Thomas Bradwardine. They all clearly incorporate a medieval understanding of the precepts of *memoria*, which has wrought a thorough sea-change upon the classical mnemonic described in the *Ad Herennium*. I have chosen to discuss them out of chronological order because neither Bradwardine nor John of Garland show any close affinity to the *Ad Herennium*, but Albertus does – therefore, John of Garland and Bradwardine are good examples of medieval mnemotechnical principles, not derived directly from the classical text of Tully. Albertus wrote about one generation after John of Garland did, and Bradwardine some ninety years after Albertus.

It is often the confused student who can teach one the most about unstated general assumptions. One of the most revealing accounts of memory training from the early thirteenth century is the garbled account of the *Ad Herennium* on memory, found in John of Garland's *Parisiana poetria*. John seems to have acquired his education in Paris, and to have taught there except for a brief sojourn at Toulouse. He wrote in the 1230s, by which time the Aristotelian winds were blowing the *Ad Herennium* on memory into greater respectability, if not quite to comprehension. John recommends as most necessary for poets organizing their material for invention (composition) the "ars memorandi secundum Tullium," "the art of remembering according to Tully." But it is evident from what he says that John of Garland had little idea of what the first-century B.C. Tully was about. His confusion is instructive, however, for it is that of a man educated in a rather different memory keying system, trying to relate the strange terms of *Ad Herennium* to those with which he is familiar.

What he is familiar with is the system of keying mnemonically on "locus, tempus, et numerus," as we found those terms used by Hugh of St. Victor – page design, memory "occasion," and an ordering system that places items to be remembered in a grid design.[3] To this basic knowledge, acquired as part of his own early grammatical training, John of Garland tries to add the learned rules of the architectural mnemonic. The discussion occurs in Book II, devoted to what John calls selection, literally the "binding-together," of readings ("alligare lecta"), John's psychologically suggestive term for invention. Having discussed what sorts of material to select and the various tropes and figures (mostly drawn from Geoffrey of Vinsauf's *Documentum*), all in terms of a vaguely defined notion of stylistic levels, John proceeds to the art of remembering. The discussion is brief and wholly geared to comprehending what John thinks is being said in *Ad Herennium*. After his discussion of *memoria*, John of Garland proceeds immediately to give examples of well-composed letters, the subject-matter of the "ars dictaminis," "art of the dictamen" (whose intimate basis in the arts of *memoria* I will discuss in chapter 6). *Ars dictaminis*, and the related *ars notataria* or *notaria*, the "art of notes" or "shorthand," in which the system of Latin abbreviations was taught to students of law, are both closely associated with discussions of *memoria*, as these begin to reappear in handbooks of rhetoric in the later Middle Ages.[4] I describe the setting of this discussion in the *Parisiana poetria* because its placement underscores one of John of Garland's basic assumptions, namely that selecting and gathering material one has read is the heart of successful composition, and that this can occur only because one has a trained memory.

John of Garland says that the art of remembering is essential for selecting ("electio") and organizing material. So, as Cicero says, we should place ("disponere") in our minds an open space ("area"), in a place neither too bright nor too gloomy, because these qualities are harmful to retaining and selection. The area should be thought of as divided into three principle parts and columns ("per tres partes principales et columpnas"). In the first column, subdivided in three, we place "courtiers, city dwellers, and peasants," together with their particular concerns, duties, and the things pertaining to them. If one's teacher (of rhetoric, in this instance) should say something in class having to do with these three levels of audience, we place it in the appropriate section of the first column. In the second column we mentally mark off ("intelligi distingui") authoritative texts, "exempla et dicta et facta ['deeds'] autentica,"[5] including the source of each, which we have read in a book or hear in class. To aid in recalling a particular text, we should also mentally note the circumstances under which we first heard it, "the place in which, the teacher from whom, his dress, his gestures," or the page upon which we read it, whether it was light or dark (referring to the hair- or skin-side of the parchment), "the position on the page and the color of the letters."

Finally, in the third column we should imagine written the sounds of all sorts of languages and the characteristics of animals ("omnia genera linguarum sonorum et vocem diuersorum animancium") and etymologies, interpretations, and distinctions ("ethimologias, interpretationes, differentias").[6] These should be in alphabetical order ("secundum ordinem alphabeti"). So when the teacher makes an etymological explanation or we hear a word in a language we do not know we put it in this column, together with something that marks it. Word and sign together we gather ("collocemus") in the third column. Whenever we hear an unfamiliar word, we relate it by sound to one we know and so, associating one with the other, store the unfamiliar safely in our memory.

Now it is clear that John does not understand the *Ad Herennium*, but he does understand the system he learned himself. And so the *Ad Herennium*'s rule of using "intercolumnia" for backgrounds is understood as the columnar design of a manuscript page, rather like the design Hugh devised for his pupils to help them memorize those seventy folio pages of the most important data for their study of Scripture. There are more examples of medieval "misreadings" in this text. The *Ad Herennium* advises architectural locations with few people in them, meaning "open" in that sense, but John misreads this rule. The open space ("area") is like a vacant page to be written upon in columnar format, with sub-divisions upon it for the various categories of subject. And on this vacant page we write in three columns the material we learn: first, what is relevant to decorum and style; second, all the authoritative texts we read or hear, which we write down as though they actually were on a page, marked and colored, each with its source and each also with whatever associative detail of *locus* or *tempus* (in Hugh of St. Victor's sense) help us to recall them. The making of John's second column itself would require all the mnemonic utilities that Hugh of St. Victor counsels by way of dividing, marking, and gathering authorities.

The third column is of particular interest. It is ordered alphabetically in the memory, as *distinctio* collections and concordances were on the page. To help us remember hard words and words in languages we do not know (such as Hebrew and Greek) and the etymologies, interpretations, and *distinctiones* requiring such material, we should associate words we do not know with those we do. Although there is irreduceable imprecision in John of Garland's language here, I think informed guesswork will help us through some of the murk. The two chief memory aids (*notulae* of a sort) which John mentions are "omnia genera linguarum sonorum et vocem diuersorum animancium," or "all kinds of sounds of languages and the *voces animantium* of diverse animals."[7] Using the "sounds of languages," that is coincidental homophony between sounds in a known tongue and the sound of unknown words, is a simple and effective mnemonic (by "omnia genera" John probably means to include vernaculars as well as Latin). Robert of Basevorn's advice to use the syllables of the chant or the five vowels to recall texts in a sermon division is a slight variation of what John counsels here. And we recall that Luria's subject, S., recalled the words of Dante's unknown Italian by associating their sound with words familiar to him in Russian.

The *voces animantium* is a list of the habits and physical features thought to characterize the animals and birds; it was disseminated both as a simple listing (the form it takes in such sources as Isidore) and, in an expanded semi-narrative form, as the Bestiary, versions of which were a standard feature of Western culture from at least Alexandrine Greece.[8] Scholars have not entertained the possibility of a mnemonic function for the Bestiary, but what John of Garland says concerning the usefulness of "voces animantium" to help mark material is very suggestive, especially taken in conjunction with other evidence. As we will shortly see, Thomas Bradwardine also uses mental "pictures" from the Bestiary and from the traditional depictions of the Zodiac signs for mnemotechnical purposes.

The Bestiary was thought of as a beginner's book, an entertaining way of retaining moral precepts. This does not exclude it from being of use to learned readers too, but its primary audience was the relatively unlearned novices and the monks who taught them. Despite its puerile and pleasurable contents, it was found commonly in monastery libraries, even those of the Cistercian reform. This fact is particularly significant, for the Cistercians frowned on idle image-making, and are responsible for an unadorned style both of architecture and manuscript painting. In such an apparently hostile environment, only some over-riding perception of its utility could account for the Bestiary's continuing presence and dissemination among these monks.[9]

A book from the English Cistercian library of St. Mary's, Holmecultram, makes a particularly interesting study from the standpoint of mnemonic technique. It is an early copy of an Anglo-Norman version of the Bestiary, composed about 1130 by Philippe de Thaon (or Thaün) for Adelaide of Louvain, Henry I's queen. The manuscript is in the British Library now, MS. Cotton Nero A. v, and the first eighty-two folios of it are the original, twelfth-century book from Holmecultram. The Bestiary is preceded by a mnemonic rhyming poem on the dating of Easter, and by several doggerel stanzas, also in Anglo-Norman, describing the traditional images of the Zodiac and the Calendar. The fact that this book is in Anglo-Norman indicates that it was for the "pueri" of the monastery, the novices, many of noble families, beginning their studies, and not for the adult scholars, who would have known Latin (it is the only Anglo-Norman book in Holmecultram's library).

Philippe de Thaon's Bestiary is presented as a memory-book. In each of its "pictures" of the animals, its verses admonish the reader to remember particular pieces of the description as well as the whole: "Aiez en remembrance · ceo est signefiance," "Hold in memory · this is important." The Bestiary is described by its author as a "gramaire," or elementary book, derived from "Physiologus" (supposed to have been the original author of the Bestiary) and Isidore of Seville, whose *Etymologiae* contained a listing of the *voces animantium*. Thus the contents of this book were understood to be among the "puerilia" of a medieval education, and, along with the grid-layout described by Hugh of St. Victor, the Bestiary and the Calendar/Zodiac images were also elementary mnemotechnical tools.[10]

But how were they used? Here John of Garland supplies an important clue. The Bestiary descriptions are laid away so that one can use them later to mark material for recollection. They do not themselves supply an orderly memory grid, nor (probably) were the Zodiac signs used for a grid. Instead, one uses the rigid order of numbers and/or alphabet to lay out one's basic grid, but then one uses these sorts of vivid images to further mark the material for immediate, secure recollection. What the Bestiary taught most usefully in the long term of a medieval education was not "natural history" or moralized instruction (all instruction in the Middle Ages was moralized) but mental imaging, the systematic forming of "pictures" that would stick in the memory and could be used, like rebuses, homophonies, *imagines rerum*, and other sorts of *notae*, to mark information *within* the grid.

It is important that the Holmecultram Bestiary is not in fact illustrated – the "pictures" are entirely verbal, they are not drawn on the page. This forced the students to make the pictures carefully in their minds, to "paint" mentally, thus learning one of the most critical of mnemonic techniques. (As we will see in chapter 7, "decoration" of one's mental "book" remained basic in mnemotechnique, even after pictorially graphic images became a much commoner feature of medieval books, including Bestiaries.)

John of Garland counsels that the *voces animantium* are to be laid alphabetically on one's memory-page. We may recall from chapter 3 how Peter of Ravenna says that he had alphabetized lists of all sorts of material stored in his memory places, which he used to mark the thousands of textual "bits" he had collected. Visual alphabets, in which the letters are given the shapes of animals, birds, or tools, are very common, as Frances Yates observed, in fifteenth century treatises on memory, but derive "almost certainly . . . of an old tradition."[11] Often, the name of the animal or bird also begins with the letter it is made to represent.

The most elaborate drawings that I have seen are in Host von Romberch's *Congestorium*,[12] the product of a late-fifteenth-century German Dominican, whose "congestion" (and it certainly is that) of lore concerning memorial heuristics seems to conserve the traditions of his order. Romberch's schemes incorporate what is in the *Ad Herennium*, but add to it an enormous amount of advice on how to fashion complex grid systems based both on alphabetical and numerical orders. Several of the alphabetical ones involve animal images;

in one case, the letters are associated with animals whose names begin with those letters, so that for A one might think of an eagle (*aquila*), for B an owl (*bubo*), for N a bat (*noctycorax*), etc. Peter of Ravenna, we recall, could pull forth a string of beasts beginning with A or B or whatever letter of the alphabet. In another case, Romberch suggests using animals or various implements whose figures are bent into the shapes of the various letters. The printed text (1533) offers several pages of these, a number of which look very like the twisted shapes of birds and other beasts used to decorate initials in manuscripts from the early Middle Ages on. Romberch evidently sought to preserve the mnemonic efficacy of such manuscript decoration, attested to by Hugh of St. Victor. But instead of seeing these drawn on a page, one used them mnemonically to mark a text or *distinctio* (which is basically a "common place," a set of texts remembered *ad verbum* or *ad res*, which together define a moral topic).[13]

A remarkably fierce animal suddenly looms into a Biblical *interpretatio* by the Dominican scholar, Hugh of St. Cher, which may help to shed light on how the *voces animantium* could be used for organizing material in the memory. It occurs in his comment on the phrase "in medio umbrae mortis," Ps. 22:4.[14] "Et nota," he says in a phrase which, I have already suggested, is both an invitation to remember (in reading) and a trigger for recollection (in composing), "quod inter omnes peccatores, detractores proprie dicuntur umbrae mortis," "among all sinners detractors are most fittingly called of the shadow of death." For death indeed spares no-one but carries off everyone equally; likewise detractors detract everything. Wherefore, a detractor is signified by a bear (*ursus*). A bear has a great big voracious mouth, just like a backbiter or detractor. And it has three rows of teeth, which Hugh of St. Cher proceeds to moralize in terms of a backbiter's nasty characteristics.

Where did the bear come from? Judson Allen, who carefully studied this matter, says that Hugh's comment is found in no other Psalter gloss; it is his own. Hugh of St. Cher cites the most famous bear in Scripture, the one with all the teeth in Daniel's dream (Dan. 7:5). This text supplies the details of the image: "tres ordines erant in ore ejus, et in dentibus ejus," "three rows were in his mouth, and in his teeth" (the King James Version so differs from the Vulgate that I have translated the Latin directly).

The bear has a wide, devouring mouth, as does death, as do backbiters – the "moralizing," hermeneutic connections are reasonable enough. And the connection of death with biting is clear, basically by means of the homophony of Latin *mors*, "death," and *morsus*, "bite." Furthermore, though Latin *detractor* has no homophonic or etymological connection to *mors* or *morsus*, the late Latin participle *mordentem*, from *mordere* "to bite" and, by a metaphorical extension, "to make a caustic comment," clearly connects to "detractors" in meaning, and to "death," "biting," and "teeth" in sound. The Old French word, *mordant*, "bitter speaking," would have been familiar to Hugh for he was French; he may well also have known the word *backbiter* from English students at Paris. Such a mnemonically useful tissue of homophonies accords with John of Garland's advice regarding the use of the sounds of all kinds of languages to help fix etymologies and interpretations in the memory. But none of these words requires a bear.

I suspect that the reason why a bear entered Hugh of St. Cher's compositional memory is because the word *ursus*, like *umbra*, starts with a U. *Ursus*, together with its *voces* – the most vivid of which is its big mouth, according to Isidore, who derives *ursus* from *os*, "mouth" – and texts relevant to it, such as this obvious one from Daniel, would be stored in Hugh's memory under "U," helping to mark etymologies, distinctions, and interpretations of words and texts which also start with "U." And so, when composing his *distinctio* on *umbra*, the U-animal comes to mind, and it has characteristics (*voces*) which, happily, can this time be pressed into service of the point he wishes to make. In other words, what first led Hugh to a bear was not its hermeneutical aptness, but the simple fact that *ursus* and *umbra* have the same initial letter. *Ursus* leads to its etymology in *os*, *oris*; hence "teeth," and the happy homophony of *mors* and *morsus* that I sketched out earlier. So the bear's appearance in the written text is a vestige of Hugh's mental organizational scheme. That it also serves his interpretation is, of course, why that connection is preserved in the final composition.

John of Garland's memory advice confirms certain features as standard in medieval mnemotechnique. In particular, treating the memory as though it were a flat area divided linearly into columns within a grid seems clearly medieval. Hugh of St. Victor describes the elements differently, but he too says to treat memory as a "linea," a "line" of bins in a numerically-addressed grid. The earliest source of such a lay-out is unclear to me at this point, but linearly formatted diagram pages, such as Eusebius's Canon Tables, were widely known and used from earliest times.[15] Almost certainly the development of tabular layouts and the advice to use them mnemonically went hand in hand, since there is a clear, persistent theme in all medieval mnemonic advice, to take advantage of the presentation of the physical page as a fixative for memory. Roman mnemonics were not so closely tied to the grid; as we have seen, the classical mnemonic ties the "places" to an architectural setting. This changed understanding of the nature of the mnemonic "locus" – from a three-dimensional room, in which perspective changes as one "walks" through it mentally, to a two-dimensional cell within a grid on a flat surface – may account for some of the confusion medieval writers had in understanding Tully's rules about the making of backgrounds (these gave them more trouble than the ones about the making of images). "Locus" for Cicero was a space with depth and variable perspective; for Hugh of St. Victor, "locus" was a position on a page that could be "viewed" only frontally. The words which Hugh uses for the mental locations into which material is inventoried are *sedes* ("seats") and *conditorium* (originally meaning "tomb," but here something like "a rectangular box," the shape of a Roman tomb).

John of Garland's presentation of *memoria* in his *Parisiana poetria* is too informal to be a true "art" of memory, in the Aristotelian, scholastic sense of that word. A proper art requires general principles and a system which one can apply to a variety of circumstances, and these are not features of John of Garland's mnemonic advice. But a medieval treatise on memory that does meet the criteria for an "art," yet owes as little to Ciceronian sources as does the advice of John of Garland, is the *ars memorativa* attributed to Thomas Bradwardine, mathematician and theologian at Merton College from 1325 to 1335. Subsequently, he was chancellor of St. Paul's and prebend of Lincoln, then a royal chaplain to Edward III, and finally he died of the plague in August, 1349, a month after his confirmation as Archbishop of Canterbury. Bradwardine is best known for his participation on the orthodox side in the debate regarding the roles of predestination, grace, and free will, through his theological tract, "De causa Dei contra Pelagios"; his other work is mathematical in nature – a tractatus on proportions, one on the problem of squaring a circle, a "speculative" arithmetic and a "speculative" geometry. And then there is the tract we are concerned with here, "De Memoria Artificiali."

This treatise belongs to Bradwardine's Merton years.[16] It is of considerable interest that it was not composed by a professional teacher of rhetoric, like John of Garland, nor for elementary-level students, but by a theologian for university students. The work exists in three manuscripts, Fitzwilliam Museum (Cambridge) MS. McClean 169, and British Library MSS. Harley 4166 (a text closely related to that of McClean 169, but missing the last third of the treatise) and Sloane 3744. All three of these copies are English in origin, written during the fifteenth-century, and they have been collected in students' books that contain other natural science materials. The Sloane manuscript version is a summary digest of Bradwardine's advice. It is also incomplete, missing the discussion of "memory for syllables" and "memory for words," and containing a different, abbreviated conclusion. The McClean manuscript contains a version that is nearly three times the length of that in Sloane 3744. Because the McClean version is much fuller, I have based my discussion on it; the other adds nothing to its material. Unfortunately, no reliable transcription of either version has been published; the translation I offer as appendix C to this study is of my own transcription of McClean 169.

Bradwardine's treatise is interesting on two grounds; first, it codifies mnemonic advice of the sort that exists piecemeal in a few sentences in other medieval documents, and secondly, though some of its precepts resemble ones in the classical architectural mnemonic, Bradwardine obviously draws on a different tradition. His *ars memorativa* has been treated by some modern scholars as though it were in the *Ad Herennium* tradition, but it is not.[17] It articulates a completely medieval art of "images in places," which owes nothing directly to Tully and is not associated by Bradwardine with any classical authority. The incidental similarities between Bradwardine's rules and those of Tully are explained by two factors, one being certain enduring requirements of human recollection (such as having a rigid, easily-reconstructable order to the backgrounds; making visually-remarkable and emotionally-laden associations through images· and the rule of Seven Plus-or-Minus Two), and the other being a few continuous pedagogical traditions. For, as in the case of the advice given by Hugh of St. Victor, there is no reason to believe that Bradwardine created a wholly new art of memory. At most, he was drawing together in a single manual advice that had been practically, if not so systematically, available for centuries. And, as we will see, these same conventions are to be found not in a textual tradition but in manuscript painting traditions from the early Middle Ages. This suggests to me that the mnemonic role of book decoration was consciously assumed from the beginnings of the book in the West; we have seen other evidence of this close link in the lexicography (if I may call it that) of memory as well.

It is in a few generalities rather than specifics that Bradwardine's system resembles that described in the *Ad Herennium*, written 1,400 years earlier. Bradwardine distinguishes many of the basic terms of memorial art: memory for "things" and memory for words, natural and artificial memory, the archetypal metaphor of memory as a surface onto which letters are written, and the very idea of "places" and "images." But both the manner and specifics of his presentation are quite different from what is in Tully. He begins by describing six general properties of places or "locations" (*loci*): the size, shape, and characteristic features of a single location, and the number, order, and distance away that characterize a set of such background locations.

A *locus* should be of a size neither greater nor smaller than what the eye can take in at a single glance – a small garden or a cloister are ideal in their extent. In shape it should be rectangular, like a page or a tablet. This is a striking and significant difference between Bradwardine's rules for the *loci* and those of the architectural mnemonic. It clearly is related to both John of Garland's and Hugh of St. Victor's use of the word *locus* to refer to the presentation on the page of the textual matter to be remembered.

The *locus* should be a lighted, completely open space, with no distracting detail of its own. It must be neither too dark nor too glaringly illuminated. One should not image to oneself a crowded location, such as a church or marketplace. One should use real places, which can be visited and re-inspected frequently, in preference to wholly imaginary ones, which are trickier and would require greater mastery to keep clearly and unchangingly in mind.

The places in their ordered sets should contrast with one another in color as well as content. Bradwardine describes making a first set of five locations on the theme of a field: the first might be a waste field, the second a green garden, the third the same field at harvest, the fourth the field after harvest when only the stubble remains, and the fifth the field blackened by burnt stubble. (It is of some interest, I think, that Bradwardine uses the common motif of the seasonal changes as a set of memorative locations.) One multiplies one's available locations in such sets of five, Bradwardine counsels, working upward from ground-level to the upper storeys, as though of a building. After the set of fields, he describes a set of flat raised locations: a large couch, an armoire, a table, a tomb, an altar. Then come roofs (wood shingles, thatch, slate, tile, and of lead) and terraces (floored with earth, greenstone, tiles, straw, or carpeting). By multiplying sets of five in this manner, one never has to think of more than five closely-related locations at any one time, but one can also extend the multiplying process as much as one chooses, though Bradwardine suggests that no more than ten related sets be constructed at one time, lest the fabrication become too unwieldy.

For one must be able to keep track exactly of each location in relation to the others in its own and related sets. So the places must have "contiguity" (or "neighborliness," to use Aristotle's word) and "direction" – as the order of numbers and alphabets have both of these basic features. Without such a rigid schematic order, one cannot "find" a "place" easily, nor can one "move about" or "gather" them together. I have stressed before the "shuffling" requirement which a memory system must address – Bradwardine's method of multiplying sets in fives does this. These "locations" are the mental bins of one's inventory, each of similar size, shape, and illumination, and each of a monochromatic color but the colors contrasting with those of the other locations in its set (the carpeted flooring of the fifth member of Bradwardine's fourth set suggests that a simple pattern within the monochrome was tolerable). One relates these to one another basically in the manner in which people construct a grid or matrix, as "sets" of empty boxes, "built" one on top of the other, and "addressed" individually by means of a pair of coordinates that places them within the matrix.

One final feature of the locations concerns what Bradwardine calls "distancia" and "distancia intercepta." By this term he seems to mean what we call "perspective," both with respect to the position of the observer and with respect to the "distance" depicted *in* the location itself, foreground and background. The observation point is frontal, and far enough away from the scene so that everything in it can be seen clearly, fully, and at once. There is no suggestion here, as there is in the *Ad Herennium*, that the mental eye's perspective will change as one "walks" – in the Bradwardinian account, the eye is positioned "optimally," so that one takes in the whole location at one glance. Additionally, within the location whatever detail (a hill, perhaps, or a tree or a couch) is needed to set the "image" in it is depicted, but no *distant* background is shown, for this might distract from the clarity of the mnemonically-important "image." Thus, a mnemonic scene in its "background" may have some shallow suggestions of setting, but no deep perspective. Bradwardine says that the "distance" in the location should be void – a single color or a simple design. Both of these perspectival conditions are common in early medieval painting. Indeed the "picture-page" of the sixth-century Gospels of St. Augustine (figure 29) provides an excellent illustration of such a locational arrangement, frontal perspective, and "emptiness" of distance. One finds such features still in late medieval painted scenes.

Into the cell-like arrangement of locations in tiers, one places the *imagines*. Bradwardine gives several general rules for the construction of memorial images for content ("things") and images for words. This organizational feature of his treatise is another significant difference from the *Ad Herennium*, for it clarifies the fact that as images, those employed for various mnemonic functions do not differ significantly in their characteristics. Memorative images should be of moderate size, but that is their only moderate feature. Because the memory retains distinctly only what is extraordinary, wonderful, and intensely charged with emotion, the images should be of extremes – of ugliness or beauty, ridicule or nobility, of laughter or weeping, of worthiness or salaciousness. Bloody figures, or monstrosities, or figures brilliantly but abnormally colored should be used, and they should be engaged in activity of a sort that is extremely vigorous.

These figures are to be grouped against the plain background in an active scene, their relative positions acting as cues to the order of the material with which they are associated. So, the image for the first matter to be recalled is placed towards the front of the location, its torso occupying the center, rather in the manner which art historians call hierarchical spacing. The word which Bradwardine uses, *torus*, signifies, in classical Latin, an enlarged rounded form, like a bolster; it can also mean "muscle." It survived in the Middle Ages as a technical term in architecture, to refer to the rounded, doughnut-shaped "pillow" on which a column rested. As used here by Bradwardine, it must mean the same thing as modern "torso," but perhaps a torso enlarged in size. Then the second image is placed on its right hand, and it is helpful if the central image has limbs or some means of attaching the other images to itself physically. The third and fourth images (if they are needed) are attached serially to the right of the second. A fifth image is attached to the left side of the central image, with the following ones joined serially to it. To "read" this composite, one begins in the center, then looks right as far as one can, and then "returns" to the center and looks left. The figures are joined to one another in an active, even violent, manner. The first image is to strike or hold the second with its right hand, the third to ride around the second, and so on, so that these vigorous activities act "like a kind of gluing-together of the order among them." One can have three or five or seven images in a single group but not many more, because one tends to lose track over seven. And within each image the order of precedence is rigid: central front, then right, then left, and foreground over background figures. It is clear from Bradwardine's description of these groupings that the locations have some depth to them; the figures do not occupy just a flat plane, but are "impressed" memorially in the manner of a carved relief.

Bradwardine's chief example for grouping images in locations is the twelve signs of the zodiac. It is an odd group for him to pick in a sense, because the zodiacal signs are examples neither of memory for content nor of memory for words; it is tempting to find a reason in the use, mentioned in antiquity, of memorial systems based on the zodiacal signs.[18] If this were the case, the twelve signs themselves would be used only as markers for other material. Bradwardine does not in fact use them for anything other here than as examples to illustrate the basic principles he has already given for the characteristics and arrangements of images in a location. He could, most likely, expect all his students to be familiar with them already, not as "concepts" (they are hardly that) but as images of the purely fictive, associational kind that is basic for memorative heuristics.

He groups the twelve images in two mental locations. Aries, the ram, is figured in the center of the first location, with the second sign, Taurus, to its right. In front of Taurus is Gemini, the Twins, born either from a woman or from the Bull (in order to avoid having an extraneous image). One of the twins plays with a Crab. To the left of Aries is Leo, who attacks Virgo. Virgo holds Libra in her right hand, while with her left she tries to balance Scorpio in the scales. These eight images, whose order and linkage in the scene cues their actual order, in the manner which Bradwardine earlier defined, are all in the first location. The remaining four form a scene in a second location: Sagittarius is placed in the center, shooting arrows at Capricorn, who holds Aquarius in his right foot and Pisces in his left, while pouring forth water "in a wondrous manner" from the water-vessel for the fish. The images are brilliantly colored, especially with red, white, and gold, and every color is described as the superlative of its type in hue and intensity.

But what is most surprising, to a puritan-formed sensibility, is the emphasis on violence and sexuality which runs through all the interaction of the figures in each scene. A super-white ram is kicked by a super-red bull with super-swollen testicles (so one will be sure one is not looking at a cow or a heifer), which the ram in turn kicks so hard that blood flows copiously. To its left, the ram is also kicking a rampant lion in the head, causing another wound. The lion is attacking a beautiful maiden, whose whole left arm is dreadfully swollen from the wound inflicted by a scorpion, which she is trying to balance in her scales. The twins are ripped from the womb of a woman whose parturitional wound extends to her breast. Or they are being born grotesquely from the bull. The twins are most beautiful, but one is being pinched dreadfully by a horrible crab, and is weeping while trying to free his hand, while his heartless twin caresses the monster "in a childlike manner." The images of the second location are less violent but no less grotesque, as a rampant goat, shot with arrows (and so bleeding profusely) by a bowman, carries a water-jug in one front foot and fish in the other, for which it pours out water from the jug. And the whole account concludes, matter-of-factly, with Bradwardine's comment that, having constructed such scenes, one can recite their contents "in the order he wants, forwards or backwards."

Not all of Bradwardine's images are violent, though all are vigorously "extreme," in conformity with a basic principle for memory images, namely, that what is unusual is more memorable than what is routine. One remembers abstract concepts by a concrete image: "sweetness" by an image of someone happily eating sugar or honey, "bitterness" by an image of someone foully vomiting. Wholly abstract ideas like God, angels, or the Trinity, can be attached to "an image as painters make it" or, later in the treatise, "as it is usually painted in churches." This is more direct evidence that every sort of image, whatever its source or placement, was considered to have memorial utility. But we will consider this matter further in a later chapter.

Images are used for memorizing *verbaliter* or *sententialiter*. In accord with elementary pedagogical practices, Bradwardine considers the method for remembering "for words" as being essentially a matter of building upon a method of remembering by syllables. He discusses memory-for-words as both "memoria sillabarum" ("memory-by-syllables") and "memoria oracionis" (by which Bradwardine does not seem to mean "oration" but "[textual] theme"); the one is basically an extension of the other. First one analyzes the whole number of possible syllables, for each of which one finds an image of something whose name begins with that same syllable. These syllable-hooks can come either from Latin or vernaculars, even from dialects of a vernacular.

As an example, Bradwardine takes the sentence (alluding to the English victory over the Scots in the second battle of Berwick in July, 1333): "Benedictus Dominus qui per rege Anglie Berewicum fortissimum et totam Scotiam subjugavit," "Blessed be God who by the English king subjugated mightiest Berwick and all of Scotland." To remember the first phrases of this sentence, he says, one might make a scene composed of St. Benedict ("Benedictus") in the center, with St. Dominic to his right ("Dominus"); to the left of Benedict is a cow ("qui," a bilingual pun), who holds a partridge (*perdix*) in her foot; this "will give the word 'per' to your memory." The scene in the second location comprises a king ("rex"), holding an eel in one hand ("anglia") and a mighty bear ("Bere-wic") in the other. For the last phrase of the sentence, one might construct a scene of someone named Thomas ("totam"), who is subduing a Scot as he would a beast, and who holds a wondrous yoke ("sub-*juga*-vit").

Many of the puns in Bradwardine's examples are bilingual, depending on homophonies from Latin, English, and English dialect words. For instance, the Latin syllable "qui" sounded to him like the northern dialect pronunciation of English "cow," which was [ki]. Actually Northern [ki], spelled "cy" or "ci," is the plural form, but Bradwardine was, after all, a southerner. What is also apparent is that he pronounced Latin like a Frenchman, so that *qui* comes out as [ki] instead of [kwi]. This is a fine instance of using the sounds of every sort of language as a memory aid, the advice we found in John of Garland.

The syllable images obey rules of calculation rather than any sort of naturalism, by which I mean that their function in a particular context takes precedence over their realistic nature. For example, to remember the syllable "ab-," one might picture an *abbatus*, "abbot." For the reverse syllable, "ba-," one can either remember a separate object, whose name starts with "ba-" (Bradwardine suggests *balistarius*, "crossbowman") or one can simply reverse the position of the abbot, so he appears upside-down. For a three-letter syllable, such as "bal-," one adds to the "ba-" image a feature which stands for the added letter. "L" is readily associated, for an Englishman, with a bent elbow, which both forms an "L" and sounds like English "elbow." The position of the elbow-image in relation to the "abbot" establishes whether the syllable is "bla-" or "bal-" or "lab-." When the "l" comes first, it is shown at the abbot's head; "lab-" is an abbot with an elbow held over his head. If the "l" is medial, the elbow is held in the middle of the image; "bla-" might be an upside-down abbot holding his elbow at his waist (or a rightside-up crossbowman doing the same). If the "l" is last, as in the syllable "bal-," it figures at the bottom of the image. "Bal-" is figured, humorously, as an upside-down abbot chewing on an elbow. It is interesting that a style of marginal "drollery" in use in England at about this time (seen for example in the Rutland Psalter) features several images of dismembered limbs, some being chewed on by grotesque creatures. I explore the general connections between manuscript marginalia and memory images in chapter 7; there are a number of specific parallels between the changing styles of the two that argue for a closer link than scholars have entertained, and this is one of them.[19]

Such image-making is governed by positional concerns, a kind of additive calculation in which the position of the elbow (in Bradwardine's example) relative to the rest of the image functions algorithmically, as does the position of a number in the columns of tens in the algorism itself. The same locational calculative principles are at work in Bradwardine's advice on using memory-images for numbers, such as a unicorn for "one," or a lamb with seven horns for "seven," or a dismembered hand with only nine digits for "nine," or – interestingly from the standpoint of mathematical history – either a zero or a Greek *chi* for "ten." One works with these images according to one's ability in the algorism, the methods of calculation based upon tens which we commonly use today, but which was then relatively new to Europe. This calculational bent is appropriate to Bradwardine's personality, but it is quite different from what the *Ad Herennium* has to say about making images "for words." And it is fascinating to contemplate a mathematician like Bradwardine calculating mentally through the use of such lively pictures; after all, the much simpler system of "Arabic" notation was then commonly in use. The algorism itself was part of this new system; Bradwardine nonetheless counsels the use of these vigorous calculational "pictures." Apparently he thought that their vigor made them more useful for mental work than the more abstract notational system. The sources of these "number-pictures" are interesting too: the unicorn is from the Bestiary, most of the other images are from the Bible and/or the common iconography of church painting and sculptures, and the images involving fingers most likely derive from their common use in daily calculation.

Most of Bradwardine's images are the stuff of Grand Guignol, but they can also be funny. The abbot's image, already subject to imaginative indignities by being reversed each time one wants to remember "ba" instead of "ab," is ridiculous when we encounter the sainted Benedictine dancing to his left with a white cow with super-red teats who holds a partridge, while with his right hand he either mangles or caresses St. Dominic ("Benedictus Dominus qui per"). Or the imperial king holding a struggling eel in his right hand and a bear by its tail with his left ("rege Anglie Berewicum"). The puns move easily between Latin (*anguilla*, "eel" and *Anglie*) and English (*ursus*, "bear" and "Bere[wic]"). It is like a mental game of charades, or children's rebus games, utilizing several languages and every source of image. But for Bradwardine and his contemporaries, such games have serious scholarly utility because their culture was still profoundly memorial. No opprobrium of childishness or frivolity or obscenity or inappropriateness attaches to such image-making. The disgusting and the silly, the noble and the violent, the grotesque and the beautiful, the scatalogical and sexual are presented, one after another, and usually as part of the same scene, just as memory dictates.

The one thing that cannot be tolerated is dullness or quietude or any failure to rivet the attention. These are shocking images but their shock value is useful. And while the very notion of *useful* sex and violence would be, for our own post-puritanical age, an ultimate jadedness, titillation (and it is that) for Bradwardine is a necessary component of the art of memory, serving pious functions such as meditation and preaching. I suppose we could consider the use of such images as a kind of extreme instance of St. Augustine's dictum that the things of this world are to be enjoyed as they prove useful to the good, rather than as ends in themselves. But one can certainly also understand, from this context, the motive for St. Bernard's admonition to the Benedictines of Cluny that monks should have no need of grotesque figures to help them meditate, and the continuing caution throughout the period against the sin of *curiositas*, especially in meditation.

Bradwardine's approval of lively images in memory-work can be paralleled in other medieval texts. One of the most striking features of Albertus Magnus's analysis of memory is his enthusiastic commendation of the usefulness of vivid metaphor to secure recollection. Albertus treats the nature of recollection and the architectural mnemonic specifically in his treatise "De bono," Question II, article 2, written about 1245 while he was at Paris. Albertus's precepts (which we might think of as prefatory explanations of an art of memory) thus were composed 115 years later than Hugh of St. Victor's elementary advice, twenty years later than John of Garland's unsystematic account of *memoria*, and predate by eighty-eight years Bradwardine's fully-fledged art of memory. Albertus is one of the earliest medieval philosophers to argue systematically for the ancient architectural art as the best of all arts of memory. He is also about the earliest to speak of an *art* of memory ("ars memorativa") rather than just to use the general term "memoria" for an eclectic collection of empirical advice. Finally, Albertus sets his art of memory in the context of moral philosophy rather than in a discussion of rhetoric; this too represents a shift from earlier pedagogical treatises, as we will see later in this chapter.

Albertus's discussion is set up in the usual scholastic manner, queries and responses both being drawn in part from the discussion in the *Ad Herennium* itself. Albertus is concerned specifically to recommend this art: "ars memorandi optima est, quam tradit Tullius." His justification is made on moral grounds as well as practical ones. Tully's memorial art especially is valuable for the ethical life and judgment as well as for a rhetor ("ad ethicum et rhetorem"), since moral judgments are expressed in particular acts and it is therefore necessary that their basis (i.e. prudence) be incorporated in the soul in corporeal images (Q. II, a.2, *solutio*). They cannot be retained in images, however, except by the memory. "Unde dicimus, quod inter omnia quae spectant ad prudentiam, summe necessaria est memoria," "Wherefore we say that, among all the matters which pertain to prudence, the most necessary is *memoria*."

It is important to recognize that Albertus is defending not memory training, which he takes for granted, but this particular system. Certain of his questions address either insufficient definition in Tully (e.g. objection 10) or apparent contradictions between what is found in *Ad Herennium* and in Aristotle (e.g. objections 3 and 7) or in Aristotelian psychology, as already commented upon by Albertus in his own treatise on the soul (e.g. objections 2 and 13). He also addresses an apparent hostility to the whole scheme as being altogether too curious and elaborate. Such hostility did in fact exist among previous generations of Parisian masters, as we will see.

Albertus is much interested in the ancient system's use of vivid visual images against precisely visualized backgrounds set in order; it is this feature that makes Tully's system the best. He is obviously working with Tully's text, trying to adapt it to thirteenth-century circumstances and the memory training with which he is familiar; the results are instructive. He considers, for example, what the phrase "aut natura aut manu" (*Ad Her.* III.16.29) means, since Tully does not clearly define it, and suggests (probably correctly) that it refers to kinds of *loci*, a field ("pratum") being an example of a natural place, a house or intercolumnar space of an artificial ("handmade") one (resp. 10).

Judging by his comments on the five principle characteristics given for desirable background images, Albertus clearly understands that they are designed for ease in perception as one walks through one's places in memory, seeing images on backgrounds. "Confusion," he writes, "is engendered either in respect to the background-place or the matters located in it or to that which by its action makes visible the background and what is in it."[20] If one crowds too much into one location, one will confound one's images: "it heaps up a great many images, and so these images break up in the soul and do not remain, just as a great number of waves break up in water."[21] This effect, however, is not what the *Ad Herennium* gives as the reason to avoid crowds; the concern there was with the initial making of backgrounds, and to avoid imprinting crowded places because of their adverse effect on the clarity of the backgrounds.

One can also be confused if one's places are too much alike, too close together or far apart, or improperly lit. Images must be seen clearly, for "something glaring confounds sight" whereas obscurity impedes it; in either case the images are not properly imprinted and therefore cannot be seen with the inner eye. Following these general guidelines, each person can form his own places from diverse sources. A comparison of the sources enumerated by Albertus with those in the *Ad Herennium* again indicates that Albertus had adapted his source. Tully mentions these specific examples: "aedis" (a house), "intercolumnium" (the space between columns, a colonnade), "angulus" (a recess), "fornix" (an arch), all clearly Roman architectural items. Albertus's examples are equally clearly medieval: "templum" (a church), "intercolumnium," "pratum" (cloister-garden), "hospitalis" (hospice or hospital). The only shared word is *intercolumnium*, though Albertus surely had a different sort of columned space in mind (perhaps a cloister or a columned church interior) than did the author of *Ad Herennium*. In fact, "intercolumnium" is the only specific kind of "location" in the architectural mnemonic that has an unbroken history – perhaps this is due to the continuing use of columns to mark off memory groups in the various tabular formats, such as the Canon Tables. These columnar formats feature images of architectural columns, often joined by arches, to frame the textual material.

Albertus's account of the *Ad Herennium* advice concerning image making shows his fascination with the procedural details of this system. He gives first a complete account of the technique for creating images-for-things. He uses the examples given in the *Ad Herennium*, but it is clear that not all of its details are familiar to him:

we place in our memory "a sick man in bed, who is a figure of the deceased, and we place the defendant standing by the bed, holding in his right hand a cup, in his left hand tablets, and a physician standing upright holding the testicles of a ram," so that certainly in the cup should be the memory-cue of the poison which he drank, and in the tablets should be the memory-cue of the will which he signed, and in the physician may be figured the accusor and by the testicles the witnesses and accessories, and by the ram the defense against matter being adjudicated.[22]

Albertus's attempts to comprehend this scene show his editorial efforts to understand the Latin of a culture far outside his experience. Most notable is his change of the original "medico testiculos arietinos tenentem" to "medicum astantem tenentem testiculos arietinos." In the original text, the defendant and the sick man are the only two human figures in this scene, the defendant holding cup, tablets, and on his fourth finger (*medicum*, used in the ablative singular, is an abbreviated noun-form of the phrase *digitus medicinalis*) the ram's testicles (in ancient Rome money bags could be made from the skin of ram's testicles).[23] Albertus adds a third figure to this scene, a physician (*medicus*, used in the accusative singular) who is standing also by the bed, and he holds the ram's testicles. And why a ram? Since they are noted for their territorial defensiveness, the ram can signify the proceeding against the defendant. What is clear from this ingenious adaptation is Albertus's effort clearly to visualize a "similitudo rerum." His particular misunderstanding here, it seems to me, proves precisely his understanding of the general method.

But a more taxing passage awaited him, the description of the technique of "similitudines verborum" or memory for words, using as its example the line, apparently cited from a popular Roman play, "Iam domum itionem reges Atridae parant," "Now for their journey home the kings, sons of Atreus, prepare." Every commentator on the *Ad Herennium* has floundered about here. A major portion of the difficulty is attributable to the fact that the images which the *Ad Herennium* suggests one use to remember these Latin words are visual puns which depend entirely on contemporary allusions – a reference to two celebrated Roman families, in one instance, and to two well-known contemporary actors in the other. To remember the first half-line one thinks of Domitius "raising hands to heaven while he is whipped with thongs by the Marcii Reges [*iam domum itionem reges*]," both Domitius and Rex being names of distinguished Roman families. Caplan, the Loeb translator, comments that the scene "is doubtless our author's own creation," and it is difficult to understand why it involves whipping, except as an instance of the general principle of forming images related to one another through violent activity. The second half-line is recalled by a scene of the two famous actors, Aesopus and Cimber, making ready for their roles as Agamemnon and Menelaus in a play about Iphegenia ("Atridae parant").

Albertus's attempt to deal with this passage is complicated by a bad manuscript reading, although the correct one seems also to have been available to him. For "domum itionem," "journey home," he has "domi ultionem," "revenge at home." So in Albertus's account (see appendix B) somebody named Domitius is being whipped (for revenge before being exiled) by Marcian (that is, "warlike") kings. But having made a certain sense of the scene in the first memory location, he makes hash of that in the second. The original text advises that, to remember the phrase "Atridae parant," one should imagine the two actors, Aesopus and Cimber, making ready for their roles in a play of "Iphegenia" as Menelaus and Agamemnon ("the sons of Atreus"). Here again Albertus was not helped by faulty manuscripts which left out the explanatory reference in the *Ad Herennium* to Menelaus and Agamemnon as the "sons of Atreus."[24] All that Albertus found in his manuscript of the text was a reference to two people named Aesopus and Cimber who prepared Iphigenia for wandering, or incited her to wander. The mnemonic association is made by linking the notion of "preparing" with that of "wandering," for, as Albertus observes, one who prepares ("parat se") for something wanders about.

Those who have also struggled with obscurities in ancient texts cannot help admiring Albertus for plunging into this crux instead of silently reporting it, though in this case discretion might have served him better. The nature of his effort indicates again his grasp of the essential features of the method and purpose of image making, if not of this particular example of it. He raises these two specific instances of image-making from *Ad Herennium* as the basis for others' objection to the whole method (objection 10), on the grounds that it is metaphorical and obscure, and therefore a hindrance rather than a help to memory. Better to remember the things themselves (the actual words of a text) than to adopt this cumbersome, confusing method.

Albertus defends the method with vigor precisely because it is metaphorical, grounds that must be of interest to students of medieval fictional literature. He quotes almost in full the advice of *Ad Herennium* on the making of striking and unusual images, and replies at length to possible objections (objs. and resps. 16–21). The images one composes must be striking and vivid, rare and unusual, "quae quasi mirabiles sunt, imagines nobis constituamus" (obj. 20). What is unusual and marvelous strikes us and is retained in the memory more than what is ordinary ("mirabile plus movet quam consuetum"); moreoever, what is marvelous by its forceful impression on us causes us to remark it, and that engenders both inquiry and reminiscence. For this purpose, fabulous metaphorical images, composed from marvels ("compositae ex miris") are best: "metaphorica plus movent animam et ideo plus conferunt memoriae." For as Aristotle says (in *Metaphysics*, I.1, where he also says that experience is made of many memories), this was why the earliest philosophers wrote their ideas down in poetry, because fables composed of marvels were more moving to the memory and to inquiry ("fabula, cum sit composita ex miris, plus movet"). All inquiry begins in wonder ("ex admirari"), he continues, quoting the *Metaphysics* again (I. 2), for the start of philosophical thought is in wondering about causes, about befores and afters and whys. Though he does not explicitly invoke it, Albertus clearly makes an etymological connection between *miris* and *admirari*, and thus a relationship of some compatibility between *fabula* and *philosophari* – the link between them being through the requirements of memory.

Some of his work shows Albertus's use of a technique of composing vivid visual images that incorporate the principle of the marvelous and active. It must be admitted that this quality is, in the final public version of a text, a matter of personal style, although it is found commonly enough even in the prose of scholastic Biblical commentary, I think, to make the dry, non-metaphorical style of Aquinas, Ockham, or Bradwardine (in his theological work) exceptional rather than not. And even when a writer does not use vivid images in his finished products, this is no ground for supposing that he did not use memory images, for Aquinas, like Albertus, particularly advocates them and we have seen already the liveliness of Bradwardine's imagination in forming memory images. Genre may well be a critical element; mathematical and logical writing provides its own compositional mnemonic in the rigid order of its propositions, whereas commentary on a text like the Bible may need more frequently an "artificial" mnemonic heuristic to help "fix" its points in order.

I think it is the case that familiarity from memory training with the technique of "vigorous" image-making, even in the context of theological debate (where it becomes a useful tool for keeping any sort of discourse in mind), provided the scholarly audience with a habit of encountering such imagery even in the context of commentary and treatise, without finding it inappropriate. And Albertus's stress upon the mnemonic *usefulness* of what is marvelous and unusual gives a crucial ethical justification for using even fantastical or salacious or violent images. Albertus makes it clear that the criterion for creating mnemonic images is not decorum but utility. Because the memory is physiologically constituted in such a way that it better retains what is unusual and emotionally charged rather than what is expected or routine, material must be marked with those sorts of images. Students of literature have always remarked the penchant for strikingly peculiar allegory in many of the pre-modern arts. But it may well be that much of what we suppose to be "allegory," and thus to have a specifically iconographic meaning (if only we knew what it was) is simply a mnemonic heuristic.[25]

Albertus's *Postilla in Isaiam*, of which a reliable modern edition exists, affords several interesting examples of Albertine imagination. First, as is also true of Aquinas's work, quotations from pagan authors, including the poets, are much in evidence. In this commentary he quotes from Cicero twenty-three times, most frequently from *De inventione*; he also quotes "Homer," Horace (five times), Ovid (seven times), Martial, Vitruvius, and Virgil, among several others. Moralized stories of the pagan gods, including Jupiter, Priapus, Venus, and the jackal-god Anubis, also find their way into his commentary. Frequently these tales are used to point the Augustinian moral that the pagan gods were no better than devils, corrupt; indeed one of Albertus's richest sources is *The City of God*. Another is evidently from some sort of early version of *Ovide moralisée*, so popular later in the century and into the following one. Commenting on the phrase "in auribus meis" (Is. 5:9), Albertus says:

Wherefore in the fables of the poets in Ovid [*Met.* II, v, 47ff.] great Jupiter, who represents the god of gods, when he needed to strike down Phaeton, who was burning up the sky and earth and all therein, took up his javelin beside his ear, that he might clearly teach that it is judicious first carefully to listen and weigh the merits of the persons and their causes, and then to smite the killers.[26]

But not all of Albertus's vivid visual images are so self-evidently literary in character. For example, commenting on Is. 35:6, "Then shall the lame man leap as an hart," Albertus moralizes the verse with an unusual image rather like the "curious, emblem-like 'pictures'" found by Beryl Smalley in Holcot's *Moralitas*.[27] "The soul," Albertus says, "has two feet, that is intellect and emotions. When they are equal, and emotion is made equal in truth to the intellect, then a man walks well. If however one or the other is bent, the intellect through error or emotion through desire, a man is lame."[28]

Two other examples are also curious. In commentary on Is. 47:2, Albertus writes of the phrase *revela crura*, "make bare the thigh," that it is a custom of prostitutes to reveal their legs in order to incite desire. "Wherefore Venus was painted with her skirt raised to reveal her leg that she might provoke lust."[29] Smalley discovered this passage and comments on it that its source is not in any pictorial tradition for "the mythographers all represent Venus as naked . . . Curious and of an observant turn of mind, [Albertus] may have seen or read some study of her wearing a dress. Maybe he simply invented her as a personification of harlotry."

Then there is the ram which runs amok in the middle of Albertus's commentary on Aristotle's *De memoria*. Invoking the *Ad Herennium* on the making of memory images as a practical instance of Aristotle's understanding of how memory works by association, he comments on the phrase "testiculos arietinos" (*Ad Her.*, III, 20, 34). Frances Yates translates the passage as follows:

For example, if we wish to record what is brought against us in a law-suit, we should imagine some ram, with huge horns and testicles, coming towards us in the darkness. The horns will bring to memory our adversaries and testicles the dispositions of the witnesses.[30]

Yates wonders wittily whence such a vigorous beast could appear: "How has it managed to break loose from the lawsuit image to career dangerously around on its own in the dark?" She suggests perhaps the connection had something to do with the zodiac or perhaps was just the result of too many lonely nights of study. I rather think that in this early effort to understand the *Ad Herennium* text, Albertus had not quite grasped its meaning and thought at once in terms of the *voces animantium* memorial images with which he was familiar. And so he figures for us a full-sized ram charging with lowered horns in its traditionally adversarial manner. The testicles are in Tully of course, but as we see from Bradwardine's memory pictures, the familiar images of the zodiac (and the Bestiary, as well) are used as memory pictures, and the macho of this ram is certainly in keeping with the qualities Bradwardine gives to his own images. And to the *Ad Herennium*'s statement that the testicles are a pun on "testes," "witnesses," he adds that the ram charging with its great horns recalls adversaries. By the time he came to comment again on this text in *De bono*, he understood better what was meant in the original. But this ram has, as an image, a vigorous lot in common with Hugh of St. Cher's open-mouthed bear. The liveliness of these images, indeed, indicates why the advice in *Ad Herennium* to make active and marvelous *imagines* fell onto such fertile ground, for the usefulness to memory of *imagines rerum*, vivid mental pictures, seems never to have entirely been forgotten.

Before proceeding to discuss the circumstances within which the architectural mnemonic was revived, let me summarize the features which seem to be distinctively medieval in the memory advice we have examined in John of Garland, Bradwardine, and Albertus Magnus. With respect to the memory *locus*, these are: 1) a plain colored or simply patterned background, with just enough suggestion of depth to be able to position the images in relation to one another; 2) the observer positioned frontally in respect to the scene, at a distance from which the whole composition can be taken in completely at a glance; 3) the "hierarchical" arrangement of the images, which enables them to be "read off" in sequence – this sequence can be from the center to either side, or, in a circular arrangement, clockwise or counterclockwise (we will see examples of these in chapter 7). With respect to the *imagines*: 1) their grouping in a scene in which the order among them is expressed through physical action; 2) the use of vivid, unusual, and extreme images; 3) the use of images from a variety of sources, including the Bestiary, the Kalendar, and all other sorts of painted or sculpted forms, such as those found commonly in churches.

The placement of the "locations" is two-dimensional, diagrammatic, and frequently within a grid. As I have observed before, this is a dominant feature of medieval mnemonics. One of the most popular of late medieval ethical manuals was an allegorical treatment of the game of chess, composed by the Dominican friar, Jacopo da Cessola, around 1300. It was one of the works printed by William Caxton. In an excellent essay on this work, Raymond DiLorenzo commented that it uses mnemonic technique to integrate the ethical material which the friar has composed as a set of "things-to-be-remembered." The mnemotechnique used is the chessboard, a grid, into which *imagines* (the chess pieces, described with vivid and unusual detail) are fitted. Jacopo prefaces the work, which is basically a florilegium, by saying that chess was invented by a philosopher who sought to correct a tyrannical king. As they played the game, the philosopher instructed the king in the virtues and vices that attached to each piece. Thus the game itself became for the king a mnemonic of kingly virtue and responsibility, a "Rule for Princes" presented in a form that embeds its own mnemonic – the form of a grid filled with images, familiar to medieval audiences as a basic format for the page of memory.[31]

The earliest medieval *artes memorativae* belong to the thirteenth century – or, more precisely, the earliest written medieval *artes* belong to this period. In Alcuin's dialogue with Charlemagne on rhetoric (ninth century), the king asks his magister, Alcuin, if there are any specific precepts for *memoria* (trained memory), which is the noblest aspect of rhetoric ("nobilissima . . . rhetoricae parte"). There are none, replies Alcuin, except disciplined exercise in memorizing ("ediscendi exercitationem"), practice in writing, and the discipline of cogitation or mental composition. One should also avoid drunkenness (which is harmful to any discipline of soul or body). *Memoria* is a storehouse, custodian of invention and cogitation, of "things" and "words," and without it "even the most eminent of the speaker's other talents will come to nothing." Charlemagne's question about precepts is another way of asking whether *memoria* is an art or not. Alcuin takes for granted that *memoria* is a study, involving discipline, training, and practice. But he apparently saw no need (at least for Charlemagne) for a complex set of related precepts in addition to the elementary principles of memory training, the *puerilia*. He thought of memory as a consciously constructed inventory, a library, a storehouse of material in the form of both "words" and "things." But his advice to the emperor does not go farther, to suggest a systematic art of memory.[32]

This bias, if that is what it is, against an art of memory can also be found in Quintilian and in the late Roman rhetoricians of the fourth and later centuries. In *De oratore*, Cicero speaks of the architectural mnemonic art as so well-known that it needs no elaborate description. But Quintilian, while not rejecting it totally, plays down its utility and that of other such *artes*. Evidently a fashion favoring practice and discipline in the elements of memory training over more elaborate, curious (and Greek) *artes* had begun to dominate Roman memorative pedagogy; this bias seems to me consistent with Quintilian's judgments against using "canned" lists of ready-made *imagines* and all other quick prescriptions for memory training. Of course, *Ad Herennium* also counseled against substituting the schemes of others for one's own; this is a traditional pedagogical caution, the basis of Plato's warning in *Phaedrus* against substituting textbooks and methods for teachers and discipline. But Quintilian's bias towards philosophical rhetoric and against the sophistical excesses he saw in his contemporaries like Seneca seems to me reflected again here in his remarks about the limited usefulness of *artes memorativae*. Instead, he stresses the elementary aspects of memory training, reserving the various arts for it to those of advanced ability and to teachers of dubious reputation (or so he implies).

This emphasis on the elements rather than on an "art" of *memoria* is found still in the fourth century. Julius Victor wrote that "for impressing memory some teach observations of a great many places and images, which do not seem effective to me."[33] Since he took a great deal from Quintilian, it is not surprising to find this opinion, and it also indicates that during the centuries after Quintilian wrote, his judgment continued to predominate, despite the fact that Cicero himself spoke favorably of the architectural art in *De oratore*, and despite the detailed description of it in the *Ad Herennium*, a text whose influence seems to have been greatest from the fourth century on, after it was attached to the works of Cicero.[34] Julius Victor in turn greatly influenced Isidore of Seville and Alcuin. Yet, as we have seen, Julius Victor does give instructions in the basic mnemonic preparations: division, memory "for things" and "for words," using memorial *notae*, meditation, and composition. So it seems that in later antiquity and the earlier Middle Ages the memorial *artes* were regarded in standard pedagogy as marginally helpful at best, and that the focus of memory training was on its elements, instilled through practice and discipline, but without emphasizing a universal body of principles. To use the traditional categories, *memoria* was taught as a *studium*, a collection of empirically-proven guidelines, but it was not a systematic *ars*, as it apparently had been regarded in the time of Cicero and would be again in the thirteenth century. The distinction I am making is between what we would call a "craft," learned by apprenticeship, and a "scientific discipline" that must be taught from a text-book.

Although arguments from silence are not worth much without positive, corroborating evidence, it is interesting that Augustine makes no mention of an art of memory, though trained as a teacher of rhetoric and though he is one of the great philosophers of memory. Frances Yates attempted to make a case for his having been a practitioner of the architectural art, on the basis of his descriptions of memory's power in Book x of *Confessions*, of which the following is typical:

Behold, in those innumerable fields, and dens, and caves of my memory, innumerably full of innumerable kinds of things, first, either by images, as all bodies are: secondly, or by the presence of the things themselves, as the arts are: thirdly, or by certain notions and impressions, as the affections of the mind are . . . through all these do I run and flit about, on this side, and on that side, mining into them so far as ever I am able, but can find no bottom. So great is the force of memory, so great is the force of life, even in man living as mortal.[35]

But the metaphors Augustine uses here are archetypal: one did not need to practice the architectural art to believe that memory was locational in nature, like a vast cave with many inner caverns in which all experience was inventoried, and that it had immense power which training could enhance. Indeed, though copied as one of Cicero's works, the *Ad Herennium* was not much commented on or quoted until after the eleventh century.[36]

And when it was first revived, its memory advice was received with some skepticism. John of Salisbury (who knew Quintilian's *Institutio* better than most of his contemporaries) alludes to arts of memory: "Seneca most readily promised to teach the art for furnishing memories, of which I certainly wish I were a master; but as far as I know, he did not actually teach it. Tullius seems to have applied himself to this in [*Rhetorica ad Herennium*] but the latter is not of much help to me."[37] And Geoffrey of Vinsauf, writing at the turn of the thirteenth century, dismisses Tully's art completely: "Tullius relies on unusual images as a technique for training the memory, but he is teaching himself; and let the subtle teacher, as it were in solitude, address his subtlety to himself alone."[38]

Instead, Geoffrey counsels the elements of memory training: divisions, placing the pieces in a rigid locational order (one, two, three, etc.), marking material with mental *notae* for secure recollection from the storage-bin ("cella") of memory, respecting the limits of short-term memory ("brevitas"), and not stuffing too much in at one time, for the store-room of memory responds well only while it is having fun, and so must be treated well ("Cellula quae meminit est cellula deliciarum"). The problem with a method like Tully's is that it is gimmicky and ready-made, whereas no single group of markers (*notae*) will work equally well for everyone. Everyone should make little markers of his own choosing and devising, for those are "safer [*tutior*]" for recollection. One should note the concern Geoffrey expresses for the *safety* of a recollective scheme – Thomas of Waleys has the same concern.[39]

The arts of memory

One other early medieval writer on memory should be considered here, because he is credited by Frances Yates as being the one who "handed on the art [of memory] to the Middle Ages."[40] This is Martianus Capella, a fifth-century teacher whose allegorical encyclopedia on the seven liberal arts, *The Marriage of Mercury and Philology*, became influential after the turn of the millennium. Martianus treats *memoria* in the traditional way, as a part of rhetoric. But he is rarely mentioned as a proponent of an art of memory and never, to my knowledge, linked with the precepts of Tully. What Martianus describes under *memoria* are some of the elementary rules of ancient mnemotechnique, but nothing that constitutes an art of memory, let alone repeats what is peculiar to the architectural art.

So, Martianus says that while memory is a natural talent, it may be assisted by training. The craft of memory has only a few rules but requires much practice; but by it words and things can be grasped quickly and surely. Memory for "things" is easier and less time-consuming than memory for "words." Simonides invented the art from his experience when a banqueting-hall collapsed, and he was able to identify the victims because he had attached their names to the places where they were seated. Order is thus the key to the precepts of memory training. The order is memorized as a set of distinctive mental locations into which one puts images of things to be recalled – for example, if one wants to remember a wedding, one would place the image of a girl in a saffron wedding veil; if a murderer, a sword or other weapon. "For just as what is written is contained in wax and letters, so what is committed to memory is written into areas as if on wax and in page-form [*in cera paginaque signatur*]."[41] But since much labor is required for remembering, we should write down what we wish readily to retain. If the material is long, divide it into shorter sections for ease of memorizing. It is useful to mark with *notae* things we want particularly to recall. When memorizing, one should not read aloud but meditate upon the material in a low murmur. It is best to exercise the memory at night, when silence aids concentration.[42]

The sources for all of this lore are *De oratore* and Quintilian's *Institutio*, not the *Ad Herennium*. Martianus himself provides the particular examples. An order is "memorized into" the mind ("Is [ordo] . . . meditandus est") as distinctive, well-known (and "-lighted") locations ("in locis illustribus"). Into these locations the likenesses of objects ("species rerum") and images of abstract content ("sententiarumque imagines") are gathered ("collocandae sunt"). Rather than a procedure like that for forming "places" advised in the architectural mnemonic, what Martianus counsels is a prototype of advice like that of Hugh of St. Victor (and others, as we shall see) – to form a "line," "linea," in one's mind that acts as a schematic ordering device (like a diagram) for material that is then put into it. This is the commonest type of medieval description for what one does in forming "places," and it is not the same kind of procedure as that described in the *Ad Herennium*. Bradwardine's sets of places in fives, one on top of another as in a matrix, is more like constructing a diagram than like the memorizing of a street or house; that quality seems distinctively medieval.

From the time of Quintilian, then, *memoria* seems to have been commonly taught only as an elementary study, consisting of a few basic rules and some common-sense advice, eclectic, empirical, pragmatic, but not a unitary discipline with a full methodology. This study concentrated on the essentials and was suspicious of what seemed to be shortcuts. Are there precepts? Charlemagne asks Alcuin. None, is the reply, only discipline, training, and exercise. *Memoria* was a practice and a procedure rather than a subject. In this practice, the importance of *notae*, or *signa* as they are also called, was universally acknowledged – including *imagines* of every sort which could be used for mnemonic associations.

Boncompagno da Signa, writing in 1235, discusses no "art" of recollection, no principles for constructing such *notae*. Instead he lists virtually everything made as a potential memory aid, for somebody in some circumstances. Every sort of sign, starting with language itself, helps us to remember something – indeed, for Boncompagno, any interpretative activity is essentially a matter of recalling something to memory. So, the cock which crowed when Peter betrayed Jesus was a memorial sign ("memoriale signum") by which Peter recalled Jesus's prophetic words. All books, all pictures, images, sculptures, all cruciforms, all insignia of rank and station, banners, alphabets, methods of calculation, notches cut into sticks to record loans and repayments, the stories told to children which record the events of history, even the jargon of thieves – everything has a memorative function by which God reminds us of Himself, and we remember the world. Boncompagno's version of Neoplatonism, which is evident, interests me less in this context than the fact that his list is so completely eclectic. He has a philosophy of memory (of a sort) but he has no *ars memorativa*, no principles on which to explain how these diverse kinds of *signa* work.

Another specialized term, in addition to *nota* and *signum*, that defines a function of images used memoratively, is the phrase "imagines rerum." These terms, I think, belong to the common pedagogy of *memoria* and are not specific to a version of an *ars memorativa*. They are distinguished by function, *nota* being reserved for any sort of mental marker one uses to file and cue stored material. *Imagines rerum* traditionally seem restricted to the function of public speaking, declamation, and hence composition. Though no admirer of memory arts, Quintilian does favor the making of *imagines rerum* when preparing a speech. Eloquence, he writes, depends upon the orator's emotional state; the mind of the speaker must be emotionally engaged and moved to adapt itself to the things of which we are speaking, and to conceive "imagines rerum."

Quintilian uses the term again when he discusses in greater detail how emotions are stirred in the orator. To do so one is much helped by vivid images, "which the Greeks call *fantasiai* . . . whereby images of things absent are again presented in our minds" (VI, 2, 29). These *imagines* generate the very emotions in the orator which he seeks to awaken in his audience, and cause him to re-experience (vicariously make present again) what happened:

shall I not see the assassin burst suddenly from his hiding-place, the victim tremble, cry for help, beg for mercy, or turn to run? Shall I not see the fatal blow delivered and the stricken body fall? Will not the blood, the deathly pallor, the groan of agony, the death-rattle, be indelibly impressed upon my mind?[43]

But "imagines rerum" are also critical for retaining the order and flow of a speech – a mnemonic function. Unless one can speak with order, copiousness, and style one is not speaking but only ranting. To produce such ordered pattern:

those vivid conceptions [rerum imagines] of which I spoke, and which, as I remarked, are called *fantasiai*, together with everything that we intend to say, the persons and questions involved, and the hopes and fears to which they give rise, must be kept clearly before our eyes and admitted to our emotions.[44]

It is the *imagines* that can be fixed by the mind's eyes and that arouse again one's emotional response ("intentio") to the initial matter, so these are the key to holding any discourse in our memories. One is not trying to store away written texts by their agency (even if one were so unskilled an orator as to have written one's complete speech down in advance), for words alone are easily lost and cannot be reconstituted if one were to stumble or need to depart suddenly from one's prepared theme. We find Martianus Capella advising the use of such vivid "thematic" images to help remember a speech (the veiled bride, the sword). And though related to the phrase "memoria rerum" (another basic concept of mnemotechnique), "imagines rerum" seems restricted more especially to the context of declamation. "Memory of things" can refer also to a method of memorizing texts in the first place.

For Bradwardine, what he calls "memoria orationis" does not consider how to remember a whole speech but rather how to recall a single thematic sentence word-for-word, a "theme" of the sort about which one might develop a speech extemporaneously. In addition to the rebus-like "syllable-memory" one uses to remember one's theme word-for-word, he advocates using "imagines rerum," vivid images which mark the main points one will develop extemporaneously in one's talk. Thus, the art of forming "imagines rerum" in memory places addresses a somewhat different task and set of problems than do the indexing heuristics. They act as focal images for the speaker's meditation. The "places" order the major stages in the speech; the "imagines rerum" in each location (supplemented, perhaps, by themes remembered in "imagines verborum") trigger the memory through their emotional force to recall various parts of its mental library. "Places" and "images" are certainly heuristic – they maintain order – but they are more than that, for they are memorial in the meditative sense too.

Unlike a simple matrix of numbers and letters, "imagines rerum" can act as compositional sites and associational cues that can "gather in" much related material laid down elsewhere in memory, because they invite the orator's "eyes" to stay and contemplate. This function is also distinctively medieval, most likely developed in monastic meditational practices. It accounts for the curiously medieval use of the verb "remember" to describe what one was doing when one meditated, in vivid "picture"-form, on hell and heaven, places one had never oneself visited and thus could not actually "remember," in our sense. But meditation, as we will see in the next two chapters, was thought to be intense memorial activity. The use of "imagines rerum" as "sites" for memorial composition ("compositio") is therefore a kind of "remembering." This also helps to explain the curious nature of a medieval diagram; rarely is it a diagram *of something*, as ours are. Rather, it requires one to stay and ponder, to fill in missing connections, to add to the material which it presents. It is a meditational artifact, an "imago rerum," and not primarily informational in its usefulness.[45]

Memory became an art again (while continuing to be an elementary skill) about the year 1240. Of the three writers whose mnemotechnique I discussed earlier in this chapter, only John of Garland was a teacher of rhetoric. Albertus Magnus was a professor of theology and logic; so was Thomas Bradwardine. Yet it is John of Garland who produces an old-fashioned pragmatic of mnemonic advice, having no pretensions to *ars memorativa*, if he knew what one was. A generation after John of Garland, in the same university setting though in a different faculty, Albertus Magnus wrote his sympathetic and philosophically systematic discussion of the *Ad Herennium*'s precepts for an art of memory based upon images in places, giving it a seriousness which it did not lose again until well after the Renaissance. The conclusion seems to be that professional rhetoric teachers had little role in the initial development of medieval arts of memory.

Commenting on the intellectual situation of *memoria* at the end of the twelfth century, Gillian Evans remarked that "[t]he elements of a formal art of memory and of a formal study of the faculty of memory, based on older authorities, are all present in the twelfth century schools ... What was missing was a stimulus – perhaps in the form of an individual scholar with a special interest in the topic – to bring the elements together."[46] I think we may safely conclude that this "individual scholar" was Albertus Magnus. Though we know very little about his early life, it seems probable that he studied at Padua during the first decade of its foundation as a *scolium* around 1222. Padua was founded by scholars from Bologna – indeed the influence of Boncompagno da Signa on its rhetoric curriculum was strong from the start. But Padua was also noted as an early center for the study of Aristotle's *libri naturales*, including the brief essays of the *Parva naturalia*, and if Albertus was there, it was the "natural history" books that he studied, rather than rhetoric.[47]

Indeed, the only extensive commentary on the memory section of the *Ad Herennium* written before the thirteenth century (there are more commentaries on the other parts of Tully's work) appears to be the work of Thierry of Chartres, and to have been composed in the 1130s, a full century before

Albertus Magnus's commentary on Aristotle's *De memoria*. Thierry was a teacher at Chartres, and later chancellor, in the first half of the twelfth century, a contemporary of Hugh of St. Victor and of John of Salisbury's teacher, Bernard of Chartres. His interest in rhetoric is primarily in its organization of topics; he is best known for his studies in the "Old Logic" of Aristotle and in Plato. His commentary on the *Ad Herennium* is preserved only in a single manuscript of the twelfth century. It has been edited recently by Karin Fredborg, probably its first publication since then.

What Thierry has to say about Tully's mnemonic techniques "hardly goes beyond mere paraphrase," as Fredborg notes, and only one of his remarks about the memory section – an explanation of the characters Domitius and the "Martii reges" which figure in the example given by Tully for *memoria ad verbum* – is picked up by any of the writers who immediately followed him and used his comments in their own work.[48] Like his contemporaries, then, Thierry seems to have been little interested in the architectural mnemonic, or in contributing to its revival as a practical tool for oratory, nor does he appear to have understood significantly better than they did what it was all about. He comments on it because it is part of Tully's text, paraphrasing almost exactly what it already says, glossing words, explicating grammar, explaining the mythological allusions.

Nonetheless, Thierry's commentary is not without interest, because of the intelligence of his comments and his generally positive stance towards the subject. He exhibits none of the outright scorn for artificial memory schemes that we find in John of Salisbury and Geoffrey of Vinsauf, though they both wrote a good deal later in the twelfth century than he did. He expands the skepticism, already apparent in the *Ad Herennium*, concerning the utility of memory for words – this sort of thing, he says, is useful as an exercise only, and to remember verses from the poets.[49] The difference between Thierry's mistrust of "memoria verborum" and Bradwardine's adoption of it for what he calls "memoria orationis" is probably a mark of the change in sermon style between the twelfth and fourteenth centuries, the dominant model being the so-called "thematic" sermon. Interestingly, this style comes into prominence about 1230 – about the same time as the full revival of the *Ad Herennium*'s mnemonic advice.

Thierry then rehearses in paraphrase the example in the *Ad Herennium* of how to remember the verse "Iam domi ultionem [*sic*] reges Atridae parant." And he adds an example of his own: if you should want to remember the first two lines of Book II of the *Aeneid* ("Conticuere omnes intentique ora tenebant / cum pater Aeneas lecto sic orsus ab alto est [*sic*]"), you might imagine someone sitting on a couch ("sedentem in lecto") and reciting something, while surrounded by many intent listeners ("multos intentos ad audiendum").[50] This is a perfectly sensible image – rather more sensible than those given as examples in the *Ad Herennium* – but it does not, in fact, exemplify the advice of Tully to construct visual homophonies that will cue a line for you word-by-word. It is much more like an image *ad res* than an image *ad verbum* in the manner of the *Ad Herennium*.

Yet the vocabulary of the ancient mnemonic advice in general does not seem foreign to Thierry. He gives a sympathetic and comprehensive explanation of "imagines rerum" and their value to orators, of the reasons why "artificial memory" can benefit natural talent, and of the need for practice and disciplined exercise in making sets of numbered locations. He is clear about what the locations are and how the images are fitted into them, why the locations remain stable while one changes the images to suit the needs of each particular orational "cause." He understands the reason for a fixed order among the locations, so that one can go backwards as well as forwards, or in whatever order one likes. He knows that "intervalla" refers to "locorum distantias," the distance from which one views a location in the mind's eye, for one's view of the content will be confounded if one's view-point is situated too close or too far away.[51] He understands that grotesque, unusual, wonderful images excite the memory, and need to be used instead of ordinary or routine ones. And he approves the advice in Tully against relying entirely on ready-made images instead of finding one's own. It is only in regard to "memoria verborum" that he seems dubious, and in this he is in the company of Quintilian and the anti-Sophist Roman tradition, as we have seen.

Yet Thierry's commentary seems to have had virtually no influence on either his contemporaries or later writers – certainly Albertus Magnus was not influenced by Thierry's clear explanation of that wretchedly difficult crux concerning Aesopus, Cimber, Iphegenia, and the sons of Atreus. Had he known Thierry, who seems to have had a slightly better manuscript than he did, Albertus would not have given such a muddled gloss of this passage. So Thierry's commentary has no important role in the revival of the architectural mnemonic. This means that Albertus and the other later memory writers got their understanding of "locations," "images for things," and "images for words" in other ways. For this reason in particular, the fact that Thierry is so clear about most of the *Ad Herennium*'s memory terms and descriptions of technique is of greater significance than the few moments of hesitation he displays, for it supports the conclusion that many of the basic concepts of memory advice from late antiquity remained current in the twelfth century – current enough for an exceptionally intelligent commentator, like Thierry of Chartres, to explain the gist of the *Ad Herennium* on memory with clarity, if without enthusiasm.

The reassessment of memorial art was given a crucial intellectual impetus by the translation into Latin of Aristotle's *De anima* and its related treatises, including the one on memory and recollection. This material was first translated by James of Venice (the Old Translation), and had begun to circulate widely by about 1200.[52] Albertus commented on it during his years at Paris. As we have seen, he connects Aristotle's comments on the associative nature of memory and the principles by which it operates with the example of the advice and images adduced in *Ad Herennium*. He is the first

Western scholar to have done so. His pupil, Thomas Aquinas, does the same, both in his own *De memoria* commentary and in the *Summa* (1272). By mid-century the art of making memorial "images in backgrounds," and more importantly, the idea that *memoria* could be treated as an "art," with principles and structure, even though its specific application varied so much with individual experience, had been accepted as philosophically and logically reputable. As a result of this circumstance of its revival, the art of memory is often found dissociated from the study of rhetoric in the later Middle Ages, and treated as a part of logic or moral philosophy. Separate memorial *artes* and essays on strengthening memory were typically composed and circulated as independent treatises, often in anthologies of works on "natural philosophy," a description that fits well both of the manuscripts in which copies of Bradwardine's treatise are found, and the essays of Mattheolus of Perugia and even Peter of Ravenna.

It was Aristotle who made these rules comprehensible through his analysis of the visual and associative working of recollection. A manuscript of the first decade of the fifteenth century (Ambrosiana MS. R.50.supra) appends a forty-line heroic poem setting forth the rules for the art of memory to the Latin translation of Aristotle's *Nichomachean Ethics*. Though it does not go so far as to attribute these verses to Aristotle himself, it is clear that the connection – even a sort of authorship – of Aristotle with the art of memory had become something of a commonplace.

Just as important as his analysis of memorial associations is the fact that Aristotle also described the process of recollection as a variety of reasoning, not just a practical craft. This setting of the art of memory in the context of logic rather than rhetoric "put . . . artificial memory on an altogether new footing," as Frances Yates rightly observed.[53] It did more than that. It resurrected the very idea of memory as an art, more systematic and scientific than the simple if effective "puerilia" described by Hugh of St. Victor and taught in generations of elementary classrooms. It is one of those ironies of history that Peter Ramus, who, in the sixteenth century, thought he was reacting against Aristotelianism by taking *memoria* from rhetoric and making it a part of dialectic, was essentially remaking a move made 300 years before by two Dominican professors who were attempting to reshape memorial study in conformity with Aristotle.

But rhetoric did not simply give over the study of *memoria* to the logicians. The recovery of Aristotle's major psychological texts is not sufficient to explain the immediate popularity of *ars memorativa* in circles that included theology students and professors, students of law, friars, and (especially in Italy) bureaucratic clerks, merchants, physicians, and notaries. A translation of the memory section of *Ad Herennium* appeared in Italian not later than 1266, only a few years after Albertus Magnus's discussion of it in *De bono*, and before Thomas Aquinas commended it in the second part of his Summa. And a French version was made by Jean d'Antioche at the end of the thirteenth century, as part of a translation of the *Ad Herennium*.[54] The explanation for this popularity, I think, lies in cultural and educational factors that greatly increased people's needs and opportunities for speaking publicly, to a variety of audiences both clerical and lay. These came into prominence during the latter twelfth century, and were fully developed during the thirteenth and fourteenth centuries.

Unlike the situation in the earlier Middle Ages, when public oratory was the responsibility primarily of abbots and bishops, addressing one another or monks in their cloisters or a few aristocrats, the culture of the medieval university called for public disputations, sermons, and other forms of oral address on the part of all students as well as professors. Lawyers had always needed to retain quantities of detailed material and to be able to speak disputationally; the study of law expanded greatly after the twelfth century. The Fourth Lateran Council of 1215 encouraged greater participation by the laity in the life of the church, the chief vehicle for which was to be vernacular sermons. The lay culture of courtiers and merchants also incorporated the need to speak well publicly during the thirteenth and fourteenth centuries.

We can trace these social developments in the rapid proliferation from the thirteenth century on of memorial *artes* – some based mainly upon Tully, some (like Bradwardine's) clearly not. They are written in Latin and in the vernaculars, especially Italian and French. Often they are the work of Dominican friars, though other orders and even laymen (especially in the fourteenth century) were also active transmitters. Whatever their content and provenance, however, they are all called *artes memorativae* after the twelfth century, though the term is rarely used before then during the Middle Ages when *memoria* is discussed.

It is a phenomenon of the very greatest importance to this study of what I have called "memorial culture," that the Dominican order, which was responsible for developing many of the most useful tools for the study of written texts during the thirteenth century, was simultaneously the most active single proponent and popularizer of memory as an art, and especially of the principles of Tully. The Dominicans developed the written concordance to the Bible, devised indexing schemes for texts that were to continue in use for centuries (they are responsible, for example, for the referential scheme of dividing a column of text into areas marked A through G), and compiled many collections of *distinctiones*, *quaestiones*, and other scholars' and preachers' aids. Of course the Franciscans and other fraternal orders compiled similar reference tools, and practiced techniques of traditional *memoria* that eventually also came to be called *artes*. But Albertus Magnus and Thomas Aquinas are the two earliest theologians to commend particularly the art of memory which Tully taught as being the best of all; these two great saints exercised their influence for several centuries in ensuring Dominican sponsorship of the architectural mnemonic.[55]

But, as I have observed, preaching friars and theology students were not the only groups in the thirteenth century who took up *ars memorativa* with enthusiasm. The mid-thirteenth-century Italian translation of Tully, the earliest vernacular one, was probably made by a Florentine jurist, Bono Giamboni,[56] who also translated Brunetto Latini's *Trésor* into Italian from French. It is closely associated in the written record with a collection of rhetorical precepts, chiefly from the *Ad Herennium*, made by a Dominican, Guidotto da Bologna. Brunetto Latini himself was a great "Ciceronian"; his *Trésor* is a compendious florilegium of things to be remembered from classical writers on a variety of ethical and rhetorical subjects. Though it does not include Tully's memory art, there is some basis for thinking that such compilations were thought of specifically as memory books, and their compilers revered at this time in Italy as major exponents of *ars memorativa*. Bono Giamboni's translations soon became attached to an early Italian ethical florilegium, *Ammaestramenti degli Antichi*, compiled around 1300 by the Dominican friar, Bartolommeo, of the convent of San Concordio in Pisa.

The author of the *Ammaestramenti* preface makes clear why he considers an art of memory to be necessary for all educated men, including laity:

if a man has the wisdom to know well how to understand things, and also has wisdom and justice, which is the firm desire to want to arrange things well, and to want to do it rightfully, he must know how to speak . . . for without speech his goodness would be like a buried treasure . . . We have already seen the first thing a speaker must know, how he is to learn to speak good, ornamented, and ordered speech, as I have shown you. Now I wish to show you the second thing a speaker must know in order to speak perfectly, which is how his speech may be held in memory, for no one will speak well if when he speaks he does not have it clearly in mind.[57]

The art of memory is specifically an aid for speakers, not for learners, for composers, not for readers. This distinguishes it most clearly from the elementary rules of memory training. But, like all memory training, it was considered to be an ethical as well as a practical imperative.

Memory and the Ethics of Reading

There is no questioning the fact that written material came increasingly into use from the eleventh century on; the reason that more manuscripts survive from the later Middle Ages is because more were made. The making of scholarly compendia is a response to this increase, and the larger educated, book-needing public that created it. There is an increase not only in bulk, but in the complexity of indexing and classifying schemes that one does not see before the late eleventh century, and it is evident that, though they derive from mnemonic principles in use for centuries, they seem much too technical to have served directly as a mnemonic – to be useful as memory devices, a user would need some prior training and familiarity with basic mnemonic principles.

But these facts do not seem to have altered significantly the value placed on memory training in medieval education, nor to have changed the deliberate cultivation of *memoria*. Medieval culture remained profoundly memorial in nature, despite the increased use and availability of books for reasons other than simple technological convenience. The primary factor in its conservation lies in the identification of memory with the formation of moral virtues. Writing, as we have seen, was always thought to be a memory aid, not a substitute for it. Children learned to write as a part of reading/memorizing, inscribing their memories in the act of inscribing their tablets. Writing itself was judged to be an ethical activity in monastic culture. A twelfth-century sermon says, in part: "Let us consider then how we may become scribes of the Lord. The parchment on which we write for Him is a pure conscience, whereon all our good works are noted by the pen of memory." The orator then proceeds to moralize the various implements of writing: pumice, knife, pen, ruler, chalk, ink, and so on.[1]

In 1330, the Franciscan friar William of Ockham, virtually interdicted from the intellectual community of Western Europe by Pope John XXII for his teachings challenging papal power, found himself living at the Franciscan convent in Munich. There he spent the rest of his life. Having been a member of university communities at Oxford, Paris, and in Italy, where he had access to the best libraries in Europe, his isolation at Munich was distressing to him, not least because there he had virtually no books, nor means of obtaining them, for the Pope had warned that nothing was to be sent to him. Ockham makes this quite clear at several points in his *Dialogus*, the long dialogue on the limits of papal power between a master and his pupil, which contains a few pieces (chiefly Part II) written earlier, and much new material.[2] The work was in circulation by 1343; it appears to have been unfinished, because, while Ockham names the matters he intended to include in Part III, the manuscripts all break off in that part, each at different places and none complete.

Ockham's situation as a scholar is a dramatically extreme case that demonstrates quite clearly the necessary role that memorial training and transmission continued to play in both education and scholarly dialogue throughout the Middle Ages, even as the number of books increased.[3] In the first part of *Dialogus*, "Magister," Ockham's persona, tells his pupil that, in order to conduct his arguments properly, he needs various books and materials he cannot get, a theme sounded frequently throughout the work, "but you know I do not have any of [various writings he has just spoken of] and according to the [papal] order they absolutely refuse to communicate them to me."[4] He complains again in the prologue to the third part of not having the books he wants: "if it seems to you that I in no way get immersed beyond the prefatory material [that is, do no more than skim the surface of the subject]: it is the best I can do when I am not able, as I would like, to come by the books I need." To which his pupil, the other member of the dialogue, responds that he has no fear but that "Magister" will draw what he needs from his memory.[5]

The Master counsels his disciple whenever he can to extract and memorize material from a wide variety of sources; indeed, if the Master had not done so when he had the opportunity, he would now have no hope of access to even the most fundamental texts, the Bible and the collections of canon law. The pupil asks how one gets knowledge of a subject like imperial rights and powers? "Complete knowledge of them, – which in making tracts you recall [*tractanda commemoras*] from books of sacred theology, and of both kinds of law, that is canon and civil, of moral philosophy, and from the histories of the Romans, and especially of the emperors, and of the greatest pontiffs, and of other peoples – should be most patiently extracted and solidly built up. By which means alone I have hope of obtaining the Bible and the Decretum together with the four books of decretals." And he again apologizes if, under the circumstances, he seems to make an imperfect or awkward book. His pupil responds by saying that even though in these days circumstances prevent the making of a perfectly complete work, "it is still useful not to remain wholly silent, because we may provoke those with a good supply of books into perfecting and completing the work."[6]

Professor Miethke has observed that polemical writing, a genre that requires the utmost currency for its effectiveness, was often composed, even in the fourteenth century, on the basis of a scholar's memory of the work to which he was responding, or even on hearsay accounts of texts, rather than on written copies. Written copies of new work, treatises, disputations, and the like, were difficult to obtain, even if one lived close to their origin in both place and time. There are very few fourteenth-century manuscripts of

Dialogus, yet it is clear that Ockham's ideas had tremendous currency and occasioned bitter controversy throughout Europe, even in his own lifetime. In 1343, Duke Albert of Austria is said to have supported the position of the Emperor, Lewis of Bavaria, against the Papacy, because he was persuaded by the emperor's report of the ideas in a "dialogus" produced by Master William of Ockham. Obviously papal interdict did not in fact prevent even Ockham's current work from circulating out of Munich, and given the conditions, the chief method of such circulation, Miethke thinks, would have been oral, well in advance of written copies.[7]

It is important to recognize that Ockham's memorial training occurred as a part of his ordinary education, and that he expects his students to fill their memories as a part of their ordinary education. (The Magister in *Dialogus* has no reason to suppose his student will be exiled as he was, yet he urges him to fill his memory just the same.) Ockham did not educate himself with the idea that he might go to Munich, nor was he, as a student, the captive of provincial schools having, in consequence, infrequent access to libraries. His whole scholarly life until 1330 was spent in the greatest of European universities, his circle the most "bookish" of the time. And still it is clear that he read to memorize, that in composing he was able at will to draw extensive resources from his memorial library. He does indeed ask those with access to a supply of books to "perfect" his work, but what Ockham meant by "perfect" is not "correct" in our sense (as a modern scholar, forced into similar circumstances, might beg indulgence for "inexact" citations, pleading a faulty memory). Ockham means "complete" or "fill out"; he apologizes for only "skimming the surface" of his analyses and expositions of the subject ("de prefatis . . . nullatenus intromittam"), for if he had the latest material he would be able to fill out the contents he had earlier stored in his memory. This incomplete and prefatory work composed from memory fills 551 folio pages with material that is certainly not of an elementary nature.

Evidently Ockham's memory did not contain dim recollections of a few commonplaces learned in grammar school, and evidently too he did not pause frequently during composition to find references in his books, for he had none. Nor could he consult extensive indices in the library of the Munich Franciscans, or thumb through his own books for marginal *notae* marking passages pertinent to "imperial power" in order to do his research. And the thought of Ockham and his companions escaping down the Rhône from Avignon to Italy with a trunkful of parchment slips (to say nothing of persuading his papal jailors, who were suspicious precisely about his opinions, to let him keep such a heap of slips during four years of imprisonment) is simply silly. Yet exactly these activities – frequent consultation of indices, thumbing books to pick up previously marked passages, writing citations on to parchment slips, even "scissors-and-paste" composition – have all been presumed by many medievalists to have been the methods by which scholarship was conducted during this period. We are even solemnly told that

Hugh of St. Victor was the last teacher to recommend a good memory as a scholarly necessity.[8]

It has been known for a long time that the publication of information during the medieval period often occurred by means of sermons and such oral forms. So Bernard of Clairvaux's preaching of the Crusades was disseminated quickly through western Europe both by direct preaching on his part and by others preaching what he had said.[9] This was also an early Church custom; Cyril of Alexandria composed many sermons which he sent to all the bishops of Greece, who, in turn, memorized them and preached them to their own congregations.[10] All sorts of material was disseminated in this way; a famous example is the invention of eyeglasses, first disclosed in a sermon preached in February of 1306 by the Dominican friar Giordano (who belonged, incidentally, to the same convent at Pisa as did Bartolommeo da San Concordio).[11]

Observations by modern scholars that many full commentaries, such as that on Tully's *Ad Herennium*, sprang up virtually fully formed in the late eleventh and early twelfth centuries (as did so many other written scholarly tools) are best explained by their compilers having been able to draw upon a stock of glosses and comments, developed and disseminated orally over a long time from one generation of masters to the next in monastery classrooms, and from one monastery to another via travelling scholars. John Ward aptly describes this as a "gloss potpourri ... the accumulating mass of rhetorical wisdom [which] came to form a kind of anonymous pool, from which pitchers were drawn almost at random." The schoolroom, as he says, was a very conservative place, in which particular glosses might have a life of a millennium or more. It was also one of the most important locations for the preservation and dissemination of eclectic oral lore, for in it students learned to lay down pieces of text and commentary together memorially via the sorts of heuristics I discussed earlier. Indeed, the piece by piece nature of memory storage may help to account for the line by line nature which most of the earliest commentaries took.[12] In an important sense, every "ordinary gloss" was essentially a florilegium of Important Things To Remember, at least in the judgment of its compiler, arranged for easy storage and recollection.

The astonishing precision with which Richard and Mary Rouse have been able to date the emergence of complex glossating apparatus within a couple of decades in the twelfth century suggests strongly that the written versions express an existing oral tradition.[13] They were written down then rather than at an earlier time because a large, new public of university scholars needed to be accommodated. University activity heavily depended on oral forms, from the lecture itself, to the oral (and orational) nature of examinations, *disputationes*, and *sermones*. In lecture, students studied from books open before them, but it is significant, I think, that the manuscript illuminations typically show them without pens.[14] They would have mentally marked the important passages, as Hugh counsels, by memorizing them from the same codex each time (a problem solved when students owned their own copies of major texts), noting the shapes of the letters, the position of the text on the page, and then filing segments of it appropriately away, with the teacher's comments "attached" to the textual image. By contrast, a modern student in class or the library without a pen is a lost soul.

But in the minds of modern scholars oral transmission raises the question of accuracy; we tend to dismiss memory as a reliable disseminator and instead look solely to writing (manuscript copies or letters) as the agent for all varieties of accurate transmission. Yet, as I have observed before and will again here, medieval scholars simply did not share our distrust of memory's "accuracy." Remembering Ockham's desire for "perfection," (and his comment can be multiplied endlessly in scholarly works throughout the Middle Ages) what was valued was completeness, copiousness, rather than "objective" accuracy, as we understand and value it now. In this as in much else, medieval assumptions about the "occasionalness" and "plenitude" of literature are at odds with modern textual fundamentalism.

Richard de Bury's love for books was not that of a mere bibliophile, but a scholar's love (as Petrarch recognized).[15] Yet it is not at all clear in *Philobiblon* that every volume he saved from dust and dirt was saved physically. Some – how many we cannot know – he "collected" in memory and later had his secretaries write out from dictation. He tells us this directly, but it is also clear from the way he talks about books, what they are, and of what use, that trained memory and the book are closely linked – even for him, in the mid fourteenth century, the avid collector of one of Europe's greatest private libraries.

Bury closes his first chapter with a catalogue of metaphors for books, many of which we have already encountered as metaphors primarily for memory: *thesaurus, scrinium, favus* ("honey-comb"), and a couple that suggest he had encountered Hugh of St. Victor in some form (or at least shared some of his commonplaces): "arca Noe," "lignum vitae," and "scala Jacob."[16] Most of these reappear elsewhere in his treatise as motifs for both books and the memorial activities of scholarship. For in Bury's prose, as in that of so many other writers, the two are practically interchangeable. Having a good memory is virtually as good as having the book itself, and better than having an untrustworthy written copy of it. Such play, it seems to me, can be found in a passage such as the following, when Bury describes his collecting habits in Paris, "the paradise of the world."[17] There, he says, are to be found delightful libraries, "super cellas aromatum redolentes" (p. 70, line 2), which include the meadows ("prata") of the Academy, the lounges ("diverticula") of Athens, the walks of the Peripatetics, the promontories of Parnassus, and the porches ("porticus") of the Stoics. And then follows a catalogue of classical and Christian authors, after which Bury says that "having unbound the strings of our treasuries and our *sacculi*, we distributed coinage with a joyful heart, and we recovered by this ransom priceless books from mud and sand."[18] I do not wish to argue that Richard de Bury bought no books, for it is evident both from *Philobiblon* and contemporary accounts that he bought and transported for his personal library a great many, though it may be wondered whether there were really five cartloads, as the Durham chronicler has it.[19] But I do wish to point out that the language in this passage plays heavily with common metaphors for memory training as well as with the literal action of buying books. *Thesaurus, sacculus,* and the actions of redeeming the words of authors with a payment and of dispensing coins from one's *sacculus,* joyous heart (memory) and all, are all metaphors we commonly encounter in works about memory, and it seems to me that Bury may well be engaging in a playful scholarly conceit here, meaning perhaps that where poorer scholars depended upon the *sacculi* of their memories to redeem books, he had tangible coin to pay. Or perhaps he means (for I do not think he was mean-spirited) that he depended on both the *thesaurus* of his purse and that of his memory to ransom wisdom from dirt and neglect; he uses the plural forms of both *thesaurus* and *sacculus,* after all.

Twice Bury comments directly on how he depended on the industry of others to collect books, especially the most recent of works. In chapter 4, the neglected books are made to complain of how shabbily they have been treated, but comment favorably on virtuous clerks who use them properly, that is, memorize them:

First of all it behooves you to eat the book with Ezekiel, that the belly of your memory may be sweetened within ... Thus our nature secretly working in our familiars, the listeners hasten up gladly as the magnet draws the willing iron. What an infinite power of books lies down in Paris or Athens, and yet sounds at the same time in Britain and Rome! In truth while they lie quietly they are moved, while holding their own places they are borne everywhere in the minds of their listeners.[20]

Later Bury describes his network of clerical searchers, who reported to him orally every new discourse and argument, no matter how half-baked and unfinished, from every part of Christendom, exactly the correspondents denied by edict to Ockham. They are like keen hunters after rabbits, like men setting nets and hooks for every little fish ("pisciculus"):

From the body of Sacred Law to the notebook of yesterday's bits of sophomoric discourse, nothing could escape these searchers. If a devout sermon sounded in the fountain of the Christian faith, the holy court of Rome, or if a new question was aired with novel arguments, if the solidity of Paris ... or English perspicuity ... had set forth anything concerning the advancement of knowledge or the explanation of faith, this immediately was poured into our ears still fresh, unerased by any word-scatterer and uncorrupted by any idiot, but from the purest pressing of the wine-press it passed directly into the vats of our memory for clarifying.[21]

These two passages demonstrate clearly that oral transmission from one memory to another was still an important and respected aspect of the dissemination of learning in academic and administrative circles during Bury's time. Books can stay physically on their shelves in Paris and yet move to the centers of England and Rome, if they have been transmitted by one who imitates the prophet Ezekiel and first consumes (memorizes) their contents. Everything from authoritative canons to the latest controversy is reported directly to him orally, memory to memory – not having to go through the unreliable medium of scribal copying. It is worth pausing over this last statement, for it is so foreign to modern assumptions that one may slide over it. The ignorant, word-scattering, cloudy-headed idiots who would erase ("denigratum") or otherwise spoil the texts in transmitting them are the professional copyists and secretaries into whose charge the copying of books for university scholars had now passed. Bury is saying that he regards the memorial transmission of a trained cleric as more reliable than the written copy produced by one of these scribes.

When one's first relationship with a text is not "to encounter another mind" (or subdue it, as one suspects sometimes) or "to understand it on its own terms," but to use it as a source of communally experienced wisdom for one's own life, gained by memorizing from it however much and in whatever fashion one is able or willing to do; when one's head is constantly filled with a chorus of voices available instantly and on any subject, how does such a relationship to the works of other writers differently define the meanings of such literary concepts as "reader," "text," "author"? In the next part of this chapter I would like to examine in some detail just what a medieval scholar meant when he said that he had read a book. I am not focusing here on the activity called *lectio*, "study," though that is the word actually derived from *legere*,[22] but rather the activity which, in each individual reader, must succeed *lectio* in order to make it profitable, that is, *meditatio*.

Hugh of St. Victor well defines the difference between *lectio* and *meditatio* in his *Didascalicon*. *Lectio*, "reading" or "study," trains one's natural *ingenium* by the order and method ("ordo et modus") of exposition and analysis, including the disciplines of grammar and dialectic. Meditation begins in study ("principium sumit a lectione") but

is bound by none of study's rules or precepts. For it delights to range along open ground, where it fixes its free gaze upon the contemplation of truth, drawing together now these, now those ideas, or now penetrating into profundities, leaving nothing doubtful, nothing obscure. The start of learning, thus, lies in *lectio*, but its consummation lies in meditation.[23]

In Hugh of St. Victor's *De arca Noe morali*, the ark of studies which one builds board by board in one's memory, the entire process of learning centers in meditation. The Ark of Wisdom/Prudence ("arca sapientiae") has three storeys, which represents three stages of moral judgment: correct, useful, and habitual ("rectus, utilis, necessarius"). I am in the first storey of the ark when I begin to love to meditate (that is, memorize) Scripture, and my thoughts freely ("libenter") and often consider thereby the virtues of the saints, the works of God, and all things pertaining to moral life or to the exercise of the mind. I can then say that my knowledge is correct, but it is not yet useful, for of what use is knowledge hidden away and inactive? But if I not only know but act in a way that is good and useful, so that the virtues I have learned to admire in others I make my own ("meas faciam") by disciplining myself to conform at least outwardly to right living, then I can say that the understanding of my heart is useful, and I will then ascend to the second storey. When the virtue I display in works is mine internally as well, when my goodness is completely habitual (that is a state of being) and necessary to me, then I ascend to the third storey, where knowledge and virtue become essential parts of me (become "familiar" or "domesticated," to use another common metaphor).[24] What Hugh describes here is a process of completely internalizing what one has read (and one must remember that *habitus* is used like Greek *hexis* in all these discussions), and the agency by which this is accomplished is *meditatio*, the process of memory-training, storage, and retrieval.

Petrarch supplies one of the most revealing analyses of reading in the late Middle Ages. Like Ockham, Petrarch was clearly no backward provincial, clinging to outmoded ways of study. Yet Petrarch's name is linked with those of Cicero and Thomas Aquinas in many Renaissance memory texts as one of the chief proponents of an artificial memory system, a reputation that seems to be based not on his having written a book of memorial technique but on his copious florilegial collection of commonplaces, *Rerum memorandarum libri*.[25]

Petrarch was greatly devoted to the writing of St. Augustine. He carried a pocket-sized copy of the *Confessions* everywhere with him, and used it on at least one occasion for *sortes Augustinianae* exactly on the model of Augustine's own *sortes Biblicales* in the garden, recounted in *Confessions VIII*.[26] The very custom of using books for *sortes* is an interesting example of regarding books as personal sources whose function is to provide memorial cues to oneself, divine influences being able to prophesy through the images of letters on the page just as they can during sleep through the images written in the memory.

Petrarch composed three dialogues with Augustine which he called his *Secretum*, not designed for publication until after his death.[27] In these he confesses his doubts and sins to the saint through the mouth of his persona, Francesco. "Francesco" bewails the frailty of his body, the disgust he feels for Milan, "the most melancholy and disorderly of towns" which assails his soul daily with its clamor and dirt. Augustine reminds him of many literary works addressing this problem, including one of his own; do these not help him? Well, yes, says Petrarch,

at the time of reading, much help; but no sooner is the book from my hands than all my feeling for it vanishes. *Aug*: This way of reading is become common now; there is such a mob of lettered men . . . But if you would imprint in their own places secure notes [*suis locis certas notas impresseris*] you would then gather the fruit of your reading. *Fran*: What notes? *Aug*: Whenever you read a book and meet with any wholesome maxims by which you feel your soul stirred or enthralled, do not trust merely to the powers of your native abilities [*viribus ingenii fidere*], but make a point of learning them by heart and making them quite familiar by meditating on them . . . so that whenever or where some urgent case of illness arises, you have the remedy as though written in your mind . . . When you come to any passages that seem to you useful, impress secure marks against them, which may serve as hooks in your memory [*uncis memoria*], lest otherwise they might fly away.[28]

The margins of Petrarch's books are full of such marks.[29] This passage makes quite clear that Petrarch used them, at least in part as did Grosseteste, to construct his mental concordances of texts, each "hooked" into its own place in his memory by a key. There they provide the matter for prudence, the experience upon which "Francesco" can draw in need, a remedy for distress written in the mind ("velut in animo conscripta"). The process whereby what he takes from his texts is imprinted ("impressere") is meditation.

And it is clear from what he says that such memorizing is done according to a learned and practiced technique. One does not rely upon *ingenium*, "aptitude," one hides the fruits of reading in the recesses of memory ("in memorie penetralibus")[30] and through practice makes one's reading familiar to oneself, domesticates it (to use Albertus Magnus's word), makes it one's own. Perhaps no advice is as common in medieval writing on the subject, and yet so foreign, when one thinks about it, to the habits of modern scholarship as this notion of "making one's own" what one reads in someone else's work. "Efficere tibi illas familiares," Augustine's admonition to "Francesco," does not mean "familiar" in quite the modern sense. *Familiar* is rather a synonym of *domesticare*, that is, to make something familiar by making it a part of your own experience. This adaptation process allows for a tampering with the original text that a modern scholar would (and does) find quite intolerable, for it violates most of our notions concerning "accuracy," "objective scholarship," and "the integrity of the text." Modern scholars learn all they can about a text, making sure they know the meaning of every word in it. So did medieval scholars; that was what *lectio* was for. But a modern scholar is concerned primarily with getting the text "objectively right," treating it as an ultimate and sole authority. We are taught to "legitimate" our reading (by which we mean our interpretation or understanding) solely by the text; we see ourselves as its servants, and although both the possibility and the utility of such absolute objectivity have been called into question many times during this century, this attitude remains a potent assumption in scholarly debate, even for those most wedded to reader-response theories.

But the medieval scholar's relationship to his texts is quite different from modern "objectivity." Reading is to be digested, to be ruminated, like a cow chewing her cud, or like a bee making honey from the nectar of flowers. Reading is memorized with the aid of *murmur*, mouthing the words subvocally as one turns the text over in one's memory; both Quintilian and Martianus Capella stress how murmur accompanies meditation. It is this movement of the mouth that established rumination as a basic metaphor for memorial activities.[31] The process familiarizes a text to a medieval scholar, in a way like that by which human beings may be said to "familiarize" their food. It is both physiological and psychological, and it changes both the food and its consumer. Gregory the Great writes, "We ought to transform what we read into our very selves, so that when our mind is stirred by what it hears, our life may concur by practicing what has been heard."[32] Hugh of St. Victor writes of walking through the forest ("silva") of Scripture, "whose ideas [*sententias*] like so many sweetest fruits, we pick as we read and chew [*ruminamus*] as we consider them."[33]

The various stages of the reading process are succinctly described at the end of Hugh of St. Victor's Chronicle preface (appendix A). All exegesis emphasized that understanding was grounded in a thorough knowledge of the *littera*, and for this one had to know grammar, rhetoric, history, and all the other disciplines that give information, the work of *lectio*. But one takes all of that and builds upon it during meditation; this phase of reading is ethical in its nature, or "tropological" (turning the text onto and into one's self) as Hugh defines it. I think one might best begin to understand the concept of "levels" in exegesis as "stages" of a continuous action, and the "four-fold way" (or three-fold, as the case may be) as a useful mnemonic for readers, reminding them of how to complete the entire reading process. "Littera" and "allegoria" (grammar and typological history) are the work of *lectio* and are essentially informative about a text; tropology and anagogy are the activities of digestive meditation and constitute the ethical activity of making one's reading one's own.

The ruminant image is basic to understanding what was involved in *memoria* as well as *meditatio*, the two being understood as the agent and its activity. Though monastic theology developed the idea of meditation in terms of prayer and psalmody its basis in the functions of memory continued to be emphasized. *Ruminatio* is an image of regurgitation, quite literally intended; the memory is a stomach, the stored texts are the sweet-smelling cud originally drawn from the meadows of books (or lecture), they are chewed in the palate. Gregory the Great says that in Scripture "venter mens dicitur," thereby adding *venter* to *cor* as a synonym for memory in Scripture.[34] Six centuries later, Hugh of St. Victor, discussing *memoria* in *Didascalicon*, says that it is imperative to replicate frequently the matter one has memorized and placed in the "arcula" of one's memory, and "to recall it from the stomach of memory to the palate."[35]

Composition is also spoken of as *ruminatio*. In one of his sermons, Augustine says that he has not prepared formally but desires that he be allowed to ruminate upon the day's Scriptural reading.[36] Another example, the most famous of all, is in Bede's account of the English poet, Caedmon, who changed ("convertebat") what he learned by hearing in *lectio*, or sermons, into sweetest poetry by recollecting it within himself ("rememorandum rerum") and ruminating like a clean animal ("quasi mundum animal ruminendo").[37] Caedmon's rumination occurs at night, the optimal time for such activity; the fact that he was a cowherd may be coincidental to the story, but Bede emphasizes it so much that one suspects he thought the detail significant in the context. Philip West has suggested that his profession suits his ruminative activities; perhaps the ancient link between poets and ruminative animals, found in many cultures, has some connection with the rumination of composition.

Metaphors which use digestive activities are so powerful and tenacious that "digestion" should be considered another basic functional model for the complementary activities of reading and composition, collection and recollection. Unlike the heart, no medical tradition seems to have placed any of the sensory-processing functions in the stomach, but "the stomach of memory" as a metaphoric model had a long run. Milton, his biographers agree, mentally composed a store of verses each day, which he then dictated to a secretary. John Aubrey comments that while Milton had a good natural memory, "I believe that his excellent method of thinking and disposing did much to help his memory," a clear reference to the kind of training, disciplined practice, and deliberate design ("disposing") that had always been features of classical memory-training. And Milton's anonymous biographer, speaking also of his mental composition, remarks that if the poet's secretary were late, "he would complain, saying he wanted to be milked."[38]

Likening the products of mental rumination to those of digestion led to some excellent comedy; one thinks at once of Rabelais and of Chaucer's Summoner's Tale. But the metaphor was also realized seriously. There is a remarkably graphic statement of it in the *Regula monachorum* ascribed to Jerome, though composed probably in the twelfth century. The writer speaks of the various stomach rumblings, belchings, and flatulence that accompany the nightly gathering of the monks in prayer. But, he continues, as a famous pastor has said, just as smoke drives out bees, so ructation caused by indigestion drives away the inspiration of the Holy Spirit. Belching and farting, however, are caused by the preparation and digestion of food. "Wherefore, as a belch bursts forth from the stomach according to the quality of the food, and the significance [to health] of a *flatus* is according either to the sweetness or stench of its odor, so the cogitations of the inner man bring forth words, and *from the abundance of the heart the mouth speaks* (Lk. 6:45). The just man, eating, fills his soul. And when he is replete with sacred doctrine, from the good treasury of his memory he brings forth those things which are good."[39] No comment is needed on this text, so very odd and even irreligious to us, except to observe that I can think of few more cogent statements of the curious consequences deriving from ancient and medieval notions of the soul's embodiment than this serious, pious linking of the sweetness of prayer and of the stomach. Though the immediate notion of the Spirit as a breath or wind ("flatus") is Biblical, moderns, accustomed to thinking of this trope as a mere figure of speech, would never make the connection this medieval writer did. It stems from exactly the psychosomatic assumptions that directed medical writers to prescribe foot-soaking, head-washing, and chewing coriander to improve memory, sweetness of the mouth and stomach being evidently as necessary to the healthy production of memory as a stress-free body (with relaxed feet and a non-itching scalp) is to productive concentration.

The monastic custom of reading during meals is described in some texts as an explicit literalizing of the metaphor of consuming a book as one consumes food. A late *Regula* for women adapted from the writings of St. Jerome makes the connection clear: there should be reading during meals "so that while the body is fattened [*saginatur*] with food, the mind should be filled [*saturetur*] with reading."[40] Benedict's *Rule* says that "while the brothers are eating they should not lack in reading";[41] the contemporaneous (sixth century) *Regula magistri* gives the reason why in words much like those of the later rule I just quoted. Every brother who has learned his letters should take his turn reading during meals, "so that there should never be a lack of restoration for the body nor of divine food, for as Scripture says, man does not live by bread alone but in every word of the Lord, so that in two ways the Brothers may be repaired, when they chew with their mouths and are filled up through their ears."[42] The Rule for women continues by characterizing how each sister should follow the reading. With absorbed, intent mind ("mens sobria intenta sit") she should actively, emotionally enter into the reading. She sighs anxiously when, in prophecy or historical narrative, the word of God shows enmity to the wicked. She is filled with great joy when the favor of the Lord is shown to the good. "Words do not resound, but sighs; not laughter and derision but tears."[43] This last comment is a reformation of one of Jerome's dicta, that "the preacher should arouse wailing rather than applause,"[44] itself an idea that accords with the advice given by Quintilian and others that an orator must above all arouse the emotions of his audience. This *Rule* admonishes against laughter because, like applause, derision is associated in the writer's mind with detachment and disengagement from the material, tears with the opposite; the state of being "engaged with" and "totally absorbed in" the text (as I would translate the adjectives *sobria* and *intenta*) is necessary for its proper digestion.

Commentary on the two moments in Scripture (Ezekiel 3:3 and Revelation 10:9–11) in which a prophet is given a book to eat that is sweet as honey in the mouth underlines the need to consume one's reading.[45] "Therefore we devour and digest the book, when we read the words of God," says Hugo de Folieto in the twelfth century. "Many indeed read, but from their reading they remain ignorant . . . but others devour and digest the holy books and are not ignorant because their memory does not let go of the rules for life whose meaning it can grasp."[46] And Jerome, commenting on the Ezekiel text, says "when by assiduous meditation we truly may have stored the book of the Lord in the treasury of our memory, we fill our belly in a spiritual sense, and our bowels are filled, that we may have with the Apostle the bowels of mercy (Coloss. 3:12), and that belly is filled concerning which Jeremias said: 'My bowels, my bowels! I am pained at my very heart' (Jer. 4:19)."[47]

Biblical study provides a model for other literary study. In the same part of the second dialogue in *Secretum* we looked at earlier, Augustine says that one needs a store of precepts from one's reading, in order to guard against sudden emotion and passion – anger for instance. Yes, replies "Francesco," he has found much good on this matter not only in philosophers but in poets as well. And he proceeds to give an interpretive reading of *Aeneid* 1, 52–57, the description of Aeolus in the cave of the winds:

As I carefully study every word, I have heard with my ears the fury, the rage, the roar of the winds; I have heard the trembling of the mountain and the din. Notice how well it all applies to the tempest of anger . . . I have heard the king, sitting on his high place, his sceptre grasped in his hand, subduing, binding in chains, and imprisoning those rebel blasts.[48]

And he demonstrates his interpretation by appealing to the last line of the description, "mollitque animos et temperat iras" (1. 57); this, says Petrarch, shows that this passage can refer to the mind when it is vexed by anger.

Augustine praises the meaning which "Francesco" has found hidden in the poet's words, which are so copious and familiar in his memory. For, "whether Virgil himself meant this while he wrote, or whether, entirely remote from any such consideration, he wished only to describe a maritime storm in these verses and nothing else,"[49] the lesson which "Francesco" has derived concerning anger is truthful and well-said. Extraordinary as this opinion is to a scholar brought up on notions of the inviolate authority of the text, we should not assume on the other hand that Petrarch's words, in the mouth of his revered mentor, indicate only an extreme subjectivity. Virgil's words remain significant themselves as the subject of the disciplines associated with *lectio*, and a source of wisdom and experience (via memory) for anyone who cares to read and remember them. The focus for Petrarch at this point is rather what the individual reader makes of those words, and that focus is not scientific but ethical.

Virgil's words having been devoured (or one might say "harvested"), digested, and familiarized by "Francesco" through *meditatio*, have now become *his* words as they cue the representational processes of his recollection. It is as though at this point the student of the text, having digested it by re-experiencing it in memory, has become not its interpreter, but its new author, or re-author. Petrarch has re-spoken Virgil; "re-written Virgil" we would say, with strong disapproval. But the re-writing which is acknowledged in what both Augustine and "Francesco" say, is seen as a good not for Virgil's text, which is irrelevant at this point except as it has occasioned Petrarch's remembrance, but for "Francesco's" moral life.[50]

Hugh of St. Victor's preface to the *Chronica* (appendix A) gives usefully succinct definitions of the three "levels" of Biblical exegesis which indicate quite clearly which belong to the activity of *lectio* and which to *meditatio*. *Littera* is the subject of grammatical and rhetorical study; *historia* is the foreshadowing relationship of one event in the Bible to another, and is what is often also called *allegoria*. After these disciplines comes *tropologia* (which is more like what we think of as "allegorical"); it is what the text means to us when we turn its words, like a mirror, upon ourselves, how we understand it when we have domesticated it and made it our own, and that is the special activity of memorative *meditatio*, the "culmination" of *lectio* but bound by none of its rules, a free play of the recollecting mind. "Holy Scripture," wrote Gregory the Great, quoting Augustine, "presents a kind of mirror to the eyes of the mind, that our inner face may be seen in it. There truly we learn our own ugliness, there our own beauty."[51] As we do this, the text's initial sweetness may well turn to indigestion and pain, as it did for St. John, but such *dolor* is to be welcomed. For, as Hugo de Folieto comments on Revelation 10:11, "He certainly suffers pain in his stomach who feels affliction of mind. For this can be understood because, while the word of God may begin by being sweet in the mouth of our heart, before long the *animus* grows bitter in doubt against itself." And he quotes Gregory, "We devour the book when with eager desire we clothe ourselves with the words of life."[52]

The psychology of the memory phantasm provides the rationale for the ethical value of the reading method which Petrarch describes. A properly-made phantasm is both a "likeness" (*simulacrum*) and one's "gut-level response" to it (*intentio*), and it is an emotional process that causes change in the body. The insistently physical matrix of the whole memorative process accounts for Petrarch's slow, detailed refashioning of Virgil's description. The active agency of the reader, "discutiens," "breaking up" or "shattering" (one could even translate "deconstructing") each single word as he recreates the scene in his memory, is emphasized: "Ego autem audivi . . . audivi . . . audivi." He re-hears, re-sees, re-feels, experiences and re-experiences. In this way, Virgil's words are embodied in Petrarch's recollection as an experience of tumult and calm that is more physiological (emotional, passionate) than "mental," in our sense. Desire underlies the whole experience, changing from turmoil through anger to repose.[53] The re-created reading becomes useful precisely because in the heat of passion Petrarch's emotions replay that process of change, for he can remember what right action *feels* like. That is not a rational decision process, but one of desire and will guided through the process of change by remembered habit, "firma facilitas" or *hexis*.

I have noted before that the medieval understanding of the complete process of reading does not observe in the same way the basic distinction we make between "what I read in a book" and "my experience." This discussion by Petrarch, I think, makes clear why, for "what I read in a book" *is* "my experience," and I make it mine by incorporating it (and we should understand the word "incorporate" quite literally) in my memory. One remembers the boast of Chaucer's eagle in *The House of Fame* that he can so palpably represent "skiles" to his students that they can "shake hem by the biles" (*HF*, II, 869–870), the avian manner of making them one's dear friends.

In this way, reading a book extends the process whereby one memory engages another in a continuing dialogue that approaches Plato's ideal (expressed in *Phaedrus*) of two living minds engaged in learning. Medieval reading is conceived to be not a "hermeneutical circle" (which implies mere solipsism) but more like a "hermeneutical dialogue" between two memories, that in the text being made very much present as it is familiarized to that of the reader. Isidore of Seville, we remember, in words echoed notably by John of Salisbury, says that written letters recall through the windows of our eyes the voices of those who are not present to us (and one thinks too of that evocative medieval phrase, "voces paginarum," "the voices of the pages.")[54] So long as the reader, in meditation (which is best performed in a *murmur* or low voice), reads attentively, that other member of the dialogue is in no danger of being lost, the other voice will sound through the written letters. Perhaps it is not inappropriate to recall again, having just spoken of Petrarch, the Greek verb, *ànagignósko*, "to read," but literally "to know again" or "remember."

A great deal has been written on the subject of audible reading in antiquity, and its apparent replacement by silent reading at some later time. Reading aloud is assumed to have been the more common method, and those who believe that there is sharp contrast between orality and literacy have made much of a "change" from one form to the other, seeing it as a shift of sensibility from the "earmindedness" of orality to the "eyemindedness" of literacy. Judicious scholars of this school have always known that silent reading to oneself was also practiced in antiquity, but have insisted that it was regarded as strange and uncommon.[55] It seems to me, however, that silent reading, "legere tacite" or "legere sibi," as Benedict and others call it,[56] and reading aloud, "clare legere" in "voce magna" or "viva voce," were two distinct methods of reading taught for different purposes in ancient schools and both practiced by ancient readers, and that they correspond roughly to those stages in the study process called *meditatio* and *lectio*. They clearly acquire additional meanings, perhaps even a whole theology, in medieval monastic culture;[57] and university library statutes suggest that reading silently ("legere tacite") may have become more noiseless in a university reading room than the phenomenon of the same name may have been in a monastic cell.[58] But I think these developments themselves were founded in and continued to be based upon these distinctive but complementary, elementary pedagogical procedures, the "viva voce" of lecture and the "voce tenui," as it is called sometimes, of memory and meditation.[59]

The *locus classicus* for any discussion of ancient reading habits is, in fact, from late antiquity: Augustine's description in the *Confessions* VI, 3 of Ambrose reading:

I regarded Ambrose himself as a man who was fortunate in the view of the world, greatly honored, as he was, by many men of importance . . . As to the hope he bore within him, the struggles he had with temptations associated with his lofty position, his consolation in adversities, the sweet joy with which the secret mouth within his breast-hoard [memory] chewed over Thy Bread [*occultum os eius quod erat in corde eius, quam sapida gaudia de pane tuo ruminaret*], I had no inkling or experience . . . I was unable to seek what I wanted from him . . . since there were throngs of busy people who cut me off from his ear and mouth. And when he was not with them, which was a very little part of the time, he was either refreshing [*lit.* remaking] his body with sustenance or his mind with reading [*aut corpus reficiebat necessariis sustentaculis aut lectione animum*]. As he read, his eyes scanned the pages and his heart searched out the meaning, but his voice and tongue were silent [*lit.* stilled] [*sed cum legebat, oculi ducebantur per paginas et cor intellectum rimabatur, vox autem et lingua quiescebant*]. Often, when we were present . . . we saw him reading quietly in that way and never in the other [*sic eum legentem vidimus tacite et aliter numquam*]. After sitting silently for a long time [*sedentesque in diuturno silentio*] (for who would dare to impose a burden on one so engrossed [*tam intento*]) we would depart, thinking that in the small time he had to refresh his mind [*reparandae menti suae*], free from the noise of other people's troubles [*feriatum ad strepitu causarum alienarum*], he preferred not to be distracted by something else; that, perhaps, he was afraid lest some listener following it with great interest [*ne auditore suspenso et intento*] might ask him about some obscure passage which he was reading – and then it would be necessary to explain it or to discourse upon the more difficult problems, and, having given time to this task, he would read fewer volumes than he desired. However, it was quite possible that the more correct reason for his silent reading was for the sake of keeping his voice, which in his case, was easily made hoarse. Anyhow, whatever his purpose was in doing this, this man had a good reason for doing it.[60]

I have quoted this description at length because I think it is often misread. It presents an excellent contrast between the two kinds of reading, *lectio* and *meditatio*. Ambrose withdraws over a book into silence, *meditatio*, even though others are present; Augustine contrasts it specifically here with the activity of *lectio*, delivered in a loud voice to a listener who freely asks questions. In meditational reading, Ambrose, the reader, is *intentus*; in the other kind, the listener is *suspensus* and *intentus*.

In a scholarly tradition going back to the late nineteenth century, Augustine's response is characterized as one of "surprise and wonder" at Ambrose's "strange" habit.[61] I do not find these traits in what Augustine says, however. Instead this seems to me a sympathetic portrait of a very busy man's efforts to make time for the kind of scholarly study that refreshes him, written (we should remember) by a man who by then was himself a very busy bishop, subject to exactly the interruptions and demands he shows us in Ambrose. This situation helps to explain the slight defensiveness of Augustine's last remark, responding to what might be seen as Ambrose's rudeness or failure in duty. (Saving the voice is a reason given for using *vox tenuis*, in addition to its usefulness for memorizing, in the rhetoric of Fortunatianus, who was more or less Augustine's contemporary.) What surprises Augustine is that Ambrose never read in the *other* way, though others were present ("et aliter numquam").

The basic contrast in Augustine's portrait of Ambrose is carried in the two words *stepitus* and *tacitus*.[62] Meditative reading is Ambrose's means of acquiring *silentium* amid the *strepitus* of his daily activities, even in the common room where his petitioners gathered. To repair his mind ("reparandae menti suae" – we notice again the underlying motif of building), Ambrose refrains from *lectio* and engages instead in *meditatio*.

Strepitus, especially for Augustine, means "loud noise, confusion, rumbling," and other sorts of disordered, unconcentrated, "busy" noise, the interruption that daily congress creates. At the end of Book IX of the *Confessions*, Augustine laments the contrast between the meditative conversation between Monica and himself, as they talk alone ("soli") and gradually ascend to mystical contemplation ("venimus in mentes nostras et transcendimus eas, ut attingeremus regionem ubertatis indeficientis, unde pascis Israel in aeternum veritate pabulo"),[63] and descend back to the chattering noise of the mouth where words are born and die ("ad strepitum oris nostri, ubi verbum et incipitur et finitur"). The contrast here is exactly that made in his description of Ambrose, and casts some additional light on it. For Augustine never says that his conversation with Monica ceases; all the verbs continue to be in the first person plural, indicating shared activities. Being *soli* and *taciti* does not mean being "solitary" or "private" in a modern sense, nor does it mean "quiet" in our sense; it has rather to do with the difference between their concentrated, attentive, meditational conversation and *strepitus*, between rumination and chit-chat. Indeed, *while they are speaking* ("dum loquimur"), they touch a little ("modice") that eternal life, "toto juctu cordis," "with an all-out thrust of our hearts." The heart-thrust here should, I think, be understood as a figure for a particular effort of recollection, as Augustine plays on the root of Latin *recordari* (*cor, cordis*).[64]

Whether or not the vocal chords are used is a secondary difference between the two methods of reading. This distinction is well defined by Isidore of Seville in some brief memory advice that he gives in his *Sententiarum*. After advising that one divide a long text in order to memorize it according to the memorial principle of *brevitas*, he says that memory is also much better aided by silent reading than by reading aloud: "Silent reading is more acceptable to the senses [meaning here the interior senses engaged in making memories] than full-voice; the intellect is better trained [*lit.* constructed] when the voice in reading is quieted, and in silence the tongue is moved. For by voiced reading the body is tired and the voice's sharpness is dulled."[65] Ambrose's "silent" reading is not a function of whether his lips move or not, but of his single-minded concentration, his "solitude" and "silence."

Augustine begins his description of Ambrose with the metaphor of rumination; Ambrose's "hidden mouth" which is in his heart (memory) "ruminates" the texts of Scripture. Such reading was nourishment for his mind, as food was for his body (yet another instance of the digestion-rumination metaphor associated with *meditatio*). When he read for this purpose, his eyes were led over the page as his recollection ("heart") "poured over [*rimabatur*]" the meaning. The verb *rimor* is related to the noun *rima*, meaning "crack, fissure," and was used originally in an agricultural context to mean "turn up" or "tear open" the ground. *Rimor* is used by Virgil of a vulture feasting on entrails, and by Juvenal of an auger pouring over the heart of a sacrificed chicken.[66] All of this indicates that meditative reading, "legere tacite," was a slow, thorough process in keeping with its memorative function, one in which each word was examined thoroughly ("broken into pieces") as one stored a piece of text away together with its heuristic associations. *Rimor* is an intensely energetic, suspenseful, concentrated, and meticulous activity, which gives a vigor to meditation that the placid image of cud-chewing may not.

This concentration is described as *tacitus, intentus*, a state in which, in this scene, both Ambrose and his companions are in long-lasting silence ("diuturno silentio"). *Silentium* is also a word found in late-antique rhetorical texts, those of the tradition Augustine was educated in, in connection with the *meditatio* necessary for *memoria*. Thus, Martianus Capella advising on the techniques of memory describes how to produce the state of concentration necessary for firm recollection: texts to be learned are not "read in a loud voice, but are more usefully meditated in a murmer; and it is clear that the memory is stimulated more readily at night than during the day, when also the silence everywhere helps, nor is concentration interrupted by sensory stimuli from outside."[67] *Silentium* is the accompaniment and also the result of being *intentus*, of *meditatio*, and *memoria* (which is why memory is easier at night) but it is evidently not incompatible with the vocal *murmur* which, together with writing on one's *tabulae*, helps greatly in memorizing.[68]

Intensity is also part of the attitude the student needs listening to his master's *lectio*; Augustine describes how such a listener would respond, if only Ambrose were reading "magna voce." Since listening students had to memorize the commentary as they heard it, clearly the *intentus* necessary to remember had to be part of their mental attitude as well. In both *lectio* and *meditatio*, *intentus* refers to the absorbed, suspenseful attitude, "hanging on each word," which the memory needs for success. This is mental silence, lack of noise (*strepitus*), mental solitude; modern students certainly recognize the state, but we associate it with "individual creativity" rarely achieved, rather than with an ordinary requirement for reading, or indeed most kinds of writing. Antiquity and the Middle Ages associated it with memory and recollection, and when they speak of silence and solitude in such a context, this state of attentive concentration is what they usually mean. They also thought that it could be taught, and encouraged practice and techniques for achieving it.[69]

This understanding of silence is still evident towards the end of the Middle Ages in the work of a scholastic rather than monastic writer, Thomas Aquinas. When, in the *Summa theologica*, he digests for his readers Tully's memory rules, Thomas alters one of them in a significant way. The *Ad Herennium* states that "solitude" conserves the sharp outlines of memory-images ("solitudo conservat integras simulacrorum figuras"); Thomas changes the reading to "solicitude" ("sollicitudo conservat integras simulacrorum figuras").[70] He does so, I think, because he understood the essential importance of a memory's being an *affectus* or *pathos*, that is, he knew the sensory-emotional nature of the state we call concentration (and think of as entirely "mental"). *Sollicitudo* is best translated in English as "worry," as a dog is said to "worry" a bone; it is conceptually like Augustine's use of *rimor* and Petrarch's of *discutere*. After nearly a millennium of monastic development of the twin ideas of "solitude" and "silence," the quality of intense, aroused attention implied in *meditatio* even in ancient pedagogy, and its fundamental necessity in the disciplines of memory, was completely apparent to Thomas Aquinas. For him, *solitudo*, in the context of memory training, is synonymous with *sollicitudo*, that attitude of mind which vexes or "worries" the emotions and the sensations in order to engage in the activity of making, storing, recalling memory images, to the exclusion of outside *strepitus* and bustle even when it is going on immediately around one. Thomas's success at producing this state in himself is attested to by the many stories of his peers. And without that degree of emotional concentration, memory fails.

Thomas Aquinas's biographers associated his deep concentration with his prodigious memory; Francis of Assisi's biographers do as well. Thomas of Celano writes: "whenever he read in the Sacred Books, and something was once tossed into his mind, he indelibly wrote it in his heart. He had a memory for [whole] books because having heard something once he took it in not idly, but with continued devout attention his emotion-memory [*affectus*] chewed on it. This he said was the fruitful method for teaching and reading, not to have wandered about through a thousand learned discussions [*tractatus*]."[71] *Affectus* in this description is the agent by means of which rumination and memorization takes place; in other words, remembering is an activity in which the emotions must be engaged in order for it to occur at all.

"The method of reading consists in dividing [*modus legendi in dividendo constat*]" says Hugh of St. Victor.[72] Reading fundamentally proceeds by *divisio*. This meant that every text one learned was stored and recalled basically as a series of short sequences, *cola*, whether one knew it from start to finish, as many ancients knew Virgil and Homer, and many Christians knew several books at least of the Bible; or whether one learned a number of set passages from it, as I learned Shakespeare's plays; or whether one learned only its aphorisms and maxims. The ordering of these texts, their *compositio* or *collatio*, was a function of the mnemonic heuristics one imposed on them (I am speaking purely in terms of how a student learned, not of how texts were copied by scribes). It is this fundamental feature of the memorial design and its method that made it possible for a single segment of information to be cross-filed, so that one could, for example, find Psalm 1, verse 2 in the "file" containing the words of Psalm 1 in complete textual order and in the "file" dealing with the subject of *lex Domini*. One could thus think of it in several different settings, leading to the process of "composition" in the modern English sense. It is no wonder that early writers considered building metaphors to be so apt both for reading and composing, for each memorized "bit" is like a plank or brick one "places" in a design.

From at least Alexandrine times, a favored form of elementary textbook was the florilegium, or compilation of extracts and maxims derived from the great writers of the past. It was as popular with Christians as it had been with pagans. I have alluded to this literary form many times during my study, but I now want to look at the genre in greater detail. Its essence is well defined by the title of Petrarch's contribution to it, *Rerum memorandarum libri*. A florilegium is basically the contents of someone's memory, set forth as a kind of study-guide for the formation of others' memories. The contents are what Hugh of St. Victor called *sophismata*, others more commonly called *dicta* or *dictiones*, and they are presented either *ad verba*, or *ad res*.

The most familiar variety brings together ethical topics, vices and virtues and socially useful habits, such as those for study or for civic behavior. Such compilations are common in antiquity; Cicero says, attributing Aristotle, that Protagoras was the first to gather together and write down the "rerum illustrium disputationes" or commonplaces (communes loci).[73] Aristotle's word for the "special topics," as distinct from the general categories such as antithesis or similarity, is eithê, a word related to "ethics," and they were so called because they belong to the practical, particularized realm of political and ethical life, and furnish rhetoric with its enthymemes and propositions. In Roman rhetoric, the commonplaces were moral in nature; Quintilian must warn his readers that he is using the word in an unusual sense when he applies communis locus to the "place of argument" (Inst., v, 10, 20–21). Most often, they were arranged by moral categories, "in adulterium, aleatorem, petulantem," or categories of evidence, "de testibus, de tabulis, de argumentis."[74]

A good example of a scholar's florilegium is the Carolingian encyclopedia of Rhabanus Maurus, De universo. In the preface to it which he addresses to his former colleague, now bishop, Haimon, Rhabanus describes his motive for undertaking the work. He recalls that they were students together, reading a multitude of books not only of divine learning but also of natural history and liberal arts. Since then, divine providence has released Rhabanus from external cares, but called Haimon to pastoral duties as bishop, where he must contend not only with the pagans to the east, but with a fractious populace. Wherefore I thought, says Rhabanus, "that I might be able by writing to create something pleasing and useful for Your Holiness: in which you might have briefly in a few [extracts] for the purpose of being able to recollect [ob commemorationem] those things which previously you had read completely in many large codices in the stylish discourse of orators."[75] All this material "having been drawn forth carefully by me, it came into my mind that, according to the custom of the ancients who put together many things concerning natural history and etymologies of names and words, I might myself compose for you a sort of minor work in which you would have written [extracts] not only concerning natural history and the literal meanings of words, but also concerning the spiritual sense of those same things, so that you could find, continuously placed together, both the literal and spiritual meaning of each single thing."[76] And that is exactly what De universo is, a web of interpretationes of the various matters relevant to Scripture, arranged by key-words that are themselves organized not alphabetically but "logically" (starting with God and the angels). Much of it, including the organizational key-words, is taken directly from Isidore's Etymologiae. But collated continuously in one place ("continuatim") with Isidore, as Rhabanus promises, are interpretations or sensus, both litterales and mystici of the various Scriptural items. These are most likely Rhabanus's own lecture notes here collated for Haimon; much of their content was also used in the elementary Scriptural gloss compiled for beginning students in the early twelfth century called the Glossa ordinaria.[77]

The purpose of Rhabanus's compilation is not to substitute for the study of original texts, but to provide cues for recollecting material read earlier. This is a convention of the genre, florilegia being understood to be volumes only of extracts, the notes which students took on their reading. And these notes are memorative both in origin and purpose. Rhabanus describes himself as a student carefully extracting ("mihi sollicite tractandi") from his studies, and the sources from which he gathers are much like those William of Ockham "tracted" 500 years later, and recommends that his students "tract" in turn – books of sacred learning, moral philosophy, and histories (but, as one would expect, Ockham's "meadows" included a great deal of law as well). Perhaps more concretely than any other genre, the florilegium is the essential book of memory.

But why bother to write them? Especially if one is expected to be familiar as well with the full works from which these flowers are plucked? The reason has everything to do with the difference between reading as lecture and reading as meditation, meditation being an activity of "dividing" and "composing." We must remember that a trained and well-provided memory was regarded throughout this long period not as a primitive learning technique but as the essential foundation of prudence, sapientia, ethical judgment. The choice to memorize or not is not like deciding to trade in one's old typewriter for a word processor. Composition was considered to be a memorial activity too; a preacher making a sermon must draw upon his memorial storehouse. It is, after all, for the purpose of composing that Ockham advises his student to stock his memory, so that he may recall what he needs.

As a compositional and devotional aid, a florilegium is a promptbook for memoria; that is clearly how Rhabanus Maurus understood it. Such compilations provide the materials (and in some cases also suggest a format) for the memoria of those who must lecture publicly and extemporaneously, as Bishop Haimon needed to do in his sermons. Isidore of Seville succinctly articulates this requirement by remarking aphoristically that "Lectio requires the aid of memory."[78] The various types of florilegial books have been intensively studied recently, and it is clear that those of the scholastic centuries (the thirteenth and fourteenth centuries primarily) differ in format and in type of content from earlier ones, and from the late medieval and Renaissance compilations of the humanists. Monastic compilations are primarily meditational in nature, designed for an audience of varying sophistication, whereas the scholastic florilegia, like the Manipulus florum or "Bunch of Flowers" studied by Richard and Mary Rouse, are often highly technical, even jargonish textbooks for clerics composing sermons. These arose to fill a particular market demand to which I have already alluded: the greatly increased population of university scholars and preachers. Many of these scholastic florilegia are organized so technically that they would be hard to memorize as such, but their usefulness assumes an already well-trained memory. They are thus still memorial promptbooks, "ob commemoratione," but a derivative sub-genre for specialists. Indeed as Christina von

Nolcken has shown, the specialization of preachers' florilegia into collections of Scriptural "distinctions" (or scholastic definitions) and sermon *exempla* was reorganized in the fourteenth century in a more compendious form of various sorts of material from an array of sources. Their entry-headings were moral topics.[79] The resulting composition was one that a late twelfth-century cleric approvingly characterized as "adorned with flowers of words and sentences and supported by a copious array of authorities. *It ran backwards and forwards on its path from its starting-point back to the same starting-point*" (my emphasis). The memorial principle of such organization is evident, and as von Nolcken comments, these features remain impressively constant.[80]

In a careful study of pre-scholastic florilegia, Munk Olsen notes that monastic collections follow a number of different principles of order, sometimes even in different sections of the same compilation.[81] These range from clear ordering schemes by moral topic, some even alphabetically arranged by topic or *incipit*, to those in which extracts are arranged by author, to ones showing no discernible order at all, including those "mini-florilèges" which are nothing but short pieces copied onto margins or the blank pages of manuscripts. Extracts themselves range in length from single lines to lengthy passages. The audience intended is sometimes beginning students; several address "pueros" in their prefaces, but (as we saw with Rhabanus) adult scholars are mainly addressed. This fact again confirms their nature as meditational prompts or sources for a memory already basically trained rather than as a primary-school text. The compiler of *Florilegium Duacense* says that because there are so many books and human memory is so yielding ("madida memoria"), "from a multitude of books I have plucked a few [matters] among a great many, which seemed to me most useful and necessary"; these one can read and meditate and learn by heart, for they are kept "non scriniis aut armariis, sed archa pectoris," "not in treasuries nor in bookcases but in the chest of memory."[82] By these extracts, the needy soul is cured, the healthy preserved, the weary recreated, the hungry fed, the simple soul may be instructed, the scholarly one aroused, the impoverished one gain something worth noting down.

It is interesting that rigidly structured compilations exist side by side with those that seem totally nonstructured, for it confirms again that the form itself of a work like this cannot be trusted as an indication of whether or not its contents were to be memorized, nor in what manner. An unorganized compilation could hardly be used unless it were to cue an already formed *memoria*, readers "slipping" the material into their own heuristic schemes, as they had been taught to do. But collections that come with their own organization were also designed to stock or cue the memories of their users, as is apparent from such a late, vernacular, Dominican product as Bartolommeo's *Ammaestramenti*. Moreover, it is not clear always that the compilers themselves distinguished their audiences carefully; the author of *Florilegium Duacense* clearly thought his readers would include both adults and beginners.

Florilegia retained their immense popularity until this present century. The justification for their use goes back to ancient pedagogy, and is well described by Quintilian. Once a child learning to read progressed from syllables to whole words, his writing exercises (which kept pace with his reading) consisted of writing out words, especially hard words, on the ancient principle that one should always concentrate on what is difficult, for then the mastery of what is easier is also accomplished. He was also set to copy lines, which he memorized for reciting during this task, repeating them in a murmur while he wrote.[83] Because memory was so intimately and constantly involved, Quintilian urges that "the lines, which he is set to copy, should not express thoughts of no significance, but convey some sound moral lessons. He will remember such aphorisms even when he is an old man, and the impression made upon his unformed mind will contribute to the formation of his character. He may also be entertained by learning the sayings of famous men and above all selections from the poets ... For memory is most necessary to an orator."[84] Such an exercise, in other words, is not useful *except* as these bits of reading are memorized, or as they recall to mind matter previously stored away. In providing the maxims for discourse, they provide the materials of character too.

Texts such as Cato's *Distichs* provided such elementary material, as did the Psalms.[85] Quintilian's advice is echoed by Julius Victor, and we see the same practice centuries later in the teaching of Bernard of Chartres, described by John of Salisbury:

Bernard used also to admonish his students that stories and poems should be read thoroughly, and not as though the reader were put to flight like a spurred horse. Wherefore he always insistently demanded from each one, as a daily debt, something committed to memory.[86]

Cassiodorus provides one of the best medieval statements of the virtue of acquiring such material, the "topica" as he calls them, stored in memory. "Clearly [*memoria* is] a remarkable sort of work – that in one place could be gathered together whatever the mobility and variety of the human mind was able to learn by inquiring about the sensible world through various postulates – it contains the free and willful mind; for wherever it turns itself, whatever thoughts it enters into, of necessity the human mind falls into some one of those common places earlier mentioned."[87] The commonplaces are understood here to be habits of thought, habits of character as well, the *hexis* or "firma facilitas," "complete mastery" of subject and self, that Quintilian understood *hexis* to mean. One cannot think at all, at least about the world of process and matter ("in sensibus ... per diversas causas"), except in commonplaces, which are, as it were, concentrated "rich" schemata of the memory, to be used for making judgments and forming opinions and ideas.

This is really no more astonishing than saying that one cannot think without opinions, or without categories. But it is true that the nature of those opinions for medieval students was more consciously literary in origin than is the nature of most of our received opinions, which we like to think are "factual" instead (some people I know even claim to have "factual opinions"). And this memorized chorus of voices, this everpresent florilegium built up plank by plank continuously through one's lifetime, formed not only one's opinions but one's moral character as well. Character indeed results from one's experience, but that includes the experiences of others, often epitomized in ethical commonplaces, and made one's own by constant recollection.

Abelard relates the following famous and instructive anecdote about Heloise:

I admit that it was shame and confusion in my remorse and misery rather than any devout wish for conversion which brought me to seek shelter in a monastery cloister. Heloise had already agreed to take the veil in obedience to my wishes and entered a convent. So we both put on the religious habit, I in the abbey of St. Denis and she in the Convent of Argenteuil which I spoke of before. *There were many people*, I remember, who in pity for her youth tried to dissuade her from submitting to the yoke of monastic rule as a penance too hard to bear, but all in vain; she broke out as best she could through her tears and sobs into Cornelia's famous lament:

> O noble husband,
> Too great for me to wed, was it my fate
> To bend that lofty head? What prompted me
> To marry you and bring about your fall?
> Now claim your due, and see me gladly pay . . .

So saying she hurried to the altar, quickly took up the veil blessed by the bishop, and *publicly* bound herself to the religious life.[88] (My emphasis)

Heloise quotes from Lucan's poem, *Pharsalia*, the verses with which Pompey's wife, Cornelia, greets her husband after his shameful defeat in battle, offering to kill herself in sacrifice to placate the gods. In his study of the episode, R. W. Southern states the parallel: as Cornelia offers herself to death to save her husband at the moment of his greatest shame, so Heloise sacrifices her life that Abelard might overcome his shame, for "[l]ong before Abelard had seen himself as the modern Jerome, Heloise had seen herself as the modern Cornelia."[89] It was a natural thing for her to do, because these lines from Lucan were in her memory, they helped to make up her experience. Since Heloise read in the medieval way Hugh of St. Victor describes, she did not "see herself as" Cornelia, in the sense of acting a role; rather, Cornelia's experience, given voice by Lucan, had been made hers as well – so much her own that she can use it, even, perhaps, with irony, in such an extreme personal situation.

Literary fragments of florilegial length, "dicta et facta memorabilia," are a frequent (though to our eyes peculiar and somewhat embarrassing) accompaniment to medieval moral decisions. Augustine, at the very moment of his greatest personal anguish, thinks immediately of the hermit, Anthony, as he hears the mysterious command "Tolle, lege," and picks up the Book to read whatever his eye chances on.[90] One sometimes gets the impression that a medieval person, like Chaucer's Dorigen, could do nothing (especially in duress) without rehearsing a whole series of exemplary stories, the material of their experience built up board by board in memory, and, as Gregory says, transformed into their very selves, so that even in moments of stress the counsel of experience will constrain a turbulent and willful mind. If the task is properly done, as Cassiodorus says, the mind of habitual necessity (a meaning of *hexis*) will have a "place" for anything it may encounter, whatever the circumstances.

A modern woman would be very uncomfortable to think that she was facing the world with a "self" constructed out of bits and pieces of great authors of the past, yet I think in large part that is exactly what a medieval self or "character" was. Saying this does not, I think, exclude a conception of individuality, for every person had domesticated and familiarized these *communes loci*, these pieces of the public memory. It does underscore the profound degree to which memory was considered to be the prerequisite for character itself. The link is suggested in the fact that Greek *charaktér* means literally "the mark engraved or stamped" on a coin or seal; by transference, the word came to mean "distinctive mark" and hence the "distinctive quality" of a person or thing, and ultimately also "type" (of person) or "style."[91] The word's literal meaning continued to be recognized, however; in *Orator*, Cicero translates it with the Latin word *forma*, which had a similar range of meanings.[92] One basic conception of a memory phantasm, as we have seen, employs exactly the same model, that of "seal" or "stamp," in wax most commonly, but also on a coin (as in Hugh of St. Victor's *Didascalicon*). The Greek concept of *hexis*, crucial to an understanding of moral behavior, is a predisposition that "stamps" or "forms" the embodied soul towards behaving in certain ways rather than others. Perhaps here as clearly as anywhere else in ancient and medieval culture, the fundamental symbiosis of memorized reading and ethics can be grasped, for each is a matter of stamping the body-soul, of *charaktér*.

Heloise's moment of moral decision is articulated as a rhetorical action. This is the most telling feature of the entire incident. It gives us a clear way of understanding just how ethics and rhetoric were thought to coincide, and as there has been a great deal of misunderstanding about this, especially in the modern school of "Exegetical" criticism, I want to analyze her action carefully.

Exegetical critics believe that literature is ethical in nature, but they think of the ethical use of texts in entirely normative and definitional terms. All medieval literature, they believe, was thought to promote charity, and the only value of the "specifics" of a text, its "literal level," is as an instance of a universal and normative moral principle. But the direction of this analysis runs exactly counter to that of any rhetorical situation. Rhetorically conceived, ethics is the application of a *res* or generalized content (most often expressed in a textual maxim) to a specific, present occasion *which is public in nature*, because it requires an audience. Rhetoric "makes" commonplaces by a process of adaptation. Normative or transcendental analysis, in contrast, "discovers" a universal, timeless principle amid the detritus of the event, and its moral truth is unconditioned by audience, occasion, speaker, or text. But rhetoric does not normalize an occasion, it occasionalizes a norm.[93]

What is so striking, and so strikingly medieval, in Heloise's action is her articulation of her own present dilemma and decision by means of her memory of a text in the public domain (as we would say). She re-presents Cornelia in her own present situation; the text from Lucan provides a temporal and spatial meeting-ground, a "common place," between a "public memory" and her personal situation, and gives her "a way of talking about" herself in the present. Heloise is "making a commonplace" even as she speaks to her grieving friends and relatives, and in the process she is "re-presenting" Cornelia. Or rather, she implies, both Cornelia's action and now her own are part of a definitional "copiousness," which can be usefully held together within a common memory locus – that is why the presence of an audience is so crucial. And "copiousness," as I argued in chapter 1, is not a process of analytical definition so much as it is compiling a memory place that is most like a florilegial entry, an indefinitely expandable grouping of "dicta et facta" on some common theme or subject. And, as I also have said, these themes ("Justice," "Wifely Chastity," "Disgraced Husbands") do not function as *a priori* definitive norms, but as labels, the mnemonically necessitated listing of the memorial "bin." And, of course, sayings and stories can be listed in more than one bin, for, like ethics itself, they are "copiously" – rhetorically – defined.

The presence of an audience would appear to be crucial to the making of the ethical action. This simply reminds us that a rhetorical conception of ethics requires that its social and public nature be stressed. But it is remarkable that instances of moral judgment in medieval literature seem so often to require both a literary text and an audience to complete them, whether the audience is in the work itself or is created by a direct address to readers (Petrarch speaks to Augustine about Virgil, Dorigen utters a formal complaint "as ye [that is, we readers] shal after heere").

The function of this audience, however, is not to supply a norm. It is to supply a memory. Heloise's friends and relations try to dissuade her "in pity for her youth"; sobbing so that she can scarcely speak, Heloise breaks out "as best she could" with Cornelia's lament and takes the veil. The scene is deliberately made memorable – perhaps even contrived to give the appearance of spontaneity, in the best traditions of Ciceronian rhetoric – and speaker and audience together collaborate in this. Memorableness, enabled for this occasion by the quality some writers have called "performance" (and to which we might apply the rhetorical term, "delivery") would, in fact, seem to be the necessary source of the ethical nature and efficacy of Heloise's act.[94] And the mediator of the action is a piece of a literary text. Why? Because it is that which is common to both the subject and the audience, a piece of their common memorial florilegium. If the audience did not recognize Heloise's quotation, the scene would lose its ethical effectiveness. Instead of talking about ethical rules in medieval culture, it would be truer to speak of ethical memories, "contained" in texts, "dicta et facta memorabilia"; they are not ethical algorithms or universal definitions, but are "copious," like literature. And they require not to be applied (like a theorem) but to be "read," interpreted.

This brings us back to the third element in the complete ethically-valorized action – Heloise herself. For it is her memory that is the "first mover," as it were, of the whole incident. Clearly, she is not "expressing herself." Self-expression is a meaningless term in a medieval context – on that point I agree with the Exegetes, for there was no concept of an autonomous, though largely inarticulate "individual self," to be defined against social norms. Heloise is not expressing herself, but neither is she simply expressing Lucan. She is "expressing her character," a function of *memoria*.

So instead of the word "self" or even "individual," we might better speak of a "subject-who-remembers," and in remembering also feels and thinks and judges. In other words, we should think of the apprehending and commenting individual subject ("self") also in rhetorical terms. Her subjectivity is located in Heloise's memory, including her whole florilegium of texts, one of which she "invents" (in the ancient sense) for this occasion, thereby investing it, the occasion, and her own action with "common" ethical value, and giving her audience "something to think about."[95]

It seems to me that the basic notion of a memory-place as a commonplace into which one "gathers" a variety of material is essential to understanding how the process of ethical valorizing occurs. In considering what is the ethical nature of reading, one could do much worse than to start with Gregory the Great's comment, that what we see in a text is not rules for what we *ought* to be, but images of what we *are*, "our own beauty, our own ugliness." It is this which enables us to make these texts our own. We read rhetorically, memory makes our reading into our own ethical equipment ("stamps our character"), and we express that character in situations that are also rhetorical in nature, in the expressive gestures and performances which we construct from our remembered experience, and which, in turn, are intended to impress and give value to others' memories of a particular occasion.

Thus, the entire ethical situation in Abelard's account is socially and rhetorically conceived: it requires a recollecting subject, a remembered text, and a remembering audience. These, of course, are also the three ingredients found in virtually all medieval narrative literature. What makes a poem like Chaucer's *Book of the Duchess* ethical is its construction: a recollecting subject (the dreamer, the Man in Black), remembered "dicta et facta" (the dream itself, fair White, the Ovidian tale of Ceyx and Alcyone), and the remembering audience (the dreamer who listens to the Man in Black, and we readers). That the poem also talks generally about death, love, or honor does not in itself make it an ethical poem. Rather, the ethical content is made by both the common and specific "topics" of death, love, and honor, recollected and spoken by somebody to somebody else in this poem, which thereby lodges as an experienced event in the memories of its audience, memories that are made up equally of *imagines* ("likenesses") and *intentiones* ("responses"). Ethics is inseparable from the "copiousness" of the text itself and its effect upon the *memoria* of its audience and witnesses.

It is interesting to reflect that the psychoanalytical situation is in some respects parallel to the one I have just described, for the same three ingredients are present: recollecting subject, remembered "dicta et facta" in all their copiousness, and a remembering audience. But psychoanalysis is neither public nor social in its occasion, and it is therefore not truly rhetorical, despite these structural similarities. Nonetheless, psychoanalysis often presents itself as a modern version of *memoria* (and sometimes as a modern version of ethics too), though in fact by privileging the concept of "private" it is greatly different from medieval *memoria*. Jacques Lacan sounds very much like Cassiodorus when he writes that: "[Psychoanalytic] recollection is not Platonic reminiscence – it is not the *return* of a form, an imprint, an eidos of beauty and good . . . coming to us from the beyond. It is something *that comes to us from the structural necessities, something humble*" (my emphasis).[96] But of course the "structural necessities" that Cassiodorus meant when he spoke of the "containers" of trained memory that give shape to the uneducated mind (I would have used the adjective "private," but it is too anachronistic) were neither generic attributes of humankind nor infusions from some vague cultural "mentality," but were the publicly held commonplaces laid down according to a manner and method that everyone knew and approved.

Italian and French humanism of the thirteenth and fourteenth centuries is studded with vernacular florilegia, including Brunetto Latini's *Trésor*, written in French for the circle at Avignon (*c.* 1266) but soon translated into Italian. A modern editor of *Trésor* writes disparagingly of it as a compilation of compilations, which "contains no element of imagination, no artistic pretension."[97] Yet Dante has memorialized it as Brunetto's chief work, the fame of which will live forever. And Petrarch did not disdain to produce an ethical florilegium (in Latin, to be sure, but for a lay audience), derived mainly from Valerius Maximus's very similar compilation (known by its medieval title, *Dicta et facta memorabilia*), though Valerius Maximus was also much admired and studied at this time.

It is certainly true to observe that ethically-directed florilegial compilations are distinctive (though not original) products of the early Renaissance, from *Trésor* (1266) to such an Erasmian product as *Adagia* (1508). As Thomas M. Greene has observed in a fine essay on the *Adagia*, "the impulse, whatever it was, that produced this [florilegial] text and its thousands of companions, has to be regarded with some curiosity."[98] Clearly it was an impulse distinct from, though not in conflict with, the equally typical humanistic one to restore the original purity and wholeness of ancient texts.

I myself regard the two activities as, fundamentally, humanistic adaptations of the two kinds of reading, *lectio* and *meditatio*, which had been developed in medieval schools. The desire to establish true texts evolved from the scholarship of grammar and rhetorical study, a careful restoration and analysis of textual *litterae*. This sort of study – together with commentary and the questions it invokes and responds to – were traditionally the tasks of *lectio*, a master reading a text aloud to his students, responding to questions, elucidating hard passages, and, above all, "establishing the text." In monastic tradition, *lectio* encompasses all the disciplines of the sacred page; Hugh of St. Victor makes this clear in the program he sets forth in *Didascalicon*. But *lectio* is the preface to, and must be completed by *meditatio*, if study is to be a truly moral, useful activity. This link between studious reading and meditative composition based upon the flowers culled from reading goes back to the Rome of St. Jerome and is very much a heritage of ancient rhetoric. Jerome wrote to Pope Damasus that "to read without also writing is to sleep."[99] The humanist impulse to compile florilegia directs the literary enterprise specifically to forming, from humanist sources, the ethical character of the laity, while at the same time confirming one's own memory and providing an occasion for meditative composition. Making florilegia is an unbroken tradition of medieval pedagogy; these humanist examples in the genre broaden it to include exactly the audience to whom the humanist memory-texts are also directed: lawyers, physicians, merchants, aristocrats, and clerical bureaucrats of all sorts, the components of the extensive secular society coming into existence in southern, and then later northern, Europe.

And in this enterprise, the florilegial books of ethical instruction compiled by the regular clergy also played their part.[100] Even in fourteenth-century England at least one such compendium was made for personal meditation and not primarily as a preachers' manual. At the very end of the century, John of Mirfeld, an Augustinian canon of St. Bartholomew's, Smithfield, made his *Florarium Bartholomei*, which he prefaces by saying that it provides a "storehouse" of material "which every Christian soul needs for its virtuous behaviour and its salvation . . . Understand, however that [these texts] are not to be read amidst tumults, but in quiet; not speedily, but one subject at a time, with intent and thoughtful meditation."[101]

I find Bono Giamboni's role as *translateur* of both *Trésor* and Tully on memory to be revealing, for it connects both *Trésor* and the *Ammaestramenti* with memory training, for which Tully's precepts offered a humanistically-approved method, more authentically classical (perhaps this is what was thought) than methods such as those which Thomas Bradwardine taught, associated with university training. Bartolommeo, the Italian Dominican, begins his florilegium with the passage (cited "ad res" and in the vernacular) from Cassiodorus which I quoted earlier in this chapter: "Siccome dice Cassiodoro: Lo senno umano se egli non è ajutato e restaurato per le cose trovate d'altrui, tosto puote mancare del suo proprio," "As Cassiodorus says: human judgment if it is not adjusted and restored by things found in [the works of] others, promptly will fall short of its true nature."[102] There are few clearer statements of this eminently florilegial formulation concerning the nature of human character, and the role which public memory, enshrined in books, must play in the development of individual ethical behavior.

Human beings are born imperfect, needing to be perfected. To be sure this Augustinian doctrine is thought of in terms of vice and virtue, but it is very easy, especially if one thinks in modern popular-Freudian terms, to fall into an essentially Manichaean understanding of the process as a kind of war between the superego and the unconscious. It is truer to the assumptions driving the compilers of florilegia to think of character in terms of "completion" or "filling-out" or "building" (the root concept in Latin *instruo*, "instruct"). Public memory is a needed ethical resource, for its contents complete the edifice of each individual's memory.

Therefore, says Bartolommeo, it behoves a wise man not to rest content with his own ideas, but by diligent study to search out those of others. Of course, not all of their wisdom can be contained in a little book, and so, he says, he has taken pains to "gather" or "pluck" (like flowers) [*raccogliere*] their wisdom, as he best can.[103] Bartolommeo then describes the basic order he has followed in his compilation; clearly, however, Bono's translation of Tully was soon also considered to be an appropriate appendix to it. Memory technique was attached to such florilegia not as an afterthought but as an integral part. It provided the method whereby the flowers of study could be made not only *recti*, but *utiles* and *necessarii* too. Bono's translation is clearly designed for such a collection, not as a self-standing piece; this is apparent from his prefatory remarks, which address the ethical nature of learned discourse, regarding mnemotechnique as an essential means to that greater end.

I would like to close this chapter by examining for a moment the reading-seduction of Paolo and Francesca in Canto v of Dante's *Inferno*. This scene brings together in a particularly compressed and fruitful manner several of the aspects of reading that I have discussed, and I would like to meditate on it in terms of three of its key words: memory, desire, and reading. Francesca begins with memory, re-presenting her past, "the time of your sweet sighing," in response to Dante's request. "There is no greater pain than to recall the happy time in misery [*ricordarsi del tempo felice / nella miseria*]." Her recollection is of reading, itself a memorative, recollective activity:

We read one day for pastime [*diletto*, "delight"] of Lancelot ... Many times that reading drew our eyes together and changed the colour in our faces, but one point alone it was that mastered us; when we read that the longed-for smile [of Guinevere] was kissed by so great a lover, he who never shall be parted from me, all trembling, kissed my mouth. A Galeotto was the book and he that wrote it; that day we read in it no farther.[104]

Modern readers, concentrating on the failings of the lovers' judgment, tend to see in this story only an example of passion overmastering reason, and to blame Francesca for her self-serving words that put the onus for her actions on the book and its author. Or, if they are keener moralists, they blame the lovers for wasting their time on such trash in the first place when they should have been reading sterner stuff. Or the story is read as a caution against leaving a young man and woman alone together at all. In any case, the consensus seems to run, Paolo and Francesca are to be blamed for improperly reading the book by allowing it to arouse their emotions.

This interpretation accords well with modern notions (usually attributed to "Augustine") that medieval people thought texts to be authoritative maps for their actions, readers being totally passive in the face of what they read.[105] But as I hope my study has helped demonstrate, this scholarly fiction is manifestly untrue. Medieval reading was highly active, what I have called a "hermeneutical dialogue" between the mind of the reader and the absent voices which the written letters call forth, at times literally in the murmur of ruminative meditation. In this scene, it is not an idle detail that Paolo and Francesca read together, and thus aloud. If such activity does not occur, reading has not truly taken place for the memory has not been engaged. Thus, reading is first a sensory activity ("diletto"); when the senses and emotions are engaged, when imagination forms its images and cogitation responds affectively to them, memory and recollection can occur. And *only* when memory is active does reading become an ethical and properly intellectual activity. What therefore activates Paolo and Francesca's desire? The activity of reading itself, just as Francesca says.

Recall for a moment Hugh of St. Victor's description of the three-stage process of reading-meditation. First, one focuses on the example, next one acts in imitation of it, and then one internalizes the imitation so that one's own vital power (*virtus*) is permanently changed. The moment such a change occurs is the moment of desire, and with it, of will. It is also the moment during which the full process of meditative study is completed; when, in Gregory the Great's words, what we read is transformed into our very selves, a mirror of our own beauty or ugliness, for we have, like Ezekiel, eaten the book. The end of Francesca's remembering to Dante, and the end of the lovers' desire, is also the end of their reading ("that day we read no farther").

This understanding of what medieval reading was supposed to be complicates the pathos of this tale as no mere moralism can. No wonder that Dante swoons "like a stone," emotionless and thus memoryless, from the effort of his remembering (both at the time, listening to Francesca, and later writing it down) of her remembering of their remembering of the story memorialized in the book. *Ricordare* and *leggiare* and *amare* are simultaneous activities, necessarily accompanying each other. Paolo and Francesca are reading properly here, recreating the exemplary scene, rewriting it in their own memories. But having eaten the book with Ezekiel and St. John, they find in the experience a fitting echo of the Revelation account, as its sweetness turns bitter. Their fault is not in having read the *Lancelot* in the first place, nor is it simply in allowing their reading to create desire; it is in reading "no farther," "imperfectly" in the medieval sense.

Memory and the ethics of reading

In the ongoing hermeneutical dialogue that the process of reading was understood to be, the question of when and how to "divide" looms rather large. This is another aspect to the irony and pathos of Francesca's last words, to their reading imperfectly, "no farther." Comments like this are fairly common in medieval literature; one instructive parallel occurs in *Piers Plowman*, when Lady Meed boasts to Conscience that she has read the Bible and lives by the text "Omnia autem probate," "try out all things" (I Thes. 5:21). To which Conscience replies that she should have read the rest of the sentence, "quod bonum est tenete," "hold fast to that which is good."[106] Similarly here, Paolo and Francesca are not wrong to utilize Lancelot and Guinevere as instructive examples, nor to re-write their story in their own memories, but they did not finish the sentence. This presents their fault as one of poor *divisio* and incomplete reading, rather than of "wrong" interpretation according to some transcendental norm. "One point alone" is the problem – "solo un punto."

In the *Inferno*, the pair read the scene from the French prose *Lancelot* to the moment when Guinevere kisses her lover. Also present with the two main characters in *Lancelot* is Galahot (Galeotto), Lancelot's faithful companion, who has arranged the meeting and actually suggested the kiss. To one side, out of earshot, are Guinevere's lady-companions, including the Lady of Malohaut, and Galahot's seneschal. The kiss is described in a paratactic sentence, made up of several clauses or *cola* marked in the manuscripts with a point, "punto" in Italian. Each *punto* marks out a memory-sized "bit," in the traditional manner of textual punctuation.

The sentence begins thus: "Et la roine voit li cheualiers nen ose plus faire · si le prent par le menton & le baise deuant galahot asses longement ·" That is presumably where Paolo and Francesca stopped reading. Had they read the next clause of the sentence after the point, they would have read that Lancelot and Guinevere's illicit love-making was instantly discovered: "si que la dame de malohaut seit quele le baise."[107] Now the Lady of Malohaut is in love with Lancelot herself, has just imprisoned him and tried to seduce him (unsuccessfully), and she is Big Trouble. Guinevere, immediately after the kiss, swears Lancelot and Galahot to secrecy (of course), but it is by then too late – for the Lady of Malohaut has already seen and comprehended, and cannot be trusted. Indeed (to learn from this example) every illicit love affair has its "Lady of Malohaut," and it is only a matter of time (often not long) before she shows up; thus their fear of her watchful and dangerous eyes, to those who have read far enough in their book to be concerned about her, should be enough to check passion. But Paolo and Francesca failed to get to the crucial "point."

I am not really suggesting that the lovers' only fault was one of punctuation – yet they did not punctuate wisely. "Solo un punto" did them in, says Francesca, one little mark of punctuation. But "modus legendi in dividendo constat." And since *divisio* produced the building-blocks of memory, and hence of education and character, punctuation was not an altogether trifling affair. It was crucial, as it still is, to the intelligibility of a text, but it was also crucial ethically, given the role that reading and memorizing played in the formation of moral judgments. We recall that Stephen Langton spent over thirty years "coting" the Bible, and that Robert of Basevorn reserves the practice of "quotation" only to the most learned and skilled of doctors. Scholastic "quotation" is a form of punctuating, as all textual division is. In a letter describing his own habits of study, Ambrose writes of working long into the night to punctuate perfectly the ancient teaching of the Fathers, and to fix it firmly in his memory by continual, familiar practice and in slow increments – as an aid to which he writes down his studies with his own stylus. "Ad unguem distinguere" is the verbal phrase he uses, meaning to "mark off, divide up" or "punctuate" or "decorate," "to a hair" (literally "to a finger-nail") or "exactly." Since what he says of the nature and circumstances of his studies rules out the possibility that he was decorating the "senilem sermonem" that occupied him, he seems to have been doing what the scholastics called quoting his texts, and making them familiar and habitual to himself at the same time in leisurely stages ("lento quodam figere gradu"), using his own hand and stylus, in the best school fashion, to fix the impression in his memory. In that way he is sure not to just blow the words about ("deflare") to an attendant scribe taking dictation, but to hide them away ("abscondere"), in his memory-receptacle where all *lectio* should be hidden safely.[108] Thus Paolo and Francesca's failure to read further, even one *punto* more, is one that reverberates within the whole tradition of the methods of reading developed in the elementary schools of antiquity and the Middle Ages. The "Lady of Malohaut" in the person of Francesca's husband, Giovanni Malatesta, discovers them instantly and fatally, just as the book warned – if only they had not "divided" at the "point" where they did. It is not the least of the many pathetic ironies in Dante's scene that lovers who failed to divide perfectly in life will never be parted in death.

6

Memory and Authority

In this chapter, I want to explore the connections between *memoria* and medieval assumptions about the nature of authority and authorship. Composition is the activity which links them, and I will spend most of my time discussing in detail the process itself of composing texts designed for oral or written delivery, as it was taught and practiced in schools. Composition is one of the two activities of meditation, and the complement to *divisio* in memorial practice. As division is the mode of reading, as Hugh of St. Victor says, so composition – the "placing together" of bits laid away by division – is the mode of text-making, what we call "writing." The memory bits culled from works read and digested are ruminated into a composition – that is basically what an "author" does with "authorities."

It is also important to recognize that there are two distinct stages involved in the making of an authority – the first is the individual process of "authoring," and the second is the matter of "authorizing," which is a social and communal activity. In the context of memory, the first belongs to the domain of an individual's memory, the second to what we might conveniently think of as public memory. Texts are the primary medium of the public memory, the archival *scrinia* available to all, from which, by the methods I examined in my last chapter, an individual stores, *ad res* or *ad verba*, the chest of his or her own memory.

The distinction between *res* and *verbum*, as we have come to understand it in the context of memorial practices, is at the heart of medieval views of how one should deal with the texts that make up public memory. For *memoria ad res* is an adaptation of the original language for mnemonic purposes rather than a simple iteration of it. Thomas of Waleys, we recall, distinguished between "reciting" and "retaining and speaking"; "recitare" is the word-for-word repetition of a text "verbaliter," whereas "retinere et dicere" is performed "sententialiter," according to the meaning signified in its principal words. In terms of this distinction, reciting is what children do when first learning to read; "retaining" – the function of rhetorical *memoria* – is associated, as always, with the more advanced activities of composition, the domain of rhetoric.

We will consider in some detail what the *res* was taught to be in the compositional process; this will make its role somewhat clearer. But I would like to emphasize here that the *res* of a literary text was something extra-linguistic, for which words are "found" from one's memorial store as one translated it into speech. These words mediate the public appearance of the *res*, rather as clothes may be said to mediate the public appearance of a person (to use a favorite metaphor) – they suggest and conceal, they give clues and cues, they reveal but never completely. The notion that a text has both *res* and *verba* posits an "idea" or "meaning" that lies "within" or "behind" speech as some sort of construct partly independent of and greater than the words from which it is constructed. There is, as it were, *an intention of the text* which can, and indeed must, be translated from one mind to another and adapted to suit occasions and circumstances. This adaptation was not believed to substantively alter the enduring *res* (or "sentence," as it was called in English), which is in a continual process of being understood, its plenitude of meaning being "perfected" and "corrected." The adaptation process, which is the work of interpretative commentary and meditative reading is crucially what makes the public, the "authorized" text.

In considering medieval views of textual authority, one needs always to keep in mind that *auctores* were, first of all, texts, not people. When the old woman in Chaucer's Wife of Bath's tale, in order to win an argument vows that "auctors can I fynde, as I gesse," she means that she can find in her memory store specific quotations from textual sources, not that she can find people who write. The "intentio auctoris" or "author's intention" – a common category of the scholarly "introduction to the text," which was known as the *accessus ad auctores* – was defined by Albertus Magnus in a tautology that equates the author's intention with the words in the text: "the intention of the speaker as expressed in the letter is the literal sense."[1] Consequently, there *is* no extra-textual authorial intention – whatever *intentio* there is is contained in the textual signs alone. All meaning develops from there. Albertus's definition invokes the commonplace of Isidore of Seville, that the *litterae* of writing are representations both of a voice ("speaker") and of words spoken. But the words ("voces") in turn are signs "of things" – *res*, the concept one keeps coming back to in all pre-modern discussions of rhetoric, language, and the role of *memoria*.

The word *auctor* was thought to be derived from the verbs *agere*, "to act," and *augere*, "to grow." A second word, *autor*, was related through etymology to Greek *autenthein*, "authentic," but medieval dictionary-makers distinguished the two words, one spelled with a c and one without, quite carefully. *Auctoritas* derived from *auctor*, and was defined by Hugutio of Pisa in about 1200 as "sententia digne imitatione," "a saying worthy of imitation." Thus, both "authority" and "author" were conceived of entirely in textual terms, for an "auctor" is simply one whose writings are full of "authorities." And an "author" acquires "authority" only by virtue of having his works retained "sententialiter" in the memories of subsequent generations.[2]

Author-texts are retained and imitated "ad res" because it is there, not in their actual words, that their authority lies; this is the assumption in

Hugutio's definition. It is related directly, I think, to the memorial distinction between iteration and imitation, *recitare* and *retinere*, "memoria verborum" and "memoria ad res." Both the word *auctor* and the later synonym, *originalis*, are related closely to the traditional metaphor of literature as a great river flowing over time from a *fons* or "source." So, when Jerome wrote of the Bible as "originales libri," he meant something like "originating texts," "progenitors" of a whole family of textual descendants, especially commentaries and other adaptations, which are the indication, or "authorization," of a work's institutional standing in the public, communal memory.[3]

Let us look again at Petrarch's comment, through the mouth of "Augustine," concerning the meaning he finds in the Cave of the Winds passage in the *Aeneid*, for Petrarch a major "auctor":

I cannot but applaud that meaning which I understand you find hidden in the poet's story, familiar as it is to you; for, whether Virgil had this in mind when writing, or whether without any such idea he only meant to depict a storm at sea and nothing else, what you have said about the rush of anger and the authority of reason seems to me expressed with equal wit and truth.[4]

Petrarch has responded to this text's *res*, amplifying it through first familiarizing it in his memory (by *divisio*) and then writing it anew in words that do not reproduce the actual language of the *Aeneid*, but rather adapt its "sentence" to Petrarch's own situation (*compositio*). Were we to think of this exegetically, we could say that Petrarch gives these lines a tropological interpretation. But the point is that his interpretation is not attributed to any intention of the man, Virgil, but rather to something understood to reside in the text itself. Authorial intention in itself is given no more weight than that of any subsequent reader who uses the work in his own meditative composition; the important "intention" is in the work, as its *res*, a cluster of meanings which are only partially revealed in its original statement.[5] Petrarch supports his reading by appealing to some of the words in this passage that suggest anger and turmoil, but he does not suggest that these meanings were ever Virgil's intent – they may or may not have been, it is unimportant. What keeps such a view of interpretation from being mere readerly solipsism is precisely the notion of *res* – the text has meaning within it which is independent of the reader, and which must be amplified and "broken-out" from its words, as they are processed in one's memory and re-presented in recollection. Amplifying is an emotional, image-making activity as we have seen, and it is just this quality that makes it ethically profitable. More importantly than growth in knowledge, reading produces growth in character, through provisioning – in *memoria* – the virtue of prudence.

Composition starts in memorized reading. The commonest way for a medieval author to depict himself is as a reader of an old book or a listener to an old story, which he is recalling by retelling. At this point it might be well to consider the commonplace of the reader/author as a bee. This trope came most familiarly to the Middle Ages in the form given to it by Seneca, whose letters were a standard item in the medieval curriculum of rhetoric, or *ars dictaminis* as it came to be more commonly called during the twelfth century.[6] Seneca wrote: "We ought to imitate bees, as they say, which fly about and gather [from] flowers suitable for making honey, and then arrange and sort into their cells whatever nectars they have collected."[7] Composition begins in reading, culled, gathered, and laid away distinctively in separate places, "for such things are better retained if they are kept separate"; then, using our own talent and faculties, we blend their variety into one savour which, even if it is still apparent whence it was derived, will yet be something different from its source ("ut etiam si apparuerit unde sumptum sit, aliud tamen esse quam unde sumptum est appareat").

I mentioned this variation of the storehouse metaphor for memory in chapter 1; like the rest of those metaphors, this one too should be understood not as a mere decoration but a complex model of the process of composition and authorship. As a model it is a variant also on that of digestion, as indeed Seneca realized: "the food we have eaten, so long as it retains its original character and floats in our stomachs as a mass, is a burden; it passes into tissue and blood only when it has been changed from its original form. So it is with the food which nourishes our mind ... We must digest it; otherwise it will only come into our acquired memory-store [*memoria*] and not pass on to become part of our own abilities [*ingenium*]." Merely to store memory by reading is an incomplete process without composition, for composing is the ruminative, "digesting" process, the means by which reading is domesticated to ourselves. Indeed the two tasks require one another – Jerome echoes this same principle when he says that there is no point to reading if one does not also compose and write.[8]

This familiar trope of the bee has been extensively analyzed as a model for classical, medieval, and Renaissance assumptions concerning the nature of literary imitation, the relationship of authors to their antecedents, and the changing way in which these assumptions have been understood.[9] I have no desire here to rehearse work which has been so ably and thoroughly done. But the scholars who have analyzed it most comprehensively have started from the preoccupations of Renaissance writers defining themselves against a medieval world which they sought to reject (while often unaware, inevitably, of the extent to which they were themselves still its products), and in the course of such analyses a particular medieval understanding of the trope has, I think, been rather slighted and misrepresented. To get at this particular medievalness, I must emphasize that in this trope composition, like reading, is assumed to depend on a memory properly stored with discrete, immediately recoverable *loci*. For Seneca, *memoria* is not an alternative to creativity (which is how I would understand his use of "ingenium" in this passage) but the route to it. He does not disparage *memoria*, but only its undigested, parrot-like use.

Memory is the matrix of all human temporal perception. This too is a medieval commonplace, nowhere so eloquently explored as in the final books of Augustine's *Confessions*. *Memoria* makes present that which is no longer so in actuality; indeed, as we have seen, this temporal understanding of memorial representation is more emphasized, at least in medieval analyses, than its mimetic one. Prudence, the ability to make judgments in a present context about both present and future matters, is founded upon *memoria*, and traditionally was represented with three eyes, looking to past, present, and future. But memory remains, by its nature, of the past – a thing cannot be in memory until it is past. This insistence is basic in medieval Aristotelian (and Augustinian) psychology, as I emphasized in chapter 2. Therefore, to say that memory is the matrix within which humans perceive present and future is also to say that both present and future, in human time, are mediated by the past. But "the past," in this analysis, is not itself something, but rather a memory, a representing of what no longer exists as itself but only in its memorial traces.

It seems to me that this is quite different from insisting, as Renaissance and modern scholars have done, that the past is mediated by the present. The change in emphasis, in the direction of mediation, if you will, is critical. It seems to be typical of modern (Renaissance) consciousness to give the past, like other scientific subjects, objective status apart from present human memories. As a result, perhaps, a Renaissance scholar worried that the past had been "distorted" through the mediation of the present, and sought to recover or resuscitate the dead past itself. In his book on Renaissance literary imitation, Thomas M. Greene has emphasized how the language of necrology and revival is woven into those scholars' antiquarian and philological projects.[10] By contrast, Augustine journeyed through his memory not to find his past but to find God, his present and future. And it is clear that Augustine assumed that the way to God lay only through the re-presenting of his past in memory; he has no interest in his past except as it provides him with a way and ground for understanding his present.

Few features of medieval scholarship are so distinctive as an utter indifference to the pastness of the past, to its uniqueness and its integrity "on its own terms," as we would say. Ordinarily, medieval scholars show no apparent interest in archaeology or historical philology, and the representation of classical or Biblical figures in medieval dress is continually amusing to modern audiences of their art and literature. Yet it is evident as well that medieval scholars realized that language and societies had changed significantly over time; Chaucer and Dante commented famously on the phenomenon, but the acknowledgement is found often much earlier as well. Indeed, the division of "modern" from "ancient" was first formulated at the beginning of the Middle Ages.[11] It simply does not seem to have been thought to be of paramount importance.

This "omnitemporality" in medieval thought, as Erich Auerbach called it, is usually attributed to a prevailing belief in the eternity of God and consequent emphasis upon divine continuity in human history. The dogmatic cause is surely important, but no more so, I think, than the particular character of the medieval institution of *memoria* by means of which texts of past authors are constantly related in and through present minds (the dual meaning of the English verb *relate* is important here, for it captures both the positioning and re-speaking of these texts). The sole relic of the ancients with which medieval scholars vigorously concerned themselves was written texts; this choice itself is interesting, for there were other artifacts of antiquity still readily visible. But the letters which compose texts alone can speak (for letters are the signs of voices no longer present); only they can be related to the present and future, and thus become the material of prudence.

The most comprehensive model of the medieval view of what constituted *memoria* is the medieval book itself, especially those fully "marked up" codices, punctuated and ornamented to the last, precise hair ("distincti ad unguem," to adapt what Ambrose said of his labors). As codicologists speak of paper or parchment or stone as a "support" for writing, so the book itself is the chief external support of *memoria* throughout the Middle Ages. In its lay-out and ordering, it serves the requirements of readers who expected to engage it in their own memories. It also often records the memorial gatherings of a whole community of readers over time, presenting in its multiple margins the graphic display of a *catena* or chain of comments upon the source-text. The distinctive format of the glossed book, used especially for Biblical texts and law, but later also for secular authors, is the most satisfying model of authorship and textual authority which the Middle Ages produced (see figures 5 and 6), as many scholars have recognized. Let me emphasize once more, that I do not believe that the book mimes memory; its relationship to *memoria* is not that of a mirror or copy, any more than letters on parchment mime their contents. The relationship is functional; the book "supports" *memoria* because it serves its requirements, some of which are biological, but many of which, in the memorial cultures of the Middle Ages, were institutional and thus conventional, social, and ethical.

But before examining the finished product, the book itself that both results from and furnishes *memoria*, it will be helpful in the rest of this chapter to consider in detail how the act of making a text was thought to proceed, in order to stress its origins in the activities of memory. I think it will become clear during my discussion that the terms "oral" and "written" are inadequate categories for describing what actually went on in traditional composition. I would propose the term "memorative composition" instead, and stress its close affinity to the metaphors of digestion and rumination which I examined in my previous chapter.

It is clear both from descriptions of pedagogy and from the practices of individual writers, that much of the process of literary composition was expected to occur mentally, in mature authors, according to a well-defined method that had postures, settings, equipment, and products all its own. The drafts that resulted were designated by different names, which do vary a bit according to the particular writer, but each of which denotes a fairly well defined stage of composition. These are, first, *invention*, taught as a wholly mental process of searching one's inventory. It involves recollection primarily, and occurs with postures and in settings that are also signals of *meditatio*; indeed, it is best to think of invention as a meditational activity. It results in a product called the *res*, a term we are familiar with from the pedagogy of memory training, and which means about the same thing in this context. The *res* is the "gist" of one's composition; more complete than what modern students think of as an outline, it should, according to Quintilian, be formed fully enough to require no more than finishing touches of ornamentation and rhythm. In other words, the *res* is like an early draft or even notes for a composition, still requiring much shaping and adjustment.

The post-invention stage is, properly, composition itself. Its products are called *dictamen*; it might, but need not, involve writing instruments. As will become clear, the *dictamen* is most like what we now call a "draft"; a number of versions, each unfinished, could be involved. *Compositio* covers three closely-related activities: *formalization*, or taking one's *res* and giving it final form as a composed piece; *correcting*, both by adding and emending, but also by comparing and adjusting the revisions to make sure the words fit one's *res* in intention and accuracy as much as possible (changing one's *res* drastically at this stage would indicate a lack of proper invention); *polishing*, artfully adjusting one's expression to make it striking and memorable in all its details (the medieval *ars dictaminis* addresses this specifically). For *compositio*, a set of waxed tablets or other informal (easily correctable) writing support could be used, on which one might write down all or parts of one's *res* to make stylistic tinkering easier. But, depending on one's maturity and experience, this process could, like invention, be completely mental.

When the *dictamen* was shaped satisfactorily, the composition was fully written out on a permanent surface like parchment in a scribal hand; this final product was the *exemplar* submitted to the public. (Usually, as we shall see, the scribal fair-copy was submitted once again for a final corrective collation by the author or author's agent before the exemplar was made available for further copying.) The word "writing" properly refers to this last inscribing process, which the author might do himself, but usually did not. Saint Anselm's biographer, Eadmer, clarifies this when he describes how he wrote his biography of Anselm:

When I had first taken the work in hand, and had already transcribed onto parchment a great part of what I had drafted in wax [*quae in cera dictaveram pergamenae magna ex parte tradissem*], Father Anselm himself one day called me to him privately and asked what it was I was drafting and copying [*quid dictitarem, quid scriptitarem*].[12]

Eadmer was reluctant to obey, knowing Anselm's humility, but showed his work in the hope that Anselm would correct it. In fact, Anselm did so, deleting some things, approving others, and reordering some material. But, as Eadmer feared, Anselm's reticence showed itself a few days later when he called Eadmer in and told him to destroy all "the quires in which I had put together the work." Eadmer obeyed the letter of Anselm's order and destroyed the quires after first copying their contents into others.

In this admission of guilt, Eadmer makes clear the distinction between the composing and copying stages. Of the first, he uses the verb *dictare*, of the second *scribere*. *Dictare* is done "in cerae," "on wax"; *scribere* is the action whereby the *dictamen* is *traditum*, "transcribed," to parchment. Since Eadmer did his own copying the distinction is an interesting one, for it indicates that Eadmer thought of the two activities as different, even when the same person performed them. *Dictare*, for Eadmer, evidently simply means "compose," without any suggestions of oralness (one can "dictate" with one's stylus on wax); *scribere* is what a scribe does, even when the scribe is also the author. One needs to be careful not to over-generalize Eadmer's consistent distinction, for there are instances when the verb *dictare* means "dictate to a secretary," as Thomas Aquinas did, sometimes from a written *dictamen* (in *littera inintelligibilis*) and often directly from memory.[13] And *scribere* is used in contexts when the author is still composing. But the fact that these two verbs sometimes overlap in meaning does not indicate that the two processes, of composing and of transcribing in secretarial hand, were undifferentiated. The author produces a *res* or *dictamen*; that which is a *liber scriptus* is in a formal hand on parchment, and the product of a scribe.

The distinction is long-lived. Chaucer makes it, in English, when he begs his scrivener, Adam, that he should "after my makyng . . . wryte more trewe!"[14] Once the work was written out, it was corrected by the author (Chaucer complains of the amount of rubbing and scraping of parchment he must do after Adam's work), as Anselm corrected Eadmer's written composition, and equally, as Bernard of Clairvaux and Augustine corrected the *reportationes* of their oral sermons. It is important to realize that the written version of a text was considered to be a scribal or secretarial product, not an authorial one *no matter who the scribe was*. As such a written text was presumed to need emendation and correction; *emendare* is also a stage of the composition, formation, "authoring" of a text, which follows the fair-copy product. This is very different from the status which a printed text has now, for a medieval text was not presumed to be *perfectus*, "finished," even though it had been *scriptus*, "written." The first task which both ancient and medieval elementary students performed in school when they had written copies of texts before them was *collatio*, in which the *grammaticus* read aloud from his text while the pupils emended theirs; thus the introduction a child had in school to a written text was as something that needed to be checked and corrected.[15]

Having sketched these stages out, I now want to examine in more detail how they are related to the procedures of trained recollection. In Book x of his *Institutio*, Quintilian describes an unskilled student in the throes of starting a composition (the stage of invention), as lying on his back with eyes turned up to the ceiling, trying to fire up his composing power ("cogitationem") by murmuring to himself, in the hope that he will find things in his memorial inventory to bring together into a composition. (That Quintilian does not approve of such desperation, preferring that one compose more calmly, is not germane to my present concern.)[16] If a modern teacher were to describe such a scene of typical desperation, she would not do it in these terms. Instead, someone would be described with pen in hand, seated at a desk amid heaps of crumpled paper. And while the person might have a desperate or vacant look, while he might get up to pace the floor and stare out a window, he would be silent, returning constantly but silently to his pen and sheets of paper (or her computer screen). And when composition finally began, that too would be silent (even though, in fact, many people still subvocalize while actually composing). What Quintilian describes, however, is a student murmuring during recollective meditation in order to compose. And this he regards as the typical initiating activity of composition – what one does in order "to get an idea."

The mental activity which Quintilian's desperate author is attempting to stimulate is *cogitatio*. This is one of the functions of the "inner sense," and, as we have seen, while it gets defined with somewhat different emphases in the various accounts of human psychology, it is the ability to compose. To summarize my earlier description, *vis cogitativa* is closely allied in medieval psychology with *vis aestimativa*. According to Avicenna, who defines it most stringently, it is the compositive human imagination, or the activity of taking the individual phantasms produced by *vis imaginativa* or *vis formalis* and putting them together with other images, mainly those previously stored in memory. It corresponds to what Aristotle calls the "deliberative imagination," a combination of *phantasia* with *dianoia*, or the power of constructing with conscious judgment a single image out of a number of images.[17] Some medieval psychologists distinguished the simple act of putting images together from the act of judging the result, and use *imaginativa* for the former, reserving *cogitativa* for the judging faculty.[18] But throughout its long history, *cogitatio* is basically the activity of putting images together in a consciously recollected, deliberative way. Though it is often translated into modern English as "thought," one should never forget that the *vis cogitativa* is an activity of *animus*, the sensory-emotional soul; it therefore is never as abstractly rational as the modern word "thought." Its judging power is emotional, the sort of thing that causes a lamb, seeing a wolf, to run in fear. For Aristotle, the cogitative activity ("dianoêtikê psychê") is "the faculty which judges what is to be pursued and what is to be avoided," what is good and what is evil, not "rationally" but as an initial emotional judgment; cogitation, he says, also comprises the functions of combination and separation.[19] So the act of invention, carried out by cogitation, was thought to be one of combining or "laying together" in one "place" or compositive image or design the divided bits previously filed and cross-filed in other discrete *loci* of memory. The result was a mental product called the *res*, the model of one's composition. It is this that an orator or preacher would lay up in *imagines rerum* when preparing to speak, and its close kinship is apparent to the technique of memorizing texts according to their *res*, which one would then shape into words to suit a particular occasion.[20]

For composition is not an act of writing, it is rumination, cogitation,

The book of memory

dictation, a listening and a dialogue, a "gathering" (*collectio*) of voices from their several places in memory. The fifteenth-century Italian physician, Mattheolus of Perugia, wrote that *meditatio* is derived from "mentis dictatio."[21] The ancient writers frequently speak of the importance of listening to what one is composing. In *Heroides*, Ovid's Leander writes that "having spoken in such words to myself in a low murmur, the rest my right hand talked through with the parchment."[22] Thus, the *vox tenuis* which accompanied meditative reading seems to have accompanied composition as well; we might recall the story of Thomas Aquinas's conversations with Saints Peter and Paul that so disturbed his *socius*. I have used the phrase "hermeneutical dialogue" to describe the relationship between a reader and his reading in *meditatio*; it applies also to composition, for indeed that hermeneutical dialogue constitutes the process of composing, as reading and other experience is gathered together and domesticated in memory.

But what exactly was this process of *collectio* thought to be as it relates to our own acts of composing? One of the boldest and most complete accounts comes from Augustine, as one might expect. During his meditation on *memoria* in Book x of the *Confessions*, Augustine speaks of how the sense impressions are "impressed" in the mind as images stored up in the wonderous cells of memory.[23] Then he proceeds to discuss *cogitatio* and *collectio*, as the power and particular activity involved in making ideas, creating thoughts. "Cogitando," ("thinking") is "nothing else but by meditating to gather together those same things which the memory did before contain more scatteringly and confusedly." Augustine's use of *colligere*, deriving from the verb which means both "to lay down" and "to read," carries in this context a specific meaning of gathering together the memories of what one has read and stored in separate places earlier, as well as a general meaning of "collecting" earlier experiences of all sorts.

We discover ("anvenimus") such things as concepts and ideas when by an act of cogitation (*cogitendo*) we collect ("colligere"), and by the act of turning our *animus* we attend to ("animadvertendo curare") those things which the memory has held here and there ("passim") and unarranged together in any particular design ("indisposite"). These we place ("posita") gathered together in our memory, so those matters which formerly lay scattered from each other and unnoticed ("ubi sparsa prius et neglecta latitabant") now easily come together in a "familiar" opinion ("iam familiari intentioni facile occurrant"). The process Augustine describes is generally recognizable to us from other writers too, for this is Aristotelian *vis cogitativa*. *Cogitatio* finds ("invenire") things held in various memory-places and collects them ("colligere") into one place ready at hand ("ad manum posita").[24]

"How many things of this kind my memory holds," Augustine continues, "placed ready at hand . . . things which we are said to have learned [*didicisse*] and to know [*nosse*]." If I stop recollecting them ("recolere") then they again break up and slip away ("dilabantur") into the remoter recesses of my memory ("in remotiora penetralia"), whence I must draw them together again ("cogenda rursus") in order to know them again. Knowing, *cogitan-dum*, derives its name from this action of continually gathering dispersed images and *res* together ("ex quadam dispersione colligenda"). For *cogo* (draw together) and *cogitatio* (cogitate) are derivative one from the other, as are *ago* (do) and *agitatio* (do continually) and *facio* (make) and *facito* (make frequently)."[25] But the action of gathering is a particular property of the mind's activity, so that what is collated in the memory ("in animo colligitur") is now said literally to be cogitated, *cogitari*.

So learning is itself a process of composition, collation and recollection. But the result of bringing together the variously stored bits in memory is "new" knowledge. It is one's own composition and opinion, *familiari intentio*. This is the point at which collation becomes authorship. Augustine understood this quite well in his own composing experience, for he speaks of the process of *cogitatio/collectio* as an expansive one; paradoxically perhaps, the act of bringing memory images together into a single, compositive design is the path to greater, more comprehensive understanding. "I know but I do not understand," he says in one of his sermons, drawing a characteristic distinction, "but cogitation makes us expand, expansion stretches us out, and stretching makes us roomier."[26] For Augustine, the pieces brought together in *cogitatio* make a sum greater than its parts. Knowledge extends under-standing not by adding on more and more pieces, but because as we compose our design becomes more capacious, it dilates. "New" knowledge, what has not been thought, results from this process, for dilation leads ultimately even through the deepest "cavi" of memory to God. Augustine characteristically speaks of this as a "going through." How shall I reach God? he asks. "I shall pass through [*transibo*] even this power of mine which is called memory; I shall pass through it to reach Thee, sweet Light." God is indeed beyond memory, but the only way there is through and by means of it, "ascendens per animum meum ad te." Augustine gives it a metaphysical twist, but his description of how invention occurs as an activity of *memoria* belongs clearly to the ordinary pedagogy of rhetoric.[27]

In practice, invention was an intensely emotional state, more so than we now associate with thinking. We have very few specific medieval accounts of people doing what we call composing. Among the best are those of Thomas Aquinas, and Eadmer's description of Anselm, written around 1100.[28] The work in question was the *Proslogion*; Eadmer reports what Anselm told him of the great difficulty he experienced composing it:

partly because thinking about it [*haec cogitatio*] took away his desire for food, drink and sleep, and partly – and this was more grievous to him – because it disturbed the attention [*gravabat intentionem ejus*] which he ought to have paid to matins and to Divine service at other times. When he was aware of this, and still could not entirely lay hold on what he sought, he supposed that this line of thought [*hujusmodi cogitationem*] was a temptation of the devil and he tried to banish it from his mind [*repellere a sua intentione*]. But the more vehemently he tried to do this, the more this thought pursued him [*tanto illum ipsa cogitatio magis ac magis infestabat*]. Then suddenly one night during matins the grace of God illuminated his heart, the whole matter [*res*] became clear to his mind, and a great joy and exultation filled his inmost being. Thinking therefore that others also would be glad to know what he had found, immediately [*ilico*] and ungrudgingly [*livore carens*] he wrote it on writing-tablets [*rem . . . scripsit in tabulis*] and gave it to one of the brethren of the monastery for safe-keeping.[29]

There are a number of interesting features to this description. Eadmer describes the activity of composition as one of profound concentration, a meditative withdrawal that takes one from food, sleep, and even the most sacred routines of the day. This activity is described in the repeated terms *intentio* (concentration) and *cogitatio* (mulling over). This *cogitatio* is spoken of initially as an enemy; Anselm wants to repell it ("repellere"), but it more and more aggressively and hostilely takes over ("infestabat") his *intentio*, even when he turns it to the liturgical office (which is to be performed also with *intentio*). So obsessed is he that he fears the devil is tempting him. Then, of a sudden, *cogitatio* is completed (Eadmer attributes the grace of God) and only at that moment is a product, called the "res," committed to a writing surface – but to one that is traditionally associated with unfinished work and with the formation and functions of memory. By no means has it yet been "authorized," that is, become an "auctor" or source-text for other minds and memories to use.

I have already stressed that *cogitatio* involves recollection since it uses memorial images; however, it is a pre-rational process even though it involves making judgments, for these are emotionally and intuitively based at this point rather than logically so. Like meditative reading, invention is not, to use the categories of medieval psychology, a process of the "intellectual" soul, but primarily of the "sensory-emotional" one, dependent upon the images stored in memory and the effectiveness of the heuristic structures in which they have been laid down there.

This antiquated language conceals from us an important characteristic of memorial cultures, one I have stressed before but that is worth pointing to again. Alexander Murray has reminded us that what constitutes "rational behavior" is, to some considerable extent, a matter of culture. His *Reason and Society in the Middle Ages* traces how "reasonableness" as a category of thought was influenced in the later Middle Ages by a tension between "monastic culture," whose roots were in the disciplines of meditational prayer (among other things), and "intellectual culture," which developed in the urban ambiance of the universities. These tendencies existed equally in the same institutions and even the same individuals. They were not often perceived as tensions in conflict, but their eventual incompatibility is reflected in our sharp division now between "reason" and "emotion," to the point of assuming them to be incompatible altogether.[30] In the teaching and practice of composition, however, the monastic cultivation of meditational prayer, itself evolving from practices in the ancient schools, remained dominant. This stressed emotion, the basis of memory, as the key to "creativity," as we can readily see from the fact that medieval *cogitatio*, translates, as I emphasized in chapter 2, not as our phrase "reasoning out" (with its emphasis on logical connections) but as "mulling over," a process that depends heavily on free association and one's "feeling for" a matter.

Quintilian assures his students that *cogitatio* can be greatly helped by an orderly consideration of the case, but that order is not necessarily what we would call "logical" or "intellectual." It is an heuristic structure which we follow by habit rather than "deducing" it anew from each separate occurrence; that is, we follow a set form or procedure we have memorized (for example, we might apply an invention procedure like the "adverbial question" which my school-teachers taught me: who, what, where, when, how, why? Or, were we medieval clerics needing a sermon on a text, we might use the heuristic of the "four levels" of interpretation.) Reason alone cannot help that frantically murmuring student, for he has not yet gathered his memorial images to the point where reason can process them. All that can help is a recollected heuristic, a trained memory which proceeds by habit and emotion, pre-rationally.

The highly emotional state described by Quintilian is very like that of Anselm as he desperately sought what he could not quite find ("nec adhuc quod quaerebat ad plenum capere valens"). We recall also what Thomas Aquinas's biographers said of his habit of intense prayer: "At night . . . he would rise, after a short sleep, and pray, lying prostrate on the ground; it was in those nights of prayer that he learned what he would write or dictate in the day-time. Such was the normal tenor of his life – a minimum of time allowed to sleeping and eating, and all the rest given to prayer or reading or thinking or writing or dictating."[31] Such physical accompaniments of *cogitatio* are apparent in all the accounts of composition, prostration being its common posture; Quintilian's student lies down on his back, Thomas Aquinas face-downwards. It is a position designed to shut out external stimuli, especially visual ones, which would serve to confuse or distract one's recollective eye as it looks through its inventory of places, for both *strepitus* and *turba* are great mnemonic enemies.

The emotions (*affectus*) are the starting-point, as they must be in order to engage *memoria* and *cogitatio*. Reginald, Thomas Aquinas's *socius*, said of him that "in his soul, intellect and desire [*intellectus et affectus*] somehow contained each other . . . his desire [*affectus*], through prayer, gained access to divine realities, which then the intellect, deeply apprehending, drew into a light which kindled to greater intensity the flame of love."[32] Desire begins the ascent to understanding by firing memory, and through memory's stored-up treasures the intellect is able to contemplate; the higher its understanding, the more desire flames in love as it both gets and gives more light. It is a sentiment worthy of Dante himself. So Anselm, searching his memory places for the pieces he cannot quite find to complete the design which his *cogitatio* is constructing fears the devil, fears the intense emotion that has invaded his body as well as his thoughts, keeping him from food and sleep as well as from liturgical prayer. So Thomas falls prostrate in tearful prayer. But the products of this non-logical, obsessive, emotional activity are closely-reasoned monuments of scholastic logic, the *Proslogion* and the *Summa theologica*.

It is significant that the times when both Anselm and Thomas Aquinas are described as being particularly distraught are when they are stuck, searching for connections they can't quite get hold of. "Once at Paris," writes Gui of Thomas Aquinas, "when writing on Paul's epistles, he came upon a passage which quite baffled him until, dismissing his secretaries, he fell to the ground and prayed with tears; then what he desired was given him and it all became clear."[33] Thomas wept in order to solve an intellectual difficulty; Anselm behaved like a monk in love until his rational problem came clear. A modern scholar similarly stumped would go to the library or thumb through notes. By such transports of fear and desire, Thomas and Anselm expected to stimulate their memorial libraries. Gui reports that Thomas never set himself to compose without tearful prayer, and "[w]hen perplexed by a difficulty he would kneel and pray and then, on returning to his writing or dictation, he was accustomed to find that his thought had become so clear that it seemed to show him inwardly as in a book the words he needed." It is clear also from Gui's account that Thomas deliberately and habitually cultivated the posture of prostrate prayer in order to produce a solution to a specific compositional problem.[34]

After invention comes the process of shaping the *res* into the version called *dictamen*. The mental activity required is still what the philosophers called *vis cogitativa*, but rhetoricians appear to use *cogitatio* for the revision stage of composition. (This is a bit confusing because Eadmer speaks of Anselm's invention stage as "cogitatio," perhaps because he was not a teacher of rhetoric.) One is still composing, but working on a much more complete form of the text than at the start of *inventio*. There seem to be a number of terms used for this stage – Fortunatianus and Julius Victor both call this "compositio"; Quintilian reserves the word "cogitatio" for it; Augustine calls it "collectio"; for Hugh of St. Victor, as we shall see, it was a kind of "collatio." In any event, the root concept is still a recollective one, bringing together, "collecting" from different "places," into a designed text (*res*) which now exists in a common place in one's memory. A related distinction is made in the scholastic terms for these two stages, invention and composition, called respectively *forma tractatus* and *forma tractandi*. The "forma tractatus" corresponds to the *res* of a text, the content arrived at during invention, or the "drawing" – both "out" and "together" – (the root meaning of *traho*) of material into a fully coherent textual argument. The "forma tractatus" can then be shaped up and refined stylistically in a "forma tractandi." The continuous, polishing nature of this latter activity is indicated in the fact that a present participle is used for it (*tractandi*), whereas the *res* is finished (*tractatus*) when invention is complete. A tract (*tractatus*) is philosophical or moral argumentation without stylistic embellishments or "figures"; the basic expression of reasons, ideas, logical connections and all structural elements such as divisions, belong to the "forma tractatus" and the various figures of style to "forma tractandi." Such definitions follow naturally from the pedagogy and practice of composition I have described. The distinction is correlative to that between "memoria ad res" and "memoria verborum," and also to the emphasis given to the former in the pedagogy of *memoria*.[35]

Fortunatianus says that *memoria* has two essential objects: that material be securely retained, and that it be directly (*cito*) retrievable. This is essential not only for *compositio* that uses writing (*scripta*) but "immo et cogitatio," "especially cogitatio."[36] Later, speaking of Simonides's system, he remarks that for "scripta vel cogitatio" we should place together orderly heuristic cues and memorial *similitudines*. Julius Victor makes a similar distinction between composition during which we write ("scribimus") and that we do in cogitation ("cogitamus") both of which depend on the same processes of *divisio* and *compositio* that characterize a trained and designed memory.[37] Both these writers are distinguishing between methods of composition, one which involves writing on a physical surface and one which is entirely mental, involving no written draft at all.

One should take careful note that neither writer suggests that the two styles of composing require different mental preparation or procedures, or that one involves memory and the other not. Indeed, as presented, the difference is no more significant than our individual preferences for revising in longhand or at a machine. We see similar idiosyncrasy of choice in the compositional aids of writers throughout the Middle Ages. The same writer may choose sometimes to work with a wax tablet and other times not. Thomas Aquinas, we recall, wrote out portions of his *res* of the *Summa contra gentiles* in *littera inintelligibilis*. These pages show the signs of revision and tinkering that characterize the shaping up of a *dictamen*. But for the composition of *Summa theologica* (a longer and more complex work) he worked most often without writing anything down at all, calling a secretary in when he was finished to take down his dictation in fair hand. Quintilian, advising that prose rhythm is an effect to be worked on carefully, relates approvingly that Plato tried out the first four words of the *Republic* in a variety of orders on his wax tablets in order "to make the rhythm as perfect as possible," because this small elegance could be better worked on with the help of a tablet. Quintilian himself, however, does not encourage dependence on such physical aids. It is important to keep in mind that Quintilian was addressing the requirements of orally-delivered compositions, the need to be able to revise and change, digress and add, freely and confidently during delivery itself. So the various techniques he discusses are derived in response to such a situation. But these same techniques were applied to compositions designed to be read, and the drafting stages in the production of a final exemplar are virtually the same; the production of a *res* and then a *dictamen* follows the same successive steps, whether the *dictamen* was then read to a scribe or delivered publicly.[38]

When was the stylus to be used? Here again individual habits obviously varied, but Quintilian describes in detail the received pedagogy that lies behind the distinctions made by later teachers and practitioners. The elementary preparation for eloquence is writing, he says in Book x (on composition); a beginner must write out maxims and sayings on wax tablets "as much as possible and with the utmost care." Writing is crucial because it forces us to concentrate and its slowness makes us careful: "as deep ploughing makes the soil more fertile . . . so, if we improve our minds by something more than superficial study, we shall produce a richer growth of knowledge and shall retain it with greater accuracy [*fidelius continet*]."[39] In other words, one writes solely as an aid to memory: "it is writing that provides that holy of holies where the wealth of oratory is stored and whence it is produced to meet the demands of sudden emergencies."[40] "Illic opes velut sanctiore quodam aeraris conditae," "there the riches are hidden away as in a kind of most sacred treasury"; the phrase could serve as summary of Hugh of St. Victor's opening paragraph in his preface on memory-training, composed ten centuries later.

A beginner must also learn how to cultivate the circumstances needed in all meditational activity. Young students should seek out solitude, silence, and seclusion, and learn to pursue their task with utmost concentration and involvement.[41] Gestures accompanying strong emotion will likewise serve to stimulate the mind (*animus*), and so important is this gestural stimulus that one should not follow the example of those foolish authors who start dictating right away to scribes, lest the presence of another inhibit us (recall how Gui says Thomas Aquinas sent his secretaries away before he prostrated himself in tears).[42] The author should learn not to compose in "the heat and impulse of the moment," dashing off a speedy draft as some do, who call such a thing their "silva," literally meaning "forest" but used metaphorically here for "unformed matter." One should exercise care from the outset "to form the work . . . in such a manner that it merely requires to be chiselled [*caelandum*] into shape." Here Quintilian advises that the *res* of one's composition be carefully planned out in one's mind before it is committed in any way to written form; "chiselling" is what one does on one's tablets (and a scribe is not appropriate until the very last stage).[43] Finally, even as beginning students, we should "train ourselves so to concentrate our thoughts [*intentio*] as to rise superior to all impediments to study. If only you direct all your attention to the work which you have in hand, no sight or sound will ever penetrate to your mind."[44] Therefore, wherever we are, in a crowd, on a journey, at a party, we must practice fashioning a secret inner sanctuary ("secretum") for *cogitatio*.

Quintilian stresses one matter in regard to the layout of the waxed tablets. Waxed tablets best serve excision and correction (though people with poor eyes may have to use parchment in order to see the letters better – parchment slows down the writing process, however, and so may hinder thought). Excision and correction were, of course, vital in revision but so was addition and what we might think of as digression. Dilation, *dilatatio*, allowing space for matter that might occur to you while you revise, is just as necessary as excision. As a beginner writing one's *res* onto tablets, one should, says

Quintilian, be sure to allow such space physically, in the form of blank leaves, and also be sure not to cover all the space of the tablet page, but leave generous margins.[45] The practice seems self-evident, and I don't wish to belabor it, but it underscores how the original text, the *res*, was conceived of as a common "place" into which new material is "collected" from other "places" in the tablets as one refines one's *dictamen* for delivery to an audience. For Quintilian does not recommend that one continuously recopy one's revised text in a "clean copy" in order to incorporate such additions – thus a set of written tablets would show visually just what was original and what was added (erasures are not so apparent on wax as on paper because the end of the stylus smooths the wax out). This is the visual image of his text which a student would imprint in memory before delivering it – not that of a clean, fixed document but rather the memorandum of a text, a palimpsest of the series of one's compositional drafts. It is a procedure that invites additional digression and commentary.

Having learned to revise with stylus and tablets, a student advances to the technique of *cogitatio* proper, the ability to revise mentally (Quintilian is using the word *cogitatio* to refer to a technique, not simply to the natural psychological process). "Proxima stilo cogitatio est," he writes, "next in order [of mastery] after writing with a pen is cogitation." *Cogitatio* "derives force from the practice of writing and forms an intermediate stage between the labors of the pen and the more precarious fortunes of improvisation," and is more frequently used by mature orators than either of the other two compositional methods.[46] Eventually, through practice, we will develop to the point where we can rely as surely on what we have prepared by *cogitatio* alone as what we have written out word for word and memorized. *Cogitatio*, however, requires an especially careful conception of the order of the composition, so that we may take advantage of things occurring to us at the moment (those which we would put in the margin if we were using a tablet). Such a composition "must be conceived on such lines that we shall find no difficulty either in departing from it or returning to it at will."[47]

"But the crown of all our study and the highest reward of our long labors is the power of improvisation," especially for an advocate who cannot always count on having time to prepare himself, and must instead rely on the agility and readiness which he has acquired by practice and training. *Ex tempore dicendi*, "improvisation," calls first of all for knowing the order in which the points of an argument proceed, from first to second to third and so on. *Divisio* is absolutely essential to establish the "modus et finem," "method and conclusion," of a composition. The mind must be so trained that it can pay attention to the invention, arrangement, and style both of what we are saying at the moment and what we will say next, for an extemporaneous speech must especially exhibit "an orderly, ornate, and fluent manner" and have "regular pattern" – "in plures simul continuas," "among many different things continuing design at the same time."[48]

To ensure such facility, Quintilian counsels that, together with all the relevant questions, persons, and arguments, we must keep before our mental eyes "rerum imagines" or *phantasiai*. The phrase is used technically here, to refer to those vivid images of "the thing[s]," those which we have associated with the *res* of our composition. Their function is not only to keep track of the composition's form (as it is in *Ad Herennium*) but to awaken the emotions of the orator.[49] "Maxima enim pars eloquentiae constat animo. Hunc adfici, hunc conspicere imagines rerum . . . necesse est."[50] The greatest part of rhetorical activity involves the functions of the sensory soul, forming, combining, reacting to, storing, and recollecting sense images. Quintilian more particularly describes the value of the *phantasiai* to the orator, for thereby "things absent are presented to our *animus* with such vividness that they seem actually to be before our very eyes."[51]

The mature orator will use all three methods of composition. He will write out and memorize some of his speech (perhaps the beginning) and may use his tablets as he is composing to perfect particular phrases, he will above all carefully plan out and prepare the bulk of his oration by *cogitatio*, and be able to adapt to sudden turns of a case, or to sudden inspiration, by speaking extempore when he wants to. Cicero himself kept "notebooks" (*libellos*) of memoranda; Quintilian will allow, he says, the use of such jottings, which may even be held in the hand and occasionally glanced at. But "I think we should never write out anything which we do not intend to commit to memory."[52]

Throughout the Middle Ages, preaching included much *ex tempore dicendi*, as one might expect. The Dominican friar, Giordano of Pisa (he who first publicized eyeglasses), can be quite frank about his freedom. "I thought of preaching to you not about this, but about something else; but when it pleased Him that I should be so fluent in this, thank God this has really been a good sermon. But anyway I want to tell you a little about what I had planned to say."[53] On another occasion, "I am so full, and I have so much in me, and I am so rich that I do not know what to say to you: I have said nothing of what I prepared, not a thing."[54] The friar's sermons were taken down by reporters, whose comments are preserved;[55] this *reportatio* represented the first written version of the work, which Friar Giordano seems not to have subsequently corrected.

The written *reportatio* was customarily submitted to the author for emendation before being published. Deferrari quotes from Gregory Nazianzenus's farewell sermon: "Farewell, ye lovers of my discourses, in your eagerness and concourse, ye pencils seen and unseen, and those balustrades, pressed upon by those who thrust themselves forward to hear the word."[56] These "pencils" continued to be a fact of life in both the lay and learned circles throughout the Middle Ages; it is, I think, worth noting that Gregory refers to them as simple machines. He is, of course, being witty but his wit tells us something quite profound about the way in which the reporter's role was regarded. The scribe as such is not a thinking being, a reader or scholar, certainly not an *auctor* himself, but a mere "pencil," performing the humble and subservient task of writing.

Christian sermons were thus composed and published in the manner of all ancient orations, worked out mentally in the ways that Quintilian describes, written down at the time of delivery by reporters and then often corrected by the author before being made available for further dissemination in an exemplar. The Greek church historian, Socrates, says of Atticus, bishop of Constantinople: "Formerly, while a presbyter, he had been accustomed after composing his sermons, to commit them to memory, and then to recite them in church; but by diligent application, he acquired confidence and made his instruction extemporaneous and eloquent. His discourses, however, were not such as to be received with much applause by his auditors, or to deserve to be committed to writing."[57] Atticus demonstrates exactly the sequence of training and proficiency which Quintilian describes, even though his results were disappointing to his congregation. And we must also notice that a sharp distinction is made between Atticus's "writing out" and memorizing *ad verbam* for oral delivery (regarded as a mark of ineptitude) and the exemplar written by a scribe which marks a text deemed worthy to be preserved.

St. Augustine composed mentally with much happier results than poor Atticus. In a 1922 article, R. J. Deferarri gathered much of the extensive evidence in Augustine's sermons which indicates the cogitative and extempore nature of their composition, among which this remark may stand as typical. In an Easter sermon on the text "et Verbum erat apud Deum" (Jn 1:1), Augustine speaks of how the "inner word" (God's *res*, as it were, which by grace informs human speech) is translated into ordinary discourse. The speaker has planned his sermon in his mind as an "inner word," which he will varyingly express to fit the occasion. "For I who speak with you," he says of his own habitual practice, "before I come before you, I mentally compose [*cogitavi*] in advance what I will say to you. When I have composed what I will say to you, then the word is in my memory. Nor would I speak to you, unless I had previously composed in my mind."[58] This mixture of prior *cogitatio* and purely *ex tempore dicendi* is a common feature not only of Augustine's sermons but of those of his contemporaries, Roman and Greek, and clearly continued throughout the Middle Ages. Not only does Augustine's *De doctrina christiana* assume that preachers will compose in this way; so, as we have seen, do the late medieval *artes praedicandi* of Robert of Basevorn and Thomas of Waleys. The reason for numerically dividing sermons is to allow the preacher to take off extempore without losing his place in his premeditated sermon (he would have no need for such an aid if he were reading from a written text), or to speak in terms of memory-design, to allow him to "gather together" material from other memorial *loci* into the *locus* where the "eye of the mind" is "reading" its text. Friar Giordano's admittedly extemporaneous sermons employ numerical *divisiones* just like pre-planned ones, pulled in from the numbered bins of his memorial treasury.[59]

Yet we must be careful not to regard the informal style of the popular sermon as caused by its predisposition to extempore composition. Quintilian, speaking for the central tradition of classical rhetoric, does not associate particular compositional methods with any of the three kinds of style distinguished in that tradition, nor with any particular genre of discourse. There are, however, two fatal errors in delivery which an orator can make (and these cautions are repeated by every writer on the subject through the Middle Ages). The first is to lose one's way in one's oration, hesitate, or be reduced to the need of a prompt. The second is to appear in any way to be reciting word for word a pre-written text. Quintilian counsels various ways of avoiding this, such as seeming to grope for a word, pausing, perhaps wondering aloud how to answer an opponent's charge, and other devices which give the effect of spontaneity. But genuine spontaneity is equally bad if one cannot achieve the same level of crafted eloquence one attains by careful *cogitatio*; that is why *ex tempore dicendi* is reserved only to masters whose memories are fully stored and effectively designed.[60]

This ability to appear unrehearsed despite elaborate preparation is what the Romans seem to have considered the crowning achievement of rhetorical *memoria*, regarded in the context of performance. In all the rhetorical textbooks, *memoria* preceeds *pronuntiatio* or "delivery" and the discussion concerns how to achieve facility and the mastery of memorial design necessary for this end. The assumption that writing is handmaid and servant to memory is once again demonstrated in this ancient prejudice against any composition appearing to have been written down in advance of delivery. Cicero says of the great orator Marcus Antonius: "he always gave the appearance of coming forward to speak without preparation, but so well prepared was he that when he spoke it was the court rather that often seemed ill prepared."[61] Cicero particularly stresses the orator's memory: "Erat memoria summa, nulla meditationis suspicio", "When he spoke his trained memory was of the best kind, giving no hint of prior meditational composition." I know of no more succinct demonstration of how greatly we misunderstand when we reduce ancient and medieval *memoria* to our word "memorization."

I would now like to consider two case studies of medieval authorship, which indicate in practice the distinctions I have drawn so far. The first is Hugh of St. Victor's "De arca Noe morali," a wide-ranging commentary on Genesis 6–7; the second continues Eadmer's account of Anselm composing his *Proslogion*. In his preface to "De arca Noe morali," Hugh describes how the work began as an exchange "in conventu fratrum," "in a gathering of the brothers," while he sat once with them responding to their questions. His *sermones* on that occasion so pleased them that he decided to write down what he had said: "However, because I knew certain things to have been especially pleasing to the brothers, I specially wanted to commit them to the care of my pen in a *collatio*, not so much because I thought them worthy to be written but because I recognized that material new to that occasion [*literally* 'unheard before then'] would be yet more pleasing in this way [i.e. written down]."[62] In other words, "De arca Noe" began as an oral exchange between

Hugh and a gathering of his fellow canons of St. Victor, the sort of *lectio* that Augustine hoped he might (but did not) have with Ambrose. Such a discussion session, during which the master responds to questions, and comments on the base text in the Bible by extending its meaning with reference to other texts, is called *collatio* by Isidore of Seville.[63]

Hugh's oral "collatio" on that occasion becomes then the basis for the composition which he commits to writing. This written version is what he actually calls his *collatio*, a word which was also used for the communal reading of the monks under their abbot and for the communal meal. Again, the link of reading, composition, and food is apparent; "De arca Noe" itself was certainly read at monastic *collationes* of various sorts, the mental meal to accompany the physical one. Evidently, in its many uses, "collatio" retained the idea of "gathering together," of texts with one another, of masters and students, and of monks over their reading at meals. It is also an informal stage of composition, between purely oral exchange and something that has achieved the finish which makes it "worthy" of the scribe's ministrations. In short, it has the status of a *dictamen*, something with which Hugh felt free to fiddle even as he wrote it out.

At the end of Book II of this work, Hugh introduces a tree-figure, the "arbor [or 'lignum'] sapientiae," which grows in holy hearts as in an invisible Paradise, and which embodies allegorically both the Tree of Knowledge in Eden and the Tree of Life in Revelation. It is introduced in characterizing epithets, a series of fifteen rhyming phrases of three words each (one is actually six words made up of two apposite phrases),[64] and having given the list, Hugh announces to his audience that he intends to rest for a little while, since an overly long sermon is not profitable.

He takes the matter up again in Book III. He will expand each item in the series announced at the end of Book II: "[h]ic ipsius incrementi gradus, quos ibi breviter et summatim perstrinximus, latius per singula prosequendo explanabimus."[65] We remember the phrase "breviter et summatim" from his advice on reading in *Didascalicon*; this third book of "De arca Noe morali" may be considered a practical application of what Hugh advised there. Each *summatim* phrase is expanded in a *capitulum* in Book III, in the same order announced at the end of II. So the first phrase of the passage in II, 18, describing the tree as "per timor seminatur" is the subject of III, 1: "De seminatione arboris sapientiae per timorem." The second, "per gratiam rigatur," is the subject of III, 2: "De rigatione arboris sapientiae per gratiam," and so on, in unviolated order. The order of the phrases themselves follows that of the growth of the tree and its fruit: planting, watering, the seed sometimes being sterile, sometimes rooting, germinating, opening, growing, strengthening, greening, leafing and branching, flowering, fruiting, ripening, being harvested, and finally eaten.

This compositional structure is mnemonic. The rigid steps (*gradus*) in the growth of a tree provide Hugh's heuristic as he composes. To each stage of growth, Hugh has attached a Biblical *dictum* concerning wisdom, usually a verse or two defining the word *sapientia* as a virtue or quality (*timor Domini, gratia, dolor, fides*, etc.). So the basic mnemonic order is the stages of tree-growth to which the thematic texts on wisdom are "attached." Each growth-stage with its primary text is the subject of one chapter, and is stated in a rubric at the start. Within this essential structure, a number of excursive topics are developed from a phrase or word of the rubric; these may "bring in" other texts. Basically the structure is that of a concordance, or *catena*, in which the parts are associated by key-words, each of which pulls other texts and sayings with it, "compounding with interest," as Hugh's Chronicle preface promises. It is also easy to understand, considering such a compositional plan, how the metaphor of fishing came to be commonly associated with mnemonic work.

We know that Book III is extempore because Hugh tells us so at its end. He apologizes that the whole thing has been a digression from his real subject, which was the building of the *arca sapientiae*. He says that it ballooned (or blossomed) from his discussion in the second Book, and that he had not planned it:

But now, while we have been following out the by-ways of our exposition, we have digressed a long way from what we had proposed. Wherefore for this also we beg your indulgence, because, as I truly confess, most often in this treatise we have invented many things while writing than we have written down having already worked them out. So likewise in this matter I blush to confess my foolishness. Now, however, we will continue by returning to our plan, concerning the making of the ark of wisdom.[66]

Despite his assurance to us in the Prologue that the version he is setting before us is, though informal, a *written* composition, Hugh includes this lengthy extemporaneous digression, for which he apologizes with red face as being "longius a propositio nostro." Are we are to conclude from this that Hugh was as prone to spontaneous digressions when he was writing as we would expect a speaker to be? And that the heuristic structures of his memory-library are as apt to show (or be disguised) in a written composition as in a spoken one? It is evident that we must.

A great deal has been made of what is called the "oral style" of medieval sermons, and its supposed differences from "written style" or "authorial style." Oral style, in this theory, is characterized by repetition, verbal formulae, digressions, especially of a colloquial or "informal" kind, and parataxis above all. Written style, by contrast, is hypotactic and "periodic" in the Latin manner, marked by subordination and subdivisions; it contains longer and more unusual words, is "non-repetitive," and self-consciously artful. This distinction has been raised in this century to the status of a truism in literary analysis, but, unlike many truisms, this one is not true. It rests upon a genuine tautology, which causatively associates the stylistic features of a particular text whose compositional conditions are known with its method of composition; these features are then used to "prove" that the text was composed in a particular way.[67]

What can we deduce from style alone about the methods by which a work was composed? Nothing at all. Medieval writers extended the classical canons of stylistic decorum by applying them not just to content and genre but to types of audience. Thus a sermon preached to the "people" would require a popular style in order to be understood, while one preached to a learned audience would require a more elevated, *gravis* style. But medieval writers did not associate the levels of style with compositional methods. Hugh clearly had no real objection, despite his blushes, to leaving his meditation on *arbor sapientiae* as Book III of his written text; indeed, if he did not confess it himself, there is no way from its style that one could tell he was composing extempore, so little does the third book differ in terms of sentence structures, vocabulary, complexity and artfulness of expression, from the others. The composition of "De arca Noe morali," from what Hugh tells us, involved at certain points all three of the compositional methods described by Quintilian: it is a premeditated *collatio* with an orderly *praepositum*, it is written with a stylus, and it is also at times at least *ex tempore dicendi*. Moreover, it is typical that medieval composition involved all of these methods.[68]

Eadmer's account of Anselm tells us some interesting things about the status or "authorization" of the various products of the compositional stages. The written product of Anselm's lengthy and arduous *cogitatio* (which we have already examined) is called by Eadmer a *res*. This Anselm wrote onto tablets as soon as ("ilico") he had finished his completed design. Eadmer tells us that Anselm gave these wax tablets to the brothers for safe-keeping. After a few days, he asked for them again but they could not be found. So, "Anselm wrote another draft on the same subject [*aliud de eadem materia dictamen*] on other tablets, and handed them to the same monk for more careful keeping."[69] But these tablets were found thrown on the floor, their wax broken and scattered. The monks collected the pieces and brought them to Anselm, who was able to piece the wax together and with difficulty ("vix") recover the writing. "Fearing now that by some carelessness it might be altogether lost, he ordered it, in the name of the Lord, to be copied onto parchment [*pergamenae jubat tradi*]."[70]

Eadmer calls what was on the first set of tablets "res" and the second "dictamen." Anselm's "res," when lost, is easily recovered by him from memory; he asks for the tablets after some time has elapsed, finds they are missing, but is untroubled by their loss. But the second set, called "dictamen," he pieces together with difficulty, and decides to have copied onto parchment at once to prevent their loss. This suggests that the "dictamen" was a much revised, expanded, and polished version of the "res," which cannot be as readily reconstructed. (It would also seem that Anselm, in the eleventh century, was more inclined to use a stylus and wax tablets for composition than was Thomas Aquinas in the thirteenth. I mention this simply as a caution against interpreting the differences in their techniques as influenced by something more than individual choice.)

Eadmer tells these stories of Anselm's difficulties in composing *Proslogion* not to talk about his compositional methods – for to him there was nothing noteworthy in them – but as moral tales, to indicate that Anselm's work was not taken seriously at first by his fellows, when it was in its pre-exemplary state. The long time that *Proslogion* spent on wax tablets before it went on to parchment is meant to convey this undervaluing, as also is the astonishing carelessness of the monks entrusted with it. (Only the devil – if he were responsible for the breakage – seems to have understood its significance.) But on parchment the text will become safe – it is worth noticing that the motive for making the exemplar is safety.

This initiates another stage in the full composition of *Proslogion*. Parchment support makes the text not only safe but public. This decision by Anselm was made, Eadmer says, "livore carens," "ungrudgingly," invoking a venerable commonplace that attributes the publication of a work to the author's generosity, humble spirit, and freedom from envy. It is interesting that the sin resisted is envy. We moderns with our firmly-held assumptions about intellectual "ownership" and the consequent possibility of "theft," might be inclined to attribute non-publication to avarice, miserliness. Attributing envy, however, suggests that the motive was thought to be pure "malice," an act against society itself. So an author who does not share his work and launch it, as it were, into the stream of literature, is thought to be guilty of a sin against community. The last step of authorship is to overcome such envious feelings and submit one's work to the communal process of "authorization" through public comment and readerly response.[71]

The end of Eadmer's story of the finishing of *Proslogion* comes with Gaunilo's criticism of its arguments, and Anselm's further response, both of which he incorporated into the text itself:

This work came into the hands of someone who found fault with one of the arguments in it, judging it to be unsound. In an attempt to refute it he wrote a treatise against it and attached this to the end of Anselm's work. A friend sent this to Anselm who read it with pleasure, expressed his thanks to his critic and wrote his reply to the criticism. He had this reply attached to the treatise which had been sent to him, and returned it to the friend from whom it had come, desiring him and others who might deign to have his little book to write out at the end of it the criticism of his argument and his own reply to the criticism.[72]

Anselm's humility is exemplary, but, unlike Eadmer, that is not what I find interesting in this account. In the first place, we note that an unknown reader, Gaunilo, composed a criticism of Anselm's text which he simply wrote out as though it were a continuation of it. Moreover, he is not the one to send it to Anselm; a friend of Anselm's does this, sending a copy of the text with Gaunilo's addition that has come into his possession. This behavior would get a modern reader a stiff fine, if not jail, but Eadmer finds it unremarkable, not reproving Gaunilo's manner of publication in the least. And indeed scholars familiar with medieval readers' habits of simply adding material as the spirit moves them to texts by someone else will not be surprised either. It is a mark that one's work has been truly read, and made his own, by someone else, and this in turn is another way of indicating that it is gaining "authority," as it generates further texts.

We can watch, in this history of the *Proslogion*, the initial stages of its "socialization," as it were, as it enters public memory and becomes "literature." The authority of the original work, to come into full being, requires that there be a Gaunilo, as it also requires Anselm's reply to him – and the many comments, pro and con, that it has generated since. For a text achieves full authority not by closing debate but by accumulating it – that, I think, is what we can learn from Eadmer's tale, about what constituted the "originality" of a text for a medieval public. Notice that Anselm, welcoming Gaunilo's response (I see less humility in this than joy at being finally taken seriously), simply adds his own comments to Gaunilo's comments and instructs that both sets of comments be incorporated as the end of the text in all subsequent copying. His behavior suggests to me that once his work was made public (in an exemplar) Anselm saw himself as a co-equal reader along with other readers like Gaunilo, adding to the readerly flow that keeps the work alive and "original" in its proper sense. A modern author, responding to critics (let us say in a revised preface) relegates them to the footnotes or to selective quotation; and we expect this because, to us, his "authority" attaches to him personally, *he* is author. But the way Anselm treats it, "authority" is a property of the text, proven by its ability to generate other work; once the original exists, he places himself with Gaunilo as equally its reader, and what he thinks of the merits of Gaunilo's comments is given the status simply of more commentary, further dialogue.

This same observation concerning Anselm's attitude toward his written work is made by Brian Stock in his fine analysis of Anselm's description of the way he came to compose the *Monologion*, which began and was carried out in a way like that of Hugh of St. Victor's "De arca Noe morali."[73] Stock emphasizes two matters: first, that Anselm regards his written version as the result of a process that is "reductive" not complete; secondly, that the text both results from and remains the focal point of a "dialogue" Anselm has in his own mind (in *cogitatio*), with his clerical brethren (*Monologion* began as "sermones" which his brethren requested him to write down in an exemplum), and finally with "a putative reading public."[74] In the case of Gaunilo's response to *Proslogion*, that public was putative no longer, and it is both significant and as typical as anything can be of the Middle Ages, that Anselm immediately invited it, in writing, into his text. If his first written exemplum is "reductive" (in Stock's word) it is so only as it offers the germ *in pagina* of subsequent dialogue – indeed, it requires dialogue in order to achieve its proper textual function. Anselm says that *Monologion* began "in familiar conversation" ("sermones colloquendo") with his brother monks, thus, like Hugh, emphasizing the communal talk that started and will sustain his work. This is not just a monkish peculiarity, I think, though the ideal of such a dialgoue-text could be well realized in such a setting. The principle behind it is fundamental in the rhetorical tradition of text-making. As a "composition," the written exemplum is expansive; it offers a "common place" which collects subsequent comments, glosses, references, as readers apply, adapt, restate, meditate upon it. Truly it is commentary and imitation which make a text an "auctor" – not the activities of its writer but of its readers. This has little to do, I think, with literacy, but everything to do with the institutional nature of literature in a memorial culture.

The author's *dictamen*, whether scribally transcribed or not, was thus a sort of memorandum of his composition at a particular stage, which he might reconstruct or revise almost continually, as he worked to perfect his *res*. In this sense, the modern notion of a "finished" work is quite foreign to medieval authorship. Authors would issue versions of a work which they still intended to perfect to scribes for copying onto parchment, perhaps in an effort to make them "safe," as Anselm wanted to do. Chaucer's *Troilus and Criseyde* circulated in at least one shorter version than the one we now possess, as Root demonstrated long ago. A note by the scribe before several blank lines on one folio page in the St. John's College, Cambridge, manuscript indicates that "her faileth thyng þᵗ is nat yt made."[75] And the two versions, F and G, of the Prologue to *The Legend of Good Women* clearly represent different "publications." The visions and revisions of *Piers Plowman* were once thought to be so unusual as to constitute *prima facie* evidence that multiple authors were responsible, but in fact the phenomenon is not uncommon in kind, though perhaps Langland was unusual in the degree of his revisions.[76] Petrarch habitually continued to revise autograph copies of his works after he had sent a version off for transcription and circulation; this is true both of his poetry and prose works.[77] And the revising process was not limited to the first author. Readers, in the course of familiarizing a text, became its authors too. No modern reader would think of adapting and adding to the work of someone else in the way that medieval readers freely did, sometimes indicating the difference by writing their own work in margins, but often not. The results plague every editor of a medieval text.

Perhaps because of the familiarity of their language, readers seem especially to have recorded in vernacular texts the ways in which they had made them their own, by adding passages, incorporating comments, respecting the *res* but not necessarily the *verba* in the manner in which *memoria* expands during meditation. The more amateur a production (one can really only use such a word after the twelfth century) the more apt one is to find this, since these were made for private use. Among English works, the manuscripts of *Piers Plowman* are particularly notorious. Unlike the professional scribe, whose job was to copy not to read, an amateur writing for him- or herself was writing as a reader, whose task was to make one's own what one finds in texts. Rather than condemning them for this, we should understand that such wholesale private commentary is a form of compliment, a readerly contribution to the text's continuation, and a judgment that it is worthy to be a public source for *memoria*.

I have spoken of the medieval book as a support for the various activities of *memoria* – no format shows better its compositional, cogitational, *catena* characteristic than the lay-out of the glossed books, which developed during the course of the twelfth century in France, particularly in Paris. They have been the subject of a penetrating study by Christopher de Hamel, who has demonstrated how they came into being just after the compilation of the line by line Biblical commentary known as the *glossa ordinaria*.[78] This "standard commentary" was "simply a practical aid for students beginning on their study of the Bible," as G. R. Evans calls it, "distilling out the essence of the work of previous centuries" to present "a manageable and reliable" introduction in brief, summary, *ad res* form that was keyed specifically to the Bible text itself and did not try to address large questions or explore difficult matters.[79]

The glossed book's layout, difficult to set up and copy, was reserved for works that were among the most fully institutionalized (that is, "authorized" in the sense I have been developing in this chapter) – the Bible, especially the Psalms and the Pauline Epistles, books of canon law, and (by the late fourteenth century) the works of certain classical authors. The layout presents graphically the process of this authorization, for the compiled comments are written all around the author-text, keyed into it, *catena* fashion, via red underlinings, heuristic symbols, and other punctuation (in one early layout the Biblical words being commented on were written out in red and the commentary in ordinary dark ink).[80] They are also among the most fully decorated of books – and they are those which must be fully memorized. *Catena* is a mnemonic layout, elementary in memory training, in which the source text itself serves as the ordered set of "backgrounds" into which material is keyed. The complete format was developed for the commentary compiled by Peter Lombard for the Psalms and the Epistles, a revision of the older compilation by Anselm of Laon. It is possible that Peter Lombard himself devised the format, leaving it to professional scribes to carry out; this would not be unusual for a master to do, though the format is extremely complex in execution – one thinks of Hugh of St. Victor's design for his *Chronica*, and of Peter of Poitiers's diagrammatic *Genealogia*, both also twelfth-century French products.[81] The source-text is written in the center of the page on alternate lines in the large, careful hand known as *textualis formata*, and the commentary, hooked into it via key-words and phrases, is written in a smaller hand around it. One immediately sees the textual relationship of source to commentary; one is also provided with a mnemonically useful image to help to place the commentary safely in one's memory, *catena*-style. Recall how Hugh of St. Victor advises his students to pay close attention to the shapes of the letters and the colors on the page in order to fix a memorial image of the text – the glossed format seems deliberately designed to present memorable variations of letters (the different hands) and colors, for each page is unique. These different hands became conventionally used for these different kinds of text; the large hand developed into fully-formed Gothic script; the smaller, squatter hand was used for commentary, even in books that did not reproduce a source text. Clearly, they were used to form a visual cue to the sort of text with which one was dealing.[82]

One of the best written of the glossed books of Psalms was made for Herbert of Bosham, a confidant of Thomas Becket, probably in the late 1160s (figure 5).[83] It was made in two large books, so extensive was the project; it presents the texts of both Jerome's "Gallican" and "Hebrew" translations of the Psalms, and Peter Lombard's commentary. The first volume is now in the library of Trinity College, Cambridge (MS. B.5.4) and the second in Oxford (Bodleian Library, MS. Auct. E inf.6).[84] One of their more original features is the use of painted figures to help fix the page as a mnemonically functional visual image. These figures usually inhabit the outermost margins of the page. The gloss itself is carefully annotated, with the sources of the commentary identified (Jerome, Augustine, Casiodorus) and a system of patterned dots is established as a unique additional "signature" for each of the main sources (such indexing patterns seem to be quite common in glossed layouts; one thinks of the use of similar systematic *notae* for concording purposes which we see in Grosseteste's books, for example). The painted figures are a part of this apparatus: so, a bearded man labeled Augustinus (or Cassiodorus or Hieronimus) points a javelin at the commentary text. He holds a banderole on which is written a warning such as "Ego non probo" or "Hic michi caveat" or "Non ego"; it is significant that these figures seem only to mark disagreement among commentators. In addition to these figures, several of the psalms have emblematic pictures painted next to their opening words; unlike the citational figures, these can occur in the inner margin where the gloss itself is written, as well as in the outermost one, suggesting that they too were considered essential in the gloss, and acted as markers for these particular psalms. Unfortunately, both manuscripts were badly mutilated by someone who cut many such figures out of their pages, so that whatever system there may have been is now lost; it is apparent, however, that certain of these figures were deliberately repeated. A figure of "Ethica" holding a dove and a serpent, for instance, appears at the beginning of Psalms 4 and 11; the figure of a soul in flames, with the legend "Homo in igne, Deus in homine" is repeated at the beginning of Psalms 2, 8, and 81.

This textual format, serving the memorial layout of *catena*, is thus an applied mnemonic containing numerous visual helps to memory in its features, and also laying out graphically the relationship of the "auctor" and all its progeny, including their disagreements. The way in which the commentary is woven together around the "auctor" illustrates how the authority is understood as source-word rather than as final-word, the way we tend to understand it now. In a properly designed memory, just as on these pages, the verses of the source will be like a line with many hooks on it, and as one pulls in one part of it, all the fish will come along. To pull in one text is to pull all the commentary, as well as other texts concording with it. Source, glosses, citations, punctuation, and decoration are all married up together in a single memorial image which constitutes "the text"; one cannot meaningfully talk for long about one of these strands in isolation from the others, for that is not how they were perceived. They all serve *memoria* practically (they help to form the heuristics of order, unique address, division, and composition needed for safe storage and retrieval) and they also image its institutional nature. A work of literature was not taught in isolation, as an artifact produced by some person long dead whose intention we must now "recover," but as an ever-rolling stream accumulating and adapting over time as it is "collated" with its multitude of readers. *Collatio* means all these things: bringing together of texts, conversations about texts, and feeding upon texts as one feeds at a community meal.

The format remained very popular, especially for university use. A copy of the Gregorian Decretals with two distinct levels of identified commentary in it (law commentary was usually signed with the initials of the master responsible for it) plus additional comments in other hands shows in a wonderfully visual manner how the source text has been wound about with generations of commentary. In this manuscript (Bodleian Library MS. Lat. th. b. 4, originally completed in July of 1241 at Bologna) the originating text is written in a large formal hand in two columns down the center of the page, with the commentary about it on all four sides (figure 6).[85] Margins have been left between the two parts of the book and between the two columns of text; these contain ink decorations and comic drawings, such as a fox chasing a rooster (f. 37) and a cat with a mouse (f. 84v). But these margins have themselves been written over with other commentary (though the drawings are usually left alone); in addition there are interlinear glosses in the main text. So the page presents a "text" that consists of a great many margins, those margins traditionally left for the memorial activities of readers over time. And these responses form an integral part of the public presentation of "the text"; indeed, in this manuscript, the original text seems almost overwhelmed by its margins, as is perhaps suitable for a legal book. In earlier glossed books, scribes ruled an extra margin for current readers when the complex of written text and gloss threatened to crowd out the blank space of the page. Blank space is needed both to ensure a clean, crisp image of the text (for *turba*, "crowding," is a great enemy of memory) and to allow one to make one's own *notulae*.[86]

There are manuscripts in which the commentary has been written out in the margins, while blank space has been left for the main text, unfinished by the scribes. One such is Newberry Library MS. 31.1, intended for a text of Fulgentius's allegorical paraphrase of pagan myths, with Pierre Bersuire's "On the features of the pagan gods" used as a commentary.[87] It is an odd way for a manuscript to be left, for usually the source text was written first with the commentary fitted in. This manuscript was used despite what to us would be an insurmountable handicap, presumably by those who had the source so well memorized that they attached the commentary to it mentally. In this regard, it is significant, I think, that this empty page space has been respected by readers, whose own notes are written in the expected place, outside the margins of the commentary, as though the unwritten space was also required in some way for the making of a proper memory image keyed to the mentally-supplied text – perhaps as a surface onto which textual cues could be projected in memory. In doing this they were following what had been the standard before the invention of the glossed layout, when line by line commentary on the Bible text was written out continuously, without all the keys supplied in a glossed book, and a reader had to supply the appropriate Bible text from the grid in his memory.

So important is the acquiring of commentary to establish an "auctor," that at least one medieval vernacular writer supplied an exemplar of his work in the form of a glossed book. There is a manuscript of Boccaccio's romance epic, *Teseida*, written entirely by Boccaccio himself, which is now in Florence, Biblioteca Medicea Laurenziana MS. Acquisti e Doni 325 (figure 7). It is on parchment, of course, written out with rubrics, initials, and even a few decorations, and space has been left for additional miniatures. It is obviously an exemplar, not a dictamen, so that its format was intended by Boccaccio to be copied by others. But it is a glossed book. The stanzas of the source text are written in the large display hand reserved for "auctors," and commentary, written in the appropriate script, surrounds it in the margins. These annotations, comments, and corrections are also Boccaccio's. As Pasquali says of this manuscript, "[Boccaccio] began and continued in fits and starts to add notes at one or another point in his poem (at times brief interlinear interpretations, at times erudite excursus), without having completely compiled a running commentary," though he seems headed in that direction. In *Teseida*, Boccaccio is both the originator of his text, and its reader; his own commentary invites commentary from others. And, of course, *Teseida* itself is a re-presenting of the classical legend, with Statius quite clearly remembered – so Boccaccio as composer is also, simultaneously, a reader.[88] Evidently, Boccaccio considered the heart of the process of making literature to be not the production of a beautifully written out "final" text, but the unending collocation which the author-text conducted with its readers in the margins, the "background" for memory. By giving his new work all the trappings of a glossed book, Boccaccio was claiming for it the immediate institutional status of an "auctor."

In conclusion, I would like to look at the matter of plagiarism, as pre-modern centuries defined it. It is sometimes said that there was no plagiarism before there was a law of copyright; this is not true. But plagiarism was differently defined, as a matter essentially of poor *memoria*. Composition cannot occur without "auctors," used in the way we have seen in these last two chapters. One's audience will, of course, recognize them and their translation to the occasion of one's own design, for they are in the public memory. The *memoria* of the composer and the *memoria* of the audience are thus bound in a dialogue of textual allusions and transformations, and not to engage in it is the mark of a dolt.

Thus Quintilian scorns orators who simply repeat the words of others, or who boilerplate their own speeches, as much as he scorns those who appear to be rehearsing a word-for-word memorized speech. How shamed they should feel, he says, "at displaying this miserable piece of furniture to an audience whose memory must have detected it so many times already: like the furniture of the ostentatious poor, it is sure to show signs of wear through being used for such a variety of different purposes."[89] *Ad res* memorizing supposes that the reader will recreate the original's *sententiae* in words that are at least partly his own; this freedom respects the fruitful *auctoritas* of one's source as ignorant parroting cannot. John of Salisbury, describing Bernard of Chartres's custom of making his students recite daily from the works which were to serve as their models, suggests a distinction between true and false imitation that is close to Quintilian's, and instructive:

if, to embellish his work, someone had sewed on a patch of cloth filched from an external source,[90] Bernard, on discovering this, would rebuke him for his plagiary, but would generally refrain from punishing him ... if an unsuitable theme had invited this, he would, with modest indulgence, bid the boy to rise in [true] imitation [*ad exprimendam auctorum imaginem ... conscendere*]."[91]

In a letter to Boccaccio in 1359, Petrarch writes of how he had thoroughly familiarized Virgil, Horace, Livy, Cicero, and some others:

I ate in the morning what I would digest in the evening; I swallowed as a boy what I would ruminate upon as an older man. I have thoroughly absorbed these writings [*michi tam familiariter ingessere*], implanting them not only in my memory but in my marrow ... But sometimes I may forget the author, since through long usage and continual possession I may adopt them and for some time regard them as my own; and beseiged by the mass of such writings [*turba talium obsessus*],[92] forget whose they are and whether they are mine or others'. This then is what I meant about more familiar things deceiving us more than others; if at times out of habit they return to the memory, it often happens that to the preoccupied mind, deeply intent on something else, they seem not only to be yours but to your surprise, new and original ... I grant that I like to embellish my life with sayings and admonitions from others, but not my writings [*Vitam michi alienis dictis ac monitus ornare, fateor, est animus, non stilum*] unless I acknowledge the author or make some significant change in arriving at my own concept from many and varied sources in imitation of the bees. ... I much prefer that my style [*stilus*] be my own, uncultivated and rude, but made to fit, as a garment, to the measure of my mind, rather than to someone else's ... each [writer] must develop and keep his own [style] lest ... by dressing grotesquely in others' clothes ... we may be ridiculed like the crow.[93]

I would like to suggest that this eloquent characterization of his own practices is less a manifesto of a new Renaissance spirit of individuality and freedom from the dead authority of some mythical "paradigm text" than a restatement of the very medieval description of reading and composing we encountered, also eloquently, in Hugh of St. Victor on the ark of wisdom. The life is adorned with others' maxims so that by the process of domestication their character stamps the character of the man and becomes that of his style (and here we must remember that *stylus* means both "pen" and "style" in our sense), cut, like good clothing, to one's own measure of ability, "ad mensuram ingenii mei." How the words of others become the measure of one's own mind is described earlier, the digestion and rumination by which they are made mine, "michi tam familiariter ingessere." Familiarizing makes the wholesale appropriation of one's sources "honorable," for, like a bee, one has transformed the many nectars of the reading-flowers in one's memorial storehouse into a single honey, "e multis et variis unum faciat." If they have not been so processed, then the imitation is dishonorable.

We, of course, would still regard the results as plagiarism, so long as the "idea" was recognizable. Perhaps that is because we think of plagiarism as theft and authors as owners with final rights to their work. But for Petrarch, as for Bernard and Quintilian, plagiarism occurs only when one unwittingly or from laziness quotes *verbaliter* because one's memory-design has been overwhelmed by the *turba* of all the pieces of one's improperly stored reading. That is a failure of memory, due to one's own neglect and sloth (including the kind of sloth that overworks the body); it is not perceived as a matter of theft. Plagiarism is to be avoided because it makes oneself appear ridiculous and shameful, like a clown in ill-fitting clothing, whose garments are not "familiar" to him. It is a failure of invention because it is a failure of memory, that educated *memoria* of the trained author, who knows how to speak without appearing to have memorized at all.

1. Pearl and gold jewellery used as a border, an allusion to the common trope of the precious jewels of memory, using as an example the "pearls" of Christian wisdom. From "The Hours of Catherine of Cleves."

2. Noah's Ark, in the shape of a four-legged wooden storage chest, floating atop a sea of drowned people, animals and giants. From 'The Ashburnham Pentateuch.''

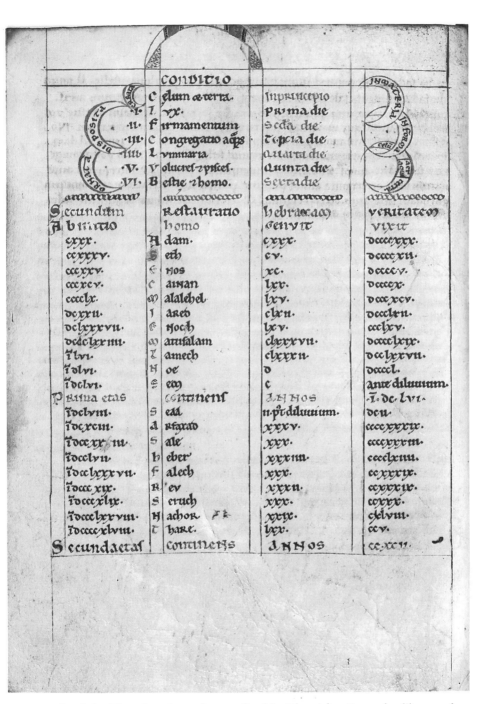

3. Hugh of St. Victor's column format for his *Chronicles*. From the library of St. Victor.

4. A page of Canon Tables from a late ninth-century Gospels made in the monastery of St. Martin in Tours.

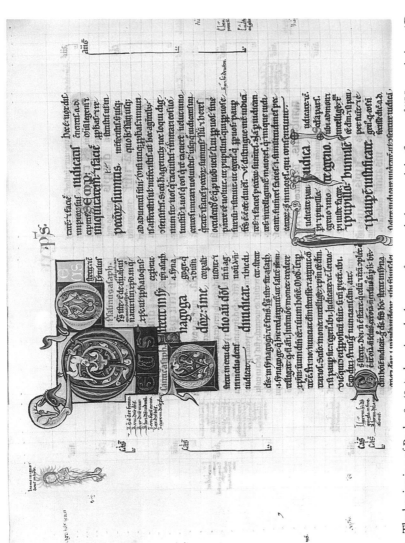

5. The beginning of Psalm 81 (82), showing the layout of text and gloss, and the figure of "Homo in igne / Deus in homine," "Man in fire / God in man". From Herbert of Bosham's Psalms with the gloss of Peter Lombard.

6. Fully glossed page from a Decretals. Notice how various readers have expanded the number of "margins" with their own glosses. In the center margin are drawings of long-necked creatures, and a fox chasing a rooster.

7. A page of Boccaccio's autograph of his *Teseida*; he wrote the text and gloss in different hands, and also made the large initials.

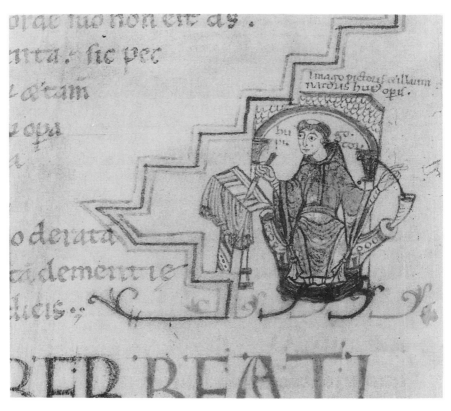

8. The inscription above the drawing of the scribe reads "Imago pictoris et illuminatoris huius operis. Hugo pictor," "The image of the painter and illuminator of this
work. Hugh the Painter".

9. Verse-illustration for the text of Psalm 148. From "The Utrecht Psalter."

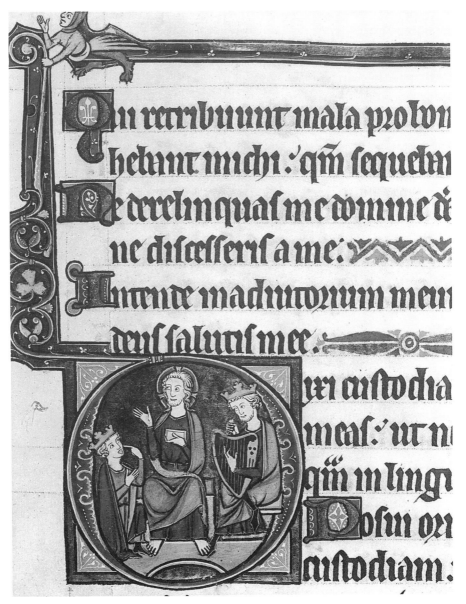

10. Initial of Psalm 38 (39). From "The Cuerden Psalter."

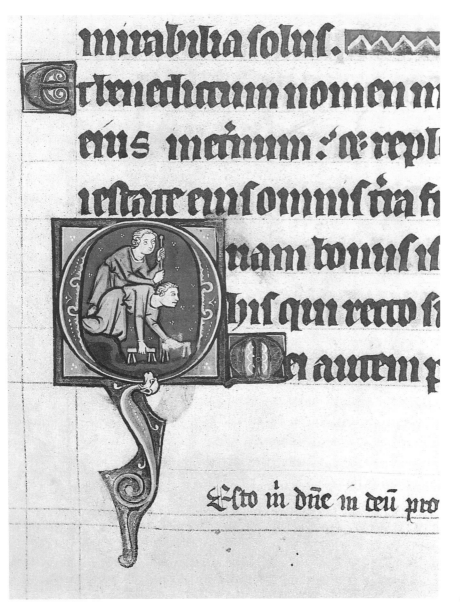

mirabilia solus.

Et benedictum nomen m

eius   magnum : & reple

iestate eius omnis tra h

nam bonus u

his qui recto si

si autem p

Esto in dne in deu pro

11. Initial of Psalm 72 (73). From "The Cuerden Psalter."

12. Initial of Psalm 79 (80). From "The Cuerden Psalter."

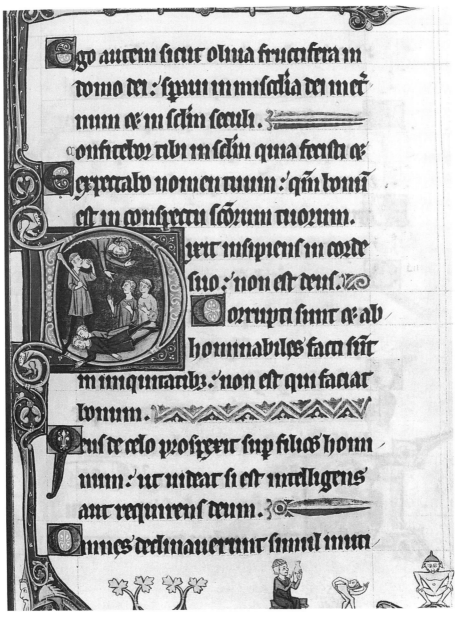

Ego autem sicut oliua fructifera in domo dei : speraui in misedia dei meorum & in selm seculi.

Confitebor tibi in selm quia fecisti & expectabo nomen tuum : qm bonum est in conspectu sanctorum tuorum.

Dixit insipiens in corde suo : non est deus. Corrupti sunt & abhominabiles facti sunt in iniquitatibus : non est qui faciat bonum.

Deus de celo prospexit sup filios hominum : ut uideat si est intelligens aut requirens deum.

Omnes declinauerunt simul inutiles

13. Initial of Psalm 52 (53). From "The Cuerden Psalter."

14. The drawing of a man on a gibbet cues the text, "And þeues loueþ and beleuþ hateþ and at þe last be hongyt" (line 138). Over the figure's legs seems to be written (the ink is badly rubbed) "Nota de mandatu," "make a note concerning the commandment," in reference to the underlined verses in Latin, lines 140a–c. From *Piers Plowman*, C. XVII. 118–148.

15. Hugo de Folieto's picture of his Preface to "Concerning the Dove and the Hawk."

16. Hugo de Folieto's picture of the chief themes of "Concerning the Dove and the Hawk."

17. Detail of dogs' heads and a banner marking a *titulus*, "Quid sit proprie spes,"
"what is properly hope," keyed to Augustine's *Enchiridon*.

18. Drawing of a dog and a rabbit, marking a notation that reads: "Signa humanam
benevolentiam," "mark human goodness," also for Augustine's *Enchiridon*. It seems
apparent from the grammar that "Signa," like the common "Nota," is an imperative
directed to the reader.

19. Detail of a dragon, marking the *Enchiridon*, with the annotation, "Signa utilissimam sententiam breuemque," "Mark this most useful and brief aphorism."

20. The start of a sequence of *bas-de-page* narrative pictures from "The Smithfield Decretals." A hunting dog is wounded by a rabbit-archer.

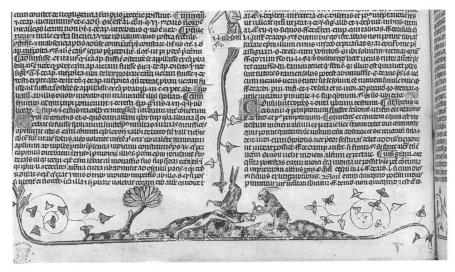

21. Two rabbits tie up the dog.

22. The dog is tried before a rabbit judge.

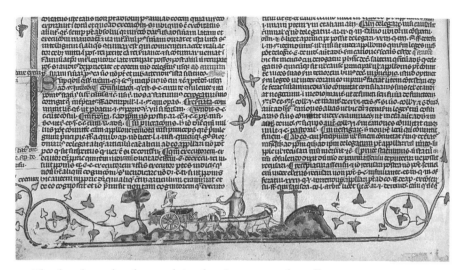

23. The dog, bound and gagged, is taken in a cart to the gallows.

24. The dog is hanged. A rabbit thumbs its nose at the corpse, while brandishing a victory banner.

Audite gregori comes in
dite. angelou gloria ro
manorum specialis a
postole. per thesum xpistum et
per virtutes quibus mirabilis
papa sedis apostolice fulsisti:
et venerandus patriarcha vni
uersalis ecclesie. Adiuua me va

25. Coins used as a border, an allusion to the common trope of memory as coins to be laid away in one's memory treasury. From "The Hours of Catherine of Cleves."

26. Bees in a hive and gathering nectar from flowers in the border, an allusion to a common trope of memory as the flowers of reading ("flori-legium") to be gathered by readers as bees gather nectar from their hives. From "The Hours of Catherine of Cleves."

27. Caged birds used as a border, an allusion to a common trope of memory as birds caged or penned in coops. From "The Hours of Catherine of Cleves."

Anctissime ac beatissi
martir laurenti. sup
plicter ego peccator fer
uus tuus pietatem tuam exoro
ut pro me spurcissimo multis
q̃ vittorum ponderib; oppresso
preces effundere digneris ad õ
nipotentem deum quatinus

28. Fish used as a border. Notice that they form a "chain," one fish fastening itself to the next, and that the chain is drawn by fishhooks, an allusion to the "hook" that draws a *catena* or "chain" of texts. From "The Hours of Catherine of Cleves."

30. The first page of the Gospel of Matthew (the text is Mt. 1: 18: "Christi hic generatio"), showing "Chi-rho-i" in large letters. Two sedentary cats and several mice, two of which are nibbling a communion wafer, can be made out at the right of the bottom of "Chi." To their right, at the base of the stem of "rho," is a black otter eating a salmon. From "The Book of Kells."

29. A picture-page, showing a grid format and frontal perspective towards figures set against a plain background. Compare the instructions for forming memory locations in Thomas Bradwardine's "De Memoria Artificiali." From "The Gospels of St. Augustine."

7

Memory and the Book

"PAINTURE" AND "PAROLE"

The importance of visual images as memorial hooks and cues is a basic theme in all memory-training advice and practice from the very earliest Western text we possess, the *Dialexeis*. In that pre-Socratic fragment, one is advised to fashion rebuses, or visual riddles based on homophonies, to recall the sound of particular words (*ad verba*) such as personal names, and heraldic images, such as Ares for anger, to remember themes (*ad res*). In a study of the architectural mnemonic, Herwig Blum sought to link this technique to the plentiful use of decoration, such as mosaic, frieze, and painting, in ancient buildings, both domestic (as at Pompeii) and monumental.[1] We have always known that certain classes of allegorical images, such as those in Renaissance emblem books, were to be used for meditational reminiscence, for their authors tell us so.[2]

The function of *picturae* in medieval cultures has been, I think, rather misunderstood. In 600 Pope Gregory the Great wrote a letter to the hapless bishop, Serenus of Marseilles, who had become concerned that some of his flock might be engaged in superstitious worship of the holy images in his church. To prevent this, he destroyed all the pictures, thereby scandalizing his entire congregation, which deserted him on the spot. This story has been understood as an early indication that medieval images were a strict form of iconography, pictorial writing. The art historian Emile Mâle analyzed the function of Gothic images as "the literature of the laity" ("laicorum litteratura").[3] The Gothic cathedral, Mâle argued, was essentially a Bible in stone and glass, its images designed to substitute for the written word in communicating the stories of the Bible to a lay congregation which could not read and therefore, Mâle assumed, had no other access to their content. The notion that the medieval laity as a group could not read has now been largely discredited by the accumulation of contrary evidence, from even the earliest medieval centuries. Such explanations also play down the fact that books and churches made for learned groups and liturgical use were also profusely pictured. But Mâle was not wrong in saying that the cathedral was a form of literature, only in his understanding of what that statement meant to a culture that did not share the bias ingrained in our notion of representational realism.

For that is a non-medieval bias. "Representation," as we have seen, was understood not in an objective or reproductive sense as often as in a temporal one; signs make something present to the mind by acting on memory. Just as letters, *litterae*, make present the voices (*voces*) and ideas (*res*) of those who are not in fact present, so pictures serve as present signs or cues of those same *voces* and *res*. Gilbert Crispin, the abbot of Westminster from 1085–1117, says this of *pictura*: "Just as letters are the shapes and signs of spoken words, pictures exist as the representations and signs of writing."[4] The Latin verb *repraesentare*, "represent," is derived from the word meaning "present in time," *praesens*. Abbot Gilbert's is not a mimetic definition but a temporal one, in keeping with the traditions of both ancient and medieval philosophy and pedagogical practice; the letters and other images are signs not primarily by virtue of imitating an object but by virtue of recalling something that is past to memory. This understanding requires that pictures themselves function "textually," as a type of writing and not something different from it in kind.[5]

With reference to this very medieval notion of what a picture is for, we may look at what Gregory wrote to Bishop Serenus:

It is one thing to worship a picture, it is another by means of pictures to learn thoroughly [*addiscere*] the story that should be venerated. For what writing makes present to those reading, the same picturing makes present [*praestat*] to the uneducated, to those perceiving visually, because in it the ignorant see what they ought to follow, in it they read who do not know letters. Wherefore, and especially for the common people, picturing is the equivalent of [*pro*] reading.[6]

Several aspects of this characterization require comment. First, Gregory says that the picture is for learning a story, "historia." It is not, in our sense, a picture of some thing but rather the means for memorizing and recollecting the same matter or story that written letters also record. Like Abbot Gilbert, Gregory insists that *picturae* are essentially textual in the way that they function. What writing makes present, pictures also present, namely "quod sequi debeant," "what [their viewers] ought to follow through on [in their own behavior]." Looking at pictures is an act exactly like reading. And reading, as we have seen, is a complex activity involving both an oral phase, that of *lectio*, and a silent one, of *meditatio*, committing the substance of the text to memory, re-presenting it in order to make it one's own. That is the nature of learning it (*addiscere*). So, as reading letters "praestat," "makes present," a story – and the Latin is emphatically temporal in its meaning – so too does seeing a picture. "[P]ro lectione pictura est" – picturing is the equivalent of reading and so can stand in for it (the force of "pro" in this formulation) *because it is also a rhetorical activity*.

Both textual activities, picturing and reading, have as their goal not simply the learning of a story, but learning it to familiarize and domesticate it, in that fully internalized, even physiological way that medieval reading required. But in order to profit from *pictura*, one must understand it rhetorically, as directly referential not to an object but to a text ("historia") and thus to the human memorative processes called reading and composition. The images' auxiliary nature with respect to writing keeps them from being used idolatrously. Bishop Serenus was scandalized by his flock, before he scandalized them, because they failed to recognize exactly this distinction. They took the images to be directly representational of things themselves, and, having thus objectified them, they reified and mystified them.

Pictura and *litteratura* remain intimately linked in the later Middle Ages. A good example is the work of Richart de Fournival, who was a canon of Amiens cathedral in 1240, and its chancellor in 1246; later he became a canon of Rouen, and chaplain to Cardinal Robert de Sommercote. He died not later than 1260. He is remembered for a work that exists in many manuscripts of the thirteenth to fifteenth centuries, *Li Bestiaires d'Amours*; so popular was it in its day that it acquired a sequel, *Li Response du Bestiaire*.[7] Richart designed his text as a picturebook, the writing and seventy-plus drawings of animals forming a unit. He explains his plan in a preface. All people by nature desire knowledge, he says, and because they live so short a time, they must rely upon the knowledge gained by others as well as their own experiences. To gain such knowledge, God has given the human soul the ability of memory.[8] Memory has two gates of access, sight and hearing, and a road particular to each of these portals. These roads are called *painture* and *parole*.[9]

Painture serves the eye and *parole* the ear. Both are equal means of access to the "house of memory," which holds all human knowledge of the past, and each has cognitively the same effect. But the "painture" of a text is not confined only to the pictures painted on a page, as Richart de Fournival makes clear. Its "painture" also includes the mental images which it raises in its readers'/listeners' minds: "When one sees painted a story, whether of Troy or something else, one sees those noble deeds which were done in the past exactly as though they were still present. And it is the same thing with hearing a text, for when one hears a story read aloud, listening to the events one sees them in the present."[10] It is significant that Richart uses the verb *veir* of what happens in memory both from something received from sight and from hearing. Because it is translated into predominantly visual images by the mind, even *lectio*, "lire," (reading-aloud) creates "painture." Thus, "seeing" is not confined to silent reading, any more than "speaking" is to reading aloud.

Because memory has these two gates, Richart says, he has designed his book to be especially memorable by enhancing both its *painture* and *parole*. In saying this he does not mean simply that he has put together a book with illustrations, although he has done this as well. "And I will show you how this text has both *painture* and *parole*," he continues: "For it is clear that it has *parole*, because all writing is made in order to signify *parole* and in order that one should read it: and when one reads it aloud, writing returns to the nature of *parole* [speech]. On the other hand, it is clear that it also has *painture* because the letter does not exist unless one paints it [that is, unless one gives it a visible form]."[11]

"And when you read," continues Richart, "this writing with its *painture* and *parole* will make me present to your memory, even when I am not physically before you."[12] This is a remarkable restatement of the idea, found in Isidore, that letters are signs of sounds (*voces*) which in turn signify things. Thus a written word has visual shape (its *painture*) and calls to mind sound (its *parole*); which one of these two senses affords the "gate" to memory thus depends not on whether a text was composed orally or in writing, but on how it is presented to its audience on a given occasion, whether by being read aloud or silently to oneself. The distinction Richart makes here is related to the long-standing, and at this time universal one between "legere clare" and "legere tacite," with their varying connotations concerning the readers' tasks. And in either case, the sensory gateway is always dual (though the proportions of "seeing" and "hearing" differ according to the two types of reading), for all words are both shape and sound by their very nature, and all sensory impressions are processed so as to act upon memory in the same way, making what is no longer physically before one present to the mind's eye. "On les veïst," says Richart of the events in the story of Troy, whether one comes to "see" them through looking at their pictures or reading of them in words.

Thus the visual presentation of a text was considered, at least by the learned, to be a part of its meaning, not limited to the illustration of its themes or subjects but necessary to its proper reading, its ability-to-be significant and memorable. Malcolm Parkes has spoken of punctuation and other aspects of lay-out as the "visual grammar" of language, as necessary to comprehension as the pauses and accents of spoken language.[13] This is another way of saying, in essence, that language has both *painture* and *parole* in its nature, precisely what Richart is talking about.

And the idea is articulated often. When, at the beginning of *La Vita Nuova*, Dante addresses his readers to explain the genesis of his work, he says that "in the book of my memory" he found "a rubric which says: Incipit Vita Nuova. Under which rubric I find written the words which it is my intention to copy into this little book; and if not all, at least their substance."[14] Somewhat later, he refers to "words written in my memory under large paraphs [that is, paragraph markers]." Charles Singleton has written cogently on Dante's use of this conceit to govern the progress and nature of his work, and the extent to which the image of himself as the scribe and glossator of a previously extant text is exploited.[15] What I want to emphasize here is that Dante, in composing, sees the work in visual form, written in his memory as pages with text, rubrics, and paraphs.

In a similar fashion, the English poet, John Lydgate, begins a poem on "The Fifteen Joys and Sorrows of Mary" by describing how he came to write it. First, he saw a Pity "sett out in picture," that is, the painted scene we now call the Pieta. As he inspects this "meditacioun" closely (and notice that the picture itself is termed the meditation) it resolves itself into "Rubrisshes departyd blak and Reed / Of ech chapitle a paraf in the heed / Remembryd first Fifteene of her gladynessys / And next in ordre were set hyr hevyness-ys."[16] Like Dante, Lydgate thinks of his poem as laid out in his memory like a written page, with an illumination, text, rubrics, and paraphs, a page of the book of his memory that seems in lay-out very like that of a fifteenth-century Book of Hours, which is the sort of memory book that a fifteenth-century poet's readers would know best. *Memoria* is stored and inventoried in such divisions, inscribed as visual images; this was the elementary pedagogy which Dante and Lydgate shared, and which long predates them both.

I have already mentioned a passage from Chaucer's *The House of Fame*, in which all the voices, the *parole*, of human beings are described as rising from earth to Fame's house, where they assume the shape of those who spoke them. It is an exceptionally exact realization in poetry of the traditional medieval understanding of what words are. These human *paroles* do more than just represent (in form and time) the *voces* of those who spoke them, they also come clothed in language's graphic form, its manuscript *painture*:

> Whan any speche ycomen ys
> Up to the paleys, anon-ryght
> Hyt wexeth lyk the same wight
> Which that the word in erthe spak,
> Be hyt clothed red or blak,
> And hath so very hys lyknesse
> That spok the word that thou wilt gesse
> That it the same body be,
> Man or woman, he or she.   (1074–1082)

The figures are clothed in red or black, according to the ink in which the letters forming these words were written. Chaucer has peopled his House of Fame with literature that has both *painture* and *parole*. He also gives us a precise image of how *litterae*, written in black and red, are signs of *voces* (both "voices" and "words") and *voces* re-present in our memories those no longer immediately present to us.[17]

The scribe who wrote out the letters was often identified as the "painter" or "picturer" of the manuscript. For example, a late eleventh century English manuscript from Exeter (figure 8) pictures a monk named Hugo, with his scribal pen and knife, identifying the portrait as "imago pictoris et illuminatoris huius operis." Very similar is a portrait of a monk named Isidore in a manuscript of 1170 written for the cathedral at Padua, which calls him the painter of the manuscript, and shows him in the act of writing. And the nun Guda wrote in her colophon, "peccatrix mulier scripsit et pinxit hunc librum."[18] Indeed, the earliest medieval evidence suggests that at that time, too, the scribe was most often also the book's decorator, and that often when an author wrote out his own text he also punctuated and decorated it in a scheme that he intended copyists to preserve. The Latin verb, *distinguere*, means "divide up," "mark," "punctuate," and "decorate," all activities pertaining to the fundamental task of *divisio*. Thus, Jerome admonishes later copyists to preserve his punctuation of the Bible. There is evidence that Eusebius himself designed the canon tables named for him; the decoration of the fourth-century *Virgilius Augusteus* (Vatican MS. lat. 3256) was done by the scribes. The earliest illustrations in books occur at the beginning of sections of the text in order to mark its divisions, thus serving as what Nordenfalk calls "a kind of pictorial rubrics."[19] The Augusteus manuscript of Virgil has colored initials, the earliest surviving examples of this feature, at the beginning of the first line occurring on each page, but such large initials were soon used to mark the beginning of each major division of a text. The monks at St. Albans in the twelfth century described the finishing of a text by decorator and rubricator as a task of exacting division, "ad unguem," which they were proud to have done "irreprehensibiliter."[20] Though the forms of decoration and rubrication they put in their book were very different from those in fourth-century use, their phrase recalls that of St. Ambrose laboring over his books *distinguendam ad unguem.* Nordenfalk observes that book decoration was born of "the necessity of providing a dividing and supporting framework for tabular texts," such as lists of numbers, or names of persons and places, or "words divided into syllables by punctuation."[21] Such phenomena need the "visual grammar" that lines and columns provide because they have no grammar of their own. But whereas the earliest kind of decoration one finds in papyri is of this sort, I do not think that decoration was generated solely to organize lists. It is rather a subspecies of punctuation itself, and thus basic to reading and retention, for to quote again Hugh of St. Victor's succinct aphorism: "Modus legendi dividendo constat." Manuscript decoration is part of the *painture* of language, one of the gates to memory, and the form it takes often has to do with what is useful not only to understand a text but to retain and recall it too.

One of the continuing themes in medieval manuscript illumination is the use of what some art historians call "word-pictures," or images that cue the text they accompany. The technique seems to me clearly related to the practice of making mnemonic *imagines*, and examples of it can be found which pre-date by many centuries the thirteenth-century revival of the *Ad Herennium.* The best known example is the Utrecht Psalter, of which a number of medieval copies seem to have been made.[22] Though the manuscript is ninth century, the style of its drawings reflects older models, Byzantine and even late classical. This suggests that these images belong to a long tradition of *imagines verborum* associated with the psalm texts; it seems to me that if the images were thought to be especially useful – for example, mnemonically – that would help to account for the longevity of the style, and for its continued copying.[23]

One example, adapted from DeWald's facsimile of the manuscript, will suffice as an illustration of the technique used for each of the psalms.[24] Psalm 148, "Laudate Dominum," calls upon the various parts of creation to praise the Lord. It is fairly long, and need not be quoted in full, but a summary of its constituent verses is useful for understanding the picture-scene which accompanies it in the Psalter (figure 9). The following are invited to praise the Lord: angels, hosts, sun and moon, stars, heavens of heavens and waters above the heavens (1–6); dragons and deeps, fire and hail, snow and vapours, stormy wind (7–8); mountains and hills, fruitful trees and cedars, beasts and cattle, creeping things and flying fowl (9–10); kings and all people, princes and judges, young men and maidens, old men and children (11–13), for God exalts "the horn of his people," Israel (14). The picture shows, at its upper center, a large figure of Christ ("Dominus") the Creator, in a mandorla (the globe of the created universe) – He is flanked by "angels." At each end of this upper space, or "heaven," is a half-figure, one holding up the "sun" and the other the "moon." Below the Christ are "mountains" and "hills." A "fire" is burning on them, and they are covered with "fruitful trees, and all cedars." On the ground, and in the tree branches, are "beasts, and all cattle, creeping things, and flying fowl." Beside the mountains and hills are two people, each with an open book (verse 6: "he hath made a decree which shall not pass"). They are at the head of four groups of people, "kings," "princes and judges" (dressed as soldiers), "young men and maidens," and "old men and children." At the bottom of the picture is shown "all deeps" and "dragons."

The picture of each psalm in this psalter provides a set of cueing images for its principle words (and I use the adjective in its original meaning, "beginning," as well as its modern one – these are the words that will "start off" the recollective chain). Both the *picturae* and the *litterae* together make up the *litteratura*, the "text," as presented in this book, and both address the ocular gateway to memory. The words, however, can also be sounded aloud, and so can also address its aural gateway. I think the pictures of the Utrecht Psalter provide an excellent example of what Gregory the Great meant when he said that images are a form of *litteratura*, which, like graphemes, recall not meanings directly but the words ("voces") which are the signs of meaning.

Another example, painted in a style quite different from the Utrecht Psalter though still using "word-pictures," is a Psalter now in the Morgan Library (MS. M 756), sometimes called the Cuerden Psalter, made in England, probably Oxford, around 1270. The use of word-pictures is unusual in thirteenth-century English art, more typical at this time of French art. There is a donor picture in the book, which would indicate the involvement of a lay patron, but Dominicans are also pictured frequently in its pages, suggesting that this Order had a role as well in its making.[25]

Each psalm in this book has an initial which is a rebus-like "picture" of some key words in the psalm text. Psalm 38 begins, "Dixi custodiam vias meas ut non delinquitur in lingua mea. Posui ori meo custodiam cum consisteret peccator adversum me," "I said I will take heed to my ways, that I sin not with my tongue: I will place a guard on my mouth when the sinner comes before me". The initial of this psalm in the Cuerden Psalter ("D") shows a nimbused Christ seated at the center of the picture (figure 10). David with his harp is shown to His right, and Christ covers David's foot with His own (this is a way of joining these two figures in their "location," as memory advice prescribes). The Christ figure looks to His left, where the same David figure is shown kneeling, and pointing to his extended tongue. The position of these figures suggests the mnemonic principles which

Bradwardine's treatise expounds, even though they were drawn some seventy years earlier. Christ is in the middle, and to His right is David, who is the subject of the first word in the text, "Dixi." Christ steps on David's foot, thereby joining the two figures in an action of hitting, touching, striking, or something similar. The left side of the scene provides an image of chief words in the second and third phrases of the psalm, "non delinquitur in lingua mea" and "posui ori meo custodiam." To remember the correct order of the words, one first looks to the right and then to the left of the central figure, their orderly joining being indicated by the actions of the central image, covering a foot in one case and looking in the other.

Another good example of the sort of "imagines verborum" that occur in the Cuerden Psalter is the initial to Psalm 72 (figure 11), which shows a crippled man moving about on his knees, while balanced by two low stools which he holds in his hands, while a second stooped figure with a staff goes behind him. This image refers to verse two of this psalm, "mei autem pene moti sunt pedes, pene effusi sunt gressus mei," "but as for me, my feet were almost gone; my steps had well nigh slipped". Psalm 79's initial (figure 12) shows two men imploring a large, kingly figure who holds a lamb in one hand; this is the first verse, "Qui regis Israel intende: qui deducis velut ovem Joseph" (sic in manuscript).

The initial of Psalm 52 (figure 13), which begins "Dixit insipiens," shows, on the left, a figure of the fool with a club, eating a round loaf of bread. This figure is often found in Psalters, to mark the initial of Psalms 13 and 52, which are virtually identical texts. (The round loaf refers to verse 4 [modern numbering], in which the "workers of iniquity" are said to "eat up my people as they eat bread.") But other figures appear in the initial as well as the fool. These refer to verses two and three; at the bottom of the round space inside the "D" are two male figures lying on the ground together in what appears to be a homosexual embrace: they are those who "are corrupt and are made abhominable in their inquities" (verse 2). To the right and top of the space, a nimbed Christ looks down and points to two other male figures, one of whom is tonsured: these refer to verse 3, "God looked down from heaven on the children of men to see if there were any that did understand, or did seek God." Reading this scene counter-clockwise from the top produces the correct order of the verses: "Dixit insipiens," "Corrupti sunt," and "Deus de celo prospexit."

One sees this impulse to provide textual pictures in late medieval manuscripts produced by lay amateurs, so it is not confined, at least by the end of this period, to learned productions. These amateur productions are often done in a style that is idiosyncratic and bears little relationship, either in iconography or in execution, to the books produced by professional workshops. This makes their use of pictures all the more interesting as an indication of what readers thought they needed in order to profit from a book.

Among amateur manuscripts, a copy of *Piers Plowman* in the Bodleian

Library (MS. Douce 104, written in 1427) contains drawings on almost every page, which relate to the poem in several different ways. Some are "imagines rerum," related to the content in a way that we seem to recognize easily, such as the drawings of the Seven Deadly Sins. So, opposite the text's brief description of the courtesan, "Pernel prout hert," is drawn a woman-dandy who wears a gorgeous robe and a belt with golden balls on it (f. 24). The text describing Gluttony is actually written (or rewritten) over a drawing of a figure with cup and a swollen belly (f. 29) – here the relationship of word and picture is made concrete. Others of the pictures are associated with marginal *tituli*; for example, opposite text discussing the duties of knights is a knight with the words "nota de kny3thod" written across it (f. 35v).

Still other images follow the precepts for "imagines verborum" by cueing either chief words or concepts of the text with which they are associated. For example, opposite a discussion of Charity appears the figure of a young man in hose and doublet holding a round mirror – this evokes (but does not explain) the line "Ac I seygh hym neuere sothly but as my-self in a miroure" (f. 74). A speech by Free-Will (Liberum Arbitrium) on how Holy Church is a love-knot of loyalty and faithful belief is accompanied by a drawing of a man hanged on a gibbet, an allusion not to the theme of the speech but to one line in it, "And þeues loueþ and beleuþ hateþ and at þe last be hongyt" (manuscript reading, (f. 79; see figure 14). Finally, a number of images are not obviously related to particular texts but recur at intervals in the margins, probably according to the reader's own system; chief among these is a figure suggesting meditation, shown either as a seated man holding his head on his hands (ff. 54, 63) or a male head shown gazing pensively at the text (f. 65). Douce 104 is an entirely personal production, written and decorated by one individual for his personal use; its text is basically that which modern editors recognize as C, but it contains a number of odd and idiosyncratic readings, suggesting that it may have been at least partly a production of *memoria*.[26]

MENTAL PICTURES

Painture, as Richart de Fournival's comments make clear, is primarily a function of words themselves. One could "paint" with words alone, making pictures solely from words that never seem to have been realized in what we would consider to be a pictorial way. Such purely verbal *picturae* are addressed directly to the memory of the reader, for it is only in one's own *vis imaginativa* and *memoria* that they are given picture form. The author is a "painter," not only in that the letters he composes with have shapes themselves, but in that his words paint pictures in the minds of his readers. And by the same token, all the visual forms in a book "speak," they have *parole*, sometimes literally represented in the form of a voice-scroll, the cartoon-like banner that emerges from a figure's mouth. In his translation of the *memoria* advice in *Ad Herennium*, Bono Giamboni adds to the Latin original the rule that memory images should not be "mute," "silent." They must speak. This carefully fabricated aural-visual synaesthesia (sometimes including the olefactory too) articulates and supports the physiological need to make "rich" images; one recalls how crucial a role synaesthesia played in the mnemonic successes of Luria's "S."

Examples of word pictures, which are described as "paintings" even though no drawing accompanies them are frequent in medieval literatures, both Latin and vernacular. Some interesting examples from the fourteenth century were described by Beryl Smalley in her book on the English "classicizing" friars, especially Robert Holcot, the Dominican who was closely associated with Richard de Bury.[27] Smalley discusses the "pictures" of two friars in particular, Holcot and John Ridevall, a Franciscan who lived somewhat before Holcot. Ridevall's pictures are found in his *Lectura* and Holcot's in his "Commentary on the Minor Prophets," both works addressed to clerics, who would have used the material in composing their own sermons. Smalley includes an index of seventy such pictures, culled from these works and others, and also prints a partial transcription of the ones in the Bodleian Library manuscript (MS. Bodley 722) of Holcot's commentary.[28] Smalley was concerned particularly with the sources of these images; it is clear from her discussion that some of their attributes are conventional, found even in classical literature, and some were apparently invented. My concern here is with the form in which they are presented.

Ridevall calls his images "poetica pictura," which are "painted according to the poets [*pingitur a poetis*]."[29] But they are not extracted from earlier authors, for they cannot be found in the sources he cites. They are, however, pictorial in their details, not abstract or simply narrative. And Ridevall insists that these pictures are images that he and his sources "painted." If we take what Richart de Fournival has to say about the way words paint pictures and apply it here, it will help us to understand Ridevall's meaning. His classical authors did indeed "paint" these images in a sense, but as the mental pictures which Ridevall has formed from their content. They arise from earlier texts but through the medium of his own image making, as a means for remembering. Smalley comments of the pictures that "[t]heir many . . . traits could hardly be illustrated," and concludes that they were never intended to be other than textual in form, "aural aids" to be used in preaching to keep up audience interest.[30] She is quite right in observing this. A textual picture, however, is as good as a painted one in addressing *memoria*, for it can be painted in memory without the constraints of paint and parchment. These are emblematic pictures. They function as compositional aids, the use which Ridevall's intended clerical audience would most readily have for them. They are "imagines rerum," which relate the parts of a theme like Faith or Sloth through a set of images, each of which is associated with one of its aspects (or divisions, in scholastic language).

A good example is Holcot's picture of Charity:

This is said according to Augustine's seventh sermon on John [vii, c. 4]: no one can say what sort of face love has, what shape, what stature, what sort of hands or feet she has.

Nonetheless she has feet, for they lead to the church. Whence from this image, it is possible to describe charity or love as a queen "placed" [*collocata*] on a throne, of elevated stature, of a well-made shape, married to Phebus, strengthened by children, nourished with honey, with a four-sided face and gold-appearing clothing, having hands stretched out dripping with liquid, ears open and straight, eyes flaming and devoted in wifely fashion, and goat-like feet.[31]

In other of Holcot's pictures, the attributes are also numbered, and the images are partially developed as a sermon might be, with texts, *exempla*, further definitions, and explanations. As Smalley notes, each attribute of the image is moralized by Holcot with a "string of quotations"; indeed, as she also observes, the *distinctio* is a "precursor of the 'picture.' Holcot's Child [one of these images] could be rewritten as a *distinctio*."[32]

The manuscript calls each of these allegories "pictures," indicating them by the word "pictura" written into the margin, but it is itself completely without decoration beyond the essentials of punctuation. These pictures are evidently entirely addressed to mental imagining, an aspect of the memory-directed "painture" which any text has. Holcot says as much himself. Of the picture of Idolatry, which is associated by him with the text of Osee (Hosea) 9:1, he writes that he places the painting of Idolatry "over" the letters "Noli letari," which begin the verse.[33] He says the same thing about his other pictures – each is placed "above" ("super") a particular text with which it is associated. These mental pictures organize the glosses to these verses and, as in a glossed book, are painted "above" or "upon" the author-text, "super illam litteram," exactly in the way written glosses are made "upon" an author-text. And the image has been mentally projected onto the letters of the page, as a way of remembering and organizing not simply a text but a whole apparatus of glosses from which one could develop a sermon.

One of the most characteristic features of twelfth-century pedagogy (which comes to us chiefly in the form of Biblical commentary, sermons, and meditational works) is the describing of mental pictures that are often, but not always, like diagrams which serve to consolidate, summarize, and "fix" the main contents of the commentational text. In the rest of this section, I would like to examine two of these in particular, which are roughly contemporary, and both of the mid twelfth century: Hugh of St. Victor's "De arca Noe mystica" and Hugo de Folieto's "De columba et acciptre," a part of his Bestiary-style treatise "De avibus." Only one of these (Folieto's) was drawn, presumably to an exemplar made by the author.[34] The other (Hugh of St. Victor's) was never drawn, and despite the diagram's elaborate "visualiza-tion" through it author's descriptive words, no scribe of its fifty-three surviving manuscripts seems to have attempted even a crude approximation of it. Evidently a medieval reader did not need to have pictures drawn on a parchment page in order to understand that a book or text had "picturae."

Hugh of St. Victor's text is called in various manuscripts "De pictura archae" or "de visibilia pictura archae" or "depinctio archae," as well as by what has become its modern title, "De arca Noe mystica." It is also frequently presented as the fifth book of Hugh's other commentary on this same subject, "De arca Noe morali."[35] Modern editors present the commentary *mystica* as a separate treatise, but it does share many of the same themes as its longer companion-commentary. Beryl Smalley called it a diagram, and she was clearly correct.[36] "De arca Noe mystica" is a cosmography – a combination of *mappa mundi* and *genealogia*, together with mnemonics for the vices and virtues (including the monastic virtues), the books of the Bible, a calendar, and other assorted categories of information – all put together as an elaborate set of schematics imposed upon the Genesis description of Noah's Ark. Hugh had likened the building of the Ark to the building of a medieval education, all tucked away in its various compartments with the pathways between them clearly marked – this treatise is a kind of demonstration of this governing figure, the archetypal memorial *arca*. Hugh himself calls it a "machina universitatis" (col. 702A), containing both a "mappa mundi" and a "linea generationis." And it organizes for mental storage the chief themes of Hugh's commentary *morali*, here presented both "summe" ("in summary") and "breviter."

The ark is presented in two projections, one as a flat plane seen from above (called the "planus," "plan"), the other an elevation ("altitudo") or cross-sectional view, and Hugh moves between these two as his purpose changes. Moreover, the details of the model are often incoherent, impossible to graph completely (I have tried) because they shift and change – indeed, this "picture" only works as a mental encyclopedia, whose lineaments can merge and separate and shuffle about in the way that mental images do, but two-dimensional ones fixed on a page cannot.

On a flat, rectangular surface – like the page of a book or a tablet, the page of memory – Hugh says that he "draws" and "paints" ("depingere," "pingo") a diagram.

First of all, in order to delineate the religious significances of Noah's ark, on the plane [which is also the plan] where I intend to paint it, I seek the midpoint, and there, having fixed that point I draw around it a small square, in the form of those cubits in which the Ark was measured. At the same time, I draw another square around this one, a little bigger. And so the space between the inner and outer square can be seen as the border of the cubit. Having done this, I paint a cross in the inner square, so that its horns touch each side of the square, and I draw over it in gold. Then I color in those spaces which are left on the surface of the square between the four angles of the cross and of the square: the two above in flame-color, the two below in sapphire. Thus the one half of the cubit in flame-color seems to represent fire, and the other half, in sapphire color, to represent cloud. After this, in the border of the cubit above the cross I write α, which is the beginning. Opposite it, under the cross, I write ω, which is the ending. On the right horn of the cross I write χ, which is the first letter of the word Christ, and also signifies the Ten Laws which were initially given to the ancient people, [who were] partially elected and so are, with justice, gathered on the right. On the left horn, however, I place ϲ [for final ϛ], which is the last letter in the word Christ, and signifies, in the number 100, the completion of grace, which was given to the gentiles, who seemed at first, because of their total paganism, to be gathered together on the left. Then I cover the space in the border on all sides with the colors of purple and green, the outer-side with purple and the inside with green, and in the middle of the golden cross which I made, I paint a year-old lamb standing upright.[37]

Aspects of this diagram are fashioned in accordance with familiar mnemonic advice of the most elementary sort. An empty, rectangular space is marked off into distinct compartments, each in turn "painted" with coded information recorded in both writing and pictorial images. These images function as cues, "imagines rerum," for remembering highly complex material; both the images themselves and their relationship to one another are mnemonically important. Once he has described its basic construction, Hugh then gives a lengthy "moralization" of the features he has placed in his mental diagram. The nature of this moralization is crucial to understand; Hugh himself explains it at the end of this treatise:

We have said these things about the configuration of our Ark, so that for whoever wishes to gaze mentally [*intueri*] upon the decoration of the house of the Lord and His wonders (of which there is no fixed number), this may sometimes stimulate his emotions [*affectus*] by way of example. (cols. 702D–703A)

Notice first that Hugh is clearly describing his own compositional image, "our Ark." Since much of the content is similar, but in an abbreviated form, to the concerns of Books I, II, and IV of "De arca morali," this diagram would appear to be at least a version of the mental plan or "imago rerum" from which he spoke his *collatio*.

Hugh had spent quite a lot of time in "De arca morali" on the details of lodging within the Ark, and he refers to this previous discussion. Concerning the raven, for example, he says: "These matters I have sown altogether more completely in that book which I have already dictated concerning the Ark." (col. 698D) From remarks of this sort, it seems clear that Hugh regarded his "pictura archae" as related to this other treatise, the "De arca morali," which preceded its composition and to whose themes and concerns this diagrammatic treatise refers. Hugh's "pictura archae" is thus not a picture of the Ark in the sense of being an illustration, even in allegory, of that object in Genesis; it is rather a "picture" of Hugh's earlier colloquies, and aids the related rhetorical processes of memory and invention. The diagram of the Ark *mystica* does not include the material in Book III of "De arca morali"; of course we remember that Book III, which I examined in my previous chapter, is a digression from his original plan. This diagram is thus personal to Hugh, and is presented to others as an example which may provoke someone else's imagination and memory, their "affectus."

Thus the diagram and its values are not seen by Hugh as prescriptive, nor are they exactly what we think of as "iconographical," if by iconography we understand the images to represent fixed, generally accepted meanings. Rather, it employs just that kind of associational heuristic which the scholastic writers distinguished from "universal" logic, and defined as particular to reminiscence. Basic to the pedagogy of memory is the caution that each individual must make up his own set of associations – what works for one will not automatically work for all. Because of this, the values which the images are given by one author can only be exemplary, not universally normative (as mathematical images are). In his moralization of the images in his diagram (and by "moralization" Hugh meant the process of giving something personal valuation or signification, "making it mine"), Hugh explains what his own associations with them are, but these are not consistent.[38]

So, for example, the purple color of the border of the central cubit may represent the blood of Christ's passion, and the green the rewards of grace which it made possible. Or, the purple may signify Christ's blood and the green the water by which, in Noah's day, the world was judged. Or purple might be the damnation of the wicked and green the liberation of the good. The moralizing procedure gathers an increasingly dense store of associations around the hook-image (purple, green), as the composer "looks" mentally at his images, down different chains of thought and in different contexts. It is important to notice how these associational chains vary – they may even be contradictory, as they are in the example I have just given. That is because the technique addresses the task of reminiscence. Hugh's memory diagram of the Ark is a meditational and compositional device, and it employs a scheme of "images" in "places" that Bradwardine would have recognized, even though the concept of an art of memory, as we have seen, was not something with which Hugh of St. Victor was likely to be formally familiar.

Having completed his "picture" of the central cubit (its importance to the Ark based on Genesis 6:16), Hugh turns to the plan of the whole structure that extends out from it. A quadrangular figure is drawn again around the midpoint, but this one corresponds in the ratio of its sides to the dimensions of the Ark itself, being six times as long as it is wide (Hugh admits, however, that this is an awkward ratio, and so for convenience' sake four to one is more easily managed). Across this area four lines are extended, two laterally and two vertically, forming a cross in the middle. The distance between each pair of lines corresponds to the dimensions of the central square, so that they cross exactly under the cubit. The rectangle of the Ark itself is oriented east and west in its long dimension, east being directed to the top ("sursum") of the mental page and west to its bottom ("deorsum"). The north side is also called the right ("dextera") and the south the left ("sinistra"), though this nomenclature is not consistent.[39]

Within the perimeter of the large rectangle, two others are drawn about the central cubit, one inside the other in such a way that their angles are formed at points equidistant along the diagonals of the outermost rectangle. Thus there are four quadratures in the planar projection: the central square or cubit, and the three rectangles, each four to six times as long as it is wide. The three rectangles are the three main decks or "mansions" ("mansiones") of the three-storey Ark. And drawn across the whole plan are the two sets of double lines described earlier, which meet under the middle cubit.

Hugh then turns to a description of the elevation. In this projection, the double lines which are drawn latitudinally across the Ark and under the central cubit are seen to represent the halves of a central column that runs up the middle of the Ark, through the center of each of its storeys. Atop it, the central cubit sits like a crown or capital, and forms a lantern window, the only source of light for the structure beneath. From the lantern, beams extend downwards to the exterior walls of the Ark, forming the roof. The bottom of the column is the Ark's entrance. The whole structure looks like a cut-off pyramid, exactly as Hugh describes the Ark in Book I of "De arca morali": "ad similitudinem curtae pyramidis" (c. 633A).[40] The description of these three basic models – of the central cubit and of the Ark's plan and elevation – comprises chapter 1 of the "pictura" of the Ark.

Chapter 2 describes the central column. It signifies the Tree of Life and the Book of Life together, the Book being its northern hemisphere and the Tree its southern; its north also represents Christ's human nature and its south half His divinity. These associations summarize Hugh's lengthy moralization of the column of the Ark in Book II, 9 of "De arca morali." On the plan, however, the column is shown splayed out, as it were, so that the arms of the cross which are directed towards the north and the south represent these two faces of the column. They are differentiated by color also, the north being green, the south sapphire. Floor beams extend across each of the three rectangles to meet the roof beams which extend diagonally from under the lantern to the largest perimeter; these form the three decks.

Next, Hugh focuses on the longitudinal "belt" ("zona"), which extends from one end to the other of the plan. This belt represents the "longitude" of the Church, that is, its life in time. The upper half of the figure, from the top of the Ark to the central cubit represents history from Adam to the Incarnation, the lower half, time since the Incarnation. In the upper half are written the names of the generations from Adam to Christ; in the lower the succession of Apostles and Popes.

Within this diagram, Hugh singles out the twelve patriarchs and the apostles for a particular mnemonic. Midway down the upper half, the name "Judah" is written – centrally, because he was the first-born. About it and to right are written the names of the next three patriarchs; to the left, the remaining seven, from Dan to Benjamin. Superimposed on these names are busts of the twelve, what Hugh describes as "likenesses from the chest up" of the sort which the Greeks called *eikones*, and sometimes are seen carved in stone tablets.[41] Thus the twelve appear in order in their places, name and image together in a semicircle, "like the Senate of the city of God," "quasi quidam senatus Dei civitas."

Just below the central cubit is written "Peter," and to left and right about him, also in a semicircle, the names of the rest of the Apostles, six to the right and five to the left. We recall that in Bradwardine's memory-art the order of items in series depended on groupings to the right and left of a central figure. To each apostle's name is also attached an "icon" – "cum suis iconibus." When completed, the rank of Apostles together with the rank of Patriarchs "should be constituted in the likeness of the twenty-four Elders of the Apocalypse, seated around the Throne" (col. 687A), that is, the central cubit pictured with the Cross and Lamb. Following this figuring of the Apostles is written the succession of Popes, through Honorius (d. 1130), and the remaining space is for those who will live after us, through the end of time.

But the historical diagram has more refinements. It is also divided into three unequal parts, one extending from Adam to the Patriarchs, the second from the Patriarchs to the Incarnation, and the last through the bottom half of the whole figure. These correspond to the times of the natural law, the written law, and grace. Hugh marks these by painting three border stripes down the long sides of the Ark. But the stripes are not of equal width, for the outermost is broader than the two others, and the middle one is narrowest of all. They are painted in three colors: green, yellow, and violet, whose relative position in the lines corresponds to the division of time being represented. Green is outermost (the broadest line) during the time of natural law, yellow during the written law, violet during the time of grace. Violet is in the middle (the narrowest) at the time of natural law, yellow in the time of grace, and green in the time of written law. The innermost stripe is yellow during the time of natural law, violet in that of written law, green in that of grace. The three colors represent, says Hugh, the three kinds of moral action possible to human beings – motivated by natural goodness, motivated by God's revealed law, and motivated by grace. All three sorts have been present on earth in every period of history, but the proportions have varied, in the manner recalled by the distribution of the colors in the border stripes. One could easily use this color-code as a mnemonic basis for a meditation on the nature of human moral action throughout history; indeed, Hugh starts to do just that in this part (chapter 5) of "De arca mystica."

The elevation of the Ark shows the ship's ladders, by which one mounts from one storey to the next. These, says Hugh, are placed about the center column at the intermediate points of the compass, called by Hugh the east- and west- "frigor," "cold," and "calor," "heat" (north-east and north-west and south-east and south-west). These associate the storeys with ascents from vice to virtue and to holiness. So, from "the cold of the east" (the north-east) which Hugh calls "pride," one ascends first to fear, then to sorrow, then love. From the "cold of the west," which is ignorance, one ascends to knowledge, meditation, and finally contemplation. From "the heat of the east," which is fervid zeal of spirit, one ascends to temperance, to prudence, and finally to fortitude. There are twelve ladders in all, four about the column, on each of the three decks. Each ladder has ten steps, for a total of 120, or sixty plus sixty. On the steps, alternating by sex, are placed sixty men and sixty women, who represent the sixty warriors of Israel who surround the bed of Solomon (Cant. 3:7) and the sixty queens (Cant. 6:8) who mount up to his embrace.

But the ladders contain far more detail than this. Those three on the north-east are inscribed with the thirty books of the Bible, in order, ten on each as though each step of the ladder were a book.[42] And each book is divided on the outside (as it were, on its spine – books were still usually stored flat in their cupboards at this time) into three "grades" or "stages," corresponding to the three modes of Biblical interpretation: literal narrative, allegory, and tropology or "moralizing." Each of the ladders also has an inscription, appropriate to its role in the three stages of virtuous ascents which Hugh analyzed previously. For the north-east, the ascent from pride, the three stages were fear, sorrow, and love. So the first ladder has inscribed on it: "Here ascend those fearing hell-fires, calling out with Isaiah and saying, 'Their worm is not dead, nor their fire extinguished.' (Is. 66: 24)" This is the last verse in Isaiah. At the top of the first ladder is the book of Lamentations, tenth in Hugh's Bible. On the second ladder is written, "Here ascend those mourning the exile of their present life, who are led captive in Babylon, on account of the desertedness of the house of the Lord." At the top of this ladder is the book called Paralipomenon or Chronicles; the last event it tells of is the beginning of the Captivity. The third ladder in the series is labelled, "Here ascend those sighing for their homeland, awaiting the return of the bridegroom, and saying 'Come, Lord Jesus Christ.' (Revelation 20: 21)" This verse is, of course, the last verse of the Apocalypse, and the last in the Bible.

In the next three chapters of Hugh's treatise, the ladders are pressed into the service of a greatly elaborated moralization of the vices and virtues. The details of this are a bit hard to describe, so a translation of part of it may provide a useful sampling of this section. Hugh "gathers in" material by using the four directions, the boxing of the compass, which he introduced earlier:

In the four corners of the Ark the four evangelists are also pictured: the lion in the north-east, that he might terrorize the proud; the eagle in the north-west, that he might illuminate the blind; the bull in the south-west, that he might slay the flesh; and in the south-east the man, that he might recall mankind to its beginnings. [Hugh previously says that the south-east, the direction of zeal, is where man was created – these compass points are part of a geographical-historical-moral "mappa mundi".] Throughout the Book of Life, which looks to the north, some ascend from the north-east and some from the north-west, and as a result on every part from the surface inward of the lower ladder a hand extends downward with a open volume, as though coming from the Book of Life, here it chides, there it teaches. In one [page] is written a reproof: "Vae, vae, vae." On the other is written the teaching of Judah: "In the beginning God created the heavens and the earth." Throughout the Tree of Life others ascend, some from the south-east and some from the south-west, wherefore in every part of the surface of the lowest ladder a branch extends downwards, here having leaves, here fruit, and, as though coming from the Tree of Life, it feeds some and shades others.

Then the virtues are painted in this way opposite each ladder on the part to the inside. First, from the north-east, fear ascends naked towards the scroll, having thrown down the spoils of pride because of the fire and worms, which are shown under the foot of the ladder. On the second ladder, sorrow is painted and next to him the crossing to Babylon with Joachim, and so obliquely descending to the foot of the second ladder and in this way exiting from the Ark into Babylon, whose situation on the world-map is in that place. Next to the third ladder love is pictured like one of the virgins with a burning lamp and a flask of oil, expecting the arrival of the Bridegroom.

The book of memory

Every one of the virtues, having extended one hand upwards, expresses a gesture of ascent. (col. 696B–C, cap. 8–9)

Other *imagines* of the virtues inhabit the other ladders. The ladder of desire ("concupiscentia") starts in the bottom of the Ark's hold, on the south-west quadrant of the column, with a figure of a pubescent naked girl covered with branches from the Tree (of Life), towards whom a seducer ("incentor vitiorum," "an exciter of vices") blows fire from his nostrils and mouth. Higher up on this same ladder a naked boy cuts green switches from the branches, in order to express, in the manner of an *imago rei*, the virtue of patience. The figures on the ladders to the north-west, the direction of knowledge, begin with a cloaked person, his face veiled, who falls down at the foot of the ladder, striking a rock and shattering the vessel he is carrying – this is the image for ignorance, "which through various errors shatters the wholeness of the soul." On the second ladder sits meditation, "collecting the fragments of the fractured vessel." And on the third ladder, contemplation, depicted as a *faber* ("smith") conflates the fragments and liquifies them in the pipe-shaped furnace, which is what Hugh imagines the top of this ladder to be, making of the fragments newly-minted coins reformed in the likeness of God (now, although not earlier, the top of the ladder of contemplation is painted in a single, simple color which extends over the whole so that no divisions or steps can be seen in it). On another set of ladders, those on the south-east, temperance is painted like a father seated at his family table; prudence like a journeying pilgrim who flees the world; and finally fortitude, dressed in a cloud, like one who would reject the world and be elevated above.

Hugh allows his Ark-diagram to complicate almost endlessly, as it develops in his recollective meditation. There are many roomettes ("mansiuncules") within the Ark itself, which the Bible refers to but does not describe. But Hugh thinks that some were built like nests ("nidos") into the outer wall of the Ark, for the amphibious animals who can live neither entirely in water nor entirely on dry land. The rooms within the Ark itself, of which there are a great many (though again, the Bible says nothing about them), represent places mentioned in the route of the Exodus, from Rameses in Egypt to Jericho on the bank of Jordan. This "map" is fitted mnemonically onto the various temporal and moral categories which Hugh has already associated with the directions and areas of the main figure.

Surrounding the whole Ark are ellipses, which diagram Hugh's cosmology. The innermost of these represents the zone of air, and is divided into quadrants that correspond to the four "parts" of the world which is the rectangular Ark itself (these four are the areas formed when the cross is laid out onto the largest rectangle). In each quadrant of this ellipse a figure is painted to recall one of the four seasons, and the twelve winds are disposed on it as well at the appropriate compass points. Another zone is projected outside this one and divided into twelve parts; in it are represented the twelve months together with the twelve signs of the Zodiac (Hugh points out that each sign begins and ends in the middle of a month – he did not, in this diagram, follow the convenient convention of other Kalendar artists and collapse the two systems into one). Surrounding the calendar ellipse, is the figure of divine Majesty, His shoulders and head rising above the top of the whole figure and His feet extending below it, thereby seeming to contain all things in His embrace. About Him are two seraphs with extended wings, between whom and the figure of Majesty are painted the nine orders of angels, forming a semicircle about the Throne. Included also is a line of six circles extended from the top of the "linea generationis" to the Throne; in each of these is written a rubric which summarizes in order the work of a day of creation.[43]

Though Hugh of St. Victor's diagram of the Ark was never painted, a simpler textual "picture" of the same sort as "De arca Noe mystica" does exist in painted form. It is part of the treatise by Hugo de Folieto now called "De avibus" ("On Birds"), the first nineteen chapters of which are actually a separate composition concerning the dove and the hawk (indicated quite clearly in the manuscripts by the phrase "Explicit de columba et accipitre," though Migne's edition does not show this). Hugo de Folieto entered the priory of St.-Laurent-au-Bois in the village of Fouilloy (Folieto) near Corbie in 1120, became its prior in 1152, and died about twenty years later.[44] This priory was absorbed in 1223 by the large Benedictine foundation at Corbie; as a result Hugo de Folieto was forgotten and his work – which remained popular – was attributed to his contemporary, Hugh of St. Victor, until the eighteenth century. In addition to his book of birds, he wrote several other short treatises which focus on picture diagrams, including "The Wheels of True and False Religious" and "Concerning Shepherds and Their Sheep." Carlo de Clercq, the modern historian who has worked most extensively on Hugo de Folieto and his picture treatises, has concluded that while he did not probably execute any of the existing manuscript drawings himself, Hugo did supply the design for them and intended them to be an integral part of his texts. Indeed, in his two "wheel" treatises, the wheel diagrams are identified as "capitulum 1," the explication forming the succeeding chapters of the works. In other words, the picture is not an illustration of the text or even a diagram accompanying it, but as much a part of it as the words themselves. Modern editors who do not pay attention to this are violating what Hugh composed, for they are in essence arbitrarily deleting chapters from his work.[45]

Hugo's treatise on the dove and hawk and other birds was soon attached to another treatise, on animals, and so became part of one of the chief versions of the Bestiary. An independent section of anonymous authorship was also added, which lists the *voces animantium* in alphabetical order (and chapter 11 of Hugo's own treatise on the dove and hawk also lists the dove's *voces* in summary form). Hugo's drawings for his own treatise were often partially and poorly copied by later scribes and illuminators, but several manuscripts preserve the whole cycle.[46] For our purposes here, the most interesting of these pictures are the first two, each containing a good bit of text in addition to drawing. Both are summary *picturae* of, respectively, the first prologue and the first eleven chapters of the treatise.

The first summary picture (figure 15) is a simple "imago rei" of the first preface, which Hugo addresses to a fellow monk, Hugo Rainerus, who is known only from this text. He describes how this Hugo has begged him to write what follows concerning the dove and the hawk, and how, while he, Hugo de Folieto, has come to the contemplative life from a clerk's vocation, his fellow monk came from the military life – thus in his own life, Hugh Rainerus has combined the features of the hawk and the dove, which flies far away into solitude. Both the hawk and the dove share the same perch, and so "I from the clergy, you from the military, turned in conversion that we might sit in the life of the [Benedictine] Rule as though on a perch."[47]

The "imago" which Hugo devised for this text shows a cleric and a knight in two locations within a frame of dual arches separated by a column through which runs a single pole or perch. Over the knight is perched a hawk, over the clerk a dove. On the archway is written "Ecce in eadem pertica sedent accipiter et columba," "Behold on the same perch sit the hawk and the dove." On the perch is written "Hoc pertica est regularis vita," "this perch is the life of the Rule." Above the knight is written "miles," above the clerk "et clericus," and on the column which separates the two is written "activa" (next to the knight) "et contemplativa vita," next to the clerk. On the external wall of the knight's location is written "paries ['wall'] bonorum operum," and on the other external wall "paries sanctorum cogitationum."[48] The motto about "good works" on the knight's wall refers to a sentence in which Hugo characterizes his fellow as one who "[was] used to carrying off domestic birds [but] now draws woodland birds (that is secular clergy) to conversion with your hand of good works."[49] So the first of Hugo de Folieto's *imagines* presents in this simple fashion the *res* or *sententia* of this first Prologue. The images are set in two locations, architecturally characterized, and they "speak" the chief points of the text which they represent. They are *paintures* with *paroles* in the manner which Richart de Fournival describes, for the "parole" of the painting is taken from the accompanying text, and the painting derives directly from the "painture" in the text's metaphoric, "picturing" language.

The next "picture" in the treatise (figure 16) is more complex, as the text it summarizes is longer, but the composition follows these same principles. The treatise on the dove is an exegesis of Psalm 65:14 (Vulgate): "Si dormiatis inter medios cleros, pennae columbae deargentatae, et posteriora dorsi ejus in pallore auri." This dove, which occurs in a psalm recalling the Exodus, is collated with two other doves – the one which Noah sent out from the Ark, and the dove of the Holy Spirit. The word "cleros" in this verse is understood by Hugo to be a Greek word meaning, in de Clercq's phrase, "attitudes . . . selon les circonstances de la vie."[50] *Cleros* is translated into Latin by Hugo as *sors, sortis*, usually translated in modern Latin dictionaries as "fate," but better translated in this context as "outlook on life," or "mentality."

Several features of this picture show some affinity with Hugh of St. Victor's verbally-described diagram of the Ark *mystica*. First, there is a large central image of the dove, which relates all the various *res* of this treatise as the Lamb draws together those in Hugh of St. Victor's work. Though this diagram is circular rather than rectangular, one notices that it is a circle imposed upon a rectangle that is enclosed in a colored frame – the basic shape of the tablet of memory. The chief themes of the treatise are written in summary phrases or *tituli* in locations within this framed rectangular space. It would be too tedious for this chapter to show exactly the correlation of these phrases with the full text; briefly, those written immediately about the wheel-like circle surrounding the dove are taken from chapters 2–4, which have to do with defining relationships among the "attitudes" ("sortes") of the Old and New Testaments, and the contemplative life. The two rectangular locations just outside the wheel and the four smaller circles in the corners summarize the color symbolism of the dove, which Hugh discusses in chapters 5–10 (chapter 11, as I said earlier, is a summary listing of the traditional attributions of the dove). Around three sides of the margin just inside the outer frame is written the fourteenth verse of Psalm 67; across the bottom of this margin is a title for the picture: "Exprimit hanc mundam sine felle columbam," "[the picture] portrays the pure dove without bitterness [or 'taint']." The words in this picture are all written in red, at least in the Lyell manuscript, confirming their status as mnemonic rubrics for the text which the diagram accompanies.

Hugo de Folieto says that his treatise is directed to an audience of "illiterati." But the context in which he uses this word affords one of the better chances we have to understand its meaning for a learned, monastic writer like Hugh. Obviously, as de Clercq astutely has remarked, given the amount of Latin writing in Hugo's pictures, most of it employing abbreviated forms, they cannot have been intended for "illiterates" in our present understanding of that word. Nor can his audience have been laity who knew no Latin, or who could only mouth the syllables and sound the words, without being able to comprehend them. Hugo says that he writes in order to satisfy the wish of Hugo Rainerus "to paint the dove whose 'wings are silvered and whose back is pale gold,' and to build minds through a picture [*per picturam mentes aedificare*] . . . so that what the mind [*animus*] of simple people would scarcely be able to capture with its mental eye at least it can discern with its physical one, and what it can barely conceive from hearing it will perceive by seeing."[51] In a second preface, Hugo restates this point: "What writing signals to the more learned, picturing does to those less educated. . . . I therefore labor more that I may please the unlearned than that I might speak to those who are more learned and, so to speak, pour my milk into a vessel already full."[52] Hugo restates the old idea which we find in Gregory, that picturing and writing are the same, only in different media. To this, he adds the observation, also very traditional, that the memory (that is, the whole process which takes place in the "animus") more readily retains something seen than something only heard – an observation which seems to me clearly derived from the experience of an education which was mostly presented in an aural form. It is worth emphasizing Hugo's concern here for those beginning students who have not yet learned how to do this, how to "see" mentally the "painture" in the textual "parole" which they receive in class. This concern, in turn, reflects a fundamental belief that in the mind, for memorial retention, all input had to be transformed into visual, readable form.

But the term "illiteratus" involves yet one more, related, assumption, basic to the medieval epistemology of signs.[53] The notion that we are all, in varying stages, "illiteratus" in respect to the perfect knowing of God is a common medieval trope. It derives immediately, in its choice of words, from the belief that *litterae* are a category of signs; this being so, like all signs, they are necessary to mediate truth to the limited and incomplete minds of human beings. Hugo defends himself for making a treatise on such a mundane subject as the dove by noting that he is not being silly or merely entertaining, for both David and Job left divinely truthful lessons for us through metaphor when they wrote of birds. Isidore noted, in a basic definition, that "figures are extremely useful in 'gathering.' For subjects [*res*] which by themselves are least comprehensible, are easily grasped by a comparison of things [*comparatio rerum*]." This comment occurs in his chapter "De collatione" (to which I have referred before) in which he discusses various aids to memory, including reading a text frequently, breaking a long piece into short bits, and reading "sub silentio," in a murmur.[54]

The comparative terms in which Hugo de Folieto defines his audience ("simplicior" as against "doctior") makes it clear that his audience is the beginning students of the monastery, postulants for whom the treatise with its pictures will serve both as a way of organizing for mnemonic effectiveness some basic exegetical material on the dove and the hawk, and also as an exemplary model of how to make *imagines* for remembering other exegetical collations. The picture reduces the words to their *res*, the outline of topics and principle words, which, in speaking, one would elaborate. The verb Hugo uses for his pictures, in addition to *pingere*, "paint," is *decrescere*, "reduce in size," that is reducing prolixity to memorable *brevitas*, according to the principle of storing mnemonically "rich" units. Hugo de Folieto's remarks point to an elementary pedagogy of making such compositional images as a technique for remembering.

"DISTINGUISHING" THE BOOK

I would like now to suggest a few additional ways in which the requirements of mnemonic technique may have specifically influenced the decoration of medieval books. It seems to be a fact that medieval book decoration was thought to provide sources of mnemonically valuable images, and examples to encourage the making of other such images, mentally at least. But influence sometimes also went the other way, as we have seen in the case of word-pictures, where mnemonic principles of "imagines rerum" and even "imagines verborum" directly influence the making of an image. The symbiotic relationship between memorial effectiveness and the layout of books throughout the Middle Ages is apparent at the level of principle and general rules; the more difficult problem is to know to what extent the selection of images and decorative elements reflected particular mnemonic techniques and themes. My remarks here are very incomplete, for the subject is large and any treatment of it will need to address changes as well as continuities of style and presentation, and relate these to vogues of mnemonic training, insofar as these existed. A few outstanding themes do emerge, however, even at this preliminary point in my investigations.

I have grouped my observations into three general categories: marginalia, classroom diagrams, and compositional "imagines rerum," though it should be kept in mind that the three kinds do not always neatly sort out from one another. Perhaps it could be said that marginal images serve the function of textual heuristics, "finding," and mnemonic storage – the need for *divisio* – while the diagrams invite further "gathering" and meditational recollection. Yet, having said this, one must instantly qualify the statement by noting that *inventio* and the mnemonic task it serves, *compositio*, are tasks equally of "finding" and "gathering" material into one place from a number of previously stored places. The tasks of "finding" and "gathering" are no better distinguished from one another than "memory" is from "recollection." Still, one must start somewhere (a fundamental mnemonic principle); and having said that, I have acknowledged that my definitional structures (like a great many others) are more useful as mnemonic devices than reflective of "fact."

In his general advice on memory training, Quintilian emphasizes three basic mnemonic principles: first, the utility of *imagines*, often of the rebus variety, for both memory-for-words and memory-for-things; second, the absolute essentialness of proper *divisio* and *compositio* both to memorizing and to composing, for "one who correctly divides cannot possibly get lost in the order of his speech" (XI, ii, 32); and third, always to use the same tablets when one first sets out to commit something to memory, because the appearance of writing, its visual image including any *notae* that may accompany it, is crucial to success.

A book made some fifty years after Hugh of St. Victor wrote indicates, as clearly as any medieval book I know of, a conscious effort by its makers to use images solely because they are mnemonically valuable. It is a copy of Augustine's *Enchiridion*, which was made and decorated in England at the end of the twelfth century for the Cistercian abbey of St. Mary's in Holmecultram, Cumberland. It is now Huntington Library MS. HM 19915. There are several other texts in this book, but it is the *Enchiridion*, an elementary primer of Christian faith, that I want to consider here.

In most respects, HM 19915 is an ordinary medieval book of its period (though no less interesting for that). It has summarizing *tituli* in the margins, which seem to be written in the same hand as the main text. Each chapter is numbered, and has a descriptive heading. The initial letters are written large and colored alternately in red, green, and light blue, the colors used in other Holmecultram books of this same period.[55] Most of these initials have some simple filigree pen-work either in or surrounding them, of a sort compatible with the generally sober style which art historians have associated with the Cistercians. The text is divided into *cola* and *commata*, and is rubricated appropriately. And highly stylized forms of the word *nota*, written in black ink, each distinct, appear in several of the margins opposite important text; these seem to be contemporary with the text itself, and indeed it is most likely that the same scribe, most likely a monk of the house in whose library the manuscript was housed, wrote, punctuated, decorated, and "annotated" it.

The unusual feature of this manuscript is that its marginal notations and *tituli* are each enclosed in an elaborately drawn image, each one unique, each colored in washes of several hues (figures 17–19). Several of the enclosing forms are geometrical (a square, a lozenge), some are architectural (steps surmounted by a column and tablature), some are banners on which the *titulus* is written, and some – the most surprising of all – are animals.[56] There is one showing two dogs' heads ringing each end of a banner, on which is written the *titulus* which summarizes that part of the text (figure 17); one is a dragon breathing forth a pall of smoke on which is written a command to the reader to mark ("signa") a particularly apt bit of text (figure 19); another shows a dog chasing a hare, their tails forming a ring in which is written the notation, "Signa humanam benevolentiam," "Mark human benevolence." (figure 18).

The function of *tituli* as mnemonic helps, a part of the rubrification of a written text, is well understood. They are found from antiquity onward and they present the longer content of a text, the "prolixitas," in a brief summary form (its "brevitas"), a "resumé des chapitres," as Berger calls it in his history of the Vulgate Bible.[57] Written in the margin, *tituli* became part of the apparatus of the Bible at an early period; they could be either summaries, as we understand that word, or a quotation of the first few words in a textual division. In other words, they present the text according to the principles of *memoria ad res*, in which the "sentence" (to use the Middle English word) or principle (that is, "starting-off") words are used to cue the memory.

Enclosing the *tituli* in images, as in HM 19915, was evidently done to enhance their mnemonic function, by adding to something which was already understood to be mnemonic in function (the *titulus*), an attribute (the lively image) known particularly to impress memory. There is no other plausible reason for adding such images, because they are not related iconographically or as "imagines rerum" to the text they accompany, nor do they serve mechanical needs of a scribe or binder, as catchwords do. I have examined all of the manuscripts still extant from Holmecultram (there are eleven); others have marginal titles, sometimes enclosed in geometric or architectural forms, but none have the elaborate designs of HM 19915. Furthermore, these designs occur in only one of the works copied in this manuscript, Augustine's *Enchiridion*. As a primer of faith, the *Enchiridion* was a text that beginning students, whose mental imagining skills were not well developed, needed to learn. These vividly decorated *tituli* and notes would help them. The cultivation of images as recollective devices in such a basic book is an important link in the evidence which establishes that one of the earliest tasks taught in learning to read was learning to mark text with mnemonically useful mental images.

Marginal notations, glosses, and images are an integral part of the "painture" of literature, addressing the ocular gateway to memory and meditation. Indeed, the margins are where individual memories are most active, most invited to make their marks, whether physically (as in the ubiquitous NOTA command or a pointing finger, sometimes drawn with a string around it, or crudely-sketched human and animal heads, or, especially in later manuscripts, implements such as shovels) or only in their imagination.[58] But the images in medieval books function in other mnemonically significant ways. These include rebus-like images which pun visually on certain words or themes of a text, all sorts of diagrams, and pictures that are of the type which Lydgate suggestively called "meditaciouns," focal images like the "pity" which he "saw" in his mental book, and which can stimulate a recollective "composicioun" of texts.

As we have seen, the observations that memory is easily overwhelmed by too solid or lengthy a diet, that it requires pleasing, that it retains best what is unusual and surprising, that memorizing is best served when one fixes what one is learning within a fully synaesthetic context, are standard features of mnemonic advice in the twelfth and thirteenth centuries. It is significant that the style of painting "drolleries" in manuscript margins comes into widespread use in the mid-thirteenth century, along with the fashion for the "thematic" sermon (the sort of composition served by Bradwardine's "memoria orationis"), and at the same time that the mnemotechnique described in the *Ad Herennium* was revived, under the twin sponsorship of the early humanists and the Dominicans.[59] The grotesque creatures, the comic images of monkeys and other animals mimicking human behavior, images that are violent, ugly, salacious or titillating, noble, sorrowful, or fearful possess the qualities recommended for memory images by the *Ad Herennium*. This may represent an instance where a particular mnemotechnique did influence a new style in book decoration, though one should remember that the general principle of making extraordinary images to influence memory was known all along.

In addition to discrete marginal images, some manuscripts employed *bas-de-page* (bottom margin) pictorial narratives. These, commonly, refer either to saints' lives or to well-known comic cycles like the Renart stories or Aesop's fables, or to fabliaux such as "the squire who laid eggs."[60] A

fourteenth-century manuscript of the Decretals, written in Italy but illuminated in England, provides a virtual feast of such narratives, most carrying
over several pages. It belonged to the priory of St. Bartholomew's, Smithfield
(where John of Mirfield was a canon) and it is now in the British Library, MS.
Royal 10. E. iv. The Decretals are a digest of canon law, and required
memorizing in order to be fully useful. It was one of the essential books that
William of Ockham insisted his "pupil" store away. The bottom margins of
the Smithfield Decretals are filled with stories told entirely through pictures,
like a running cartoon. These have no apparent relationship to the material in
the text which they accompany. There are saints' lives, with their usual
complement of grotesque incident; a salacious story of a friar who seduces a
miller's wife and murders her husband (ff. 113v–117); and a number of
animal fables, some involving characters from the Renart cycle, and some
seemingly made up. Two involve a group of killer-rabbits, who track down a
human hunter and truss him up, and then capture a hunting dog, try him in a
rabbit-court, and hang him (figures 20–24).[61]

But there is yet another sort of marginal image, both more ancient and
more persistent than the drolleries and grotesques. Certain classes of images
appear over and over in the margins from the earliest decorated books
through hand-painted printed books. These include jewels, coins, birds, fruit,
flowers (sometimes shown with insects sucking their nectar), and scenes of
hunting and fishing, both by animals and humans. Examples of several of
these, from a Book of Hours made around 1440 in Utrecht for Catherine of
Cleves, the Duchess of Guelders (Pierpont Morgan Library MSS. 917 and
945), are shown in figures 25–28 and figure 1.[62] As metaphorical tropes, these
same classes of image figure persistently in the pedagogy of invention and
memory, those two processes for which books are the sources and cues. Of
course there were major shifts in painting style and in the market for books as
they became more numerous and widely available. But, as we have seen, the
assumption that writing is the servant of memory persisted over a long time.
Trained memory is a storehouse, a treasure-chest, a vessel, into which the
jewels, coins, fruits, and flowers of texts are placed. The reader gathers nectar
from these flowers to furnish the cells of memory, like a bee (figure 26). Coins
and other treasure are perhaps the most common of memory tropes; they also
have a complementary association (as do gold, pearls, and rubies) with the
Biblical "treasures" of the Kingdom of Heaven (figure 25). Some Books of
Hours have pilgrims' badges as a marginal decoration; a book such as this was
traditionally thought of as a scrinium, a "shrine," the pilgrim's object.[63]

Birds, a common and long-lasting element in book decoration from the
early programs for the Canon Tables to the elements of Insular interlace to
the margins of Psalters and Books of Hours, have also a very long association
with thoughts and memories, as we saw in chapter 1. Birds, like memories,
need to be hunted down (by a fowler or hawker, a common variation on the
general motif) or stored up in a cage or coop, as in figure 27. They are also part
of the Christian motifs of the "Tree of Life" and "Book of Life," so clearly

linked to one another exegetically, as in Hugh of St. Victor's "De arca Noe mystica." Jesus likened the kingdom of Heaven to a mustard seed that grows into a tree so large that all the birds of the air come to rest in its branches: "et fit arbor, ita ut volucris caeli veniant, et habitent in ramis ejus" (Mt. 13:32). This tree is also, by the mnemonic technique of collation, the Tree of Life, or the Wood of Life ("lignum," the word Hugh of St. Victor uses) and this association links it to the "Book" of Life, as Hugh says.

Such images, it seems to me, are not iconographical, nor do they illustrate or explain the content of a particular text. They serve the basic function of all page decoration, to make each page memorable, but they also serve to remind readers of the purpose of books as a whole – that they contain matter to be laid away in their memorial storehouse, shrine, fiscal pouch, chest, vase, coops, pens, or bins, a task especially suitable in connection with the sorts of books these images most often accompany – Bibles, psalters, decretal collections, prayer books, and other books that especially need to be remembered. A very early example makes my point. The Codex Alexandrinus, a fifth-century Greek Bible, has drawings of an empty vase into which a *titulus*, written in increasingly shorter lines, seems to fall as though in a stream. This simple image serves as a reminder that the words of God pour forth in a stream from the book into the vessel of memory (an ancient commonplace for *memoria*), and that one's task is to be sure they are laid away there properly.[64]

Metaphors of fishing, hunting, and tracking down prey are also traditional for recollection. Aristotle speaks in *De memoria* of how people recollect from some starting-point: they "hunt successively," (451^b 19). The verb he uses is *ther-âma*, "to hunt or fish for." The same image is incorporated into the very definition of recollection by Albertus Magnus: "reminiscenti[a] nihil aliud est nisi investigati[o] obliti per memoriam," "recollection is nothing but the tracking-down of something hidden away in memory."[65] The metaphor is also used, elaborately, by Quintilian, who, defining the "places" of argument laid down in memory, likens a skillful orator to a huntsman or fisherman who knows exactly the habits and haunts of his game (*Inst.*, v, x, 20–22). The metaphor in the word *error*, both "error" and "wandering," is an aspect of this same idea, for the one who wanders through the pathless *silva* (meaning both "forest" and "disordered material") of an untrained memory is one who has either lost the footprints (*vestigia*) that should lead him through, or never laid them down in the first place.

Hunting and fishing go together in this trope of memory. The mnemonic *notae* which one uses to get around one's storehouse are called both tracks (*vestigia*) and hooks (*unci*). Geoffrey of Vinsauf, discussing *memoria*, advises students to be diligent and practice the contents of their memorial store, laid away with markers of whatever sorts of *notae* suit them. Otherwise, they will be like a cat, which wants the fish but not the fishing.[66] Fish are fairly common in a number of manuscripts, sometimes drawn crudely by a reader opposite a portion of text, thus functioning like a "NOTA" admonition.[67]

Many manuscripts' margins contain images that seem to grow out of the words and into the margins, a kind of emphasizing bracket that becomes the shape of a hand or a head. Heads are very common, possibly because the head is the seat of memory. Heads also can be differentiated more easily than pointing hands (which can be provided with a string or a cuff, but not much else), for they can wear a variety of headdress, be male or female, frontal or in profile, and so on. A head, drawn with a text-balloon such as modern cartoonists use, as though it were "thinking" the words of a *titulus*, occurs in a margin of the Winchester manuscript of Malory.[68] This image clearly indicates that this reader understood drawings of heads to be a part of a book's mnemonic apparatus.

A prominent feature of medieval book art is the use of diagrams. The Canon Tables, written "intercolumnia" – between arched columns that are decorated with birds and floral motifs – are one very early example, which we find in books from the earliest medieval centuries (figure 4). The typical layout of the Kalendar, marked by images of the Zodiac and (later) the labors of the months, is another. In fact, one of the more intriguing aspects of Hugh of St. Victor's Ark-picture is its "gathering" of many common medieval diagrams into one "place," and, if one adds the columnar format he employed for his *Chronicle*, it is clear that Hugh was accustomed, both in teaching ("lectio") and in his own meditational composition, to use virtually every major genre of diagram common in the twelfth century – ladders, trees, circles, columns, maps, and genealogical charts – all enclosed within the rectangular shape of the memorial page. Even more interesting is Hugh's assumption that basic pedagogy consists in the ability to use such structures readily to perform tasks of mnemonic calculation (collating texts, for example). His own practice indicates that such recollective skill is, in large measure, what he is referring to in his aphorism, "the whole usefulness of education consists only in the memory of it [*In sola enim memoria omnis utilitas doctrinae consistit*]".

In many ways, Hugh of St. Victor is a twelfth-century version of Quintilian, not an innovator of technique so much as an admirably clear, practical guide to the best pedagogy of his time. This pedagogy employed visual aids and diagrams to an extent that many modern historians have noted. For example, in his descriptive catalogue of English Romanesque illuminated manuscripts, C. M. Kauffmann writes that "the pictorial diagram . . . became one of the typical features of Romanesque art."[69] But most of these diagrams had been in common use for centuries before the twelfth, as mnemonic compositional aids – one thinks, for example, of the "ladder" with which Benedict organized the "rungs" (*gradus*) of humility in the seventh chapter of his Rule.

Indeed, it is a much-remarked medieval characteristic to treat the space in a full-page drawing diagramatically, that is, with images placed in specific locations, often grouped about a large central figure, often in an architectural setting, often with related images enclosed in roundels or other geometric forms, usually with a border, and commonly with inscriptions, like *tituli* or rubrics, to be associated with the figure and to help associate the figures with one another. The justification for this practice is mnemonic necessity. The framework of the page provides a set of orderly *loci*; furthermore, this frame remains constant while the images in it change from page to page – that is the manner of a diagram, and it is also the manner of the page of memory, "imagines rerum" imposed upon set of "places" in an orderly framework or grid.

Examples of this format span the whole period that we call the Middle Ages. The Gospels of St. Augustine (Cambridge, Corpus Christi College MS. 286), made in Italy in the sixth century, was at Canterbury during the Middle Ages, and is thought to have been brought to England from Rome by St. Augustine himself. A full-page "picture" (figure 29) groups figural scenes, many containing textual tags, into a gridwork of twelve "places," each set in a border. The whole rectangular construction is enclosed in another border painted around the vellum page. The outer border demarcates the "area" of the page, just as the memory-page in Hugh of St. Victor's "pictura" has a border enclosing it. The *loci* are small quadratures within this, three across in each of four tiers, and clearly separated from one another by a red-colored border. Some of the individual *imagines* are given a rudimentary background; others are set in what has been called "hierarchical space," wherein the figures are grouped in such a way that the main figure, the first in the order, appears in the center and larger than the subsidiary figures grouped to its right and left.

The background is simple, a single color without any distance to it, more than the barest suggestion of a setting for the figures. And the perspective of the viewer is from the front and central, the qualities that define "distancia" in the mnemonic advice that has survived from later centuries. In fact, this page exemplifies so many of the rules of making mnemonic locations described by Bradwardine that one might, at first, wonder if he must have seen it; the manuscript was, after all, at Canterbury. Yet the details of Bradwardine's examples are not those of the drawings in the Gospels of St. Augustine. Their similarity in principle, however, suggests strongly that the same general rules that governed the making of the sixth-century Gospels' page were still a part of medieval mnemonic pedagogy in the fourteenth century.

The picture-page in this Gospels provides a complete set, in order, of "imagines rerum" for the events of the Passion, drawn not from a particular gospel but synthesizing all four accounts. The picture-page comes between the gospels of Mark and Luke; it is thought that similar pages, with images from the earlier life of Christ, were placed before Matthew and between Matthew and Mark, and that a page showing events from the Passion to the Ascension preceded John. Such a placement is usual in early medieval Gospels, which were large books designed for community use in a monastery.[70]

Picture-pages in medieval books had cycles of popularity. A much later example is a Flemish Psalter of the second half of the thirteenth century (Pierpont Morgan Library MS. M 183), which contain four such pages. M. R. James's catalogue decription of this manuscript demonstrates clearly how the individual subjects of the images are inserted into a framework that is stable in all four of these pages – stable not only in shape and configuration, but in the type of content that occupies the different parts of the frame.[71] Again, the "places" in the frame are separated clearly from one another by borders; the "imagines rerum" refer to sixteen main events in the life of Christ and to various saints. This framework is quite elaborate, though its relationship to the common grid-format is evident.

Such "imagines rerum," painted only mentally or also on parchment, share many features with the teaching diagrams which the later Middle Ages produced in abundance. Diagrams were a common feature of medieval classrooms. One of the better known, and most widely used, was in a tree form, composed by Peter of Poitiers in the twelfth century. It is the genealogy of Christ, called "Compendium Historiae in Genealogia Christi" or, simply, the "Genealogia," and it is quite like the "linea genealogia" we encounter in "De arca Noe mystica."

Beginning with Adam, the names of Christ's predecessors are listed in order, with a brief biographical sketch. The names and their relationships are indicated by lines and, usually, circles, with pictures of the chief events, such as the Temptation and the Flood – often also the diagram known as the Tree of Jesse is included. A version of the diagram seems to have had an independent existence early in the twelfth century, for Stephen Langton reports that a genealogical diagram, "a historical tree of the Old Testament," was painted on skins (parchment) and hung on the wall in Paris classrooms; a manuscript of it was in the library at St. Victor.[72] It was much copied, often incorporated into universal chronicles from the twelfth through the fifteenth centuries; it was also translated into several vernaculars, including English, and had an exceptionally long run in the classroom.

Frequently, the "Genealogia" was written on a continuous roll of parchment rather than in a codex. Three examples in the Bodleian Library are of some interest. An English codex of the second quarter of the thirteenth century (MS. Laud Misc. 151), which contains both this text, in Latin, and Peter Comestor's *Historia scholastica*, belonged to Cardinal Morton (d. 1500) at one point in its history, and the first leaf pictures both his coat of arms and a rebus for his name, a drawing of a cask, or "tun," with the letters "mor" written on it. A roll (MS. Barlow 53), dating from the early fifteenth century, is an English translation of the "Genealogia," with its preface. And finally, another roll, MS. Lat. th. b. 1, also English and from the first half of the thirteenth century, is especially interesting because its companion roll (MS. Lat. th. c. 2), which may have been attached to it at one point, contains diagrams of the Seven Deadly Sins, the Seven Gifts of the Spirit, and so on. The genealogy roll begins with a drawing and exposition of the seven-branched candlestick, proceeding to enumerate a number of "sevens" and also "threes" before it gets to Peter's diagram itself. Such a digest of preaching aids would be a useful tool for classroom lecture.[73]

Peter of Poitiers's preface makes it clear that his format is a memory aid. Considering the length of holy writ, he says, he has digested the genealogical information and presented it in this form so that students may retain it in memory, as in a treasure-bag ("quasi in sacculo"). He uses the same image for memory used by Hugh of St. Victor in his *Chronica* preface, that of a *sacculus* or compartmentalized money-pouch, in which coins of various sizes can be carried, each in its place without loss or confusion. As I showed in my first chapter, this image is a common variant of the archetype of memory as *thesaurus* or *arca*. And Peter goes on to say that his scheme, though useful for all, is particularly so for those students who feel overwhelmed by the bulk of historical material, since for them, "lengthy subject matter, because [it is] adjusted to the visual sense [by means of the diagram], is committed to the habit of memory."[74]

In his section on "memoria," Geoffrey of Vinsauf (who was Peter's contemporary) emphasizes the mnemonic value of *formae*: "'loca, tempora, et formae' and other similar 'notulae' are sure ways to lead me to [what I have stored away]."[75] He does not define what these "formae" are. The word can mean "shape" or "outward appearance." But it can also mean "geometric shape" or "outline" – the sort of thing that a diagram is,[76] and given the fondness of the twelfth-century classroom for diagrams, I am inclined to think that this was what Geoffrey probably meant. Diagrams formed of concentric circles, rose diagrams (which are not confined to windows), the primitive chart that forms the *Genealogia*, Hugh of St. Victor's columns of persons, places, and dates for his *Chronica*, ladder diagrams, and the veritable forest of "trees" to illustrate the relations of parts of a subject whether it be preaching or vices and virtues – all such *formae* are common features in manuscripts too, especially in the twelfth and thirteenth centuries.[77]

There is one more famous diagram worth considering here, described by John of Garland. I discussed in chapter 3 John's instructions for composing a three-columned memory tablet that was to include all the *voces animantium*, "sounds from various languages," and so on, in alphabetical order; some manuscripts of John's text include a partial schematic drawing of this, but it was clearly designed as a mental structure, infinitely expandable as such schemes are. John also mentions, however, a diagram "quam pre manibus habimus," "which we have in our hands," the so-called Rota Virgili or Virgil's Wheel.[78] This circular diagram is also drawn in some manuscripts of the *Parisiana poetria*, and it shows a series of concentric circles divided into three wedges, within which comparisons, likenesses, occupations, animals, plants, and implements are written that pertain to John's subject, the three different kinds of audience to be considered in determining stylistic decorum. Virgil's Wheel was clearly a mnemonic diagram that this students held; it is likely that it could be physically manipulated, as its concentric circles suggest.

The figure of the rhetorical "rota Virgili" may provide the connection between the Latin word *rota*, "wheel," and the English phrase "by rote." *Rote*, according to the OED, is "of obscure origin," although it appears as though it should be derived either from Latin *rota*, "wheel," or from French *rote*, "way, route." As the OED states, however, there has been "no evidence to confirm the suggestions."[79] My review of the evidence does not confirm a derivation either, but it may help to strengthen the suggestion in favor of the Latin over the French.

"By rote" appears in English in the fourteenth century meaning both "reciting (prayers, speeches, and the like) from memory" (an essentially neutral usage) and, in a pejorative way, "reciting unintelligently or by formula." For Chaucer, the word on its face is neutral, meaning "from memory exactly," a synonym of *memoria ad verba*. The first clearly pejorative uses of the word (which are from the fifteenth and sixteenth centuries) modify "rote" with "mere" or "pure." "Rote" had also a generalized meaning of "habit" or "custom," that which memory produces. The earliest OED citation, in a poem by William Shoreham written probably in the 1330s, refers to a bad habit as a "wikked rote"; habitual knowledge is what the classroom *rotae* were designed to instill. John Gower speaks of the pagans' "rote" ("custom") in his *Confessio amantis* (VI, 1311), interestingly in the context of knowing magical arts and sorcery (things that scholars, whose memories were sure to be trained, would dabble in).

The clearest link between English "by rote" and the rhetorical tradition which included using the "rota Virgili" diagram is in Chaucer's Pardoner's Tale, when the Pardoner describes his rhetorical tactics and how he adopts his speech to his audience:

> Lordynges, quod he, in chirches whan I preche,
> I peyne me to han an hauteyn speche
> And rynge it out as round as gooth a belle,
> For I kan al by rote that I telle.
> My theme is alwey oon, and evere was:
> *Radix malorum est cupiditas.* (VI, 329–334)[80]

The "rota Virgili" showed schematically how to adopt one's speech to particular kinds of audiences, something at which the Pardoner is especially adept. Notice how he distinguishes between his "theme," which is always the same, and his ability to vary it to suit the particular occasion and congregation, *ex tempore dicendi*, a boast he repeats in lines 412–420 when he describes how he has insulted particular enemies in his sermons. To repeat my earlier disclaimer, I have hardly settled the etymological puzzle here, but the possibility of a link with memory devices like the Rota Virgili is suggestive. It is also easy to see how, if it referred to a mnemonic schoolroom diagram, "speaking by rote" could come to mean "speaking by mere formula."

Wheel-diagrams were not limited to the teaching of rhetoric. Wheels that move and are intended to be manipulated are common enough artifacts in manuscripts. For example, two moving wheels are found in Bodleian Library

MS. Bodley 177, a collection of scientific pieces made up of four separate manuscripts written in the last part of the fourteenth century. On f. 63v there is a simplified astrolabe, made of two freely-moving concentric parchment disks, and on f. 62r a wheel that reveals the letters of the Latin alphabet in various combinations. This latter is constructed from vellum disk in which holes have been cut, its center pierced, and a thong tied through it to the back of the leaf on which it is placed, allowing it to move freely. Hugo de Folieto's wheels imply movement, most obviously those of his treatise on "True and False Religious," which depict the rising and declining patterns of the lives of a good and a false monk.

One medieval figure in the subject of memory design and arts, about whom I have had little to say because he has been thoroughly studied by Frances Yates and R. J. Hillgarth, is the late thirteenth-century Spaniard, Ramon Lull (1235–1316; the last version of his art was written 1305–08).[81] Lull's art was designed to be both a key to universal knowledge and a memory art. Though he did have some influence in the late Middle Ages, he is probably more important in the context of Renaissance figures like Giordano Bruno and Camillo, with whom Yates is most occupied. Lull's is an extremely subtle, complex, and learned system, not at all for beginners. Nor is it, as Yates points out, at all like the system of *loci* and *imagines* described in *Ad Herennium*. Yet it did not come out of nowhere. Yates relates it to the Neoplatonism of Scotus Eriugena. But I think many of its characteristic uses of symbol and figure have much commoner origins.

Frances Yates attributes two apparent innovations to Lull. First, he "designates the concepts used in his art by a letter notation, which introduces an almost algebraic or scientifically abstract note into Lullism." And secondly, he uses diagrams extensively, such as concentric circles, rotating triangles within a circle, ladders (steps), and trees, to "introduc[e] movement into memory."[82] But diagrams such as these, which all imply the sort of movement and manipulation of which Yates speaks, were a common feature of the medieval elementary classroom, precisely for the purpose of memory training. So was the use of letter notation to organize concepts. Moreover, Hugh of St. Victor's "Ark" is also a universal diagram, designed to organize a large amount of disparate information in a readily available, mnemonically effective, way. This fact suggests that such diagrammatic *machinae universitatis* were encouraged in medieval pedagogy well before Lull. Whether their source can be specifically derived from medieval Neoplatonism remains to be seen; I am inclined to look for major influences in the practical disciplines of monastic prayer, rather than in either "Platonic" ("Augustinian") or "Aristotelian" doctrine.[83]

For mnemonic purposes, diagrams, like other sorts of images in medieval books, can have either (or a combination) of two functions: they can serve as "fixes" for memory storage, or as cues to start the recollective process. The one function is pedagogical, in which the diagram serves as an informational schematic; the other is meditational. There are a number of diagram-like pages in liturgical and devotional books throughout the Middle Ages, whose function is of this latter sort. In his classic study of a much-copied sequence of such theological "diagrams" from the late Middle Ages, Fritz Saxl commented: "A wealth of wisdom is displayed, which slowly reveals itself to the patient reader who does not mind the absence of a well-defined general lay-out. . . . Each picture . . . must be pondered again and again."[84] Such diagrams are like the seventeenth-century "emblems" – indeed, they may well be their medieval predecessors. They compose a "place" for a meditative recollection by "picturing" various theological and devotional themes. Their obscurity and partialness are deliberate; as deliberate as is the clarity of a pedagogical diagram such as the "Genealogia."

The most easily accessible now of the late medieval diagram-encyclopedias is the De Lisle Psalter (British Library MS. Arundel 83–II), published in a facsimile edited by L. F. Sandler. Only the drawings now exist, but in the original book they preceded a psalter made for an English layman, Robert De Lisle. These drawings, made in the early fourteenth century, are copies of a group of "pictures" devised towards the end of the thirteenth century by a Franciscan friar, John of Metz. The group was called the "Speculum theologiae" or, in England, the "Orchard of Consolation," names which suggest both the encyclopedic intention of their maker and their contemplative purpose. (Recall Gregory the Great's admonition that, in our true reading, we see as in a mirror, "speculum," our own vices and virtues.) The word "orchard" was used in the title of other medieval English vernacular works of devotion, such as "The Orchard of Syon"; it is a variant on the ancient "flowers of reading" trope, these being the "fruits" of meditational *memoria*. Three of the diagrams in the "Orchard of Consolation" are known to have originated from texts, as "pictures," *imagines* of their *res*: a "Tree of Life," a "Tree of Vices and Virtues," and a "Cherub," the diagram-picture of the "res" of a sermon-treatise by Alain of Lille, "On the Six Wings of the Cherubim."[85]

These theological "pictures," textually derived, are realizations on parchment of the kind of meditative, *compositional* mental imagining we encounter in Hugh of St. Victor's "De arca Noe." They have more in common with mnemonic rebuses than with the kind of schematic to which we now restrict the word "diagram." But they are rebuses of a very elaborate type. An ordinary rebus is an image-for-the-word, like the rebus of "Morton," which I described earlier in this section. These, however, are "imagines rerum," designed to call to mind the framework of a composition that each individual should ponder and elaborate further. They provide "places," as it were, for memorial "gathering," *collatio*, in the manner which Hugo de Folieto provided for his treatise "On the Dove and the Hawk."

The spectacular pages of some of the earliest books of the Middle Ages, the Insular liturgical books designed to be used by an entire community of monks and kept often in the cloister for general reading, can be considered in this way. The "carpet-pages" of interlace that grace such Gospels as the Book of Durrow (late seventh century) or the Book of Kells (late eighth century; figure 30) are most like diagrams in the way in which they treat space. For example, Jacques Guilmain has demonstrated the simple, orderly geometry upon which the forms of ornament in these carpet pages rests. As he comments, the making of these pages "is an art that cannot be described simply as a catalogue of its component parts, for just as significant is the syntax of those parts . . . all details relate to the wholes as completed fabrics."[86] Moreover, they are not pages which one can easily digest; like the texts they accompany they must be looked at and looked at again, ruminated, absorbed and made one's own. The figures that peek through the interlace are not apparent until one looks long enough to begin putting together what seems at first fragmentary. It is a process such as the one Hugh of St. Victor describes as the journey from ignorance to contemplation; one first sees only an overwhelming jumble of fragmentary detail, then as one meditates one begins to collect the pieces, and then in contemplation forges a meaningful pattern.

In a famous description, which some scholars think may be that of the Book of Kells itself, the twelfth-century Welsh historian, Giraldus Cambrensis, recounts his encounter with such a book. It is remarkable to me not so much because of its apparently realistic depiction of the artistry of one of these Insular manuscripts as because of its articulation of a process of seeing, reading, and meditation that, Giraldus says, fulfilled his ordinary expectations to an extraordinary degree:

Look at [the forms in this book] superficially with an ordinary casual glance, and you would think it is an erasure, and not tracery. Fine craftsmanship is all about you, but you might not notice it. Look more keenly at it and you will penetrate to the very shrine of art. You will make out intricacies so delicate and subtle, so exact and compact, so full of knots and links, with colors so fresh and vivid, that you might say that all this was the work of an angel and not of a man. For my part, the oftener I see the book, and the more carefully I study it, the more I am lost in ever fresh amazement, and I see more and more wonders in the book.[87]

What Giraldus described is not an act of picturing or illustration, but an act of reading, in the monastic understanding of what "reading" is. It is basically a rhetorical practice, an act of *memoria* in which the figures grouped in the picture are designed both to recall and to stimulate further mental image-making in the reader. Pages that consist of a framework alone, without super-imposed images, are especially suggestive. An example is the carpet-pages of the Book of Durrow, which, like all the early-produced Gospels, was designed for community use. Here empty rectangular panels are set in a framework of interlace, some panels having a plain-colored background, some a simple interlace design, like the empty "places" into which particular "imagines rerum" may be projected, and then erased and used again for other occasions and other texts – and by a variety of people, as is fitting for a communally used book.[88]

I do not believe that the ornamentation of a medieval page consists of images to be memorized exactly, but is instead presented as an exemplary aid to the making of such images. Nothing could prevent a lazy user from rote memorization, but all memory advice is clear that one should not rely on ready-made images, one should learn to fashion one's own, for only this exercise will concentrate the mind enough to ensure clear, safe traces. A true memory image is a mental creation, and it has the elaboration and flexibility, the ability to store and sort large amounts of information, that no pictured diagram can possibly approximate.

There is also a built-in indeterminacy of meaning, and even of relationship of parts, to medieval diagrams, for they follow the "logic" of recollection – which is associative and determined by individual habit – and not the "universal" logic of mathematics. Like the *tituli*, the rubrics, and the punctuation, the picture-diagrams are a part of the apparatus of a text – aiding its mnemonic *divisio*, surely, but deliberately inviting memorial *compositio* as well, the recollective process by means of which a particular reader engages a particular text (with all that includes) on a particular occasion.

The idea that manuscript decoration had a practical use has begun to be broadly adopted by codicologists and art historians; as De Hamel says, "Decoration is a device to help a reader use a manuscript."[89] But, as I hope this chapter has shown, if we take a wholly utilitarian approach to decoration, especially if we identify it with some preconceived notion of "literate" as opposed to "oral" culture, we will misunderstand its full function as much as we did when we thought of it as "only" decoration, or as a help for those who couldn't read. Like reading, of which it is a part, decoration is "practical" in the medieval understanding of that word, having a basic role to play in every reader's moral life and character because of its role in the requirements of memory.

Every medieval diagram is an open-ended one; in the manner of examples, it is an invitation to elaborate and recompose, not a prescriptive, "objective" schematic. Hugh of St. Victor did not think that he had produced a model of what the Ark was "really" like, whether at the literal, allegorical, or moral levels; this is apparent from the way in which he freely adds to the Genesis account of its lineaments and freely contradicts his own previous interpretations. Once again, we can see how his whole attitude towards a text differs from ours; it is not to him, a definitive "statement" of fact or experience but an occasion for rumination and meditation, for the engagement of *memoria*. Invitations to meditate further are found throughout his "pictura." After describing his elaborately "painted" ladders, for example, Hugh remarks, "There are a great many other things which might be said respecting these [figures] which, necessarily, we cannot bring into this place" (col. 697D). But the reader may stay to meditate and contemplate and learn from the examples which Hugh has provided.

The rhetorical indeterminacy of a medieval diagram extends as well, I think, to all the elements that "distinguish" a medieval page. Iconography, in art as well as literary criticism, treats images as direct signs of some thing, as having an inherent meaning that will be universal for all readers. But, like the painted letters, all the other decorative elements are signs that act directly only upon memory. In the memory of a particular reader they will become meaningful as I make them mine. And memories, as we have seen, are differently stored, having different tracks and associative paths. The one thing that a manuscript image must produce in order to stimulate memory is an emotion. It must be aesthetic in the Aristotelian sense of this word. It must create a strong response – what sort is of less importance – in order to impress the user's memory and start off a recollective chain. That combination of image and response makes up the memory image, and *only then*, when the fully formed image is in memory, can it become a subject of interpretation.

Let me take as an example of this distinction the famous black otter eating a salmon that is tucked into the bottom border of the "rho" of the Chi-rho page at the beginning of Matthew in the Book of Kells (figure 30). It is very hard to find amid the myriad and apparently fragmentary forms on this page. But as I suggested earlier, the page is designed to make one meditate upon it, to look and look again, and remake its patterns oneself; the process of seeing this page models the process of meditative reading which the text it introduces will require. The letters on this page are virtually hidden away in the welter of its other forms; indeed, thinking of this aspect of its design, Françoise Henry calls it "a sort of rebus" (p. 182). Yet it is not a true rebus, as are the visual puns suggested for remembering proper names by the author of *Dialexeis*. Nor is the Chi-rho page by any means a diagram-picture for the gospel of Matthew, even to the extent that "De arca mystica" is of "De arca morali." It helps instead to initiate the divisional and compositional process that is required to read Matthew, and it is this that makes it valuable to memory. In that process, the discovery of the successful otter, and – next to it – the two cats surrounded by mice they are too lazy to catch, surprises us with a shock of delight, whether or not we know the proverbs about lazy cats, or care to make a meditational link between industrious fishermen and cats who will not work for their food.[90] And, as Geoffrey of Vinsauf says, repeating a cliché of long standing, the memory-cell needs to be delighted as it works, lest too much heavy food give it indigestion. The emotion of surprise in itself makes the page effective in memory, whatever the meanings we may later give to its many forms.

Afterword

A number of years ago, I decided to write a little book about time in medieval narrative poetry. Since temporal relationships typically are a function of their narrator's recollection, I moved quickly to memory as a focusing theme. I thought I would compose an introductory survey of how *memoria* was defined in rhetoric and as a philosophical concept, and also how memory training had been practiced in medieval schools. I knew that several intellectual historians had written essays on the philosophy of memory in the Middle Ages, and I assumed that historians of rhetoric had covered the topic in their field too. What I discovered was a seeming consensus among those scholars that learned people of the Middle Ages had no particular interest in *memoria* at all, despite the acknowledged fact that books were in relatively short supply until the very end of the period, and that oral forms of discourse, such as sermons and disputations, continued – even increased – throughout the entire span of time as major social activities.

Historians of rhetoric concentrated on the changing classification of tropes and figures, while intellectual historians seemed agreed that Augustine had settled the matter once and for all, as far as medieval thinkers were concerned – at least until Aquinas came along and corrected a few of his notions. Before 1960, no historian, with the exception of Helga Hajdu, had written at any length about medieval mnemonic practices (though one could find dismissive references to them). Harry Caplan's concern was with the medieval transmission of the *Rhetorica ad Herennium*. Edmund Gardner wrote an essay about "imagination and memory," but only in reference to Dante. After 1960, the two historians who wrote the most about *memoria* were students of the Renaissance. Paolo Rossi's concern was with Renaissance logics; his interest in medieval sources began with the late thirteenth-century Italian translations of ancient memory advice. And Frances Yates left the firm (though perhaps unintended) impression that any learned interest in artificial memory during the Middle Ages resulted from involvement with the occult, and not from a commonplace tradition.

My "introductory survey" grew into the present book. I do not regard it as a definitive treatment of *memoria* in the Middle Ages. It is still an introductory chapter to a subject that seems only to open up each time one thinks one has pinned it down. Much remains to be done. For example, a great many "arts of memory" and treatises "for increasing memory," chiefly from the thirteenth through fifteenth centuries, remain unstudied. They should be collected and classified before a full history of medieval memory training can be written. For the earlier Middle Ages, I think one will find the traditions of memorial art not in separate treatises but in the practices of monastic prayer. The way in which these practices were translated for the pious laity of the late Middle Ages – the same audience that read the late medieval arts of memory addressed to lawyers, merchants, and other gentlemen – may illuminate a neglected source of early humanism. The relationship between all this material and the features of medieval books, both in general and at particular times and places, is a topic I barely touched in my last chapter. A number of art historians and codicologists have begun to study it in more particular detail than I could here, and it seems to me an obvious next step.

Interpreters and historians of literature are concerned just now with a host of issues raised by the present emphasis on general theory in the study of literature. For them, recognizing the role which *memoria* played in the making and reception of literature during the Middle Ages has immediate consequences. Students of medieval literature have for some time now realized that modern literary theory has intriguing parallels to the concerns and assumptions of medieval poets and readers. Indeed, it is remarkable how many of the most insightful of Continental theorists began as students of medieval or ancient literature.

Yet modern literary theory, when applied directly to medieval literature, has tended to obscure the very medievalness of that literature, and to present Dante, Chaucer, the French writers of romance and fabliaux, as crypto-moderns, subverters and deconstructors of tradition in an anti-establishment mode. Understanding the fundamental role of *memoria* – with all the various strands that cultural modality gathers up – redresses the imbalance in this view. For deconstruction, as we have seen, is at the heart of meditation and the assimilation of literature. Indeterminacy of meaning is the very character of recollective gathering. Emotions are the matrix of memory impressions, and so – of course – desire moves intellect, as all learning is based in remembering. These themes of deconstruction and psychoanalytic criticism are not socially subversive when we detect them in medieval literature; they are the tradition itself. Adaptation, the essential conduct of *memoria ad res*, lies at the very basis of medieval literary activity. Eustache Deschamps, the late-medieval French poet, called Chaucer a "graunt translateur": a great rememberer of traditions and famous stories that, like all good medieval readers, he had made fully his own. It is an epithet one might apply fittingly to the medieval centuries as a whole.

I have spoken frequently of *memoria* as a social institution, as essential to medieval paideia as it was to ancient. But one might equally – and perhaps more inclusively – speak of it as a "modality" of medieval cultures in the West, using a term from anthropology. A. J. Greimas argues that all cultural "values" are in fact "modalities" rather than absolutes. Clifford Geertz, arguing that cultures can be understood as "symbol-systems," and that culture is a public and social phenomenon, neither a private neurosis nor a transcendental norm (and he draws upon Wittgenstein in saying this), also speaks of the "modalities" which enable such symbol-systems to operate. Symbols are matters of relationships which must in some way be publicly recognized and remembered – they are not absolutes, but function entirely within social life.

Using such a view of culture, *memoria* can be considered as one of the modalities of medieval culture (chivalry might be another). It has identifiable and verifiable practices and procedures that affect a variety of cultural phenomena (the making of books, the compositional structures of sermons, the layout of the Bible, citational habits, classroom diagrams, the prevalence of certain tropes in poetry), and it also is a value in itself, identified with the virtue of prudence. As modalities, values enable certain behavior, and also give greater privilege to some behaviors over others (this could be construed as an anthropological way of stating the scholastic idea that all virtues are *habitus*). They thus become conditioners of a culture, which is a very different thing from regarding them as cultural "mentalités," in the same way that an identifiable and describable practice differs from a definitional "idea." It is in this way that I think we can meaningfully speak of the Middle Ages as a memorial culture, recognizing that, as a set of institutionalized practices, *memoria* was adapted, at least to a point, as these institutions changed, and yet that as a modality of culture it had a very long life as a continuing source and reference for human values and behavior.

As I sought to understand the texts I was studying, they became stranger to me than I had thought them to be, yet their strangeness, I discovered, lay in my expectations. I had continually to adjust my preconceptions, not only about the sixth- or twelfth- or fourteenth-century Middle Ages, but about unexamined basics, such as the nature of "memory," "mind," "imitation," and "book." Many things I had believed could not be done, such as composing difficult works at length from memory, had to be entertained as possibilities – even as expected and much admired behavior. The assumptions that I had been making had taught me that such feats occurred in primitive societies but were lost to literate, logical scholars.

I found, too, that I was dealing in large measure with unstated assumptions on the part of the medieval writers I was studying, chiefly their belief that all human learning is memorative in nature. It is that continuing belief that has led me to emphasize the memorial basis of the medieval cultures of the West. I call them "memorial," knowing that to modern readers the word has connotations only of death, but hoping that I can adjust their understanding of it – as I have had to do my own – to a more medieval idea: making present the voices of what is past, not to entomb either the past or the present, but to give them life together in a place common to both in memory.

Appendix A

Hugh of St. Victor
"De Tribus Maximis Circumstantiis Gestorum"[1]

Children, knowledge [sapientia] is a treasury [thesaurus] and your heart is its strongbox [archa]. As you study all of knowledge, store up for yourselves good treasures, immortal treasures, incorruptible treasures, which never decay nor lose their look of brightness. In the treasure-house of wisdom are various sorts of wealth, and many filing-places in the storehouse of your heart. Gold is put in one place, in another silver, in another precious jewels. Their orderly arrangement is clarity of knowledge. Dispose and separate each single thing into its own place, this into its and that into its, as you learn where this or where that should be gathered. Confusion is the mother of ignorance and forgetfulness, but orderly arrangement illuminates the intelligence and firms up memory.

You see how a money-changer who has unsorted coins, divides his one pouch into several compartments, just as a cloister embraces many separate cells. Then, having sorted the coins and separated out each type of money in turn, he puts them all in their proper places, since the differentiation [distinctio] of his compartments preserves the separation and distinction of the items, and thus keeps them unmixed. Additionally, you observe in his display of money-changing, how his ready hand without delay follows wherever the commanding nod of a customer has caused it to extend, and quickly, without delay, it brings each thing which he either may have wanted to receive or promised to give out, into a separate place without confusion. And it would provide on-lookers with a spectacle silly and absurd enough, if, while his money-bag should pour forth so many varieties without muddle, this same bag, its mouth being opened, should not display on its inside an equivalent number of separate compartments. And so this particular schematic arrangement [discretio] of places, which I have described, at one and the same time eliminates for the on-lookers any mystery in the action, and, for those doing it, an obstacle to their ability to perform it.

Now as we just said by way of preface, a classifying-system for material makes it palpable and visible to the mind [discretio rerum evidentiam facit]. Truly such a visual scheme for one's learning both illuminates the soul when it perceives and knows things, and confirms them in memory [Evidentia vero

rerum animum simul et in agnitione illuminat et in memoria confirmat].
Return, therefore, children, to your heart [Redi ... ad cor tuum][2] and
consider how you should dispose and collect in it the precious treasures of
wisdom, so that you learn about its individual repositories, and when for
safe-keeping you place something in them, dispose it in such an order that
when your reason asks for it, you are easily able to find it by means of your
memory and understand it by means of your intellect, and bring it forth by
means of your eloquence. I am going to propose to you a particular method
for such classification.

Matters we have learned are classified in the memory in three ways; by
number, by location, and by occasion. Thus all the things which you may
have heard you will both readily capture in your intellect and retain for a long
time, if you will have learned to classify them according to these three
categories. I will demonstrate one at a time the manner in which each should
be used.

The first means of classifying is by number. Learn to construct in your
mind a grid numbered from one on, in however long a sequence you want,
extended as it were before the eyes of your mind.[3] When you've heard
enumerated a group of items of a certain numerical size, get in the habit of
quickly turning your mind there [on your mental grid] where the sum-total
[of items enumerated] is marked off, as to that location [on the grid] at which
the group's full numerical complement is marked off all the way up to its last
member. For example, when you hear about a group of ten things, think of
the tenth place [along the grid], or the twelfth for a group of twelve things, so
that you conceive of the whole group following in order up to its limit, and
similarly for other numberable groups. Make this method of thinking and
this way of imaging it practiced and habitual, so that you conceive visually of
the extent and limit of all numerical groups, just as though [they were] placed
in particular places. And listen to how this mental visualization [consideratio]
could be useful for learning by heart.[4]

Suppose for example that I wish to learn the psalter word for word by
heart. I proceed thus: first I consider how many psalms there are. There are
150. I learn them all in order so that I know which is first, which second,
which third, and so on. I then place them all by order in my heart along my
[mental] numerical grid, and one at a time I designate them to the seats where
they are disposed in the grid, while at the same time, accompanied by voicing
[prolatio] or cogitation, I listen and observe closely [attendo] until each
becomes to me of a size equivalent to one glance of my memory: "Beatus
vir," with respect to the first psalm; "Quem fremuerunt," with respect to the
second; "Domine quid multiplicasti sunt," with respect to the third; this
[much] is kept in the first, second, and third compartments.[5] And then I
imprint the result of my mental effort [consideratio] by the vigilant concentration of my heart so that, when asked, without hesitation I may answer,
either in forward order, or by skipping one or several, or in reverse order and
recited backwards according to my completely-mastered scheme of places,

what is first, what second, what indeed 27th, 48th, or whatever psalm it should be. In this manner [disputants] demonstrate [that] the scriptures confirm their own arguments when, in order to get compound interest for the authority of some one psalm, they say this is written in the 63rd, this in the 75th, or whatever other psalm, fetching forth for reference not its name but its number. For surely, you don't think that those who wish to cite some one of the psalms have turned over the manuscript pages, so that starting their count from the beginning they could figure out what number in the series of psalms each might have? Too great would be the labor in such a task. Therefore they have in their heart a powerful mental device, and they have retained it in memory, for they have learned the number and the order of each single item in the series.

Having learned the [whole order of] psalms, I then devise the same sort of scheme for each separate psalm, starting with the beginning [words] of the verses just as I did for the whole psalter starting with the first words of the psalms, and I can thereafter easily retain in my heart the whole series one verse at a time; first by dividing and marking off the book by [whole] psalms and then each psalm by verses, I have reduced a large amount of material to such conciseness and brevity. And this [method] in fact can readily be seen in the psalms or in other books containing inherent divisions. When however the reading is in an unbroken series, it is necessary to do this artificially, so that, to be sure according to the convenience of the reader, [at those places] where it seems [to him] most suitable, first the whole piece is divided into a fixed number of sections, and these again into others, these into yet others, until the whole length of material is so parcelled up [restringatur], that the mind easily can retain it in single units. For the memory always rejoices both in brevity of length and fewness in number, and therefore it is necessary, when the sequence of your reading tends toward length, that it first be divided into a few units, so that what the mind [animus] could not comprehend in a single expanse it can comprehend at least in a number, and again, when later the more moderate number [of items] is subdivided into many, it may be aided in each case by [the principle of] minuteness or brevity.

So you see the value to learning of a numerical division-scheme; now regard and consider of what value for the same thing is the classification-system according to location. Haven't you ever noticed how a boy has greater difficulty impressing upon his memory what he has read if he often changes his copy [of a text] between readings? Why should this be unless it is because, when the image-receiving power of the heart is directed through the exterior sense into so many shapes from diverse books, no specific image can remain within [the inner sense] by means of which a memory-image may be fixed? For when something is brought together to be fashioned into an image [informari] from all [the copies] indiscriminately, one superimposed upon another, and always the earlier being wiped away by later ones, nothing personal or familiar [domestica . . . aut familiaris] remains which by use and practice can be clearly possessed.

Therefore it is a great value for fixing a memory-image that when we read books, we study to impress on our memory through our mental-image-forming power [per imaginationem] not only the number and order of verses or ideas, but at the same time the color, shape, position, and placement of the letters, where we have seen this or that written, in what part, in what location (at the top, the middle, or the bottom) we saw it positioned, in what color we observed the trace of the letter or the ornamented surface of the parchment. Indeed I consider nothing so useful for stimulating the memory as this; that we also pay attention carefully to those circumstances of things which can occur accidentally and externally, so that for example, together with the appearance and quality or location of the places in which we heard one thing or the other we recall also the face and habits of the people from whom we learned this and that, in so far as they are the kind by which they accompany their performance of a certain activity. All these things indeed are rudimentary in nature [puerilia], but of a sort beneficial for boys.

After the classifications by number and place follows the classification by occasions [discretio temporibus], that is: what was done earlier and what later, how much earlier and how much later, by how many years, months, days this preceeded that and that was followed by this other. This classification is relevant in a situation when, according to the varying nature of the occasions on which we learned something, at a later time we may be able to recall to our mind a memory of the content [ad rerum memoriam], as we remember that one occasion was at night and another by day, one in winter another in summer, one in cloudy weather another in sunshine.

All these things truly we weave as a kind of prelude [to our learning], bringing together these elementary foundations, lest we, disdaining the least element of our studies, start little by little to ramble incoherently [diffluere]. Indeed the whole usefulness of education consists only in the memory of it, for just as having heard something does not profit one who cannot [pituit, sic, for potuit] understand, likewise having understood is not valuable to one who either will not or cannot remember. Indeed it was profitable to have listened only insofar as it caused us to have understood, and to have understood insofar as it was retained. But these are as it were basics for knowledge, which, if they are firmly impressed in your memory, open up all the rest readily. We have written this [list of names, dates, and places] out for you in the following pages, disposed in the order in which we wish them to be implanted in your soul through memory, so that whatever afterwards we build upon it may be firm.

All exposition of divine scripture is drawn forth according to three senses: story, allegory, and "tropology," or, the exemplary sense. The story is the narrative of actions, expressed in the basic meaning of the letter. Allegory is when by means of this event in the story, which we find out about in the literal meaning, another action is beckoned to [innuitur], belonging either to past or present or future time. Tropology is when in that action which we hear was done, we recognize what we should be doing. Whence it rightly receives the name tropology, that is, speech that has changed direction or discourse folded-back on itself [sermo conversus sive locutio replicata], for without a doubt we turn [convertimus] the word of a story about others to our own instruction when, having read of the deeds of others, we conform our living to their example.

But now we have in hand history, as it were the foundation of all knowledge, the first to be laid-out [collocandum] in memory. But because, as we said, the memory delights in brevity, yet the events of history are nearly infinite, it is necessary for us, from among all of that material, to gather together a kind of brief summary – as it were the foundation of a foundation, that is a first foundation, which the soul can most easily comprehend and the memory retain. There are three matters on which the knowledge of past actions especially depends, that is, the persons who performed the deeds, the places in which they were performed, and the time at which they occurred. Whoever holds these three memorially in his soul will find that he has built a good foundation for himself, onto which he can assemble afterwards anything by reading and lecture [per lectionem] without difficulty and rapidly take it in and retain it for a long time. However, in so doing it is necessary to retain it in memory [memoriter] and by diligent retracing to have it customary and well known, so that his heart may be ready to put in place everything he has heard, and apply those classification-techniques which he will have learned now to all things which he may hear afterwards by a suitable distribution according to their place and time and person.

While time and number measure off the long side in the chest of memory, place extends the area transversely, so that, following along sequentially, the rest of the material may be disposed in its places. First, therefore, we will place our persons with their dates in order, extending them from the beginning along the long side of the grid [in longitudinem lineam]. Next, we will mark off our places adequately to whatever number the extent of our summary, gathered up out of all the material, will require. Now indeed you have enough to do to imprint in this fashion in your memory the matters which are written out below, according to the method and diagram for learning-by-heart demonstrated to you earlier, so that by experience you will know the truth of my words, when you perceive how valuable it is to devote study and labor not just to having heard the lectures on the scriptures or to discussion, but to memory-work.

The creation of nature was perfected in six days and the renewal of man will be achieved in six stages. The world was made before time began, fashioned in six days, in the first three days it was put in order, and fitted-out and decorated in the three following. On the first day light was made, on the second day the firmament between the waters above and the waters below. On the third day the waters which were under the firmament were gathered together in one place, and dry land appeared, and produced green plants and germinating fruits. Behold the arrangement of the elements in four. The heaven was stretched out above, next the air was made clear, next the waters were gathered together in one place, then the land was revealed. Its equipping and decoration followed. On the fourth day lights were created for ornamenting the heaven, sun and moon and stars. On the fifth day fish were created from the waters, and birds, birds for decoration of the air, fish for equipping the waters. On the sixth day were made the beasts of burden and [wild] beasts and the rest of living creatures, for ornament of the dry lands.[6] At the very last, in fulfillment of all, humankind was created, Adam and Eve. When he was 130 years old Adam engendered Seth. And Adam lived after he engendered Seth 800 years. Thus it is found in the Hebrew. However the authors of the Septuagint place 230 years before the birth of Seth, 700 after. And in all the period of Adam's life was 930 years. And likewise the others follow along [in the columns of the diagram] according to the true disposition of the Hebrew.[7]

Appendix B

Albertus Magnus
De bono, Tractatus IV, Quaestio II "De Partibus Prudentia"[1]

Next, the properties of prudence are investigated. And we follow the three categories of three philosophers, namely Tully, Macrobius, and Aristotle.

First Tully says at the end of his First Rhetoric [*De Inventione*]: "there are three parts to prudence, memory, intelligence, foresight." Macrobius, however, says in his *Commentary on the Dream of Scipio*: "the knowledge of prudence lies in intellect, circumspection, foresight, a willingness to learn, and caution." And Aristotle at the end of the first Book of his *Ethics* says that the intellectual virtues are prudence [sapientia], *phronesis*,[2] and intelligence [intelligentia].

Article One: What "Memoria" Might Be[3]

Let us inquire first concerning the word "memoria," which Tully only mentions. And we will inquire in two ways, namely concerning what it might be in itself, and concerning the art of memory which Tully teaches. First therefore let us examine what memory is. Tully says that "memory is the faculty by which the mind recalls things that were in the past." [*De inv.* II, 53, 160].

1   But it seems that according to this definition memory would not be a part of prudence. Memory, by means of which what has happened is recalled, is a function of the soul and not a characteristic capable of being developed by education and training [habitus], as is demonstrated in the questions *De anima* [Albertus Magnus, *De homine*, Q. 40, a. 1]; every part of prudence, however, is a matter of learning [habitus]; therefore memory is not a part of prudence.

2   Also, it was asserted above, that memory is a part of the sensory soul and not of the rational *per se*; prudence however is *per se* in the rational soul; therefore memory is not a part of prudence.

3   Moreover, to recollect things that have occurred is the action of a cognitive power; prudence, however, is a characteristic of ethical judgments [moralium]; therefore again memory is not a part of the virtue of prudence.

267

4   Likewise everything is directed and guided by something which is or can be; nothing of what has been, insofar as it has been, is or can be; therefore no direction is possible from past things, insofar as they are past. Whence this final conclusion follows, thus: All prudence is guided by present things, those things which are, or to future ones, those which can be; therefore no memory is a part of prudence.

5   Moreover, the recollection of something which happened comes about either by means of reason proceeding from a definite principle, or only by means of the forms of sense-objects. If it comes about in the first way, then to recall something past will be an act of reminiscence and not of memory, as appears from what was demonstrated earlier in my tract *De anima* [Albertus *De hom.*, Q. 41, a. 1]. If however, it is by the second method, then the action of memory will not accord with the rational soul, and thus it will not be a part of prudence.

But on the contrary: Prudence is the knowledge of the good and evil of actions; this knowledge, moreover, is greatly aided by events that have already happened, because by means of the past it will know in what way it should manage itself in the future; therefore memory should be a part of prudence.

Likewise, in a certain decretal, Pope [Gregory IX] says: "From your past life we separate out what we should anticipate concerning the future." [Greg. IX, Decret. 2.23.6 i. f.] So memories of the past direct us regarding the future; therefore, memory is a part of prudence. Likewise the Philosopher says that "an intellectual power stands in need of experience and time." [*Eth. Nic.*, I, i, 1103a 16–17]. The Philosopher says elsewhere in the beginning of *Metaphysics*: "memory creates experience among men; many memories of the same thing make effective the power of a single experience" [*Meta.*, 1.1, 980b, 20–981a 1]. Therefore it seems that memory should be generative of prudence and a part of it.

SOLUTIO: We say that memory is a part of prudence, insofar as memory comes under the definition of reminiscence. When prudence distinguishes those things by which it is assisted from those by which it is impeded in its work, it is necessary for it to proceed by a process of inquiry, and thus necessary for it to progress from a pre-determined starting-point, and through intermediate probabilities to arrive at a working hypothesis; and likewise since prudence proceeds from things that happened in the past, it uses memory, insofar as it is a function of reminiscence.

1   We reply therefore, that to recollect [repetere] things which are past comes about in two ways, that is from our natural predisposition, and this sort of recollection is only a psychological potential and imperfect in that it has no habitual method whence it might proceed. And there is recollection from trained habit, by which the past is recalled, whenever one wishes to recollect. And this can be a part of cognitive training [in

habitu cognitivo], and then it is theoretical, or it can be part of moral training [in habitu morali], and then it is practical and is the virtue pertaining to prudence.

2 Replying to the next that "memoria," insofar as it mixes itself up with reminiscence, belongs more to the rational soul than to the sensible soul, because reminiscence is as it were a kind of logical reasoning [syllogismus], as the Philosopher says, and so then "memoria" is a habit of the rational soul.

3 Replying to the next, that memory has two functions, that is, it is a condition for what we know rationally [habitus cognitivorum], and a condition for making ethical judgments [habitus moralium], and here it is discussed as a condition of making moral judgments, as I said.

4 Replying to the next, that the past so far as it is past brings nothing to our guidance in the present or the future. But memory takes in an event that is past as though it stayed ever-present in the soul as an idea and as an emotional effect on us, and so this event can be very effective for providing for the future. Moreover, I say "to stay in the soul as an idea," meaning an idea of good and evil, and "as an effect," meaning how much it affected positively or harmed those performing it.

5 Replying to the next, that "memoria" is understood by Tully as the trained habit and not as the psychological faculty. However, "habit" does not fall under the heading of reminiscence so much as it does of memory, and so it is more readily discussed as memory than as reminiscence. Both memory and reminiscence indeed proceed from past events when they are past. But a past event when past creates no habitual effect except in memory, and so it is called "memoria" by Tully. There are those, nonetheless, who say along with John Damascene and Gregory Nixenus, that memory is the accumulation of both sensible objects and of intellectual ones, and so they say there are two faculties of memory, that is, one of the sensible soul and the other of the rational. But this is not said in the natural philosophy which Aristotle taught, or the other following him. What indeed appears to us concerning this matter can be expressly discovered in our treatise *De anima*.

Article Two: Concerning the Art of Memory

Secondly, let us inquire concerning the art of memory which Tully treats in his Second Rhetoric, at the end of Book III.

Let us determine what "artificial" memory might be. For Tully divided the memory into natural and artificial, and he said our native memory was "something which is imbedded in our minds, born simultaneously with thought." And he says artifical memory is that "strengthened by a kind of inductive reasoning [inductio quaedam] and a system of rules."[4]

1 But it seems this is not so at all, because what he calls "natural memory" is either the activity of the soul, which is memory, or a particular

habitualized action, by which this power is made fully effective. If it is the first sort of thing, then he speaks nonsense, because a power of the soul cannot be classified together with some one habitual characteristic and above all of the very same power. But the artifical memory is a habit and it cannot be a habit except of a power, which is memory. If it is the second sort of thing, then it would not seem to be of our nature, because habitualized training in remembering things is not inborn in us.

2 Moreover, what he says – that ["'memoria'' is] "what is imbedded in our minds, born simultaneously with thought" – seems to be opposite to what is good for our native memory. I showed indeed, in my treatise *De anima* [*De homine*, Q. 40 a. 3] that the best conditions for memory are cold and dry, whence we say the melancholics are the best at remembering. But the worst condition for thought lies in cold and dry, because thinking [cogitatio] is the repeated working-over [coagitatio] and running back and forth [discursus] of reason on the objects of memory [memoribilia], and for the operation of reason warmth and pliability or dampness work better. For what is warm moves vigorously and what is damp best responds to all movements. Therefore the best condition for natural memory is not generated together with thought.

3 Moreover, we should inquire concerning what this same person [Tully] says about the artificial memory, that analogous argumentation [inductio] and a system of rules strengthen it, because these proceed from some reasoned principle by analogy or example or enthymeme or syllogism, when none of these is proper to memory but more to reminiscence, as Aristotle says in his book "De memoria et reminiscentia."

4 Moreover, it should be asked what is the difference between an induction and a general rule. An inductive argument comes about when entirely from single cases a universal principle is inferred, and in such a case a whole memory is generated as much of the natural as of the artificial. For the Philosopher says that out of many things, regarding which an example [instantia] is not already inventoried in the mind, "memoria" is created by the experience of the intellect. Thus the whole memory is made by the experience of generalizing from single cases [ab inductione experimento] among those things we have taken in [acceptorum]; thus this is not specific to the artificial memory.

5 Moreover, it appears from this that he should be wrong when he says "memoria" is made from a system of rules when induction suffices.

6 Likewise, a system of rules is a logic of universal principles; but a universal is generated by memory, as the Philosopher says; therefore what is generated by memory generates memory, which is impossible. Therefore Tully says wrongly that "memoria" is created by a system of rules.

7 In connection with this latter point, we should inquire concerning the rules, which he teaches, that are attendant on this artificial memory. He says indeed that among them it is necessary above all to pay attention to

those on which it is based: "the artificial memory consists of backgrounds and images." And he defines what he calls backgrounds thus: "By backgrounds [loci] I mean such scenes as are naturally or artificially set off on a diminished scale, complete, in a visually striking manner, so that we can grasp and embrace them easily by the natural memory – for example, a house, an intercolumnar space, a recess, an arch, or the like. An image is, as it were, a figure, mark, or portrait of a thing we wish to remember, such as the general class [genus] of horse, lion, eagle" and by this method it is sought. So when time is said to be more of the essence of memory than space, as something which falls within its very definition, why does not Tully say that time is as necessary to pay attention to as place is?[5]

8   Likewise, a background represented "on a diminished scale" is a truncated and mutilated place; "completely" represented however is a background equivalent to the thing itself. Therefore it seems that "diminished in scale" and "complete" are contradictory with regard to the same object of memory, and thus by saying one thing about something the other will be false.

9   Moreover, to represent "in a strikingly visual manner" does not seem suitable for the background of all memory-objects, because not every sort of object-for-remembering is made in a visually-marked place.

10   Moreover, what is a memory-place set off "naturally" and one "completely artificial"? These indeed ought to be defined but Tully does not do so, either earlier or later.

11   Further, let us inquire concerning the rules which he makes to be observed about background-places and there are five in general. The first of them is that "it will be more advantageous to obtain places in a deserted than in a populous region, because the crowding and passing to and fro of people confuse and weaken the impress of images, while solitude keeps their outlines sharp." The second is that "places differing in form and nature must be secured, so that, thus distinguished, they may be clearly visible; for if a person has adopted many intercolumnar spaces, their resemblance to one another will so confuse him that he will no longer know what he set in each background." The third is that "the places ought to be of moderate size and medium extent, for when excessively large they render the images vague, and when too small often seem incapable of receiving an arrangement of images." The fourth is that "the places ought to be neither too bright nor too dim, so that the images may not grow obscure in shadows nor be dazzling from brilliant light." The fifth is that "the interval between the places should be of moderate extent, approximately thirty feet; for like an external glance [aspectus], so the inner glance of thought [cogitatio] works less well when you have moved too near or too far away."

12   So, let us inquire concerning these background-places. It seems indeed at first when he speaks concerning the faculty of reminiscence, that

physical places are of no value for that which reminiscence deduces by a rational method. But physical backgrounds, at least ones of this sort, are in the image-making faculty.

13 Further, I held in my tract *De anima*, in the question "On memoria," that memory indeed retains for the soul not so much the images of sense objects but the reactions [intentiones] received from these images. Therefore it seems that images of physical places would not be especially valuable, but he ought to teach an art of such a kind as we should arrive at the responses abstracted from them.

14 Likewise, to imagine is from *imaginatio*, which according to the Philosopher is the treasury of forms, and therefore is also called *(vis) formalis*. Thus it seems that these things are more of *imaginatio* than of *memoria*.

15 Further it seems that he has taught incompletely the rules for the backgrounds in which the images of things to be remembered are deposited, because many other things are useful as places for remembering besides those he defined, solitude, distinctness, intervals neither too great nor too small. Many people indeed remember at sometime by the opposite characteristics of places.

Further, this same Tully himself adds a little further on: "if we are not content with our ready-made supply of backgrounds, we may create a region for ourselves and obtain a most serviceable distribution of appropriate backgrounds."

16 Additionally to this, let us inquire further concerning the images gathered in the places we spoke of. Tully says indeed that in two ways we must hold likenesses for remembering, one way according to things, the other according to words. "Likenesses of things [rerum] are formed when we enlist images that present a general view or summation of the matter with which we are dealing; likenesses of words are established when the record of each single name or word is kept by an image." Yet this technique which Tully speaks of does not seem to be a useful skill but more of an impediment to remembering, for two reasons. Of which one is that there will be as many images according to his method as there are matters and words. Therefore their multitude would confound the memory. The second reason is because metaphors represent things less well than do the words themselves. If therefore we should refer the literal content in our material and words to images, as he teaches, we will be less quick to remember. For he thus teaches us to have recourse to images: "[if] the prosecutor has said that the defendant killed a man by poison, has charged that the motive for the crime was an inheritance, and declared that there are many witnesses and accessories to this act," we place in our memory "a sick man in bed, who is a figure of the deceased, and we place the defendant standing by the bed, holding in his right hand a cup, in his left hand tablets, and a physician standing upright holding the testicles of a ram," so that certainly in the cup should be the

memory-cue of the poison which he drank, and in the tablets should be the memory-cue of the will which he signed, and in the physician may be figured the accusor and by the testicles the witnesses and accessories, and by the ram the defense against the matter being adjudicated. The same method is observed regarding images for words. But what is literal would affect any one more easily than what is non-literal, and so literal words will stimulate the memory more than metaphorical ones.

17 Moreover, Tully himself says that "when we wish to represent by images the likenesses of words, we shall be undertaking a greater task and exercising our ingenuity the more; this we ought to effect in the following way." Suppose we wish to recollect these words: "Now their revenge at home [*domi ultionem*]" or "their "home-coming [*domum itionem*, the right reading]," which is better, "the kings, sons of Atreus, prepare [*Iam domum itionem reges Atridae parent*]." In a background we must place Domitius, raising hands to heaven, while he is whipped with thongs by the Marcian kings; this will be "now the kings their revenge at home." In the next place, Aesopus and Cimber preparing wandering Ephigenia; this will be "Atridae making ready." That is, we should imagine someone who is beaten with sharp thongs by the Marcian kings, that is the sons of Mars, that is who aid Mars the god of war, for his own exile or for revenge, and because he who prepares himself for something wanders about, we represent wandering Ephegenia preparing Aesopus and Cimber [*sic*].[6] These indeed are metaphorical words and obscure things not easy to remember.

18 Finally, let us inquire concerning those rules which Tully gives for gathering images in such background-places. Indeed Tully says that "the backgrounds are very much like wax tablets or papyrus, the images like the letters, the arrangement and disposition of the images like the script, and the delivery is like the reading." This does not seem possible. For letters are few in number compared to the number of elements, and according to the diverse arrangements they express, whatever may be needed for speaking, as Democritus said happens in tragedies and comedies; but it would be necessary to have a great many images or they could not express the content in its literal kind.

19 If it is said definitely that a few images are enough, this indeed will be contrary to Tully, because it appears from the above examples that it is necessary to have one's own likenesses of things.

20 Next after Tully has taught what kinds of places we ought to employ, in a similar way he teaches what sorts of images we must seek out, that is, "we should set up the mental images of our likenesses to be as striking as possible, though not multiform or diffuse and changeable in nature, but we shall select images that are doing something; if we attribute to them exceptional beauty or singular ugliness; if we dress some of them with crowns or purple cloaks so that the likeness may be more distinct to us; or if we somehow disfigure them as by introducing one stained with

blood or soiled with mud or smeared with red paint, so that its form is more striking, or by assigning comic effects to our images. For that too will ensure that we are able to remember more easily." From this it appears that it is not sufficient to have a limited number of images, so that according to their diverse arrangement each single one expresses a meaning to us, but we must have many, and these will not be less difficult to recall than the matters or universals themselves. Therefore the rules of Tully are useless.

21 Moreover, even Tully himself says regarding the images, that in order to recollect by their means, we need two conditions to be met, that is, that they be for studying and equally, that they be strange and unusual, ones which are almost marvels. And he touches on the reason for each of these conditions, saying of the first thus: "But such an arrangement of images succeeds only if we use our notation to stimulate the natural memory, so that we first go over a given verse twice or three times and then represent the words by means of images." Likewise, in the same place: "art will supplement nature; for neither by itself will be strong enough, though we must note that theory and technique are much the more reliable." He also touches on the reason for the second condition, saying: "Now nature herself teaches us what we should do. When we see in everyday life things that are petty, ordinary, and common, we generally fail to remember them, because the mind is not being stirred by anything novel or marvellous. But if we see or hear something either incredibly decent or base in human beings, also unheard of, great, incredible, dangerous, that we are likely to remember for a long time."[7]

Likewise in the same place: "things which are immediate to our eye or ear we commonly forget; incidents of our childhood we often remember best, nor could this be so for any other reason than that ordinary things easily slip from the memory while the striking and novel stay longer in the mind." Again, in the same place: "Thus nature shows that she is not aroused by the common, ordinary event, but is moved by a new or striking occurrence. Let art, then, imitate nature, find what she descries, and follow where she directs. For in invention nature is never last, education never first; rather the beginnings of things arise from natural talent, and the ends are reached by discipline."

From all these quotations it appears that for the artificial memory disciplined practice in images and contents [negotiis][8] and words and much else besides is required, so that our images may be rare and eyecatching, and thus it seems that these may not be predetermined images which we employ for remembering all sorts of things, as we employ letters for signifying every sort of thing in writing. If because of this it is said that the images ought to be as numerous as the matters and words, Tully says the contrary about what is good for memory, in the same book just before the end: "I know that most of the Greeks who have written on the memory have taken the course of listing images that correspond to a great many words, so that persons who wished to learn these images by heart would have them ready without expending effort on a search for them. I disapprove of their method on several grounds." And he puts forth in general six reasons why what they say is wrong. Of which the first is thus stated by Tully: "first, among the immemorable [*sic* for 'innumerabile'] multitude of words it is ridiculous to collect images ['mille' *omitted*]. How meagre is the value these can have when out of the infinite store of words we shall need to remember different ones [*second* 'aliud modo' *omitted*]?" The second reason is "why do we wish to rob anyone of his initiative, so that, to save him from making any search himself, we deliver to him everything searched out and ready?" The third is because "one person is more struck by one likeness, and another by another. Often in fact when we declare that some one form resembles another, we fail to receive universal assent, because things seem different to different persons; the same is true with respect to images, one that is well defined to us appears relatively inconspicuous to others; everybody, therefore, should in equipping himself with images suit his own convenience." The fourth reason is because "it is the instructor's duty to teach the proper method of search in each case, and, for the sake of greater clarity, to add in illustration some one or two examples of its kind, but not all, as for instance, when I discuss how to find an introduction, I give a method of search and do not write out a thousand kinds of Introductions. The same procedure I believe should be followed with respect to images." The fifth cause is because since memory is of two kinds, that is of things and of words, "lest we make memorizing too difficult, we should be content with memory for things," lest the number of words overwhelm what is memorized. The sixth and final reason is that we do not have training in memorizing-for-words unless it makes our *res* more readily memorable, indeed, "that by such training memory for things is confirmed in us, which alone principally is of practical use. In every discipline artistic theory is of little avail without unremitting exercise, but especially for memorizing theory is valueless unless made good by industry, devotion, toil, and care."

SOLUTIO: We say that art of memory is best which Tully teaches, above all with respect to those things-for-remembering which pertain to how we live and to justice, and these memories chiefly relate to ethics and rhetoric because since the action of human life consists in particular events, it is necessary that this art be within the soul through corporeal images; in these images however it will not remain except within the memory. Whence we say that among all those things which point towards ethical wisdom, the most necessary is trained memory, because from past events we are guided in the present and the future, and not from the converse. Indeed that necessity be in trained memory to the highest degree, Tully proves by this argument, saying: "While an engrossing preoccupation may often distract us from our other pursuits, from memorizing nothing whatever can divert us. Indeed there is never a moment when we do not wish to commit something to memory, and we wish it most of all when our attention is held by business of special importance. So, since a ready memory is a useful thing, you see clearly with what great pains you must strive to acquire so useful a faculty, so that you will be able to judge having learned its utility." Therefore we say with Tully that the kind of "memoria" which relates to human life and justice is two-fold, that is, natural and trained or "artificial." That is natural which by virtue of its talent for finding-out things remembers easily something it knew or did at an earlier time. The "artificial" however is one which is made from an orderly arrangement of images and places, and, as in everything else art and virtue are a perfection of natural talent, so also in this. What is natural is completed by training. This however should be noted, that in all these matters I have been discussing, the word "memoria" is posited instead of "reminiscencia," for the reason determined above.

1   We reply to that which was questioned in the first place, by saying that Tully defines "natural memory" as a power perfected by a natural habit and not an absolute power of the soul. Those people are called naturally good at remembering who have that ability either completely or mostly by nature, which others have by exercise of the art of memory, just as philosophers have said with regard to the divine intelligence, which knows all things by its very nature. And this kind of talented memory is with regard to its own disposition very well able to be compartmentalized and divided up exhaustively [condividi], in that it is itself a trainable power.

2   To the next I respond, because the word "memoria" is posited in place of "reminiscencia," likewise the condition beneficial for it accords more with what is beneficial for mental ingenuity than for the memorative power, in the way that reminiscence uses rational method and ingenuity in proceeding from one or many definite principles accepted in advance. And so this objection is not tenable.

3   I reply to the next, especially as it is most often the case that "memoria" is used in place of "reminiscencia" by Tully, that since there is no recollection without memory, what is good for memory works also for recollection.

4   Replying to the next, that memory can be thought of in two ways, that is in respect to its objects or the neuropsychological condition [habitus] left by these objects, and thus it is true that all memory is generated by inductive reasoning. But ready aptitude for memory-work is observed both in the action of memorizing and in retaining things-to-be-remembered, and thus remembering is like a certain category of that art which is called the art of remembering, and thus it is generated not so much from inductive reasoning but by the many rules of organization for doing it. There are however these two in general for doing it, that is, an induction on the basis of one's memorial images, and a rule based on an organizational starting-point, from which the memory begins to proceed rationally in its action of remembering. As I said in the question

Appendix B

"Concerning recollection" [*De homine*, Q. 41] recollection starts its procedure from a beginning determined by something acquired before or in respect to something forgotten. Whence it is necessary that within the soul there be something out of which it proceeds and something in terms of which it progresses. What it proceeds from is the starting-point, which Tully calls rules. What it progresses in terms of are images, which are like letters within the soul, as Tully says.

5 From this appears the solution to the next objection, which is that a rule is not useful in memory-work.

6 I reply to the next, that a rule is generated out of the materials of memory on the basis of the things-worth-remembering from among those we acquired earlier, but it aids in the same activity, insofar as in the act of remembering it goes over the very same thing-worth-remembering, and thus nothing prevents memory from engendering something that previously was produced in itself.

As something closely connected to this, let us inquire concerning the rules which Tully taught, in saying that these are the best, as he himself says, and one of them is accepted as a starting-principle, in terms of which first of all a matter [res] worthy-of-remembering moves along in the process of recollection, because, as Boethius says, every particular thing is created or has being in some place. But "place" [locus] is construed by Tully here as that which the soul itself makes for storing-up images, and this also follows because, since reminiscence has no storehouse except only the memory, and reminiscence is part of the rational soul, it is necessary that something which exists as part of reason be stored-up in corporeal images. Since however, something which exists as part of reason cannot, by means of its own nature, exist in corporeal images, it is necessary that it exist there in them through likeness and translation and metaphor, as for example, for "joy" the most similar mental "place" [locus] is a cloister-garden, and for "feebleness" an infirmary or hospital and for "justice" a courtroom, and so for the rest. And Tully talks about "backgrounds" in such a way. The image however serves the memory as a likeness appropriate to a sentiment remembered through its separate parts, as afterwards will appear in the examples which Tully gives.

7 In response to the problem concerning time, it appears of easy solution for, since all things remembered are past in time, time does not serve to classify things-worth-remembering and thus does not lead one more to one thing than to another. But a formal background mainly classifies through this feature, that not everything remembered is in one place, and it affects memory by this means, that it is formally composed [solemnis] and spare [rarus]. Indeed the mind more firmly latches onto things formally composed and sparely-constructed, and likewise such things more strongly are imprinted in it and more strongly affect it.

8 Replying to the next, that a "small-scale" or "curtailed" space is so called

by Tully not literally nor certainly meaning smaller than the image of the things stored, but meaning more that the mind should not be spread excessively by traversing through imaginary spaciousness, like a field or a city; but the "place" is "small-scale" when the soul at once flies swiftly around its corners seizing the images hidden away in them. And through this appears the solution to the following objection because "small-scale" and "complete" are not contradictory, but being "small-scale" more ably restricts the straying of the mind, and "completeness" facilitates the whole matter being remembered.

9   I reply to the next by saying that because a conspicuous background more affects the soul, and although not every memorable thing is formed in a conspicuous place, nonetheless each thing-worth-remembering has to be put away in a likeness having a conspicuous background; so indeed this background-place is mentally grasped, as was said.

10   To that which was objected next, I say that Tully by means of his examples does define the difference between natural backgrounds and those which are artificial. A meadow is a "natural" place, a house or intercolumnar space, on the other hand, is "artificial."

11   To the previous query concerning the rules for places which Tully taught, I say that there are five, as he says, which especially create the best condition for remembering, and all are construed to prevent confusion in remembering. But confusion is engendered either in respect to the background-place or the matters located in it or to that which by its action makes visible the background and what is in it. And if confusion arises in respect to the matters in the location, then it will be the sort covered by the first rule, because a background, in which one has frequent encounters while on one's mental tour [obambulatio], heaps up a great many images, and so these images break up in the soul and do not remain, just as a great number of waves break up in water. If however confusion exists with regard to the background-place only, this is of three kinds, insofar as what affects its relative position. There is certainly the task of distinguishing one location from another, and on this principle the second rule is interpreted. Then, there is its comparableness and proximity to the matter to be remembered, and in this way the third precept is understood. There is next the extent [spatium] of the material, in terms of which the closeness or remoteness of one position from another is determined, and as far as this the fourth rule is interpreted.[9] If however the confusion results from the quality which on both sides makes us able to see what's going on, then it is a matter of obscurity or brightness, for something glaring certainly confounds sight and so it escapes from the mind and is not strongly imprinted; something obscure however does not sufficiently present things to view, and so again not much is imprinted by the one imagining. And thus it is clear through definition in what ways these rules are interpreted.

12   To the next objection the solution appears through what was said earlier,

because although reminiscence is situated within the rational soul, nonetheless it subjects itself to memory, and thus they bring together at the backgrounds the things-we-make-images-of [imaginabilia].

13 Replying to the next, the reactions [intentiones] which memory stores do not exist absolutely apart from the images of particulars, as is demonstrated in the same part of that treatise [*De homine*, Q. 40 a. 1]. And so these reactions are taken in at the same time along with the images, and therefore there is no need to have special rules for them.

14 Replying to the next, that imagination understood as the calculus of things-imaged, according to what the Philosopher says, by definition is slave to memory, because it is called "imagination" from its imitating an object, in that in shaping an object it causes us to have imitated that object, and that is, when by means of this imagining-action we arrive at what we earlier had taken in. The image-making-action however, which more properly is called *vis formalis*, contains the likeness according to what is received from the object into ourselves, and so more characteristically holds it insofar as it is a shape rather than a mental image. Because of this it is called *formalis* by the philosophers.[10]

15 I respond to the next problem, that Tully did not teach imperfectly; it is necessary that he who learns about "place" should understand it under these different headings. But Tully wished to say that various people will place for themselves different backgrounds, those indeed which move them more. For some will place a church, from having turned their minds to churches, others to an intercolumnar space, others a cloister-garden, others a hospital, because they are affected by these; nonetheless it is necessary that anyone learn his background-place according to these five categories, because otherwise they will not engender memory but the confusion of mind which leads to forgetfulness.

16 Replying finally to the question concerning images for things and for words, that in truth these images convey much to the memory and are as much for the purpose of making the thing intelligible, as they are for producing copies.

To that other objection, I reply that there are many individual things, but by transference a few are used in speaking about many [others] having similarity, and so although literal words make for more accuracy about the thing itself nevertheless the metaphors move the mind more and thus convey more to the memory.

17 Replying to the next, that what is marvelous [mirabile] is more moving than what is ordinary, and so when images of this metaphorical sort are made up out of marvels [ex miris] they affect memory more than commonplace literal matters. So indeed early philosophers translated their ideas in poetry, as the Philosopher says [*Metaphy.*, 1.2 982b 15–20; cf. 1.3 983b 28–32 and Aristotle's quotation of Hesiod at 1.4, describing him as an early philosopher], because a fable, since it is composed out of marvels is more affecting. From this it appears that "from wondering [ex

admirari] about befores and afters then and now is the beginning of philosophical thinking" [*Metaphy.*, 1.1 982b 11–12], because what is wonderful [mirum] by its vigorous motion causes questioning, and thence gives rise to investigation and recollection.

18 Replying to a further question concerning the rules for images of things and of words, that metaphors define many things in one, in that there are many likenesses within the one metaphor, and thus they are like letters, but it is true that the literal things themselves are many and confusing.

19 Replying to the next, that what Tully means by "appropriate images" are ones which define by express and notable likenesses and not ones which are particular for each of one's memory-matters separately.

20 Replying to the next that in his examples Tully touches on those which strongly move us and not those which are appropriate; those which strongly move us adhere in our mind for a longer time and more quickly occur to us.

21 Replying to the next that Tully teaches that for study we require that every particular [proprium] bit of information adhere in our mind and indeed that each particular be attached to it by a metaphor, but even so such a way of studying will not sufficiently cause us to recollect, in that particulars of our education are excessively numerous and one effaces another. And therefore the art of remembering is executed by means of a few rules for backgrounds and images. Through this appears indeed the solution to the whole objection, and that which Tully presents contrary to it clearly is to be conceded.

Appendix C

Thomas Bradwardine
"De Memoria Artificiali"
(Translated from Fitzwilliam Museum, Cambridge, MS. McClean 169, by
permission of the Syndics of the Fitzwilliam Museum.)[1]

For trained memory, two things are necessary, that is, firm locations and also images for the material; for the locations are like tablets on which we write, the images like the letters written on them; moreover, the locations are permanent and fixed, whereas the images are now inked on like letters and are then erased; and the locations are fundamental to the images, just as I earlier said of them. With regard to these locations, then, six matters are distinguished, that is, size, configuration, characteristics, number, order, and distance-away [distancia intercepta].[2] Each location should be of moderate size, as much as one's visual power can comprehend in a single look, such as a small garden or arcaded space [like a cloister]. Indeed memory is most powerfully affected by sensory impression, most strongly by vision; wherefore something occurs in memory as it customarily occurs in seeing.

Truly a location's configuration should be like a four-sided oblong. Concerning its characteristics, four things are known: to wit, that the places should not be made so dark that then they cannot be taken easily nor readily from memory, nor with great brightness, for then they will impede the perception of the inscribed images. Secondly, it is known that the places should not be formed in a crowded place, such as a church, the market, etc., because the crowding into one place of content-images which frequently occur in memory will crowd out other content-images. But they should be formed in regions deserted by men and empty. Thirdly, it is known that it helps a lot that the places should be real rather than mostly imagined or made-up, for real places one can frequently inspect, and thus through repetition shape and firm-up an habitual knowledge of them. Nevertheless by means of imaginary places properly made one can work if one chooses.

Fourthly, it is useful that contrasting locations be formed (as also might similarly be said in connection with the number of places). And so the first place might be like land unused and empty; the second like a green garden; the third like land having hay lying about or fruits as in time of harvest; the fourth as having stubble after gathering the fruits; the fifth like black ground after the stubble is completely burned. Then make for yourself another five places higher up, if you want, such as a large and high couch; then a cupboard; then a table; then a tomb; then an altar. Then if you want to climb more through another five places, first place the roof of a house made of wood, secondly of thatch, thirdly of stone, fourthly of red tile, and fifthly [*lacuna* in the text]. Then if you want perhaps another five floors of upper-rooms, the first as though of earth, the second as though paved in green stone, the third paved with tile, the fourth spread with grasses or straw, and the fifth furnished with carpets or cloths. These four times five backgrounds should suffice for all things to be remembered, or perhaps ten of them or somewhat fewer, unless a man should want to make unheard-of marvels.

Truly order requires that the places have contiguity and direction, so that memory may with facility find all the inscribed images in their places easily, in forward order or backwards. Concerning the depiction of the background within the locations [locorum distanciam] two things are determining, that is, extent and detail [qualitas]. The extent will be moderate when the location is clearly distinguished; the detail of its background, however, should be none, but it should be an empty void. With regard to the rememberer who mentally perceives the locations, three things are required for effectiveness, that is, a clear and firm habitual memory of these locations, which one should make by their frequent inspection or at least should turn them over and over in one's mind. Secondly, that one should know promptly without counting whichever number in the order of places it may occupy. Thirdly, when one must use one of the locations for a memory task, one imagines oneself positioned at the optimal distance from it [fingat se positum in distancia optima] and from there reviews the location.

These precepts suffice us in regard to the locations; now we go on to the images, where four considerations occur, that is size, quality, order, and number. The size should be average, as was said above regarding the backgrounds. Their quality truly should be wondrous and intense, because such things are impressed in memory more deeply and are better retained. However such things are for the most part not average but extremes, as the most beautiful or ugly, joyous or sad, worthy of respect or something ridiculous for mocking, a thing of great dignity or vileness, or wounded with greatly opened wounds with a remarkably lively flowing of blood, or in another way made extremely ugly, strange of clothing and all bizarre of equipment, the color also very brilliant and intense, such as intense, fiery red, and the whole color strongly altering the appearance. The whole image also should have some other detail or movement, that thus more effectively than through what is routine or at rest, they may be commended to memory.

The ordering of images should be done thusly. For the first thing which you want to remember, fashion for yourself an image of the size and character just described, which you place in the front of the first location. And if you can, make for the image a right hand and left hand, and constitute the image that comes next in order on the right hand of the first. Then position it so that the first image with its right hand holds, drags, strikes the following image, or does something of this nature to it, or the second holds itself opposed to the first; thus the procedure should be like a glueing together of the order among them [quasi quedam colligacio ordinis inter illas]. And this method of linking should be observed among all the images in the same way consistently. And, if you can, position the third as though riding around the second or doing something other to it, and to the third join the fourth, if you can; and to the left hand of the image relate the fifth, and to the fifth the sixth, if you can.

If truly you don't want to gather so many images into one location, place the first image as was said, the second to its right, and the third to its left, and crossing over to the second location, in it and any following ones you will collect as many images as is agreeable. But you should pay diligent attention especially to this, that the torso of any image is the first thing in any order to look at. Then, the hand or foot with its appendages that is nearer to the front of the location comes in order before the more remote part and its contents.

As to the number of images, it is notable that in one place three images in fitting positions are possible, or five or seven, but not many more, lest a superfluous multitude of them should blur their distinctiveness. With respect to the images, moreover, two things are helpful for the rememberer. First he should not make his images for himself too quickly and inquisitively, but a little at a time he imprints whatever portion he wants for himself profoundly and stablely by cogitating. The second thing is that not just the image itself but equally its order with relation to what most immediately precedes and what follows he should equally diligently commit to his memory, so that wherever he may wish, forwards or backwards, he may recollect easily regarding this one particular.

But one achieves recollection in two ways: in one easy way, that is, by the content itself only; in another difficult way, that is according to the exact words as well. It is necessary to have this double method of memorizing, and in the first place the memory for content should be treated. I say the *res* for memory are twofold, some sensory and concrete, and some abstract. Of the sensory things, some are visual and some not. Of those visible some are overly large, some overly small, and others are average. I will speak in the first place about those that are average.

Suppose that someone must memorize the twelve zodiacal signs, that is the ram, the bull, etc. So he should make for himself in the front of the first location a very white ram standing up and rearing on his hind feet, with (if you like) golden horns. Likewise one places a very red bull to the right of the ram, kicking the ram with his rear feet; standing erect, the ram then with his right foot kicks the bull above his large and super-swollen testicles, causing a copious infusion of blood. And by means of the testicles one will recall that it is a bull, not a castrated ox or a cow.

In a similar manner, a woman is placed before the bull as though laboring in birth, and from her uterus as though ripped open from the breast are figured coming forth two most beautiful twins, playing with a horrible, intensely red crab, which holds captive the hand of one of the little ones and thus compells him to weeping and to such signs, the remaining child wondering yet nonetheless caressing the crab in a childish way. Or the two twins are placed there born not of a woman but from the bull in a marvellous manner, so that the principle of economy of material may be observed. To the left of the ram a dreadful lion is placed, who with open mouth and rearing on its legs attacks a virgin, beautifully adorned, by tearing her ornate garments. With its left foot the ram inflicts a wound to the lion's head. The virgin truly holds in her right hand scales for which might be fashioned a balance-beam of silver with a plumb-line of red silk, and then weighing-pans of gold; on her left is placed a scorpion wondrously fighting her so that her whole arm is swollen, which [scorpion] she strives to balance in the aforesaid scales.

Then in the front of the second location is placed an archer with suitable equipment, holding a wonderous bow fully extended, in which more marvellously should be an arrow, and he strives to shoot arrows at a goat standing erect slightly farther back in the same location, grotesquely and disgustingly hairy, having a fanciful horn and a golden, luxuriant beard. And he holds in his right foot a remarkable jug full of water, in his left foot unusual fishes, for which he pours copiously very clear water from the water-vessel. And if it should be necessary to remember more things, one places their images in the following locations in a similar manner. Having done so, the rememberer is able to recite these things in the order he wants, that is forwards or backwards.

If however you wish to recall things of extreme size, whether large or small, of the sort such as the world, an army, a city, a thousand, an iota, or the smallest of worms, one makes average-sized images of them, perhaps of the sort that are depicted by manuscript decorators [a pictoribus], either by means of something contrary to them, similar, or that will in another way match up a related memory of such kinds of things. If however you want to recall abstractions by sensible things, as for instance "sweetness," place someone feeding himself with something sweet, like sugar, honey, milk, or something else of this sort tasting pleasant. But for "bitterness," place someone feeding himself on something bitter and immediately vomiting it up in a disgusting manner. For "foulness," place someone smelling bad in the presence of someone else, who closes his nostrils with one hand as though against the bad odor and with the other gestures contemptuously towards this thing. For a thing entirely abstract, of the sort as God, an angel, infinite space, and such matters are, place an image as the painters make it [ut faciunt depingentes], or secure its recollection by means of something that is contrary to it, similar, or analogous in another manner.

Having spoken concerning memory-for-things, now memory-for-words occupies us, for which I demonstrate the following precept [conclusio] for remembering given syllables [de memoria sillabarum propositarum]. To commit a syllable artificially to memory, the rememberer should have for himself an immediate image for any syllable always stored away by habit, which whenever he wants he is able freely to use, and this he does in this manner. He should consider and write down for himself the whole possible number of syllables, and should also consider the same number of easily visualizable things known to him, whose name in Latin or in his own language or in another language known readily to him may start with or completely coincide with those syllables, whichever is more useful. And because among diverse languages, and even among different speakers of the same language several names for the various things are used frequently, which may occur more readily to memory, it is not fully possible to give specific advice that applies to all people. But each should take pains to adapt this advice to his memory in his own way, and most prudently to conserve his version without variation.

Whenever you should want to remember according to a particular syllable, place something whose name begins with that syllable or is totally coincident with it in a particular location, as was taught above, by means of which one may immediately recall the name of that thing whose first syllable it appropriates, and one should work in a similar way with regard to any syllable. But whoever wants to shorten this labor should do this only in the language known to him whose ready memorableness will seem to him more useful, for in one language of whatever sort, I maintain, there are fewer syllables than all the ones which might possibly be of use. But certainly practical instruction in this technique is in the long run more economical and more useful [than a general conclusion].

Every syllable is a vowel or composed of a vowel and a consonant. For the five vowels make for yourself five images in this way: for "A" make for yourself gold [aurum], a communion wafer [azimus], or Adam naked covering his genitals with leaves, or something else of this sort whose name begins with A or is in like manner found in a language [other than Latin] which occurs to you more easily. For "E" place Eve naked hiding her genitals with green leaves, or something else of the sort as was said earlier. And for the remaining vowels you should make for yourself the remaining images in a similar fashion.

For any syllables made in the minimal way therefore, that is constituted only from one vowel and a consonant, work in like manner. So, for the "ab" syllable, make for yourself a well-known abbot [abbatus] costumed appropriately; for "ba" a crossbowman [balisterius] with a belt and the other things that are required, and with respect to the other syllables work likewise in the same way. If however you should wish to work more economically, signal to yourself an erect abbot for "ab," an upside-down one for "ba"; an upright crossbowman "ba," an upside-down one "ab." And in similar fashion you can place only one image for pairs of syllables, according to its various positions.

For syllables of three letters, with two consonants at the extremes and a vowel in the middle, here is an example that will serve for all such cases. So, for the syllable "bar" you make Bartholomew, flayed; for "rab," indeed, Rahab the well-known harlot, and for other paired syllables you fashion one thing or another in such a manner, according to one likeness or another, as I said. If however you wish to make the technique still easier, fashion for yourself images for all the syllables,[3] or at least for those which occur alone as many times before as after syllables of two letters; to pick out a few, of this sort are "r" and "l" with those like them. For the "l" consonant, therefore, if you are English, you can make for yourself an elbow, which accords with the aforesaid consonant both in name and shape. So therefore, if you want to recall "bal," you station the image of the "ba" syllable, an upside-down abbot (or an erect crossbowman, if you want to use that) and he holds the elbow in his mouth transversely through its middle (or in the other method it is attached to the uppermost extremity of the crossbowman) in order to signify that the "ba" syllable must be followed by an "l." Then the "lab" syllable may be signified by the same image having the contrary situation. But for retaining memorially the syllable "bla," position a crossbowman holding his elbow in the middle in his hand, if you like, or under his belt, which should signify to you that "l" ought to be in the middle of the "ba" syllable, and so it will figure for you the syllable "bla." There are indeed other syllables of more letters, and for them a prudent person is able satisfactorily enough to extend this art. These [rules] however suffice for the memory of syllables.

Using this technique we may also treat the memory of quotations or sayings [de memoria dictionum], concerning which a general rule [conclusio] like this might be permitted for remembering a saying to be recalled artificially. This precept follows from the previous one, for any saying has syllables in serial order, and therefore by having memory for syllables one also gains memory for quotations. Another way however is shorter and more handy, although more uncertain. This involves mixing content-memory with word-memory [miscendo realem memoriam cum verbali]. If you need to recall a certain quotation which may be associated by you with a content-image [rem ymaginabilem], place for yourself the image for that content [rei illius ymaginem] instead of using this other memory technique for a saying. And if an image of content already known to you may occur which would also serve the quotation you propose to remember, the name for the content is selected whose name in two or more syllables is concordant with the quotation. If however you should not be able to find one, at least seek out something whose name in the first syllable sounds like the quotation, which you are able to fashion according to the previous rule; and it is a further rule that at the same time the matter be constituted so that through its parts it connects up the recollection of the whole and just the reverse, and from the beginning of the quotation to anywhere in its totality, and by means of one likeness to another likeness, or by means of one of its contraries to the rest, and by means of any association whatever or pertaining in whatever manner you like, it will connect all the rest to be recalled.

Appendix C

Having expedited these things in such a way, it remains to speak concerning the memory for themes [memoria oracionum];[4] the following general rule [conclusio] may be allowed. To deliver whatever theme you have proposed, the method follows from the next example: "Benedictus Dominus qui per rege anglie Berwicum fortissimum et totam Scotiam subjugavit." ["Blessed be the Lord who by the English king subjugated most strongly-fortified Berwick and all Scotland."] For the first phrase, therefore, if you should know someone named Benedict or even St. Benedict the abbot place him at the front of the first location; and if you should have a certain lord known to you who by his real name is called Dominus, place him wounded in the face, drawn by the hair, mangled, or, alternatively, caressed by the hand of Benedict; or you might place there Saint Dominic or the Emperor Domitian or someone known to you called by such a name. For the third word and the fourth, which are monosyllables, proceed according to the rule concerning syllables; or for "qui" place a very white cow with teats as red as possible, erect upon her hind legs, whose right front foot Benedict holds while dancing to her left. A cow truly is called a "qui" [=ki] among the northern English. Moreover, the cow holds a partridge [perdix] in her left front foot in a curious manner, which will give the word "per" to your memory.

Truly in the foreground of the second location you should bring together a king, crowned and shining with other majestic signs of kingship, or if you should know well any king, or someone called or surnamed King, or one who in some game was a king, place him there, and he holds in his right hand an eel [anguilla] greatly agitating itself, which will give you "England" [Anglia]. To his left indeed he holds a bear by the tail or foot, which in English would signify the two first syllables of this word "Ber[e]wick," and consequently the whole name. From the other side of the bear comes most powerful Samson or a lion, and strikes that bear; and so this will figure to you the word "fortissimum." Finally, the remainder of the example should be fashioned in a third location in a similar manner, placing there someone named Thomas, subduing on his right hand like a beast, a Scot, or someone thus named or surnamed, or someone whom you knew to have campaigned vigorously in Scotland; placing indeed on his left hand a wondrous yoke.

This example concerns memory for things-listened-to [de memoria auditorum]; but truly, concerning memory for things-seen [de memoria visorum], as likewise for memory of things-written [de memoria scripture], anyone may help himself according to similar rules. Now my pen turns in addition to recollection for numerical calculation [ad memoriam numerorum]. So, for "one" you form a unicorn; for "two," Moses with his two horns, perhaps, or two tablets; for "three," a tripod, or the Trinity as it is usually painted in churches; for "four," one of Ezekiel's creatures having four faces; for "five," Christ crucified with his five wounds; for "six," the angel with six wings; for "seven," the lamb having seven horns or eyes; for "eight," the emperor Octovian; for "nine," an angel clothed in a very white garment having nine very red transverse stripes, three above, three below, and three in the middle, which may signify to you the nine orders of angels, or likewise a man having cut off his thumb, holding his wound with the other hand so then indeed only nine digits remain; for "ten," is formed a zero or a full hand, et cetera, to work with according to your skill in the algorism [secundum algorismi peritiam operare]. However, one who will learn the notary art may attain the highest perfection of this craft.

Here ends the treatise of Master Thomas Bradwardine on acquiring a trained memory. Thanks to God says R. Emylton.[5]

Notes

Introduction

1 Quoted from Miller, "Information and Memory," pp. 44–45.
2 Infeld, *Quest: An Autobiography*, pp. 263, 267, 272, 274–275.
3 "The Life of St. Thomas Aquinas" by Bernardo Gui, and Bartholomew of Capua, "Testimony at the First Canonization Inquiry." Translated by Foster, *Biographical Documents*, pp. 50–51, 37; 107.
4 These sources are available in the *AASS*, March vol. 1, pp. 655–747, in Prümmer, *Fontes vitae*, and in an English translation by Foster, *Biographical Documents*. See Foster's excellent bibliography, pp. x–xii. The relationship between the various accounts is surveyed also by Mandonnet, "Pierre Calo et la légende de S. Thomas."
5 Dondaine, *Les Secrétaires de St. Thomas*, esp. pp. 10–25.
6 Dondaine, *Les Secrétaires*, p. 25.
7 See Foster, *Biographical Documents*, pp. 44–45; Gui, sect. 25; Tocco, c. 43.
8 Foster, *Biographical Documents*, p. 73, note 59.
9 Chenu, *Introduction à St. Thomas*, p. 245; see also Dondaine, *Les Secrétaires*, pp. 20–22, and plate 37.
10 Foster, *Biographical Documents*, p. 38; Gui, c. 16; Tocco, c. 31.
11 Foster, *Biographical Documents*, p. 51; Gui, c. 32.
12 Chenu, *Introduction à St. Thomas*, pp. 248–249.
13 The technique is described by Leclercq, *Love of Learning*, esp. pp. 76–77.
14 Dondaine, *Les Secrétaires*, p. 19.
15 Foster, *Biographical Documents*, pp. 38 (Gui, c. 16), 51 (Gui, c. 32), and 37 (Gui, c. 15).
16 Gui, c. 15.
17 Dondaine, *Les Secrétaires*, p. 51; Gui, c. 32; *Fontes*, p. 89.
18 Dondaine, *Les Secrétaires*, p. 18. Walz, *San Tommaso d'Aquino*, pp. 167–168, explains Evan the Breton's story as an oblique reference to a practice of leaving notes to a secretary to write up while the author slept; but this is not what the sources say took place. The typical postures of profound concentration and sleep were remarkably similar; see my discussion in chapter 6.
19 "Epystolas de rebus maximis quaternas dictabat aliis, ipse manu propria quintam scribens." Petrarch, *Rerum memorandarum libri*, II. 2; p. 43. There does not seem to be a contemporary source for this story, though Cicero flatters Caesar as one who "forgot nothing except his injuries"; "Pro Ligario," xii, 35. The story is told to illustrate Caesar's superior memory in the elder Pliny's *Natural History*, VII, xxv, 92. Petrarch quotes from both of these sources in his own recounting of the story.

20 *ST* 1, Q. 24, a. 1. resp.

21 Smalley, *Study of the Bible*, p. 148.

22 Jaques Legrand, *Archiloge sophie:* "pourtent est ce que on estudie mieulx es livres enlumines, pour ce que la difference des couleurs donne souvenance de la difference des lignes et consequamment de celle chose que on veut impectorer "; Paris, Bibliothèque Ste. Genéviève MS. 2521, ff. 96–99v. The quotation is from f. 96r–v, and is cited by Hajdu, *Das Mnemotechnische Schriftum des Mittelalters*, p. 114. The English translation is mine, based on my own independent transcriptions of this manuscript.

23 John Wycliff, "De veritate sacrae scripturae," cap. 6 (quoted by Smalley, "The Bible and Eternity"): "sed quinto modo sumitur scriptura sacra pro codicibus, vocibus aut aliis artificialibus, que sunt signa memorandi veritatem priorem, quomodo loquitur Augustinus."

24 Hildegard of Bingen (eleventh century) dictated her mystical visions in the best Latin she could muster to a scribe, who took them down; then she had the written version corrected by a priest for inelegancies of Latin. It is apparent from the descriptions of how she worked that she composed first probably in German, then translated that to Latin herself, dictated this version, and then had it finally corrected for solecisms. It is also apparent that she could understand Latin well enough to know whether the priest's corrections fairly represented her meaning. This represents a very different situation from that commonly assumed when moderns use the word "illiterate." See Albert Derolez, "The Genesis of Hildegard of Bingen's 'Liber divinorum operum'." On the meaning of the term "illiterate," see also Clanchy, *From Memory to Written Record*, esp. pp. 175–185.

25 The excellent studies by Clanchy, *From Memory to Written Record*, and Stock, *The Implications of Literacy*, are cases in point.

26 See Brian Stock's fascinating dissection of the fundamentalist aspect of various eleventh century heresies in his *Implications of Literacy*, pp. 88–240. He does not identify this as fundamentalism, but rather associates it with literacy *per se*; the conjunction seems to me a bit of a red herring, however, because the determining distinction has to do with views of literature, which can exist among either oral or literate groups.

27 Smalley, "The Bible and Eternity," p. 89.

28 For example, see Kennedy, *Classical Rhetoric*, p. 98.

29 Greimas defines cultural values not as absolutes but as cultural and psychological modes, which allow adaptation and changes of behavior; see *On Meaning*, esp. chapter 8, "On the Modalization of Being."

Chapter 1

1 The phrase occurs in the beginning of *La Vita Nuova*, although the intimate connection of memory with writing is evident throughout his work (compare *Paradiso*, 17, 91–92, where Cacciaguida tells Dante he shall carry things told to him about the future "scritto nella mente"). For a brief discussion of the memory-as-book metaphor, see Curtius, *European Literature and the Latin Middle Ages*, pp. 326–332, but his whole previous discussion of "The Book of Nature" (chapter 16) is pertinent. E. G. Gardner has an excellent study of Dante on memory and imagination, in which he especially notes that for Dante memory was "mental writing"; "Imagination and Memory in the Psychology of Dante," esp. pp. 280–282.

2 Havelock, *Literate Revolution*, p. 57. Elizabeth L. Eisenstein rightly emphasizes the cultural effects of the "democratization" of the reading public made possible by numerous, cheap, printed materials; *The Printing Press*, esp. vol. 1, 71–159, and

The Printing Revolution, chapter 4. Good summary discussions of the state of current knowledge of literacy among the medieval laity at various times and in various places are Parkes, "The Literacy of the Laity," D'Avray, *The Preaching of the Friars*, pp. 29–43, and Clanchy, *Memory to Written Record*, pp. 151–201.

3 *Partitiones oratoriae*, 26.

4 Black, *Models and Metaphors*, pp. 219–243.

5 450a 25; Sorabji translation, *Aristotle on Memory*, p. 50. Hett (LCL) translates: "for the movement produced [by a phantasm] implies some impression of sense movement, just as when men seal with signet rings." The Greek is "katháper oi sphragizómenoi toîs daktylíois"; text ed. Hett, Loeb Classical Library. *Daktyliós* (Liddell and Scott, s.v.) is a "signet-ring," a word used also by Plato in his version of this metaphor; Aristotle's verb is a synonym of the one Plato uses, meaning "to authenticate with a seal" (Liddell and Scott, s.v. σφραγ-ιζω).

6 Sorabji, *Aristotle on Memory*, p. 5, note 1; Plato uses the image in *Theaetetus*; see following discussion.

7 Sorabji, *Aristotle on Memory*, p. 5, note 2.

8 Richardson, *Mental Imagery and Human Memory*, contains a helpful review of current experimental work in this field, set within a solid philosophical framework. Two interesting books which attempt definitions of "representation" within the context of verbal and cognitive functions are Norman Malcolm, *Memory and Mind*, and Jerry Fodor, *The Language of Thought*.

9 H. S. Chaytor makes much of these distinctions, *Script to Print*, pp. 6–10. See also Eisenstein, "Clio and Chronos."

10 *Postilla super Isaiam*, p. 11, lines 6–9, *Opera omnia*, vol. 19, on Is. 1.1, *quam vidit*: "Auditu enim satis certus non fuit, sed visu certificabatur, sicut dicit Horatius." The lines from Horace are *Ars poetica*, ll. 180–181: "Segnius irritant animos demissa per aurem, / quam quae sunt oculis subiecta fidelibus" (ed. A. S. Wilkins; trans. S. P. Bovie).

11 Liddell and Scott, s.v. ειχοσ.

12 *Commentarium in Ezekiel*, xii, 40; PL 25, 373D–374A: "Nihil enim prodest vidisse et audisse, nisi ea quae videris et audieris, in memoriae reposueris thesauro. Quando autem dicit, *omnia quae ego ostendam tibi*, intentum facit auditorem, facit et cordis oculis praeparatum, ut memoriter teneat quae sibi ostendenda sunt, *quia ut omnia ostendantur tibi, adductus es huc*."

13 Letter to Brother Michael: "Sicut in omni scriptura xx. et iiii. litteras, ita in omni cantu septem tantum habemus voces." Gerbert, *Scriptores ecclesiastici*, vol. 2, p. 46.

14 A summary discussion of "mental imagery" as a concept in modern psychology is in. Richardson, *Mental Imagery and Human Memory*, pp. 4–24; he mentions 'dual coding theory," in which pictures and verbal processes are considered to be alternative, independent methods of symbolic representation, and a "common coding theory," in which "a single system of abstract propositional representations" underlies "all cognitive and mnemonic processes" (p. 6). See also Norman Malcolm's remarks on "The Picture Theory of Memory," pp. 120–164.

15 *De natura et origine animae*, iv.vii.9; CSEL, 60, p. 389, lines 7–19.

16 The diagram is pictured in the *New Grove Dictionary* s.v. *Solmization*. The twelfth-century chronicler, Sigebert of Gembloux, writes of Guido:

Guido, Aretinus monachus, post omnes pene musicos in Ecclesia claruit, in hoc prioribus praeferendus quod ignotos cantus etiam pueri et puellae facilius discant vel doceantur per ejus regulam quam per vocem magistri, aut per visum [usum] alicujus instrumenti, dummodo sex litteris vel syllabis modulatim appositis ad sex voces, quas sola musica recipit, hisque vocibus per flexuras digitorum laevae manus distinctis per integrum diapason, se oculis et auribus ingerunt intentae et remissae elevationes vel depositiones earumdem vocum. (*PL* 160, 579C)

Of interest in this account is not only the emphasis upon the eyes' importance to the success of Guido's two schemes, but also the specific mention of girls learning chant. Alan Baddeley, *Psychology of Memory*, pp. 235–254, describes current experiments on the nature of "auditory memory": these tend to focus on the ability to reproduce and recognize rather than to manipulate and adapt – a clear example of how different modern psychological understanding of "memory" is from medieval *memoria*.

17 Most current psychological experimentation points to the conclusion that the visual is indeed most important for the ability to recollect, whether "visual" includes "pictorial" or not. As Richardson puts it, "stimulus imageability is an excellent predictor of memory performance" (p. 99). As a corollary to this, however, Richardson points out that mere "vividness" in a pictorial mental image is insignificant; what counts is its ability to create "relational organization" in the memory. Memory pictures need to be brought together in a coherent image or "scene" to be useful for accurate recollection; numbers, diagrams, and the alphabet are images with their own built-in organization, of course. For a cogent critique of problems that can arise from using words like "image" and "picture" to talk about what the brain actually contains, see Malcolm, *Memory and Mind*. Malcolm particularly warns against an "isomorphic" notion of "mental image," the idea that the "shape" of such an "image" is in some way like the form in which it is received; a version of this notion is assumed in assertions that the structure of thought is changed by the way in which text is presented to the memory; see esp. pp. 143, 244–245.

18 See the first chapter of Baddeley, *Psychology of Memory*, discussing Ebinghaus in particular. Some psychologists now are re-interesting their discipline in the phenomenon of recollection, or "long-term" memory.

19 "[R]eminiscentia nihil aliud est nisi investigatio obliti per memoriam"; *Liber de memoria et reminiscentia*, tr. 2, c. 1 (p. 107). In c. 3 of this same commentary on Aristotle's *De memoria*, Albertus distinguishes iteration from recollection, as I have described in the text. A succinct statement is the following: 'Et ista est differentia in qua reminisci differt ab eo quod est iterato addiscere, cum reminiscentia possit moveri quodam praedictorum modorum in id principium quod est ante quaesitum jam in memoria, sive ex parte rei, sive ex parte consuetudinis. Iterato autem addiscens a talibus non movetur. Cum vero non investigat et movetur per aliquod principium, tunc non recordabitur vel reminiscetur" (p. 112). When writers talk about *memoria*, in virtually every context other than defining distinctions among the "inward wits," they mean *memoria* as trained reminiscence, as in the phrase "ars memoriae." Simple iterative ability, or rote, doesn't seem to interest them, and they rarely speak of it except disparagingly.

20 For a full discussion of the derivation of the English word "rote," see chapter 7 below.

21 Thomas Aquinas is clearer than is Albertus on this point. In his commentary on Aristotle's *De memoria*, Thomas Aquinas states that recollection, even when seeming to reconstruct logically, always proceeds from humanly-originated associational habits rather than from anything necessitated by the nature of its object. See my further discussion in chapter 2.

22 191D–E; cf. 194–195; translated by F. M. Cornford (*Collected Dialogues*, p. 897). Cf. the notes on this passage and pp. 194–195 by John McDowell, trans.,

Theaetetus. See also the discussion of F. M. Cornford, *Plato's Theory of Knowledge*, pp. 21–22 and 124, who particularly notes that non-sensory objects like thoughts are also said by Plato to be "stamped" upon (or "modeled in") the memory.

23 Liddell and Scott, s.v. εκμαγειον.

24 See the discussion and plate in Roberts and Skeat, *Birth of the Codex*, p. 111 and plate I. The *tabulae* they show measure 9.1 × 5.7 cm., or about 3.5 × 2.3 inches. Needless to say, one could not get a great deal of fully-formed writing onto one at one time.

25 The text is that of H. N. Fowler, Loeb Classical Library. Liddell and Scott, s.v. σημε-, also note the word was used to gloss Latin *clavis*, and with the adjective γραφε to mean "written characters."

26 *De orat.*, II, 86–87. Quotations in this paragraph are all from this passage; LCL text and translation.

27 Fodor, *The Language of Thought*, p. 191; see also Gombrich, *Meditations on a Hobby Horse*, pp. 1–11, and Ellis, *Theory of Literary Criticism*, esp. pp. 36–45. J. T. E. Richardson's discussion of the philosophical problem is in pp. 25–42. An important discussion of the ancient meaning of "representation" is Richard McKeon, "Literary Criticism and the Concept of Imitation in Antiquity," especially pp. 155–157 in which McKeon distinguishes, vitally for the subject, between "copy" and "phantasm." More recent and complete is the discussion of imitation and representation by Wesley Trimpi, *Muses of One Mind*, especially part 2.

28 Norman, *Learning and Memory*, p. 61.

29 I have used Sorabji's translation, *Aristotle on Memory*, p. 51. Commenting on Aristotle's characterization of the memory "image" in itself, Nussbaum writes that his calling it both a *theorema* and a *phantasma* suggests that he thought its "pictorial" nature to be somewhat metaphorical, for a *theorema* "is most unlikely to be pictorial" (p. 250). Thomas of Moerbeke translates the Greek text as follows: "Secundum quidem seipsum speculatum et phantasma est. Inquantum vero alterius ut imago et memorabile"; (Aquinas, *Commentarium in Aristotelis De memoria*, Lectio III, 176; ed. Spiazzi, p. 95). Thomas Aquinas comments on this that an "image" can be either something seen or thought of in itself ("aliquod in se") or as an image of something else ("phantasma alterius"). Insofar as it is *of* some other thing ("alterius") which we have experienced in the past, it is considered as an image which leads-to (or "finds," heuristically) something other than itself and a starting-point for recollection ("sic consideratur ut imago in aliud ducens, et principium memorandi"). Aristotle himself seems to have believed, as did Plato, that the *eikones* had to be "reasonably similar to the original," though the limits of this criterion are decidedly unclear when Plato can write, in the *Timaeus*, that time is an *eikón* of eternity. Sorabji, *Aristotle on Memory*, p. 4, note 1, has a good discussion of the philosophical uses of the Greek work *eikón*.

30 In this context, it may be helpful to consider Augustine's remark that, when we speak of things past or of anything not immediately in our presence, "we do not speak of the things themselves, but of images impressed from them on the mind and committed to memory." He claims here that our knowledge of anything, except when we recognize an object immediately before us, is not direct but is only of our memory of it. What we "know," therefore, is a mnemonic likeness (as signs are functional reminders), not the object itself. Remarks like this one should, I think, be considered in discussions of Augustine's much-vexed "Neoplatonism," because they do qualify what might appear from other parts of his work to be an unqualified belief in the Neoplatonic "realism" of memory and all signs. This

comment is in *De magistro*; see Gareth B. Matthews, "Augustine on Speaking from Memory."

31 Among the basic ancient discussions are Aristotle, *Rhetoric*, and Cicero's *Orator*, a work better known to the later Middle Ages than any of Plato's several dialogues which comment on the matter. The changing ancient perception of the relationship of rhetoric and philosophy forms a continuing theme in Trimpi's fine study, *Muses of One Mind*. Gerald Bruns, in a discussion of Descartes (*Inventions*, pp. 63–64 esp.), observes that the modern era is characteristically epistemological, "wherein everything is thought to be determined or made intelligible by the workings of the [individual] mind"; ordinary speech is too error-prone and equivocal, too conditioned by the history of its usage to be of use to knowledge, and instead one seeks "a mathematical or systematized speech," which is pure precisely because history, time, and occasion have been purged from it. Such language would also be purged of memory, and recollection rendered useless in favor of a "purified" method.

32 For the development of this definition, see *Thesaurus linguae Latinae*, s.v. *adaequatio*.

33 Aristotle makes this clear especially in *Nichomachean Ethics*, 2, 6; the "mean" is not an arithmetically or statistically determined quantity but rather the principles of healthful diet or of virtue adapted to individual physiology and circumstances: "By the mean which is relative to ourselves I denote that which is neither too much nor too little, and this is not one and the same for everybody . . . an expert in any field avoids excess and deficiency, and seeks and chooses the mean – that is, not the objective mean but the mean relatively to ourselves"; (trans. Wheelwright). The passage is cogently discussed by Trimpi, *Muses of One Mind*, esp. pp. 267–270. See also Tracy on the physiological foundations of ancient ethical ideas about the "mean" and "decorum." Unlike Trimpi, Tracy does not discuss its applicability to works of art and to the use of words.

34 See *Thesaurus lingua Latina* and the *Dictionary of Medieval Latin from British Sources*, s.v. *adaequatio, adaequate*, and, for classical usage, Lewis and Short, s.v. *adaequo, adaeque, aequatio, aequalis*, and the form from which these concepts seem ultimately to derive, *aequus* and the adverb, *aeque*. The earliest surviving occurrence of *adaequatio* seems to be in Tertullian. The classical Latin adverb *adaeque*, "in like manner," glosses the Greek prepositional phrase "pros to ison," "towards the same." The development of the word in medieval philosophy towards an idea of greater and greater formal (logical) identity can perhaps be seen in the following citations given s.v. *adaequatio* in the *Thesaurus linguae Latinae*: 1) Grosseteste: "veritas propositionis est adaequatio sermonis et rei"; 2) Duns Scotus: "omnis propria racio intelligendi aliquid objectum per adaequationem representat illud objectum"; 3) Wyclif: "relatio adaequationis signi ad suum signatum, que relacio est 'ipsum esse verum,' cum sit adaequatio vel correspondencia ejus ad suum significatum." Wyclif uses the adverb to mean "fully" in this citation: "sic enim Deus uult, intelligit vel intendit rem esse, sic res est adaequate." One should note that relationship and thus "adjustment" is basic in all these uses, even when it is God who does the "adjusting" (God's "adjustment" results in perfection or completion of being, however). Even a perfectly adjusted "relationship" is not, it seems to me, the same thing as "objectivity" in knowledge, for the latter seeks to exclude from consideration anything but the-thing-in-itself, whereas the former always acknowledges the role of the knower in knowing the object.

35 The action of recollection is characterized as "interruptus" and "diversificatus": Albertus Magnus, *Liber de memoria et reminiscentia*, tract. II, cap. I (ed. Borgnet, vol. 9, pp. 107–108).

36 This discussion owes a great deal to Markus, "Augustine on Signs," and Gerald Bruns, *Inventions*.

37 See especially Chenu, *Nature, Man, and Society*; Colish, *The Mirror of Language*; Markus, "Augustine on Signs"; Kenny, "Intellect and Imagination in Aquinas."

38 Kenny, "Intellect and Imagination in Aquinas." See also Markus, "Augustine on Signs," esp. pp. 76–82.

39 *De trinitate*; see Markus, "Augustine on Signs." Augustine's use of "word" to refer both to the words humans use and to truth interiorized through grace, Christ the Word, has created a lot of confusion. Discussing the ideas of the *verbum qui intus lucet*, R. A. Markus has noted that Augustine never did explain how this was related to human language. His analysis amounts, in fact, to "two theories of language," for the "inner word" is not a sign, as speech is, but is "essentially meaningful, and presents to the mind what it means . . . [It is] the place of the mind's encounter with the object of its experience" ("res quam videndo intus dicimus," "the thing which by seeing inwardly we speak"); Markus, "Augustine on Signs," p. 78, quoting from *De trinitate* 14, 24. The inner *verbum* in Augustine seems to have more in common with the *res* spoken of in classical rhetoric and thus in rhetorical discussions of *memoria*; *decorum* and *adaequatio* are concepts which apply to it, as to all *res* when spoken in human discourse. This Augustinian "inner word" should probably be thought of as having a phantom capital letter: the *Verbum* of St. John's gospel; see Nash, *The Light of the Mind*.

40 Bruns, *Inventions*, is very good on this matter, pp. 17–43. It will be clear that Neoplatonism, especially in its most rationalist variety, differs markedly from this "practical" analysis. For a clear and most interesting account of how Neoplatonic rationalism exacerbated the "quarrel" between philosophy and rhetoric, see Trimpi, *Muses of One Mind*, pp. 200–240, and Bundy, *Imagination*, esp. pp. 131–145.

41 Nussbaum, *Aristotle's De motu animalium*, esp. pp. 241–255.

42 *PL* 66, 215D.

43 *De memoria* 452b; see Sorabji's discussion, *Aristotle on Memory*, pp. 18–21. The passage was commented on extensively in the scholastic Middle Ages. Augustine discusses also how the memory perceives time-lapses by a measuring mechanism located in memory-images (see especially *De musica*, VI. 7–8; cf. *Conf.*, XI, 27). On the sharp differences between Aristotle and Augustine concerning the existence of time as a phenomenon also external to memory, see Janet Coleman, "Late Scholastic Memoria et Reminiscentia," esp. pp. 23–30.

44 II, 86, 354: "atque ut locis pro cera, simulacris pro litteris uteremur."

45 Translated and discussed by Frances Yates, *Art of Memory*, pp. 29–31; another English translation is that of R. K. Sprague in *Mind* 77 (1968): 155–167. The text is in H. Diels and W. Kranz, *Fragmente der Vorsokratiker*, no. 90, vol. 2, 416 (section 9 of *Dialexeis*). H. Blum discusses the possible mnemonic usefulness of Roman architectural design and ornamentation, pp. 3–12.

46 John of Salisbury, *Metalogicon*, I, 13 (*PL* 199, 840C): "Litterae autem, id est figurae primo vocum indices sunt, deinde rerum, quas animae per oculorum fenestras opponunt, et frequenter absentium dicta sine voce loquuntur." This definition is an adaptation of Isidore of Seville, *Etymologiae*, I, 3, 1, but Isidore says letters are themselves "indices rerum"; Clanchy suggests the change is due to John of Salisbury's care in the nominalist-realist controversy (p. 202, note 1).

47 *De orat.*, II, 87, 360: "tanquam litteris in cera sic se aiebat imaginibus in eis locis quos haberet quae meminisse vellet perscribere."

48 *Ad Her.*, III, 17: "item qui mnemonica didicerunt possunt quod audierunt in locis conlocare et ex his memoriter pronuntiare. Nam loci cerae aut chartae simillimi

sunt, imagines litteris, dispositio et conlocatio imaginum scripturae, pronuntiatio lectioni." See Caplan's note in his LCL edition of this text (pp. 208–209), and his essay on "Memoria," collected in his *Of Eloquence*, which contains a good list of occurrences of this metaphor in both classical and later writing. Renaissance use of the metaphor is discussed in Carroll Camden, "Memory: The Warder of the Brain."

49 *De nuptiis*, trans. Stahl and Johnson, vol. 2, 204. Ed. Dick, p. 269, lines 537–538 (v, 538): "sic quod memoriae mandatur, in locis tanquam in cera paginaque signatur." For an additional possible meaning of the phrase *in pagina*, see chapter 3 below.

50 "Misericordia et veritas te non deserant; circumda eas gutteri tuo, et describe in tabulis cordis tui." Cf. Jeremiah 17:1: "The sin of Judah is written with a pen of iron, and with the point of a diamond; it is graven upon the table of their heart, and upon the horns of your altars."

51 On the close conceptual relationship of the "topics" of rhetoric, logic, and mnemonics in antiquity, see Evans, "Two Aspects of *Memoria*" and Sorabji, *Aristotle on Memory*, esp. pp. 26–34. The matter of memorial organization and design has received a great deal of attention from cognitive psychologists recently, particularly those involved in "cognitive science." D. A. Norman, *Learning and Memory*, is concerned with "the design of a memory," and notes that artificial memory systems (computers) are designed according to a "locus system," in which one first stores and then retrieves information by an addressing (heuristic) system. Gordon H. Bower ("Selective Review", 1972), who has done some work on human retrieval schemes, notes that "pegword" systems are "powerful retrieval systems," the pegword acting as a "hook" for information. He has also noted success with various others of the schemes in use since antiquity – architectural locations, alphabetical orders, and hierarchical systems, in which a sub-set of categories is organized into a supercategory, and those into still others; this is an efficient way to retrieve large numbers of items. On the success of such grouping or "clustering" systems, see also Miller, "Information and Memory." Versions of all these heuristics were also part of ancient and medieval memory design. See also Feigenbaum, "Information Processing and Memory," and Reitman, "What does it take to Remember." What I find most interesting about the similarities between ancient and modern memory design is not that the ancients anticipated modern artificial memories (for they did not) but that human beings, faced with the problem of designing a memory (whether their own or a machine's), should repeat many of the same solutions.

52 *Topica*, 1, 5: "Therefore, since I had no books with me, I wrote up what I could remember on the voyage and sent it to you." This remains an authorial trope even in the late Middle Ages, suggesting its continued relevance to compositional technique; see the discussion of William of Ockham's *Dialogus* in chapter 5 below.

53 Cicero, *Topica*, 1, 7–8: "Ut igitur earum rerum quae absconditae sunt demonstrato et notato loco facilis inventio est, sic, cum pervestigare argumentum aliquod volumus, locos nosse debemus; sic enim appellatae ab Aristotele sunt eae quasi sedes, e quibus argumenta promuntur. Itaque licet definire locum esse argumenti sedem, argumentum autem rationum quae rei dubiae faciat fidem." The *Topica*, along with a similar work by Boethius, was influential in the teaching of dialectic during most of the Middle Ages. See also Quintilian, *Inst.*, v, x, 20–22. The best discussion of the ancient understanding of *topos* is still that of E. M. Cope, *An Introduction to Aristotle's Rhetoric*, pp. 124–133.

54 Sorabji's discussion of the text is on pp. 31–34 and in his notes to this passage.

55 *De memoria*, 452a 17; trans. Sorabji, *Aristotle on Memory*, p. 56.

56 Liddell and Scott, s.v. αναγιγνωσκω, and Lewis and Short, s.v. *lego, legere*.

57 275D; *Collected Dialogues*, p. 521.

58 276D; p. 522.

59 Jacques Derrida has written at length on this passage from *Phaedrus*, from a viewpoint similar to the one I have taken here, though with his own particular objectives; see "Plato's Pharmacy," in Derrida, *Dissemination*, pp. 61–171.

60 274D–275A; *Collected Dialogues*, p. 520.

61 The suggestion that this story reflects a survival of oral traditional cultures was made by Notopoulos, "Mnemosyne in Oral Literature," and is often repeated in the writing of proponents of the "oral survivals" model for both ancient and medieval culture – see, e.g. Ong, *Orality and Literacy*, pp. 59–61. But it is clear in the passage itself that Socrates is disparaging mere book-learning which pretends to substitute for learned truth. Socrates' own approval of writing books for the proper reasons is evident as well. See Curtius, *European Literature and the Latin Middle Ages*, p. 304, and Hackforth, *Plato's Phaedrus*, pp. 162–164. Hackforth notes that Plato seems to have invented this story himself for this particular context, p. 157, note 2. Yates, *Art of Memory*, p. 53, notes that this myth was used in the Renaissance to justify extreme Neoplatonist schemes for an ultimately powerful "artificial memory"; on the admiration of the Greeks for Egyptian memories, see Havelock, *Literate Revolution*, p. 10. Egypt was the "mother of the arts" in one tradition passed along by Hugh of St. Victor; in another, the Hebrews are said to have taught the arts to the Egyptians; see *Didascalicon*, III, 2. Martianus Capella says Thoth discovered all the arts; he was perhaps remembering the *Phaedrus*. See J. Taylor's note to his translation of *Didascalicon*, pp. 210–211, note 34.

62 Clanchy, *Memory to Written Record*, p. 7. But later in his book, Clanchy seems to contradict this position when he writes that "Literacy is unique among technologies in penetrating and structuring the intellect itself" (p. 149). I agree with Clanchy's earlier statement, which seems also to accord with the findings of Scribner and Cole, *Psychology of Literacy*. This book reports a study of the introduction of script into a traditionally oral culture, and concludes that no general effects upon abilities to memorize or to think rational thoughts resulted.

63 Ong, *Ramus*, p. 108.

64 Cassiodorus, *Inst.*, II, 3, 17, ed. R. A. B. Mynors: "[M]irabile plane genus operis, – in unum potuisse colligi quicquid mobilitas ac varietas humanae mentis in sensibus exquirendis per diversas causas poterat invenire, – conclusit liberum ac voluntarium intellectum; nam quocumque se verterit, quascumque cogitationes intraverit, in aliquid eorum, quae praedicta sunt, necesse est ut humanum cadat ingenium."

65 *Epist.*, LX, 10 (*PL* 22, 595): "Lectioneque assiduo, et meditatione diuturna, pectus suum bibliothecam fecerat Christi."

66 *CT*, I. 3115, and X. 26.

67 Liddell and Scott, s.v. θησαυρ-ίζω. In *Phaedrus*, 276D, the phrase translated by Cornford as "collecting a store of refreshment for his own memory," which Plato uses when discussing the usefulness of writing books, is "eauto te hypomnemata ["memoranda"] thesaurizomenos"; text edited H. N. Fowler, Loeb Classical Library. It is noteworthy that for Plato his book is a store-house for his memory, its extension, not its substitute.

68 "Lay not up for yourselves treasures upon earth . . . But lay up for yourselves treasures in heaven."

69 "And when they had opened their treasures, they presented unto him gifts; gold, and frankincense, and myrrh."

70 Lewis and Short, s.v. Citations are to Columella, *De re rustica*, 8, 8, 1; 8, 8, 3; and 8, 9, 3; at 8, 14, 9 the pens for geese are also called *cellae*.

71 *Georgics*, 4, 163–164 (LCL). Virgil repeats this language in *Aeneid*, 1, 432–433, where he likens the builders of Carthage to bees who "strain their cells to bursting with sweet nectar"; "cum liquentia mella / stipant et dulci distendant nectare cellas."

72 *De re rustica*, 8, 9, 3; see also, for *loculamenta*, 8, 8, 3. Columella uses *loculamenta* for a bee-hive in 11, 5, 2.

73 *Epigrams*, 1, 117 (LCL): "De primo dabit alterove nido / rasum pumice purpuraque cultum / denaris tibi quinque Martialem." Cf. *Epigrams*, 7, 17: "Hos nido licet inseras vel imo / septem quos tibi misimus libellos" (you may place the seven little books I send you even in your lowest pigeon-hole). Seneca uses *loculamenta* in *De tranquillitate animi*, when, inveighing against those who collect books for show, he complains that such idlers have "bookcases built up as high as the ceiling" (tecto tenus exstructa loculamenta). These Latin words for Roman library fittings are discussed, together with citations, by John Willis Clark, *The Care of Books*, pp. 32–36.

74 *Georgics*, 4, 250.

75 Clark, *The Care of Books*, p. 35.

76 OED, s.v. *pigeon-hole* (sb.), 7e.

77 Liddell and Scott, s.v. περιστερ-. Aristotle distinguishes between this bird and other species.

78 *Theaetetus*, trans. Cornford, 197d–199.

79 Philosophy speaks of the "pennas etiam tuae mentis quibus se in altum tollere possit adfiguram." On the development of the winged soul from this image in Boethius, see Courcelle, *La Consolation de philosophie dans la tradition littéraire*, pp. 197–199 and plates 119–124. As used by Boethius the image is Neoplatonic, as the soul, remembering, rises to its forgotten glory and perfection. Courcelle stresses this connection, but the evidence does not, I think, support a conclusion that the notion is exclusively Neoplatonic.

80 Sandys (ed), *Aristotle's Constitution of Athens*. Clark calls attention to this note (*The Care of Books*, p. 34, note 1) as suggesting that a "pigeon-hole" arrangement was used also by the Greeks for filing written material.

81 Cf. Hugh of St. Victor, "De arca Noe morali," II, 1 (*PL* III, 636B) says the dove sent forth is the mind: "Quod autem per avem anima significetur."

82 Clark, *The Care of Books*, p. 35; cf. the portrait of Ezra editing the Old Testament in the seventh century Codex Amiatinus, discussed by Cahn, *Romanesque Bible Illuminations*, pp. 33–34, and shown in plate 12, p. 31. The deep wall-recesses that sometimes housed the wooden *armaria* of the later Middle Ages can been seen in a number of places. Clark has several pictures of them; see esp. figures 20 and 25. Two good illustrations of self-standing wooden *armaria* are in figures 27 and 28.

83 *Inst.*, 1, x, 7: "muta animalia mellis illum inimitabilem humanae rationi saporem vario florum ac sucorum genere perficiunt; nos mirabimur, si oratio, qua nihil praestantius homini dedit providentia, pluribus artibus egeat."

84 The authorship of *Philobiblon* is discussed by Thomas, pp. xliii–xlv.

85 Prologue, 7; ed. E. C. Thomas, p. 7.

86 This is Thomas's reading; earlier editors, however, read "per spirituales vias oculorum," a reading that makes better sense in terms of scholastic perception-psychology; see my discussion of Thomas Aquinas's description of ocular perception, chapter 2, below.

87 1, 25 (Thomas, p. 13, trans. p. 163, with some alterations by me). It is interesting to notice the sexual metaphor that Bury uses to describe how reading acts upon the memorial store during meditation. Sexual metaphors for how reading acts

upon the reader are common in clerical writing on the subject from the thirteenth century on, most familiarly in Jean de Meun.

88 *De universo*, 22, 1; (*PL* 111, 594C): "favus Scriptura est divina melle spiritualis sapientiae repleta."

89 Ch. 8, 136; ed. Thomas, p. 76: "apes argumentosae fabricantes jugiter cellas mellis."

90 *Didascalicon*, 1, i.

91 *PL* 77, 172B: "Super semetipsum sacros codices in pelliceis sacculis missos dextro laevoque portabat latere, et quocunque pervenisset, Scripturarum aperiebat fontem, et rigabat prata mentium." On another occasion, Equitius revealed that a monk in his monastery named Basil was really a devil, and had him expelled from the convent; afterwards this same Basil tried to annoy Equitius through magical arts by levitating his cell but could not harm the holy abbot. Soon thereafter, Basil was burned to death by a zealous Christian mob in Rome.

92 Lewis and Short, Du Cange, s.v. *scrinium*; see also the Ox. Lat. Dict. The *scrinium memoriae* may have been "of historical records"; cf. Lewis and Short, s.v. *memoria*. In a letter to a newly installed bishop, Gregory the Great gives instructions to make an inventory and put it in his church *scrinium*: "de quibus etiam secundum rerum inventarum paginam desusceptum te facere volumus, et in scrinium ecclesiae tuae transmittere," "concerning which, according to the brief of the things inventoried, we want to make for you a receipt and to transmit it to the shrine of your church." Gregory had from the previous bishop such a receipt, which he sent "in scrinio nostro"; *Epist.*, III, 50; *PL* 77, 646.

93 Spenser, *FQ*, II, ix. 65.

94 Du Cange, s.v. *scrinium*.

95 "Epistle" 32; *PL* 61, 338: "If desire should seize one for meditating on the holy law / Staying here he may concentrate upon the sacred books."

96 Beeson, *Isidorstudien*, pp. 162–163. The oldest manuscripts state that these and several other such verses which he composed were written on Isidore's book-presses ("scripta sunt in armaria sua"); Clark, *The Care of Books*, p. 47, note 2. The word *cupa*, "enclosure," usually means a "coop" or "barrel" but can also mean "a niche in a *columbarium*"; the word is related through a common Indo-European root to Old English *hyf*, modern "(bee-) hive." A *columbarium*, as its name indicates, is a "pigeon-coop"; Lewis and Short, and Ox. Lat. Dict. s.v. *cupa, columbarium*.

97 Beeson, *Isidorstudien*, p. 157; "Sunt hic plura sacra, sunt mundialia plura; / Ex his si qua placent carmina, tolle, lege. / Prata vides plena spinis et copia floris; / Si non vis spinas sumere, sume rosas." Note the allusion to the words of the voice to Augustine, "Tolle, lege." For a demonstration of Isidore's intimate familiarity with Augustine's *Confessions*, see Courcelle, *Les Confessions … dans la tradition littéraire*, esp. pp. 235–253.

98 *PL* 100, 175C: "O quam dulcis vita fuit, dum sedebamus quieti inter sapientis scrinias, inter librorum copias, inter venerandos Patrum sensus." Here Alcuin calls the books themselves *scrinia*. Compare Richard de Bury, *Philobiblon*, ch. 7, 107, who calls the books burned with the Alexandrine Library, "scrinia veritatis."

99 Henry, *The Book of Kells*, p. 150.

100 See, for example, the exhibition catalogues, *Medieval Manuscripts and Jewelled Book-Covers*, of the John Rylands Library, Manchester.

101 MED cites legislation that includes makers of "males" with other leather-workers.

102 OED, s.v. *mail*, etymological note.

103 *Sir Bevis of Hamptoun* 1297; "Prima Pastorum," 224–225, in the edition of A. C. Cawley.
104 *Havelock*, 48; Chaucer, *CT*, A. 694; *Piers Plowman*, B, V. 230; Layamon, *Brut*, ll. 1769–1770 (EETS 250, 1963). See also the Towneley "Magnus Herodes," where the king's soldiers boast they have "mych gold in oure malys," ed. Cawley, line 453.
105 MED, s.v. *male* (a), cited from a fifteenth-century cookery-book.
106 On this portrait, painted on an oak panel and dated 1532, see John Rowlands, *Holbein*, pp. 82–83 and plate 74. The strongbox rests against the wall behind the merchant's arm.
107 *The Tale of Beryn*, lines 701–702.
108 Stephen Hawes, *The Pastime of Pleasure*. On Chaucer's probable acquaintance with the architectural mnemonic, see my "Italy, *Ars memorativa*, and Fame's House."
109 *Didascalicon*, I, 2; cf. John of Salisbury, *Metalogicon*, I, 11.
110 See Riché, *Education and Culture*, p. 461. Aldhelm, who died in 709, composed a sort of riddle on the subject of his books, which is called "De arca libraria"; the text is in Thompson, *Medieval Library*, pp. 114–115.
111 Cited by Riché, *Education and Culture*, p. 461, note 99, from *Regulae magistri*, 17, p. 206: "Simul etiam arcam cum diversis codicibus membranis et chartis monastherii."
112 *Metalogicon*, I, 11; "[M]emoria vero quasi mentis arca, firmaque et fidelis custodia perceptorum." (*PL* 199, 839A.)
113 "Tollite librum istum, et possite eum in latere foederis Domini Dei vestra."
114 The manuscript is discussed by Cahn, *Romanesque Bible Illumination*, pp. 26–29.
115 Smalley, *Study of the Bible*, p. 5 quotes Philo. A full analysis of architectural metaphors for exegesis is de Lubac, *Exégèse médiévale*, vol. 4, pp. 41–60. Authority for this idea may be found in texts such as Proverbs 24: 3–4: "Through wisdom is an house builded; and by understanding it is established: And by knowledge shall the chambers be filled with all precious and pleasant riches."
116 *Moralia in Job*, PL 75, 513C: "Nam primum quidem fundamenta historiae ponimus; deinde per signaficationem typicam in arcem fidei fabricam mentis erigimus; ad extremum quoque per moralitatis gratiam, quasi superducto aedificium colore vestimus."
117 Du Cange, s.v. *mens*. Hugh says in "De arca Noe morali" that *mens* holds time; that makes it synonymous with memory (Bk. II, 1). Dante's use of *mente* is synonymous with *memoria* (for example, *Inferno* 2, 7–9); and Chaucer says of the dying Arcite: "For he was yet in memorie and alyve," in a context where we would use the word "conscious" (*CT* I. 2698).
118 The various titles given to this work are listed in Goy, *Die Uberlieferung der Werke Hugos von St. Viktor*, p. 212. The treatise has been translated into English by a Religious of C.S.M.V., *Hugh of St. Victor: Selected Spiritual Writings*.
119 "Commentarium in Ezechielem," esp. Bks 12–14.
120 I, 2; *PL* 176, 622B: "Hujus vero spiritualis aedificii exemplar tibi dabo arcam Noe, quam foris videbit oculus tuus, ut ad ejus similitudinem intus fabricetur animus tuus."
121 I, 2; 626C: "quam sapientia quotidie aedificat in cordibus nostris ex jugi legis Dei meditatione."
122 *Commentarium in Ezekiel*, 40: 4 (*PL* 25, 573D).
123 *Commentarium in Ezekiel*, 3: 5 (*PL* 25, 35D): "Principia lectionis, et simplicis historiae, esus voluminis est. Quando vero assidue meditatione in memoriae

thesauro librum Domini considerimus, impletur spiritualiter venter noster, et saturantur viscera."

124 II, 1; *PL* 176, 635B: "ita etiam in mente nostra praeterita, praesentia, et futura per cogitationem simul subsistunt. Si ergo per studium meditationis assidue cor nostrum inhabitare coeperimus, jam quodammodo temporales esse desistimus, et quasi mortui mundo facti intus cum Deo vivimus."

125 II, 1; 636A: "Haec est arca, quam aedificare debes."

126 "De arca morali," IV, 9; 680B: "Haec arca similis est apothecae omnium deliciarum varietate refertae. Nihil in ea quaesieris quod non invenias, et cum inveneris unum, multa tibi patefacta videbis. Ibi universa opera res-taurationis nostrae a principio mundi usque ad finem plenissime continentur, et status universalis Ecclesiae figuratur. Ibi historia rerum gestarum texitur, ibi mysteria sacramentorum inveniuntur, ibi dispositi sunt gradus affectuum, cogitationum, meditationum, contemplationum, bonorum operum, virtutum et praemiorum."

127 Du Cange, s.v. *apotheca, apothecarii*. At least by the thirteenth century, the word seems sometimes to have meant specifically drugs and medicines (s.v. *apotheca-ria*). In great houses in France, the "dessert chef" seems to have been called *apothecarius* (s.v. *apothecarii*, 4). It is worth recalling that sugars were relatively scarce and often considered to have healing properties.

Chapter 2

1 Evans, "Two Aspects of *Memoria*," p. 263. I discuss this matter at greater length in chapter 4.

2 Wolfson's essay is both philosophical and philological in nature, tracing the usage of the Latin terms and how they translate Greek and Arabic (and Hebrew, where appropriate). The essay should be read in conjunction with Bundy, *Theory of Imagination*, whose pioneering and deservedly influential study it corrects in some important aspects. A more recent, useful overview of Arabic-medieval medical doctrine is Harvey, *Inward Wits*. Alastair Minnis has briefly surveyed the function of *vis imaginativa* in "Langland's Ymaginatyf and Late Medieval Theories of the Imagination" – his essay begins to provide a corrective to overly stringent interpretations of medieval faculty psychology, though like many characterizations of what medieval people thought about imagination, it suffers from being too narrowly focused both in topic and in sources con-sidered.

3 Wolfson, "The Internal Senses," p. 115.

4 See Richard Rorty's comments in *Philosophy and the Mirror of Nature*, esp. pp. 3–13.

5 See Matson, "Why Isn't the Mind-Body Problem Ancient?," p. 93.

6 *De memoria*, 415b 10ff.

7 Aristotle talks about the heart as the seat of perception in *Parts of Animals*, 666a 14ff., and *Generation of Animals*, 781a 20ff. What he says in *De memoria* about the processing of memory images, however, might be interpreted as qualifying these other statements.

8 Wolfson, "The Internal Senses," esp. pp. 69–74; see also Harvey, *Inward Wits*, pp. 4–8. Early medicine and the contributions of the Alexandrine anatomists (3rd century B.C.) are discussed in standard histories, such as that of Charles Singer, *A Short History of Medicine*, pp. 36–41.

9 Varro, *De lingua Latina*, VI, 46; LCL, vol. 1, pp. 214–215.

10 Bosworth-Toller, *An Anglo-Saxon Dictionary*, s.v. *heorte*.

11 Rorty has a fine discussion of how the "mind-body problem" was created in the Renaissance, *Philosophy and the Mirror of Nature*, esp. pp. 39–69.

12 Aristotle, *De anima*, II, 1; cited by Matson, "Mind-Body Problem," p. 97.

13 Both quotations from Matson, "Mind-Body Problem," pp. 96–97; the whole essay is an excellent, succinct analytic description of the matrix surrounding classical discussions of soul and body. A more complete analysis of the essentially biological nature of sensation and memory, ethical behavior, and political life is in Theodore Tracy, *Physiological Theory*, who concludes that for Aristotle, and also Plato, the essential model for understanding is physiological, based upon notions of health in the organism. See the remarks by Martha Nussbaum on the nature of Aristotle's understanding of the so-called "practical syllogism" in ethical judgment, *De motu animalium*, pp. 165–220.

14 Sorabji, *Aristotle on Memory*, p. 16. "Affection" and "emotion" are both words that must be understood physiologically – they affect and move the body. Nussbaum discusses the fact that for Aristotle emotion and judgment both can also be described in physiological terms; pp. 146–158. References to *De memoria et reminiscentia* in this paragraph are by Bekker number (I will use the short title *De memoria* from here on). Except where otherwise noted, I have used Sorabji's translation throughout.

15 Either the weight itself on perceptual organs or the excessive fluidity which Aristotle associated with dwarfism, or both, hinder the persistence of images and make it difficult for the motion set up by a sensory impression in a human receiver to stop and be "fixed" as a memory-image; see Sorabji, *Aristotle on Memory*, p. 114.

16 Tracy's book contains a full explication of this physiological theory, which indeed provides the central model for Aristotle's thought about mind, knowledge, politics, and ethics.

17 Sarton, II–II, pp. 893–900, gives Arnaldus's bibliography and the printed editions of his work; Arnaldus is discussed by Lynn Thorndyke, *History of Magic and Experimental Science*, vol. 22, pp. 841–861.

18 Arnaldus, *Opera omnia* (Basle, 1585), in which see esp. "Aphorismorum," cols. 243–244, "De bon. mem." cols. 837–838; the latter appears to be a recension of the advice in "Aphorismorum," together with some recipes for memory enhancement "praised by the authorities", "Laudata ab autoribus."

19 "Supervitet coitum superfluum et carnes facilis digestionis" (One especially avoids unnecessary intercourse and easily-digested meats); Mattheolus Mattheoli, "De augenda memoriae," (Rome, [1494]) iv. r. Advice against drunkenness is also given by Alcuin in his dialogue on rhetoric (ninth century); undoubtedly, some of these prescriptions were passed along orally, and some are based on continuing observation. It is well to remind ourselves that Avicenna's work is compendious; he is an "originator" in the pre-modern sense, not in our own.

20 That is, "gaudium temperatum et honesta delectio" ("Aphorismorum," col. 244D); the likening of feeding memory to feeding the stomach is most fully expressed by Geoffrey of Vinsauf, but the memory-stomach metaphor is quite pervasive; it lies behind the standard monastic (and patristic) metaphor of *meditatio* as "rumination"; see chapter 5, below.

21 *Guy de Chauliac*, pp. 617, 620, and 627. Pepper is also of fourth-degree hotness, and so would presumably not be good for memory, although it is rarely mentioned as a specific prohibition.

22 Mattheolus, 4.v.: "Corpus teneatur mundum a superfluitatibus vnde quottidie ventris beneficium et si non naturale fiat artificiale."

23 "Aphorismorum," col. 244E.

24 Arnaldus, col. 244: "Solicitudo et visorum seu auditorum frequens recordatio, memoriam corroborat et confirmat."
25 See Wolfson, "The Internal Senses," pp. 120–122.
26 *De memoria*, 450a 10–15; Wolfson, "The Internal Senses," pp. 74–76.
27 *De memoria*, 449b 30. Nussbaum comments that it is not clear what sort of image Aristotle thought one utilized for concepts like "goodness" or "truth"; see pp. 266–267. Unlike Aristotle, Thomas Aquinas says that intellect itself is retentive of "knowledge-forms" ("conservativa specierum"), concepts and other things composed for thinking. Though this is a crucial difference in certain contexts (it is a major difference between Aristotle and Neoplatonism, and important as well in Christian descriptions of how an individual soul can be immortal), for the purpose of my discussion of memory in this chapter it would only be confusing to emphasize it.
28 That is, "centrum omnium sensuum et a qua derivantur rami et cui reddunt sensus, et ipsa est vere quae sentit"; Avicenna, *Liber de anima*, IV. 1; p. 5, lines 57–59.
29 Aristotle, *De anima*, III, ii, 425b 12ff. Aristotle and indeed the whole classical–medieval tradition did not distinguish between sound-as-heard and as vibration of air; for them, sound was sound and was not pertinent to the human mind unless some abstraction was involved. As Matson points out, this is one reason why they had no mind-body *problem*.
30 I realize that the concept of "raw feels" is a spin-off of the mind-body problem, and so on the historical grounds I argued earlier I should not even introduce the language here; but I hope I will be forgiven. On "raw feels," see Rorty, *Philosophy and the Mirror of Nature*, esp. pp. 24, 88–98.
31 Harvey summarizes al-Razi's account (*c.* 900), pp. 9–13, which in turn depended largely upon Galen. Four ventricles are described, a pair in front and two behind them, one following the other. *Imaginatio* is located in the front pair, *cogitatio* in the middle one, and *memoria* in the last one. It is hard to know just what, in a normal brain, the ancients were describing as such "cavities"; is it possible that this is an instance of a metaphoric archetype (the brain as a compartmentalized storage-place) helping to shape observation?
32 IV, i, p. 6, 11. 66–68; Van Riet text: "Formam enim sensibilem retinet illa quae vocatur formalis et imaginatio, et non discernit illam ullo modo."
33 Wolfson, "The Internal Senses," p. 92.
34 *De anima*, III, xi, 434a, 9–10.
35 Wolfson, "The Internal Senses," pp. 86–95.
36 Wolfson, "The Internal Senses," pp. 118–119.
37 Janet Coleman has some acute remarks on the importance of *intentio* and memory in "Late Scholastic Memoria."
38 This crucial, much cited passage, is also found in *Posterior Analytics*, II, xix (100a).
39 As is apparent from Tracy, the notion of "embodiment" is elementary in Aristotle, and Aquinas rejects any modification of this idea in the area of how human beings know, specifically the implications in Avicenna and Averroes that direct knowledge of abstractions is possible. See also Kenny, "Intellect and Imagination in Aquinas."
40 *In De anima*, Lectio 13 on Bk III, par. 792. I quote the translation by Kenelm Foster; the Latin text is that of the Marietti edition (Turin, 1949).
41 Sorabji, *Aristotle on Memory*, pp. 14–17; the image, from Aristotle's *De anima*, is commented on by Thomas in par. 26 of Lectio 2 on Bk I.
42 *In De anima*, Lectio 14 on Bk II, par. 417.
43 Lectio 1 on Bk III, par. 570–574.
44 Lectio 14 on Bk II, par. 418.

45 Lectio 14 on Bk II, par. 417.
46 Lectio 14 on Bk II, par. 416.
47 Lectio 14 on Bk II, par. 406–414.
48 Lectio 24 on Bk II, par. 553–554.
49 Lectio 24 on Bk II, par. 552. The nature of Aristotelian "hylemorphism," that is, the idea I have been describing that perception occurs by causing physical changes in the organ that make it "like" what it perceives, is well analyzed by Tracy, who sees it as a consequence of Aristotle's idea that the body is a balanced compound of the four elements, animated by a soul. These elements and their associated qualities (heat, cold, moisture, dryness) occur in paired opposites, which react when contact between them is established. "If the objective quality is strong enough, the qualitative change which it sets up in the medium evokes a corresponding change in the sense organ, i.e. the organ responds in the direction of that quality in proportion to its intensity. In so doing, the organ becomes *like* the objective quality" (Tracy, *Physiological Theory*, p. 207). See also Nussbaum's discussion of hylemorphism and Aristotle's concept of *pneuma*, pp. 146–164. Thomas Aquinas, like Galen, located the *sensus communis* in the first ventricle of the brain. He also seems to make a sharper distinction than Aristotle does, between a sense like touch, which is directly affected by its object, and sight, whose "likeness" is "immaterial," in the way I am attempting to describe. For Thomas, sight is "like" its object as the imprint of a seal in wax is "like" the sealing-ring, an image which links the product of sight directly to the nature of the memorial phantasm. Clearly, the analogies between the external and inner "eyes" were far-reaching in Thomas's thought.
50 Lectio 6 on Bk III, par. 669.
51 Lectio 13 on Bk III, par. 792.
52 Quoted from Averroes, *Epitome of the parva naturalia*, II, i; Blumberg trans., p. 30.
53 For analysis of Aristotle's account, see Sorabji, *Aristotle on Memory*, pp. 14–17; also Tracy, *Physiological Theory*.
54 Lectio 2 on Bk I, par. 19–20; see also *ST*, Ia, Q. 76, art. 1.
55 Lectio 12 on Bk III, par. 783.
56 Lectio 12 on Bk III, par. 782.
57 Sorabji, *Aristotle on Memory*, p. 17.
58 Lectio 12 on Bk III, par. 776.
59 Lectio 12 on Bk III, par. 773.
60 *ST*, Ia, Q. 85, art. 1, obj. 4.
61 *ST*, Ia, Q. 75, art. 5; also Q. 76 passim, but esp. arts. 1 and 3.
62 See *Paradisio*, 29, 76–81.
63 Gardner, "Imagination and Memory," esp. pp. 280–282. The quotation is from p. 282. This passage has received some recent comment from Guiseppe Mazzotta, who sees the "failure" of Dante's memory as part of a conscious "deconstructionist" enterprise in the poem (*Dante: Poet of the Desert*, pp. 260–267). Insofar as Dante's term "failure" is understood by modern interpreters to carry a negative *moral* connotation, it seems to me a wrong emphasis, and somewhat perverse, to label as a *moral* fault what is the intrinsic limitation of a biological mechanism (memory). See the comments of John Freccero on "The Final Image" in his *Dante: the Poetics of Conversion*, pp. 245–257.
64 *ST*, Ia, Q. 77, art. 8.
65 *ST*, Ia, Q. 79, art. 6, resp. obj. 2.
66 Sorabji discusses the difference very clearly, pp. 11–12. Aristotle's discussions of the matter in both "On Divination in Dreams" and "On Dreams" are relevant.

67 Aristotle calls them "the movements of the senses when one is asleep"; *On Dreams*, 462a 15–30. Averroes says that sleep is the "sinking of [the] common, perceptive faculty into the interior of the body"; *Epitome*, II, ii, p. 33.

68 "[H]aec est propria prophetia virtutis imaginativae"; *Liber de anima*, IV, ii; *Avi. lat.* vol. 2, p. 19, line 61.

69 "[A]liquando est ab intellectibus et aliquando est a divinationibus et aliquando est ex versibus, et fit hoc secundum aptitudinem et usum et mores." IV, ii, *Avi. lat.*, vol. 2, pp. 19–20, ll. 68–70.

70 *Liber et anima*, IV, ii; *Avi lat.* vol. 2, p. 20, ll. 71–75: "quae adiuvant animam plerumque incognitae et plerumque sunt sicuti apparitiones subitae, quae non sunt residentes ita ut rememorari queant nisi eis succurrerit anima cum retentione appetita."

71 Quotations in this paragraph are all from *Epitome*, II, i, p. 28. These comments also occur in Albertus Magnus's commentary on Aristotle's *De memoria*, evidence of how widely spread this tradition was in teaching. Albertus follows his discussion of the image-forming ability's role in reminiscence by adducing the advice for making vivid memory images found in the *Rhetorica ad Herennium*.

72 Oliver Sacks, *The Man Who Mistook His Wife for a Hat*, discusses the phenomenon now restrictively called "reminiscence"; he suggests that to restrict the term as modern neuropsychology has may be an error of an overly-mechanistic science, and comments that memories may be more like scripts or scores than algorithms; see pp. 138–142, and the interesting case-study that is the title-essay of the book. Certainly both Aristotelian analysis and practical mnemonics recognized that recollection proceeds via a network of associations, the "richer" the better and the more secure.

73 *De memoria*, 449a 9ff.

74 Averroes, *Epitome*, II, i, p. 30. Aristotle stresses the emotional accompaniment of recollections in *De memoria*, 453a.

75 *Rerum memorandarum libri*, II ("De memoria"), 13: "Vidisse semel vel audisse sat est, nunquam obliviscitur, nec res modo meminit, sed verba tempusque et locum ubi quid primum accepit. Sepe totos dies aut longas noctes colloquendo transegimus: audiendi namque cupidior nemo est; post annos vero suborta earundem rerum mentione, siquid forte plus minus ve aut aliter dixissem, submissa voce confestim admonebat hoc me aut illud verbum immutare; mirantique et unde hoc nosset percunctanti non solum tempus quo id ex me audivisset, sed sub cuius illicis umbraculo, ad cuius undam fluminis, in cuius maris litore, cuius montis in vertice – longinquas enim secum oras circuivi – me singula recognoscente memorabat."

76 *Inst.*, XI, 2, 20: "Ita, quamlibet multa sint, quorum meminisse oporteat, fiunt singula conexa quodam choro, nec errant coniungentes prioribus consequentia solo ediscendi labore."

77 *Inst.*, V, 10, 20–22. Alterations of the Loeb translation, which I have made in order better to reflect the spatial nature of the mental search which Quintilian describes, are indicated in square brackets.

78 *De memoria*, 451b 18ff; in this instance I have used the Loeb translation by W. S. Hett.

79 *De memoria*, 451b 29; see Sorabji's discussion of how recollecting (the mnemonic search) differs from remembering (the object of memory), *Aristotle on Memory*, pp. 41–48.

80 Sorabji, *Aristotle on Memory*, p. 31.

81 Sorabji, *Aristotle on Memory*, pp. 29–30. I discuss this important passage in the

Topics at greater length in connection with ancient method of using numbers as a recollective scheme; see chapter 3.

82 *ST*, Ia, Q. 78, a. 4, *resp.*

83 Quintilian comments that "we must, of course, invent for ourselves" the mnemonic images we use; *Inst.*, XI, ii, 22.

84 Thomas Aquinas, commenting on this passage, defines the associative nature of recollection clearly: *De memoria et reminiscentia commentarium*, Lectio VI, 379–383.

85 *ST*, Ia, Q. 93, art. 7, ad. 3. See also Q. 79, art. 7, ad. 1.

86 *ST*, II–I, Q. 50, art. 5, *resp.*

87 See especially Rand, *Courtroom*, pp. 25–33, 103–112; in the matter of the cardinal virtues, Rand observes, Cicero was Thomas Aquinas's "constant companion and one of his respected authorities" (p. 32).

88 Douay translation of Vulgate "sobrietatem enim et prudentia docet, et justitiam et virtutem, quibus utilis nihil est in vita hominibus."

89 Rand, *Courtroom*, pp. 26–28; see also Loeb note on *De inventione*. The word *phronésis*, sometimes also translated as *prudentia*, has a complex medieval history. Aristotle often links it with *doxá* or "judgment," but says that while animals also have *phronésis*, only humans have *doxá*. Sorabji translates the word as "intelligence" (pp. 77–78), and the word clearly describes a sub-conceptual and sub-judgmental ability rather like what we mean when we say that our dog is "intelligent." But in the Middle Ages, *intelligentia* appears as one of the parts of prudence (along with memory and providence), following the definition of prudence given in *De inventione*, II, 160. This use of *intelligentia* is rendered as *phronesis* by Albertus Magnus, perhaps following the twelfth-century vogue for Greek.

90 *Ad Her.*, III, ii, 3.

91 *De inventione*, II, 53, 160.

92 *ST*, I–II, Q. 57, art. 3, ad. 3.

93 *ST*, I–II, Q. 57, art. 1, *concl.*

94 *ST*, I–II, Q. 57, art. 4, *resp.*

95 *ST*, I–II, Q. 57, art. 5, *resp.*

96 *ST*, II–II, Q. 48, *resp.*

97 Brunetto Latini, *Livres dou Trésor*, II, 59, lines 2–5 (ed. Carmody, pp. 233–234). On prudence as containing all teaching, see II, 56–58; for example, "Mais ki bien consire la verité, il trovera que prudence est le fondement des unes et des autres; car sans sens et sans sapience ne poroit nus bien vivre, ne a Dieu ne au monde"; II, 56, lines 4–5 (pp. 230–231). The "Seneque" referred to is probably Martin of Braga (sixth century), Pseudo-Seneca, whose brief moral treatise, "Formula honestae vitae," was widely known during the Middle Ages: "Si prudens est animus tuus, tribus temporibus dispensetur. Praesentia ordina, futura praevide, praeterita recordare" (*PL* 72, 24C). I am indebted to Paul Gehl for this citation.

98 *ST*, II–II, Q. 49, art. 1. Notice how Thomas Aquinas has brought together the texts on *ethos/éthos* from the *Ethics* and *Metaphysics*.

99 See Tredennick's translation of the Greek text in the Loeb edition.

100 My quotation is from Rand, *Courtroom*, pp. 61–62. A list of Thomas's pagan sources is on pp. 17–18 of this same book.

101 *ST*, II–II, Q. 49, art. 1, obj. 2.

102 Tracy, *Physiological Theory*, p. 251. Tracy gives an excellent exposition of the somatic-emotional basis of Aristotle's ethics, based chiefly on *De anima* with reference also to *Nichomachean Ethics*: see esp. pp. 247–261. My discussion here is much indebted to his.

103 See the first sentence of Moerbeke's text, in Thomas Aquinas, *In de memoria et reminiscentia commentarium.*

104 *De memoria,* 450a 25–30.

105 *De memoria,* 449b 24; for discussion see Sorabji, *Aristotle on Memory,* pp. 1–2 for other uses of *hexis* and *pathos* in this sense in *De memoria.*

106 Sorabji, *Aristotle on Memory,* p. 1.

107 *Nichomachean Ethics,* 1103a 17ff.

108 *Nichomachean Ethics,* 1104a 27–30. In his commentary on this passage (*In decem libros ethicorum commentarium,* Bk II, Lectio 1, 247), Thomas Aquinas notes the pun in Greek *ethos,* and concludes, "Just so for us the noun *moralis* signifies something formed from habit, whenever it pertains to vice or virtue [*sicut etiam apud nos nomen moralis significat quandoque consuetudinem, quandoque autem id quod pertinet ad vitium vel virtutem*]." *Consuetudo* is defined as synonymous with *mos,* "custom." Furthermore, the *virtutis moralis* is described as "in parte appetitiva," and as such is based in something more like what we would call "physiological" than what we might call "rational" or even "mental."

109 Tracy, *Physiological Theory,* pp. 229–231; the quotation is from p. 230.

110 *Posterior Analytics,* II, 19; 100a 1–5.

111 Norman, *Learning and Memory,* pp. 74–80.

112 Thomas Aquinas, *De memoria,* Lectio 1, 298.

113 Tracy, *Physiological Theory,* p. 229.

114 Averroes II. i, p. 30; cf. also *De memoria,* 453a 15–30.

115 *ST,* I–II, Q. 56, art. 5, obj. 3.

116 The *Rhetorica ad Herennium* and the *De inventione* were copied together during the Middle Ages; the *Ad Her.* was not proven to be not by Cicero until the sixteenth century. Though classicists refer to the author of *Ad Herennium* as "auctor ad Herennium" or as "pseudo-Cicero," for the sake of brevity, I have adopted for him his medieval English name of Tully. I use Tully only for this author, however; Cicero gets credit for those things that are genuinely his.

117 *De bono,* II, art. 2: "Dicimus ergo cum Tullio, quod memoria pertinentium ad vitam et iustitiam duplex est, scilicet naturalis et artificialis. Naturalis est, quae ex bonitate ingenii deveniendo in prius scitum vel factum facile memoratur. Artificialis autem est, quae fit dispositione locorum et imaginum, et sicut in omnibus ars et virtus sunt naturae perfectionis, ita et hic. Naturalis enim perficitur per artificialem."

118 *ST,* I–II, Q. 58, art. 1.

119 "Figura namque quae in sigillo foris eminet, impressione cerae introrsum signata apparet, et quae in sigillo intrinsecus sculpta ostenditur, in cera exterius figurata demonstratur. Quod ergo aliud in isto nobis innuitur, nisi quia nos qui per exemplum bonorum, quasi per quoddam sigillum optime exsculptum reformari cupimus, quaedam in eis sublimia et quasi eminentia, quaedam vero abjecta et quasi depressa operum vestigia invenimus?"; Hugh of St. Victor, "De institutione novitiorum" (*PL* 176, 933B), translated by Caroline Walker Bynum, *Jesus as Mother,* pp. 97–98. According to his biographer, Anselm of Canterbury used this same trope for moral education, alluding as well to the ancient belief that the wax of memory is softer and better able to take impressions in youth than in age (Southern, *Eadmer's Life of Anselm,* pp. 20–21).

120 Its composition is discussed by Caplan in the Loeb edition, pp. vii–xxxiv.

121 Cicero says he will not insult his audience by describing the scheme in detail: "ne in re nota et pervulgata multus et insolens sim" (my emphasis).

122 This idea was familiar to the early Middle Ages through Boethius, who articulates

it in his translation of Porphyry's *Isagoge*. The relationship between mnemonic places or topics and what came to be known as "topics" in logic is a vexed one since, to many ancient philosophers, there did seem to be some sort of relation and yet the mnemonic "place" has a physical and physiological "location" that seems more ontologically "real" than the logical or even rhetorical topics do, both of which seem to be "entities" of language rather than of occupied space. Ancient and medieval philosophers worried the question of the ontological status of the logical "topics" without reaching any consensus; for a review of the problem at several stages in its life, see the final chapters of Eleonore Stump, *Boethius's De differentiis topicis*. Though the problem is more one of philosophy than of practical pedagogy, uncertainty about it seems to be reflected in the way in which Aristotle's *Topica* and Cicero's work on the same subject are claimed by some writers on the topics of rhetoric and writers on mnemotechnique as well as thought to be works of dialectic. I discuss this somewhat more in chapter 3.

123 The translation is that of Rackham, for the Loeb edition of *De oratore*, with two of my own modifications, indicated in square brackets.

124 Quintilian's method is discussed in Yates, *Art of Memory*, chapter 2, to which I am much indebted, and also in Harry Caplan's essay, "Memoria," in *Of Eloquence*.

125 Luria, *Mind*, p. 33, note. The connection between this case study and the rules of the architectural mnemonic was first made by Sorabji, to whom I am indebted. A number of mnemonists' techniques are discussed by Alan Baddeley, *The Psychology of Memory*, pp. 347–369.

126 Luria, *Mind*, pp. 33–34.

Chapter 3

1 Most of these are described at least briefly by Helga Hajdu, *Das mnemotechnische Schriftum*, passim. A digital mnemonic from an early fourteenth-century Anglo-Norman manuscript is described in Geneviève Hasenohr, "Méditation méthodique et mnémonique." The syllogism mnemonic is keyed, by the vowels of its various syllables, to the types of proposition that a syllogism can contain. A commonly-used mnemonic verse for the ecclesiastical calendar, "Cisiojanus," is discussed by Rolf Max Kully in *Jeux de mémoire*, pp. 149–156. Several of these content-specific mnemonics are discussed in a recently-translated (1988) essay by Umberto Eco, "An *Ars Oblivionalis*? Forget It!"

2 Thompson, *The Medieval Library*, p. 613. He describes an interesting verse-catalogue from St. Albans abbey of "all those [books] which are placed in the windows," p. 379.

3 A portion of the *Chronica* without the preface was published in the *MGH*, vol. 181. The prologue is discussed as a mnemonic text by Grover A. Zinn, "Hugh of St. Victor and the Art of Memory." A list of contents written on the end-paper of an early fourteenth-century manuscript of the text (B.N. lat. 14872) calls it an art of memory ("Tractatus, vel potius artificium memoriae"); this characterization of it was dismissed as "adventitious" by R. Baron (Zinn, "Hugh of St. Victor and the Art of Memory," p. 211, notes 2 and 3). For reasons that will become apparent in my next chapter, it is significant that the phrase "artificial memory" was used by a post-thirteenth century reader to describe this text, though it was not called that in the twelfth century, when it was first composed. (Goy, *Die Uberlieferung*, p. 40, ascribes this manuscript to the late thirteenth–early fourteenth century; it had been ascribed to the twelfth by Delisle.) That the number scheme was understood to constitute an "art of memory" by late medieval and Renaissance writers is

apparent from the title of a manual for confessors by the Augustinian friar, Anselmo Faccio: *Memoria Artificiale di Casi di Conscienza . . . disposto artificiosamente per via di numeri* (Messina, 1621).

4 Green, p. 486.

5 Goy, *Die Uberlieferung*, pp. 36–43.

6 "In sola enim memoria omnis utilitas doctrinae consistit"; Green, p. 490, lines 39–40.

7 "[U]t interrogatus sine dubitatione respondere possim, sive ordine prolatis, sive uno aut pluribus intermissis, sive converso ordine et retrograde nominatis ex notissa locorum dispositione, quis primus, quis secundus, quis etiam xxvii, xlviiii, sive quotuslibet sit psalmus. Hoc modo scripturas se affirmasse ostendunt qui, auctoritate psalmi alicuius usuri, hoc dixerunt in lxiii, hoc in lxxv, sive alio quolibet psalmo scriptum est"; Green, p. 489, ll. 36–41.

8 This is one of Thomas Bradwardine's mnemonic principles – see appendix C, and compare what both Hugh of St. Victor and Albertus Magnus have to say about "brevity" (appendices A and B). The rules for forming backgrounds given in the *Rhetorica ad Herennium* are governed by the need for the person remembering to see at a glance, clearly and without confusion, what is there.

9 "Memoria enim semper gaudet et brevitate in spatio et paucitate in numero, et propterea necesse est ut, ubi series lectionis in longum tenditur, primum in pauca dividatur, ut quod animus spatio comprehendere non potest saltem numero comprehendat"; Green, p. 490, ll. 6–9.

10 Trans. J. Taylor, p. 87. The standard edition of the Latin text is that of Buttimer; I cite it only when I think Taylor's translation needs to be modified.

11 "An putas eos, quociens aliquem psalmorum numero designare volebant, paginas replicasse, ut ibi a principio compotum ordientes scire possent quotus esset quisque psalmorum? Nimis magnus fuisset labor iste in negotio tali"; Green, p. 489, ll. 42–44.

12 Taylor, p. 93. "Colligere est ea de quibus prolixius vel scriptum vel disputatum est ad brevem quandam et compendiosam summam redigere"; III. 11; Buttimer, p. 60, lines 16–18.

13 "Memoria hominis hebes est et brevitate gaudet"; III. 11; Buttimer, p. 60, lines 24–25.

14 "Debemus . . . in omni doctrina breve aliquid et certum colligere, quod in arcula memoriae recondatur"; III. 11; Buttimer, p. 60, lines 26–27.

15 Miller, "Information and Memory." The limits of short-term memory have been known and studied for some time experimentally; some of the earliest experiments recorded in modern psychological literature are from the eighteenth century; see Miller and also Norman, *Memory and Attention*, pp. 98–124.

16 Miller, "Information and Memory," p. 45. On the role of "gathering" in complex learning, see also Norman, *Learning and Memory*, esp. pp. 80–116, and Bower, "Organizational Factors."

17 *Chronica*, Preface, p. 489, line 41.

18 Murphy, *Rhetoric in the Middle Ages*, pp. 65–66, 80, 195–196.

19 C. Julius Victor, *Ars rhetorica*, cap. 23: "Memoria est firma animi rerum ac verborum ad inventionem perceptio"; Halm (ed.), *Rhetores latini minores*, p. 440, line 11. The twelfth-century gloss on Cicero's *De inventione* by Thierry of Chartres echoes this paraphrase: "[Memoria est] firma animo percipere, memoriter retinere que sunt apta ad inventione sive verba sive res, i.e. sententie"; (Ward, *Artificiosa eloquenta*, vol. 2, pp. 226–227, transcribed from Brussels MS. Bibl. Roy. 10057–10062).

20 "[N]am qui recte conpegerit orationem, numquam poterit errare"; (p. 440,

ll. 25–26). This is an interesting modification of Quintillian's original: "nam qui diviserit, numquam poterit in rerum ordine errare" (*Institutio*, XI, 2, 36). Both "dividing" and "composing" are thought of as specific, definite tasks performed to ensure against error (failure of memory) by imposing a numerical order (one, two, three, etc.).

21 "In his autem, quae cogitamus, et in his, quae scribimus, retinendis proderit multum divisio et compositio . . . Et si prima et secunda deinceps cohaereant, nihil per oblivionem subtrahi poterit, ipso consequentium admonente contextu"; ed. Halm, p. 440, ll. 24–25, 27–29. Cf. Quintilian, *Institutio*, XI, 2, 36ff, and notice again the utter confidence that if one memorizes properly in order, one cannot err or forget.

22 The comment is made in Remigius's commentary on Donatus; see Minnis, *Theory of Authorship*, pp. 19, 226 (notes 75, 77).

23 "[Q]uos per ordinem ex integro legant"; *PL* 66, 704A.

24 Fortunatianus, *Artis rhetoricae libri*, III, 13; ed. Halm, p. 129, ll. 17–18; "Quid vel maxime memoriam adiuvat? Divisio et conpositio: nam memoriam vehementer ordo servat."

25 Ed. Halm, p. 129, ll. 25–26; "Semper ad verbum ediscendum est? si tempus permiserit: sin minus, res ipsas tenebimus solas, dehinc his verba de tempore accomodabimus."

26 John of Salisbury, *Metalogicon*, I, 24: "he diligently and insistently demanded from each, as a daily debt, something committed to memory"; trans. McGarry, p. 69.

27 Riché, *Education and Culture*, p. 200, note 146.

28 A good review of the role of memorization in medieval pedagogy, which clearly sets forth the changing balance in late medieval university education from recitation and purely oral forms to reliance on books made available to students through the cheaper and faster copying methods of the university stationers' *pecia* system, is Pierre Riché, "Rôle de la mémoire dans l'enseignement médiéval"; he also notes the "paradox" that written arts of memory proliferate in step with the greater availability of books. I discuss this matter further in chapter 5.

29 *Love of Learning*, p. 90; see also pp. 18–22, and cf. Riché, *Education and Culture*, pp. 120–121.

30 "Omnis qui nomen vult monachi vindicare, litteras ei ignorare non liceat; quin etiam psalmos totas memoriter teneat"; *Rule of Ferreolis*, ix (*PL* 66, 963D); cited by Riché, *Education and Culture*, p. 115.

31 Riché, *Education and Culture*, p. 464; on the length of time needed to memorize, see note 117 on that page.

32 Pierre Courcelle, *Les Confessions*, Part II, chs. 1–3. On Gregory's indebtedness to Augustine, see esp. pp. 225–231.

33 Riché, *Education and Culture*, pp. 461–464.

34 "Hoc ideo constituimus ut frequentius aliqua meditentur et memoria teneant scripturas, Fratres, ut quando in quovis loco codix deest textum lectionis vel pagine si opus fuerit memoria recitetur": *La règle du Maître*, XLIX, ed. H. Vanderhoven and F. Masai, p. 241.

35 Smalley, *English Friars*, p. 154.

36 Charland, pp. 335–6; "Verba enim de facili memoria excidunt, et ex levi actione sic turbatur dicentis memoria quod verba prius concepta non occurrunt. Immo, saepe cadens syllaba, cadit a toto. Tunc praedicator confunditur, quia se verbis plus quam sententiae alligavit." The brief quotations from Thomas of Waleys in my next few sentences are all from p. 336.

37 Charland, p. 336; "Et si qua sunt verba in auctoritatibus illis quae sunt merito

singulariter ponderanda, illa singulariter conetur memoriter retinere et dicere, de aliis minus curans. Et pro certo hoc habeat quod [multae] sunt auctoritates sanctorum quas propter sui prolixitatem vel obscuritatem melius est et utilius solum sententialiter dicere quam verbaliter recitare. Et dato quod verbaliter recitentur, ubi sunt auctoritates obscurae omnino, earum sententia est sub verbis claris aliis exponenda, ne, dum ab auditoribus non intelliguntur, careant omni fructu."

38 Isidore of Seville, *Etym.*, I, xx.

39 Silverstein, "Adelard, Aristotle, and the *De natura deorum*"; quotations are from pp. 82 and 84. Silverstein sets the two passages up in parallel columns, but they are too long to reproduce here, and I refer the reader to them for a textbook example of *memoria sententialiter*.

40 "But as for me, my feet were almost gone; my steps had well nigh slipped. For I was envious at the foolish, when I saw the prosperity of the wicked." In *De arca Noe morali*, III, iv (*PL* 176, 650C).

41 "Rejoicing in the habitable part of the earth; and my delights were with the sons of men." In *De arca Noe morali*, III, v (*PL* 176, 652C).

42 Miller, "Information and Memory," p. 46.

43 In Latin the word commonly means "a fallacy." But it does not mean that here; for instance, Richard de Bury in *Philobiblon* contrasts the permanence of sacred law to "yesterday's sophismata written in quaterni" (unbound pamphlets or memo-books). De Bury means that such things are "unauthoritative" or "ephemeral," rather than merely "false," in our sense. Once again, we have encountered a case where "false" means something more like "impermanent" or "incomplete" than absolutely "wrong." The use which Hugh of St. Victor makes of the word in the passage quoted links *sophismata* with the modern meaning of its derivative, "sophomoric," meaning "the sort of wisdom young students with lots more to learn have."

44 *Didascalicon*, VI, 3: "Quoties sophismatum meorum, quae gratia brevitatis una vel duabus in pagina dictionibus signaveram, a memetipso cotidianum exegi debitum, ut etiam sententiarum, quaestionum et oppositionum omnium fere quas didiceram et solutiones memoriter tenerem et numerum"; Buttimer, p. 114, ll. 18–22. My translation differs significantly from Taylor's here, for I understand this passage in the context of Hugh's *Chronica* preface.

45 On ancient writing tablets, see Roberts and Skeat, *Birth of the Codex*, pp. 11–14.

46 Lewis and Short, s.v. *pagina*.

47 The entries in the *Thesaurus linguae Latinae* make this dual meaning clear; see s.v. *pagina*.

48 s.v. *paginare*, from Ambrose, *Epist.* 50 (*PL* 16, 1159C): "Hoc munusculum sanctae menti tuae transmisi; quia vis me aliquid de veterum Scriptorum interpretationibus paginare."

49 "Vel quas ipse Deus leges interprete Mose / Condiderat, sacri quas servat pagina saxi."

50 Du Cange, s.v. *paginator* and *rubrica, rubricare*.

51 "Ego puto ad memoriam excitandam etiam illus non nichil prodesse"; Green, p. 490, line 25. This point is discussed in much more detail in chapter 7.

52 The most thorough study of the Canon Tables is Carl Nordenfalk, *Die Spätantiken Kanontäfeln*, 2 vols. Hugh took much material for his own chronicle from Eusebius's chronicle, also laid-out in tabular form.

53 On the Eusebian and other early divisional schemes, see H. Wheeler Robinson, *The Bible in its Ancient and English Versions*, p. 23, and also the *DTC*, s.v. Hugues de Saint Cher.

54 Herwig Blum, *Antike Mnemotechnik*, p. 8: "Doch darf man sagen, dass der grösste Teil der römischen Malerei sich zur Einrichtung mnemonischer Stellen eignet"; see also Saenger, "Silent Reading," p. 375.

55 "Nunc ergo satage ut ea quae subter describentur ita memoriae tuae imprimas, secundum modum et formam discendi superius tibi demonstratem"; Green, p. 491, lines 29–31.

56 See esp. Riché, *Education and Culture*, pp. 460ff. As lay devotions became an increasing concern in Europe after the thirteenth century, the Psalms were among the texts translated into the vernaculars, evidence of their ethical importance in meditational *memoria*. This period of vernacular translation needs to be distinguished carefully from the much earlier period, which produced translations of the Bible into Old English and other Germanic vernaculars, primarily for the use of clergy and a small audience at court; see Micheline Larès, "Les traductions bibliques: l'exemple de la Grande-Bretagne," in *Le Moyen Age et la Bible*, pp. 123–140.

57 On the character of the thirteenth-century pocket Bibles, developed as one of the tools for scholars "faced with the task of composing sermons" (p. 280), see Laura Light, "The New Thirteenth-Century Bible and the Challenge of Heresy." On the development of the various versions of the Bible during the whole Middle Ages, see Laura Light, "Versions et révisions du texte biblique," in *Le Moyen Age et la Bible*, pp. 55–93.

58 "Ego puto ad memoriam excitandam etiam illud non nichil prodesse, ut eas quoque quae extrinsecus accidere possunt circumstantias rerum non neglegenter attendamus, ut verbia gratia, cum faciem et qualitatem sive situm locorum reminiscimur ubi illud vel illud audivimus, vultus quoque et habitus personarum a quibus illa vel illa didicimus, et si qua sunt talia quare gestionem cuiuslibet negotii comitantur. Ista quidem omnia puerilia sunt, talia tamen quae pueris prodesse possunt"; Green, p. 490, ll. 25–31.

59 See Frances Yates's various discussions of Lull in *Art of Memory* and *Collected Essays*. Whether Roger Bacon actually wrote an art of memory is a matter more of persistent rumor than surviving documentation, but he seems to have been keenly interested in the subject. I discuss Bradwardine in chapter 4.

60 *DTC*, s.v. Hugues de Saint Cher. *CHB*, volume 2, pp. 102–154, contains a good brief account of the development of chaptering in the medieval Bible; see also S. Berger, *Vulgate*, pp. 316–327, especially with regard to early punctuation and stichometry of the texts. St. Jerome's use of *cola* and *commata* was much studied by medieval and Renaissance commentators; see his remarks in his preface to Isaiah, quoted by Berger, p. 317, note 3 (*PL* 28, 825B).

61 Smalley, *Study of the Bible*, pp. 222–224; she transcribes, p. 224, MS. Cambridge, Peterhouse College 112 f. 107a, which I have translated here. Jerome's text is: "Monemusque lectorem ut . . . distinctiones per membra divisas diligens scriptor conservet" (*PL* 28, 504B–505A). The Latin of Langton's gloss is: "*Per membra* id est per capitula . . . que valde necessaria sunt ad inveniendum quod volueris et ad tenendum memoriter."

62 *Enarrationes in Psalmos*: "partim sermocinando in populis, partim dictando exposui, donante Domino, sicut potui; psalmum vero centesimum octauum decimum, non tam propter eius notissimam longitudinem, quam propter eius profunditatem paucis cognoscibilem differebam." (*CCSL* 40, p. 1664).

63 *CCSL* 40, p. 1844: "Sicut iam meministis ex ordine nobis tractantibus iste psalmus est centesimus uicesimus quintus, qui inter illos psalmos est, quorum est titulus, *Canticum graduum*."

64 *CCSL* 38, p. 35.

65 *Commentarium in Isaiam*, *PL* 24, 289B.

66 *Commentarium in Isaiam*, *PL* 24, 229A.

67 *PL* 22, c. 542. He refers to Ps. 72 by number in a letter to Marcella; *PL* 22, c. 425.

68 *PL* 24, 289D: "sextus et septimus superiores libri allegoriam quinti voluminis continent."

69 Bede, *De schematis et tropis Sacrae Scripturae liber*, *PL* 90, 175–186. It is, of course, possible that some of these numbers, especially since they are written in numerical notation (which is easier to insert) rather than written out in full (as Augustine's are), were added in copies made somewhat later than Bede's death: Richard and Mary Rouse, *Preachers, Florilegia and Sermons*, discuss briefly the citational style found in Carolingian manuscripts, which they describe as less than systematic, especially compared to the elaborate indices and marginal cross referencing one finds in later medieval manuscripts (p. 29).

70 *CHB*, vol. 2, p. 119, note 2.

71 *CCSL* 38, p. 29; in the body of this text, he refers to "verso primo" and "verso secundo."

72 Saenger, "Silent Reading," esp. 376–377.

73 Alcuin, *Expositio in Psalmos poenitentiae*, *PL* 100, 571C: "Sed primo omnium numerorum eruendas rationes ratum putavi, id est, cur etiam psalmi poenitentiae septenario numero consecrati essent? aut quare centes[i]mus decimus octavus viginti duabus periodis divideretur, quorum singuli octo haberent versus? Aut quid rationis sit, quindecim esse psalmos, qui cantico graduum titulo praesignarentur?"

74 Huntington Library MS. HM 26052, an English manuscript of Augustine's *Enarrationes super Psalmos*, contains numbers in its margins which are apparently the verse numbers of each Psalm as Augustine discusses them in order. This is the only instance I have seen in which the verse numbers are written in. The text dates from the late twelfth century, and is rubricated; the Biblical texts are underlined in red. Opposite each of these, in the margin, the verse number is written, though this notation does not continue throughout the manuscript. The red underlining and verse numbering were evidently written in quite a bit later, probably in the fourteenth century. The verse divisions and numbers used are very like those found in printed versions of the Vulgate. A few other such instances undoubtedly also exist, but these rare exceptions do indeed prove the rule.

75 "Tunc enim quandoque signatur ipse psalmus, et dicitur: *Psalmus xl*^{us} vel *xxx*^{us}, vel aliquo alio modo simili. Aliqui tunc omittunt signationem talem, et solum dicunt: *Istud habetur in Psalterio*, et ratio est quia psalmi sunt communiter satis noti"; Charland, pp. 346–347. One should note that the large, illuminated Psalters intended primarily for liturgical use usually contained the Psalm numbers, though not the verse numbers; this is true of such an early book as the Utrecht Psalter.

76 The citational conventions are explained in Xavierus Ochoa and A. Diez, *Indices canonium, titulorum, et capitulorum corporis juris canonici*, and the similar volume by the same authors covering civil law, *Indices . . . corpus iuris civilis*. I am grateful to Professor James A. Brundage for teaching some rudiments of legal citation to a Fellows' seminar at the Newberry Library in 1984.

77 "Ex signatione capituli accidit saepe inconveniens, nam saepe accidit, quando multae allegantur auctoritates, quod excidit a memoriis praedicatorum in quibus capitulis continentur auctoritates, et tunc allegant unum capitulum pro alio. Unde, ad vitandum istud inconveniens, recordor quod illo tempore aliquo pauci praedicantes actu signabant capitula; librum tamen signabant unde auctoritas fuit sumpta. Tamen, quando scribebant sermones, bene consueverunt signare libros et

capitula. Credo quod modus iste fuit melior, quia tutior quam sit modus iste modernus quo capitula cum libris signantur." Charland, p. 347.

78 It is quite common to find space left in the written version of a sermon or devotional text for the citation to be filled in; even so late a composition as Reginald Peacock's *Donet* shows this. On the relationship among the stages of composition leading to the scribally-produced text, see chapter 6, below.

79 Rouse, *Preachers, Florilegia and Sermons*, p. 16. The Dominican concordance, a project overseen by Hugh of St. Cher, is described in *DTC*, s.v. Hugues de Saint Cher. See also R. and M. Rouse, "La concordance verbale des Ecritures," in *Le Moyen Age et la Bible*, ed. P. Riché and G. Lobrichon, pp. 115–122.

80 Rouse, *Preachers, Florilegia and Sermons*, note 30, p. 16.

81 *Preachers, Florilegia and Sermons*, p. 4. On the usefulness of *divisiones* for the composition of sermons, see also Minnis, *Theory of Authorship*, pp. 155–157, who quotes the Dominican Master-General, Humbert of Rouen, to the effect that collections of these are "the arms of preachers" (p. 156).

82 Charland, pp. 268–269: "Magistris autem et professoribus sacrae theologiae licet, immo eos decet, omnia exquisite quotare, quia quantum ad istud defertur eis ab aliis propter protestationem excellentiae magistralis et ostentionem humilitatis in deferentibus, et propter dignitatem gradus et honorem."

83 *OED*, s.v. *quote* and *MED*, s.v. *cote(n)*, *cote*.

84 Smalley, *Study of the Bible*, p. 224.

85 See Thomas of Waleys's remarks about the mnemonic value of citation (Charland, p. 347), quoted above. Christina von Nolcken, "Some Alphabetical Compendia," prints a typical example of a *distinctio* on a moral theme intended for use in preaching.

86 Charland, p. 370; "Dato vero quod tantum una fiat divisio thematis, adhuc illa divisio erit bene ut illis, tam praedicatori quam etiam auditori. Non enim propter solam curiositatem, sicut aliqui credunt, invenerunt moderni quod thema dividant, quod non consueverunt antiqui. Immo, est utilis praedicatori, quia divisio thematis in diversa membra praebet occasionem dilatationis in prosecutione ulteriori sermonis. Auditori vero est multum utilis, quia, quando praedicator dividit thema et postmodum membra divisionis ordinate et distinctim prosequitur, faciliter capitur et tenetur tam materia sermonis quam etiam forma et modus praedicandi; quod non erit si praedicator indistincte ac sine ordine et forma confuse procedat."

87 Charland, p. 110; on the overlap in form and method between "university" and "popular" sermons, see D. L. D'Avray, *Preaching of the Friars*, pp. 123–125.

88 See for example the sermons preached on Feb. 23, 1305 in Sta. Maria Novella; Delcorno (ed.), *Quaresimali Fiorentino*, numbers 3 and 4.

89 Sorabji, *Aristotle on Memory*, pp. 28–30; see also the comments by Eleonore Stump in her edition of Boethius's *De differentiis topicis*, esp. pp. 15–17.

90 Aristotle, *Topics*, VIII, 13 (163b), trans. W. A. Pickard-Cambridge. The Renaissance development of memory arts in conjunction with logical systems is the subject of Paolo Rossi's *Clavis universalis*. On the development of the idea of Topic in medieval logic, and its relationship to the general method of mnemonic topics, see Stump, *Boethius' De Differentiis Topicis*, pp. 18–26, and especially G. R. Evans, "Two Aspects of *Memoria*."

91 *Formae praedicandi*, 48; Charland, p. 311: "Take note of these divisions: the utility of the Passion, 'Jesus'; the power of His suffering, 'crying out'; the truth of His humanity, 'in a loud voice'; His freedom to suffer, 'sent forth'; the pain of separation, 'His spirit.'"

92 Charland, p. 311–312: "Then [the theme] is subdivided as follows: There are five

vowels, AEIOU, which make up every word [with a pun on the double meaning of *vox*, 'word, voice']. Just so the five wounds of Christ make up every cry whether of joy or of sorrow. Behold 'in His hands' the A and the E: 'with loving-kindness I have drawn thee' [beginning with A in Latin] and Isaiah, 'Behold, I have graven thee upon the palms of my hands' [beginning with E in Latin]; 'in His side' the I: such a mark the wound of the lance imprinted, that is 'the door of the Ark' which [was] 'in the side', etc. in Genesis; and in John: 'reach hither thy hand and thrust it into my side' [a verse which begins with an I in Latin]; the O and U 'in His feet': 'thou hast put all things under his feet' [the Latin text begins with O]. So as you follow out [these links] you may say in fact: 'My foot has held his steps' [the Latin begins with U]." A translation of Basevorn's text was published in Murphy, *Three Medieval Rhetorical Arts*, though I have given my own here in an effort to stress the mnemonic form of the advice.

93 In his *ars memorativa*, Thomas Bradwardine advises associating the number five with the five wounds which Christ suffered on the cross; see appendix C.

94 Charland, pp. 311–312: "1) Walk as children of light [Eph. 5: 8]; 2) Return, return, o Shulamite, return, return, that we may look upon thee [Cant. 6: 12]; 3) To comfort your own soul is pleasing to God [Ecclus. 30: 24]; 4) Bring forth therefore fruits meet for repentance [Mt. 3:8]; 5) Loose thyself from the bands of thy neck, o captive daughter of Zion [Is. 52: 2]; 6) Wash ye, make you clean [Is. 1: 16]."

95 On Guido's solmization scheme and its development, including diagrams displaying how the full gamut was expressed in its syllables, see Reese, *Music in the Middle Ages*, pp. 149–151 and *New Grove Dictionary*, s.v. "Guido d'Arezzo" and "Solmisation."

96 "Habebis ergo argumentum ad inveniendum inauditum cantum facillimum et probatissimum . . . Namque postquam hoc argumentum cepi pueris tradere, ante triduum quidam eorum potuerunt ignotos cantus leviter canere, quod aliis argumentis nec multis hebdomadibus poterat evenire"; Martin Gerbert, *Scriptores ecclesiastici de musica sacra*, (1794) vol. 2, p. 45.

97 "[P]ro unaquaque voce memoriae retinenda"; Gerbert, *Scriptores*, vol. 2, p. 45. The whole letter (pp. 43–50) is a very interesting account of the building and extending of a simple, rigid mnemonic to increasingly complex material. The scheme began with a particular melody and text (the hymn to John the Baptist and a melody that Guido either composed or adapted in such a way that the initial syllables of the lines in the hymn matched their musical values) but was extended to signify all the notes of the gamut in every variety of combinations, independent of the text or melody of a particular chant. It worked so well, as Guido himself recognized, precisely because, unlike rote reiteration, it created "informationally rich" units.

98 *PL* 177, 135–164. Only two items are listed under "undecim" (col. 164C) – compare the copious listings for all the other numbers, through "duodecim." There are no listings for numbers greater than 12, or for 1, evidently because "one" does not constitute a mnemonic "division."

99 *Preachers, Florilegia and Sermons*, p. 69. A good example is Alanus's sermon "In adventu Domini" *PL* 210, 214–218, though many of the sermons contained in his "Art of Preaching" (which consists of examples rather than general principles, like those of Robert of Basevorn and Thomas of Waleys) observe the same principle. Alanus also composed an alphabetically-arranged index of distinctions.

100 *Inst.*, XI, 2, 29: "It is useful to place marks ("notae") against those passages that prove especially difficult, the remembrance of which will refresh and excite the

memory; for almost no-one could be so dull as to be unable to recollect a mark ("signum") which he had chosen for a particular passage."

101 Bodleian Library, MS. Bodley 722. The textual pictures are indexed at the end of this manuscript of Holcot's commentaries, indicating that they were intended to be particularly valuable heuristics to users of the book. A full discussion is in Smalley, *English Friars*, pp. 165–183; see also Saxl, "A Spiritual Encyclopaedia," pp. 101–103. I will further discuss the function of marginal images in chapter 7.

102 Peter of Ravenna, *Fenix* (Venice, 1491/2), c.iv.verso: "omnes enim lectiones meas Iuris canonici sine libro quotidie lego: ac si librum ante oculos haberem, textum et glossas memoriter pronuncio ut nec etiam minimam syllabam omittere uidear." (*Textum* in this context would refer to a cross-referential "web" of passages which a lecturer would concord as he commented on a passage of law, rather than to the "text" in the way we commonly use it.) He continues, "In locis autem meis quae collocauerim hic scribere statui et quae locis tradidi perpetuo teneo, in decem et nouem litteris alphabeti vigintamilia allegationum Iuris utriusque posui."

103 Peter of Ravenna, *Fenix*, b.iv.verso: "pro litteris alphabeti homines habeo et sic imagines vivas." The quotation which follows is also from this page. The need for vivid images to serve as mnemonic cues is a common-place of mnemonic technique from antiquity onward, not depending, as we will see, solely on the *Rhetorica ad Herennium* for its dissemination.

104 The manuscript is mentioned by McCulloch, *Bestiaries*, p. 42, and in *Survival of the Gods* (exhibition catalogue, 1987, Brown University Department of Art), no. 44, pp. 158–159. A color reproduction of two of its Bestiary pages is in the Pierpont Morgan Library exhibition catalogue, *Early Children's Books and Their Illustration* (1957), pp. 19 (illustration), 22.

105 Boncompagno, p. 279: "Per illam siquidem imaginationem alphabeti, memorie naturalis beneficio preeunte, in xxx diebus quingentorum scholarium nomina memorie commendavi. Refero etiam, quod mirabilius videbatur, quia unumquemque nomine proprio, non omissa denominatione cognominis vel agnominis et specialis terre de qua erat, in conspectu omnium appelabam: unde cuncti et singuli admiratione stupebant." On Boncompagno's personality ("[c]ompletely non-self-reflective," p. 2) and work, see Witt, "Boncompagno and the Defense of Rhetoric."

106 Bischoff, pp. 232–233.

107 *Etym.*, I, 3, 2: "Vsus litterarum repertus propter memoriam rerum. Nam ne oblivione fugiant, litteris alligantur. In tanta enim rerum varietate nec disci audiendo poterant omnia, nec memoria contineri." See also I, 21, I.

108 *Inst.*, I, 1, 25–26. On early training in ancient schools, see Marrou, *L'Histoire de l'education*, pp. 211–214, 364–366. The learning of the alphabet in late medieval schools, which had changed little from ancient times, is discussed by Nicholas Orme, *English Schools in the Middle Ages*, pp. 60–63.

109 *Inst.*, I, 1, 25: "It is for this reason that teachers, when they think they have sufficiently familiarised their young pupils with the letters written in their usual order, reverse that order or rearrange it in every kind of combination, until they learn to know the letters from their appearance and not from the order in which they occur.'"

110 *Inst.*, I, 1, 19: "initia litterarum sola memoria constant."

111 *Inst.*, I, 1, 37.

112 *Inst.*, I, 1, 36.

113 Marrou, *L'Histoire de l'education*, p. 366. The stress on syllables as a basic unit for teaching reading, and for organizing materials in monastically-produced *artes*

lectoriae is discussed by Paul Gehl, "Mystical language models"; this essay shows clearly some of the particular ways in which the pedagogy of grammar in antiquity was adapted to the Christian education of the monasteries.

114 Marrou, *L'Histoire de l'education*, p. 553, note 30.

115 Quintilian discusses punctuation in *Inst.*, IX, 4, 122–125; the quotation is from section 125.

116 Quoted from *Inst.*, IX, 4, 123. "Number" (rhythm) is analyzed in IX, 4, 52–57, where Quintilian distinguishes the "numbers" in prose from the more formal meters of verse, and defines prose-rhythm as informal but certainly present. The development of the prose cursus, a topic much discussed by literary historians, and used in administative and legal writing especially, is probably a related mnemonic aid for the trained notarius.

117 On the stability over time of the Latin Bible's cola and commata divisions see S. Berger, *L'Histoire de la Vulgate*, pp. 317–318.

118 "Memoria vero quasi mentis arca, firmaque et fidelis custodia perceptorum." (I, 11; *PL* 199, 839A); cf. "Quare retentione et frequenti revolutione, quasi thesaurum memoriae sibi format" (IV. 9; *PL* 199, 921D).

119 "Sunt et *notae*, quae scripturarum distinguunt modos, ut deprehendatur, quid in eis lucidum, quid obscurum, quid certum, quid dubium; et in hunc modum, plurima. Pars haec tamen artis jam ex maxima parte in desuetudinem abiit; adeo quidem, ut studiosissimi litteram merito querantur, et fere lugeant, rem utilissimam, et tam ad res retinendas, quam intelligendas, efficacissimam, majorum nostrorum invidia aut negligentia, artem dico deperisse notariam. Nec miretur quis, tantam vim fuisse in notulis: cum et musici cantores, paucis characteribus, multas acutarum et gravium differentias indicent vocum. Et ob hoc quidem, characteres illos musicae claves dicunt. Si tamen tanta scientiae clavis fuit in notulis, mirum est nostros, licet plura scierint, non agnovisse majores, aut tantae scientiae perditas esse claves" (I, 20; *PL* 199, 850D–851A).

120 "[E]t si totius haberi non potest, ad instructionem legendorum, plurimum confert ipsius memoriter vel hanc tenuisse particulam" (I, 20; *PL* 199, 851B).

121 See Caplan, "A Medieval Commentary on the *Rhetorica ad Herennium*," in his *Of Eloquence*.

122 Caplan, *Of Eloquence*, p. 256

123 Leclercq, "Love of Learning," p. 73.

124 Edited by Rossi, *Clavis universalis*, pp. 286–289. I have worked from the Huntington Library copy of the first edition of *Fenix*; the work (minus its preface) was translated from a French version into English by Robert Coplande, a pupil of Wynkyn de Worde, and printed in London around 1545 (= *STC* 24112).

125 Rossi, *Clavis universalis*, p. 289.

126 In the form in which it came to be attached to later medieval Bibles, the fully-alphabetized index became a sort of generalized dictionary of Biblical Hebrew, into which Jerome's original work was incorporated; it is described, and attributed to Stephen Langton, by Laura Light, "Versions et révisions du texte biblique," pp. 85–86. On Jerome's knowledge of Hebrew, his work on the compilations, and his astonishingly accurate concording memory, see *CHB*, vol. 2, pp. 91–101 especially.

127 Preface to "Liber de Nominibus Hebraicis": *PL* 23, 815B: "et rei ipsius utilitate commotus [*var.* novitate commotus] singula per ordinem Scripturam volumina percucurri." If the variant reading, "excited by its novelty," is at all authentic, it suggests that Jerome thought this way of organizing Biblical glosses to be especially innovative as well as useful.

128 The Book of Durrow's glossaries are discussed by A. A. Luce in the facsimile

edition, edited by A. A. Luce, *et al.*, vol. 2, pp. 7–14 and esp. p. 10. A general discussion of alphabetical habits during the Middle Ages is Lloyd W. and B. A. Daly, "Some Techniques in Medieval Latin Lexicography."

129 Daly, *Alphabetization*, esp. pp. 93–96; the ancients did know how to alphabetize absolutely, for examples of fully-alphabetized lists survive. A common partial alphabetizing scheme used in the Middle Ages is by the first syllable of a word (e.g. ba- words, then be- words, then bi-, bo-, bu-). This most likely reflects early reading-recitation training, in which students proceeded from letters to syllables, before learning complete words; see the discussion below of a similarly alphabetized fourteenth-century index.

130 Quintilian, *Inst.*, iv, 5, 3.

131 First described in S. Harrison Thomson, "Grosseteste's Topical Concordance of the Bible and the Fathers," pp. 139–144.

132 Hunt, "The Library of Robert Grosseteste," p. 132.

133 Hunt, "The Library of Robert Grosseteste," pp. 121–122.

134 Thomson, "Concordance," p. 140.

135 Hunt, "The Library of Robert Grosseteste," p. 124, note 4.

136 Hunt, "The Library of Robert Grosseteste," p. 124. Another transcribed entry was printed by Thomson, together with a description of MS. Lyons 414, in his *Writings of Robert Grosseteste*, pp. 122–124, and see also "Grosseteste's Topical Concordance." R. W. Southern discusses the use of this index, and Grosseteste's motives for making it, in *Robert Grosseteste*, pp. 186–204.

137 Hunt, "The Library of Robert Grosseteste,"; see also Hunt's "Manuscripts Containing the Indexing Symbols of Robert Grosseteste," 241–244. To those which Hunt lists might be added Huntington Library MS. HM 26061, a Bible and missal of the mid thirteenth century, containing what appear to be indexing symbols, especially in the center margin of the book of Proverbs. It is not clear that these correspond to Grosseteste's system, however, and they might be those of a reader with his own version of notae having shapes similar to some used by Grosseteste. See the reference to this MS. in R. and M. Rouse, *Preachers, Florilegia and Sermons*, p. 18, note 34, and the description of it in the Huntington Library's *Guide to Medieval and Renaissance Manuscripts*.

138 Thomson, "Grosseteste's Topical Concordance," p. 144; cf. *Writings*, p. 124.

139 I have somewhat modified the translation of Hunt, "The Library of Robert Grosseteste," p. 127 from the Latin quoted in Callus, "The Oxford Career of Robert Grosseteste," p. 46: "Sed quando aliqua ymaginatio notabilis sibi occurrebat ibi scripsit ne laberetur [sic] a memoria sua, sicud et multas cedulas scripsit que non omnes sunt autentice. Non enim est maioris autoritatis que dissute scripsit in margine libri phisicorum quam alie cedule quas scripsit, que omnia habentur Oxonie in libraria fratrum minorum, sicut oculis propriis vidi" (from MS. Vat. Palat. lat. 1805, f. 10v).

140 Hunt, "The Library of Robert Grosseteste," pp. 128–129.

141 Compare the typical entries transcribed by Hunt, "The Library of Robert Grosseteste," p. 124, and those transcribed by Thomson, "Grosseteste's Topical Concordance," p. 142, and *Writings*, p. 123.

142 There has been a suggestion made, amounting in some accounts now to a fact, that Grosseteste used parchment slips as well as margins to record notes; some scholars have speculated that these slips formed the basis of his concordance. The suggestion was based on William of Alnwick's reference to Grosseteste's having written marginal notes and "multas cedulas" (and on another manuscript reference to Grosseteste's *cedula*: "Hanc demonstracionem inveni Oxonie in quadam cedula domini Lincolniensis"; see Hunt, "Library," p. 127). Latin *sceda*

or *scida*, diminutive *scedula* or *cedula*, does indeed mean "a strip of papyrus" or "a small leaf or page." (Lewis and Short, s.v. *scida*.) But, like Latin *pagina*, a word with which it is often associated (as in Martial, *Epigrams*, IV, 89), it carries the connotation of something composed or put together in haste and informally, the sort of thing one would write on the last little bit of a book. So, Latin *schedium* is "an impromptu poem or speech" (Lewis and Short, s.v. *schedium*). Quintilian refers rather contemptuously to scholars who toil away reading even worthless notations ("indignos lectione scidas" *Inst.*, I, 8, 9). In other words, *cedula* like Latin *pagina* and English 'note," can refer both to a kind of writing surface and to a genre of composition. It seems to me likely that William of Alnwick (and the writer of the marginal note mentioned by Hunt) was characterizing all of Grosseteste's marginalia as *cedulae*, that is "impromptu, disjointed memoranda of ideas," and not necessarily referring to actual little scraps of parchment. Indeed the parallelism of his reference tips the balance for me in favor of this interpretation ("what he wrote . . . in the margin of his *Physics* is of no greater authority than the other ['alie'] 'cedulae' which he wrote"). One must also wonder whether it is plausible that the library of the Friars Minor at Oxford had kept stacks of little parchment scraps, though they were thought to have no authority, as well as Grosseteste's books – for it is in that library that William Alnwick says he saw Grosseteste's marginal "cedulae."

143 The text has been edited by Borgnet, vol. 5, pp. 30–47.
144 The Rouses, *Preachers, Florilegia, and Sermons*, pp. 20–21, talk briefly about the citational system used in this index, but not its alphabetizing scheme. The index is on ff. 318–322 of the manuscript.
145 The catalogue of Titchfield Abbey in Hampshire calls its cases "columpnae"; R. M. Wilson, "The Medieval Library of Titchfield Abbey," pp. 150–177, 252–276. A translation and sketch, reconstructed from the manuscript description, is given by J. W. Clark, *The Care of Books*, pp. 77–79.
146 Thomson, *The Medieval Library*, pp. 613–629. See also the account of press-marks in Ker, *Medieval Libraries*, pp. xviii–xix, and for individual libraries.
147 Daly, *Alphabetization*, pp. 18–26.

Chapter 4

1 The standard studies of the medieval *Ad Herennium* commentation traditions are still those of Harry Caplan, reprinted in his *Of Eloquence*. Further references can be found in J. J. Murphy, *Medieval Rhetoric: A Select Bibliography*.
2 I have outlined this development in my esssay, "Italy, *Ars memorativa*, and Fame's House."
3 The text I have used is Traugott Lawler, *John of Garland's Parisiana poetria*. Lawler says that John of Garland's system was "applied only to what is said in the classroom" (p. 237, note on lines 87–115), but this is not so, for lines 103–105 counsel paying attention to the page design in order to remember what one reads. John's treatise was probably addressed to fairly elementary students; see Lawler, pp. xviii–xix.
4 Murphy, *Rhetoric in the Middle Ages*, pp. 194–268.
5 In general, I quote Lawler's translation of the Latin text, but I have made certain changes which reflect the meaning of certain words in the context of memory advice. *Distinguo* means to "mark" or "set off" by a distinctive color or mark, as well as having the vaguer meaning "separate." It also means "punctuate." This phrase in this context is unambiguous advice to make mental *notae*, perhaps even in color, as is done in written texts. *Autentica* means "original" or "belonging to

the sources," not "authentic" in our sense; see M. D. Chenu, *Introduction à St. Thomas*, pp. 109–113.

6 *Differentias* is an alternative word for *distinctio*; see Lawler, *Parisiana poetria*, p. 239, note to line 108.

7 Lawler places a comma in this text between "linguarum" and "sonorum," but I think the sense of the passage requires that it not be there; the phrase translates into English as "the sounds of languages," that is, familiar words associated mnemonically with strange ones by homophony, as Bradwardine in his art of memory (see appendix C) uses English words to remember Latin.

8 The standard study of the development of the Bestiary is Florence McCulloch, *Medieval French and Latin Bestiaries*.

9 See John Morson, "The English Cistercians and the Bestiary." Morson especially discusses the use of material from the Bestiary in the writings of Aelred of Rielvaux and other English Cistercians.

10 Philippe de Thaon's Bestiary is discussed by McCulloch, *Medieval French and Latin Bestiaries*, pp. 47–56.

11 Yates, *Art of Memory*, 118.

12 Host von Romberch, *Congestorium Artificiose Memorie*, Venetiis, per Melchiorem Sessam, 1533. The writing of the treatise is dated to 1513. Romberch was a Dominican friar from Cologne; the work is thoroughly discussed by Yates, *Art of Memory*, pp. 122–130, who reproduces some of the many schematic drawings in it.

13 Clark Hulse has suggested to me that this habit may help explain why even in the sixteenth century the decoration of many books could be left incomplete; if readers were encouraged to supply a memorial image of their own projected into the printed text like decoration, they might not have objected to having books left incomplete, with missing decoration. Romberch's advice is aimed at an audience of readers wishing to retain written material – there is a brief chapter at the end on how to retain aurally-presented material, but he begins by saying that he has little to offer on the subject beyond the fact that it is the speaker's duty to speak clearly and to use vivid gestures (advice going back to antiquity), and he observes that memorizing from a book is much easier because we can read the text several times in order to imprint it clearly.

14 I found this passage in J. B. Allen, "Langland's Reading," p. 352, where it is discussed in relation to an entirely different subject.

15 Nordenfalk, "Beginning of Book Decoration," suggests an Egyptian or at least Near Eastern source for the Eusebian layout. Using a grid to relate pictorial images is a layout found first in mosaics from the Antioch region. The chapter and verse grid format for the Bible goes back at least to the Masoretic text. All of this fragmentary evidence would point to a Near Eastern milieu for the beginnings of the mnemonic use of a grid. The little we can judge of Aristotle's systems suggests that he used linear schemes, but whether they constituted a true grid or not is hard to tell. That is as far as I am able to trace a source; in any event, there is no text in the Latin tradition before the Middle Ages that advocates a mnemonic grid arrangement.

16 Obermann, *Bishop Thomas Bradwardine*, pp. 10–22. The article on Bradwardine by J. E. Murdoch in the *Dictionary of Scientific Biography* does not mention this treatise at all; it is reported as a "doubtful" work by J. A. Weisheipl, "Repertorium Mertonense," p. 182, but Weisheipl examined only in the inferior version in Sloane 3744 (which he erroneously identifies as Sloane 377). The internal evidence of the text for date and provenance, especially in the McClean MS. version, is strong, and when added to the apparently unanimous manuscript attributions,

seems to me enough to ally most of the doubts that the treatise is not Bradwardine's. I have reviewed the evidence for attribution in a note to appendix C, below.

17 Yates mentions it, *Art of Memory*, p. 114, and Beryl Rowland treats it as in the Ciceronian tradition in "Bishop Bradwardine, the Artificial Memory, and the House of Fame."

18 Quintilian says that Metrodorus of Scepsis used the Zodiac as the basis for a mnemonic system of places (*Inst.*, XI, ii, 22). Carl Nordenfalk describes a Canon Tables, each one marked with a zodiacal sign, in a tenth-century manuscript: "A 10th-Century Gospel Book in the Walters Art Gallery." There is no proof that these marks were being used as a mnemonic, but Nordenfalk comments that the use of the zodiac as part of the "decoration" of Canon Tables was rare. I would suggest that someone, knowing that the Canon Tables needed to be memorized, marked them in this instance with signs from the conventions of mnemotechnique, rather than only reproducing the usual architectural collonnade, as in figure 4 (which is itself part of an ancient convention of mnemotechnique, as we have seen).

19 The Rutland Psalter (B.L. MS. Add. 62925) is dated c. 1260. Its use of marginal grotesques is, from the viewpoint of style, "precociously early"; Kauffmann, *Romanesque Painting*, no. 112. A facsimile of the manuscript was edited for the Roxburghe Club by E. G. Millar.

20 Resp. 11: "confusio generatur ex parte loci vel locati vel eius quod actu visibilem facit locum et locatum."

21 Resp. 11: "multas ingerit imagines, et ideo confrigunt se in anima et non manent, sicut undae multae confrigunt se in aqua."

22 Objection 16: "reponemus in memoria 'aegrotum in lecto, qui est defuncti figura et reum ponemus astare lecto, dextra poculum, sinistra tabulas tenentem et medicum astantem tenentem testiculos arietinos,' ut scilicet in poculo sit memoria veneni, quod propinavit et in tabulis memoria haereditatis sit, quas subscripsit, et in medico figura sit accusatoris et in testiculis figura testium consciorum et in ariete defensio contra reum in iudicio."

23 Caplan's text, pp. 214–215, note b. No manuscripts known to us now seem to have the reading Albertus gives here; see the textual notes in F. Marx's *editio maior* of 1894.

24 Manuscripts of the E recension of *Rhetorica ad Herennium*, a twelfth-century edition based upon a rediscovered manuscript from the fourth or fifth century, omit the reference to Agamemnon and Menelaus altogether, and introduce the adjective "vagantem" for Iphigenia. Albertus almost certainly used an E-type manuscript, given his version of this passage. E reads "domum itionem" correctly, a reading which Albertus says he knows but rejects for the alternative, and wrong, reading "domi ultionem." On the E edition, see Caplan's introduction to the Loeb text, and F. Marx's preface to his *editio maior*, xii–xv.

25 This is suggested also by Raymond D. DiLorenzo, "The Collection Form and the Art of Memory," esp. pp. 206–207.

26 *Postilla in Isaiam*, p. 74, lines 70–76: "Unde in fabulis poetarum in Ovido magnus Iupiter, qui deus deorum confingitur, cum Phaethontem percutere deberet, qui caelum et terram et omnia quae in eis sunt, combusserat, iaculum post aurem accepit, ut patenter doceret, quod iudicum est prius diligenter audire et merita personarum et causarum ponderare et postea ferire feriendos."

27 Smalley, *English Friars*, p. 134. Yates suggested that these "pictures" might be related to the art of memory; *Art of Memory*, pp. 96–101.

28 *Postilla in Isaiam*, p. 374, lines 17–22: "Duos pedes habet anima, intellectum scilicet et affectum. Qui quando aequalis sunt, quod scilicet affectus adaequatur

intellectui veritatis, homo bene ambulat. Si autem vel ambo vel alter curvus est, intellectus scilicet per errorum et affectus per libidinem, homo claudus est."

29 *Postilla in Isaiam*, p. 474, lines 76–78: "Propter hoc etiam Venus pingebatur, quod veste aliquantulum elevata crus revelavit, ut ad libidinem provocaret." See Smalley, *English Friars*, p. 115.

30 Yates, *Art of Memory*, p. 79. The Latin text of Albertus's commentary is in Borgnet, vol. 90, 97–118.

31 DiLorenzo, "The Collection Form and the Art of Memory."

32 The text of Alcuin's "Dialogue on Rhetoric and the Virtues" is in *PL* 101, 919–946; the brief discussion of memory is in col. 941. See also Wilbur Howell, *The Rhetoric of Alcuin and Charlemagne*, whose text and translation (pp. 136–139) I have quoted. Notice how Alcuin stresses practice in writing as one of the disciplines of memory, an emphasis one also finds in Quintilian's advice and others, like Martianus Capella, deriving from the same tradition. No memory writer seems to have worried, with Thammuz in *Phaedrus*, that writing would undermine memory competence – on the contrary. It is worth recalling, in this context, that Luria's subject, S., discovered that writing things down was useless to him in trying to forget anything.

33 "Ad [memoriam] obtinendam tradunt plerique locorum et simulacrorum quasdam observationes, quae mihi non videntur habere effectum"; ed. Halm, p. 440, lines 15–17.

34 *Rhetorica ad Herennium*, ed. and trans. H. Caplan, esp. pp. xxxiv–xxxv.

35 x, ix, translated by William Watts, Loeb Classical Library.

36 Of early medieval references, Caplan (p. xxxv) mentions only a letter of Servatus Lupus from the early ninth century, and comments that the oldest extant manuscripts belong to the ninth and tenth centuries. Written commentaries appear about the twelfth century. The earliest classical references are in scattered sources from Jerome (in works from 395 and 402) through Priscian (early sixth century). These references are not specifically to the memory section, it should be noted.

37 *Metalogicon*, I, 20, trans. D. D. McGarry, p. 59: "Seneca se artem comparandae memoriae traditurum facillime pollicetur: et utinam innotuisset mihi, sed quod eam tradiderit, omnino non recolo. Tullius in rhetoricus operam dedisse visus est; sed similibus mei multum non prodest. Exstant autem, quae discere vix sufficimus, sed minus curamus"; *PL* 199, 851A.

38 Lines 2017–2019 in the edition of Faral, trans. M. F. Nims: "Tradit imaginibus peregrinis Tullius artem, / Qua meminisse decet; sed se docet et sibi soli / Subtilis subtile suum quasi solus adoret."

39 "[M]y own subtlety may be pleasing to me and not to [Cicero]. It is beneficial only to the one it suits, for enjoyment alone makes the power of memory strong. Therefore have no faith in these or other *notae* if they are difficult for you, or [less agreeable, 'minus acceptae']. But if you wish to proceed more securely, fashion your own signs for yourself, of whatever kind your own inclination suggests"; lines 2020–2025, trans. Nims, with my modifications.

40 Yates, *Art of Memory*, p. 50.

41 v, 538–539; edited by Aldolphus Dick; trans. by R. Johnson in volume 2 of Stahl and Johnson, *Martianus Capella and the Seven Liberal Arts*. The memory section is Book v; a translation, which differs significantly in emphasis from Johnson's, of a portion of this book appears in Yates, *Art of Memory*, pp. 51–52. Yates understands the references to memory places physically, whereas Johnson, understands them solely as "dead metaphors" and abstractions. The best definition of *topos* by a modern scholar is that of Harry Caplan: "The *topos* is the head under which arguments fall, the place in the memory where the argument is to be

looked for and found, ready to use" (*Of Eloquence*, p. 83). Cf. Cicero, *Topica*, an elementary text on the subject: "It is easy to find things that are hidden if the hiding place is pointed out and marked; similarly if we wish to track down some argument we ought to know the places or topics: for that is the name given by Aristotle to the "regions ['quasi sedes,' 'sort of seats'] from which arguments are drawn"; II, 8.

42 "[T]hings are read in a loud voice, but for meditating [memorizing] a murmur works better"; ed. Dick, p. 269, lines 19–20. Pierre Riché discusses the volume-level of early monastic students, *Education and Culture*, esp. pp. 117–119, 465–466. The association of voice-level with different reading functions is discussed at length in chapter 5, below.

43 *Inst.*, VI, 2, 31.

44 *Inst.*, X, 7, 15.

45 I will return to this point in chapter 7. The best discussion of late medieval diagrams is still that of F. Saxl, "A Spiritual Encyclopaedia of the Middle Ages" *JWCI* 5 (1942). Saxl does not make any connection of these to the mnemonic technique of "imagines rerum," however.

46 Evans, "Two Aspects of *Memoria*," p. 278.

47 On the curriculum at Padua, the influence of Boncompagno da Signa, and Albertus Magnus's possible studies there, see Nancy Siraisi, *Arts and Sciences at Padua*, esp. pp. 37–43, 109–117. Albertus need not, of course, have been at Padua to study the recent translations of Aristotle; what is important is that he was their early, influential commentator and champion. About all we know of Albertus in Italy is that he says he was there, but he does not mention where he was and what he studied.

48 Fredborg (ed.), *Rhetorical Commentaries*, pp. 27, 307n. Fredborg's introduction sets forth the evidence of composition and date, and discusses both Thierry's sources and the influence of his commentaries on later writers.

49 Fredborg (ed.), *Rhetorical Commentaries*, p. 306.20–21: "Nota ad carmina poetarum in memoria retinenda verborum memoriam plus quam ad causas valere," "Note that memory for words is more valuable for retaining the songs of poets in memory than for orational themes."

50 Fredborg (ed.), *Rhetorical Commentaries*, p. 307.31–36.

51 "*Intervalla*, id est locorum distantias. . . . Confunditur aspectus ex re visa aspectui nimium appropinquata vel ab eo nimium remota"; Fredborg (ed.), *Rhetorical Commentaries*, p. 305.70–72. In this gloss, Thierry shows he understood better than twentieth-century writers on the *Ad Herennium* what "intervalla" were.

52 See D'Alverny, "Translations and Translators."

53 Yates, *Art of Memory*, p. 61.

54 Caplan, "Introduction" to the Loeb *Rhetorica ad Herennium*, p. xxxv. Jean d'Antioche's "Rhétorique de Cicéron," from Musée Condé MS. 590, is described by L. de Lisle in *Notices et extraits* 36 (1899): 207–265.

55 The roll of Dominicans is impressive. In addition to the thirteenth- and fourteenth-century writers mentioned in this chapter (Albertus Magnus, Thomas Aquinas, and Jacopus da Cessolus) it includes Peter of Ravenna, the author of *Fenix*, which adapts the architectural mnemonic to a specifically Gothic setting. *Fenix* was first published in Venice in 1491, in an English translation finally in 1548, and it was one of the most widely published of the Renaissance treatises on *ars memorativa*. Peter began his life as a lay jurist, but became a Dominican friar. Johannes Host von Romberch, author of the *Congestorium* to which I have already alluded, was a German Dominican of the early sixteenth century. The three great authorities on the art of memory to which these Renaissance writers pay homage, are Aristotle, Cicero, and Thomas Aquinas.

56 Caplan makes the attribution to Bono Giamboni ("Introduction," p. xxxv). Rossi, *Clavis universalis*, pp. 271–272, is somewhat less direct in his opinion, saying only that the vernacular translation which circulated as a preface to the *Ammaestramenti* was probably part of the *Fiore di Rettorica* of Fra Guidotto di Bologna and Bono Giamboni.

57 "Ma se l'uomo ha in se senno di saper bene in sulle cose vedere, e ancora in se senno e guistizia, cioè ferma volontà di volere le cosse bene disporre, e diritamente voler fare, sì fa bisogno di saper favellare . . . che senza favella sarebbe la bontà sua come un tesoro riposto sotto terra . . . Già abbiamo veduto della prima cosa, che al dicitore fa bisogno di sapere, cioè come ha a imparare di favellare perfettamente in ciò, che a te ho mostrato qual è buona, qual è composta, qual è ornata, e qual è ordinata favella . . . Or ti voglio mostrare della seconda cosa, che fa bisogno al dicitore di sapere, acciocchè perfettamente dica la sua diceria, cioè ome la sua dicería si reca a memoria, acciocchè quando la dice, l'abbia bene a mente, perocchè niuno la direbbe bene, se quando la dice, bene a mente non l'avesse." *Classici Italiani* (Milano, 1808), pp. 344–345.

Chapter 5

1 Often quoted, the sermon is found in Durham Cathedral MS. B. iv, 12; it was translated in part by Mynors, *Durham Cathedral Manuscripts*, p. 9. Mynors's translation is partially reprinted in Diringer, *The Book Before Printing*, pp. 206–207.

2 Miethke, "Marsilius und Ockham: Publikum und Leser," esp. pp. 548–549; the composition of *III Dialogus* is discussed by Miethke in *Ockhams Weg*, pp. 121–125.

3 On private book-collecting and ownership, see the chapter by Roberto Weiss in Wormald and Wright *The English Library Before 1700*, pp. 112–135. One should remember, however, that some members of the lay aristocracy always owned a few books; see Riché, "Les Bibliothèques de trois aristocrats laïcs carolingiens," and *Education and Culture*, pp. 184–265. A good earlier book discussing the matter of lay literacy in the later Middle Ages is J. W. Thompson, *The Literacy of the Laity in the Middle Ages*. One should therefore more accurately speak in terms of a late-medieval extension of private book ownership rather than its beginning, though the collecting of books simply to own them or to have a "scholar's library," as Petrarch's was, is a late medieval phenomenon. Of book production and book selling at this time there are a large number of studies; John Burrow, *Medieval Writers and Their Work*, provides a recent summary account as does Christopher De Hamel, *A History of Illuminated Manuscripts*. All considerations of this matter should, however, keep in mind the studies of Margaret Deanesly, such as "Vernacular Books," which remind us that, while a few individuals owned many books, most, even those who might afford them, owned very few, if any.

4 *I Dialogus*, ii, 23 (1494 ed., f. 14): "tu autem scis quod nullum habeo predictorum et forte illi de ordine nolunt mihi communicare predicta."

5 *III Dialogus*, i, prol. (1494 ed., f. 181): "Ideo si tibi videtur de prefatis me nullatenus intromittam: maxime cum ad libros necessarios non valeam (vt estimo) peruenire. *Disc:* Timor non te retrahat memoratus."

6 *III Dialogus*, ii, prol. (1494 ed., f. 229v–230): "*Magis:* Eorum perfecta cognitio, que tractanda commemoras ex libris sacre theologie vtriusque iuris canonici videlicet et ciuilis philosophie moralis et ex hystoriis romanorum atque imperatorum et summorum pontificum et aliarum gentium esset patentius extrahenda et solidius munienda. De quibus solummodo bibliam et decretum cum quattuor

libris decretalium spem habeo obtinendi. Quare ne forsitan opus imperfectum immo ridiculosum faciamus videtur consultius desistendum. *Disc*: Quis his diebus opus perfectum facere nequeamus cum de materia tam necessaria . . . vtile erat penitus non silere vt alios copiam librorum habentes ad faciendum perfecta opera prouocemus."

7 Discussed by Miethke, *Ockhams Weg*, pp. 121–122, and esp. notes 455 and 457. The chronicler reporting this event does not say that Albert saw a written copy of Ockham's work (as an erroneous 19th-century edition had it), but that Albert was persuaded to support Ludwig against the Clementine interdict because Ludwig supported his position ("innititur") with arguments drawn from a "dialogus" which Ockham had produced ("edidit") in the form of a student asking questions and a master responding ("sub forma discipuli querentis et magistri respondentis").

8 Many otherwise excellent, careful studies reflect such assumptions. For example, Richard and Mary Rouse have said that memory ceased to be emphasized after the twelfth century, and in an otherwise fine introduction to his edition to Bartolommaeus Anglicus's encyclopedia, R. J. Long refers to a thirteenth-century "scissors-and-paste" method of composing. Several scholars have supposed the wide-spread use of parchment slips; Antoine Dondaine pictures Thomas Aquinas pausing frequently in mid-composition to check quotations in his books; other scholars, analysing the sources of florilegial compendia, have presumed it to be "self-evident" that a scholar compiling in a particular city must have had physically available to him where he was working copies of the works he cites, that he must be "quoting directly or paraphrasing" from a text physically before him, and that manuscript evidence, had it survived, could definitively tell us which written source it was. I mention these frequently made comments only to indicate how even the best of modern scholars have assumed that medieval ones worked from books exactly in our manner, though in much less convenient circumstances.

9 *Cambridge Medieval History* (short edition), p. 527. Roy Rosenstein has called attention to the crusader song of Jaufre Rudel, which clearly shows how this song was used to disseminate the Crusade; the relevant lines (29–34) are as follows: "Senes breu de pargamina / tramet lo vers que chantam / plan et en lenga romana / a N Hugon Brun per Fillol," "without a parchment document / I send the song we sing, / smoothly and in Romance language, / to Lord Hugh Brun, by Fillol" – *The Poetry of Cercamon and Jaufre Rudel*, ed. George Wolf and Roy Rosenstein (New York: Garland, 1983).

10 Deferrari, "Augustine's Method of Composing," p. 103.

11 The circumstances surrounding the first making of eyeglasses are analysed by Edward Rosen, "The Invention of Eyeglasses." Friar Giordano announced that "it is not yet twenty years since the art of making eyeglasses was discovered . . . I saw the one who first discovered and made them, and spoke with him [*E disse il lettore: io vidi colui che prima la trovò e fece, e favellaigli*]." This sermon is xv in Delcorno's edition of Giordano da Pisa, *Quaresimale Fiorentino*, preached in Santa Maria Novella, Wednesday, February 23, 1305 (1306).

12 John Ward, "Cicero's *Rhetorica*," pp. 59–60. It is important to remember that the "authors" of most medieval commentaries of the twelfth century were in fact mainly compilers of a pre-existing store; a number of studies have brought this out, but one might especially mention those of Beryl Smalley. After the eleventh century it was more usual for the glossator to sign his contribution, perhaps because – in the cases of both the Bible and the law – an "ordinary gloss" had been compiled from the mainly anonymous stock of glosses that existed before.

13 See R. and M. Rouse, "Statim invenire."

14 Occasionally, especially in late manuscripts, one or two individuals are shown with pens – these are the reporters, those "pencils" of the Middle Ages.

15 In *Familiares*, III, i, Petrarch recounts a conversation he had in Avignon with Richard de Bury, regarding the nature of "ultima Thule," and says of him that he was "not ignorant of letters"; the remark is patronizing, of course, but no more than that.

16 I, 27–29; pp. 14–15. On Hugh of St. Victor's diagrammatic ladders, see my discussion of *De arca Noe mystica*, in chapter 7 below. Bury calls the books burned in the fire of the Alexandrine library "scrinia veritatis," (VII, 107; p. 59, lines 9–10) which he recalls "with a tearful pen [*stilo flebili memoramus*];" VII, 106; p. 58, lines 8–9). Later, invoking the motif of *translatio studii*, he describes how Aristotle transferred the ancient wisdom of Egypt to his own (memory) treasuries in good Greek, "quos omnes diserta Graecia in thesauros suos transtulerat"; X, 160; p. 92, lines 3–4.

17 VIII, 126; p. 69, line 16: "paradisum mundi Parisius."

18 VIII, 128: "apertis thesauris et sacculorum corrigiis resolutis, pecuniam laeto corde dispersimus, atque libros impretiabiles luto redemimus et arena"; p. 71, lines 4–7.

19 This has been estimated at 1,500 books; the largest documented collections made by other men of Richard de Bury's time were on the order of 100 or so. Humphrey, Duke of Gloucester, a most avid collector of manuscripts a century later may have collected as many as 500; he gave Oxford about 300 of those. Only four surviving books have been identified as belonging to Richard de Bury, all returned to St. Albans after his death (whence he had bought them – perhaps extorted them – in the first place). See Wormald and Wright, *The English Library*, esp. pp. 113–115.

20 IV, 58; pp. 29–30: "Primum oportet volumen cum Ezechiele comedere, quo venter memoriae dulcescat intrinsecus ... Sic nostra natura in nostris familiaribus operante latenter, auditores accurrunt benevoli, sicut adamas trahit ferrum nequaquam invite. O virtus infinita librorum iacent Parisius vel Athenis simulque resonant in Britannia et in Roma! Quiescentes quippe moventur, dum ipsis loca sua tenentibus, auditorum intellectibus circumquaque feruntur."

21 VIII, 134, pp. 74–75: "A corpore sacrae legis divinae usque ad quaternum sophismatum hesternorum, nihil istos praeterire potuit scrutatores. Si in fonte fidei Christianae, curia sacrosancta Romana, sermo devotus insonuit, vel si pro novis causis quaestio ventilabatur extranea, si Parisiensis soliditas ... si Anglicana perspicacitas ... quicquam ad augmentum scientiae vel declarationem fidei promulgabat, hoc statim nostris recens infundebatur auditibus nullo denigratum seminiverbio nulloque nugace corruptum, sed de praelo purissimi torcularis in nostrae memoriae dolia defaecandum transibat." *Seminiverbio* is from the Vulgate of Acts 17: 18 (as Thomas's note indicates); *denigrare* is a synonym of *detergere*, "to wipe clean," as Du Cange notes, s.v.; *corrumpere* in the context of literary texts means "falsify" or "spoil" (Lewis and Short, s.v.). Anyone who has worked with medieval manuscripts will recognize the aptness of Bury's fears; I am reminded of Chaucer's warning to Adam, his scrivener, not to "wryten newe" his *Troilus*.

22 Much has ably been written on the content and methods of medieval *lectio* in both monastic and university settings; among the best studies are those of Smalley, *Study of the Bible*, Evans, *Language and Logic of the Bible*, de Lubac, *Exégèse Médiévale*, Chenu, *Introduction à St. Thomas*, and Leclercq, *The Love of Learning*. In *Metalogicon*, I, 24, John of Salisbury defines the distinction very clearly, though his terminology for it is somewhat different from the more common one I have adopted here: "The word 'reading' [*legendi*] is equivocal. It may refer either to the activity of teaching and being taught, or to the occupation of

studying written things by oneself [*ad scrutinium meditantis*]" (trans. McGarry, pp. 65–66). He calls the former *praelectio*, following Quintilian (*Inst.*, II, 5, 4), and the latter *lectio*. He who aspires to philosophy, says John of Salisbury, "must learn reading, organized study, and meditation, together with the exercise of good works [*apprehendat lectionem, doctrinam, et meditationem, cum exercitio boni operis*]"; Latin text *PL* 199, 853D.

23 *Didascalicon*, III, 7–10; trans. J. Taylor, pp. 92–93.

24 This paraphrase-translation is of II, 6 (*PL* 176, 693D–640C).

25 Frances Yeats notes this reputation in her 1955 essay on "The Ciceronian Art of Memory"; the suggestion was adopted enthusiastically by Rossi, *Clavis universalis*, pp. 292–294.

26 Petrarch's veneration for Augustine is discussed fully by Courcelle, *Les Confessions*, pp. 329–351. The story of Petrarch's sortilege on the summit of Mont Ventoux is in *Familiares*, VI.1. There have been a number of discerning studies recently of this famous incident; see Thomas M. Greene, *The Light in Troy*, pp. 104–111, and Kahn, "The Figure of the Reader."

27 Petrarch writes in the prologue: "So, little Book, I bid you flee the haunts of men and be content to stay with me." He may have begun *Secret* at Vauclusse, but the main part was added in Milan, where Petrarch lived from 1353–1358; see Hans Baron, *From Petrarch to Leonardo Bruni*, pp. 51–101.

28 *Secretum*, Dialogue Two; translated Draper (with my alterations), pp. 97–100, 102. The Latin text is from Petrarch, *Prose*, pp. 120–122, 126.

29 Petrucci, *La Scrittura*, pp. 38–57; see also E. Pellegrin and G. Billanovich, "Un Manuscrit de Cicéron annoté par Pétrarque" (B.L. MS. Harley 2493). Like most scribes, Petrarch used a different hand for glosses than for the main text.

30 *Penetralia* means "recess" or "interior" generally, but specifically "the innermost chamber of a shrine or temple" (Lewis and Short, s.v. *penetralium*), an image that links up with that of memory as *scrinium*, and perhaps colored also for Petrarch by the architectural mnemonic scheme he certainly knew. Italian *penetrali* still carries the Latin meanings.

31 See Leclercq, *Love of Learning*, p. 73, who cites a number of writers. *Ruminare* was used metaphorically to mean "meditate" in pagan writing also; the earliest citation in the *Ox. Lat. Dict.* is third century, B.C. (s.v. *rumino*). Quintilian, though he does not actually use the verb, says that meditation (by which he means memorizing) is like rechewing one's food (*Inst.*, XI, 2, 41). See also Philip West, "Rumination in Bede's Account of Caedmon."

32 *Moralia in Job*, I, 33 (*PL* 75, 542C): "In nobismetipsis namque debemus transformare quod legimus; ut cum per auditum se animus excitat, ad operandum quod audierit vita concurrat."

33 *Didascalicon*, V, 5: "cuius sententias quasi fructus quosdam dulcissimos legendo carpimus, tractando ruminamus"; Buttimer, p. 103, lines 26–27. Notice Hugh's use of the gerundive form of *tractare*, in a context similar to that in which Ockham also uses it (see p. 000 above). It seems to be a scholastic use, "tracting" for the process of making "tracts" by mentally collating extracts during meditational composition (recall the account of Thomas Aquinas's composing habits – I have more to say about his whole matter in chapter 6). On the genre called *tractatus*, see Kristeller, "The Scholar and His Public" in *Medieval Aspects of Renaissance Learning*, esp. pp. 4–12.

34 *Cura pastoralis*, III, 12 (*PL* 77, 69).

35 *Didascalicon*, III, 11; "hoc etiam saepe replicare et de ventre memoriae ad palatum revocare necesse est"; Buttimer, p. 61, lines 1–2. The quote from Gregory is found in *PL* 77, 69B.

36 *Sermones*, 352, 1 (*PL* 39, 1550): "Unde cum sermonem ad vestram Charitatem non praepararemus, hinc nobis esse tractandum Domino imperante cognovimus. Volebamus enim hodierna die vos in ruminatione permittere, scientes quam abundantes epulas ceperitis."

37 *Historia Ecclesiastica*, IV, 24. Philip West has discussed this passage and its context in the monastic traditions of *ruminatio* in "Rumination in Bede's Account of Caedmon."

38 See Darbishire (ed.), *The Early Lives of Milton*; my thanks to James Thorpe of the Huntington Library for bringing this material to my attention.

39 *Regula monachorum*, cap. 14 (*PL* 30, 365B): "Ad orationem nocte consurgenti non indigestio cibi ructum faciat, sed inanitas. Nam quidam vir inter pastores eximius: sicut fumus, inquit, fugat apes, sic indigesta ructatio avertit Spiritus sancti charismata. Ructus autem dicitur proprie digestio cibi, et concoctarum escarum in ventum efflatio. Quomodo ergo juxta qualitatem ciborum de stomacho ructus erumpit, et vel boni, vel mali odoris flatus indicium est, ita interioris hominis cogitationes verba proferunt, et *ex abundantia cordis os loquitur* (Lk. 6: 45). Justus comedens replet animam suam. Cumque sacris doctrinis fuerit satiatus, de boni cordis thesauro profert ea quae bona sunt." This passage was cited by West, p. 220, note 11, from the 1984 reprinted edition, in which it is on column 353D.

40 *PL* 30, 435C: "ut dum corpus saginatur cibo, saturetur anima lectione."

41 *Regula Benedicta*, cap. 38 (*PL* 66, 601–602): "Mensis fratrum edentium lectio deesse non debet."

42 *Regula magistri*, cap. 24 (p. 217): "ut nunquam desit carnali refectioni et aeca [= esca] divina, sicut dicit Scriptura, non in solo pane vivit homo sed in omni verbo domini, ut dupliciter Fratres reficiant, cum ore manducant et auribus saginantur."

43 *PL* 30, 435C–D: "Tunc uniuscujusque mens sobria intenta sit dulcedini verbi Dei, suspiret anxia, cum propheticus aut historicus sermo Dei saevitiam monstrat in pravos. Gaudio repleatur immenso, cum benignita Dei annuntiatur in bonos ... Non resonent verba, sed gemitus: non risus et cachinnus, sed lacrymae."

44 *Epist.*, 52. 8 (*PL* 22, 534): "Docente te in Ecclesia, non clamor populi, sed gemitus suscitetur. Lacrymae auditorum, laudes tuae sint." See Riché, *Education and Culture*, pp. 82–83.

45 The two accounts differ in one important particular, which the commentators noted. In Ezekiel, the prophet is presented with a roll and "written therein lamentations, and mourning, and woe"; he is commanded "Son of man, cause thy belly to eat, and fill thy bowels with this roll that I give thee. Then did I eat it; and it was in my mouth as honey for sweetness." At that moment, he receives his commission to prophecy. In Revelation, the angel tells the prophet that the "little book" will be sweet in the mouth but bitter in his belly; "And I took the little book out of the angel's hand and ate it up; and it was in my mouth sweet as honey: and as soon as I had eaten it, my belly was bitter."

46 *De claustro anime*, IV, 33 (*PL* 176, 1171D): "Librum ergo devoramus et comedimus, dum verba Dei legimus. Multi enim legunt, et ab ipsa lectione jejuni sunt ... [alii] sanctum librum devorant, et comedunt, et jejuni non sunt, quia praecepta vitae quae sensus capere potuit, memoria non amisit."

47 *Commentarium in Ezechielem*, I, 3 (*PL* 25, 35D): "Quando vero assidua meditatione in memoriae thesauro librum Domini condiderimus, impletur spiritualiter venter noster, et saturantur viscera, ut habeamus cum apostolo Paulo viscera misericordiae, et impleatur ille venter, de quo Jeremias loquitur: *Ventrem meum, ventrem meum ego doleo: et sensus cordis mei conturbant me* (Jer. 4: 19)."

48 "Ego autem, singula verba discutiens, audivi indignationem, audivi luctamen, audivi tempestates sonoras, audivi murmur ac fremitum . . . Audivi rursum regem in arce sedentem, audivi sceptrum tenentem, audivi prementem et vinclis ac carcere frenantem"; *Prose*, p. 124.

49 "Sive enim id Virgilius ipse sensit, dum scriberet, sive ab omni tali consideratione remotissimus, maritimam his versibus et nil aliud describere voluit tempestatem"; *Prose*, p. 124.

50 R. W. Southern has written of John of Salisbury "patiently picking over the literary deposit of the past. The names of Lucan, Macrobius, Martianus Capella, Ovid, Cicero, follow each other in his pages with a fine impartiality, each in turn pointing a doctrine or adorning a sentence. Once the nectar had been extracted, John of Salisbury passed on like a bee to another flower, diligently, unemotionally, not stopping to consider whether it was a cowslip or a clover, so long as it gave up its treasure"; *Medieval Humanism*, p. 126. I would disagree with Southern's adverb "unemotionally" (for a memory cannot be stored without an emotion), but otherwise he precisely describes the attitude of a medieval scholar towards his sources. As he also writes of twelfth-century authors, they looked backward to the past "only for the quite practical purpose of equipping themselves to look forward" prudently. In this passage from his *Secretum*, Petrarch, devoted textual scholar though he was, shows himself, *as an interpreter of texts*, to share John of Salisbury's attitude. Here again one can distinctly see the difference between the activities of *lectio*, or textual commentation and scholarship, and *meditatio*, the application of reading to individual moral life.

51 *Moralia in Job*, II, 1 (*PL 75*, 553D): "Scriptura sacra mentis oculis quasi quoddam speculum opponitur, ut interna nostra facies in ipsa videatur. Ibi etenim foeda, ibi pulchra nostra cognoscimus." He is quoting "ad res" Augustine, *In Psalmo 103*, ser. 1, n. 4. On the activities of *lectio* and *meditatio* in monastic textual study, see Leclercq, esp. pp. 15–17.

52 *De claustro anime*, IV, c. 33 (*PL 176*, 1172A): "Ventrem quippe doluit, qui mentis afflictionem sensit. Sed sciendum est quia, cum sermo Dei in ore cordis dulcis esse coeperit, hujus procul dubio contra semetipsum animus amarescit." From Gregory he quotes, "Librum devoramus cum verba vitae cum aviditate sumimus" (1171C).

53 Since the will acts from desire, a total loss of desire would also mean a loss of free will. This idea belongs in the category of "essential" Augustine, but it is best defined in *De trinitate*. The fullest literary expression of it is the whole *Divine Comedy*, but perhaps one moment especially captures it. At the end of *Purgatorio*, Dante finds himself able to do whatever he desires because his will is completely good; however he has not, one should notice, been *purged* of desire. "Take henceforth thy pleasure for guide," Virgil tells him; "Free, upright and whole is thy will and it were a fault not to act on its bidding" (*Purgatorio*, 27, 131, 140–141).

54 For the texts from John of Salisbury, Isidore, and others, see above, ch. 1. Balogh, "Voces Paginarum," lists several variants of this phrase, including "sonus litterarum" (Ambrose), "vox antiqua chartarum" (Cassiodorus); Paulus Diaconus wrote that "pagina canit," "the page sings" or "chants," perhaps an allusion to the murmur of memorative meditation.

55 See esp. the remarks of Hendrickson, "Ancient Reading," McCartney, "Notes on Reading and Praying Audibly," and Saenger, "Silent Reading."

56 Leclercq, *Love of Learning*, p. 19; the phrase is from the *Rule*, c. 48 (*PL 66*, 703A). Benedict orders that the monks should pause in complete silence after the daily meal, although those who strongly desire to read may read to themselves in a way that does not disturb others: "sibi sic legat, ut alium non inquietet." See the

comments of Riché on evidence for the use of the voice in monastic reading, *Education and Culture*, pp. 465–466, and see also the essay on monastic reading by Jacques Dubois, "Comment les moines du Moyen Age chantaient et goûtaient les Saintes Ecritures."

57 See Leclercq, *Love of Learning*, esp. chapter 2. Paul Gehl, "Competens Silentium" provides an excellent recent discussion of monastic silence, and a useful bibliography. See also his essay "Mystical Language Models."

58 Saenger, "Silent Reading," pp. 396–398. The degrees of what passes for "quiet" are apparent in any library; see the judicious remarks of Hendrickson, "Ancient Reading," pp. 194–195.

59 See Hugh of St. Victor, *De arca Noe morali*, IV, 4 (*PL* 176, 669C), where the Bridegroom in the Canticles is said to call his Spouse "sono depresso, voce tenui," that is, in a whisper. This is the traditional voice of meditation, as befits this text's having become the great meditational text of monasticism. Interestingly, the Bible itself does not so characterize the Bridegroom's voice. Perhaps the association was aided by the reference to God's voice calling the prophet Elijah, not in an earthquake or fire, but through a whispering, weak, breath of wind (I Kings 19: 12).

60 Trans. V. J. Bourke, *Fathers of the Church*, with a few alterations of my own, based on my understanding of the Latin text in the edition of Gibbs and Montgomery.

61 The quoted words are from Hendrickson, "Ancient Reading." The adoption of this passage from the *Confessions* as "best evidence" that the ancients normally read out loud on all occasions actually goes back to Nietzsche (1885), as Balogh makes clear (p. 85).

62 The same contrast is made by Hugh of St. Victor, who knew Augustine very well as many scholars have noted, in his characterization of *meditatio*: "Ea enim maxime est, quae animam a terrenorum actuum strepitu segregat, et in hac vita etiam aeternae quietis dulcedinum quodammodo praegustare facit" (*Didascalicon*, III, 10; Buttimer, p. 59, lines 23–25). Notice also the metaphor of eating, *praegustare*, which is so commonly associated with meditation.

63 *Conf.*, IX, 10: "we came into our minds and passed through them, that we might reach the region of unfailing pasture, where you graze Israel on the eternal true food." Again, notice how strong the image of feeding ruminants is; of course Augustine is echoing the Bible here, but the physical activity of working the jaws that habitually accompanied ordinary *meditatio* pulls the literal conversation of mother and son together with the character of their discourse (as ruminative, recollective study) and with the Biblical grazing-motif.

64 See chapter 2; here again I think it is interesting that Augustine thinks of memory ("'mens" and "'cor") in terms of a physiological activity, even when it is the path to true mystical rapture; it is through the *affectus*, that is, by way of sensory memory, that one ascends.

65 *Sententiarum libri*, III, 14, 9 (*PL* 83, 689), a chapter entitled "De collatione": "Acceptabilior est sensibus lectio tacita quam aperta; amplius enim intellectus instruitur, quando vox legentis quiescit, et sub silentio lingua movetur. Nam clare legendo et corpus lassatur et vocis acumen obtunditur." *Silentium* has connotations of reverence as well as concentration; it is the state that prevailed when the auspices were being read (Ox. Lat. Dict., s.v. *silentium*). As Isidore uses it here, with *sub*, it seems to be an independent state of being rather than describing a person's behavior.

66 Ox. Lat. Dict., s.v. *rimo, rimor*; citations from Virgil (*Aenid*, VI, 599) and Juvenal (6, 551). Quintilian uses the word to mean "study thoroughly" in *Inst.*, III, 4, 6,

"cuncta rimanti"; we might translate this phrase into English as "thoroughly dissecting the matter." Interestingly here, Augustine uses the verb *rimor* to describe Ambrose's rumination of sacred text and the noun *silentium* (also used in connection with augury) to describe his own reverent and attentive notice of him.

67 Martianus Capella, v, 539, (ed. Dick, p. 269): " nec uoce magna legenda sunt, sed murmure potius meditanda; et nocte magis quam interdiu maturius excitari memoriam manifestum est, cum et late silentium iuuat, nec foras a sensibus auocatur intentio."

68 Cf. Fortunatianus on the same matter. That the activities requiring meditation were done best at night is apparent in the Latin word for them, *lucubratio*, "night-work"; Ox. Lat. Dict., s.v.

69 Quintilian counsels at some length the need to practice achieving *silentium* in crowds, and cites the story of Demosthenes studying by the seashore in the roar of the breakers, to train himself not to be disturbed by crowd-noises ("meditans consuescebat contionum fremitus non expavescere," "meditating he trained himself not to be afraid and distracted by the noisy assembly"); *Inst.*, x, 3, 26–30.

70 This change is discussed by Yates, *Art of Memory*, pp. 75–76, who seems to find it a curious medieval "misreading" of a classical concept; she is partly right, in that it is a particularly medieval change, though I think it is an obvious development in Christian hands of features already implicit in ancient teaching on memory. The *Ad Herennium* text is from Bk. III, 19, 31; Thomas Aquinas is from *ST*, II–II, Q. 49.

71 "Legebat quandoque in sacris libris, et quod animo semel iniecerat, indelebiliter scribebat in corde. Memoriam pro libris habebat, quia non frustra semel capiebat auditus, quod continua devotione ruminabat affectus. Hunc discendi legendique modum fructuosum dicebat, non per millenos evagari tractatus"; quoted by Balogh, p. 209, who also notes a change from Thomas's text when Bonaventure adapted it: "semel iniecerat, tenaciter imprimebat memoriae, quia non frustra mentalis attentionis percipiebat auditu, quod continuae devitionis [*sic*] ruminabat affectus." Balogh thinks this is significant in expressing a disdain for hearing in favor of the written word on Bonaventure's part; perhaps it is, but I wonder if Bonaventure's concern isn't to contrast Francis's mental attentiveness (concentration) with vain listening, a variation of the *silentium/strepitus* opposition. The use of *ruminare* in the following clause would bear this interpretation out, I think.

72 *Didascalicon*, III, 9; ed. Buttimer, p. 58, line 25.

73 Cicero, *Brutus*, 12, 47.

74 *Inst.*, II, 4, 22 and v, 13, 57. See Cope, *Aristotle's Rhetoric*, pp. 130–131.

75 (*PL* 111, 11–12D: "cogitabam, quid Tuae Sanctitati gratum et utile in scribendo conficere possem: quo haberes ob commemorationem in paucis breviter adnotatum quod ante in multorum codicum amplitudine et facunda oratorum locutione disertum copiose legisti."

76 (*PL* 111, 12D–13A: "Haec enim omnia mihi sollicite tractanti venit in mentem ut juxta morem antiquorum qui de rerum naturis et nominum atque verborum etymologiis plura conscripsere, ipse tibi aliquod opusculum conderem in quo haberes scriptum non solum de rerum naturis et verborum proprietatibus, sed etiam de mystica earumdem rerum significatione ut continuatim positam invenires historicam et mysticam singularum expositionem."

77 The making of this complete line-by-line gloss of the Bible was a culminating labor of monastic scholarship, completed by Anselm of Laon and his many helpers by 1117. G. R. Evans sees this as the labor that ended one phase of Biblical scholarship and helped to enable another, the general considerations of Bib-

lical doctrine that we associate with the scholastics. See her *The Language and Logic of the Bible*, esp. chapters 1–3.

78 Isidore, *Sententiarum libri*, III.14.7: "Lectio memoriae auxilio eget" (*PL* 83, 689).

79 C. von Nolcken, "Some Alphabetical Compendia." On the genres of medieval florilegia, see R. and M. Rouse, *Preachers, Florilegia and Sermons*, esp. pp. 3–42. See also their "Florilegia of Patristic Texts."

80 The opinion is that of Peter, Prior of Holy Trinity in Aldgate, with my emphasis added. It was first adduced by R. W. Hunt, "English Learning in the Twelfth Century," and subsequently by Smalley, *Study of the Bible*, p. 248, and von Nolcken "Some Alphabetical Compendia," p. 282. In such ways modern scholarship also depends on the florilegial reading of others.

81 Munk Olsen, "Les classiques Latins dans les florilèges medievaux," esp. pp. 47–57.

82 Quoted by Munk Olsen, "Florilèges," p. 56. Cf. p. 52, note 2, in which the verses of one Hadoard are quoted, explaining how when he was in charge of the book-cases, he gathered together extracts of material he wished to recollect; having preserved and gradually built up this store, he will now pay out its image in the form of a book. Munk Olsen discusses the purposes of Carolingian florilegia which contain extracts from classical texts in "Les Florilèges d'Auteurs Classiques."

83 On vocalizing while writing, see Josef Balogh, "Voces paginarum," pp. 214–216, Eugene McCartney, "Notes on Reading," pp. 184–187, and T. C. Skeat on ancient scribal dictation. The most famous ancient allusion is in Ovid, *Heroides* 18, 19–20, discussed in chapter 6, below.

84 *Inst.*, I, 1, 36.

85 Riché, *Education and Culture*, p. 464. Though a great deal has been written recently on the subject of reading and ethics in the Middle Ages, the importance of pedagogical practices, especially at the elementary level, has not been sufficiently stressed. The work of Judson B. Allen, *Ethical Poetic*, and A. J. Minnis (for example, in "John Gower, *sapiens* in Ethics and Politics") has focused on theoretical statements and advanced practices, chiefly in university or court settings; this, I think, is to start at the end of the matter not the beginning, although their work provides essential explorations of the issues.

86 *Metalogicon*, I, 24: "Historias, poemata, percurrenda monebat diligenter quidem, et qui velut nullis calcaribus urgebantur ad fugam; et ex singulis, aliquid reconditum in memoria, diurnum debitum, diligenti instantia exigebat"; (*PL* 199, 855C). On the long pedagogical tradition of such memory-work to build character and learn both reading and writing, see Nicholas Orme, *English Schools*, chapter 3.

87 The quotation from Cassiororus is given above, chapter I, note 64.

88 *The Letters of Abelard and Heloise*, trans. Betty Radice, pp. 76–77 ("Historia calamitatum," *PL* 178, 136B). The quotation is *Pharsalia*, 8. 94b–98a. A recent case against accepting Abelard's letters, including this one, as genuine has been made by John Benton, "The Correspondence of Abelard and Heloise"; Benton's case concerns whether or not Abelard actually wrote the account himself, or whether it was a retelling of the events by at least two later writers. For my purposes, the question of "authentic" authorship, while of interest, is not an exhaustive one. Whether Abelard wrote this letter or someone else, what is important to my discussion is that this supreme ethical moment is narrated not as a private, but a public one – designed to enrich the public memory. And it succeeded, for the story became a medieval "classic," helped along in part by its retelling in the *Roman de la Rose*.

89 Southern, *Medieval Humanism*, pp. 86–104, esp. 93–94. Professor Southern also

points out that Heloise's irony in choosing these words is lost on Abelard, for Pompey shows his moral greatness in not accepting his wife's offer, a crucial difference between Cornelia's fate and that of Heloise.

90 *Conf.*, VIII, 29. Augustine elsewhere expresses disapproval of using Scripture for sortilege, though only because divine words shouldn't be asked to provide answers to mundane business affairs; still, he says, it would be better to consult Scripture than "demons"; *Epist.*, 55, 37 (*PL* 33, 222).

91 Liddell and Scott, s.v. χαρακτερ; for an interesting discussion of the use of the word in rhetoric, see Hendrickson, "Characters of Style." On the memorial physiology of habit-building, see my discussion in chapter 2, above.

92 Cicero, *Orator*, 36 (edited Hendricks, LCL); Ox. Lat. Dict., s.v. *forma*.

93 The most recent and careful attempt to articulate the Exegetical school's position on the moral function of medieval literature, which starts from the basic medieval premise that literature is a part of ethics but ends up in conclusions quite opposite to those I argue here, is Allen, *Ethical Poetic*. On the importance of the rhetorically achieved negotiation of norm and occasion in ethics, see Trimpi, *Muses of One Mind*.

94 Huizinga was one of the first historians to emphasize the theatre or performance aspect of late medieval culture (which he viewed, in *The Waning of the Middle Ages*, as a sign of decadence); the concept of performance in terms of the "oral" character of vernacular literature has been developed especially by Paul Zumthor – see his *Essai*, and especially *La poésie et la voix*.

95 A great deal has been written recently on the changing concept of the "individual" in medieval culture. See Robert Hanning, *The Individual in the Twelfth Century Romance*, John Benton, "Consciousness of Self," and Caroline Bynum, "Did the Twelfth Century Discover the Individual?" (chapter 3 of *Jesus as Mother*). The term "subjectivity" I have taken from Lee Patterson, *Negotiating the Past*, esp. pp. 182–184.

96 Lacan, *The Four Fundamental Concepts of Psychoanalysis*, p. 47; my thanks to my colleague, Ned Lukacher, for this citation.

97 "Introduction," p. xxiii (my translation of the French).

98 Greene, "'Festina lente'," p. 134.

99 Smalley, *The Study of the Bible*, p. 29 and note. The quote is from *Epist.*, 36.

100 Paul O. Kristeller characterizes the culture of Renaissance humanism as basically "a lay culture," its religion "supported by laymen and secular clerics rather than by monks and friars" (*Medieval Aspects of Renaissance Learning*, p. 114), though Kristeller outlines certain important contributions of the religious orders in the final essay, with its extensive bibliography, of this same volume. The relationship of artificial memory books and these florilegial collections, esp. in a lay context and in southern Europe, is well set out by Yates, *Art of Memory*, and Rossi, *Clavis universalis*.

101 Cited by von Nolcken, "Some Alphabetical Compendia," p. 272, note 8, from the preface to *Florarium Bartholomei*, ed. and trans. by P. H.-S. Hartley and H. R. Aldridge, *Johannes de Mirfeld of St. Bartholomew's, Smithfield: His Life and Works*.

102 *Ammaestramenti*, p. 1.

103 1808 edn., p. 1.

104 Canto v, lines 121–138; edited and trans. John D. Sinclair.

105 This assumption is made by many of Professor D. W. Robertson's students; though it is unfair to attribute to Robertson the original of it, he is perhaps its most expressive modern proponent. See also the recent essay by Terence Cave, "The Mimesis of Reading in the Renaissance," in *Mimesis*, ed. Stephen Nichols

and John Lyons, in which the claim is made that before the Renaissance the reader was expected to be passive: he "should, as it were, disappear or efface himself in favor of the paradigm text" (p. 155). Just where and how this single "paradigm text" was to be found in an age of few manuscripts, and those almost always corrupt, Professor Cave does not explain. Compare Richard de Bury's complaints of scribes as cloudy-headed word-scatterers, which is simply his version of a frequent, deeply-held, and empirically-based medieval bias.

106 *Piers Plowman, the B-Text*, Passus III, 338–343.

107 Text ed. Sommers (1910), vol. 3, p. 263: "And the queen saw that the knight did not dare to do more · and so she took him [Lancelot] by the chin and kissed him before Galahot for a long enough time · until the lady of Malohaut comprehended that she kissed him." Paget Toynbee transcribed and translated the text for the Dante Society a century ago, noting that the lady of Malohaut's reaction is alluded to in *Paradiso*, 16, 14–15. He transcribed the text from MS. Lansdowne 757, which is punctuated exactly as the edition I have just quoted here. Early commentary on the *Paradiso* passage, cited by Toynbee, makes it clear that the Lady's instant discovery of the lovers' fault was understood by its readers to be an essential part of this famous scene; "Dante, and the Lancelot Romance," Fifth Annual Report of the Dante Society, (1886), pp. 41–74. Susan Noakes, "The Double Misreading of Paolo and Francesca," reviews the criticism that understands reading to be a major theme in this scene, and gives a fine analysis of it of her own. Medieval readers familiar enough with the scene to understand Dante's allusion at all (and it was a famous scene) would have understood Francesca's reference to the exact *punto* that overcame them, for they memorized it in these divisions (recall Jerome's admonition to copyists to carefully preserve his *cola et commata*, essential, as Bishop Langton said, for remembering the text).

108 Ambrose, *Epist.*, 47, 2 (*PL* 16, 1150), written ca. 390. The text is quoted by Balogh, p. 219. Ambrose explains that he has sent a perfected codex to his correspondant, for his own copy-texts are not written "ad speciem," "to be looked at" but "ad necessitatem," "for utility". He does not like to dictate always to a scribe, especially when he is doing what the Romans called "night-work" (*lucubratio*): study, reading, and composition. I have freely translated the sentence that follows: "Nobis autem quibus curae est senilem sermonem familiari usu ad unguem distinguere et lento quodam figere gradu, aptius videtur propriam manum nostro affigere stylo, ut non tam deflare aliquid videamur, quam abscondere." "Senile" here refers to the "ancients" or "elders" of the Church (Du Cange, s.v. *Senex*); *deflare* is a rare verb, usually glossed as "blab," but with this citation from Ambrose being the only one given. It also means "blow about *or* around"; Ox. Lat. Dict., s.v. *deflo*, similarly Lewis and Short. Undoubtedly all sorts of textual study and meditational activities associated with it are implied by "distinguere ad unguem," not just what we think of as punctuation, but, since the way one reads is by dividing, as Hugh (and others) says, punctuation is its basis. And it is clear that Ambrose is writing as an aid to his memory (it would not have occurred to him to do otherwise), for not only is the activity of *distinguendum* the first step to memorizing, but the verbs *figere* and *affigere*, "to fix," the notions of order and habituation implied in the words "usus familiaris" and "gradus," the time of day, and the contrast between scattering or "blowing" his studies idly about by dictating to a scribe and hiding them away in storage, all suggest the memorial nature of Ambrose's activity.

Chapter 6

1 Cited by Minnis, *Theory of Authorship*, p. 247, note 4, from Albertus's *Super epistolam ad Romanos*, cap. IV, lect. I.

2 As Minnis says, "The term *auctor* may profitably be regarded as an accolade bestowed upon a popular writer by those later scholars and writers who used extracts from his works as sententious statements or *auctoritates*, gave lectures on his works in the form of textual commentaries, or employed them as literary models"; *Theory of Authorship*, p. 10. The etymologies and distinctions are described in M. D. Chenu's essay, "Auctor, actor, autor," from which all subsequent discussions of the matter, including mine, are derived. In addition, see Chenu's discussion of the matter in *Introduction à St. Thomas*, pp. 130–132.

3 Jerome, "Commentary on Galatians," cited in Lewis and Short, s.v. *originalis*; see also s.v. *auctor*.

4 Petrarch, *Secret*, II, trans. Draper, p. 102. The Latin reads: "Laudo hec, quibus abundare te video, poetice narrationis archana. Sive enim id Virgilius ipse sesit, dum scriberet, sive ab omni tali consideratione remotissimus, maritimam his versibus et nil aliud describere voluit tempestatem; hoc tamen, quod de irarum impetu et rationis imperio dixisti, facete satis et proprie dictum puto"; Petrarca, *Opere*, pp. 124, 126.

5 Some information about who wrote the work was always thought to be important in establishing the original "occasion" of its composition – this is part of *lectio*, and is usually discussed in the preface. But that first "occasion" is not determinative or authoritarian, in our sense, over the all subsequent "occasions" on which the work's *res* might "speak to" readers over time. On the importance of the author's biography, see Minnis, *Theory of Authorship* and Huygens, *Medieval Accessus*.

6 On the development of the *ars dictaminis*, considered crucial to the needs of increasing administrations both ecclesiastical and royal, see Haskins, *Studies in Medieval Culture*, and Murphy, *Rhetoric in the Middle Ages*. Training for notaries (that is, legal and administrative officials) at universities like Padua and Bologna, included both *ars dictaminis* and the *ars notataria*; see Siraisi, *Arts and Sciences*, pp. 33–65.

7 *Epistulae morales*, 84; edited by Reynolds. All references are to this edition; the translations are my own. This particular commonplace was quoted intact by Macrobius in the preface to his *Saturnalia*, and it appears frequently in later medieval collections as well. A brief history of some of its citations, beginning in seventh century, is in Rouse and Rouse, *Preachers, Florilegia and Sermons*, pp. 115–117. Thomas of Ireland used it extensively in the preface to his florilegial collection, *Manipulus florum*; this collection was one of the most widely circulated and longest lived of the florilegial collections for preachers, and is the subject of the Rouses' fine study.

8 In this same epistle, Seneca also counsels reading and writing together to blend one with the other, "so that what has been collected from our reading, our stylus may render in graphic form."

9 Most recently and profoundly by Greene, *The Light in Troy*; pp. 72–80 discuss this trope in particular.

10 *The Light in Troy*, chapters 2 and 3.

11 The late Latin formation "moderni" (to be contrasted with "antiqui") is discussed by Curtius, *European Literature*, esp. pp. 251–255. R. W. Southern has well analyzed the historical consciousness of twelfth century scholars like John of Salisbury, in contrast to that of the Renaissance – see *Medieval Humanism*,

pp. 105–132. Southern notes that twelfth century writers looked to the past "only for the quite practical purpose of equipping themselves to look forward" (p. 126). A relationship between Froissard's "careless" attitude towards fact in his chronicle of the English and French wars and the scholastic definitions of memory found in Duns Scotus is the subject of Janet Coleman's essay on "Late Medieval Memoria." Coleman runs up against a perennial problem of traditional intellectual history, however, because she cannot connect the formulations of a limited intellectual elite, represented by Scotus, to a general literary culture, represented by Froissard; that connection is to be found in rhetorical *memoria*, as I hope the present study shows.

12 The story is in Southern, *Life of Anselm*, pp. 150–151; my quotations are from these pages.

13 Dondaine, *Les Secrétaires*, p. 17.

14 OED, s.v. *maker*; cf. MED, same heading. The word *writer* could be used to mean "author" from a very early time, but this has not become its primary meaning until very recently (OED, s.v. *writer*). In Middle English, the primary meaning of "writer" was "one who writes, a penman."

15 Marrou, *Histoire de l'Education*, pp. 230–231, 375, 522 n. 13, and 553 n. 30.

16 *Inst.*, X, 3, 15.

17 *De anima*, III, 11, 434a 9–10; see Wolfson, "The Internal Senses," esp. pp. 91–93.

18 This was especially true of Thomas Aquinas; see Wolfson, "The Internal Senses," p. 122.

19 Wolfson, "The Internal Senses," p. 78, referring to *De anima*, III, 7, 431a 14–17 and *Metaphysics*, 6, 1027b 29–30: "when sensation asserts or denies that something is pleasant or unpleasant, it pursues or avoids it. In fact to feel pleasure or pain is to adopt an attitude with the sensitive mean towards good and evil as such. This is what avoidance or pursuit, when active, really means, and the instincts to pursue or avoid are not really different from each other, or from the sensitive faculty . . . Now images occur in the soul in its thinking capacity, just like feelings. But when the soul asserts or denies that something is good or evil, it avoids or pursues. Hence the soul never thinks without a mental picture." The passage in the *Metaphysics* defines the combinative and separative functions of judgment.

20 D'Avray describes the contents of small, pocket-sized books ("vademecums"), which mendicant friars carried with them; these contain sermon models and other sermon aids. In one, the "sermons" are written out only as sets of rhyming headings to which Scriptural texts are attached. This is truly a "model" for a sermon, the *res* which an individual preacher would then be able to expand extempore; *The Preaching of the Friars*, pp. 59–60.

21 *De memoria augenda*, s. 2b; I refer to the Huntington Library copy, published at Rome, c. 1493. Mattheolus was greatly influenced by Hugh of St. Victor, as well as the standard trio of Thomas Aquinas, Cicero, and Aristotle.

22 *Heroides*, 18, 19–20: "talibus exiguo dictis mihi murmure verbis, / cetera cum charta dextra locuta mea est." Cited by Balogh, "Voces paginarum," pp. 214–216; see also McCartney, "Notes."

23 *Conf.*, x, 9. I have used the Latin text of Gibb and Montgomery.

24 *Conf.*, x, 11.

25 These etymologies Augustine took from Varro; the frequentive intensifier *-ito* is added to the root in each case.

26 *Serm.*, 225; *PL* 38, c. 1097: "Et ego scio . . . nec ego comprehendo; sed cogitatio facit nos extendi, extensio dilatat nos, dilatatio nos capaces facit."

27 *Conf.*, x, 17.

28 Southern, *Life of Anselm by Eadmer*, p. x. Mackey, "*Inter Nocturnas Vigilias*: A

Proof Postponed," gives an excellent analysis of the composition of the *Proslogion*, stressing its origin in prayerful emotion.

29 Southern, *Life of Anselm by Eadmer*, pp. 29–30. I have given a part of the Latin text in parentheses because, while Professor Southern's is an excellent English translation, it cannot entirely preserve the connotations of the original.

30 Murray, *Reason and Society in the Middle Ages*, esp. pp. 6–14, 401–404.

31 Gui, cap. 14, transl. Foster (p. 37). Cf. Tocco, cap. 30 (*AASS*, 669F): "post brevem somnum in sua camera . . . in loco, quem sibi ad orandum elegerat, in oratione prostratus; ubi orando mereretur addiscere, quae oportuisset post orationem scribere vel dictare."

32 Tocco, cap. 31 (*AASS*, 670B), trans. Foster, p. 70: "ut affectus orando mereretur ad divina ingredi, et intellectus huius merito intueri, quae altius intelligeret, quo affectus ardentius in id, quod luce caperet, amore flagraret." Thomas Aquinas is one of Murray's examples of an individual in whom "monastic" and "intellectual" cultures coexisted; *Reason and Society*, p. 340. Evidently, Anselm would be another.

33 Gui, c. 16, trans. Foster, p. 38.

34 Foster, p. 37. Recall that Quintilian suggests lying on one's back to stimulate invention. A posture associated with Augustine during meditational composition is seated, bowed over with his knees drawn up, and his head in his hand; see the plates in Courcelle, *Les Confessions*. A typical posture of composition in later medieval portraiture, shows the composer sitting at a desk with his scribal pen and knife, staring into space before a *blank* sheet. I am indebted to Michael Camille for pointing this out to me.

35 The "forma tractatus/tractandi" is discussed particularly by Minnis, *Theory of Authorship*; see also Allen, *Ethical Poetic*, and J. Simpson, "Modes of Thought and Poetic Form in *Piers Plowman*."

36 *Ars rhetorica*, III, 13; Halm, pp. 128–129.

37 *Ars rhetorica*, c. 23 "De memoria"; ed. Halm, p. 440.

38 *Inst.*, VIII, 6, 64.

39 This and preceeding quotation from *Inst.*, X, 3, 2.

40 *Inst.*, X, 3, 3.

41 *Inst.*, X, 3, 25.

42 *Inst.*, X, 3, 21.

43 Inst., X, 3, 17.

44 *Inst.*, X, 3, 28.

45 *Inst.*, X, 3, 31.

46 *Inst.*, X, 6, 1.

47 *Inst.*, X, 6, 5.

48 *Inst.*, X, 7, 1–29; all quotations in this paragraph are from that chapter.

49 Quintilian uses the same phrase used also in the *Ad Herennium*, "imagines rerum." It is thus apparent that he did not despise the making of such images; on the contrary, he regards them as most necessary, but as additional associations to stir the orator's memory not as a substitute for the heuristic of numbered order.

50 *Inst.*, I, ii, 30.

51 *Inst.*, VI, 2, 29; see also IV, 2, 121ff where Quintilian describes the usefulness of *imagines rerum* to engage the *intentio* of the audience as well. But this motive is always secondary to their necessity to the author.

52 *Inst.*, X, 7, 32.

53 Cited by Rosen (p. 30), from the 1739 edition of Giordano's sermons, p. 121.

54 Cited by Rosen (p. 31), from the 1839 edition of Giordano, p. 60 of vol. 386 in the series *Biblioteca scelta di opere italiana antiche e moderne*. This passage was

subsequently quoted in the biographical preface to Narducci's 1867 edition of Giordano's *Prediche inedite*, p. xx, note 1. All of these editions are described by Delcorno, pp. xv–xvii.

55 On the editorial problems presented by a lack of "authorized" exemplars, see Delcorno's introduction to his critical edition of Giordano's *Quaresimale Fiorentino*, esp. pp. lxxii–lxxiv.

56 Deferrari, "Augustine's Composition," p. 108, who cites *PG* 36, 492.

57 Deferrari, "Augustine's Composition," p. 105; cf. *PG* 67, 741. Deferrari cites much evidence of similar practices, pp. 101–106; in *De doctrina Christiana*, IV, 62–63, Augustine recommends the practice of extempore composition of sermons but allows that some preachers may need to memorize and "deliver what others compose for them."

58 *Serm.*, 225, 3 (*PL* 38, c. 1097): "ecce ego qui vobiscum loquor, antequam ad vos venirem, cogitavi ante quod vobis dicerem. Quando cogitavi quod vobis dicerem, jam in corde meo verbum erat. Non enim vobis dicerem, nisi ante cogitarem."

59 Examples occur throughout Giordano's sermons, especially when spoken twice in a day. The reporter will note that Friar Giordano finished his sermon later, "but I was not there and so I didn't write down any more." Examples are in Delcorno's edition, pp. 105, 284, and 418.

60 *Inst.*, XI, 2, 47.

61 *Brutus*, 139; Loeb translation.

62 "De arca Noe morali", Prologue (*PL* 176, 618): "In collatione autem, quia quaedam specialiter placuisse fratribus scio, ea potissimum stylo commendare volui, non tantum ideo quod eo digna scribi existimem, sed quia quaedam ibi prius inaudita quodammodo magis grata esse cognovi."

63 Isidore, *Sententiarum libri*, III, 14; in this same chapter Isidore also defines, as part of the same topic, the difference between "aloud" and "silent" reading, and the need for *memoria*. See chapter 5 above.

64 The phrase "per circumspectionem frondet et expandit ramos."

65 *PL* 176, 647A.

66 *PL* 176, 664A: "Sed jam, dum incidentium rationum expositionum prosequimur, longius a propositio nostro digressi sumus. Unde et de hoc quoque veniam postulamus, quia ut verum fatear, saepius in hoc tractatu scribenda plura invenimus, quam inventa scribemus. Neque enim vel in hoc meam insipientiam fateri erubesco. Nunc ergo ad propositum revertentes de fabricatione arcae sapientiae prosequamur."

67 Though related to oral composition theories of poetry, the characterization of oral style in sermons is somewhat different. On oral formulaic style in poetry, see A. B. Lord, *The Singer of Tales*; the theory has been greatly modified by recent scholars – see Watts, *The Lyre and the Harp*, Curschmann, "Oral Poetry," Brewer, "Orality and Literacy in Chaucer," and Zumthor, *La Poésie et la voix dans la civilization médiévale*. On the ambivalent oral/literate nature of much medieval French poetry, see the excellent study by Sylvia Huot, *From Song to Book*.

68 See Leclercq on Bernard of Clairvaux's compositional habits in his essays "L'Art de la composition" and "Sur la caractère litteraire des sermons de S. Bernard" in *Studi medievali* 7 (1966). Leclercq quotes Robert of Basevorn on Bernard: "Sciendum quod modus ejus sine modo ... Hic semper devote, semper artificialiter procedit." (Charland, p. 247) Notice how, for Basevorn, Bernard's seeming artlessness ("modus ejus sine modo") is always the product of artfulness ("semper artificialiter"), that is, of his artful *memoria* which, when properly designed and adequately stored, allows for what one might call planned-in-

advance-spontaneous craft. That this ancient goal of oratory was not thought to be incompatible with monastic humility and "silence" is clear from a comment by an anonymous monk, who speaks of "Bernardus noster, monachorum Antonius et Tullius oratorum" (quoted by Leclercq, "L'Art de la composition," p. 153). Another twelfth century composition that was formed through internal meditation and dialogue with his community, is Anselm's *Monologion*, as he tells us in its Preface.

69 Southern, *Life of Anselm*, p. 30.

70 Southern, *Life of Anselm*, p. 31.

71 The meaning of "livore carens" is discussed by Southern, *Life of Anselm*, note 1, p. 30.

72 Southern, *Life of Anselm*, p. 31. All the earliest copies of *Proslogion* include the two additions; see Southern, *St. Anselm and His Biographer*, p. 65.

73 Stock, *The Implications of Literacy*, pp. 331–351.

74 Stock, *The Implications of Literacy*, p. 335.

75 R. K. Root (ed.), *Troilus and Criseyde*, esp. pp. lxx–lxxiii. A more recent discussion of the versions of this poem is the introduction by Barry Windeatt to his edition of *Troilus and Criseyde*, who argues that the textual revisions are not authorial but scribal editing of Chaucer's "foul papers," the state his *dictamen* might well have been left in. For a judicious overview of these matters with regard to Chaucer's texts, see Fisher, "Animadversions on the Text of Chaucer, 1988."

76 On the problems which such medieval practices present to modern editors seeking to produce an authoritative text (in the modern sense), see the editors' introduction to George Kane and E. Talbot Donaldson, *The B-Text of Piers Plowman*, and also George Kane, "John M. Manly and Edith Rickert," in *Editing Chaucer*, ed. Paul Ruggiers, pp. 207–229, and two essays by E. Talbot Donaldson, "Manuscripts R and F in the B-Tradition of *Piers Plowman*" and "The Psychology of Editors of Middle English Texts." For a consideration of the problem in terms of modern literary theory, see Lee Patterson, *Negotiating the Past*, chapter 2.

77 Discussed by Pasquali, *Storia della tradizione*, esp. pp. 437–449.

78 De Hamel, *Glossed Books*; my remarks on the format of glossed books owes much to this study.

79 Evans, *The Language and Logic of the Bible*, pp. 46–47; this book and the earlier studies by Beryl Smalley of the development of Biblical exegesis during the previous medieval centuries show how the major scholarly project of these centuries was to develop such a line by line complete commentary, and how Anselm of Laon was deliberately reductive and non-controversial in his project, as is suitable for a beginner's book. Both books also clearly show how much more sophisticated advanced commentary had become, during these same centuries.

80 De Hamel, *Glossed Books*, p. 22. In order to recapture a somewhat similar understanding about the inclusive nature of "the Text," Jacques Derrida revived the format for his meditation, *Glas*.

81 De Hamel, *Glossed Books*, p. 23. Peter of Poitiers' Biblical genealogy is discussed briefly in my next chapter.

82 De Hamel, *Glossed Books*, pp. 36–37.

83 De Hamel, *Glossed Books*, pp. 42–44.

84 The page layout and decoration of these books has been described well by De Hamel, *Glossed Books*, esp. pp. 24–27, 42–44, and 57–58.

85 The commentary sources in this manuscript are discussed in S. Kuttner and B. Smalley, "The 'Glossa Ordinaria' to the Gregorian Decretals." There are large illuminated initials at the start of each of the five books of Decretals, which makes this one of the earliest illuminated Decretals. The basic commentary is the standard

beginning commentary put together by Bernard of Parma, and first promulgated in 1234, so this is quite an early copy.

86 De Hamel, *Glossed Books*, p. 25.

87 This manuscript, in Latin, was written for a monastery in Bohemia in the late 14th century. Besides the Fulgentius/Bersuire, it also contains a poor text of Hugo de Folieto's treatise on the dove and the hawk (discussed in greater detail in chapter 7).

88 Pasquali, *Storia della tradizione*, p. 446.

89 *Inst.*, 2, 4, 27–29.

90 The image, noted by McGarry in his translation, is both from Horace, *Ars Poetica*, 16, and from Mt 9: 16, "no man putteth a piece of new cloth unto an old garment."

91 *Metalogicon*, 1, 24; *PL* 199, 855B: "Si quis autem ad splendorem sui operis, alienum pannum assuerat, deprehensum redarguebat furtum; sed poenam saepissime non infligebat. Sic vero redargutum, si hoc tamen meruerat inepta positio, ad exprimendam auctorum imaginem, modesta indulgentia conscendere jubebat."

92 Aldo Bernardo, whose translation I have used, translates "turba" as "mass" but Petrarch is using it specifically in the context of recollection, and in such a context "turba" refers not to mass as such but rather the unorganized, undesigned "crowding" of material that overwhelms memory; cf. Albertus Magnus on Tully's rules.

93 *Familiares*, XXII, 2; trans. Aldo Bernardo, p. 213.

Chapter 7

1 Blum, *Die antike Mnemotechnik*, esp. pp. 1–17.

2 See especially Hessell Miedema, "The Term *Emblemata* in Alciati." An interesting set of late Middle English meditational "emblem-poems" was described in an essay by Thomas W. Ross, "Five Fifteenth-Century 'Emblem' Verses from Brit. Mus. Addit. MS. 37049." See also Robert W. Hanning, "Poetic Emblems in Medieval Narrative Texts."

3 E. Mâle, *The Gothic Image*, esp. pp. 390–396. The phrase "laicorum litteratura" is from the twelfth-century meditational treatise, "Gemma anima," which may be by Honorius of Autun. Discussing the uses of "pictura," the author lists three: "first, because it is the reading-material of the laity; secondly, as the house is honored by such adornment; thirdly, that the life of those who lived before is recalled in memory" (*PL* 172, 586). The wide currency of such reasons for using pictures is discussed, with a number of excellent examples, in Pamela de Wit, *The Visual Experience of Fifteenth-Century English Readers*.

4 See Michael Camille, "The Book of Signs," esp. pp. 135–138.

5 On the matter of "reading" the decorative apparatus of medieval books, see especially the comments of J. J. G. Alexander, *The Decorated Letter*, M. B. Parkes, "The Concepts *Ordinatio* and *Compilatio*," and M. Camille, "The Book of Signs."

6 "Aliud est enim picturam adorare, aliud per picturae historiam quid sit adorandum addiscere. Nam quod legentibus scriptura, hoc idiotis praestat pictura cernentibus, quia in ipsa ignorantes uident quod sequi debeant, in ipsa legunt qui litteras nesciunt; unde praecipue gentibus pro lectione pictura est;" *Epist.*, XI, 10 (*CCSL* 140A, p. 874). Gregory expressed the same sentiment in an earlier letter (IX, 209, written July, 599) to Bishop Serenus regarding the same incident: "Idcirco enim pictura in ecclesiis adhibetur, ut hi qui litteras nesciunt saltem in parietibus uidendo legant, quae legere in codicibus non ualent," "For this reason painting should be used in churches, that those who do not know letters at least by looking

at the walls may read those [things] which they are not able to read in books" (*CCSL* 140A, p. 768). Notice Gregory's use of the verb *legere* both for books and painting.

7 The modern edition is by Cesare Segré. V. A. Kolve discusses Richart on the mnemonic usefulness of visual images in connection with what he argues, convincingly, to be Chaucer's use of master memory images in certain of *The Canterbury Tales*; see esp. pp. 9–27. Sylvia Huot first drew my attention to Richart; she discusses his work admirably in *From Song to Book*.

8 These commonplaces Richart could have found in Isidore; see Segré's introduction to his edition, pp. vii–viii, and note 3.

9 "Ceste memoire si a .ij. portes, veir et oir, et a cascune de ces .ij. portes si a un cemin par ou i puet aler, che sont painture et parole." (p. 4)

10 "Car quant on voit painte une estoire, ou de Troies ou d'autre, on voit les fais des preudommes ki cha en ariere furent, ausi com s'il fussent present. Et tout ensi est il de parole. Car quant on ot .i. romans lire, on entent les aventures, ausi com on les veïst en present." *Li Bestiaires d'Amour*, p. 5.

11 "Car il est bien apert k'il a parole, par che ke toute escripture si est faite pour parole monstrer et pour che ke on le lise; et quant on le list, si revient elle a nature de parole. Et d'autre part, k'il ait painture si est en apert par chu ke[?] lettre n'est mie, s'on ne le paint."

12 "Car je vous envoie en cest escrit et painture et parole, pour che ke, quant je ne serais presens, ke cis escris par sa painture et par sa parole me rendre a vostre memoire comme present." (pp. 6–7)

13 M. B. Parkes, "The Concepts *Ordinatio* and *Compilatio*."

14 Translated by Charles Singleton, *Essay on the Vita Nuova*, p. 26.

15 Singleton, *Essay on the Vita Nuova*, pp. 25–42, esp.

16 Pamela De Wit discusses this poem, calling attention to its heavy visual emphasis, "Visual Experience," pp. 24–28. The text is in *Minor Poems of John Lydgate*, ed. H. N. McCracken, pp. 268–279.

17 Similarly, in "The Second Nun's Tale," the figure of St. Paul appears in order to speak a text from Ephesians (*CT* VIII. 200–216).

18 These examples are given by J. J. G. Alexander, "Scribes as Artists," pp. 107–109.

19 Nordenfalk, *Kanontäfeln*, pp. 46–54, and the same author's "Beginnings of Book Decoration," pp. 9–15 (the quotation is from p. 10).

20 De Hamel, *Glossed Books*, p. 60.

21 Nordenfalk, "Book Decoration," p. 12.

22 The Utrecht Psalter (University Library, Utrecht, MS. 32) was made at Rheims in the ninth century. It was in England during the eleventh to twelfth centuries, and three copies of it made while it was there are extant: London, B.L. Harley MS. 603 (*c.* 1000, unfinished), Cambridge, Trinity College MS. R. 17. 1 (*c.* 1147, complete), and Paris, B. N. MS. lat. 8846 (*c.* 1200, unfinished); see C. M. Kauffmann, *Romanesque Manuscripts*, pp. 96–97. These English copies were made in the medieval manner – they are adaptations to contemporary style rather than simple reproductions although the basic groupings and features of the original are apparent. They remember the original "ad res," as it were: see D. Tselos, "English Manuscript Illustration and the Utrecht Psalter," and especially S. Dufresne, "Les Copies Anglaises du Psautier d'Utrecht."

23 The Utrecht Psalter has received a great deal of attention; among the fullest studies are those of E. T. De Wald, *The Illustrations of the Utrecht Psalter* and S. Dufresne, *Les Illustrations du Psautier d'Utrecht*; see also D. Panofsky, "The Textual Basis of the Utrecht Psalter's Illustrations."

24 De Wald, *The Utrecht Psalter*, pp. 64–65; the illustrated page is f. 82v (De Wald's plate 129).

25 See the discussion by Nigel Morgan, *Early Gothic Manuscripts*, no. 162, vol. 2, pp. 157–162, and the bibliography which Morgan supplies on this manuscript.

26 The pictures in Douce 104 are discussed by De Wit, "Visual Experience," pp. 84–88; see also the entry for this manuscript in Paecht and Alexander, *Illuminated Manuscripts in the Bodleian Library*, vol. 3, no. 886.

27 Frances Yates noticed how like "imagines rerum" Holcot's pictures were, *Art of Memory*, pp. 96–101.

28 The transcription is on pp. 172–178 of Smalley's *English Friars*.

29 Smalley, *English Friars*, p. 112.

30 Smalley, *English Friars*, p. 118. These images are also discussed by Judson B. Allen, *The Friar as Critic*, pp. 51–52; his whole discussion is of interest (pp. 29–53), though he does not mention a mnemonic connection.

31 "Hic dicendum est secundum Augustinum super Iohannem sermone 7: Qualem faciem habet dilectio, qualem formam, qualem staturam, quales manus, quales pedes habet, nemo potest dicere. Habet tamen pedes, quia ipsi ducunt ad ecclesiam. Unde ex ista imagine potest caritas sive dilectio describi sicut una regina in throno collocata, statura elevata, figura quadrata, Phebo maritata, prole vallata, melle cibata, cum facie quadriformi et veste auriformi, manus habens stillantes et porrectas, aures apertas et directas, oculos flammeos et uxorinos et pedes caprinos"; Smalley, *English Friars*, p. 173.

32 Smalley, *English Friars*, pp. 172, 179.

33 "[I]n fine capituli, super illam litteram *Noli letari*, ubi loquitur de idolatria, pono picturam antiquorum de idolatria"; Smalley, *English Friars*, p. 173. Yates also comments on this passage, *Art of Memory*, p. 99.

34 See Carlo de Clercq, "Hughes de Fouilloy."

35 Goy, *Die Uberlieferung*, pp. 237; the first two rubrics are from Bodleian Library Laud Misc. 370 and Laud Misc. 409, both twelfth-century mss. from St. Albans, the third from B.N. lat. 10631, also of the twelfth century.

36 Smalley, *Study of the Bible*, p. 96; Smalley comments briefly, but cogently, on how "the roles of text and picture, that we are accustomed to, seem to be reversed in much of the twelfth-century educational literature. You begin with your picture"; pp. 95–96.

37 Notice Hugh's two-language pun on the Greek letter *chi*, χ, the first letter in the name "Christos" and also, in Latin, the number 10, written X, and so resembling *chi* in its visual form. Migne regards the writing of *c* here as a simple error. But perhaps it is not. From the end of the Carolingian period, the final ς of the *nomina sacra* was often written as a *c* in Latin script – χος – (see W. M. Lindsay, *Notae Latinae*, p. 396), though this apparent "c" is actually final ς. I think this is the basis for Hugh's dual-language pun. The cabalistic principle that names and numerology are contained in the same forms may also have influenced Hugh here, perhaps another example of the interest in Jewish exegetical traditions that is associated by Beryl Smalley with St. Victor; see Smalley, *Study of the Bible*, pp. 103–105, 149–172, 361–365.

38 Hugh's understanding of moralizing is very well described in his definition of the tropological "level" of Biblical exegesis: "tropology . . . is the changing-direction word or the phrase folded-back, for truly we turn the word of a narrative concerning others to our own instruction when, having read of the deeds of others, we conform our lives to their example"; see appendix A.

39 In cap. 4, Hugh refers to the right arm ("cornus") of the central cross, "dextero latere, id est aquilone" (col. 686A) but in cap. 6 he speaks of its left arm, "in

sinistro, latera aquilonis" (col. 691D). The inconsistency, I would guess, stems from a difference in Hugh's mental orientation toward his figure, that is whether he imagines himself looking towards it or out from it, an inconsistency that would arise more easily if one were working with a mental "drawing" than with an actual graph.

40 A diagram of the Ark, shown as a cut-off pyramid, accompanies some manuscripts of Peter of Poitiers' *Genealogia*. An example is Bodleian Library MS. Laud Misc. 151, f. 1, a manuscript of the second quarter of the thirteenth century (a century after Hugh of St. Victor) in which the *Genealogia* precedes the texts of the Pentateuch and Peter Comestor's "Historia scholastica." Two other diagrammatic drawings of the Ark as a curtailed pyramid are in a genealogical roll written about 1420–30 in English (Bodleian Library MS. Barlow 53); this roll is prefaced by a translation of Peter's preface, discussed later in this chapter. But the Ark took many forms throughout this period.

41 "Post haec singulis nominibus suas imagines superpono semiplenas, a pectore sursum, quales nonnunquam in tabulis solent figurari, quas Graeci frequentiori Iconas vocant"; col. 686D.

42 At this time, the Bible was considered to have twenty-two books in the Old Testament and eight in the New, as Hugh of St. Victor describes them in *Didascalicon* and in Bk 1, 4 (col. 630A) of "De arca morali."

43 Robert W. Hanning argues suggestively that the Creator-Majesty image was especially employed during the twelfth century as a model for human as well as divine creativity: "'Ut enim faber . . . sic creator': Divine Creation as a Context for Human Creativity in the Twelfth Century." Hanning's notes contain an excellent bibliography of discussion of the Majesty image from the early Middle Ages onward. It seems to have peaked in popularity, judging by its survival in manuscript painting, during the twelfth to thirteenth centuries; one should, however, be careful in relying too heavily upon such evidence for a true assessment of the relative popularity of a particular mnemonic "form" since mental composition and imaging, employing such *formae*, seem to have been a feature even of early monastic culture. A good example is the use, at the beginning of Benedict's *Rule*, of the "scala Jacobis" to "place" the stages of humility.

44 *Dictionnaire de Spiritualité*, s.v. "Hughes de Fouilloy."

45 See the essays by Carlo de Clercq, "Le Role de l'Image" and "Hughes de Fouilloy."

46 Those with complete cycles are Heiligenkreutz (a Cistercian monastery) MS. 226, British Library MS. Sloane 278, St.-Omer MS. 94 (from the Cistercian abbey of Clairmarais), and Troyes MS. 177 (from Clairvaux itself). I have remarked earlier on the significance of Bestiaries forming so common a feature of Cistercian libraries, given the order's strictures against using excessive and "grotesque" decoration and ornament, especially representations of animals (in Bernard's famous sermon). These manuscripts are all of the thirteenth century. Two other manuscripts of the twenty-one still extant have a large part of the cycle – Bodleian Library MS. Lyell 71, the one I have examined most fully and the subject of de Clercq's "Le Role de l'Image," and Bibliothèque Nationale, Brussels, MS. II, 1076. On the Lyell manuscript itself, which was made in northern Italy around 1300, see de la Mare, *Lyell Manuscripts*, pp. 211–216.

47 "Ego enim de clero, tu de militia ad conversionem venimus ut in regulari vita quasi in pertica sedeamus" (*PL* 177, 13–14); the text is in *PL* 177, 13–22 (including the books not by Hugo, the text continues through column 164).

48 I have described the image in Lyell 71; Sloane 278 has the same image, somewhat less finely executed, as is true generally of this manuscript, but with identical mottoes and layout.

49 '[E]t qui rapere consueveras domesticas aves, nunc bonae operationis manu silvestres ad conversionem trahas, id est seculares."

50 "Le Role de l'Image," p. 24. In the Revised Version, where it is numbered Ps. 67: 13, the verse reads, "Though ye have lain among the pots, yet shall ye be as the wings of a dove covered with silver, and her feathers with yellow gold."

51 "Desiderii tui petitionibus, charissime, satisfacere cupiens, columbam, cujus *pennae sunt deargentate et posteriora dorsi ejus in pallore auri* (Ps. 67) pingere, et per picturam mentes aedificare decrevi, ut quod simplicium animus intelligibili oculo capere vix poterat, saltem carnali discernat; et quod vix concipere poterat auditus, percipiat visus"; *PL* 177, 13–14.

52 "Quod enim doctioribus innuit scriptura, hoc simplicibus pictura. . . . Ego autem plus laboro ut simplicibus placeam, quam ut doctioribus loquar et quasi vasculo pleno latices infundam"; *PL* 177, 15–16.

53 As Eugene Vance has remarked, "medieval sign theory necessarily involves a problematics of memory," *Mervelous Signals*, p. 304. Vance's study, especially chapter 3, is excellent on this relationship. A playful meditation by Umberto Eco upon the relationship of *artificialis memoria* and semiotics, was recently published in English some twenty-two years after it was first written; "An *Ars Oblivionalis?* Forget it!"

54 Isidore, *Sent.*, III, 14.3; *PL* 83, 688–689. I used the literal translation, "gathering," for the complex process denoted by "collatio," Isidore's word, on the example of J. Taylor's translation of Hugh of St. Victor's *Didascalicon*.

55 This is especially true of Bodleian Library MS. Lyell 2, a twelfth-century copy of a life of Jerome and of some of his Epistles, and of Harvard College MS. 27, a collection of saints' lives. Lyell 2 also contains marginal titles enclosed in geometric forms, though nothing so elaborate as HM 19915; Harvard College 27 contains a distinctive cryptogram of "NOTA" found also in HM 19915.

56 I have seen a much later manuscript in which the catchwords have been decorated in a basically similar way (Trinity College, Cambridge MS. 0.9.1; see De Wit, p. 84). Catchwords, however, are primarily for the use of scribes and binders; the phrases so decorated in HM 19915 are *tituli*, and so can only be for the use of readers needing to remember text. Some manuscripts have catchwords decorated by readers, and even scribes. Paul Gehl, "Text and Textures," discusses two examples – a Boccaccio autograph of the *Decameron*, now in Berlin (cod. Hamilton 90) and a grammar text written in Italy in the 1390s, in which the catchwords have been decorated by the scribe (probably a student at Pisa) for his own mnemonic use, probably to help him find and keep unbound gatherings in order (University of Chicago MS. 99).

57 *Histoire de la Vulgate*, p. 307; the discussion of *tituli* is in pp. 307–315. The mnemonic utility of these "lectionis tituli," "summary-phrases for reading," is clear from comments by Cassiodorus, quoted by Berger, *L'Histoire*, p. 308.

58 Tying a string around one's finger as a mnemonic help is ancient; Quintilian mentions it in his discussion of *memoria*, *Inst.*, XI, ii, 30. The many types of mnemonic images discussed by Host von Romberch include implements, animals, and birds, as well as architecture.

59 The standard study and catalogue of marginal drolleries is Lillian M. C. Randall, *Images in the Margins of Gothic Manuscripts*.

60 This story is best known to us through the version told in the beginning reading book which the Knight of LaTour-Landry made for his daughters. Randall collected a number of marginal images which refer to this tale (misidentified as "man defecating"): see esp. figures 530 and 581–584. In these latter figures, the eggs laid by the squire have been collected into a basket.

61 The mise-en-page of this volume is "altogether different . . . from any other known system of decoration of Canon Law texts"; Sandler, *Gothic Manuscripts*, no. 101, pp. 111–112.

62 The large illustrations in this book are reproduced in John Plummer, *The Hours of Catherine of Cleves*.

63 A well-known example is in the Book of Hours made for Englebert of Nassau in the fifteenth century, Bodleian Library MS. Douce 219, f. 16v. Another page (f. 40r) has a border of pearl and ruby jewelry. Both pages are reproduced in Alexander, *The Master of Mary of Burgundy*.

64 The manuscript, in four volumes (B.L. MS. Royal 1. D. v–viii), is described by E. Maunde-Thompson, *A Catalogue of Ancient Manuscripts*, vol. 1, pp. 17–20. Such drawings can be seen in vol. 2, f. 148v, and vol. 4, ff. 5v, 76r. There are also simple flowers and leaves, and baskets of fruit on other pages of this codex. A facsimile, also edited by E. Maunde-Thompson, was published by the British Museum, 1879–1883.

65 "Liber de mem. et remin.," II, iii; ed. Borgnet, p. 110.

66 "That is the way of the cat; it wants the fish, but not the fishing," *Poetria Nova*, 2028–2209 (trans. Nims). The saying is proverbial, recorded in W. W. Skeat's *Early English Proverbs* and Hans Walther's *Lateinische Sprichwörter*, esp. numbers 2490–2491, 2495, 2504. A common form is "Cattus amat piscus, sed non vult tangere flumen," "A cat loves fish, but does not want to touch the river."

67 Cf. for example, B.L. MS.. Royal 5. D. x. (English, late thirteenth century), f. 82v; in the left margin a hand pulls in a fish on a line opposite a text from Augustine, beginning "Nam gaudet et piscis." The drawing is later than the writing of the manuscript, evidently the work of a reader, not a scribe. This manuscript contains some of Robert Grosseteste's indexing symbols, and is mentioned in R. W. Hunt, "Manuscripts Containing Indexing Symbols." A famous book using fish as one of its visual elements is the Book of Kells, of which I have more to say below.

68 *The Winchester Malory* (facsimile edition), ed. N. R. Ker, f. 23.

69 Kauffmann, *Romanesque Painting*, p. 45.

70 Weitzmann, *Late Antique and Early Christian Book Illumination*, p. 112 and plate 41.

71 The Cuerden Psalter is also preceded by picture-pages in a rigid grid format. The first of the picture-pages in M 183 (f. 9v) contains in one of the roundels reserved for saints an image which incorporates a common mnemonic of the Seven Deadly Sins, the acronym SALIGIA. This is written on two sword-like shafts which pierce the bosom of the Virgin, before whom a male figure kneels. The background is plain gold leaf, the undifferentiated sort of color suggested for memory "places." It is probably an "imago rei" for the Feast of the Seven Sorrows of the Virgin. I would like to thank Dr. William Voelkle of The Pierpont Morgan Library for bringing this image to my attention.

72 Smalley, *Study of the Bible*, p. 214. The text of the *Genealogia* and its manuscripts are discussed in detail by Philip S. Moore, *The Works of Peter of Poitiers*, pp. 97–117.

73 On all of these manuscripts, see Paecht and Alexander, *Illuminated Manuscripts in the Bodleian Library*, nos. 377 (Laud misc. 171), 429 (Lat. th. b. 1 and c. 2), 883 (Barlow 53). The layout of the two companion rolls is also discussed briefly by Nigel Morgan, *Early Gothic Manuscripts*, vol. 2, p. 180.

74 Moore, p. 99: "quasi in sacculo quodam memoriter tenere narrationes hystoriarum. . . . Quod et fastidientibus prolixitatem propter subiectam oculis habita [sic] memorie commendari et omnibus legentibus utilitatem conferre."

75 Geoffrey of Vinsauf, *Poetria nova*, ll. 2013–2014.

76 Host von Romberch distinguished clearly between *similitudo, figura* and *forma*, which he defined as follows: "Forma dat esse specificum artificiato: poterit per inde abstracta rei species in loco imaginata." In other words, "forma" fulfills the function of a diagram. Romberch is much too late to serve as definite evidence for what the word meant to Geoffrey of Vinsauf, of course, but it is interesting to see that *forma* acquired so technical a meaning in later mnemonic practice.

77 The seminal discussion of later medieval diagrams is that of Fritz Saxl, "A Spiritual Encyclopaedia of the Later Middle Ages"; a recent discussion in the general context of memorial use is John B. Friedman, "Les images mnémotechniques dans les manuscrits de l'époque gothique," pp. 169–183 in the collection *Jeux de mémoire*, edited by Bruno Roy and Paul Zumthor. Finally, in her introduction to the facsimile of the DeLisle Psalter, Lucy Sandler reproduces versions of some of the more elaborate mnemonic "formae" of the late Middle Ages; of particular interest is the independently-produced "Tower of Wisdom," which utilizes an alphabet grid as its basic ordering structure. The fact that such an elaborate set of mnemonic "picturae" is Franciscan-sponsored is of interest because, we recall, one of the picture-making friars mentioned earlier in this chapter, John Ridevall, was a Franciscan.

78 It is reproduced on p. 87 of Faral; see also Lawler, pp. 40–41. Book IX of Isidore's *Etymologiae* has several of what Isidore calls "stemmata" which indicate complex degrees of kinship (and thus whom one cannot marry); most are in tree form, like modern genealogies, but one is in the form of partitioned concentric circles. Evidently such forms were later adapted to show kinship among other kinds of things as well; they still are, of course.

79 OED, s.v. *rote*. The MED, s.v. *rote*, gives additional Middle English citations, but does not substantially change the meanings given by the OED, and it does not, of course, give etymologies.

80 The phrase also occurs in the Prioress's Tale, where the "litel clergeon," just beginning his grammar-lessons, learns a hymn by listening, "And herkned ay the wordes and the noote, / Til he the firste vers koude al by rote" (*CT*, VII, 1711–1712); and in the portrait of the Sergeant of Law, who knew all the statutes from the time of King William, and "every statut koude he pleyn by rote" (*CT*, I, 327). In these two instances, the phrase simply means "by heart" or "habit," to use the commoner Middle English synonym.

81 In addition to her *Art of Memory*, see Yates's essays collected in *Lull and Bruno*, and Hillgarth, *Ramon Lull and Lullism*.

82 Yates, *Art of Memory*, p. 176.

83 That "Neoplatonism" may be overrated as a major influence on twelfth century art is the sobering conclusion of an essay by Peter Kidson, "Panofsky, Suger and St. Denis." Kidson argues that Suger was no Neoplatonist, and not much of a dogmatic theologian at all, but wrote from a practical belief that aesthetic experience and knowledge are completely intertwined, an assumption that is evident as well in mnemonic pedagogy.

84 Saxl, "A Spiritual Encyclopaedia," pp. 83–84.

85 The history of these diagrams is fully discussed in Sandler's introduction to the facsimile.

86 Jacques Guilmain, "The Geometry of the Cross-Carpet Pages in the Lindisfarne Gospels"; the quotation is from p. 52. On the keeping of such books as the Book of Kells, see Françoise Henry, pp. 149–153.

87 Giraldus Cambrensis, "In Topographia Hibernie." The translation is from the text edited by James F. Dimock for the Rolls series. The recension Dimock edited is of one of the last of Giraldus's revisions; he produced at least five, the first

composed between 1185, when he went to Ireland, and 1188, when it was read at Oxford. The account of the book is in a chapter now called "De Libro Miraculose Conscripto" (ii, 38). For the history of the text, and an edition of the first recension (which excludes the last sentence I have translated here), see John O'Meara, "Giraldus Cambrensis in Topographia Hibernie."

88 For basic information and bibliography on the Book of Durrow (Trinity College Dublin MS. A. 4. 5) and the Book of Kells (Trinity College Dublin MS. A. 1. 6), see J. J. G. Alexander, *Insular Manuscripts, 6th–9th Centuries*. Both manuscripts have been produced in recent facsimilies, the Book of Durrow edited by A. A. Luce, *et al.*, and the Book of Kells edited by F. Henry.

89 De Hamel, *A History of Illuminated Manuscripts*, p. 101.

90 A variant of the proverb about the cat who likes fish but not to fish has to do with cats who like full bellies but not catching mice. For example (one with some of the obscurity generic to proverbs): "Cattus amat pisces, sed non vult crura madere; / Isque adeo tumidus, si non vult carpere mures: / Nulla farina tamen quamvis aliud sit in urna," "A cat loves fish but not to wet its limbs; / Likewise to have a full belly, if not to catch mice: / Nonetheless, no wheat [= food?], whatever it may like, will otherwise be in its urn [= stomach?]" (Walther no. 2491).

Appendix A

1 Translated from the edition by William M. Green; I have re-paragraphed Green's text, for the sake of clarity. Readers should also consult the essay by Grover Zinn, "Hugh of St. Victor and Memory," whose paraphrase of the sense of this Preface is most useful.

The word "circumstantia" is used here in a technical sense which derives from a standard pedagogy that Hugh used to introduce his commentaries on the various Biblical books. The form goes back as far as Gregory the Great and Bede, who spoke of there being three "circumstantiae" necessary to know about each of the Biblical books, namely, "persona, locus, and tempus" or "who wrote it? where? when and for what occasion?" Hugh of St. Victor has adapted this form to history for his beginners: one needs first to know persons, places, and dates. These "circumstantiae" are the mnemonic categories which Hugh lays out in the last paragraphs of his introduction, exactly as he wants them to be put away in the strongbox of his students' memories, and for which he provided a diagram (figure 3). The three-fold principles of memory technique he expounds at such length in the first part of his treatise, however, are different, and though he uses two of the same words (*locus* and *tempus*) their meaning is different. This suggests to me that we need to look to a different source than the medieval *accessus* alone, for the origin of these words' use in medieval mnemotechnique.

"Circumstantia" may, however, also have referred to a class of paradigmatic mnemonics of the "who, what, when" variety. Albertus Magnus uses the verb "circumsto" to describe how a network of "rich" associations serve to fix something mnemonically – see appendix B, immediately following. Perhaps the title given to this preface should be translated as "The Three Chief Memory-Fixes for History." On the earliest types of the preface, and the meaning of "circumstan-tiae" in such a context, see Hunt, "Introductions to the *Artes* in the Twelfth Century," Minnis, *Medieval Theory of Authorship*, pp. 16–17, and the standard work on the subject, Huygens, *Accessus ad Auctores*.

2 Notice here Hugh's pun on the etymology of Latin *recordari* (recollect) discussed above in chapter 2.

3 The phrase, "linea naturalis numeri," occurs three times in this part of the Preface;

literally it means "a line of natural number." As Hugh develops the technique, "naturalis" seems to mean "appropriate to the particular circumstance," and "linea" means any sort of linearly-conceived diagram or graph. A "linea naturalis numeri" is thus a mentally-conceived graph, of a size determined by the total number of things to be graphed. Since it contains "seats" or "places," and since these are numbered on both the vertical and horizontal axes in order to give each place an "address," I have translated "linea naturalis numeri" in this context as "numerical grid."

4 This visualization technique becomes clearer from the example which follows, of how to store away the text of Psalms, considered both as individual items and in terms of their places in the whole Book. The task of the mnemonic is to place or mark items in such a manner that each can be uniquely recalled, and at the same time be recalled in correct relationship to the other items in its group.

5 The principle that the memory be stored in chunks of a size equivalent to the limit of short-term memory is here invoked by Hugh, as it is by every writer on the subject at some point. Each psalm is first reduced to its incipit, and this phrase is "attached" by meditation to the numbers of the psalms in order. One can then proceed to add in memory the rest of each psalm's text, in the manner Hugh describes next. The "single glance" of memory – what you can take in at one look – is the medieval memory-writer's term closest to our concept of "short-term memory." Though this is generally somewhere from four to seven things, notice how Hugh stresses that each of his students will have to observe for himself just how long a chunk is appropriate to his own mental glance; the examples Hugh cites with respect to the first "chunk" of the first three psalms are, one notes, quite short.

6 No English word captures the double and simultaneous meaning of Latin *ornatus* and *ornamentum*, "equipment, adornment." The marriage of function and beauty, use and delight, which this family of words achieves I have rendered into English alternately with words conveying usefulness and function, and words referring to decoration. But it is a distinction Hugh blurs by his choice of "ornamentum" and "ornatus" in each of these instances.

7 These last two paragraphs refer directly to the diagram which Hugh devised for his chronology. What is interesting about his language here is the picture it is designed to paint in the minds of his students; far less elaborate than the diagram in "De arca Noe mystica," one yet notes the stress on numbers, the clear, step-by-step exposition of the order of creation, put in place by God in nature and disposed by the students in the places of their mental diagram. And as God usefully ornaments his creation, so the memory-structure needs to be decorated usefully in order to achieve the mnemonic task properly.

Appendix B

1 My translation is based on the Geyer edition of the works of Albertus Magnus, vol. 28.

2 See Sorabji, *Aristotle on Memory*, pp. 77–78, and *Nichomachean Ethics*, 1139b 15.

3 Albertus's concern in this first article is to define how the rhetorical use of "memoria," which he finds in the *Rhetorica ad Herennium* can be fitted into Aristotle's philosophical discussion, and its distinction between the psychological powers of memory and reminiscence, especially in "De memoria et reminiscentia." This requires Albertus to distinguish the trained habit of "memory" from the psychological faculties Aristotle defined, and show how it requires the action of both faculties in its working. I have left the Latin word untranslated but in

quotation marks, in order to convey the fact that "memoria" is a term under discussion in this article, and not a word whose definition has no ambiguity.

4 The quotations are from *Rhetorica ad Herennium*, III, 16. 28, as Albertus continues his effort to fit the rhetorician's understanding of "memoria" to that defined in Aristotle's psychological works. "Inductio" is probably understood technically here, referring to a kind of argumentation, discussed by both Cicero and Quintilian, which proceeds by analogy from a number of specific cases to infer a general principle or universal rule.

5 Albertus may be thinking here of Aristotle's definition of "memoria," which includes the observation that a memory can be generated only after some time has passed after the event we remember. But the idea that past time is part of the very definition of memory is familiar in the thirteenth century, and does not have to relate specifically to Aristotle – recall the common figure of Prudence with three eyes, looking to past, present, and future.

6 As indicated in chapter 4, the obscurity of this segment of the *Rhetorica ad Herennium* is not helped by the fact that Albertus was using a bad edition of it. The correct reading is, in part, "Aesopum et Cimbrum subornari ut ad Iphegeniam in Agamemnonem et Menelaum," "Aesopus and Cimber being dressed as Agamemnon and Menelaus for [a drama of] *Iphegenia*". Albertus's text read something like "Aesopum et Cimbrum subornari ut vel vagantem Ephigeniam." Albertus does what he can with this senseless quotation – understanding "subornari" as "supply, prepare, equip," he has Aesopus and Cimber being supplied or fitted-out as wandering Iphegenia (though he seems to reverse the order of the characters in the last clause of his explanation).

7 Again, Albertus has an altered text: *Ad Herennium* reads "egregie turpe, inhonestum, inusitatem, magnum, incredibile, ridiculum;" Albertus has "egregie aut honestum aut turpe in homines, tum inauditum, magnum, incredibile, periculosum." Albertus allows that decency is as memorable as its opposite; did he find danger more memorable than what's funny?

8 Albertus uses *negotium* as a synonym for *res* frequently in this treatise; for earlier precedents, see Lewis and Short, s. v. *negotium*, II B.

9 In his response, Albertus reverses the order of the fourth and fifth of Tully's precepts, as set forth in his first statement of them. This reversal seems to reflect Albertus's understanding that the rule regarding "intervalla," which I discussed in chapters 2 and 4, refers not to the viewer's distance from the background (an interpretation which, as in Tully and Bradwardine, makes it a rule governing the recollector's perception, allied to the background's visibility, but to the differentiation of one location from others in its set.

10 On Albertus's distinction between *vis formalis* and *vis imaginativa*, see Wolfson, "The Internal Senses," and chapter 2 above. Basically, the "shaping-power" (*formalis*) is more simply passive than the "image-making-power" (*imaginativa*), though both are prior (and so "lower") to the "higher" functioning of memory and recollection.

Appendix C

1 A transcription of the Latin text in this manuscript was published in 1975 by Beryl Rowland, "Bishop Bradwardine." Unfortunately, there are a number of errors in it. I myself expect soon to publish an edition of this and the other surviving copy of the treatise. I would like particularly to thank Professor Derek Brewer and Mr. P. Woudhuysen, Keeper of Manuscripts of the Fitzwilliam Museum, Cambridge, for making it possible for me to examine and transcribe the text.

2 The meaning of the phrase "distancia intercepta" is explained at the end of the third paragraph of the treatise, as the imaginary position of the observer from the location. A similar definition of "distancia" is given by Thierry of Chartres. This rule corresponds to what the *Rhetorica ad Herennium* has to say about the "intervallum" of the locational backgrounds, a matter which I discussed in Chapter 2.

3 The manuscript reads "sillabarum," but given what follows, Bradwardine would seem to have intended "consonantium" (consonants).

4 The context makes it clear that by "oration" Bradwardine is really thinking only of the "theme" chosen in advance from which the preacher spins his sermon, rather than of an entirely composed speech.

5 The attribution of this treatise to Bradwardine has been termed "uncertain" by Weisheipl (who did not see the McClean manuscript in preparing his catalogue, but only the greatly inferior version in B.L. MS. Sloane 3744). Brian Fleming, however, judged that "the presumption stands in favor of Bradwardine," though he still had undisclosed "legitimate reservations" about it; *Thomas de Bradwardine*, p. 112. The internal evidence seems to me sufficiently strong to accept the attribution to Bradwardine made in both surviving versions of the text, and in the catalogue of Syon Monastery, which lists a copy of "Bragwardinus de arte memorandi," now apparently lost (see Fleming, p. 121, note 1). The scholastic form of the treatise indicates a university setting for both the author and his audience. References to the algorism and to "cifra" or "zero," suggest someone, like Bradwardine, who was familiar with university-style arithmetic. But the most convincing evidence lies in the internal indications of the treatise's date and provenance. The exemplary sentence, "Benedictus Dominus" etc., dates the work to a time just after the English victory over the Scots at the second battle of Berwick in July, 1333. The coupling of Scots with subdued beasts suggests that English jingoism was still running high, and thus argues for a date very close to the victory. Bradwardine was at Merton College, Oxford, until 1335. The English puns on "bear," "cy," and "elbow" indicate that the author was English; his discussion of "cy," moreover, indicates that he was likely a southerner, who knew of northern dialect forms but not well enough to know the singular from the plural of this dialect word – hence his mistake about the meaning of the form "cy," discussed in chapter 4. Though we do not know exactly where Bradwardine was born, contemporary accounts associate him with Chichester, in the south; he also was a prebend of Lincoln Cathedral, which would have brought him into some contact, however slight, with "northern" (actually East Midlands) dialect speakers.

Bibliography

I. Reference Works

Blaise, Albert. *Lexicon latinitatis medii aevii*. Corpus Christianorum, continuatio medievalis, vol. 28. Turnhout: Brepols, 1975.

Dictionary of Medieval Latin from British Sources. Prepared by R. E. Latham. London: Oxford University Press, 1975– .

Dictionnaire de spiritualité ascétique et mystique. Edited by Marcel Viller. Paris: G. Beauchesne, 1937– .

Dictionnaire de théologie catholique. Edited by A. Vacant and E. Mangenot. Paris: Lerouzey & Ané, 1909–50.

Du Cange, Charles du Fresne (Sieur). *Glossarium mediae et infimae latinitatis*. Originally published 1610–88. Revised edition, 10 vols. in 5. Graz: Akademische Druck, 1954–55.

Lewis, C. T. and C. Short, *A Latin Dictionary*. Oxford: Clarendon Press, 1879.

Liddell, H. G. and R. Scott. *A Greek–English Lexicon*. Revised edition. Oxford: Clarendon Press, 1968.

Middle English Dictionary. Edited by H. Kurath, S. M. Kuhn, and R. Lewis. Ann Arbor: University of Michigan Press, 1957– .

The New Grove Dictionary of Music and Musicians. London: Macmillan, 1980.

Ochoa, Xaverius and Aloisio Diez. *Indices canonium, titulorum et capitulorum corpus juris canonici*. Rome: Commentarium pro Religiosus, 1964.

Indices titulorum et legum corpus juris civilis. Rome: Commentarium pro Religiosus, 1965.

The Oxford English Dictionary on Historical Principles. Edited by J. H. A. Murray *et al.* Oxford: Clarendon Press, 1933.

The Oxford Latin Dictionary. Edited by P. G. W. Clare. New York: Oxford University Press, 1982.

Pollard, A. W. and G. R. Redgrave, compilers. *A Short-Title Catalogue of Books Printed in England, Scotland, and Ireland, 1475–1640*. Revised and enlarged edition. New York: Modern Language Association, 1972.

Previté-Orton, C. W. *The Shorter Cambridge Medieval History*. 2 vols. Cambridge: Cambridge University Press, 1953.

A Revised Medieval Latin Word List. Prepared by R. E. Latham. London: Oxford University Press, 1965.

Skeat, Walter W. *Early English Proverbs*. Oxford: Clarendon Press, 1910.

Walther, Hans. *Lateinische Sprichwörter und Sentenzen des Mittelalters*. 6 vols. Göttingen: Vandenhoeck & Ruprecht, 1962; new series, 1983.

Young, Morris N. *Bibliography of Memory*. Philadelphia: Chilton, 1961.

Bibliography

II. Catalogues of Manuscript Collections and Exhibitions

Biblioteca Medicea Laurenziana. [*Boccaccio:*] *Mostra di manoscritti, documenti e edizioni.* 2 vols. An exhibition at the Biblioteca Medicea Laurenziana. Florence, 1975.

Brown University Department of Art. *Survival of the Gods: Classical Mythology in Medieval Art.* Exhibition catalogue. Providence, RI: Brown University Press, 1987.

de la Mare, Albinia C. *Catalogue of the Collection of Medieval Manuscripts Bequeathed to the Bodleian Library, Oxford, by James P. R. Lyell.* Oxford: Clarendon Press, 1971.

De Ricci, Seymour. *A Census of Medieval and Renaissance Manuscripts in the United States and Canada.* New York: H. W. Wilson Co., 1935–40. *Supplement.* Edited by W. H. Bond. New York, 1962.

Dutschke, C. W. *Guide to Medieval and Renaissance Manuscripts in the Huntington Library.* San Marino, CA: Huntington Library Publications, 1988.

James, M. R. *A Descriptive Catalogue of the Manuscripts in the Library of Corpus Christi College, Cambridge.* Cambridge: Cambridge University Press, 1912.

A Descriptive Catalogue of the McClean Collection of Manuscripts in the Fitzwilliam Museum, Cambridge. Cambridge: Cambridge University Press, 1912.

Catalogue of Manuscripts and Early Printed Books from the Libraries of William Morris, Richard Bennett, Bertram, Earl of Ashburnham, and other Sources, now Forming Portion of the Library of J. Pierpont Morgan. 4 vols. London: Chiswick Press, 1906–1907.

The Western Manuscripts in the Library of Trinity College, Cambridge. 4 vols. Cambridge: Cambridge University Press, 1900–1904.

John Rylands Library. *Catalogue of an Exhibition of Mediaeval and other Manuscripts and Jewelled Book-Covers Arranged in the Main Library.* First exhibition catalogue. Manchester: Manchester University Press, 1910.

Catalogue of an Exhibition of Mediaeval and other Manuscripts and Jewelled Book-Covers Arranged in the Main Library. Second exhibition catalogue. Manchester: Manchester University Press, 1924.

Catalogue of a Selection of Mediaeval Manuscripts and Jewelled Book-Covers Exhibited in the Main Library. Third exhibition catalogue. Manchester: Manchester University Press, 1939.

Maunde-Thompson, E. *A Catalogue of Ancient Manuscripts in the British Museum.* 2 vols. London: British Museum, 1881.

Mynors, R. A. B. *Durham Cathedral Manuscripts.* Oxford: Clarendon Press, for the Chapter of Durham Cathedral, 1939.

Paecht, Otto and J. J. G. Alexander. *Illuminated Manuscripts in the Bodleian Library, Oxford.* 3 vols. Oxford: Clarendon Press, 1966–73.

Pierpont Morgan Library. *Early Children's Books and Their Illustration.* Exhibition catalogue. Boston: David Godine, 1975.

III. Editions and Translations

Abelard, Peter. "Historia calamitatum." *PL* 178, 115–182. Translated by Betty Radice. *The Letters of Abelard and Eloise.* London: Penguin, 1974.

Alanus de Insulis (Alain of Lille). "In adventu domine." *PL* 210, 214–218.

Albertus Magnus. "Commentary on Aristotle's De memoria et reminiscentia." *Opera Omnia*, vol. 9. Edited by August Borgnet. Paris: Ludovicum Vives, 1890.

Bibliography

"Mineralia." "Liber de apprehensione." *Opera Omnia*, vol. 5. Edited by August Bornet. Paris: Ludovicum Vives, 1890.

"De bono." *Opera Omnia*, vol. 28. Edited by H. Kuhle, C. Feckes, B. Geyer, W. Kubel. Aschendorff: Monasterii Westfalorum, 1951.

"Postilla in Isaiam." *Opera Omnia*, vol. 19. Edited by F. Siepmann. Aschendorff: Monasterii Westfalorum, 1952.

Alcuin. "De rhetorica et de virtutibus." *PL* 101, 919–946. Translated by W. S. Howell. *The Rhetoric of Alcuin and Charlemagne*. Princeton: Princeton University Press, 1941.

"Expositio in psalmos poenitentiales." *PL* 100, 596–639.

Ambrose. *Epistolae. PL* 16, 875–1286.

Anselm. *Opera omnia.* 2 vols. Edited by F. S. Schmitt. Stuttgart: Friedrich Fromman Verlag, 1968.

Aristotle. *The Art of Rhetoric.* Edited and translated by John Henry Freese. Loeb Classical Library. Cambridge, MA: Harvard University Press, 1959.

Aristotle's Constitution of Athens. Edited by John Sandys. 2nd edition. London: Macmillan, 1912.

On Dreams and *On Divination in Dreams.* See *Parva naturalia.*

De memoria et reminiscentia. See *On Memory* and *Parva naturalia.*

On Memory. Translated with interpretive essays and commentary by Richard Sorabji. Providence, RI: Brown University Press, 1972.

Metaphysics. Edited and translated by H. Tredennick. 2 vols. Loeb Classical Library. Cambridge, MA: Harvard University Press, 1961–1962.

De Motu Animalium. Edited and translated with commentary and interpretive essays by Martha Nussbaum. Princeton: Princeton University Press, 1978.

Nichomachean Ethics. Edited and translated by Horace Rackham. Loeb Classical Library. Cambridge, MA: Harvard University Press, 1934.

Posterior Analytics. Edited and translated by Hugh Tredennick. Loeb Classical Library. Cambridge, MA: Harvard University Press, 1960.

On the Soul [De anima], Parva naturalia, On Breath. Edited and translated by W. S. Hett. Loeb Classical Library. Cambridge, MA: Harvard University Press, 1935.

Topica. Translated by W. S. Pickard-Cambridge. In *The Complete Works of Aristotle.* 2 vols. Edited by Jonathan Barnes. Princeton: Princeton University Press, 1984.

Arnaldus de Villanova. *Opera omnia.* Basle: 1585.

Augustinus Aurelius. *Confessiones.* Edited, with the translation of William Watts, corrected, by W. H. D. Rouse. 2 vols. Loeb Classical Library. Cambridge, MA: Harvard University Press, 1960–1961. Also, translated by Vernon J. Bourke. Fathers of the Church, vol. 21. Washington, DC: Catholic University Press, 1953.

De doctrina Christiana. PL 34, 15–122.

Enarrationes in Psalmos. CCSL 38–40. *Aurelii Augustini Opera*, vol. 10. Turnhout: Brepols, 1954–1984.

Epistolae. PL 33.

De magistro. PL 32, 1193–1220.

De musica. PL 32, 1081–1194.

De natura et origine animae. CSEL 60, pp. 301–420. Editum consilio et impensis Academiae caesarea Vinobonensis. Vienna: 1866–

Sermones. PL 38–39.

Averroes. *Epitome of parva naturalia.* Translated by Harry Blumberg. Cambridge, MA: Medieval Academy of America, 1961.

Avicenna (Latinus). *Liber de anima seu sextus de naturalibus.* Edited by S. Van Reit. 2 vols. Leiden: Brill, 1968–72.

Bibliography

Bartholomaeus Anglicus. *De proprietatis rerum.* Edited by M. C. Seymour. 2 vols. London: Oxford University Press, 1975.
  On the Properties of Soul and Body. Edited by R. James Long. Toronto Medieval Latin Texts, no. 9. Toronto: Pontifical Institute of Medieval Studies, 1979.
Bartholommeo da San Concordia. *Ammaestramenti degli antichi.* Classici Italiani. Milan: 1808.
Bede. "De schemata et tropis." *PL* 90, 175–196.
  "Historia ecclesiastica gentis Anglorum." In *Bede: Opera historica.* Edited and translated by J. E. King. Loeb Classical Library. London: Heinemann, 1930.
[Bede]. "De loquela digitorum." *PL* 90, 685–702.
Benedict. *Regula monachorum. PL* 66, 215–933.
Bible. *Biblia Sacra juxta Vulgatam Clementinam,* nova editio. Madrid: Biblioteca de Autores Cristianos, 1985. English of the King James Version (1611), provided for the convenience of readers knowing no Latin.
Boccaccio, Giovanni. *Teseida.* Edited by Salvatore Bataglia. Florence: Sansoni, 1938. Translated by B. M. McCoy. New York: Medieval Text Association, 1974.
Boethius. *The Consolation of Philosophy.* Edited by H. F. Stewart, with the translation of "I. T.," revised. Loeb Classical Library. London: Heinemann, 1962.
  De differentiis topicis. Translated with commentary by Eleonore Stump. Ithaca: Cornell University Press, 1978.
  In Ciceronis topica. Translated by Eleonore Stump. Ithaca: Cornell University Press, 1988.
Boncompagno da Signa. "Rhetorica novissima." In *Scripta anecdota glossatoria.* Edited by Augusto Gaudenzi. *Bibliotheca iuridica medii aevi,* vol. 2. Bononiae [Bologna], 1892.
Cassiodorus Senator. *Institutiones.* Edited by R. A. B. Mynors. Oxford Classical Texts. London: Oxford University Press, 1937. Translated by Leslie W. Jones as *An Introduction to Divine and Human Readings.* New York: Columbia University Press, 1946.
Charland, T. M. ed. *Artes praedicandi.* Ottawa: Institute d'Etudes médiévales, 1936.
Chaucer, Geoffrey. *Complete Poetry and Prose.* Edited by John H. Fisher. New York: Holt Rinehart, 1977. See also "History and Criticism" under J. M. Manly and E. Rickert, and B. Windeatt.
Cicero, M. Tullius. *Brutus* and *Orator.* Edited and translated by G. L. Hendrickson and H. M. Hubbell. Loeb Classical Library. London: Heinemann, 1939.
  De inventione, Topica, De optime genere oratorium. Edited and translated by H. M. Hubbell. Loeb Classical Library. Cambridge, MA: Harvard University Press, 1949.
  De oratore, Partitiones oratoriae. Edited and translated by E. W. Sutton and H. Rackham. 2 vols. Loeb Classical Library. London: Heinemann, 1942–1948.
[Cicero, M. Tullius]. *Rhetorica ad Herennium (Ad C. Herennium libri IV De ratione dicendi).* Edited and translated by Harry Caplan. Loeb Classical Library. Cambridge, MA: Harvard University Press, 1954. Also, the critical edition (*editio major*) by Friedrich Marx. Leipzig: Teubner, 1894.
Columella. *De re rustica.* Edited and translated by H. B. Ash. 3 vols. Loeb Classical Library. Cambridge, MA: Harvard University Press, 1948–1955.
The Cyrurgie of Guy de Chauliac. Edited by Margaret Ogden. EETS, o.s. 265. London: Oxford University Press, 1971.
Dante Alighieri. *La vita nuova.* Edited and translated by M. Musa. Bloomington, IN: Indiana University Press, 1962.
  The Divine Comedy. Edited and translated by Charles Singleton. 6 vols. Bollingen Series. Princeton: Princeton University Press, 1975.
Darbishire, Helen ed. *The Early Lives of Milton.* London: Constable, 1932.

Bibliography

Dialexeis. In H. Diels and W. Kranz eds. *Die Fragmente der Vorsokratiker*. 2 vols.
II: 405–416. Translated by Rosamond Kent Sprague. "Dissoi Logoi or Dialexeis." *Mind* 77 (1968): 155–167.

Eadmer. *The Life of St. Anselm*. Edited and translated by R. W. Southern. London:
Thomas Nelson, 1962.

Faccio, Anselmo. *Memoria artificiale di casi di conscienza*. Messina, per Pietro Brea,
1621.

Ferreolus. *Ferreoli episcopi regula ad monachos*. PL 66, 959–976.

Fortunatianus. "Artis rhetoricae libri tres." Edited by C. Halm, q. v.

Foster, Kenelm trans. *Biographical Documents for the Life of St. Thomas Aquinas*.
Oxford: Blackfriars, 1949.

Geoffrey of Vinsauf. *Poetria nova*. In *Les arts poétiques du xiie et xiiie siècles*. Edited
by Edmond Faral, 1924; reprinted Paris: Champion, 1923. Translated by Margaret F. Nims. Toronto: Pontifical Institute, 1967.

Giordano da Pisa [Giordano da Rivalto]. *Quaresimale Fiorentino, 1305–1306*. Edited
by Carlo Delcorno. Florence: Sansoni, 1974.

Giraldus Cambrensis. "In topographia Hibernie." In Giraldus Cambrensis. *Opere*.
Edited by J. F. Dimock. Rolls Series, vol. 5, no. 21. London: Longmans, 1867.
Also, an earlier recension of this text, edited with commentary by John J.
O'Meara. *Proceedings of the Royal Irish Academy* 52.C (1949), pp. 113–178.

Gregory the Great. *Dialogi*. PL 77, 127–430.

Cura pastoralis. PL 77, 9–128.

Registrum epistularum. CCSL 140–140A. Edited by D. Norberg. 3 vols.
Turnhout: Brepols, 1982.

Moralia in Job. CCSL 75. Edited by M. Adriaen. Turnhout: Brepols, 1969.

Gui, Bernardo. "Life of St. Thomas Aquinas." Latin text edited by D. Prümmer,
q. v. Translated by Kenelm Foster, q. v.

Guido d'Arezzo. "Letter to Brother Martin." Edited by Martin Gerbert. *Scriptores
ecclesiastici de musica*. Vol. 2. San-Blaise, 1774.

Guidotto da Bologno. *Il Fiore di Rettorica*. Edited by Bartolommeo Gamba.
Bologna: Masi, 1824.

Halm, Carolus ed. *Rhetores latini minores*. Leipzig: Tuebner, 1863.

Havelock the Dane. Edited by W. W. Skeat. Second edition, revised by K. Sisam.
Oxford: Clarendon Press, 1915.

Hawes, Stephen. *The Pastime of Pleasure*. Edited by William E. Mead. EETS, o.s.
173. London: Oxford University Press, 1928.

[Honorius of Autun]. "Gemma animae." PL 172, 541–737.

Horace. *The Epistles*. Edited by A. S. Wilkins. London: Macmillan, 1939. Translated by S. P. Bovie. *Satires and Epistles*. Chicago: University of Chicago Press,
1959.

Hugh of St. Victor. "De arca Noe morali." PL 176, 618–680. Translated by a Religious of C.M.S.V. *Hugh of St. Victor: Selected Spiritual Writings*. London: Faber
and Faber, 1962.

"De arca Noe mystica." PL 176, 681–702.

"De institutione novitiorum." PL 176, 925–952.

"De tribus maximis circumstantiis gestorum." Edited by William M. Green.
Speculum 18 (1943): 484–493.

"De unione corpore et anime." PL 177, 285–294.

Didascalicon. Edited by Charles H. Buttimer. Washington: Catholic University
Press, 1939. Translated by Jerome Taylor. New York: Columbia University
Press, 1961.

Hugo de Folieto. "De avibus [De bestiis]." PL 176, 9–164.

"De claustro anime." PL 176, 1017–1182.

Bibliography

Isidore of Seville. *Etymologiae.* Edited by W. M. Lindsay. 2 vols. Oxford Classical Texts. Oxford: Clarendon Press, 1911.
Sententiarum libri III. PL 83, 537–758.
"Versus in bibliotheca." Edited by Charles Beeson. *Isidorstudien.* Quellen und Untersuchungen zur lateinischen Philologie des Mittelalters. Vol. 4, no. 2. Munich: Oscar Beck, 1913.
Jean d'Antioche. "Rhétorique de Cicéron (Musée de Condé MS. 590)." Excerpts, edited by Léopold Delisle. *Notices et extraits* 36 (1899): 207–265.
Jerome. "Commentarium in Ezechielem." *PL* 25, 15–490.
"Commentarium in Isaiam Prophetam." *PL* 24, 17–704.
"Epistolae." *PL* 22.
"Index rerum et sententiarum." *PL* 23, 767–804.
"Liber de nominibus Hebraicis." *PL* 23, 815–904.
"Prefaces to the Vulgate Bible." *PL* 28.
[Jerome]. "Regula monachorum ex scriptis Hieronymi collecta" and "Regula monacharum." *PL* 30, 319–386; 391–426.
John of Garland. *Parisiana poetria.* Edited by Traugott Lawler. Yale Studies in English, 182. New Haven: Yale University Press, 1974.
John of Mirfield. "Florarium Bartholomei." In *Johannes de Mirfeld of St. Bartholomew's, Smithfield: His Life and Works.* Edited and translated by P. H.-S. Hartley and H. R. Aldridge. Cambridge: Cambridge University Press, 1936.
John of Salisbury. *Metalogicon. PL* 199, 823–946. Also, edited by Clement Webb. Oxford: Oxford University Press, 1929. Translated by D. D. McGarry, 1955; reprinted Gloucester, MA: Peter Smith, 1971.
Julius Victor. "Ars rhetorica." Edited by C. Halm, q. v.
Langland, William. *The B-Text of Piers Plowman.* Edited by George Kane and E. Talbot Donaldson. London: Athlone Press, 1975. *Piers Plowman: An Edition of the C-Text.* Edited by Derek Pearsall. Berkeley and Los Angeles: University of California Press, 1978.
Latini, Brunetto. *Li Livres dou trésor.* Edited by Francis J. Carmody. University of California Publications in Modern Philology, 22. Berkeley: University of California Press, 1948.
Layamon. *Brut: or the Chronicles of England.* Edited by G. L. Brook and R. F. Leslie. 2 vols. EETS, o.s. 250, 277. London: Oxford University Press, 1963, 1978.
"Le Livre de Lancelot del Lac." In *The Vulgate Versions of the Arthurian Romances,* vols. 3–5. Edited by H. O. Sommer. Washington: Carnegie Corp., 1910.
Lydgate, John. *Minor Poems.* Edited by H. N. McCracken. EETS, e.s. 107. London: Oxford University Press, 1911.
Martial. *Epigrams.* 2 vols. Edited and translated by W. C. A. Ker and E. H. Warmington. Loeb Classical Library. London: Heinemann, 1920–1925.
Martianus Capella. "De nuptiis philologiae et mercurii." In *Martianus Capella.* Edited by Aldolphus Dick. 1925; reprinted Stuttgart: B. Teubner, 1969. Translated with commentary by William H. Stahl and R. Johnson. *Martianus Capella and the Seven Liberal Arts.* 2 vols. New York: Columbia University Press, 1977.
Mattheolus [Mattheoli] de Perusinus. *De memoria augenda.* Rome: Johann Besicker und Sigismund Mayer, 1493 [1494].
Murphy, James J. ed. *Three Medieval Rhetorical Arts.* Berkeley and Los Angeles, CA: University of California Press, 1971.
Ovid. *Heroides.* Second edition. Edited and translated by G. Showerman, revised by G. P. Goold. Loeb Classical Library. London: Heinemann, 1977.

Bibliography

Metamorphoses. 2 vols. Second edition. Edited and translated by F. J. Miller, revised by G. P. Goold. Loeb Classical Library. London: Heinemann, 1984.

Paulinus of Nola. *Works. PL* 61, 153–438.

Pecock, Reginald. *The Donet.* Edited by E. V. Hitchcock. EETS, o.s. 156. 1921; reprinted New York: Kraus, 1971.

Peter of Poitiers. *Works.* Edited by P. S. Moore. Washington, DC: Catholic University of America Press, 1936.

Peter of Ravenna (Petrus Tommai). *Foenix domini petri ravenatis memoriae magistri.* Venice: Bernardinus de Choris de Cremona, 1491 [1492]. Translated from French to English by Robert Coplande as *The Art of Memory, Otherwise Called Phenix.* London [1548?].

Petrarca, Francesco. *Le Familiari.* 4 vols. Edited by V. Rossi and U. Bosco. Florence: Sansoni, 1933–42. Translated by A. Bernardo. *Letters on Familiar Matters.* 3 vols. Baltimore: Johns Hopkins Press, 1975–85.

Prose. Edited by G. Martelotti *et al.* Milan: Riccardi, 1955.

Rerum memorandarum libri. Edited by Guiseppe Billanovich. Florence: Sansoni, 1945.

Secret. Translated by William H. Draper. London: Chatto and Windus, 1911.

Plato. *Collected Dialogues* [translated by various hands]. Edited by Edith Hamilton and Huntington Cairns. Princeton: Princeton University Press, 1961.

Phaedrus. Translated by John McDowell. Clarendon Plato Series. Oxford: Clarendon Press, 1973. Edited and translated by H. N. Fowler. Loeb Classical Library. London: Heinemann, 1914. See also "History and Criticism" under Hackforth, R.

Theaetetus and Sophist. Edited and translated by H. N. Fowler. Loeb Classical Library. London: Heinemann, 1921.

Pliny [the Elder]. *Natural History.* 10 vols. Edited and translated by H. Rackham *et al.* Loeb Classical Library. Cambridge, MA: Harvard University Press, 1938–62.

Prümmer, Dominicus, and M. H. Laurent eds. *Fontes vitae S. Thomae Aquinatis notis historicis et criticis illustrati.* Toulouse: *Revue Thomiste*, Saint Maximim, 1911–1934.

Quintilian, M. Fabius. *Institutio oratoria.* Edited by M. Winterbottom. 2 vols. Oxford Classical Texts. Oxford: Clarendon Press, 1970. Translated by H. E. Butler. 4 vols. Loeb Classical Library. London: Heinemann, 1922.

Regula Magistri (La Règle du maître). Scriptorium Publications, no. 3. Edited by H. Vanderhoven and F. Masai. Brussels: Editions Erasmus, 1953.

Rhabanus Maurus. "De universo libri xxii." *PL* 111, 9–614.

Richard de Bury. *Philobiblon.* Edited and translated by Ernest C. Thomas. London: Kegan Paul, 1888.

Richart de Fournival. *Li Bestiaires d'Amours.* Edited by Cesare Segré. Milan: Riccardi, 1957.

Robert de Basevorn. "Forma praedicandi." Latin text edited in Charland, q. v. Translated in James J. Murphy ed. q. v.

The Romance of Sir Beves of Hamptoun. Edited by E. Kölbing. EETS, e.s. 46, 48, 65. 1885–1894; reprinted New York: Kraus, 1973.

Romberch, J. Host von. *Congestorium artificiose memorie.* Venetiis: Melchiorum Sessam, 1533.

Rudel, Jaufre. In George Wolf and Roy Rosenstein eds, *The Poetry of Cercamon and Jaufre Rudel.* New York: Garland Publishing, 1983.

Seneca. *Epistulae morales.* Edited by L. D. Reynolds. Oxford Classical Texts. Oxford: Clarendon Press, 1965. Edited and translated by R. M. Gummere. 3 vols. Loeb Classical Library. London: Heinemann, 1953–1962.

Bibliography

Shakespeare, William. *The Complete Plays and Poems.* Edited by W. A. Neilson and C. J. Hill. Cambridge: Houghton Mifflin Company, 1942.

Sigebert of Gembloux. "Liber de Scriptoribus Ecclesiasticis." *PL* 160, 547–588.

Spenser, Edmund. *The Faerie Queene.* Edited by A. C. Hamilton. Third edition. New York: Longmans, 1977.

The Tale of Beryn. Edited by F. J. Furnivall and W. G. Stone. EETS, e.s. 105. 1909; reprinted New York: Kraus, 1973.

Thierry of Chartres. *The Latin Rhetorical Commentaries.* Edited by Karin M. Fredborg. Toronto: Pontifical Institute of Medieval Studies, 1988.

Thomas Aquinas. *Catena aurea in quattuor Evangelia.* Edited by A. Guarienti. Turin: Marietti, 1953.

Commentary on Aristotle's De anima. Translated by Kenelm Foster and Silvester Humphries. London: Routledge, 1951.

In Aristotelis libros de sensu et sensato, de memoria et reminiscentia commentarium. Edited by R. M. Spiazzi. Second edition. Turin: Marietti, 1949.

In decem libros ethicorum Aristotelis ad nichomachum expositio. Edited by A. Pirotta. Turin: Marietti, 1934.

Summa theologica. Blackfriars edition (Latin and English). 61 vols. New York: McGraw-Hill, 1964–1981.

Thomas of Waleys. "De modo componendi sermones." Edited by T. M. Charland, q. v.

Tocco, Gulielmus de. "Life of St. Thomas Aquinas." In *Acta sanctorum,* March, vol. I. Paris: Société Bollandists, 1648. Also edited by Prümmer, q. v. Translated by K. Foster, q. v.

Varro. *De lingua Latina.* 2 vols. Edited and translated by R. G. Kent. Loeb Classical Library. London: Heinemann, 1938.

Virgil. *Georgics, Aeneid, et al.* 2 vols. Edited and translated by H. R. Fairclough. Loeb Classical Library. London: Heinemann, 1932.

The Wakefield Pageants in the Towneley Cycle. Edited by A. C. Cawley. Manchester: Manchester University Press, 1958.

William of Ockham. *Dialogus de imperio et pontificia potestate.* In *Opera plurima,* vol. I. Lyons, 1494–1496; reprinted London: Gregg Press, 1962.

Wyclif, John. *De veritate Sacrae Scripturae.* Edited by R. Buddensieg, in. 3 vols. *Wyclif's Latin Works,* vol. 18. London: G. Tuebner for The Wyclif Society, 1905–1907.

IV. Facsimile Editions of Manuscripts

Henry, Françoise. *The Book of Kells.* New York: Knopf, 1974.

Ker, N. R. *The Winchester Malory.* EETS s.s. 4. London: Oxford University Press, 1974.

Luce, A. A., P. Meyer, G. O. Simmons, and L. Bieler. *Evangelium quattuor codex Durmachensis.* 2 vols. Olten: Urs Graf Verlag, 1960.

Maunde-Thompson, E. *Codex Alexandrinus.* 4 vols. London: British Museum, 1879–83.

Millar, Eric G. *An Illuminated Manuscript of La Somme le Roy.* Oxford: Roxburghe Club, 1953.

The Rutland Psalter. Oxford: Roxburghe Club, 1937.

Sandler, Lucy Freeman. *The Psalter of Robert De Lisle.* London: Oxford University Press for Harvey Miller, 1983.

Bibliography

v. History and Criticism

Ahern, John. "Binding the Book: Hermeneutics and Manuscript Production in Para-diso 33." *PMLA* 97 (1982): 800–809.

Alexander, J. J. G. *The Decorated Letter*. London: Thames and Hudson, 1978.

Insular Manuscripts, 6th–9th Centuries. A Survey of Manuscripts Illuminated in the British Isles, vol. 1. London: Harvey Miller, 1978.

The Master of Mary of Burgundy. New York: Braziller, 1970.

"Scribes as Artists: The Arabesque Initial in Twelfth-Century English Manu-scripts." In M. B. Parkes and A. G. Watson eds. *Medieval Scribes, Manuscripts and Libraries: Essays Presented to N. R. Ker*, pp. 87–116. London: Scolar Press, 1978.

Alexander, J. J. G. and M. T. Gibson eds. *Medieval Learning and Literature: Essays Presented to R. W. Hunt*. London: Oxford University Press, 1987.

Alford, John. "The Role of the Quotations in *Piers Plowman*." *Speculum* 52 (1977): 80–99.

Allen, Judson B. *The Ethical Poetic of the Later Middle Ages*. Toronto: University of Toronto Press, 1982.

The Friar as Critic. Nashville, TN: Vanderbilt University Press, 1971.

"Langland's Reading and Writing: *Detractor* and the Pardon Passus." *Speculum* 59 (1984): 342–362.

Auerbach, Erich. *Literary Language and its Public in Late Latin Antiquity and in the Middle Ages*. Translated by Ralph Mannheim. Princeton: Princeton University Press, 1965.

Baddeley, Alan D. *The Psychology of Memory*. New York: Basic Books, 1976.

Baldwin, Charles S. *Medieval Rhetoric and Poetic to 1400*. 1928; reprinted Gloucester, MA: Peter Smith, 1959.

Balogh, Josef. "'Voces paginarum': Beitrage zur Geschichte des lauten Lessens und Schreibens." *Philologus* 82 (1927): 84–109, 202–240.

Baron, Hans. *From Petrarch to Leonardi Bruni*. Chicago: University of Chicago Press, 1968.

Benson, Robert L. and Giles Constable eds. *Renaissance and Renewal in the Twelfth Century*. Cambridge, MA: Harvard University Press, 1982.

Benton, John F. "Consciousness of Self and Perceptions of Individuality." In R. Benson and G. Constable eds. *Renaissance and Renewal in the Twelfth Century* (q. v.), pp. 263–295.

"Fraud, Fiction and Borrowing in the Correspondence of Abelard and Heloise." In *Pierre Abélard, Pierre le Vénérable*, pp. 469–511. Paris: Editions du Centre National de la Recherche Scientifique, 1975.

Berger, S. *L'Histoire du Vulgate pendant les premiers siècles du Moyen Age*. 1893; reprinted New York: Burt Franklin, 1959.

Bischoff, Bernhard. "The Study of Foreign Languages in the Middle Ages." In B. Bis-choff. *Mittelalterliche Studien*, vol. 2, pp. 227–245. Stuttgart: Hiersemann, 1967.

Black, Max. *Models and Metaphors*. Ithaca: Cornell University Press, 1962.

Blum, Herwig. *Die Antike Mnemotechnik*. Spudasmata, vol. 15. Hildesheim: Georg Olms, 1969.

Bower, Gordon H. "A Selective Review of Organizational Factors in Memory." In Endel Tulving and Wayne Donaldson eds. *Organization of Memory*, pp. 93–137. New York: Academic Press, 1972.

Branca, Vittore. "Copisti Per Passione, Tradizione Caratterizzante, Tradizione di Memoria." In Raffaele Spongano ed. *Studi e problemi di critica testuale*, pp. 69–83. Bologna: Commissione per i testi di lingua, 1961.

Bibliography

Brewer, Derek. "Orality and Literacy in Chaucer." In W. Erzgraber and S. Volk eds. *Mundlichkeit und Schriftlichkeit im englischen Mittelalter*, pp. 85–119. Tubingen: Gunter Narr, 1987.

Bruns, Gerald L. *Inventions: Writing, Textuality, and Understanding in Literary History*. New Haven: Yale University Press, 1982.

Bundy, Murray Wright. *The Theory of Imagination in Classical and Medieval Thought*. University of Illinois Studies in Language and Literature 12. Urbana, IL: University of Illinois Press, 1927.

Burrow, John A. *Medieval Writers and Their Work*. New York: Oxford University Press, 1982.

Bynum, Caroline Walker. *Jesus as Mother: Studies in the Spirituality of the High Middle Ages*. Publications of the Center for Medieval and Renaissance Studies, UCLA, no. 16. Berkeley and Los Angeles: University of California Press, 1972.

Cahn, Walter. *Romanesque Bible Illumination*. Ithaca: Cornell University Press, 1982.

Callus, D. A. "The Oxford Career of Robert Grosseteste." *Oxoniensia* 10 (1945): 42–72.

Robert Grosseteste, Scholar and Bishop. Oxford: Clarendon Press, 1955.

Camden, Carroll. "Memory, the Warder of the Brain." *Philological Quarterly* 18 (1939): 52–72.

Camille, Michael. "The Book of Signs: Writing and Visual Difference in Gothic Manuscript Illumination." *Word and Image* 1 (1985): 133–148.

"Seeing and Reading: Some Visual Implications of Medieval Literacy and Illiteracy." *Art History* 8 (1985): 26–49.

Caplan, Harry. *Of Eloquence: Collected Essays*. Edited by Anne King and Helen North. Ithaca: Cornell University Press, 1970.

Carruthers, Mary J. "Italy, *Ars memorativa*, and Fame's House." *Studies in the Age of Chaucer*, Proceedings Series 2 (1987): 179–187.

Cave, Terence. "The Mimesis of Reading in the Renaissance." In S. Nichols and J. Lyon eds. *Mimesis* (q. v.), pp. 149–165.

Chaytor, H. J. *From Script to Print: An Introduction to Medieval Literature*. Cambridge, MA: Cambridge University Press, 1945.

Chenu, M.-D. "Auctor, actor, autor." *Bulletin Du Cange* 3 (1927): 81–86.

Introduction a l'Etude de St. Thomas d'Aquin. Third edition. Paris: Vrin, 1974.

Nature, Man, and Society in the Twelfth Century. Edited and translated by L. Little and J. Taylor. Chicago: University of Chicago Press, 1968.

Clanchy, M. T. *From Memory to Written Record, England 1066–1307*. Cambridge, MA: Harvard University Press, 1979.

Clark, Donald L. *Rhetoric in Greco-Roman Education*. New York: Columbia University Press, 1957.

Clark, John Willis. *The Care of Books*. Cambridge: Cambridge University Press, 1902.

Coleman, Janet. "Late Scholastic Memoria et Reminiscentia: Its Uses and Abuses." In P. Boitani and A. Torti eds. *Intellectuals and Writers in Fourteenth Century Europe*, pp. 22–44. London: Boydell and Brewer, 1986.

Medieval Readers and Writers. London: Hutchinson, 1981.

Colish, Marcia. *The Mirror of Language*. Revised edition. Lincoln: University of Nebraska Press, 1983.

Cope, Edward M. *An Introduction to Aristotle's Rhetoric*. London: Macmillan, 1867.

Cornford, F. M. *Plato's Theory of Knowledge*. 1934; reprinted New York: Bobbs-Merrill, 1957.

Bibliography

Courcelle, Pierre. *Les Confessions de Saint Augustin dans la tradition littéraire*. Paris: Etudes Augustiniennes, 1963.

La Consolation de philosophie dans la tradition littéraire. Paris: Etudes Augustiniennes, 1967.

Curschmann, Michael. "Oral Poetry in Mediaeval English, French, and German Literature: Some Notes on Recent Research." *Speculum* 42 (1967): 36–51.

Curtius, Ernst R. *European Literature and the Latin Middle Ages*. Translated by Willard R. Trask. 1953; reprinted New York: Harper and Row, 1963.

D'Alverny, Marie-Thérèse. "Translations and Translators." In R. Benson and G. Constable eds. *Renaissance and Renewal in the Twelfth Century* (q. v.), pp. 421–462.

Daly, Lloyd W. *Contributions to a History of Alphabetization in Antiquity and the Middle Ages*. Brussels: Collection Latomus, 1967.

Daly, Lloyd W. and B. A. Daly, "Some Techniques in Medieval Latin Lexicography." *Speculum* 39 (1964): 229–239.

Davis, Charles T. "Education in Dante's Florence." *Speculum* 40 (1965): 415–435.

D'Avray, D. L. *The Preaching of the Friars*. Oxford: Clarendon Press, 1985.

De Clercq, Carlo. "Hugues de Fouilloy, Imagier de ses propres oeuvres?" *Revue du Nord* (Université de Lille) 45 (1963): 31–42 + Plates.

"Le Role de l'image dans un manuscrit médiéval (Bodl. Lyell 71)." *Gutenberg Jahrbuch* 37 (1962): 23–30.

De Hamel, C. F. R. *Glossed Books of the Bible and the Origins of the Paris Booktrade*. London: Boydell and Brewer, 1984.

A History of Illuminated Manuscripts. Boston: David Godine, 1986.

De Lubac, Henri. *Exégèse Médiévale*. 4 vols. Paris: Aubier, 1959–1964.

De Wald, E. T. *The Illustrations of the Utrecht Psalter*. Princeton: Princeton University Press, 1932.

De Wit, Pamela. "The Visual Experience of Fifteenth-Century English Readers." D. Phil. dissertation, Oxford University, 1977.

Deanesly, Margaret. "Vernacular Books in England in the Fourteenth and Fifteenth Centuries." *Modern Language Review* 15 (1920): 349–358.

Deferrari, R. J. "St. Augustine's Method of Composing and Delivering Sermons." *American Journal of Philology* 43 (1922): 97–123, 193–219.

Delaissé, L. M. J. "The Importance of Books of Hours for the History of the Medieval Book." In U. McCracken, L. Randall, and R. Randall eds. *Gatherings in Honor of Dorothy Miner* (q. v.), pp. 203–225.

"Towards a History of the Medieval Book." *Codicologia* 1 (1976): 75–83.

Delcorno, Carlo. *Giordano da Pisa e l'antica predicazione volgare*. Biblioteca di Lettere Italiane, vol. 14. Florence: Olschki, 1975.

Delhaye, Phillippe. "L'Enseignement de la Philosophie Morale au XIIᵉ Siècle." *Medieval Studies* 11 (1949): 77–99.

Derolez, Albert. "The Genesis of Hildegard of Bingen's 'Liber divinorum operum'." In J. P. Gumbert and M. J. M. de Haan eds. *Litterae Textuales: Essays Presented to G. I. Lieftinck*, vol. 2, pp. 23–33. Amsterdam: Van Gendt, 1972.

Derrida, Jacques. *Glas*. Paris: Galilee, 1974.

"Plato's Pharmacy." In *Dissemination*, pp. 61–171. Translated by Barbara Johnson. Chicago: University of Chicago Press, 1981.

"White Mythology: Metaphor in the Text of Philosophy." Translated by F. C. T. Moore. *New Literary History* 6 (1974): 5–74.

DiLorenzo, Raymond D. "The Collection Form and the Art of Memory in the *Libellus Super Ludo Schachorum* of Jacobus de Cessolis." *Mediaeval Studies* 35 (1973): 205–221.

Bibliography

Diringer, David. *The Book Before Printing: Ancient, Medieval, Oriental.* 1953; reprinted New York: Dover Publications, 1982.

Dodwell, C. R. *The Canterbury School of Illumination.* Cambridge: Cambridge University Press, 1954.

Donaldson, E. Talbot. "Manuscripts R and F in the B-Tradition of *Piers Plowman.*" *Transactions of the Connecticut Academy of Arts and Sciences* 39 (1955): 177–212.

"The Psychology of Editors of Middle English Texts." In E. T. Donaldson. *Speaking of Chaucer*, pp. 102–118. New York: W. W. Norton, 1970.

Dondaine, Antoine. *Les Secrétaires de Saint Thomas.* 2 vols. Rome: Editori di S. Tommaso, 1956.

Dubois, Jacques. "Comment les moines du Moyen Age chantaient et goûtaient les Saintes Ecritures." In P. Riché and G. Lobrichon eds. *Le Moyen Age et la Bible* (q. v.), pp. 261–298.

Dufresne, Suzy. "Les Copies Anglaises du Psautier d'Utrecht." *Scriptorium* 18 (1964): 185–197.

Les Illustrations du Psautier d'Utrecht. Paris: Editions Ophyrs, 1978.

Eco, Umberto. "An *Ars Oblivionalis?* Forget It!" *PMLA* 103 (1988): 254–261.

Eisenstein, Elizabeth. *The Printing Press As An Agent of Change: Communications and Cultural Transformations in Early Modern Europe.* 2 vols. Cambridge: Cambridge University Press, 1979.

The Printing Revolution in Early Modern Europe. Cambridge: Cambridge University Press, 1983.

Ellis, John. *The Theory of Literary Criticism: A Logical Analysis.* Berkeley and Los Angeles: University of California Press, 1974.

Eskridge, James B. *The Influence of Cicero Upon Augustine in the Development of His Oratorical Theory for the Training of the Ecclesiastical Orator.* Menasha, WI: Banta, 1912.

Evans, G. R. *The Language and Logic of the Bible in the Earlier Middle Ages.* Cambridge: Cambridge University Press, 1984.

"Two Aspects of *Memoria* in Eleventh and Twelfth Century Writings." *Medievalia* 32 (1980): 263–278.

Feigenbaum, Edward A. "Information Processing and Memory." In Donald A. Norman ed. *Models of Human Memory*, pp. 451–468. New York: Academic Press, 1970.

Ferruolo, Stephen C. *The Origins of the University.* Stanford, CA: Stanford University Press, 1985.

Fisher, John. "Animadversions on the Text of Chaucer, 1988." *Speculum* 63 (1988): 779–793.

Fleming, Brian. *Thomas de Bradwadine.* Ph.D. dissertation, Louvain, 1964.

Fodor, Jerry A. *The Language of Thought.* 1975; reprinted Cambridge, MA: Harvard University Press, 1980.

Fontaine, Jacques. *Isidore de Seville et la culture classique dans l'Espagne wisigothique.* 2 vols. Paris, Etudes augustiniennes, 1959.

Freccero, John. "The Fig Tree and the Laurel: Petrarch's Poetics." *Diacritics* 5 (1975): 34–40.

Dante: The Poetics of Conversion. Edited by Rachel Jacoff. Cambridge, MA: Harvard University Press, 1986.

Friedman, John B. "Les images mnémotechniques dans les manuscrits de l'époque gothique." In B. Roy and P. Zumthor eds. *Jeux de mémoire* (q. v.), pp. 169–184.

Gallo, Ernest. "The Poetria Nova of Geoffrey of Vinsauf." In J. Murphy ed. *Medieval Eloquence* (q. v.), pp. 68–84.

Gardner, Edmund G. "Imagination and Memory in the Psychology of Dante." In

Bibliography

Mary Williams and J. A. de Rothschild eds. *A Miscellany of Studies in Romance Languages and Literatures Presented to Leon E. Kastner*, pp. 275–282. Cambridge: Heffer, 1932.

Geertz, Clifford. *The Interpretation of Cultures*. New York: Basic Books, 1973.

Gehl, Paul F. "Competens Silentium: Varieties of Monastic Silence in the Medieval West." *Viator* 18 (1987): 125–160.

"Mystical Language Models in Monastic Educational Psychology." *Journal of Medieval and Renaissance Studies* 14 (1984): 219–243.

"Texts and Textures: Dirty Pictures and Other Things in Medieval Manuscripts." *Corona* (Montana State University, Bozeman, Montana) 3 (1983): 68–77.

Goldschmidt, E. P. *The Printed Book of the Renaissance*. Cambridge: Cambridge University Press, 1950.

Gombrich, E. H. *Meditations on a Hobby Horse And Other Essays on the Theory of Art*. New York: Phaidon, 1963.

Goy, Rudolph. *Die Uberlieferung der Werke Hugos von St. Viktor*. Stuttgart: Anton Hiersemann, 1976.

Greene, Thomas M. "Erasmus's 'Festina lente': Vulnerabilities of the Humanist Text." In S. Nichols and J. Lyons eds., *Mimesis* (q. v.), pp. 132–148.

The Light In Troy: Imitation and Discovery in Renaissance Poetry. New Haven: Yale University Press, 1982.

Greimas, A. J. *On Meaning: Selected Writings in Semiotic Theory*. Translated by P. J. Perron and F. H. Collins. *Theory and History of Literature*, vol. 38. Minneapolis, MN: University of Minnesota Press, 1986.

Guilmain, Jacques. "The Geometry of the Cross-Carpet Pages in the Lindisfarne Gospels." *Speculum* 62 (1987): 21–52.

Hackforth, R. *Plato's Phaedrus*. Cambridge: Cambridge University Press, 1952.

Hajdu, Helga. *Das Mnemotechnische Schriftum des Mittelalters*. Vienna: Franz Leo, 1936.

Hajnal, St. "Universities and the Development of Writing in the XIIth–XIIIth Centuries." *Scriptorium* 6 (1952): 177–195.

Hanning, Robert W. *The Individual In the Twelfth Century Romance*. New Haven: Yale University Press, 1977.

"Poetic Emblems in Medieval Narrative Texts." In Lois Ebin ed. *Vernacular Poetics in the Middle Ages*, pp. 1–32. Studies in Medieval Culture 16. Kalamazoo, MI: Medieval Institute Publications, 1984.

"'Ut Enim Faber . . . Sic Creator': Divine Creation as Context for Human Creativity in the Twelfth Century." In Clifford Davidson ed. *Word, Picture, and Spectacle*, pp. 95–149. Early Drama, Art, and Music Monograph Series 5. Kalamazoo, MI: Medieval Institute Publications, 1984.

Harvey, E. Ruth. *The Inward Wits*. London: Warburg Institute, 1975.

Hasenohr, Geneviève. "Méditation méthodique et mnémonique: un témoignage figuré ancien (s. XIIIe–XIVe)." In Rita LeJeune and Joseph Deckers eds. *Clio et son Regard: Mélanges Jacques Stiennon*, pp. 365–382. Liege: Mardaga, 1982.

Haskins, Charles H. *Studies in Medieval Culture*. Oxford: Clarendon Press, 1929.

Havelock, Eric A. *The Literate Revolution in Greece and Its Cultural Consequences*. Princeton: Princeton University Press, 1982.

Hendrickson, G. L. "Ancient Reading." *Classical Journal* 25 (1929): 182–196.

"The Origin and Meaning of the Ancient Characters of Style." *American Journal of Philology* 26 (1905): 249–290.

Hillgarth, J. R. *Ramon Lull and Lullism in Fourteenth Century France*. Oxford: Clarendon Press, 1971.

Bibliography

Howell, Wilbur S. *Logic and Rhetoric in England, 1500–1700*. Princeton: Princeton University Press, 1956.

Hughes, Andrew. *Medieval Manuscripts for Mass and Office*. Toronto: University of Toronto Press, 1982.

Huizinga, Johan. *The Waning of the Middle Ages*. 1924; reprinted New York: Anchor Books, 1954.

Hunt, R. W. "English Learning in the Late Twelfth Century." *Transactions of the Royal Historical Society*, Series 4, 19 (1936): 19–35.

"Manuscripts Containing the Indexing Symbols of Robert Grosseteste." *Bodleian Library Record* 4 (1953): 241–255.

"The Library of Robert Grosseteste." In D. A. Callus ed. *Robert Grosseteste, Scholar and Bishop*, pp. 121–145. Oxford: Clarendon Press, 1955.

Huot, Sylvia. *From Song to Book: The Poetics of Writing in Old French Lyric and Lyrical Narrative Poetry*. Ithaca: Cornell University Press, 1987.

Huygens, R. B. C. *Accessus ad Auctores*. Collection Latomus 15. Brussels: Berchem, 1954.

Infeld, Leopold. *Quest: An Autobiography*. Second edition. New York: Chelsea Publishing, 1980.

Irvine, Martin. "Grammatical Theory and the House of Fame." *Speculum* 60 (1985): 850–876.

Kahn, Victoria. "The Figure of the Reader in Petrarch's Secretum." *PMLA* 100 (1985): 154–166.

Kane, George. "John M. Manly and Edith Rickert." In Paul G. Ruggiers ed. *Editing Chaucer: The Great Tradition*, pp. 231–252. Norman, OK: Pilgrim Books, 1984.

Katzenellenbogen, Adolf. *Allegories of the Vices and Virtues in Medieval Art*. Studies of the Warburg Institute. London: Warburg Institute, 1939.

Kauffmann, C. M. *Romanesque Manuscripts, 1066–1190*. *A Survey of Manuscripts Illuminated in the British Isles*, vol. 3. London: Harvey Miller, 1975.

Kennedy, George A. *Classical Rhetoric and Its Christian and Secular Tradition From Ancient to Modern Times*. Chapel Hill: University of North Carolina Press, 1980.

Kenny, A. J. P. "Intellect and Imagination in Aquinas." In A. J. P. Kenny ed. *Aquinas: A Collection of Critical Essays*, pp. 273–296. 1969; reprinted Notre Dame, IN: University of Notre Dame Press, 1976.

Ker, N. R. "The Beginnings of Salisbury Cathedral Library." In J. J. G. Alexander and M. T. Gibson eds. *Medieval Learning and Literature* (q. v.), pp. 23–49.

English Manuscripts in the Century After the Norman Conquest. London: Oxford University Press, 1960.

Medieval Libraries of Great Britain. Second edition. London: Royal Historical Society, 1964.

Kidson, Peter. "Panofsky, Suger and St. Denis." *JWCI* 50 (1987): 1–17.

Kolve, V. A. *Chaucer and the Imagery of Narrative*. Stanford, CA: Stanford University Press, 1984.

Kristeller, Paul O. *Medieval Aspects of Renaissance Learning: Three Essays*. Durham, NC: Duke University Press, 1974.

Kully, Rolf Max. "Cisiojanus: comment savoir le calendrier par coeur." In B. Roy and P. Zumthor eds. *Jeux de mémoire* (q. v.), pp. 149–156.

Kuttner, S. and B. Smalley. "The 'Glossa Ordinaria' to the Gregorian Decretals." *English Historical Review* 60 (1945): 97–105.

Lacan, Jacques. *The Four Fundamental Concepts of Psychoanalysis*. Edited by J. A. Miller and translated by Alain Sheridan. London: Hogarth Press, 1977.

Bibliography

Lampe, G. W. H. ed. *The West from the Fathers to the Reformation.* Vol. 2 of *The Cambridge History of the Bible.* 3 vols. Cambridge: Cambridge University Press, 1969.

Larès, Micheline. "Les Traductions Bibliques: l'example de la Grande-Bretagne." In P. Riché and G. Lobrichon eds. *Le Moyen Age et la Bible* (q. v.), pp. 123–140.

Lawton, Lesley. "The Illustration of Late Medieval Secular Texts." In Derek Pearsall ed. *Manuscripts and Readers in Fifteenth-Century England,* pp. 41–69. Cambridge: D. S. Brewer, 1983.

Leclercq, Jean. "L'Art de la composition dans les sermons de S. Bernard." *Studi Medievali,* 3rd series, 7 (1966): 128–153.

The Love of Learning and the Desire for God. Translated by C. Misrahi. New York: Fordham University Press, 1961.

"Sur le caractère littéraire des sermons de S. Bernard." *Studi Medievali,* 3rd series, 7 (1966): 701–744.

Light, Laura. "The New Thirteenth-Century Bible and the Challenge of Heresy." *Viator* 18 (1987): 275–288.

"Versions et révisions du texte biblique." In P. Riché and G. Lobrichon eds. *Le Moyen Age et la Bible* (q. v.), pp. 55–93.

Lindsay, W. M. *Notae Latinae.* Cambridge: Cambridge University Press, 1915.

Lord, Albert B. *The Singer of Tales.* Cambridge, MA: Harvard University Press, 1960.

Luria, A. R. *The Mind of a Mnemonist.* Translated by Lynn Solotareff. New York: Basic Books, 1968.

The Neuropsychology of Memory. Translated by B. Haigh. Washington: V. H. Winston, 1976.

McCartney, Eugene S. "Notes on Reading and Praying Audibly." *Classical Philology* 43 (1948): 184–187.

McCracken, U. E., L. M. C. Randall, and R. H. Randall. *Gatherings in Honor of Dorothy E. Miner.* Baltimore: Walters Art Gallery, 1974.

McCulloch, Florence. *Medieval French and Latin Bestiaries.* Chapel Hill, NC: University of North Carolina Press, 1960.

McKeon, Richard. "Literacy Criticism and the Concept of Imitation in Antiquity." In R. S. Crane ed. *Critics and Criticism,* pp. 147–175. Chicago: University of Chicago Press, 1952.

"Rhetoric in the Middle Ages." In R. S. Crane ed. *Critics and Criticism,* pp. 260–296. Chicago: University of Chicago Press, 1952.

Mackey, Louis H. *"Inter nocturnas vigilias:* A Proof Postponed." In Laurie A. Finke and M. B. Schichtman eds. *Medieval Texts and Contemporary Readers,* pp. 69–99. Ithaca: Cornell University Press, 1987.

Malcolm, Norman. *Memory and Mind.* Ithaca: Cornell University Press, 1977.

Mâle, Emile. *The Gothic Image.* Translated by Dora Nussey. 1913; reprinted New York: Harper & Brothers, 1958.

Mandonnet, P. "Pierre Calo et la Légende de S. Thomas." *Revue thomiste,* new series 2 (1912): 508–516.

Manly, John Matthews and E. Rickert. *The Text of the Canterbury Tales.* 8 vols. Chicago: University of Chicago Press, 1940.

Marks, Richard and Nigel Morgan. *The Golden Age of English Manuscript Painting.* London: Chatto and Windus, 1981.

Markus, R. A. "Augustine on Signs." *Phronesis* 2 (1957): 60–83.

Marrou, Henri I. *Histoire de l'Education dans l'Antiquité.* Paris: Editions de Seuil, 1948.

Saint Augustin et le fin de la culture antique. Paris: de Boccard, 1938.

Martz, Louis L. *The Poetry of Meditation.* New Haven: Yale University Press, 1954.

Bibliography

Matson, Wallace I., "Why Isn't the Mind-Body Problem Ancient?" In Paul Feyerabend and Grover Maxwell eds. *Mind, Matter, and Method*, pp. 92–102. Minneapolis, MN: University of Minnesota Press, 1966.

Matthews, Gareth B. "Augustine On Speaking from Memory." In R. A. Markus ed. *Augustine: A Collection of Essays*, pp. 168–175. New York: Anchor Doubleday, 1972.

Mazzotta, Guiseppe. *Dante: Poet of the Desert*. Princeton: Princeton University Press, 1979.

Miedema, Hessel. "The Term *Emblemata* in Alciati." *JWCI* 31 (1968): 234–250.

Miethke, Jürgen. "Marsilius und Ockham: Publikum und Leser ihrer Politischen Schriften im Späteren Mittelalter." *Medioevo: Rivista di Storia della Filosofia Medievale* (Padua) 6 (1980): 543–567.

Ockhams Weg zur Sozialphilozophie. Berlin: de Gruyter, 1969.

Miller, George A. "Information and Memory." *Scientific American* (August, 1963): 42–46.

"The Magical Number Seven, Plus or Minus Two: Some Limits on Our Capacity for Processing Information." *Psychological Review* 63 (1956): 81–97.

Minnis, Alistair J. "John Gower, *sapiens* in Ethics and Politics." *Medium Aevum* 49 (1980): 207–229.

"Langland's Ymaginatif and Late Medieval Theories of Imagination." *Comparative Criticism* 3 (1981): 71–103.

Medieval Theory of Authorship. London: Scolar Press, 1984.

Morgan, Nigel. *Early Gothic Manuscripts*. 2 vols. *A Survey of Manuscripts Illuminated in the British Isles*, vol. 4. London: Harvey Miller, 1988.

Morson, John. "The English Cistercians and the Bestiary." *Bulletin of John Rylands Library* 39 (1956–1957): 146–170.

Munk Olsen, B[irger]. "Les Classiques Latins dans les Florilèges Médiévaux antérieurs au XIIIᵉ siècle." *Revue d'Histoire des Textes* 9 (1979): 47–121.

"Les Florilèges d'Auteurs Classiques." *Les Genres Littéraires dans les Sources Théologiques et Philosophiques Médiévales*, pp. 151–164. Université Catholique de Louvain, Publications de l'Institut d'Etudes Médiévales, second series, 5 (1982).

Murphy, James J. ed. *Medieval Eloquence*. Berkeley: University of California Press, 1978.

Medieval Rhetoric: A Select Bibliography. Toronto: University of Toronto Press, 1971.

Rhetoric in the Middle Ages. Berkeley and Los Angeles: University of California Press, 1974.

Murray, Alexander. *Reason and Society in the Middle Ages*. Oxford: Clarendon Press, 1978.

Murrin, Michael. *The Veil of Allegory*. Chicago: University of Chicago Press, 1969.

Nash, Ronald H. *The Light of the Mind: St. Augustine's Theory of Knowledge*. Lexington, KY: University Press of Kentucky, 1969.

Nichols, Stephen G. and J. D. Lyons eds. *Mimesis: From Mirror to Method, Augustine to Descartes*. Hanover, NH: University Press of New England, 1982.

Noakes, Susan. "The Double Misreading of Paolo and Francesca." *Philological Quarterly* 62 (1983): 221–239.

Nordenfalk, Carl. *Die Spätantiken Kanontäfeln*. 2 vols. Göteborg: O. Isacsons, 1938.

"The Beginning of Book Decoration." In O. Goetz ed. *Essays in Honor of George Swarzenski*, pp. 9–20. Chicago: Regnery, 1951.

"A 10th-Century Gospel Book in the Walters Art Gallery." In U. McCracken, L.

Bibliography

Randall, and R. Randall eds. *Gatherings in Honor of Dorothy E. Miner* (q. v.), pp. 139–170.

Norman, Donald A. *Learning and Memory*. San Francisco, CA: Freeman & Co., 1982.

Memory and Attention. New York: J. Wiley, 1969.

Norman, Donald A. ed. *Models of Human Memory*. New York: Academic Press, 1970.

Notopoulos, J. A. "Mnemosyne in Oral Literature." *Transactions of the American Philological Association* 69 (1938): 465–493.

Obermann, Heiko. *Archbishop Thomas Bradwardine: A Fourteenth-Century Augustinian*. Utrecht: Kemink & Zoon, 1958.

Ong, Walter J. *Orality and Literacy*. London: Methuen, 1982.

Ramus, Method, and the Decay of Dialogue. 1958; reprinted Cambridge, MA: Harvard University Press, 1983.

Orme, Nicholas. *English Schools in the Middle Ages*. London: Methuen, 1973.

Pack, R. A. "An Ars Memorativa from the Late Middle Ages." *Archives d'histoire doctrinale et littéraire du Moyen Age* 46 (1979): 221–265.

Paecht, Otto. *The Rise of Pictorial Narrative in Twelfth-Century England*. Oxford: Clarendon Press, 1962.

Panofsky, Dora. "The Textual Basis of the Utrecht Psalter's Illustrations." *The Art Bulletin* 25 (1943): 50–58.

Parkes, M. B. "The Influence of the Concepts of *Ordinatio* and *Compilatio* on the Development of the Book." In J. J. G. Alexander and M. T. Gibson eds. *Medieval Learning and Literature* (q. v.), pp. 115–141.

"The Literacy of the Laity." In *The Medieval World*. D. Daiches and A. Thorlby eds. *Literature and Western Civilization*, vol. 2, pp. 555–577. London: Aldus, 1973.

Pasquale, Giorgio. *Storia della tradizione e critica del testo*. Second edition. Florence: le Monnier, 1952.

Patterson, Lee. *Negotiating the Past*. Madison, WI: University of Wisconsin Press, 1987.

Payne, Robert O. *The Key of Remembrance*. New Haven: Yale University Press, 1963.

"Chaucer's Realization of Himself as Rhetor." In J. Murphy ed. *Medieval Eloquence* (q. v.), pp. 270–287.

Pellegrin, E. and G. Billanovich. "Un Manuscrit de Cicéron annoté par Pétrarque au British Museum [MS. Harley 2493]." *Scriptorium* 8 (1954): 115–117.

Petrucci, Armando. *La Scrittura di Francesco Petrarca*. Vatican: Biblioteca Apostolica, 1967.

Plummer, John. *The Hours of Catherine of Cleves*. New York: Braziller [1966].

Rand, E. K. *Cicero in the Courtroom of St. Thomas Aquinas*. The Aquinas Lecture, 1945. Milwaukee, WI: Marquette University Press, 1946.

Randall, Lillian M. C. *Images in the Margins of Gothic Manuscripts*. Berkeley and Los Angeles: University of California Press, 1966.

Reese, Gustav. *Music in the Middle Ages*. New York: Norton, 1940.

Reitman, Walter. "What Does It Take to Remember?" In Donald A. Norman ed. *Models of Human Memory*, pp. 469–509. New York: Academic Press, 1970.

Richardson, John T. E. *Mental Imagery and Human Memory*. New York: St. Martins, 1980.

Riché, Pierre. "Les Bibliothèques de trois aristocrats laïcs carolingiens." *Le Moyen-âge* 66 (1963): 87–104.

Education et culture dans l'occident barbare, vi^e–viiie siècles. Paris: Seuil, 1962.

Bibliography

Translated by J. J. Contreni as *Education and Culture in the Barbarian West, Sixth Through Eighth Centuries*. Columbia, SC: University of South Carolina Press, 1976.

"Le rôle de la mémoire dans l'enseignement médiéval." In B. Roy and P. Zumthor eds. *Jeux de mémoire* (q. v.), pp. 133–148.

Riché, Pierre and Guy Lobrichon eds. *Le Moyen Age et la Bible. Bible de tous les temps*, vol. 4. Paris: Editions Beauchesne, 1984.

Ricoeur, Paul. *The Rule of Metaphor*. Translated by Robert Czerny. Toronto: University of Toronto Press, 1977.

Roberts, Colin H. and T. C. Skeat. *The Birth of the Codex*. London: Oxford University Press for The British Academy, 1983.

Robinson, H. Wheeler. *The Bible in its Ancient and English Versions*. Oxford: Clarendon Press, 1940.

Root, Robert K. ed. *Troilus and Criseyde: A Critical Edition*. Princeton: Princeton University Press, 1926.

Rorty, Richard. "Is Derrida a Transcendental Philosopher?" *Yale Journal of Criticism* 2 (1988–89): 207–217.

Philosophy and the Mirror of Nature. Princeton: Princeton University Press, 1979.

Rosen, Edward. "The Invention of Eyeglasses." *Journal of the History of Medicine and Allied Sciences* 9 (1956): 13–46, 183–218.

Ross, Thomas W. "Five Fifteenth-Century 'Emblem' Verses from Brit. Mus. Addit. MS. 37049." *Speculum* 31 (1957): 274–282.

Rossi, Paolo. *Clavis universalis: Arti mnemoniche e logica combinatoria de Lullo a Leibniz*. Milan: Riccardi, 1960.

Rouse, Richard. "La concordance verbale des Ecritures." In P. Riché and G. Lobrichon eds. *Le Moyen Age et la Bible* (q. v.), pp. 115–122.

Rouse, Richard and Mary A. Rouse. "Florilegia of Patristic Texts." *Les genres littéraires dans les sources théologiques et philosophiques médiévales*, pp. 165–180. Université Catholique de Louvain, Publications de l'Institut d'Etudes Médiévales, second series 5 (1982).

"The Florilegium Angelicum: Its Origin, Context, and Influence." In J. Alexander and M. Gibson eds. *Medieval Learning and Literature* (q. v.), pp. 66–114.

Preachers, Florilegia, and Sermons. Toronto: Pontifical Institute, 1979.

"*Statim invenire*: Schools, Preachers, and New Attitudes to the Page." In R. Benson and G. Constable eds. *Renaissance and Renewal in the Twelfth Century* (q. v.), pp. 201–225.

Rowland, Beryl. "Bishop Bradwardine, the Artificial Memory, and the House of Fame." In R. H. Robbins ed. *Chaucer at Albany*, pp. 41–62. New York: Franklin, 1975.

Rowlands, John. *Holbein: The Paintings of Hans Holbein the Younger*. Boston: David Godine, 1985.

Roy, Bruno and Paul Zumthor eds. *Jeux de mémoire*. Montreal: Les Presses de l'Université de Montreal, 1985.

Sacks, Oliver. *The Man Who Mistook His Wife for a Hat*. New York: Summit Books, 1985.

Saenger, Paul. 'Books of Hours and the Reading Habits of the Later Middle Ages." *Scrittura e Civiltà* 9 (1985): 239–269.

"Silent Reading: Its Impact on Late Medieval Script and Society." *Viator* 13 (1982): 367–414.

Sandler, Lucy Freeman. *Gothic Manuscripts, 1285–1385*. 2 vols. *A Survey of Manuscripts Illuminated in the British Isles*, vol. 5. London: Harvey Miller, 1986.

Bibliography

Sarton, George. *Introduction to the History of Science.* 3 vols. Washington, DC: Carnegie Institution, 1931.

Saxl, Fritz. "A Spiritual Encyclopaedia of the Later Middle Ages." *JWCI* 5 (1942): 82–137.

Scribner, Sylvia and Michael Cole. *The Psychology of Literacy.* Cambridge, MA: Harvard University Press, 1981.

"Unpackaging Literacy." In Marcia Farr Whiteman ed. *Writing: The Nature, Development, and Teaching of Written Communication,* pp. 71–87. New Jersey: Lawrence Erlbaum, 1981.

Shapiro, Meyer. "On the Aesthetic Attitude in Romanesque Art." In Meyer Shapiro. *Romanesque Art,* pp. 1–27. New York: Braziller, 1977.

Sherwin-White, A. N. *The Letters of Pliny: A Historical and Social Commentary.* Oxford: Clarendon Press, 1966.

Silverstein, Theodore. "Adelard, Aristotle, and the *De natura Deorum.*" *Classical Philology* 46 (1951): 82–86.

Simpson, James. "Modes of Thought and Poetic Form in *Piers Plowman.*" *Medium Aevum* 55 (1986): 1–23.

Singer, Charles J. and R. A. Underwood. *A Short History of Medicine.* New York: Oxford University Press, 1962.

Singleton, Charles. *An Essay on the Vita Nuova.* 1949; reprinted Baltimore: Johns Hopkins University Press, 1977.

Siraisi, Nancy. *Arts and Sciences at Padua.* Toronto: Pontifical Institute, 1973.

Skeat, T. C. *The Codex Sinaiticus and the Codex Alexandrinus.* Revised edition. London: British Museum, 1955.

"The Use of Dictation in Ancient Book Production." *Proceedings of the British Academy* 42 (1956): 179–208.

Smalley, Beryl. "The Bible and Eternity: John Wyclif's Dilemma." *JWCI* 27 (1964): 73–89.

English Friars and Antiquity in the Early Fourteenth Century. New York: Barnes and Noble, 1960.

The Study of the Bible in the Middle Ages. Third edition. Oxford: Blackwell, 1984.

Southern, R. W. *St. Anselm and His Biographer.* Cambridge: Cambridge University Press, 1963.

Medieval Humanism and Other Studies. Oxford: Blackwell, 1970.

Robert Grosseteste. Oxford: Clarendon Press, 1986.

Stock, Brian. *The Implications of Literacy: Written Language and Models of Interpretation in the Eleventh and Twelfth Centuries.* Princeton: Princeton University Press, 1983.

"Medieval Literacy, Linguistic Theory, and Social Organization." *New Literary History* 16 (1984–1985): 13–29.

Testard, Maurice. *St. Augustine et Cicéron.* 2 vols. Paris: Etudes augustiniennes, 1958.

Thompson, J. W. *The Literacy of the Laity in the Middle Ages.* University of California Publications in Education, vol. 9. Berkeley: University of California Press, 1939.

Thompson, J. W. *et al. The Medieval Library.* University of Chicago Studies in Library Science. Chicago: University of Chicago Press, 1939.

Thomson, S. Harrison. *Writings of Robert Grosseteste.* Cambridge: Cambridge University Press, 1940.

"Grosseteste's Topical Concordance of the Bible and the Fathers." *Speculum* 9 (1934): 139–144.

Thorndike, Lynn. *History of Magic and Experimental Science.* 8 vols. New York: Macmillan and Columbia University Press, 1923–1958.

Bibliography

Toynbee, Paget. *Dante, and the Lancelot Romance.* Fifth Annual Report of the Dante Society. Cambridge, MA, 1886.

Tracy, Theodore. *Physiological Theory and the Doctrine of the Mean in Plato and Aristotle.* Chicago: Loyola University Press, 1969.

Trapp, Damasus. "Augustinian Theology of the Fourteenth Century: Notes on Editions, Marginalia, Opinions, and Book-Lore." *Augustiniana* 6 (1956): 146–274.

Trimpi, Wesley. *Muses of One Mind.* Princeton: Princeton University Press, 1983.

Tselos, Dimitri. "English Manuscript Illustration and the Utrecht Psalter." *The Art Bulletin* 41 (1959): 137–149.

Van Dijk, S. J. P. "An Advertisement Sheet of an Early Fourteenth-Century Writing Master at Oxford." *Scriptorium* 10 (1956): 47–64.

Vance, Eugene. *Mervelous Signals.* Omaha, NB: University of Nebraska Press, 1986.
"Saint Augustine: Language as Temporality." In S. Nichols and J. Lyons eds. *Mimesis* (q. v.), pp. 20–35.

Vickers, Brian ed. *Occult and Scientific Mentalities in the Renaissance.* Cambridge: Cambridge University Press, 1984.

Vickers, Nancy J. "Petrarchan Lyric and the Strategies of Description." In S. Nichols and J. Lyons eds. *Mimesis* (q.v.), pp. 100–109.

Von Nolcken, Christina. "Some Alphabetical Compendia and How Preachers Used Them in Fourteenth-Century England." *Viator* 12 (1981): 271–288.

Walz, Angelus Maria. *San Tommaso D'Aquino: studi biografici sul dottore angelico.* Rome: Edizioni Liturgiche, 1945.

Ward, John O. *Artificiosa eloquentia in the Middle Ages.* Ph.D. dissertation, University of Toronto, 1972.
"From Antiquity to the Renaissance: Glosses and Commentaries on Cicero's *Rhetorica.*" In J. Murphy ed. *Medieval Eloquence* (q. v.), pp. 25–67.

Watts, Ann C. *The Lyre and the Harp.* New Haven: Yale University Press, 1969.

Weisheipl, J. A. "Repertorium Mertonense." *Medieval Studies* 31 (1969): 174–224.

Weitzmann, Kurt. *Late Antique and Early Christian Book Illumination.* New York: Braziller, 1977.
Illustrations in Roll and Codex: A Study of the Origins and Method of Text and Illustrations. Reprinted, with additions. Princeton: Princeton University Press, 1970.

West, Philip J. "Rumination in Bede's Account of Caedmon." *Monastic Studies* 12 (1976): 217–226.

Wilkins, Ernest H. *Studies in the Life and Works of Petrarch.* Cambridge, MA: Medieval Academy of America, 1955.

Wilson, R. M. "The Medieval Library of Tichfield Abbey." *Proceedings of the Leeds Philosophical and Literary Society* 5 (1940): 150–177, 252–276.

Windeatt, B. A. ed. *Chaucer: Troilus and Criseyde.* New York: Longmans, 1984.

Witt, Ronald G. "Boncompagno and the Defense of Rhetoric." *JMRS* 16 (1986): 1–31.

Wolfson, Harry A. "The Internal Senses." *Harvard Theological Review* 28 (1935): 69–133.

Wormald, Francis. "The Monastic Library." In U. McCracken, L. M. Randall, and R. Randall eds. *Gatherings in Honor of Dorothy E. Miner* (q. v.), pp. 93–109.
"The Survival of Anglo-Saxon Illumination After the Conquest." *Proceedings of the British Academy* 30 (1944): 127–149 + Plates.

Wormald, Francis and C. E. Wright eds. *The English Library Before 1700.* London: Athlone, 1958.

Bibliography

Yapp, Brundson. "The Birds of English Medieval Manuscripts." *Journal of Medieval History* (Amsterdam: University of Hull) 5 (1979): 315–349.

Yates, Frances A. *The Art of Memory*. London: Routledge and Kegan Paul, 1966.

Lull and Bruno: Collected Essays. 2 vols. London: Routledge and Kegan Paul, 1982.

"The Ciceronian Art of Memory." In *Medioevo e rinascimento: studi in onore di Bruno Nardi*, pp. 871–903. Florence: Sansoni, 1955.

Zinn, Grover A. Jr. "Hugh of St. Victor and the Art of Memory." *Viator* 5 (1974): 211–234.

Zumthor, Paul. *Essai de poétique médiévale*. Paris: Editions Seuil, 1972.

La poésie et la voix dans la civilisation médiévale. Essais et Conférences du Collège de France. Paris: Presses Universitaires de France, 1984.

Index of manuscripts

Index of manuscripts

General index

Note: Modern authors are included only when their work has received substantive discussion in the text or notes.

General index

General index

Guilmain, Jacques, 255
Guinevere, 185, 187

habit, *habitus*, 252, 260, 267–9, 270, 276;
  associational, "habitual" nature of
  recollection, 20, 48, 64; trained memory as
  habitus that makes possible moral
  judgement, 65–6, 67–8, 70–1; *see also hexis*
Hackforth, R., 297 n. 671
Haimon, Bishop, 175, 176
Hajdu, Helga, 80, 258, 308 n. 1
hands, pointing, in manuscript margins, 248
Hanning, Robert W., 343 n. 43
Havelock, Eric, 16, 297 n. 61
Havelock the Dane, 41
Hawes, Stephen, 108; *The Pastime of
  Pleasure*, 41–2
heads, as manuscript marginal marks, 248
hearing, sense of, 52, 55, 223, 224, 227, 303
  n. 29; *see also* auditory memory
heart (*cor*), association with memory, 48–9,
  85, 161, 165, 172, 330 n. 64
Hebrew(s), 297 n. 61; alphabet, 109, 110;
  language, 36; names in Bible, Jerome's
  gloss on, 115–16, 317 n. 126
Heloise (pupil of Abelard), 179, 180, 181–2,
  332 nn. 88 and 89
Hendrickson, G. L., 330 nn. 58 and 61, 333
  n. 91
Henry, Françoise, 257
Herbert of Bosham, glossed Psalter of, 216,
  figure 5
heresies, medieval, fundamentalism a
  component of, 11, 290 n. 26
"hermeneutical" and "heuristic", distinction
  between, 19, 20–1, 105; reading and
  composition conceived as "hermeneutical
  dialogue", 169–70, 186, 187, 198, 213, 218
Herophilus of Chalcedon, 48
Hesiod (Greek poet), 279
"heuristic" and "hermeneutical", distinction
  between, 19, 20–1, 105; heuristic systems,
  80, 296 n. 51
hexis, 68–9, 163, 169, 178, 180, 307 n. 105;
  see also habit
Higden, Ranulf, *Polychronicon*, 102
Hildegard of Bingen, 290 n. 24
Hillgarth, R. J., 253
historia, 222; as one of the three levels of
  Biblical exegesis, 45, 168, 264–5
historical consciousness, medieval, 193, 265,
  335 n. 11
Holbein, Hans, portrait of George Gisze,
  41
Holcot, Robert, 38, 89, 108, 230, 316 n. 101,
  342 n. 27; *Moralitas*, 142; picture of
  Charity, 230–1

Holmecultram Abbey (Cumberland), 243,
  244; Bestiary, 126–7
Homer, 21, 142, 174
homophony, puns, 143, 347 n. 2; bilingual,
  126, 128–9, 135, 137, 320 n. 7, 342 n. 37;
  visual, 28, 73, 105, 140, 151, 221; *see also*
  rebus
honey, *see* bees and honey
Honorius of Autun, 340 n. 3
hooks, hooking, as metaphor for
  recollection, 672, 114, 163–4, 216; *see also*
  fishing
Horace, 17, 142, 219 n. 10, 340 n. 90
hospitalis, as memory-place, 139
house, as memory-place, 138, 139, 148, 271,
  278
Hugh of St. Cher, 128, 129, 143, 314 n. 79
Hugh of St. Victor, 7–8, 95, 151, 153, 255,
  297 n. 61, 300 n. 117; advice on
  reading-meditation, 44, 162–3, 164–5, 168,
  174, 179, 184, 186, 219, 330 nn. 59 and 62;
  compositional habits and advice, 83, 91,
  118, 202, 208–11, 213; and connection
  between memory and moral character, 71;
  "De arca Noe morali", 43–5, 91, 162,
  208–11, 233, 235, 298 n. 81; "De arca Noe
  mystica", 44, 123, 231–9, 241, 247, 253,
  342–3 nn. 37–40; *Didascalion*, 42, 43, 81,
  83, 92, 162, 209, 343 n. 42; influence on
  Mattheolus, 51, 336 n. 21; on memory as
  basis of learning, 82, 106, 159, 248, 264;
  and mnemonic principle of "gathering",
  83–5, 102; on mnemonic value of textual
  layout and need always to use same codex,
  93, 128, 215, 263–4; and need to impress
  the circumstances under which something
  is memorized, 60, 81, 95, 12 5, 264;
  number grid system, 80–5 *passim*, 92–4,
  98, 99, 127, 129, 262–3, 265, 348 n. 7;
  preface to *Chronica* ("De Tribus Maximis
  Circumstantiis Gestorum"), 35, 80–5
  passim, 92–3, 101, 215, 261–6, 308 n. 3, 311
  n. 52; on the three levels of exegesis, 44,
  45, 165, 237, 264–5; use of metaphors for
  memory, 35, 39, 40, 43, 113, 165, 180, 261;
  use of visual aids, 93, 123, 231–9, 248, 253,
  254, 256, 311 n. 52; *see also* brevity;
  divisio; *locus*; and memory-images;
  sophismata
Hugutio of Pisa, 190, 191
Hugo de Folieto, 167, 169; *De avibus*, 107,
  231; treatise "On the dove and the hawk",
  231, 239–42, 254, *figures 15 and 16*; wheel
  treatises, 239, 253
Hugo, the "Painter", pictured on
  manuscript, 225, *figure 8*
Hugo Rainerus, 240, 241

General index

Luria, A. R., description of Russian mnemonist, *see* Shereshevski

Lydgate, John, 224–5, 245

McCulloch, Florence, 320 nn. 8 and 10

McKeon, Richard, 293 n. 27

Macrobius, 67, 267, 329 n. 50, 335 n. 7

Maimonides, 67

Malcolm, Norman, 291 nn. 8 and 14, 292 n. 17

Mâle, Emile, 221, 340 n. 3

male (leather strong-box), as metaphor for memory, 34, 39, 41–2

Malohaut, Lady of, 187, 188, 334 n. 107

Malory, the Winchester, 248

manuscripts, 322 n. 36; blank spaces left for reader's response, 205, 217–18; of lay amateurs, 228–9; medieval collections of, 326 n. 19; mnemonic value of page layout and decoration, 9, 93–5, 125, 215–17, 221–9 *passim*, 239–57 *passim*; painting conventions related to arts of memory, 123, 128, 131; "reading" the decorative apparatus of, 222, 340 n. 5; role of earliest illustrations to mark textual divisions, 226; unreliability of scribal copying, 160, 326 n. 21, 334 n. 105; *see also* marginalia

maps, 248; *mappa mundi*, 232, 237

marginalia, manuscript, 108, 215–18; *bas-de-page* pictorial narratives, 245–6; connection between memory-images and, 136, 216, 244–8, *passim*, 344 n. 56; grotesques and "drolleries", 136, 245, 321 n. 19, 344 n. 59; Robert Grosseteste's marginal notes, 117–19, 318 n. 142; space left for reader's additions, 205, 217; *see also tituli*

Markus, R. A., 295 nn. 36 and 39

Marrou, Henri I., 15, 112

Marsh, Adam, 117, 119

Martial, 36, 142

Martianus Capella, 22, 28–9, 164; *The Marriage of Mercury and Philosophy*, 147; memory advice, 86, 107–8, 147, 149, 173, 322 nn. 32 and 41

Martii reges (Marcian kings), as mnemonic image, 140, 151, 273

Martin of Braga, 306 n. 97

Matson, Wallace I., 49, 301 n. 5, 302 nn. 12 and 13, 303 n. 29

Mattheolus of Perugia, 48, 50–1, 104, 153, 198, 302 n. 19, 336 n. 21

Mazzotta, Guiseppe, 304 n. 63

meadows *see* fields

medical theory of memory, 47, 48, 50, 301 nn. 2 and 8

meditation, 50, 59, 137, 145, 162–76 *passim*, 189, 198; considered as memorial activity, 46, 88, 118, 123, 150; *see also* digestion-rumination metaphor; Hugh of St Victor; *lectio*; murmur of meditation

Meed, Lady (*Piers Plowman*), 187

Meliodorus, 33

memorandum, 92, 206

memoria orationis see themes, memory for

memory-as-book metaphor, 16, 29, 224, 290 n. 1

memory feats, prodigious, 7, 12–13, 61, 74, 75; *see also* mnemonists

memory-images, mental imagery, 16–18, 46, 123, 173, 206, 291 n. 14, 292 n. 17; for abstractions, 51–2, 56–7, 134–5, 277, 284, 303 nn. 27 and 39; advice against using ready-made, 108, 145, 152, 256, 274–5; Aristotle's theories concerning, 16–17, 23–4, 28, 49–50, 51–60 *passim*, 68, 293 n. 29, 301 n. 7, 302 n. 15, 303 n. 27; Bestiary as source of, 126, 127, 143, 144; Bradwardine's rules for, 110, 126, 132–7, 141, 143, 227–8, 235, 282–4; Cicero's rules for, 22, 28, 73; emotional component of, 54, 59–60, 67–8, 69, 130–1, 148–9, 169; grouping of, 133–4, 144, 227–8, 249, 282–3; Hugh of St. Victor's use of pieces of text as, 81, 82, 92–3; medieval book decoration as source of, 242–57 *passim*; mnemonic value of vivid and unusual, 109, 130–4 *passim*, 137, 138, 141–3 *passim*, 152, 273–4, 279–80, 316 n. 103; for numbers, 136, 287–8; physiological process by which images were thought to be made, 49–60 *passim* 302 n. 15; pictorial nature of, 18, 23, 24, 28, 291 n. 14, 292 n. 17, 293 nn. 29 and 30; power of constructing a single image out of a number of images, 53, 197; and process of recollection, 56, 61–2, 63; reading and, 223–4; representational aspect of, 22–6, 293 nn. 27 and 29; *Rhetoria ad Herennium*'s advice concerning, 63, 73–4, 130–1, 139–43 *passim*, 151–2, 173, 245, 272–5; Robert Holcot's use of, 108, 230–1, 342 n. 27; Shereshevski's use of, 75–9 *passim*; synaesthesia and, 78–9, 95, 229–30; temporal nature of, 28, 60; "visualized homophony" as principle for forming, 28, 73, 105, 151–2, 221; and "word-pictures", 226–42 *passim*, 243; *see also* Albertus Magnus; memory for things; memory for words; Quintilian; Thomas Aquinas

memory-places *see locus*

memory-storage, 46–60 *passim*, 70; *see also locus*; memory-images; seal-in-wax model; storehouse model

General index

Root, R. K., 214, 339 n. 75
Rorty, Richard, 15, 301 n. 4, 302 n. 11, 303 n. 30
rosary, 80
Rossi, Paolo, 15, 72, 258, 314 n. 90, 324 n. 56, 333 n. 100
rota, 252; rota Virgili, 251–2
"rote" memory, 61, 89, 90, 346 n. 80; distinction between memoria and, 19–20; etymology of "rote", 252, 346 n. 79; see also recitare
Rouse, Richard and Mary, 15, 100, 101, 107, 159, 176, 313 n. 69, 325 n. 8, 335 n. 7
Rowland, Beryl, 321 n. 17
rubrics, 92, 226, 244, 249, 256
rumination see digestion-rumination metaphor
runic alphabet, 109, 110
Rutland Psalter, 136, 321 n. 19

sacculus (money-pouch), as metaphor for memory, 34, 41, 84, 251; Hugh of St. Victor's use of, 39, 81–2, 92, 261; Richard de Bury's use of, 160, 161
Sacks, Oliver, 305 n. 72
St. Albans abbey, 226, 308 n. 2, 326 n. 19
St. Bartholomew's priory, Smithfield, 184, 246
St. Mary's abbey, Holmecultram, see Holmecultram
St. Victor, cathedral school of, 81, 209, 250
saints, 40, 250; lives of, in bas-de-page pictorial narratives, 245, 246; prodigious memories of, 12–13, 71
Sallust, 67
Samson, finding honey in lion's mouth, 44
Sandler, L. F., 254, 346 nn. 77 and 85
Sandys, John Edwin, 37
sapientia (wisdom, knowledge), 65, 66, 71, 83, 176, 210, 261; arbor sapientiae, 91, 209
Saussure, Ferdinand de, 32
Saxl, Fritz, 254, 316 n. 101, 323 n. 45, 346 n. 77
"scanning" (ability to move around memory instantly and securely), 7–8, 18–19, 63, 72, 112, 132, 152, 261; see also order; starting-point
scholasticism, 14, 46, 71, 137–8, 176, 202, 332 n. 77
Scotus Eriugena, John, 253
scribere, 195, 196
scribes, 4, 10, 188, 195–6, 206–7, 214, 215; as "painters", 225; unreliability of, 160, 326 n. 21, 334 n. 105
scrinium, as metaphor for memory, 34, 39–40, 160, 189, 246, 327 n. 30; scrinarius, 39–40

scripts, use of different, for text and commentary, 215–16, 218, figure 7; see also littera inintelligibilis; textualis formata
seal-in-wax model: applied to moral character, 71, 180, 307 n. 119; basic to Thomas Aquinas's understanding of knowledge, perception and memory, 55–6, 57, 304 n. 49; of memory, 14, 16–32 passim, 33, 49, 62, 72, 291 n. 5; see also wax tablets
seasons, as set of memory-places, 131
secretorium, 40
sedes, used for mental locations, 29, 86, 129, 323 n. 41
self, medieval conception of, 180, 182, 333 n. 95
Seneca, 36, 66, 67, 75, 298 n. 73; and memoria, 146, 192; Quintilian and, 75, 145; and trope of reader/author as bee, 37, 191–2
senses, sensory perception, 173, 198, 206, 330 n. 64; conception of the "interior senses", 47–8, 51; errors of perception, 76; memory as final process of sensory perception, 47–60 passim, 68, 78–9, 304 n. 49; see also hearing; sensus communis; sight; smell; taste; touch
sensus communis, 51, 52, 53, 58, 78, 304 n. 49
sententia, 90, 112, 165, 191, 219, 244
sententialiter, remembering material, 89–90, 189, 190, 311 n. 39
Serenus of Marseilles, Bishop, 221, 222, 223, 340 n. 6
sermons, 154, 159, 177; composing and publishing of, 206–8; delivery, 90, 208; extempore, 206, 207, 208; numerical division of, 85, 103–6, 107, 207, 314 n. 81; "oral" and "written" style, 210, 338 n. 67; sermon models, 197, 336 n. 20; "thematic" sermon, 151, 245; "university" and "popular", 103, 104, 314 n. 87; see also Thomas of Waleys
Servatus Lupus, 322 n. 36
"sets" of memory-places, 110; see also alphabet; numbers; seasons; voces animantium; Zodiac
Seven Deadly Sins, 229, 250, 345 n. 71
"seven plus or minus two", rule of, 84, 131
sexuality: in mnemonic images, 134, 137, 142, 245; sexual metaphors for reading, 298 n. 87
Shakespeare, William, use of term "quote", 103
Shereshevski ("S", Russian mnemonist), 14, 75–9, 83, 95, 126, 230, 322 n. 32
Shoreham, William, 252
short-term memory, 82–3, 84, 146, 309 n. 15,

390

General index

voice-level, association with different reading functions, 74, 86, 88, 147, 170–3, 198, 323 n. 42, 330 n. 59, 338 n. 63; *see also* murmur of meditation

Von Nolcken, Christina, 176–7, 314 n. 85, 332 n. 80

Ward, John O., 159
Watts, Isaac, 39
wax tablets, 21–2, 29, 72, 74, 92, 243, 293 n. 24; use in composition, 195, 196, 203, 204–5, 211, 212; writing on, to aid memorizing, 86, 112, 156, 173; *see also* seal-in-wax model
Weisheipl, J. A., 350 n. 5
West, Philip J., 165, 327 n. 31, 328 n. 37
wheel-diagrams, 239, 251–3
will, and desire, in mnemonic process, 169, 329 n. 53
William of Alnwick, 118, 318 n. 142
William of Moerbeke, 56, 68, 293 n. 29
William of Ockham, 141, 156–8, 160, 161, 163, 246; *Dialogus*, 89, 99, 156–7, 158, 324 n. 2, 325 n. 7; use of *tractandum*, 108, 176, 327 n. 33
wisdom *see sapientia*
wise men (Magi), *thesauri* of, 35
Wittgenstein, Ludwig, 22, 260
Wolfson, H. A., 47, 53, 301 n. 2, 336 n. 18
women, images of, to stimulate memory, 109

Wood of Life (*lignum vitae*), 160, 247; *see also* Tree of Life
word, *verbum*: Augustine's notion of "inner word", 26, 295 n. 39; representational relationship between word and thing, 24–7, 295 n. 39; sound (*parole*) called to mind by visual shape (*painture*) of word, 224–5; *see also* memory for words; "word-pictures"
"word-pictures", 226–42, 243
writing, 77, 156; likened to picturing, 241–2; practice in, as discipline of memory, 144, 322 n. 32; relationship to composing, 10, 195, 196, 203–5, 336 n. 14; relationship to memory, 8–9, 16, 30–2, 111, 208, 246, 322 n. 32; relationship to thought, 96; teaching of, 112, 178; vocalizing while, 178, 332 n. 83; *see also* Isidore of Seville; scribes; scripts
Wyclif, John 9–10, 294 n. 34

Yates, Frances, 15, 127, 153, 253, 258, 297 n. 61, 320 n. 12, 321 n. 27, 331 n. 70; and architectural mnemonic, 71, 72, 73, 75, 143, 146, 147, 322 n. 41, 342 n. 27

Zeno (the Stoic), 34
Zinn, G. A., 308 n. 3
Zodiac, 117, 239, 248; Bradwardine's use of, 110, 126, 133–4, 143, 283–4